CORPUS GENEALOGIARUM SANCTORUM HIBERNIAE

INSTITIÚID ARD-LÉINN BHAILE ÁTHA CLIATH

CORPUS GENEALOGIARUM SANCTORUM HIBERNIAE

EDITED BY

PÁDRAIG Ó RIAIN

DUBLIN INSTITUTE FOR ADVANCED STUDIES

1985

ISBN 901282 80 4

Printed in the Republic of Ireland by Mount Salus Press Limited

In memoriam
omnium praedecessorum meorum
qui aut recensiones aut editiones
genealogiarum sanctorum Hiberniae curaverunt
et praesertim illorum illustrium sacerdotum
Paulus Walsh (†1941) et Paulus Grosjean (†1964)

CONTENTS

FOREWORD

AMONG the 'publications suggested or in progress' of the Irish Archaeological Society (1840-1853) was 'the genealogy and history of the saints of Ireland' which was to be edited, with a translation and notes, by John O'Donovan and J. H. Todd. Despite their manifest qualifications, it is perhaps just as well that these scholars never completed the project, for they had decided to edit the text 'from the Book of Lecan', a composite source deriving, ultimately, from two twelfth-century manuscripts.

The genealogies of the Irish saints were first published in 1916-17 by the Rev. Paul Walsh who, very naturally, since its authors had already prepared it for the press in 1630, chose the recension of the Four Masters (*GRSH*). In his Preface (p.vii), however, the editor announced that he regarded the publication of this late recension as an aid to the 'further study of the whole body of genealogies of Irish saints'; this he hoped to undertake on another occasion, examining and reducing to order 'the various genealogical collections in Rawlinson B 502, the Book of Leinster, the Leabhar Breac, the Book of Ballymote, the Book of Lecan and other sources.'

So unrivalled were his qualifications in the field, that had his other occupations allowed him sufficient time to complete the work, Paul Walsh would undoubtedly have earned *'l'extrême reconnaissance des hagiographes'* promised him by the eminent Bollandist, Paul Grosjean, who recommended the inclusion of the study in the series *Monumenta Hiberniae* then envisaged as a means of celebrating the fifteenth centenary of the arrival of St. Patrick in Ireland *(Anal. Bolland.* 42 (1924) 439).

Alas, it was left to Paul Walsh's edition of the Four Masters' recension to be the only serviceable authority on the genealogies of the saints down to this day. Paul Grosjean, who remained acutely conscious of the importance of the text, published, with J. Fraser, the only hitherto printed copy of the early recension from Laud Misc. 610 (La), and in the same fasciculus of *Irish texts* (3, 1931) edited Cúchoigríche Ó Cléirigh's version of the metrical recension. By enumerating the entries of both editions, Grosjean indicated his intention of providing an index. In the current edition, by adopting the numbers of his entries, I have gone some way towards fulfilling this intention.

My edition, then, of the genealogies of the saints is a continuation and in some respects a completion of work already begun or projected by these two great scholars. In preparing it, I have been assisted in a number of ways by colleagues and friends, to all of whom I am deeply indebted. The late Anne O'Sullivan kindly placed at my disposal her photocopy and diplomatic transcript of the Book of Leinster text, and supplied me with information on the scribes and backgrounds of the Trinity College manuscripts, H.2.7 (1298) and H.2.17 (1319). Niall Buttimer made a very careful transcript of H.2.17 (1319) on my behalf, and Máirín Ní Dhonnchadha transcribed for me with equal care sections of the Bodleian manuscripts, Rawlinson B 486 and Laud Misc.610. Nollaig Ó Muraíle kindly made available to me his transcript of Dubhaltach Mac Fhirbhisigh's *naoimhsheanchas*. On matters relating to the editing of the text I have consulted on various occasions my friends, Pádraig de Brún, Rolf Baumgarten and Donnchadh Ó Corráin. The latter also kindly allowed me to use his copy of H.2.7 (1298) ff. 178-83. Máire Herbert read and made helpful comments on the whole Introduction. Tomás Ó Concheanainn helped with some of the detail given in sections 4-7. K. W. Nicholls obliged me greatly by reading the Index of Place and Tribal names, to which he added some thirty identifications. Before going to press the text was read by James Carney who very kindly drew my attention to a number of errors. Brian Ó Cuív also read the text at page-proof stage and very kindly pointed out some errors and inconsistencies. Máire Uí Chinnseala expertly saw the work through the press.

Finally, special thanks are due to Elmarie Uí Cheallacháin who, with great patience and skill, prepared a typescript of the whole work. I also wish to acknowledge gratefully a research grant from the Special Projects Section of the Arts Faculty Fund, University College, Cork.

PÁDRAIG Ó RIAIN

ABBREVIATIONS

Acta Sanctorum	The Bollandist series of that name begun by J. Bollandus, I (1643)-.
Acta SS Hib.	J. Colgan, *Acta sanctorum Hiberniae* (Louvain, 1645); reflex. facsimile published by Irish manuscripts commission, Dublin, 1948.
AFM	J. O'Donovan, *Annals of the kingdom of Ireland by the Four Masters* (Dublin, 1848-51).
AI	S. Mac Airt, *Annals of Inisfallen* (Dublin, 1951).
Anal. Bolland.	*Analecta Bollandiana* I (1882)-.
Anecd.	O. J. Bergin, R.I. Best, K. Meyer, J. G. O'Keeffe ed. *Anecdota from Irish manuscripts,* 1-5 (Halle, Dublin, 1907-13).
Arch. Hib.	*Archivium Hibernicum* I (1912)-.
AU	W. M. Hennessy, *Annals of Ulster* 1-4 (Dublin, 1887-1901).
B	The Book of Ballymote, Royal Irish Academy, Dublin.
B.Brigte	D. Ó hAodha, *Bethu Brigte* (Dublin, 1978).
BCC	A. O'Kelleher, G. Schoepperle, *Betha Colaim Chille* (Chicago, 1918).
B.Decclain	P. Power, *Life of St. Declan of Ardmore and Life of St. Mochuda of Lismore* (ITS 16, London, 1914).
B.Fenagh	W. M. Hennessy, D. H. Kelly, *The Book of Fenagh* (Dublin, 1875).
B.Moling	W. Stokes, *The birth and life of St. Moling* (Paris, 1906).
BNÉ	C. Plummer, *Bethada náem nÉrenn. Lives of Irish saints* 1, 2 (Oxford, 1922).
B.Phátr.	K. Mulchrone, *Bethu Phátraic. The tripartite life of Patrick* 1 (all published) (Dublin, 1939).
Brit. Mus. Cat.	*Catalogue of Irish manuscripts in the British Museum* 1 (1926) by S. H. O'Grady; 2 (1926) by R. Flower; 3 (1953) by R. Flower and M. Dillon.
Cáin Ad.	K. Meyer, *Cáin Adamnáin* (Oxford, 1905).
CGH	M. A. O'Brien, *Corpus Genealogiarum Hiberniae* 1 (Dublin, 1962).
Chron. Scot.	W. M. Hennessy, *Chronicum Scotorum.* Rolls Series (London, 1866).
DF	The *naoimhshenchas* section of Dubhaltach Mac Fhirbhisigh's *Leabhar Geinealach.*
Fél.	W. Stokes, *Félire Oengusso Céli Dé. The martyrology of Oengus the Culdee* (H.B.S. 29, London, 1905).
Fél.[2]	W. Stokes, *On the calendar of Oengus,* R.I.A. Trans., Irish MS. Ser. 1 (Dublin, 1880).

Gen. tracts	T. Ó Raithbheartaigh, *Genealogical tracts* 1 (Ir. MSS Comm., Dublin, 1932).
Gorm.	W. Stokes, *Félire hÚi Gormáin. The martyrology of Gorman* (H.B.S. 9, London, 1895).
GRSH	P. Walsh ed. *Genealogiae regum et sanctorum Hiberniae* (*Arch. Hib.* 5-6 (1916-17) append. and, separately, Maynooth and Dublin, 1918).
H	Trinity College MS H.2.7(= 1298).
H[1]	Trinity College MS H.2.17(= 1319).
H.B.S.	Henry Bradshaw Society.
Heist VSH	W. W. Heist, *Vitae sanctorum Hiberniae*. Subsidia hagiographica 28 (Brussels, 1965).
Hy. Fiach.	J. O'Donovan, *The genealogies, tribes and customs of Hy-Fiachrach* (Ir. Arch. Soc., Dublin, 1844).
IHS	*Irish historical studies* 1(1938)-.
Ir.lit.	C. Plummer, *Irish litanies* (H.B.S. 62, London, 1925).
Ir. texts	J. Fraser, P. Grosjean, J. G. O'Keeffe, *Irish texts* 1-5 (London, 1931-34).
IT	W. Stokes, E. Windisch, *Irische Texte mit Übersetzungen und Wörterbuch,* 2te-4te Ser. (Leipzig, 1884-1909).
ITS	Irish texts society.
JCHAS	*Journal of the Cork Historical and Archaeological Society,* second series, 1(1895)-.
JKAHS	*Journal of the Kerry Archaeological and Historical Society* 1(1968)-.
JRSAI	*The Journal of the Royal Society of Antiquaries of Ireland* 1(1849)-.
L	Book of Leinster, Royal Irish Academy, Dublin.
La	Laud Miscellany 610, Bodleian Library, Oxford.
Lb	Leabhar Breac, Royal Irish Academy, Dublin.
Lc, Lc[1]	The Book of Lecan, Royal Irish Academy, Dublin.
Lib. Hymn	J. H. Bernard, R. Atkinson ed. *The Irish Liber Hymnorum,* 1, 2 (H.B.S. 13-14, London, 1897-8).
Lis. Lives	W. Stokes, *Lives of saints from the Book of Lismore* (Oxford, 1890).
M	Book of Uí Maine, Royal Irish Academy, Dublin.
M.Don.	J. H. Todd, W. Reeves ed. *The martyrology of Donegal. A Calendar of the saints of Ireland.* (Ir. Arch. Celt. Soc., Dublin, 1864).
Misc. Celt. Soc.	J. O'Donovan ed. *Miscellany of the Celtic Society* (Dublin, 1849).
Misc. Hag. Hib.	C. Plummer, *Miscellanea hagiographica Hibernica.* Subsidia hagiographica 15 (Brussels, 1925).
M.Tall.	R. I. Best, H. J. Lawlor ed. *The martyrology of Tallaght* (H.B.S. 68, London, 1931).
NLI	National Library of Ireland.

O'Clery	S. Pender ed. *The O'Clery book of genealogies* (= *Analecta Hibernica* 18(1951)).
Onom.	E. Hogan, *Onomasticon Goedelicum* (Dublin, 1910).
Plummer VSH	C. Plummer, *Vitae Sanctorum Hiberniae* 1, 2. (Oxford, 1910).
PRIA	*Proceedings of the Royal Irish Academy.*
R	Rawlinson B 502, Bodleian Library, Oxford.
R[1]	Rawlinson B 486, Bodleian Library, Oxford.
RC	*Revue Celtique* 1(1870)-51(1934).
RIA	Royal Irish Academy.
RIA Cat.	*Catalogue of Irish manuscripts in the Royal Irish Academy.* Fasc. 1-28 (Dublin, 1926-70).
SG	S. H. O'Grady, *Silva Gadelica* 1, 2 (London, 1892).
SH	*Studia Hibernica* 1(1961)-.
T.Hom.	W. Stokes, *Three middle-Irish homilies on the lives of saints Patrick, Brigit and Columba* (Calcutta, 1877).
V.Col.	W. Reeves, *The life of St. Columba* (Ir. Arch. Celt. Soc., Dublin, 1857). A. O. and M. O. Anderson, *Adomnan's life of Columba* (Edinburgh, 1961).
V.Trip.	W. Stokes, *The tripartite life of Patrick* 1, 2. Rolls Series (London, 1887).
ZCP	*Zeitschrift für Celtische Philologie* 1(1897)-.

INTRODUCTION

1. GENERAL BACKGROUND

When Giolla Modhuda Ó Caiside boasted of knowing his saint's *senchus ... go bun gnáth a gheinealaigh,*[1] he cannot have been aware of the uniquely Celtic character of this part of Máedóc's record; so unique in fact that the eminent Bollandist and Celticist, Paul Grosjean,[2] could speak of it as a *coordonnée hagiographique* equal in importance for the Celtic saint to the two *coordonnées* — day of death and place of burial — which, since Delehaye,[3] have been accepted as the *bona fides* of the European saint. Grosjean's view requires more respect for the pedigree than its generally fictional character warrants.[4] Yet, there can be no doubt of its very real contribution to our knowledge of the Celtic saint.[5]

The particular interest in the saint's descent is an aspect of a more general Celtic concern with genealogies. In his recent work on *Les généalogies,*[6] L. Genicot concluded that the genre was a product *'des traditions "barbares" ',* without Roman or Biblical model, so rich are the remains of the Celts, followed by those of the Anglo-Saxons and Germans, when compared with the meagre genealogical record of the 'Latin' cultures of western Europe. And of the Celts it was the Irish who, orally[7] and in writing, most assiduously cultivated the genre. Already in the seventh century Irish pedigrees were being written down and when, at a much later date, the great corpus of secular pedigrees was compiled, its authors could draw on a vast quantity of written materials.[8]

Unfortunately, as yet no detailed investigation of the secular corpus

1 *BNÉ* I, 281, §266.

2 P. Grosjean, 'Notes d'hagiographie celtique', *Anal.Bolland.* 76 (1958) 379-418, p.389n.

3 H. Delehaye, *Cinq leçons sur la méthode hagiographique* (Brussels, 1934) 13-17.

4 P. C. Bartrum, *Early Welsh genealogical tracts* (Cardiff, 1966) vii, judges Welsh pedigrees 'on the whole... to be reliable', but none of them have been adequately tested. J. V. Kelleher (*SH* 3 (1963) 119) rightly states that the purpose of the pedigree was to conceal rather than to lay bare the saint's true origins, but wrongly assumes that these origins were often 'unpalatably plebeian'.

5 For other discussions of saints' genealogies see P. Ó Riain, 'Towards a methodology in early Irish hagiography', *Peritia* 1 (1982) 146-59, pp. 157-8; *idem,* 'Irish saints' genealogies', *Nomina* 7 (1983) 23-9.

6 L. Genicot, *Les généalogies* (Typ. des sources du moyen âge occident. 15, Turnhout, 1975) 14.

7 M. Dillon, 'The consecration of Irish kings', *Celtica* 10 (1973) 1-8, pp. 6-8, concludes that some of the earliest surviving fragments of Irish poems, often genealogical in character, were intended for recital at the consecration of kings.

8 J. Carney, 'Three old Irish accentual poems', *Ériu* 22 (1971) 23-80, pp. 65-73, favours a very early date for the nucleus of the Leinster poems which, he suggests, belong to the seventh century in their present form. A date in the same century is favoured by K. Meyer, 'Über die älteste irische Dichtung', I *(Abh. Preuss. Ak. Wiss.,* 1913, Phil.Hist.Cl. 6) and M. Dillon, 'A poem on the kings of the Eoganachta', *Celtica* 10 (1973) 9-14; p.13.

has been undertaken.[9] A glance suffices to show, however, that already in its earliest manifestation the composition of the Irish pedigree was governed by two characteristic and interrelated criteria, *Geblütsheiligkeit,* or pureness of pedigree, which might cause a descent to be traced back to Adam,[10] and politics whose vagaries — such commentators as Carney, Byrne, Kelleher, Dumville and Ó Corráin are agreed[11] — often found a mirror-image in ancestral permutations. The 'fine (genealogical) ladders' which the poet, praising his lord's name, was expected to scale seldom stood upright.[12] And it can hardly be a coincidence that the earliest written pedigrees are roughly contemporary with a fundamental change in the social order which, indeed, they may have been intended to legitimize, at least in part.[13]

The saint's pedigree was as much governed by these criteria as was that of the petty king; more so in fact, for its bearer had lived in a remote and otherwise completely undocumented past — the so-called Age of Saints, roughly 500-600 A.D. — which the native historians were prone to recreate in whatever image they might choose. Almost inevitably, therefore, the saint's descent became prey to those localizing forces which, as a matter of course, affected his cult, and which sometimes produced quite staggering results. Thus, a probably originally single saint Findbarr eventually acquired six or more different statements of his descent, each more or less in line with the location of one of the several churches of which he was patron.[14] Implicit in each such statement was a total claim to the saint, who was thus provided with the six or more separate and false identities by which he is known. Yet, even where the saint's original 'unity' remains unquestioned, two or more conflicting pedigrees may still dispute his origins. Molua (116), for instance, and Caimmíne (290) are each provided with three alternative descents, the genealogist being no doubt undecided as to which was the 'correct' one. Similarly, a large number of saints, including Becc m. Dé (21), Ibar (96), Moninne (98), Déclán (107), Cainnech (123), Brénainn (127) and Fursu (157), are provided with at least one variant version of their descent.

9 In the monumental *Corpus genealogiarum Hiberniae* (Dublin, 1962) M. A. O'Brien has provided an authoritative edition of the text. K. Hughes, *Early Christian Ireland: introduction to the sources* (London, 1972) 160-2, provides a general discussion of the text. E. Mac Neill, *Celtic Ireland* (Dublin, 1921) 43-63 examines its mythological content. *Idem,* 'Early Irish population-groups: their nomenclature, classification and chronology', *PRIA* 29 (1911) 59-114, treats of its early materials. J. V. Kelleher, 'The pre-Norman Irish genealogies', *IHS* 16 (1968) 138-53 comes closest to a detailed discussion of the composition of the text, but very much still remains to be done.

10 Dillon, *Celtica* 10 (1973) 12, draws attention to two early examples. See also Genicot, *Les généalogies,* 35-44.

11 Carney, *Ériu* 22 (1971) 73; F. J. Byrne, 'Tribes and tribalism in Ireland', *Ériu* 22 (1971) 128-66, pp. 146 ff; Kelleher *IHS* 16 (1968) 144-5; D. N. Dumville, 'Kingship, genealogies and regnal lists', in P. H. Sawyer, I. N. Wood ed. *Early medieval kingship* (Leeds, 1977) 72-104, pp. 73-84; D. Ó Corráin, 'Lugaid Cál and the Callraige', *Éigse* 13 (1970) 225-6. See also Mac Neill, *PRIA* 29 (1911) 93; T. F. O'Rahilly, *Early Irish history and mythology* (Dublin 1946, repr. 1964) 266-7.

12 W. Stokes, J. Strachan, *Thesaurus Palaeo-hibernicus* II (Cambridge, 1903) 295.

13 Byrne, *Ériu* 22 (1971) 153.

14 P. Ó Riain, 'St. Finnbarr: a study in a cult', *JCHAS* 82 (1977) 63-82.

In certain cases, the genealogist can be apprehended *in flagranti* as he provides his saint with local trappings. Dechoin Áed of Cúil Maine, for instance, promptly became the son of Maine as well, and *mutatis mutandis* the same is true of Berchán of Cell Ḟidne and Brandub of Tech nEchaċh. More often, however, it is the correspondence between the saint's pedigree and the location of his church that points to localization and fabrication. A society which almost invariably presented its saints as prodigious travellers saw no apparent inconsistency in providing them with very local pedigrees. Áed m. Bricc (9), for instance, whose principal church was in Mide, is given a Ceinél Ḟiachach pedigree because of the location of his church at Rahugh (Ráth Áedo), co. Westmeath, but is also assigned to the Ceinél Bóguine because Sliab Liac, which is associated with him, lay within that territory.[15] Cróine (38) is attached to the same family because of the location of her church, Tempall Cróine, in Ceinél Bóguine.[16] Dáire (39) of Mag Gamnach in Tír Amalgada is affiliated to the Uí Amalgada.[17] Fínán (7) of Tech Airthir in Uí Ercáin includes Ercán m. Déin in his descent. When taken with the comparative lateness of full-length pedigrees as such, these and many other similarly implausible correspondences suggest that *a priori* very few if any saints' pedigrees can be regarded as authentic.

Despite this general lack of authenticity, however, the study of genealogies 'may yield valuable and unforseen results' as Eoin MacNeill long ago observed.[18] The fact, for instance, that the biographer of Bairre, patron of Cork, rejected the saint's local, Uí Echach pedigree (356) — which suited so perfectly the circumstances of his birth as described in the Life[19] — in favour of a Connacht substitute (314) can hardly be dissociated from the succession to the saint of a Mayo monk in the middle of the twelfth century.[20] In this instance the adoption of the pedigree was no doubt a factor in legitimizing the presence in Cork of the Connacht monk. And, since other evidence survives of this kind of interference, the inference may well be that the form taken by the saint's pedigree often reflects that of the family which provided successors in the abbacy of his church.[21]

These then are the intrinsically important elements of the pedigree, the evidence it provides of the saint's localization, which more often than not is consistent with the location of his church, and the light it sometimes throws on the affiliations of those regarded as his

15 For the Ceinél Bóguine context see B 85b.

16 *GRSH* 39, §11.

17 *Ir.texts* 3 (1931) 2.

18 Mac Neill, *Celtic Ireland* 44. Cf. Genicot, *Les généalogies*.

19 Findbarr's mother was, allegedly, a servant of the Uí Echach king in whose household the saint was born (*BNÉ* I, 11(§5)).

20 E. Bolster, *A history of the diocese of Cork*...(Shannon, 1972) 78.

21 D. Ó Corráin, 'The early Irish churches: some aspects of organisation', in *idem* ed. *Irish Antiquity* (Cork, 1981) 327-41, p.330, cites the affiliation of Rónán mac Beraig (=325) to the Uí Chrítáin, the hereditary clerical family at Druim Inesclainn. He concludes 'that the genealogies of the saints...primarily served the needs of clerical dynasties'.

successors. The saint's real origins are generally not discoverable by means of his pedigree and even in the earlier part of the record, where the *Moccu*-formula is often used to describe the saint's tribal affiliation, examination shows that considerations of cult and not of person are likely to be involved.[22]

A brief statement of descent is the norm in the earlier part of the Irish hagiographical record.[23] Brigit's seventh-century biographer gives the names of her parents only.[24] Adamnán, writing c.700, contents himself with the names of Colum Cille's father, mother and grandfathers.[25] Patrick's seventh-century biographers, who had the saint's own statement of his descent as far back as his great-grandfather, were similarly reticent.[26] Indeed, even as late as the tenth century, no special recognition is given to the importance of the saint's pedigree either in the earliest Irish Life of Patrick, which was composed c.900, or in the Irish Life of Adamnán, to which a date of c.961-4 may be assigned.[27]

Full-length pedigrees are a feature of the later, eleventh and twelfth-century *bethada* (including the homiletic Irish Lives of Patrick, Brigit and Colum Cille) which in certain cases can be shown to have actually used the corpus of saints' pedigrees (henceforth the Corpus) as a source.[28] By implication, therefore, the Corpus, if it had been composed in any of its extant forms some centuries prior to this period, as has been suggested by J.V. Kelleher,[29] must have had a very limited circle of readers, for had it been a well-known text, it would almost certainly have been used to flesh out the already very scanty materials from which saints' Lives were composed. Furthermore, the generally full-length form of its pedigrees in all the extant versions, which seems to be a late feature, militates against a very early date for the Corpus as a whole.[30]

22 P. Ó Riain, 'Cainnech alias Colum Cille, patron of Ossory', in P. de Brún, S. Ó Coileáin, P. Ó Riain ed. *Folia Gadelica* (Cork, 1982) 20-35.

23 The same is true of the Welsh record (Bartrum, *Early Welsh gen. tracts* 22-31). See also Genicot, *Les généalogies* 11n.

24 This applies both to *Cogitosi Vita Sanctae Brigitae* and to the so-called *vita prima*. Unfortunately, Brigit's ninth-century Irish Life is acephalous (D. Ó hAodha, *Bethu Brigte* (Dublin, 1978). For a bibliography of Brigit's several *vitae* see J. F. Kenney, *The sources for the early history of Ireland: ecclesiastical* (New York, 1929) 359-62.

25 A. O. and M. O. Anderson, *Adomnan's Life of Columba* (London, 1961) 186, 546.

26 L. Bieler, *The Patrician texts in the Book of Armagh* (Dublin, 1979) 66. The later *vitae* (*secunda, quarta* and *tertia; idem, Four Latin lives of Saint Patrick* (Dublin, 1971) 51, 122) add nothing to Muirchú's statement on the saint's descent.

27 K. Mulchrone, *Bethu Phátraic* (Dublin, 1939) 5. For the Irish Life of Adamnán, of which M. Herbert and I are preparing an edition, see *Anecd.* 2 (1908) 10-20. The pedigree of Adamnán given at the beginning of the earlier text, *Cáin Adamnáin* (K. Meyer, Oxford, 1905, p.2), was probably interpolated at a much later date.

28 *Lis. Lives* 24 (Colum Cille), 35 (Brigit); *V.Trip.* 432 (Patrick). The pedigree is not found in all versions of these Lives, however.

29 J. V. Kelleher, 'The pre-Norman Irish genealogies', p. 143. He is followed by Dumville, 'Kingship, genealogies. . .', 76. More recently, D. Ó Corráin, 'The early Irish churches. . .', 330, speaks of the 'genealogies of the saints, most of which were put together in the eighth century'.

30 Patrick's pedigree with its reference to *'Britinus...in Europam venit'* and to his

Kelleher's dating of the Corpus to the ninth century was of a tentative nature, deriving not so much from a close examination of the text as from the implications of the still earlier date he had proposed for the drafting of the genealogical scheme observable in the corpus of secular pedigrees. Since he considered this scheme to be also reflected in the saints' genealogies, he can only have had in mind the recension represented by the Book of Leinster (L) and by its derivative texts, BLcLb, for, with the exception of the text in H.2.17 (1319) which is very short and completely unrelated in its arrangement to the genealogical scheme of the secular corpus, no other version of the Corpus shows evidence of a tribal grouping of the entries. Examination shows, however, that L's scheme, whatever may be said of its affinity to that of the secular corpus, is likely to have been first devised by Áed mac Crimthainn, the twelfth-century scribe and probable redactor of the recension.[31]

So much for an early dating of the Corpus on grounds of its arrangement. The earliest extant manuscript version, that preserved in Rawlinson B 502 (R), formerly known as the Book of Glendalough,[32] was written down in the early part of the twelfth century. Internal evidence suggests, however, that this recension of the text was first composed at the Columban monastery of Kells at a date not earlier, and perhaps a generation or so later, than 938, the year in which Dubthach, the final entry in its list of Colum Cille's successors, died.[33] At the earliest, therefore, a date in the middle or in the second half of the tenth century seems possible for this recension.

Comparison of this recension with that composed in Ormond, and now represented by MR[1]LaH and the *recensio minor* (pp. xxxviii-ix below), provides some slight evidence of the use of a common source whose provenance, in the case of the Ormond text, points to north-east Ulster. It may well be, therefore, that a text, possibly composed at the monastery of Bangor (whose patron, Comgall, is given particular prominence), was already in existence in the early part of the tenth century.

The grounds for an early dating of the Corpus in any form are, however, by no means very strong and, given the fact of its relatively late reception by other branches of Irish hagiography, such as the Lives of saints, it is fair to say that the scene of the text seems to be set

descent from 'Fergus Lethderg...Nóe' reveals the influence of the Leabhar Gabhála (R. A. Macalister ed., *Lebor Gabála Érenn* 1(ITS 34, 1938) 22 §10, 160 §99, 166 §102; 3(ITS 39, 1940) 126 §245, 148 §264). If, as seems likely, its 'British' content derives ultimately from Nennius's *Liber Brittonum* (*Lebor Bretnach*), then this part may not have been composed until the mid- to late eleventh century, the period of its reception and translation in Ireland (D. Dumville, 'The textual history of 'Lebor Bretnach', *Éigse* 16 (1976) 255-73).

31 It should be borne in mind that just before tackling the pedigrees of the saints Áed had finished copying the L version of the secular corpus.

32 P. Ó Riain, 'The Book of Glendalough or Rawlinson B 502', *Éigse* 18 (1981) 161-76.

33 See below (section 8).

by the otherwise demonstrable upsurge of interest in the Irish saints which made its appearance in the eleventh century.

The text of the Book of Leinster (L), more properly Leabhar na Nuachongbála, which is dated to the period after 1152, has been chosen as the basis of this edition of the Corpus for the following reasons. The only earlier manuscript, Rawlinson B 502 (R), more properly Leabhar Glinne Dá Locha, which was compiled c.1120-30, preserves the Corpus in a fragmentary form only, its lacuna being filled by the very much later (but generally reliable) Book of Lecan (Lc^1), otherwise Leabhar Mór Leacáin. Although using R as a source, L, which is followed by three other manuscripts, provides a very independent recension of the text. As such, therefore, it represents the largest single group within the eleven manuscripts containing the text. Also, L's version of the Corpus (1-326) leads off in the manuscript a collection of miscellaneous hagiographical texts of which all those not hitherto edited critically, i.e. with notes and indexes, are here annotated and indexed for the first time (663-735). In other words, the whole of the hagiographical section of the Book of Leinster, the *recueil encyclopédique classique,* as Grosjean styled it,[34] minus the texts of the martyrology of Tallaght and of the litanies of Irish saints, which have already been edited critically,[35] is covered by this edition.

With a view to completeness, two texts not contained in L are added here. These are the *recensio minor (rec.min.)* or abbreviated version of the Corpus (416-661) — here taken from the Book of Lecan (Lc) — of which Grosjean has already published the version in Laud Misc. 610 (La),[36] and the *recensio metrica* (662) or metrical recension, which is better known as *Náemshenchus náem Inse Fáil,* and which has also been published by Grosjean in its most recent form.[37] Both previous editions are limited to a printing of the text.

In the discussion which follows, each recension of the Corpus is examined with a view to identifying its provenance, sources and relationships. The miscellaneous items (663-735),[38] which follow the Corpus in L, are discussed separately in the notes to the text. In certain cases, however, e.g. 674-89, 722, these materials formed part of the main text of recensions other than L and, as such, are also taken into account here.

2. THE L RECENSION

The Book of Leinster (L), formerly Leabhar na Nuachongbhála, or the Book of Oughaval, at which church in co. Laois it was kept, is now preserved in the library of Trinity College, Dublin.[39] Its compilation

34 *Anal. Bolland.* 76 (1959) 389.
35 R. I. Best, H. J. Lawlor, *The martyrology of Tallaght* (H.B.S. 68, 1931); C. Plummer, *Irish litanies* (H.B.S. 62, 1925).
36 *Ir. texts* 3 (1931) 87-94 (§§1-205).
37 *Ibid.* 40-80.
38 L's text ends at 735; 736 is from RLc^1; 737-8 are from M.
39 In the preparation of this edition I have used R. Atkinson ed., *Book of Leinster,*

was begun in or about the year 1152 and was completed by several scribes, foremost of whom, Áed mac Crimthainn, abbot of Terryglass in co. Tipperary, was a native of the area around Oughaval in co. Laois. He wrote the greater part of the manuscript, including ff. 347-54 and 365-74 which contain the texts edited here.[40]

There is evidence to suggest that Áed not only wrote this recension of the Corpus — henceforth referred to as L — but also composed it. Thus, while the aim of the redactor was to produce a text which grouped the saints in accordance with their tribal affiliations, the different sections almost invariably begin at the heads of columns, e.g. Airgialla (347f), Déise (348b) Dál nAraide (348d), and Mumain (350c). Since there is no interruption of the text in these cases, however, nor any occurrence of blank spaces, additions must have been made at the ends of preceding columns or in the margins. And, as it happens, a good deal of material, mostly written by Áed in the smaller than normal hand which he adopted, among other occasions, when departing from his exemplar, does seem to have been interpolated. This applies to marginal additions as well as to the contents of whole columns which are characteristically written in a smaller hand. Thus entries 68-78 (= L 347-48 *in marg.*), consisting of a miscellaneous group of saints, intervene between two Airgialla saints, Énna (67) and Lúrach (79), both of whom are in sequence in the Book of Glendalough, L's likely source here as elsewhere. In the same way, entries 160-182 (= 349g-350a), which are completely out of character with the remainder of the Corpus, appear to have been added to the text, R again being the source for at least some of them, i.e. 170, 172, 173, 175, which form a sequence in that manuscript's final list of entries (R 52Ri = Lc 40Vb).

If L was constructed in the manner described, then Áed, who had a fairly critical approach to his text, must also have been the redactor. The very extensive use of reference marks, most of which single out key persons in the pedigrees, but some of which draw attention to marginal additions (e.g. 91^{u-u}, 92^{i-i}, 124^{c-c}), shows that the text was written in order to be used. In other words, its author often returned to it.

Another even clearer pointer to Áed's authorship of the recension is the manner in which he chose to arrange the saints. His main source, the Book of Glendalough (R), shows no evidence of an arrangement along tribal lines. Lacking an immediate model for this text, therefore, it is not surprising that Áed's arrangement of the saints should strike a personal note. His own family, the Uí Chrimthainn

lithographic facsimile (Dublin, 1880) as well as a diplomatic transcript of the text which was very kindly placed at my disposal by Anne O'Sullivan. I have also collated the text with a photocopy of the manuscript and, to obtain clarification on certain points, I have consulted the original manuscript.

40 For an account of the manuscript see R. I. Best, O. Bergin, M. A. O'Brien, *The Book of Leinster formerly Lebar na Núachongbála* 1 (Dublin, 1954) xi-xxvi; W. O'Sullivan, 'Notes on the scripts and make-up of the Book of Leinster', *Celtica* 7 (1966) 1-31.

(Chrimthannáin), claimed descent from Crimthann Án, son of Cathaír Mór, ancestor of the Laigin. Their lands however, were in Loígis and it is to the churches and saints of this area that Áed's first loyalties were owed.[41] Thus, despite the fact that the family had held the succession to the abbacy of Terryglass, co. Tipperary, for many centuries — long enough to impose their own pedigree on the church's patron, Colum,[42] their attachment to Clonenagh, a Fothairt foundation, appears to have counted for more. The annal which records the violent death in 845 of Áed mac Duib Dá Chrích of the Uí Chrimthannáin, styles him 'abbot of Tír Dá Glas and Cluain Eidnech'.[43] Two hundred years later, in 1069, following the treacherous slaying of Gilla Muire mac Duib, chief of the Uí Chrimthainn, at the church of Timahoe (Tech Mochua) in co. Laois, the assassin was dispatched 'in revenge of Fintan (of Clonenagh) Mochua (of Timahoe) and Colman (of Oughaval)', a triad whose composition accurately reflects the local order and distribution of Uí Chrimthannáin allegiance.[44]

The emphasis in the arrangement of Áed's version of the Corpus could almost be described as an elaboration of this annal. Following Patrick and Brigit, the two indispensable introductory entries,[45] are Fintan (3) and Mochua (5) (the intervening saint Sárnat (4) being a marginal addition) who are succeeded by two other saints belonging to the Fothairt. Colmán of Oughaval, while he is tucked away in the body of the text, is entered twice (145, 187), on each occasion in apparent response to the mention of a Loígis saint, Óenu (144) and Aduar (186). Finally, pride of place in the Laigin section goes to Colum of Terryglass (241) and to Momáedóc (242), both of whom are affiliated to Áed's own family, the Uí Chrimthannáin. In sum, therefore, a more suitable author of the L text than its scribe, Áed mac Crimthainn, could hardly be found.

The detail of the text's tribal arrangement is as follows:

1. *Patrick, Brigit* (1, 2).

2. *Fothairt;* 5 entries (3-7) including a marginal addition (4).

3. *Uí Néill, Connachta;* 54 entries (8-46, 70-75, 77, 78, 81-86, 90) including several added in the margins of col.s 347, 348 and, after some Airgialla entries, in 348a.

4. *Airgialla:* 27 entries (47-67, 69, 76, 79, 80) beginning at the top of col. 347f and including additions in the margins of 347. The sequence is disturbed by the addition of some Uí Néill saints (see 3 above).

41 For an account of Áed, including most of the detail which follows here, see O'Sullivan, *Celtica* 7 (1966) 1-2.

42 For Colum's pedigree see Corp. 241. For the evidence in favour of Colum's basic identity with Colum Cille see Ó Riain, *Peritia* 1 (1982) 150-51.

43 AU s.a. 844.

44 AFM 1069.

45 Brigit yields second place to Ruadán in the Lothra recension (Rawlinson B 486, R^1) and to Trea ingen Chairthinn in H. In all other versions (other than BLc and H^1 which omit her, and La which places her much further down the list) she follows Patrick.

5. *Déise;* 8 entries (87-89, 91-94, 107), beginning at the top of col. 348b. The sequence is broken by an addition (90) at the foot of 348b. Déclán's pedigree (107) was added at the foot of 348e.

6. *Dál nAraide;* 27 entries (95-106, 108-121, 138) beginning at the top of col. 348d (95 is added in at foot of the preceding col.). The sequence is disturbed by a Déise entry (107); 138 (Commán) duplicates 109.

7. *Ulaid, 'Síl Ír';* 46 entries (122-137, 139-154, 156-159, 184-89) beginning at the top of col. 348h. Disturbing the sequence is Commán (138) of Dál nAraide, Munnu (155) of Corco Raíde, and two columns of miscellaneous additions 160-182; 183 (Máel Anfaid) belongs to the Osraige, but it should be noted that Loígis saints are three times included in this section (144, 145, 156, 186, 187). Otherwise the section includes Dál Fiatach, Dál mBuain and Conmaicne saints.

8. *Mumain;* 51 entries (190-240) beginning at the top of col. 350c and headed *Mumnenses sancti.* The third entry, however, 192 (Mac Doborchon), is supplied with an Uí Bairrche pedigree. Pride of place goes to the Dál Cais representative, Martan (190), Colmán of the Eoganachta taking second place. Also included in the section are saints of the Cianachta, Corco Loígde, Fir Muige, Síl Chonaire and Dál Riata (cf. *CGH* 246-9).

9. *Laigin:* 54 entries (241-294) beginning at the top of col. 351d, and headed *Lagnenses sancti.* The sequence, which covers a large range of Laigin families, including Uí Chrimthannáin, Uí Dúnlainge. Dál Meisin Corb, Uí Cheinselaig and Uí Bairrche, also takes in Osraige and Uí Fáilge, but not Loíchis (see 7 above). The sequence is twice disturbed, i.e. following 263 where a number of other saints Berchán are added with a note (271) to explain their inclusion here, and at 279 where two saints of Ceinél Eogain are entered.

10. *Miscellany;* 32 entries (295-326). Included are saints of Síl Ír, Corco Loígde, Ciarraige, Airgialla, Eoganachta etc. Appropriately, however, and perhaps in imitation of R (see below), Áed completed his recension with an entry on Patrick (326).

3. SOURCES OF THE L RECENSION

Among the many books drawn upon by Áed mac Crimthainn, 'chief historian of Leinster in wisdom, knowledge, cultivation of books, learning and study',[46] and by his fellow scribes, a very important place was occupied by the Book of Glendalough, now Rawlinson B 502 (R), which was compiled c.1120-30. Examination of L's version of the corpus of secular pedigrees will no doubt bear out this statement. The composition of L's version of the corpus of saints' pedigrees already warrants it. The arrangement of the entries, their text and in some cases evidence of a palaeographical nature combine to show how heavily dependent Áed was on R.

46 Áed is so addressed in a letter from Find Ua Gormáin, bishop of Kildare; see Best, Bergin, O'Brien, *The Book of Leinster . . .*, xvi.

Within the limits set by Áed's decision to group his saints along tribal lines, there is a remarkable amount of agreement in the arrangement of entries, as the following random sequences show:

L	34	35	36	122	123	124	125	196	197	198	199
RLc[1]	79	81	87	29	30	32	33	65	69	70	72

L	243	244	245	246	247	248	249
RLc[1]	42	48	38	49	50	51	59

In a text such as the Corpus, agreement of this kind can only stem from the use of the earlier manuscript as a source. Áed's text which, drawing on his genealogical expertise as 'chief historian of Leinster,' he often changes, adding or subtracting materials, nevertheless shows a considerable amount of agreement with that of RLc[1], even down to the occasional dot over *m* and *n,* as in *ṁBechain* (175[b]). And while Áed's skill and R's generally very careful text ensured the survival of very little in the way of common error or misreadings of the source, that which does occur is all the more important as evidence.

At 37[c-c], where L's otherwise unrecorded *Dromma* is written as an alternative to *Cluana* in the placename Cluain Railgech, now, apparently, Clonrelick in co. Westmeath, the explanation may be that R's cł (i.e. *cluana*) is written almost as if the *l* were the shaft of the letter *d.* Similarly, at 72[a], L's inadmissible *m. Fiachra* for *m. Fiachna* no doubt resulted from R's tendency to allow the initial minim of *n* to dip below the (notional) line, thus resembling *r.* Finally, at 210[b], L's reading *hUriu* for the correct *hUdriu (Uidriu)*[47] is an error it shares with Lc[1], representing R for which the text is lacking at this point.

Where Áed adds a detail, he can sometimes be seen to have drawn it from a text found elsewhere in R. In adding information concerning mothers, for instance, Áed uses a text much closer to Lc[1] than to his own version of the tract on the mothers of the saints (722). The inference must be that R was again his source, although the text is now missing from that manuscript. Similarly, Áed's entries, 303, 304 occur in much the same form in R's version of the corpus of secular pedigrees (R 160b 53-5, *CGH* 311) but are not reproduced in the L version of the secular corpus. Other such possible borrowings from the R version of the secular corpus are 166-7 and 321-3. Of these, 321 is also reproduced in L's version of the same text, but Áed's placing of *sunt* before *Druimm Inasclainn,* as in R (148a 54), seems to confirm his use of that manuscript as a source.

For the rest, Áed appended a good deal of material to his version of the Corpus in the form of *disiecta membra* (663-728). Some sections, i.e. 674-89,[48] which contain biblical entries, and 707-08, which are lists of homonymous saints, may have been edited from R.[49] Others,

47 For the correct form see *CGH* 380.

48 A number of these entries are in fact confined to the BLc[1] version which used R as a source at this point.

49 See note to 707-8. Part of 690 may also have been taken from R (see note).

however, have a thoroughly independent appearance. Thus Áed's local associations with Terryglass and with Fothairt churches were no doubt responsible for the inclusion of some Terryglass items (667-8) as well as two very detailed and highly interesting tracts on saints and churches connected with the cult of St. Brigit (663, 670).

Áed's recension, with its well-thought out, if not always happily completed, arrangement of the entries, with its evidence of careful copy-reading and extensive use of references, is a monument to the 'learning and study' of its scribe and author, whose *floruit* coincided with the beginnings of a dramatic decline in the cultivation of Irish letters. A measure of the fall in the standards of Áed's successors is the mixture of carelessness and ignorance which characterizes the common source of the three manuscripts, The Books of Ballymote (B) and Lecan (Lc) and the Leabhar Breac (Lb), that reproduce his text.

4. THE COMMON SOURCE OF BLcLb

The versions of the Corpus preserved in the roughly contemporary, late fourteenth or early fifteenth-century Books of Ballymote (B), Lecan (Lc), and Duniry, otherwise the Leabhar Breac (Lb), each of which will be discussed *separatim* below, have a manifest affinity both to each other and to the Book of Leinster (L). Thus reference to the Table of Entries shows that, allowing for some exceptions, all four manuscripts are in general agreement in the number and arrangement of their entries. On the other hand, reference to the variant readings *passim* shows that, when disagreeing with L, manuscripts B, Lc and Lb tend to agree among themselves; L cannot therefore have been their immediate common source. Further examination shows, however, that this source must have been copied directly from L.[50]

The most impressive piece of evidence is at 118[c-c] where L's *Fidrui m. Diarmata* has the abbreviation ɫ (= *uel, nó*) added to its first component in BLb, which read *Fidrui ɫ m. Diarmata.*[51] Evidently, the scribe of the common source had misconstrued Áed mac Crimthainn's use of a stroke through the head of *d* in *cend* (= cend*fota*), which, while it belongs to the adjacent column, is here run on to *m. Diarmata,* taking it to represent the abbreviation ɫ. Examples of other misconstructions, which can best be explained by reference to L, are as follows:

124[j-j]; L *Duib Dechoin* (with dots as marks of reference under *Duib*); B(Lb) *Da(th)chon*. Lc omits.
209[j]; L *Fortcheirn* (*Fīcħ* MS); BLcLb *Fortchi.*
274e; L *Cormaic Et Falbe* (with *Et* interrupting a sequence of *m.* = *mac*); BLcLb *Cormaic m. Failbhi.*
670.16[i]; L *Mani* (*Man,* MS); BLcLb *Manuis.*

50 See also Ó Riain, *Éigse* 18 (1981) 162-4.
51 No doubt reacting to the ɫ, Lc omits *m. Fidrui.*

This clear lack of skill in interpreting his source is matched by the scribe's failure to comprehend Áed's arrangement of the materials and the system of references which supplements it. Thus marginal glosses are incorporated where they occur rather than where they belong (84, 85, 91, 92, 168[b-b]). Also, Áed's use of Latin is almost invariably misunderstood (122[m-m], 209[b-b] (where the corruption is translated into a saint's mother), 311[h-h], 690[a-a] etc.). Similarly, titles sometimes become part of personal names as in BLcLb's *Decoimet* for Áed's perfectly legible *Dechoin Áed* (58).

This evidence of scribal incompetence indicates a date for the completion of the work nearer to the period of the manuscripts which preserve it than to that of the original on which it is based. Yet, some features seem to belie this implication. For instance, many additions to L's text, which do not appear to have been interpolated by a very much later hand, are omitted by the common source of BLcLb, e.g. 182[a], 211[b], 242[d-d], 252[a-a] etc.[52] Also, there is some slight textual evidence to suggest that the author of the Irish Life of Findchú of Brí Gobann, which was hardly composed as late as the end of the fourteenth century, drew on the common source for his pedigree of the saint.[53]

On the whole, however, this evidence is very tenuous and it seems preferable to assume that the common source was never more than an *ad hoc* copy of L, transcribed by a copyist of no great ability who had been commissioned to do so by one or other of the 'directors' of the great manuscript compilations then in progress west of the Shannon. The fact that B, which is the most faithful copy of the common source, turned to a completely different *vorlage* for its introductory material (which Lb also obtained elsewhere) suggests that the scribe of the common source had not bothered to include L's *disiecta membra* (663-728). The suspicion must be, therefore, that the common source may never have formed part of a codex in its own right.

5. THE BOOK OF BALLYMOTE (B)

Now preserved in the Royal Irish Academy (RIA 23 p 12),[54] The Book of Ballymote (B) was compiled in the late fourteenth century (between 1383 and 1397) by a number of scribes, including the otherwise unknown 'Robeartus Mac Síthigh', who, having transcribed

52 Anne O'Sullivan informs me that while these additions tend to be 'rubbed and faint' they could have been made by the hand of the text. And, at any rate, they appear to have been made 'very early'.

53 *Lis.Lives* 84-98. The Life, which has yet to be edited critically, names the saint's father as Findlug, thus providing a composite version of the pedigree (see 78, 320.1.2.). Its readings, *Abruinn, Erca Deirg* are closest to the representatives of the common source. Kenney, *Sources* . . ., 458 suggests a date c.1100 but this seems too early.

54 *RIA Cat.* 1610-55. In the preparation of this edition I have used R. Atkinson ed., *The Book of Ballymote,* photographic facsimile (Dublin, 1887). See also T. Ó Concheanainn, 'The Book of Ballymote', *Celtica* 14 (1981) 15-25.

the text of the pedigrees of the saints (212a-225c) wrote: *Finit amen finit don naemhseanchas Robeartus Mac Sithigh scripsit.*

Of the three manuscripts based on the common source, B is by far the most faithful copy, reproducing almost all the text (unlike Lc, which regularly, and Lb, which occasionally (43, 66, 68, 132 etc.), omit entries) including of course its errors, which are frequently compounded. A somewhat careless though faithful scribe, Mac Síthigh adds almost nothing to his source beyond the occasional final generation or two. Where his source appears to have run out, however, the scribe turned to a new manuscript. Thus the introductory sections, consisting of the tract on the mothers of the saints (722) and the biblical and classical pedigrees (674-689), are drawn not from L, which relegates these materials to its *disiecta membra,* but from a source which Lc[1] also used.[55] The same applies to the copy of the lists of homonymous Irish saints (707-8), which is followed by the same invocation as was added by the scribe of the Book of Glendalough (Rawlinson B 502) to his version of the lists.[56] While in overall agreement with R, BLc[1] share a sufficient number of readings and errors in these texts to indicate their derivation from a common source which, however, appears to have been copied directly from Rawlinson B 502.

Finally, a later and very faithful copy of Mac Síthigh's text, which was not used in the preparation of this edition, is contained in the fifteenth-century part of the British Library manuscript Add. 30512 (ff. 56-67), a still later copy of which survives in the eighteenth-century Trinity College, Dublin MS, H.1.11 (= 1285), pp. 168-179, in the hand-writing of Hugh O'Daly.[57]

6. THE BOOK OF LECAN (Lc)

Now preserved in the Royal Irish Academy (RIA 23 P 2),[58] the Book of Lecan (Lc) was compiled about the year 1397 by a number of scribes, mainly, however, by Giolla Íosa Mac Fhirbhisigh who also copied its version of the pedigrees of the saints. Mac Fhirbhisigh's immediate *vorlage* was not the common source but, as a misplaced scribal note at f. 42Rd 13 shows, a composite version drawn partly, i.e. ff. 40Vc 37-46Vb 44 (Lc), from that source (here named *'slicht Liubair na Fuachongbala',* the version of the Book of Leinster) and partly, i.e. ff. 34Ra 1-40Vc 35, 47Ra 1-49Re 46 (Lc[1]), from a source

55 See also P. Ó Riain, 'NLI G 2, f.3 and the Book of Glendalough', *ZCP* 39 (1982) 29-32.

56 BLc[1] agree in omitting R's [...]*uit* from their version and share the mis-spelling *prescibit.*

57 Collation of these texts with B showed that they add nothing of interest to their source.

58 *RIA Cat.*1551-1610; cf. P. Walsh, 'The Great Book of Lecan', in C. Ó Lochlainn ed. *Irish men of learning* (Dublin, 1947) 102-118; T. Ó Concheanainn, 'The scribe of the Leabhar Breac', *Ériu* 24 (1973) 64-79; pp. 76-79. In the preparation of this edition I have used K. Mulchrone ed., *The Book of Lecan: Leabhar Mór Mhic Fhir Bhisigh Leacain,* Ir. MSS. Comm. collotype facsimiles of Ir. MSS. 11 (Dublin, 1937).

given as *'slicht Libair Glinni Da Lach'*, the version of the Book of Glendalough. This latter version, which I have identified elsewhere as Rawlinson B 502 (R), will be discussed below.[59]

The version deriving from the common source commences with an entry on *Mochua* (written *Mochuta*) (5), to which Mac Fhirbhisigh prefixed a mark of reference, no doubt following the example of his source. On the whole, Lc is a faithful copy of its source with the qualification that Mac Fhirbhisigh omitted a large number of entries, of which three only, 20, 26, 184, are not contained in the version deriving from the other source. Occasionally, Mac Fhirbhisigh drew on his fund of local knowledge to improve the text (e.g. 236), even substituting at one point a completely different descent (216).

7. THE LEABHAR BREAC (Lb)

Now in the Royal Irish Academy (RIA 23 P 16),[60] this early fifteenth-century manuscript was kept at Dún Daighre (Duniry) in south co. Galway (whence its other name Leabhar Mór Dúna Daighre), a place connected with the learned family of Clann Aodhagáin. Its single, nameless scribe refers to various places of writing, however, including the Mac Aodhagáin law school at Cluain Leathan in Múscraighe Tíre, now north county Tipperary.[61] Lb's text of the pedigrees of the saints (ff. 13a 1-23b 12) derives in the main from the common source. Unlike the other representatives of this version, however, Lb reveals evidence of a scribe who was prepared to correct (e.g. 258[a-a]) and even radically depart from his source. Thus entries are frequently rearranged, particularly in the early part of the work. (The Lb sequence on f.14 corresponds to L 86, 81, 98, 90, 15, 24, 39, 25, 37). The grounds for this kind of disarrangement are not always apparent. Elsewhere, however, the scribe has clearly been influenced by rival versions of the Corpus. Thus Baíthíne (327) follows Colum Cille (8) as in RLc^1, whose text may also have influenced Lb's versions of entries 129 and 191. Moreover, the major extraneous influence appears to have been a version of the Ormond recension (now represented by MR^{1}LaH and *rec. min.*) from which Lb drew its two introductory biblical entries, placing Christ's pedigree before that of Mary as in M and R^1.[62] Also, Lb's final group of ten entries (23ab), which do not follow the common source and are mostly omitted from L, corresponds to M 79, 73, 88, 17, 94, 95, 154, 163, 82, the implication being that Lb was using a source close to M; similarly, the entry on Cuimmíne Cadan (330) is confined to Lb and some

59 Ó Riain, *Éigse* 18 (1981) 161-76.
60 *RIA Cat.* 3379-3404. In the preparation of this edition I have used a photostat copy of the original as well as the lithographic facsimile published by the Royal Irish Academy, Dublin, 1876.
61 *Ibid.* See also Ó Concheanainn, *Ériu* 24 (1973) 64-79.
62 The original form of the Ormond recension is best preserved in R^{1}H; M's version draws extensively on L.

Ormond manuscripts. Textual evidence (20, 106, 285 etc.) tends to corroborate this inference, and changes or improvements in Lb's text are often paralleled in the Ormond recension (63^{f}, 117^{f}, 122$^{c\text{-}c}$, 126^{f,h,m}, 246$^{a\text{-}a,\ h\text{-}h}$, 249^{h}, 250$^{b\text{-}b}$ etc.).

Characteristic of Lb's scribe is his concern with 'improving' the language of his original. *Teora* and *di* regularly replace *tri* and *da; Fothartaib* and *Góedelaib* become *Fothartu* (sic) and *Goedelu* (sic). And, for some inexplicable reason, the prepositions *i* and *oc* almost invariably give way to *ó*.

8. THE BOOK OF GLENDALOUGH RECENSION (RLc^{1})

The earliest extant manuscript version of the Corpus is that fragmentarily preserved in Rawlinson B 502 ff. 51Ra 1-52Ri 56 (R), formerly Leabhar Glinne Dá Locha or the Book of Glendalough, which was compiled sometime after 1120 and probably c.1130 by an unknown but excellent scribe, and which is now in the Bodleian Library, Oxford.[63] R's lacuna, which occurs in the early part of the text, is made up by the ultimately derivative version in the late fourteenth-century Book of Lecan ff. 34Ra 1-40Vc 35 (Lc^{1}).[64] In addition to the tract on the mothers of the saints (722), the collection of biblical and classical entries (674-89), and a prose and verse tract on Patrick's household (671, 672), Lc^{1} contains seventy-eight entries (= RLc^{1} 1-78) now wanting in R. Independent evidence suggests that with the possible exception of 672, which seems late, almost all of these items were originally contained in R.[65]

The fact that R was compiled at Glendalough does not appear to have influenced its version of the Corpus. Cóemgein's pedigree (250), for instance, is given neither a particular prominence nor undue length, and equally little is made of such other local saints as those of the Dál Meisin Corb. If R's scribe had no apparent interest in introducing a local bias to the text, the same cannot be said of the author of his source who, judging by the arrangement of the initial entries, had a very obvious axe to grind. Thus Colum Cille's pedigree, which follows in third place those of the ubiquitous Patrick and Brigit,[66] triggered the pedigrees of no less than fourteen of his *comharbaí,* or successors, in the headship of the Columban *paruchia,*

63 In the preparation of this edition I have used the collotype facsimile of Rawlinson B 502 introduced and indexed by K. Meyer, Oxford, 1909. I have also consulted the original manuscript.

64 Ó Riain, *Éigse* 18 (1981) 161-76, pp. 161-66.

65 Ó Riain, *ZCP* 39 (1982) 29-32. It may be noted, however, that Lc^{1} occasionally makes an independent addition to the text.

66 Colum Cille's relegation to eighth place in L is explained by the fact that Áed mac Crimthainn's concern at this point was to intrude some Fothairt saints immediately after Brigit. Áed's lack of interest in the Columban section of the earlier manuscript is illustrated by his omission of all Colum's successors, taking Áed m. Bricc (who follows Colum's last-named successor in R) as his next entry (9).

beginning with Baíthíne, the saint's immediate successor, and ending with abbot Dubthach who died in 938. Firstly, then, R's *vorlage,* which must have been one of the earliest versions of the Corpus, cannot have been composed before c. 940.[67] Secondly, however, since the redactor obviously had a keen interest in Columban matters, we may assume that he was writing in the scriptorium of a Columban house. And this, as the evidence of subsequent entries shows, is likely to have been at Kells which, by the tenth century, seems to have become the chief church of the *paruchia.*

The last of the Columban abbots, Dubthach, is followed by Áed m. Bricc (RLc[1] 18) whose principal church, Ráth Áedo (Rahugh), lay in Mide; Kells was located in Brega. Aed qualified for inclusion here, however, by virtue of his Columban connexion, through Sliab Liac, in the parish of Glencolumbkille, co. Donegal.[68] After Áed are entered Colmán and his brothers of the Déise Breg, a family which held what is now the barony of Deece in co. Meath, and these are followed by eight saints (RLc[1] 21-8) whose common bond is their adherence to the Clann Lugdach of Ceinél Lóegaire, a family which held lands around Trim in co. Meath.

With this preponderance of Columban and Brega saints among the first twenty-eight entries, the Kells redactor must have felt that he had made his point and was now free to use other criteria in arranging what remained of his text. Midland saints, while still very common, no longer form groups as such. Also, the common feature shared by RLc[1] 29-34 (i.e. Findén of Clonard, Cainnech, Comgall, Brénainn of Birr, Ciarán and Findén of Moville) is as likely to have been their pre-eminence among the Irish saints as the fact that each is associated with Colum Cille in the early part of his record.[69] The importance of the saints as such may also explain RLc[1] 46-8 (i.e. Brénainn of Clonfert, Colum of Terryglass and Tigernach of Clones). Elsewhere, however, other considerations prevailed. Thus a group of Cork saints is formed by RLc[1] 114-7, and this is matched by a Munster series at RLc[1] 193-8. Also, female saints tend to be grouped together (RLc[1] 64-6, 68-70, 95-107, 178-81).

The recension proper ends at RLc[1] 217-25 with a series of miscellaneous entries which is appropriately rounded off by a

67 The next abbot, Dub Dúin, died in 959, by which time there is independent evidence, i.e. through the Irish Life of Adamnán, which Máire Herbert and I date to c.961-4, of a Columban interest in its saints and of hagiographical activity at Kells. It may well be, however, that the redactor was using a ready-made list drawn up some generations before his time. Finally, as M. Herbert points out to me, the list is incomplete, such abbots as Cellach (†815) the reputed founder of Kells, being omitted.

68 The scholiasts to the Irish calendars (*Gorm., Fél.* and *M.Don.*) give Áed's two churches equal prominence on his official day (Nov. 10). Elsewhere in *M.Tall* (July 30), however, Sliab Liac only is mentioned. Áed's *vita* (*Heist VSH* 167-81, *Plummer VSH* 1, 34-45) was composed in Mide: it stresses, however, the saint's relationship with Colum Cille.

69 Mentioned on several occasions by Adamnán without further identification, Finnio becomes the saint both of Moville and of Clonard in the later biography of Colum Cille. All the other saints are specifically mentioned by Adamnán.

reference to St. Patrick.[70] Lc^1, whose immediate source clearly was not R itself, added four pedigrees (226-29) — Bairre, Mac Liac, Molaise and Diarmait — from a source close to the Ormond recension; thus, in Bairre's pedigree, Lc^1 agrees with MR^1 in reading *(F)indeda* for *Ninneda.*

Other additions to Lc^1 are Attracht (RLc^1 92), which is not found in any other recension, Diarmait of Inis Chlothrann (RLc^1 147), Crónán m. Óengusa (RLc^1 148) and Colco m. Áeda (RLc^1 149). The three latter entries concern Uí Fhiachrach saints and were no doubt interpolated west of the Shannon, perhaps by Mac Fhirbhisigh himself who lived at Lecan in Tír Fhiachrach. Again, the source was a version of the Ormond recension since Lc^1 147-8 occur in precisely the same order in MR^1. Lc^1's final addition, Molaise (RLc^1 171), is also given local colour, the more usual Inis Muiredaig being replaced by Echros, now Aughris townland in the barony of Tireragh (Tír Fhiachrach). This entry is otherwise found only in the Ormond recension.

9. THE ORMOND RECENSION

The name Ormond has been chosen for want of a better term to describe a recension one of whose earliest manuscript versions, the mid- to late fourteenth-century Rawlinson B 486 (R^1), was written at Lothra (Lorrha) in north-west Tipperary, within the barony of Lower Ormond, mainly by a scribe called Mac Raith Mac an Ghabhann na Scéal. Another member of this family, Fáelán Mac an Ghabhann na Scéal, wrote the version in the Book of Uí Mhaine (M) sometime between 1378-94, and, together, these two manuscripts share an interest in north Munster with H.2.7 (= 1298) (H) and Laud Misc. 610 (La) which is reinforced by correspondences in text and arrangement. Finally, while the arrangement of its initial entries evinces no particular interest in north Munster, the *recensio minor (rec.min.)* also belongs to this group on textual and other grounds.

Reference to the variant readings throughout the Corpus reveals a generally close agreement between the texts of MR^{1}HLa; *rec. min.*'s readings are given separately (416-661). Particularly striking in this connexion is the agreement between MR^{1}La, MLa being possibly a little closer to each other than either to R^1. An independent reading is more often provided by H but, as reference to the variants of 60, 67, 99, 123^{c}, 131, 136$^{c\text{-}c,\ d\text{-}d}$ etc. shows, this manuscript must also be assigned to the group on textual grounds.

If anything, the agreement in arrangement between H and M is a more striking indication of the former's affinity to the group. Thus, the sequence M 66-109 corresponds to H 16, 18, 22, 21, 24, 25, 32, 33, 35, 36, 38, 37, 40, 8, 42, 9, 43, 44, 46-9, 52-4, 59-62, 57, 63, 67, a remarkable measure of agreement (allowance having been made for twelve omissions in the latter manuscript) when compared with the

70 These entries have been published separately by Grosjean in *Irish texts* 3 (1931) 80-1.

very infrequent similarity in arrangement between, for example, M and L or M and RLc^{1}.

M's close agreement with R^{1}La in textual matters is also reflected in the arrangement of entries. To quote two examples out of many, M 9-14 = R^{1} 59-62, 39, 63 and M 32-43 = La 247-9, 251, 253-5, 235, 256-9. Seldom, however, is there an unbroken correspondence of more than four entries between these texts, which also contain either unique entries or entries common to two representative versions only. We may infer, therefore, that the scribes of this recension tended to jumble the entries or that the various versions go back to a remote rather than to a recent common ancestor. On account of the very much abbreviated style of its entries, *rec.min.* is a special case. Nevertheless, on the basis of its arrangement and of its content, there can be no doubt concerning its place in the group.

Finally, a word on the biblical section of this recension. In its original form, which is now reflected by R^{1}H and the first two entries of M (La and *rec. min.* having lost their versions), this section consisted of the pedigrees of Christ or Joseph (675) and of Mary (674) in that order. M's scribe took the remainder of his biblical entries directly from L. As we have already seen, however, Lb's scribe, by way of contrast, took his two biblical entries from an Ormond text.

10. ORMOND'S SOURCES AND PROVENANCE

The first hundred or so entries in M, which is here taken as representative of the Ormond recension, reveal correspondences in the arrangement of saints with L and RLc^{1} which can hardly have been completely accidental in origin. M 49-53, for instance, are paralleled by L 33, 30, 34, 32, 28 and, more strikingly, M 59-61, 69-72 correspond to RLc^{1} 64-6, 73, 75, 74, 76. On the whole, more agreement of this kind is observable between M and RLc^{1}, than between M and L, and the relative closeness of the two former recensions is again borne out by comparing RLc^{1} with H. This reveals such correspondences as RLc^{1} 132-9 = H 71-3, 77, 76, 78, 80, 81 (two of the missing entries in H, i.e. 74, 79, agreeing with RLc^{1} 69, 70) to quote the most impressive example.

It should also be noted that there are several examples of textual agreement between RLc^{1} and representatives of the Ormond recension against L, i.e. $51^{a,d,m\text{-}m}$, 63^{d}, 122^{k}, $230^{e,\ f\text{-}f}$, 231^{ce}, 237^{e}, $282^{b,d,f}$ etc., but since RLc^{1} was manifestly L's main source, the latter's variant readings could have been introduced by Áed mac Crimthainn.

The immediate provenance of all versions of the Ormond recension was unquestionably the area within a radius of thirty or so miles of the monastery of Lothra, for whose prior Rawlinson B 486 (R^{1}) was written. Two representatives of the group, H and *rec.min.*, provide, however, possible pointers to a more remote provenance. Thus, while H was almost certainly composed in its present form at Killaloe, its first ten entries do not reflect an overriding interest in north Munster saints. Its tone is set by Trea of Ardtrea, near the river Bann in Ulster, who is added in after Patrick's pedigree and before those of Brigit and Colum Cille. There follows another Ulster saint, Comgall of Bangor and, while his successor is Moling of the Osraige, the next four saints are descended from Fiacha m. Máil; in other words, they belong to the Ulaid. Much the same bias is reflected in the opening section of the *recensio minor*. There, Senán of the Ulaid (417 = H 7) intrudes between Patrick (416) and Colum Cille (418) who, as in H, is followed by Comgall of Bangor. The next entry concerns Cumman of Dál Fiatach of Ulster (420 = H 13) and, while she is followed by Féichíne of the Fothairt (= H 17), the next two entries, Ciarán (= H 23) and Finnén (= H 26), likewise relate to north-east Ulster saints. Possibly, therefore, the Ormond recension started out as a 'revision' of a north-east Ulster text.

Finally, with the exception of H.2.17 (=1319) (H^1), no other recension of the Corpus exhibits such a keen interest in Connacht saints. Thus surviving uniquely in the Ormond recension are the pedigrees of Mochua of Balla (372), Colmán of Kilmacduagh (376) and Braccán of Aran (378) as well as the tracts on the saints of the Uí Maine (384, 394) and the Uí Ailella (390-3); all of these are preserved, fully or in part, in at least two representative versions of the group. Significantly, perhaps, while many of these entries are included in *rec. min.*, none survives in H. The implication may be that the Killaloe text most closely resembles the hypothetical, unrevised common ancestor of the Ormond recension.

11. THE BOOK OF UÍ MHAINE (M)

Now preserved in the Royal Irish Academy (RIA D ii 1),[71] the late fourteenth-century Book of Uí Mhaine (M) devotes almost a whole gathering, ff. 50Ra 39-53Vb 16, $54Va^2$ 36-55 Vb 58 (the intervening texts consisting of the two Irish litanies; cf. L 373b 10-374c 17) to the pedigrees of the Irish saints. The following scribal note occurs at the end of what is regarded as the most carefully written quaternion in the codex:[72] *Faelan Mac A Gabann na Scel doscrib in caidirrni seo da thigerrna carad companaig .i. don Easpog Ua Ceallaig (.i. Muircertach* above line) *7 co fogna do 7 na tabradh da charaid in caidirrne seo.* ('Fáelán Mac a' Ghabhann na Scéal wrote this quaternion for his lord, friend, companion, the bishop Muircheartach Ua Ceallaig. May it be of service to him and let him not give this quaternion to his friend').[73] Fáelán (†1423) was a member of the same

71 *RIA Cat.* 3314-56. In the preparation of this edition, I have used R.A.S. Macalister ed. *The Book of Uí Maine,* collotype facsimile of Ir. MSS 4 (Ir. MSS. Comm., 1942).
72 *Ibid.* 51.
73 *'Na Scéal',* 'of the histories', was attached as a soubriquet to this branch of the family, hereditary historians to a number of great houses including the Uí Lochlainn (*AFM* s.a. 1425) and the Uí Cheinnéidigh of Ormond (below, section 12). As I show below, however, Fáelán probably belonged to the branch which held mensal lands of the Uí Chearbhaill at Borrisokane.

family as the scribe who wrote Rawlinson B 486 (R[1]), and was already an established poet when he completed his work on the Corpus sometime between 1378 and 1394, the year in which Bishop Ua Ceallaig was transferred to the archbishopric of Tuam.[74] Either Fáelán or the scribe of his *vorlage* had difficulty in interpreting certain usages of the exemplar, notably the treatment of the minims and the letter *c*. To quote a few examples, *Coelbad* becomes *Aidilbad* (118[g]), *Cruind* becomes *Aruinn*(118[i]), *m. Moenaig* becomes *m.Inceanaig* (222[a-a]).

I have been unable to discover a statement of Fáelán's own descent. Clearly, however, his loyalties in the matter of saints were to the Cianachta, whose main representatives in or around north Munster were the Uí Chearbhaill and the Uí Mheachair, lords in post-Norman times of the baronies of Clonlisk and Ballybrit in co. Offaly and of the baronies of Ikerrin and Eliogarthy in co. Tipperary. In pre-Norman times, however, and, by Irish law, down to the sixteenth century, the Uí Chearbhaill possessions also comprised large portions of Lower Ormond, including the parish of Borrisokane which is rendered 'Buries Claniceyn', i.e. Borris of the Cianachta, in two sixteenth-century deeds.[75] Here, as late as the seventeenth century, the family of Clann an Ghabhann, later anglicized as Guinane, had their mensal lands which they no doubt originally held of the Uí Chearbhaill.[76] Fáelán's arrangement of the entries, therefore, with its particular emphasis on the saints of the Cianachta, may reflect his family's indebtedness to the Uí Chearbhaill.

Three Cianachta saints, Cianán, Fínán Lobor and Tola follow Patrick and Brigit and while these are succeeded by patrons of two Connacht churches, Termonbarry and Clonfert, the latter of which may have been the seat of Bishop Ua Ceallaigh's bishopric, two further Cianachta saints, Ultán (= M 8) and Luaithrinn (= M 10) are among the next three entries.

Apart from the Cianachta grouping, however, there is little evidence of deliberate arrangement in Fáelán's text. The heading interpolated before Molaisse m. Nadfraích (M 23), i.e. *d'Eoganachta Caisil annso,* promises more than it fulfils, for it is followed by two saints only of that denomination. Furthermore, its occurrence at the same point in La 224 means that it was already in Fáelán's source, from which a number of doublets, i.e. M 27 (132), 52 (147), 146 (178) and 167(181), and a number of homonymous pairings (M 91-2, 109-10, 179-80) were also taken over. Five more doublets M 108 (168), 155 (171) and the reduplicated sequence, M 44 (118), 45 (119) and 46 (120), are confined to M. In none of these cases, however, does Fáelán or his source appear to have turned to a different recension.

Alone among the versions of the Ormond recension, M made extensive use of the Book of Leinster (L) text of the Corpus which

74 A poem attributed to Fáelán occurs at 47Rb of the Book of Uí Mhaine. For Bishop Ua Ceallaigh's dates see Macalister's introduction to the facsimile edition.
75 D. F. Gleeson, A. Gwynn, *A history of the diocese of Killaloe* (Dublin, 1962) 151, 152n. Cf. E. Curtis, *Calendar of Ormond deeds* 5 (Dublin, 1941) 294-5.
76 *Ibid*. 212.

seems to have been available to Fáelán in the original.[77] Thus the Ormond complement of two biblical entries (675, 674) is considerably increased in M by the addition of six entries corresponding closely in arrangement and text to L (678, 682-86); so closely in fact that hEstras's title of *profeta* (683) is attached wrongly to Eimin (682), no doubt because it had been placed between the two names in L.

Similarly, only M and L reproduce the list of saints named Berchán (261-71), and from M 192 onwards, commencing at the top of folio 52V, the Ormond text shares with L thirty-seven entries one of which, Mac Erca (M 204), is placed at a point corresponding to L 171-2, thus breaking an otherwise uninterrupted sequence of correspondences. Since this entry straddles two columns in L, the confusion was again no doubt the result of direct borrowing. Something similar appears to have happened at M 200 (= L 168[b-b]) where the gloss *.i. mac Lairne* is incorrectly placed after *Dóthe* because of the scribe's failure to construe a mark of reference which, incidentally, is also misconstrued in L's other derivative at this point, the common source of BLcLb. Finally, M's source for its version of the tract on the mothers of the saints (722) — which all other Ormond texts omit — was a manuscript containing a copy of the RLc^1 recension.

12. THE LOTHRA VERSION (RAWLINSON B 486, = R^1)

Now known as Rawlinson B 486 and preserved in the Bodleian Library, Oxford,[78] this manuscript contains a version of the genealogies of the Irish saints (ff. 11(33) — 20(42)) which was written sometime in the second half of the fourteenth century by Mac Raith Mac an Ghabhann na Scéal[79] for Giolla Ruadháin Ua Macáin, prior of the house of Augustinian canons at Lothra (Lorrha), near Lough Derg

77 By Fáelán's time, the Book of Leinster, which had been compiled at Terryglass in co. Tipperary, had long since become the Book of Oughaval in co. Leix. Either the book was consulted at the latter place, therefore, or Fáelán worked from a copy.

78 *Analecta Hibernica* 1 (1930) 141-2; F. J. Byrne, *A thousand years of Irish script,* (a catalogue prepared for an exhibition of manuscripts at the Bodleian Library, (Oxford, 1979) 21. I have used a microfilm copy of the manuscript and have also consulted the original. Parts of the original were also very kindly transcribed for me by Máirín Ní Dhonnchadha. C. Plummer (*Misc. Hag. Hib.* 226) errs in his reference to the foliation of this text. An extraneous poem, interpolated at 17(39)R, interrupts the text which recommences, in a different hand(?), at 17(39)V. The final entry, at 20(42)bc, is also in a different hand. Most of the interpolated entries (R^1 3, 8 etc.) appear to be in the hand which added headings, i.e. *de genealogia Patraic* etc., to almost all the entries; (these headings are not noted separately as variant readings). The same hand wrote the bulk of the pedigrees in the secular part of the manuscript.

79 Mac Raith belonged to the same family as Fáelán, the scribe of M (see above). A religious poem, commencing *Mise ar fháesamh na finne* is attributed to him in RIA F vi 1, 78R etc. (see also note 114). He may also have been the author of the *recensio metrica* (see below) which is ascribed to him in several manuscripts. E. O'Reilly, *A chronological account of nearly four hundred Irish writers with a descriptive catalogue of their works* (Dublin, 1820; repr. Shannon, 1970) ciii, gives him a floruit of c.1380 which would suit both the date of Rawlinson B 486 and the character of the metrical recension.

in the barony of Lower Ormond, co. Tipperary, formerly the site of the monastery of St. Ruadhán.[80] The earlier and more proper title of the manuscript appears to have been Leabhar Sochair Lothra (or, simply, Leabhar Lothra (Ruadháin)), a source to which reference is made at least twice in the great manuscript compilations of the late fourteenth and early fifteenth centuries.[81] Thus, in the section given over to Múscraige pedigrees in B 142ef (= Lc 105Rd), a variant opinion is quoted as: *'sunt qui dicunt conarbo mac dō* [*i.e. do Echtgus*] *Rechtgal mac Echtgusa ut inuenietur i Libar Sochar Lothra'*. Here, as elsewhere in the text,[82] attention is drawn by the redactor to his use of more than one source. Plainly, however, he must have placed little faith in the divergent view for already copied into his text at this point were five pedigrees culminating in Rechtgal m. Echtgusa, which, presumably, had been taken from Leabhar Sochair Lothra. As it happens, these and all the surrounding Múscraige pedigrees agree very closely with the parallel text in Rawlinson B 486,[83] subject to the usual changes which occur in the course of transmission or, as in this case, when an editor drawing on at least one other source is at work. Thus generations are occasionally lost through haplography as in the pedigree of Clann Lachtna, which immediately precedes the reference to Leabhar Sochair Lothra in BLc. More frequently, pedigrees are shifted about as with that of Clann Murchon ('.i. *fear lēigind Lothra m. Folachtaig'*) which immediately follows the same reference in BLc but which, together with a number of other pedigrees, is found elsewhere in Rawlinson B 486.[84] Also, there are some omissions in the later manuscripts of explanatory, but generally superfluous, passages which occasionally occur between pedigrees in Rawlinson B 486.[85]

On account of its location within the ancient territory of Múscraige Tíre, it was only natural that it should fall to the important church of Lothra to preserve the local genealogies. Plainly, therefore, the local collection, replete with incidental topographical information,[86] used by the original redactor of the BLc tract on the Múscraige (which is much more detailed than that preserved in the twelfth-century Book of Leinster) is unlikely to have come from anywhere else, as indeed the reference to Leabhar Sochair Lothra shows. The date and provenance of Rawlinson B 486 as well as the many similarities between its text

80 Gleeson, Gwynn, *A history of the diocese of Killaloe* 210-13.

81 Leabhar Sochair Lothra was used as a source by the redactor of the tract on Múscraige pedigrees shared by B (142ef) and Lc (105Rd). Leabhar Lothra (Ruadháin) is cited as a source in the tract on the Corco Loígde (B 201a, Lc 113Ra, M 34Vb). Unfortunately, this latter tract is no longer contained in Rawlinson B 486. The use of *sochar* 'revenues' in its title may mean that the manuscript contained a rent-roll at one time. Now, Rawlinson B 486 is greatly chasmed.

82 See B 145c ('*ut dicunt alii*').

83 Rawlinson B 486 45(23)Rb — 50(28)Vb (at which point there is a break caused by two intercalated folios before the text recommences, only to finish after half a column).

84 47(25)Vab

85 e.g. between the pedigrees of 'Cóeldub' and 'Inderge' (B 141d, Lc 104Vb) or those of 'Scanlan' and 'Ailceang' (B 142a, Lc 104Vb); see Rawlinson 47(25)Rb in both cases.

86 e.g. B 143a 22-5, f 35-8, 114bc.

and that of BLc already earn it at least the title of 'Leabhar Lothra'. Before finally identifying it with Leabhar Sochair Lothra, however, one problem remains to be resolved.

Under the heading 'Uí Chainnig', pedigrees of four saints, i.e. Lachtaíne, Ciar Ascad, Grigóir and Odrán, are added to the miscellaneous section which completes the Múscraige tract in BLc and which partly corresponds to material contained in the first few folia of the Rawlinson collection.[87] There, however, only one of the four pedigrees — that of Grigóir[88] — occurs; the others are interpolated in the same hand as wrote the secular genealogies in the margins of Rawlinson's version of the saints' pedigrees (R^1). Now, if the Rawlinson scribe added in these pedigrees (which are in word-perfect agreement with those preserved in BLc) because of their occurrence in the secular collection he was copying, then, obviously, his source is more entitled to be regarded as Leabhar Sochair Lothra. But if this was the case, then why do the pedigrees not occur as a group in his collection of secular pedigrees as well? I assume that the editor of the BLc version, whose influence is clearest in the arrangement of this part of the Múscraige tract, was responsible for bringing together the four 'local' pedigrees of his source (i.e. Rawlinson B 486) which, while they were contained on different folia, had all been written in the hand of his main scribe.

As Grosjean has already suggested,[89] the provenance of this manuscript's version of the Corpus (which allots second place, after Patrick but before Brigit, to Ruadhán, and gives him a liberally glossed pedigree which is traced over one and a half folios to Adam) can hardly have been other than the monastery of Lothra. Also, in this, the second earliest extant version of the Ormond recension, no effort is made to conceal the bias of its scribe in favour of north Munster saints. Molua, who is interpolated in the top margin, and Flannán, the two patrons of the diocese of Killaloe, of which Lothra formed part, follow Brigit, only to be followed in turn by Crónán of Roscrea, Ciarán of Saigir, Odrán of Killetragh in north Tipperary, Áed m. Bricc, whose mother belonged to the Múscraige Tíre of north Tipperary,[90] Dímma Dub of the Dál Cais, Brénainn of Clonfert, Colum of Terryglass and Senán of Scattery Island (R^1 6-13). In fact, R^1's scribe found proportionately more room for north Munster saints than any other Ormond text. Unique to this version, for instance, is the pedigree of Ciar Ascad (R^1 35) of Cell Chéire (Kilkeare), barony of Upper Ormond, which takes the form of an interpolation. Likewise

87 Rawlinson breaks off at a point corresponding to B 144b 24 (Lc 106Va 28). Much of what follows in BLc, however, agrees with passages found elsewhere in Rawlinson, e.g. on ff. 45(23) *recto* and *verso* and 47(25)Va. The Uí Chainnig section in BLc (= B 145 cd) corresponds in part to material in Rawlinson 45(23)Va.

88 In the text of this pedigree Cairpre Músc is erroneously made into the son of *Dub Laige m. Dubgillai...m. Daigri*. The editor of the version used by B and Lc, noticing the error in his source, i.e. Rawlinson, compounded it by attaching this part of the pedigree to the following independent entry on Cellach m. Cormaic.

89 *Anal. Bolland.* 48 (1930) 367.

90 *Heist VSH* 167; *Plummer VSH* 1, 34.

interpolated was the pedigree of another Munster saint, Lachtaíne of the Múscraige (R[1] 34).

As with the other Ormond texts, there is little evidence of a consistent pattern in the groupings of saints, although three Cianachta (R[1] 36-8) and as many as eight Ceinél Eogain (R[1] 85-92) saints are brought together. Also, there is a group of ten female saints (R[1] 106-115). Finally, there are four unique entries (402-6) and three doublets not found in any other Ormond text, i.e. Énán (R[1] 58, 94), Dáire (R[1] 63, 103) and Molaca (R[1] 66, 102). The biblical entries (675, 674) which precede the Corpus proper reflect the original form of the Ormond text both in arrangement and in number.

13. LAUD MISC. 610 (La)

Now preserved in the Bodleian Library, Oxford, the section of Laud Misc. 610 (La)[91] containing the text of the Corpus (38a-42e) was written for 'Edmund mac Richard Butler' (†1464), nephew of the fourth earl of Ormond, as the following note, marking the first completion of the text, states: *Ni fagmait nis mo annso do naemshencus ⁊ cach nech legfes e tabrad a bennacht ar anmain Emuinn Builter oir is nemcortha uaid beth ag iarraid scribneorachta aniugh tar eis crechi do denam a nOiserge ané ⁊ airce mora.* (We find no more hagiography here: and may everyone who reads it give his blessing on the soul of Edmund Butler, for it is tireless (?) of him to ask for writing today after making a raid into Ossory yesterday with much plunder.)[92]

The text was written sometime in 1453-54 by Seán Buidhe Ó Cléirigh and Giolla na Naomh Mac Aodhagáin, who appears to have finally completed it on a Sunday, at the urging of his patron,[93] in the castle of Ráith and Phótaire (Pottlerath), co. Kilkenny whence the name of the manuscript, Leabhar na Rátha, or 'The Book of Pottlerath'.[94]

La's text of the Corpus has already been published by J. Fraser and P. Grosjean in *Irish texts* 3 (1931) 87-104 in the form of 329 enumerated entries.[95] Of these, entries 1-205 constitute a version of the *recensio minor* and, as such, are collated with the version here edited from the Book of Lecan (416-661). The remaining entries (206-329) represent another version of the full Ormond recension

Due to its composite nature, La contains only one example of Patrick's pedigree (La 1). We must assume, therefore, that Flannán

91 M. Dillon, 'Laud Misc. 610', *Celtica* 5 (1960) 64-76; 6 (1963) 135-55. A. and W. O'Sullivan, 'Three notes on Laud Misc. 610 (or the Book of Pottlerath)', *Celtica* 9 (1971) 135-51. I have collated a microfilm copy of the manuscript with the transcript published by Grosjean in *Ir. texts* 3 (1931) 87-104.

92 Dillon, *Celtica* 6 (1963) 140 (xxxv). Grosjean (*Ir. texts* 3 (1931) 104) published a part only of this note. It is followed in the manuscript by seven additional pedigrees.

93 Dillon, *Celtica* 6 (1963) 142 (xxxix).

94 A. and W. O'Sullivan, *Celtica* 9 (1971) 139, 140n, 145.

95 Occasionally, however, e.g. 237, 273, Grosjean turned two separate entries into one.

(La 206) immediately followed Patrick in the *vorlage* of the full Ormond recension. If so, then in view of the two next entries, Senán and Ruadán, there can be no doubt as to the redactor's bias in favour of Killaloe and the saints of north Munster. In fact, this emphasis is more or less maintained in the whole series of introductory entries. Thus Ruadán is followed by Cuimmíne of Clonfert, Crónán of Roscrea, Braccán and Áelchú of Aran, Beccán of Kilpeacon, near Cahir, and Liadain of the Dál Cais in that order (La 209-215).[96]

As in M, certain headings are preserved in La, i.e. *d'Eoganacht Caisil annso* (La 224) and *de Genealogia na naem Ailella annso sis* (La 312) but, again, this is as much evidence as we possess of an arrangement along tribal lines. Seven entries (La 323-9) are added in at the end but, since these are otherwise common to M only, the source must again have been an Ormond text. One entry only, La 269, is unique to La among the full Ormond texts, but it seems to have been drawn in part from the *recensio minor* (496). With R^1, La shares a number of entries omitted from M, i.e. La 227, 234, 238, 291. It also introduces four unique doublets, i.e. La 213 (215), 246 (327), 249 (328) and 250 (309); two of these, 327, 328, concern entries added in at the end.

14. TCD MS H.2.7(H) (= 1298)

Now preserved in Trinity College, Dublin, the early fourteenth-century manuscript, H.2.7. (= 1298) (H),[97] consists of three distinct sections, the first of which contains the text of the pedigrees of the saints (ff.177b-183c). The scribe of the manuscript is Lúcás Ó Dalláin, who may have written it before 1347 for Eoghan Ó Madagáin of Uí Mhaine.[98] The immediate provenance of its version of the Corpus is revealed, however, by the twelfth entry which concerns 'Domnall Ua hÉnne' (†1098), Archbishop of Cashel and 'eminent bishop of the west of Europe'.[99] The connexions of Domnall's family were with Killaloe whose patron, Flannán, immediately precedes him (H 11) in the text. It is possible, therefore, that H's version of the Corpus was composed in Killaloe at a date in or around 1100 since Domnall's reputation for sanctity would probably have best been remembered in the period immediately after his death.[100]

As already pointed out, however, the character of the initial series

96 Beccán of Kilpeacon is entered twice (213, 215).

97 I have to thank Anne O'Sullivan for kindly furnishing the reference to the manuscript's scribe and possible patron. I have also to thank Donnchadh Ó Corráin for allowing me to use his photostat copy of H.2.7's version of the Corpus.

98 I have no more information on the scribe or on his family. The date is suggested by R.I. Best, 'The oldest fragments of the Senchas Már', *Analecta Hibernica* 10 (1941) 301-3; p. 302.

99 AU s.a. 1098.

100 Gleeson (*A history of the diocese of Killaloe* 105-8; p.105) describes the bishop as 'the leading spirit' in the twelfth-century reform movement. He corresponded with Bishop Lanfranc of Canterbury.

of entries in the text points to an altogether different provenance for H's *vorlage,* and for the common ancestor of the Ormond recension as a whole. No less than six north-east Ulster saints figure among the first ten entries and, since particular prominence is given to Comgall (H 5), who follows Colum Cille here and in the related text of the *recensio minor,* it is tempting to speculate that Bangor, the most prominent of all the north-east Ulster churches, was also the place of writing of the hypothetical, unrevised Ormond text.

By comparison with other representatives of the Ormond recension, H is very brief in character; churches are seldom named, soubriquets are seldom given. Also, with very few exceptions, pedigrees tend to be short. One doublet only occurs, i.e. the pedigree of Óengus Ua Oibléin (H 66, 91). A number of entries are unique to H among the full Ormond texts, i.e. Comgall, Féichín, Domongóc, Ninnid, Ailbe, Adomnán and Baíthín (= H 5, 17, 19, 30, 39, 82, 83). Except for the last two saints, however, all of these recur in the text of the *recensio minor.*

15. THE *RECENSIO MINOR (rec. min.)*

Recensio minor denotes a recension of shortened entries (416-661) which survives in two manuscripts, Laud Misc. 610, ff. 38a-39h (La), whose text has already been published by P. Grosjean in *Irish texts* 3 (1931) 87-94 (§§ 1-205), and the Book of Lecan ff.163a-164d (Lc), containing 245 entries, which is here edited for the first time.[101]

Lc and La are manifestly very closely related; in fact, both seem to derive from the same, sometimes corrupt exemplar. Thus such errors as *Lafebe* for *Laithbe* (497), *eaxp̄r* for *epscop* (513), *Chollain* for *Colgan* (519) and *Caithlenn* for *Faithlenn* (624) are held in common. Also, each text observes an almost identical arrangement of its entries. La, however, is very much the more careless copy, frequently omitting entries and independently misinterpreting the text (480, 488, 494, 498, 519 etc.). Carelessness on the part of Lc's scribe is very much less evident (but see 492, 538, 541, 649, 650). Moreover, as in Lc's versions of the other recensions, comments of topographical interest are sometimes added (421, 526, 527).

Comparison with the other texts shows that *rec.min.* belongs to the Ormond group. Thus it shares with MR^1La excerpts from the Uí Ailella group of saints (596-99) which are not found in any other recension. Similarly, *rec.min.* 658-61 parallel M's list of aliases (M 163). Its place in the Ormond group is most clearly expressed, however, by the arrangement of its entries. Thus, to give an example, *rec.min.* 478-83, 485 correspond to M 66, 71, 70, 72, 74, 76, 78.[102] Furthermore, *rec.min.* occasionally drew twice over on the same

101 One entry is confined to La; so, together, the texts contain 246 separate entries. Giolla Íosa Mac Fhirbhisigh is again the scribe of Lc.
102 See also Appendix 1.

source, to judge by such duplicated series as 541 (615), 544 (649), 543 (616) (= M 25-7) and 478 (578), 480 (579), 482 (582) (= M 66, 70, 74), and this no doubt contributed to its excess of entries over and above the other Ormond texts. On the other hand, it contains thirty-three entries not found in any other Ormond text, and a total of twenty-two entries not shared by any other version of the Corpus. There is little, however, in these entries to reveal the redactor's bias. His interest appears to have been limited to the task of abbreviating the entries of his *vorlage* which, as has already been suggested, reflects the north-east Ulster bias of the (hypothetical) recension on which the Ormond group appears to have been based.

There is no clear internal evidence of date.[103] However, since only two manuscripts survive, at one remove from a common source, the abbreviator can hardly have been at work long before the time of the earliest extant version. We may assume, therefore, that *rec.min.*, which appears to have been used as a source by the author of the metrical recension, was composed sometime in the second half of the fourteenth century.

16. TCD MS H.2.17(H¹)(= 1319)

Now preserved in Trinity College, Dublin, H.2.17(= 1319) (H¹) is of uncertain date and provenance.[104] There are pointers, however, to a north-east Connacht origin. Thus the three other manuscripts collected by E. Lhuyd with H.2.17(=1319) came from the Leitrim-Roscommon area.[105] And, without any doubt, the manuscript's version of the pedigrees of the saints is most at home in the same general area. The usage of this area only, for instance, is reflected by the alias provided to Cruimther Fráech, i.e. *Croicheraech* (H¹ 6).[106] Then, following Patrick and Comgall (the only Ulaid saint, whose prominence may, however, reflect here as elsewhere a north-east Ulster stage in the development of the Corpus)[107] are three saints of the Síl Fergusa, one of whom, the relatively unimportant Lugaid (Lugach), had a church at Tuaim Ḟobair in co. Sligo. Five Conmaicne saints form the next group and two of these, Cruimther Fráech and Caillín, have Leitrim churches at Cluain Chollaing (Cloone) and Fidnacha (Fenagh) respectively. Finally, unique to this version of the Corpus are the following east Connacht saints; Móenacán (408) of Athleague, co. Roscommon, Cuan (409) of Ahascragh, co. Galway,

103 The text of 652 agrees very closely with Lc's version of 722.66, both adding *láech Liathmuine* to *Cuanu m. Cailchíne*. It is probable, however, that Lc's scribe, Giolla Íosa Mac Fhirbhisigh was responsible for this.

104 N. Buttimer M.A. very kindly transcribed the text for me. I have also consulted the manuscript.

105 I owe this and other information on the manuscript to Anne O'Sullivan.

106 I know of only two other instances of the alias, both from Muinter Eolais, co. Leitrim, i.e. *Celtica* 1 (1946) 66, *B.Fenagh* 192n. For another corruption of the name see *M.Don.* xliv, §24.

107 See above section 10.

the saints of the Ceinél Dobtha in co. Roscommon (410), and three saints of the Luigne, (411-3), a family which held lands in the barony of Leyney, co. Sligo.

Like the Book of Leinster version of the Corpus, H.2.17's text is arranged along tribal lines. There, however, the similarity ends for the two arrangements have almost nothing in common. In H.2.17 the sequence is as follows: Ulaid (Comgall only), Síl Fergusa, Síl Conmaic, Clann Néill, Clann Chuinn, Fothairt, Luigne and, finally, a miscellaneous group consisting of an otherwise unknown Eoganachta saint and Cianán of the Cianachta.[108]

With thirty-seven entries H.2.17 is the shortest of all the recensions. On linguistic evidence, such as the regular *ó'tát* with *cenél, dál* etc, the occurrence of such forms as *feb atfiadur* and *frisin abur* and the general character of a long note accompanying Mobí's pedigree (H[1] 31), which reads: *7 ci atbera nech combud mac do Ḟir Trí Idna Athra, ní fír són eter, ór naé meic robátur oc Fir Trí 7 ní mac díb sin Idna Athra ó nach mud eter,* the text would appear to belong to the same period as the *Passions and Homilies* of the Leabhar Breac which share most of these features.[109] The likelihood is that the text was put together at a date not earlier than the eleventh century.

17. THE *RECENSIO METRICA*

The metrical genealogies of the Irish saints, *Náemhshenchas naém Inse Fáil,* have already been discussed in detail by C. Plummer, who divided the work into three recensions.[110] Of these only the third, Cúchoigríche Ó Cléirigh's seventeenth-century revision of the text, has previously been published, by P. Grosjean in *Ir. texts* 3(1931) 40-80, and this very useful version forms the text here published, annotated and indexed (662).[111] Collation of the text with Plummer's two other recensions, the Book of Ballymote ff. 229-33 (B) and the Book of Lecan ff. 49Va-51Rb (Lc), shows that the two latter texts basically represent a single version.[112] Thus BLc share such errors as *Ronain* for *Moain* (662.40d), *Damolaisi* for *Molaise* (662.143b), *Rois o m. Erca* for *o Ros.Mac Earca* (662.146c), *Muiredaig* for *Nainneda* (662.162b) etc; Lc, however, appears to have added a number of quatrains to the original, using, it seems, its own version of the common source (section 6 above). Thus its addition at 662.74 corresponds in substance to the corrupt text of the common source at this point, which changed L's use of the Latin *soror* 'sister' into a

108 I have no other example of this arrangement.
109 I wish to thank Máire Herbert M.A. for drawing my attention to the occurence of these forms in *Passions and Homilies.*
110 *Misc. Hag.Hib.* 227-9; in place of Plummer's Book of Lecan foliation read 49Va-51Rb. A great number of later copies from manuscripts in the R.I.A., St. Patrick's College, Maynooth etc., could be added to the list of manuscripts.
111 A new edition, taking in the late copies as well, would be very welcome.
112 Plummer's division of the recensions into ABC is discarded here.

personal name. Similarly, at 662.75a, Lc's reading *Uaiti* for *Dathi* corresponds to the corrupt common source text at 90. Also, the additions at 662.71.72 and the marginal addition at 662.78 agree closely with the common source text as preserved in the Book of Lecan. Lc's version of *rec.min.* may also have been turned to account. Thus the addition at 662.153 corresponds most closely to 640.

The author of the original versification is unknown, but some conflicting ascriptions survive. Occasionally, the poet is named as Eochaidh Éigeas Ó Cléircheáin of whom little else is known.[113] In most manuscripts, however, the text is attributed to Mac Raith Mac Gabhann, who may be identical with the scribe of the Lothra manuscript, Rawlinson B 486 (R^1). In terms of background and period his authorship of the poem is very likely.[114]

Cúchoigríche Ó Cléirigh, the author of the seventeenth-century revision of the work, who rightly claims to have much improved it, refers to the original author as *'senfhilidh éiccin'*. The hundred and thirty-two saints whom he claims to have added from Féilire Óengusa and the Martyrology of Gorman appear to be mostly confined to the notes which, in view of their overall agreement with the text of the Martyrology of Donegal *(M.Don.)*, are not included here.[115]

Otherwise, Cúchoigríche's main source appears to have been a copy made by Mícheál Ó Cléirigh of the text of the Book of Lecan (Lc) which he followed wherever its readings did not require *certuccadh* or *glanadh*.[116] Where they did, and for the fifty-nine quatrains which he added to the text, Cúchoigríche's authority, his *'ughdaras seinliubar senchusa'*, was almost certainly the prose version of the Corpus in the Leabhar Breac (Lb). Thus, while the BLc text at 662.92 agrees with the prose version in the Book of Leinster (L 55), Ó Cléirigh emends in line with Lb. Similarly, the detail of the genealogical material in the fifty-nine added entries (662.30.32.37.39.53.54.60.81.82.83.86.93.96.98. 100.113.115.118.129.130.132.133.138.141.145.154.158.159.163.166. 169.173.174.176.178.189.191.193.194.200^b-202.204.206.209.210.216-18.221-24.226.227.230-32.239) regularly agrees with Lb against all

113 In RIA MS 23 M 12, p.11, *'Catha Craoibhe Tulcha'* is added to Eochaidh's name. If the early eleventh-century battle so-called is intended, then this gives a much too early date for the composition of the poem. The notice of Conaing Ua Cléirchéin's death in AU s.a. 1467 refers to his pre-eminence in history.

114 See above (section 12). E. O'Reilly, *Four hundred Irish writers* (p.ciii) gives a floruit of c.1380 to 'Mac Craith M'Gowan, who wrote genealogies of the Irish saints, and of the kings and princes of Ireland', having in mind no doubt this poem, although it does not treat of 'kings and princes' as such. The final quatrain of B's version of the metrical recension figures elsewhere as the first quatrain of a poem ascribed to Mac Craith in RIA F vi 1, 78R.

115 *M.Don.* was of course composed by another Ó Cléirigh, i.e. Míchéal, and, significantly, a copy of the notes in his hand is preserved in Rawlinson B 484, 86-7 (*Misc. Hag. Hib.* 230 (§194)). See also J. Hennig, 'A list of Irish saints in Rawl. B 484', *Éigse* 6 (1949) 50-5.

116 The original copy from the Book of Lecan dates to before 1630 (see section 18 below). The use of this copy led to such errors as *sosar* (662.74) for Lc's *soror* (itself based on a misunderstanding) which is also found in *GRSH* 63, §15.

other versions (see particularly 662.118.129.130.141.145.147.154), even to the extent of perpetuating that manuscript's errors (662.90).

Cúchoigríche's precursor, the original versifier of the collection, appears to have used the Book of Leinster (L), or a faithful copy, rather than any of its derivatives as his main source. Where BLc's reading is at variance with that of Cúchoigríche, for instance, it normally agrees with L. Thus, at 662.36c *(Aengusa),* 662.41a *(Tigernain)* and 662.92b *(Maenan),* BLc reproduce L's readings as against Cúchoigríche and each of L's derivative versions, which have *Fergusa, Tigernaig* and *Colgan* respectively. Also, at 662.102a, *Mac Liacc is Modíchu* is closer to L's *Mac Liac Dicaill* (310) than to *Mac Liac .i. Dicaill* of Lb (cf.Lc^1). Similarly, Sárnad (662.116a) is elsewhere found in L 4 only, and her associates, as listed in 662.114.116, correspond to the contents of L 6, 5, 4 in that order. Agreement in the arrangement of entries is very common, not unexpectedly perhaps since both texts arrange the saints along tribal lines. Thus 662.98-101 and 662.117-9 correspond to L 51, 57, 52, 53, 58, 59, 62, 49, 63 and L 93, 94, 92, 89, 91 respectively.

In addition to L, the original versifier used a copy of the *recensio minor.* Thus, 662.23-5 are closest to 621-3 (of which 621, 623 are otherwise confined to *rec.min.*). Similarly, 662.62, 662.105.106, 662.125.126 reflect 539, 573, 634-6 and 553-4 respectively. Finally, in drafting the section on the saints descended from Conall Gulban, the poet must have used the corresponding part of the RLc^1 recension, since this is the only other text to contain the list of Colum Cille's successors; thus 662.13.14.15.16.18 correspond to RLc^1 3.4.9.10.5. 6.7.8.

18. *GENEALOGIAE REGUM ET SANCTORUM HIBERNIAE*

'After he had been four whole years...gathering and collecting all that he could discover of the pedigrees of the saints of Ireland and of the kings from whom they were descended',[117] and after he had completed almost unaided 'the most rare and glorious' Martyrology of Donegal,[118] the poor Friar Mícheál Ó Cléirigh sat down together with three chosen companions, Fearfeasa Ó Maolchonaire, Cúchoigríche Ó Cléirigh and Cúchoigríche Ó Duibhgeannáin on October 4th, 1630, in the Franciscan Convent, Athlone, in order to compile a work which was, somewhat clumsily, to be entitled: *Seanchas ríogh Ereann...Genealuighi na naomh nÉreannach.*[119] Within one month, having worked 'days and nights', with the material

117 P. Walsh, *Genealogiae regum et sanctorum Hiberniae* (Maynooth and Dublin, 1918) (= *Arch. Hib.* 5-6 (1916-17) append.) 5, 142.
118 Colgan's words in a letter to Luke Wadding (B. Jennings, *Michael O Cleirigh* (Dublin and Cork, 1936) 97). Cf. J.H. Todd, W. Reeves ed. *A calendar of the saints of Ireland* (Ir. Arch. Soc., Dublin, 1864).
119 P. Walsh took the current title from the *approbatio* provided to the original work by the archbishop of Dublin.

support of a local patron, Toirrdhealbhach Mac Cochláin, the 'Four Masters' had prepared for the press at Louvain this first fruit of their magnificent work of collaboration in sifting and editing the materials of Irish history.[120]

In their *dedicatio, ad lectorem* and *testimonia* the editors furnished the particulars which enable a fairly precise account of the genesis and execution of their work. Very regrettably, therefore, their references to the sources on which they drew, *leabhair na seanughdar,*[121] are generally of the vaguest possible character.[122] Only once, in their statement of St. Moninne's descent,[123] do they specify a source, i.e. an tSaltair Óg, a copy they allege, of the Saltair Mór, another name for Saltair Chaisil. Ironically, this source can no longer be positively identified.[124]

In view of the prodigious preliminary work of collecting undertaken by M. Ó Cléirigh, the sources he and his colleagues used must have been both many and varied. By examining and collating each entry, however, it should be possible to identify the majority of these sources, which were not limited to previous versions of the Corpus. In chapter 2, for instance, which is devoted to the saints descended from Eoghan mac Néill Naoighiallaigh, five pedigrees (3, 13, 20, 23, 30) were extrapolated from the introductory paragraph of the Irish Life of Lasair, *Beatha Lasrach,* which M. Ó Cléirigh had copied from a manuscript belonging to Cúchoigríche Ó Duibhgeannáin in 1629.[125] Here, however, I am concerned only with the evidence the text contains of familiarity with other recensions of the Corpus.

A great influence on the text was exercised by a codex which at that time, and for most of the seventeenth century, formed part of the library of the Franciscan convent at the foot of Sliabh Auchty in the barony of Leitrim, county Galway, i.e. the Leabhar Breac or 'Great Book of Duniry'. M. Ó Cléirigh had copied a text from this codex in 1629,[126] and may have also availed of the opportunity to transcribe its version of the Corpus. In whichever form it lay before them, however, the Four Masters appear to have agreed that Lb's text was to be regarded as authoritative. Occasionally, it is reproduced name for name but, more usually, it is corrected or supplemented by comparison with other versions. Thus, to take chapter 12 (*GRSH* pp. 66-8) as an example, seven of the seventeen entries unmistakably reveal Lb's influence; of these, three (3, 5, 8) correspond *in toto,* four

120 The work remained unpublished, however, until 1916-17. M. Ó Cléirigh's autograph copy is now in the Franciscan library, Killiney (= A 16); see M. Dillon, C. Mooney, P. de Brún, *Catalogue of Irish manuscripts in the Franciscan library Killiney* (Dublin, 1969) 32-5 (cf. p.xii).

121 *GRSH* 3.

122 On the other hand, Colgan, who added numerous notes to the text, regularly names his source (*ibid.* 40(§16), 61(§§I, Ia), 62(§9) etc.).

123 *Ibid.* 47(§29a).

124 See below (section 23).

125 Jennings, *Michael O Cleirigh* 71. The Life has been edited by L.Gwynn from a later Ó Duibhgeannáin manuscript in *Ériu* 5 (1911) 73-109.

126 Jennings, *ibid.* 89.

in greater (1,2) or in lesser (6, 17) part. Two other entries (11, 12) agree as much with Lb as with any other version.

Another manuscript from which M. Ó Cléirigh had drawn hagiographical materials prior to his collaboration in the composition of *GRSH* was the Book of Leinster (L),[127] a portion of which, having become detached from the main body of the manuscript, was preserved at this time in the Franciscan convent of Donegal.[128] Five (4, 6, 13, 16, 17) of the entries in chapter 12 point to L as the main source for their readings. Of these, that of Constans (6) provides a very good example of the selective editorial method followed by the Four Masters. The text, whose forms generally agree with L, reads:

> *Constans angcoire*[a] *.i. Cuana*[b] *m. Fualascaigh m. Maoilaithcin m. Forannain m.* [c]*Maoluidhir m. Baottáin*[c] *m. Tótain m. Amhalgadha m. Niadha m. Conaill m. Fearghosa m. Murchadha*[d] *m. Aodha m. Guaire m. Amhalgadha m. Muireadhaigh m. Cairthinn m. Eirc m. Eathach m. Colla Uais.*
>
> [a]otherwise only in L. [b]otherwise only in RLc¹M.
> [c-c]otherwise only in RLc¹M. [d]otherwise only in BLcLb.

Plainly, M. Ó Cléirigh and the 'other learned historians'[129] had collated copies of at least three different versions, thus producing the kind of 'edited' text, which is characteristic of their work on the genealogies.

Sometime before he placed his collection before his three chosen colleagues for examination, M. Ó Cléirigh must have completed a copy of *Náemshenchus naém Inse Fáil,* the metrical recension of the Corpus (662), from the Book of Lecan, for this text also clearly exercised a great influence on the arrangement and on the contents of *GRSH.*[130] The 38 tribal subdivisions adopted by the Four Masters compare with some 23 only in the earlier text. Nevertheless, there is a large measure of agreement in the arrangement of both texts. Thus chapters 8-20 in *GRSH,* comprising Uí Briúin, Uí Ḟiachrach, Uí Ailella, Slicht Fergusa Cháecháin, three chapters on the Airgialla, Fothairt, Déise, Síl Conaire, Dál Riata, Dál Fiatach and Laigin, correspond, with some differences in order, to *met.rec.*'s sections on Slicht Fergusa Cháecháin, Uí Ḟiachrach, Uí Briúin, Airgialla, Fothairt, Déise, Síl Conaire (including Dál Riata), Dál Fiatach and

127 *Ibid.* 57-8.
128 Best, Bergin, O'Brien, *The Book of Leinster . . .,* xviii. Now in the Franciscan Library, Killiney, this fragment did not, however, contain the pedigrees of the saints (Dillon, Mooney, de Brún, *Catalogue...,* 5-10).
129 *GRSH* 142.
130 P. Walsh, *Irish men of learning* (Dublin, 1947) 107 states that Ó Cléirigh completed a copy of the poem from the Book of Lecan 'on 19 April, 1630'. He refers the reader, however, to Plummer's *Misc. Hag. Hib.* 227-8 where the reference is to a copy made in April, 1636. As I show here, however, Ó Cléirigh must indeed have made a copy of Lc's version prior to his work on *GRSH;* so his 1636 copy may have been a copy of an earlier copy (cf. Jennings *Michael O Cleirigh* 145-6).

Laigin. Similarly, both texts assign their concluding chapters/sections to Eoganachta, Dál Cais, Cianachta and Corco Loígde in that order.

Two entries (9, 15) in Chapter 12 of *GRSH* show direct influence of 662 (Lc) on their readings. Eochaid m. Colla's pedigree (9) is found nowhere else but in 662.105 in that form,[131] and the reading *Mac Liacc 7 Modhichu da mhac Cernaigh* (15) clearly reflects *Mac Liac is Modichu dil da mac Cernaich* ... of 662.102, the form *Modíchu* being confined to these two versions. In chapter 9 of *GRSH*, the Four Masters can also be observed extrapolating names, sometimes without an accompanying pedigree, from 662; entries 1, 7, 16, from 662.77.78, may be accounted for in this fashion.

M. Ó Cléirigh's familiarity with Lc's version of 662 means, of course, that he would also have had access to that codex's composite version of the non-metrical Corpus. Not surprisingly, therefore, the Four Masters appear to have drawn entries either wholly or in part from this source. Entries 19, 20 in chapter 22, for instance, exhibit features otherwise found only in RLc[1]. Similarly, Colum Cille's *comharbaí* (*GRSH* chapter 1), who are otherwise confined to RLc[1] 4-17, were no doubt taken from the Book of Lecan, rather than from the Book of Glendalough (R), to which, however, as I have shown elsewhere, the Ó Cléirigh family also had access.[132]

Finally, little or no use appears to have been made of the texts of the Ormond recension, including M, of whose 34 additional entries five only figure in *GRSH*, where they are presumably drawn from other sources.

19. MAC FHIRBHISIGH'S *NAOIMHSHEANCHAS*

Dubhaltach Mac Fhirbhisigh wrote his recension of the pedigrees of the saints as the eighth book of his monumental and as yet almost wholly unedited 'Leabhar Geinealach' or Book of Pedigrees mostly in the period 1649-50 (more probably during the latter year), later, in 1653, adding to it from various sources.[133] The *naoimhsheanchas* proper, which is preceded by special sections devoted to Patrick, Colum Cille and Brigit, also made up from various sources,[134] is introduced by the author at 696a as follows:

131 In fact it is also so rendered in Máedóc's second Irish Life (section 20 below) which draws on the *recensio minor* (426) at this point.

132 Ó Riain, *Éigse* 18 (1981) 166-9.

133 For an edition of the Introduction and opening chapters of the work see T. Ó Raithbheartaigh, *Genealogical tracts* I (Ir. MSS. Comm., Dublin, 1932) 1-106. An edition of the whole work is now being prepared by Nollaig Ó Muraíle M.A., and I am deeply indebted to him for placing at my disposal a typescript of the *naoimhsheanchas* as well as some detail concerning its date and author.

134 Mac Fhirbhisigh states (692.1) that he drew the material on Patrick from Fiacc Sléibte's hymn and so he did, or rather from the glosses to the poem (*Lib.Hymn.* I, 97-103). There follows (695a1) a description of Patrick's household (Corp. 671) from Lb. The remaining two items (accounts of the maternal descent of Colum Cille and Brigit) are taken from Lb's versions of Corpus 697, 722.4-6

> *Naoimhsheanchas Éreann iar sleachtaibh saine senleabhar seanchadh Gaoidhiol: gin gob' iad a n-uird suidighthe seanchusa shechmid sunn. Acht as áil linn (le toil nDé) a n-eagar, iar n-urd genealuigh agus gaire a ngaol dá chéle agus don Ríoghraidh do rémsgríobsom, gosa mbearar na naoimh.*
>
> (The pedigrees of the Irish saints according to the several versions of the old book [composed by] the historians of Ireland — although we do not follow here their arrangement of the pedigrees. But we propose (with God's help) to arrange them, in order of pedigree and the closeness of their relationship to each other and to the Kings of whom we have previously written, from whom the saints are sprung).

There are traces here of the influence of *GRSH*'s *ad lectorem* in which attention is also drawn to the previously set down 'descent of the kings'.[135] And the same earlier work may have had some influence on Mac Fhirbhisigh's arrangement of the pedigrees.[136] On the whole, however, the evidence for Mac Fhirbhisigh's familiarity with *GRSH* is slight and does not appear to be corroborated by any traces of textual influence.

Only in the most general fashion does Mac Fhirbhisigh mention his sources, using phrases such as *an senshliocht* (696c), *sliocht ele* (716b) or *iar sleachtaibh senliubhar* (746a). Examination of his text, however, shows him to have depended on a number of early manuscripts as well as on a very recent version of the metrical recension. The *senshliocht* to which Mac Firbhisigh refers at 696c (= Corpus 1.2(a)) was almost certainly the Book of Leinster (L) whose readings at this point are favoured over those of M, the only other version containing a similar text. Throughout Mac Fhirbhisigh's text L remains a major but by no means exclusive influence. Sometimes, parallel readings are supplied from other sources as in the pedigree of Epscop Maine (701c = Corp. 28) where L's version of the patronymic *Echin* is matched by *nó Enna* from one of L's derivative manuscripts. Similar additions are found throughout the book and one of the main ancillary sources used by Mac Fhirbhisigh was the Leabhar Breac which occasionally even provided the main text (e.g. 726b, Dagán, Berchán = Corp. 256, 262). It is also one of the *senliubhair* specified at 746a and from it was taken almost all the material on 750b-753b (= Corp. 161-80, 200, 301, 663-70, 690.3.4).

The other *senliubhar* specified at this point was the Book of Uí Mhaine (M) which served as the source for most of the material on 746b-748a (= Corp. 397, 703, 394) and 749b-750a (= Corp. 265, 267, 268, 271, 201, 381, 379). With L, M constituted Mac Fhirbhisigh's second major source, its version being regularly used both for the main text, e.g. Colmán Ailithir (704a = Corp. 223) and for substantial additions, e.g. Áed m. Bricc (705a = Corp. 9). Mac

135 *GRSH* 8, 143.

136 The divisions are less sharply defined in Mac Fhirbhisigh's text and the entries do not follow alphabetical order. Otherwise, the arrangement is much the same as in *GRSH*.

Fhirbhisigh's use of M is corroborated by his signature which he twice inserted in the codex.[137]

Finally, Mac Fhirbhisigh also relied heavily on a copy of Cúchoigríche Ó Cléirigh's recension of *Naoimhsheanchas naomh Inse Fáil* (662).[138] This, however, he occasionally collated with an earlier version of the metrical recension. Thus, at 707b (= 662.48) three consecutive entries, Illadan, Feirgil and Epscop Rónán, are extrapolated *in toto* from the metrical recension. Here the influence of Cúchoigríche's recension is visible in the name of Illadan's church, Ráith Libthen, and in the date of his festival, June 10 (both of which details are added in a gloss to the Brussels text) and in the form of name taken by Rónán's grandfather, i.e. *Fianchon* (= *Fiadhchon* BLc). An earlier version of the metrical recension was, however, responsible for the form taken by Feirgil's name i.e. *Fergal* and for the addition *do shíol Énna mc Laoghaire sin,* which reflects *da sil an Enda cetna* (662.48d (BLc)). Throughout the book Cúchoigríche's additions are incorporated by Mac Fhirbhisigh, who obviously held this version in the highest regard. Ironically, while a detailed study of Mac Fhirbhisigh's text may yet yield some evidence of its use, the Book of Lecan, otherwise the 'Great Book of Mac Fhirbhisigh of Lecan', with its composite text of the pedigrees of the saints, does not figure at all among Dubhaltach's main sources.

20. THE RECEPTION OF THE CORPUS IN THE IRISH LIVES OF SAINTS

The saints' pedigrees were never intended to be simple memorials of the past, to be written down lest they be lost for ever. Their original authors and later collectors were members of a 'dynastically-minded clergy'[139] who wrote in an ecclesiastical (or even secular) interest which had little to do with the persons they commemorated. The care with which Áed mac Crimthainn laid out his text, i.e. L, along tribal lines, giving due prominence to the dynasties with which he maintained ties in the ecclesiastical as in the secular sphere, and singling out key personages in the pedigrees for identification with marks of reference, shows that he was directing his text at a readership. And, as the discussion of the initial entries in most versions has shown, in this Áed was no exception. We may be sure, moreover, that biographers of saints were among the most receptive readers of the Corpus, the more so because its earliest versions concide with a burgeoning demand for saints' Lives, the materials for which were otherwise difficult enough to come by.

For various reasons, it is the *betha* rather than the *vita* which exhibits from the eleventh century onwards an interest in full-length pedigrees. Thus in the Book of Lismore collection *(Lis.Lives)*[140] all but

137 Macalister, *The Book of Uí Maine* 1.
138 At 740a he names his source as *sliocht Naoimhsheanchusa Naomh Innsi Fáil.*
139 D. Ó Corráin, in *idem* ed. *Irish antiquity* (Cork, 1981) 330.
140 W. Stokes, *Lives of saints from the Book of Lismore* (Oxford, 1890).

two of the nine *bethada* contain full-length pedigrees of their subjects, and one of the exceptions,[141] Brénainn's Irish Life, provides a full-length statement of another saint's descent.[142] On the other hand, in *Bethada Náem nÉrenn,* whose materials are mostly drawn from a collection made by Mícheál Ó Cléirigh from various sources, five of eleven Irish Lives omit the saint's pedigree.[143] *Vitae,* on the other hand, while invariably containing a statement of the saints' descent, are generally devoid of full-length pedigrees. In some collections, however, pedigrees have been added in the margins. A case in point is the Marsh's Library manuscript, Z.3.1.5, containing the so-called Kilkenniensis collection; with three exceptions, an Irish pedigree has been added to each of its *vitae.*[144] Similarly, the scribe responsible for the Rawlinson B 505 collection of *vitae* often left space vacant for the insertion of a pedigree.[145]

There is sometimes internal evidence to show that the biographer relied on a version of the Corpus for his account of the saint's descent. Cóemgein's pedigree, for instance,[146] which subject to the omission of some generations has features shared otherwise only by the Book of Glendalough recension (RLc^1), is followed directly by a statement of the saint's maternal descent, showing some verbal agreement with the B(LcM) text of 722.19.20. This tract on the mothers of the saints is now lacking in the Book of Glendalough (Rawlinson B 502), but, as I have already argued,[147] must have originally formed part of it, so that Cóemgein's biographer, a local monk, could have drawn both pedigree and maternal descent from a codex which still formed part of his own monastery's library.

The same kind of internal evidence is provided by the Irish Life of Berach of Termonbarry, co. Roscommon which again adds a statement of the saint's maternal descent to a full-length pedigree.[148] Interestingly, for it bears out the very local character of the Life, the pedigree agrees closely with that of H.2.17 (= 1319) (H^1), a Leitrim-Roscommon recension of the Corpus. The saint's maternal descent is also very close to the version in 722.101 which, however, does not survive in H.2.17 (= 1319).

Máedóc's second Irish Life, manifestly a late composition, contains a good deal of incidental genealogical information, including its subject's pedigree which has features pointing to a version of the

141 The other exception is the Life of Patrick.

142 *Lis.Lives* 104 (Iarlaithe); cf. *BNÉ* I, 47-8.

143 These are the Lives of Abbán, Brénainn, Senchiarán Saigre, Colmán Ela and Máedóc (I). Mochuta's Life is based on his *vita.* The tract on the Uí Shuanaigh also contains the pedigree of Colmán m. Duach.

144 P. Grosjean, 'Catalogus codicum hagiographicorum Latinorum bibliothecarum Dubliniensium', *Anal. Bolland.* 46 (1928) 81-148; pp. 109-11, 119-122. The three exceptions noted by Grosjean are the *vitae* of Fínán, Déclán and Malachy.

145 *Plummer VSH* I, xx.

146 *BNÉ* I, 125, §6. Cf. Ó Riain *Éigse* 18 (1981) 175-6n.

147 Above; sections 5, 8. See also note to 722.

148 *BNÉ* I, 23, §4.

Ormond recension as its source.[149] Most interestingly, moreover, the *betha* (§ 229) juxtaposes the descents of Máedóc and Dallán Forgaill, thus replicating the grouping of the *recensio minor* (425, 426) and giving to Dallán precisely that version's form of the saint's patronymic, i.e. *Colla*. The pedigrees of Ruadán (p.317), Colmán m. Duach (p.312), and the Uí Ṡuanaig (p.312), while showing differences in detail, are probably also taken from a version of the Ormond recension. The same applies to the genealogical information in the introductory paragraph to the Irish Life of Mochuta (an abbreviated version of the saint's *vita*)[150] which, while limited to a description of the saint's parents, gives sufficient detail to allow the identification of an Ormond text as its source.[151] The remaining pedigree in the collection, that of Bairre (p.11), contains evidence which points to any one of a large number of manuscripts as its source.

The Book of Lismore pedigrees are very much a mixed bag. Almost invariably an account of the saint's maternal descent follows his full-length pedigree. However, several mothers' names, i.e. those of Senán (p.54), Findchú (p.84) and Mochua (p.138), either do not occur at all or do not occur as such in the Corpus (722). And where there is agreement between both sources as regards the mother's name, as in the cases of Colum Cille (p.24), Brigit (p.35), Finnian (p.75) and Ciarán (p.119), the Lives sometimes add divergent details (Colum Cille,[152] Ciarán). The generally local character of the Life is no doubt responsible for the greater detail of its genealogical information. Ciarán's pedigree, for instance, which is unusually detailed, agrees only with the version preserved in H.2.7 (= 1298) (H), whose text no doubt reflects the tradition of the Clonmacnoise area at this point.[153]

The points of contact between the Lismore Lives and the Corpus are not always very apparent. In other *bethada,* however, they can be very obvious indeed. Thus, in *Betha Ḟorannáin,* a late production, no less than four traditional pedigrees and one *ad hoc* composition (Forannán) are given in sequence.[154] On textual grounds, these four can be quite clearly shown to have been taken from the Book of Glendalough recension, i.e. RLc[1] 61 (Cuanna), 24 (Gobrán), 27 (Colmán) and 4 (Baíthín). Similarly, the three full-length pedigrees reproduced in the first paragraph of Molaca's Irish Life correspond to a (backward) sequence in the Corpus, i.e. 219 (Cuanu), 218 (Mochuille) and 217

149 *Ibid.* 190, §I (cf. p.349n). Its addition of *m. Eirc m. Eachach* to *Carthaigh* is otherwise found only in M and Lb (Corp. 63), which latter, when it agrees with M, generally derives from an Ormond text.

150 *VSH* 1, 170-99. Cf. *Misc. Hag. Hib.* 193-4.

151 With *'Fingenn filius Gnoe'*, the saint's father, compare *Findenn m. nGnoae* of the Ormond texts ($M^1R^1La^1$) (= Corp. 126).

152 The attachment of Eithne to the Corpraige Laigen is not found in the Corpus; cf. *Lib.Hymn.* I, 182.

153 While the provenance of H's version of the Corpus appears to have been Killaloe (section 14 above), the manuscript as such has an Uí Mhaine context.

154 *Anecd.* 3 (1910) 1-7; p.2. The same source was used for the list of saints in *ibid.* p.3(§5); cf.722.7-10.

(Molaca).[155] Curiously, however, while the sequence is now preserved in full in two recensions only of the Corpus, L and RLc[1], two important variant readings in the text of 217 (Molaca), i.e. *Luchta* and *Fir Ailche,* are shared by Molaca's Life with representatives of the Ormond group only.[156]

Two other Irish Lives, those of Mac Creiche and Náile, both late productions, contain pedigrees.[157] In neither case, however, is there comparable material to be found in the early full recensions of the Corpus.[158]

Finally, the Irish pedigrees added to the *vitae* in the collection of Latin Lives in Marshs Library MS Z.3.1.5 (formerly, V.3.4), otherwise Kilkenniensis, present a more uniform character, the implication being that they represent the work of one copyist drawing in the main from a single source. This source was a representative of the Book of Glendalough recension (RLc[1]), at least fifteen of the twenty-two pedigrees agreeing with RLc[1] in all important variant readings.[159] The pedigrees added to the Insulensis (Rawl. B 505) collection are very much less numerous, numbering six in all, i.e. Énna, Colum Cille, Baíthín m. Brénainn, Áed m. Bricc, Berach and Fintan m. Gaibrín in that order.[160] Their character is, however, far from uniform and they appear to have been added from various sources at various times in the spaces left vacant by the original scribe.

21. NLI G 2, f.3 (AN INTERCALATED LEAF)

Consisting of a collection of biblical, classical and Irish saints' pedigrees, the contents of this leaf have been discussed elsewhere in great detail.[161] Suffice it here to state that the scribe of the leaf, possibly of the fourteenth century, appears to have been drawing his materials directly from the Book of Glendalough (Rawlinson B 502), thus furnishing proof of the former presence in this manuscript of the introductory entries (674-689), and simultaneously supplying second (and generally superior) copies of twelve items now lacking in it.

22. HAGIOGRAPHICAL MATERIALS IN THE CORPUS OF SECULAR GENEALOGIES

Attention has been drawn here already to the occasional use of the secular genealogical corpus, particularly in its Rawlinson B 502

155 *Ir. texts* 3 (1931) 13(§I).
156 L includes here its derivative text, B.
157 *Misc. Hag. Hib.* 13(§I), 100(§I). To these may be added the pedigree in the late Life of Molaise of Daiminis (*SG* 17) which does not correspond to any version of 117.
158 Náile's descent is given only in *rec.min.* The version in *GRSH* 118 is taken from the *betha* which had been copied by M. Ó Cléirigh in 1629.
159 An exception is that of Cainnech which is unlike the version now preserved in Lc[1] (Corp. 123). Another exception, that of Ruadán, is omitted from the RLc[1] version.
160 I am greatly indebted to Máirín Ní Dhonnchadha, M.A., who transcribed the pedigrees for me from the original manuscript.
161 P. Ó Riain, 'NLI G 2, f.3 and the Book of Glendalough', *ZCP* 39 (1982) 29-32.

recension, as a source for entries in the corpus of saints' pedigrees.[162] In later versions of the secular corpus, however, as the note to entries 246-8 shows, the position is often reversed. Thus the four pedigrees headed *'do naomhaibh Sil Colla Uais'* which are added in at Lc 81Rc 40-Rd 11, and which deal with Máedóc, Mac Liac, Colmán m. Áeda and Fergna m. Ainmirech respectively (= Corpus 63, 310, 49, 353), are drawn from a version of the Ormond recension, mostly agreeing in their variant readings with M. The same applies to the three pedigrees of Cianachta saints, Buite, Cianán and Fínán Lobar (= Corp. 231, 195, 193) which occur at Lc 223R (= B 195a^c), and which again agree most closely overall with representatives of the Ormond recension. The same recension was again used at Lc 131Vc where three pedigrees (Finnian, Brénainn and Epscop Erc Sláine) are inserted. These also form a group in H.2.7, f. 183 (= H 92-4) and generally agree with the same manuscript in their variant readings.

Finally, in the Book of Ballymote (B) groups of two and three saints are included at 85b and 164a under the respective headings of Ceinél Bóguine and Clann Chonaill Chernaig. None of the three latter saints, i.e. Ernáin m. Áeda, Mac Cainne and Sinche ingen Ḟindbairr, is contained in the Corpus.[163] Furthermore, the detail given regarding the other two saints, i.e. Báithín m. Cuanach and Áed m. Bricc (= Corp. 26, 9), is insufficient to allow the identification of the source.[164]

23. LOST VERSIONS

It stands to reason that many more versions of the Corpus than those now extant existed at one time or other only to be lost due to the ravages of time, deliberate damage or simple neglect. In the course of the Introduction several such — nameless — copies have already been adduced on textual evidence. *A priori,* however, had some or even all of these or other lost copies survived, it is unlikely that the number of recensions of the Corpus would have been increased significantly. Two versions now actually (or only apparently) lost are named in other sources. One, an tSaltair Óg, is identified by the Four Masters, who drew on it, as a copy of Saltair Chaisil.[165] Moreover, a scribal note added by Conchubhar Magaodh to a largely hagiographical collection of texts, which he copied, somewhere in Ulster, in and around 1681, names an tSaltair Óg, 'a book containing the *naomhsheanchas* of the Irish saints from beginning to end, in as much

162 See section 3 above; cf. the note to 690. A later example of a version of the Corpus drawing on a secular tract is provided by R^1 some of whose interpolated entries are taken from the tract on the Múscraige (see section 12 above).

163 For Ernáin and Mac Cainne see also *GRSH* 99, 100.

164 Elsewhere, of course, Áed m. Bricc is assigned to the Ceinél Fiachach, reflecting the location of his church in Mide (see section 8 above).

165 Doubtless this is the manuscript alluded to in the quatrain beginning *'Mogen duit a PhSaltair Og'* (RIA 23 G 4, 412) which is described as a 'daughter of the Saltair of Cormac Caisil'.

as it could be discovered in Ireland', as his source, and identifies one of the Four Masters, Micheál Ó Cléirigh as its scribe. Drawing on the 'Seanshaltair' as a source, Ó Cléirigh had collected the materials of the manuscript in 1627, the year after his return to Ireland.[166]

The other version is cited as 'Liber Sligunt [the Book of Sligo] de genealogia sanctorum Hibernorum' in a note added by a seventeenth-century hand to the *vita* of St. Declan.[167] Plainly, however, the writer had in mind the Book of Lecan (Lc) (which as the name suggests was compiled at Lecan in co. Sligo), for the page-reference accompanying the note, i.e. 48b, corresponds in terms of the seventeenth-century foliation of that codex to the modern folio 39V which, as reference to the Table of Entries (107) shows, contains Déclán's pedigree in its Lc^1 form.

Further proof of the identity of the two Books is provided by J. Ussher who quotes from the 'Book of Sligo' the tradition that St. Patrick died on a Wednesday.[168] Almost certainly, his source was Lc^1's addition to the pedigree of Patrick (1.5) which reads 'Patrick's three Wednesdays: his birth, his baptism, his death'.

I have two other references to 'Leabhar Sligigh' (The Book of Sligo). One, in a fifteenth-century poem on the king of Tír Conaill, provides no evidence towards identification.[169] The other, from Egerton 1782,[170] refers to the Book's version of *'Aided Diarmada meic Fergusa Cherrbeoil'*, which never was (or is no longer) contained in the Book of Lecan.[171] It may well be, therefore, that the Book of Sligo is indeed a lost codex whose name was mistakenly applied in the seventeenth century, perhaps by Ussher, to the well-known Book of Lecan.

24. MANNER OF EDITING

Excepting the additions from other manuscripts, i.e. 1.1, 1.2(b), 1.3(b), 1.4, 1.5, 1.6, 2.1, 2.2, 8.1, 9.1, 9.2, 327-415, 672, 675-77, 679-81, 687-89, 736-38, as well as the texts of the *recensio minor* (416-661) and the metrical recension (662), the main text is that of L, which is reproduced here more or less as it occurs in the manuscript,

166 I am grateful to Professor Brian Ó Cuív for having drawn my attention to Magaodh's manuscript. See B. Ó Cuív, 'A seventeenth-century Irish manuscript', *Éigse* 13 (1970) 143-52.

167 *Plummer VSH* 2, 35n. The hand may well be that of Ussher who used the manuscript concerned, i.e. Marshs Library MS Z.3.1.5. (Grosjean, *Anal.Bolland.* 46 (1928) 109).

168 D.A. Binchy, 'Patrick and his biographers ancient and modern', *SH* 2 (1962) 7-173; p.113. Since Lc's source at this point was the Book of Glendalough (Rawlinson B 502), this early twelfth-century manuscript probably also contained the reference to Patrick's death on a Wednesday.

169 *Ir. texts* 2 (1931) 47 (*'Leabar Sligig, Saltair Caisil, cuid dot' fhiadnaib as é a tráth'*). The poet seems to be suggesting that these, implicitly famous, compilations would be fitting repositories for a description of his patron's fame. The chieftain concerned is given an obit of 1452.

170 *SG* 72; *Brit. Mus. Cat.* 2, 273.

171 There are some chasms in the extant codex.

interference being kept to the minimum required by the word-, sentence- and paragraph-division followed in this edition. L's marginal additions and glosses are interpolated at the point intended by the scribe, if this is discoverable; otherwise, at the point of their occurrence. L's errors, which are relatively few, may usually be corrected by reference to the variant readings. Only very occasionally, e.g. 275, is a missing word or letter interpolated by the editor and, wherever otherwise unspecified, this is indicated by the use of square brackets. Square brackets are also used when illegible parts of L — which are very few in number — are made up from the readings of the derivative texts, BLcLb, if these latter agree and seem correct e.g. 287.2.4. Otherwise, and where the derivative versions do not agree or seem correct, illegible parts of the text are indicated by dots between square brackets, e.g. 75, 239. Round brackets in the text denote barely legible (or, very occasionally, superfluous) words or letters. Apart from m. (= mac, meic) and 7 (= ocus) all manuscript contractions are expanded. Unless they are uncertain, however, the expansions are not indicated.

The aim with composite name forms has been to eliminate the use of hyphens. Where two substantives are involved, the first tending to be inflected, e.g. in names having *cenn* or *máel* as their first component, the name-elements are written separately, e.g. Cenn Fáelad. On the other hand, where prefixes such as *mo-, do-, dar-* are involved, the names are written as single words, e.g. Mochonna, without regard to the stress which in these cases falls on the second syllable.

Variants have been added from other manuscripts as follows. All additions and omissions are noted. Variant forms of names are given if they constitute (a) different names, (b) differently spelt or inflected forms of the same name, e.g. Crimthann/Cremthann, Amalgaid, Amalgada, or (c) otherwise significant forms. Variant forms of the very common variety, such as B's regular Sénda for Sétna, are not always included. Similarly, the very common alternation between Eochu and Eochaid is generally left unnoticed. The equally common interchange of Fiachna, Fiachra and Fiachu is, however, generally noted. Finally, BLcLb's almost invariable corruption of L's Latin is not always placed on record.

My use of parentheses in listing variants requires explanation. Where confined to the manuscripts, e.g. Dacualein B(LbLc^1), they imply that the reading is that of the unbracketed source, or sources, the other source or sources differing in some minor orthographical or morphological respect, other than the omission of a mark of lenition. Where found in the text of the variant reading and in the list of the manuscripts, e.g. Cre(a)mthainn R(Lc^1), Neill (Noigiallaig) BLc(Lb)RLc^1, they set off the bracketed letter (letters) or word (words) as additions to the bracketed source or sources. In a very few cases, which will always be clear from the context, parentheses in the variant reading and in the list of sources draw attention to a variant within the variant noted.

Finally, where a duplicated version of the text occurs in L or in the other manuscripts, the additional source is distinguished by the affixing of ^{1}; e.g. L and L^{1}, M and M^{1} etc. Needless to say, this is not done in the case of Lc^{1} and R^{1}, whose duplicated versions are distinguished by reference to their place in the manuscript, e.g. $^{b\text{-}b}$*om.* MM^{1}R^{1}R^{1} |18| 40cLa.

In the apparatus to the *Recensio Metrica* the note $^{a\text{-}a}$*add* Brux. occurs frequently, indicating that some part of the text, most commonly a section heading, occurs in the Ó Cléirigh MS only. Occasionally the key letters $^{a\text{-}a}$ are used in the text more than once within a section, and thus they may appear out of alphabetical sequence on the second occasion. On a number of pages where they so appear (viz between pp. 82 and 100) I have added |$^{a\text{-}a}$*add* Brux.| at the corresponding point in the apparatus.

TABLE OF ENTRIES

	L	B	Lc	Lb	R	Lc[1]	M	R[1]	H	H[1]	La
1	347a	215e		13b		36Rab	50Rc	12(34)Ra	178a	428b	
2	347a			13d		36Rbc	50Rd	13(35)Ra	178a		267
3	347a				51Ve	39Rcd			181b		
4	347 *in marg. infer.*										
5	347b	215e	40Vc	13d	52Rg	40ReVa	51Rcd	17(39)Va	181d		
6	347b	215e	40Vcd	13d			51Rb		181b		
7	347b	215ef	40Vd	13d	52Re	40Rc					
8	347b	215f		13d		36Rc	50Va	|19|41Vc	178ab	430b	
9	347b	215f		13e		36Re	52Rg	13(35)Va	181d		
10	347b	215f		13e		37Rb	51Rh				
11	347b	216a	40Vd	13e			51Rh				245
12	347bc	216a	40Vd	13e							
13	347c	216a	40Vd	13e							
14	347 *in marg. sup.*	216c	41Rb	14a							
15	347c	216a	40Vd	14b							
16	347c	216a		13e		37Vb	51Rf		179a		
17	347c	216a		13ef		37Vcd	50Vh	16(38)Vb	179bc		
18	347c		40Vde	13f							
19	347 *in marg. sup.*	216c	41Rab	14a							
20	347c			23b			51Ra	|19|41Vc	180d		
21	347c	216a	40Ve				50Va				225
22	347d	216b	40Ve	13f					180a	430c	
23	347d	216b	40Ve	13f							
24	347d	216b	40Ve	14b		39Ra	51Vf 52Rb	14(36)Rb		430c	
25	347d	216b	40Ve	14b			50Rfg	17(39)Vbc		431a	
26	347d	216b		13f						430c	
27	347d	216b	41Ra	13f			50Vb	15(37)RcVa			222
28	347d	216b	41Ra	13f			50Vf	|18|40Rc			297
29	347d	216b	41Ra	13f							
30	347d						50Vf 50Vf	|18|40Rb |18|40Rc			223 294

	L	B	Lc	Lb	R	Lc¹	M	R¹	H	H¹	La
31	347d						50Vc				
32	347d	216b	41Ra	13f			50Vf 51Vd	15(37)Vc |18|40Rc			296
33	347d	216c	41Ra	13f			50Vef	14(36)Rc			290
34	347 *in marg. infer.*	216c	41Ra	13f	51Ra	37Vd	50Vf	|18|40Rc			295
35	347e	216c	41Ra	13 *in marg. inf.*	51Ra	37Vde					
36	347e	216c		13 *in marg. inf.*	51Rb	38Ra					
37	347e	216c		14b	51Rb 51Vh	38Rb 39Vc	51Rf	|19|41Ra			
38	347e				51Rc	38Rb					
39	347e	216c		14b	51Rc	38Rb	50Va	16(38)Rc |18|40Vc			
40	347e	216cd	41Rb	14 *in marg. sup.*	51Ve	39Rd			179b		
41	347e	216d	41Rb		51Vf	39Re					
42	347e	216d	41Rb	14c	52Ra	39Vd	50Vg	16(38)Rab |18|40Va	179b		216
43	347e	216d	41Rb			37Vc	50Vg				
44	347e	216d	41Rb	14a			50Vf	|18|40Rc			
45	347 *in marg. inf.*	216d	41Rb	14a							
46	347 *in marg. inf.*	216d	41Rb	14a			50Vf	|18|40Rc			
47	347f	216d	41Rbc	14c							
48	347f	216d		14c		37Re	51Ra	14(36)Va	180cd		304
49	347f	216de		14c		37Vd	50Vh	|18|40Va	179d		
50	347f	216e	41Rc	14c		37Vd	50Vg		179c		
51	347f	216e	41Rc	14c	51Ra	37Ve	51Ra				
52	347fg	216e	41Rc	14d							
53	347g	216e	41Rcd	14d							
54	347g	216ef	41Rd	14d							
55	347g	216f	41Rd	14d			50Ve 51Rf				289

	L	B	Lc	Lb	R	Lc[1]	M	R[1]	H	H[1]	La
56	347g	216f	41Rd	14d							
57	347g	216f	41Rd	14d							
58	347g	216f	41Rd	14d							
59	347g	216f	41Rde	14d							
60	347g	216f	41Re	14e	51Rb	38Ra	50Vh	[18]40Vab	179d		
61	347h	216f –217a	41Re	14e	51Rbc	38Rb					
62	347h	217a		14e	51Rc	38Rb					
63	347h	217a	41Re	14e	51Vd	39Rc	50Va	15(37)Rab	181d		226
64	347h	217a	41ReVa	14e	51Rde	38Rd					
65	347h				51Re	38Rd					
66	347h	217a	41Va		51Re	38Rd					
67	347h	217a		14e	51Vb	38Ve	51Vd	13(35)Vbc	183a		240
68	347h	217a	41Va		51Rg	38Vb					
69	347 *in marg. dext.*	217a	41Va	14e							
70	347 *in marg. dext.*	217a	41Va	14 *in marg. infer.*							
71	347 *in marg. dext.*	217b		14a	51Rc	38Rc					
72	347 *in marg. dext.*	217b	41Va	14a	51Rf	38Va					
73	347 *in marg. dext.*	217b	41Vab	14a	51Rf	38Va					
74	347 *in marg. dext.*	217b	41Vb	14a	51Rf	38Va					
75	347 *in marg. dext.*	217b	41Vb		51Rg	38Vb					
76	348 *in marg. super.*					37Va	50Vf	[19]41Ra	178a		
77	348 *in marg. sin.*	217b	41Vb	14 *in marg. infer.*			51Vbc	15(37)Rb		430cd	323
78	348 *in marg. sin.*	217b	41Vb	14 *in marg. infer.*			50Vc	16(38)Rc		430d	
79	348a	217c	41Vc	14e	51Vb	38Ve	50Vbc		183ab		243

	L	B	Lc	Lb	R	Lc¹	M	R¹	H	H¹	La
80	348a	217c	41Vc	14e		37Va					293
81	348a	217cd	41Vc	14b	52Ra	39Vc					
82	348a	217d	41Vc	15a			51Ra		180c		
83	348a	217d	41Vcd	14ab	51Rab	37Ve	52Re	⌊18⌋40b			
84	348 *in marg. sin.*	217c	41Vb	14a	52Rc	39Ve					
85	348 *in marg. sin.*	217c	41Vc	14a	52Rc	40Ra					
86	348a	217d	41Vd	14b							
87	348b	217d		15a		36ReVa					
88	348b	217e	41Vd	15a		36Va					
89	348b	217e	41Vd	15b							
90	348b	217e	41Ve	14b		37Re 39Ra		15(37)Vc		431a	
91	348c	217ef 218f		15b	51Rf 52Ra	38Va 39Vc			180d		
92	348c	217d	41Vd	15a	52Ra	39Vd					
93	348c	217e	41Vd	15cd		37Vb	50Rg	16(38)Rb	182a		250 309
94	348c	217f	41Ve	15b	52Rd	40Rb					
95	348c	217f		15b		37Vd	50Vh		180b		311
96	348d	217f		15b	52Rh	40Va					
97	348d	218a	41Ve	15c		36Vc			178b	428b	
98	348d	218a	41Ve	15c14b		37Va	50Vg				
99	348e	218a	42Ra	15c			51Rb	14(36)Vb	180d		306
100	348e	218a	42Ra	15c							
101	348e	218a	42Ra	15c							
102	348e	218a	42Ra	15c							
103	348e	218ab	42Ra	15c							
104	348e	218b	42Ra	15c			51Rc 52Ra				
105	348e	218b	42Rab	15c							
106	348e	218b	42Rb	15d 23b			51Ra				
107	348e	218b	42Rb	15d	52Rb	39Ve	50Vh		180b 182a		288

	L	B	Lc	Lb	R	Lc^{1}	M	R^{1}	H	H^{1}	La
108	348f	218b	42Rb	15d	51Ra	37Ve	51Rc				
109	348f	218bc		15d	51Rb	38Ra	52Rb	|18|40Vb			
110	348f	218c		15d	51Rc	38Rb					
111	348f	218c		15d	51Rc	38Rc					
112	348f	218c		15de	51Rd	38Rc					
113	348f	218c			51Rd	38Rc					
114	348f				51Rh	38Vc					
115	348f	218c		15e	51Va	38Ve	50Ve		182d		
116	348g	218cd	42Rb	15e	51Rh	38Vc	50Ve	13(35)Rab	182a		326
							51Rf	14(36)Vc			
117	348g	218d		15e	51Vg	39Va	50Vb	15(37)Va	180a		224
118	348g	218d	42Rbc	15e	52Rf	40Rde	50Vc	17(39)V *in*	181d		244
								marg. inf.	183b		
119	348g	218d		15e	52Rfg	40Re	50Vh				
120	348g	218d	42Rc	15e							
121	348g	218d	42Rc	15e			51Ra				
122	348h	218de		15e16a		36Vbc	51Rd	14(36)Ra	183bc		275
123	348h	218e		16a		36Vc	51Vg	|18|40Ra	180ab		301
		218f									
124	348h	218e		16a		36Vc		20(42)Rb	183c		
		218f		16a							
125	348h	218e		16a		36Vd	51Ref	16(38)Vab	179cd	428c	
								|19|41Vc			
126	349a	218fg		16b	52Rbc	37Ra	51Vd	|18|40Rab			242
						39Ve	52Re				271
127	349a	218g	42Rc	16b		37Rbc	51Va	13(35)Va	180a	429bc	
128	349b	218g		16b	51Re	38Rde					
129	349b	218g		16b	51Re	38Rde					
130	349b	218g		16b	51Vc	36Ve	51Rfg	16(38)Ra	183c		274(part)
						39Rb					
131	349b	218g	42Rc	16b			51Rb		180d		
132	349b	218g	42Rc								
133	349b	219a	42Rd	16bc			52Rg				
134	349b	219a	42Rd	16c							
135	349c	219a	42Rd	16c	52Rc	40Ra			180c		

	L	B	Lc	Lb	R	Lc^1	M	R^1	H	H^1	La
136	349c	219a	42Rd	16c		36Vde		14(36) *in marg. sup.*	179d		
137	349c	219b	42Re	16c						430a	
138	349c	219b	42Re	16c			51Rb		181a		
139	349c	219b	42Re	15 *in marg. infer.*		37Rd					
140	349d	219b	42Re	16c							
141	349d	219b	42ReVa	16c							
142	349d	219bc	42Va	16d		37Va 40Vc	51Rb 52Rg		181b		
143	349d	219c		16d		37Re 40Vc	51Rb		181b		
144	349d	219c	42Va	16d							
145	349e	219c	42Va	16d							
146	349e	219c	42Va	16d						430a	
147	349e	219d	42Vb	16d			51Ra				
148	349e	219c	42Vb	16d			50Vf			431a	
149	349e	219d	42Vb	16d						429c	
150	349e	219d	42Vb	16e	51Rb	38Ra	50Vab	15(37)Rc	183a		231
151	349e	219d	42Vb	16e	51Rd	38Rc					
152	349f	219d		16e	51Rg	38Vb					
153	349f	219d		16e	51Rg	38Vb					
154	349f	219d		16e	51Rg	38Vb					
155	349f	219de		15e	51Vc	39Ra	50Vd	16(38)Vb			248
156	349f	219e		16e	51Vc	39Rb					
157	349f	219e		16e	51Ve	39Rde		13(35)Vb			227
158	349f	219e		16e	51Rh	38Vc					
159	349f	219e	42Vb	16e17a	51Vcd	39Rb	52Va				
160	349g	219ef	42Vc	17a			52Va				
161	349g	219f	42Vc	17a			52Va				
162	349g	219f	42Vc	17a			52Va				
163	349g	219f	42Vc	17a			52Va				
164	349g	219fg	42Vcd	17ab			52Va				
165	349g	219g	42Vd	17b			52Va				
166	349g	219g	42Vd	17b			52Va				
167	349g	219g	42Vd	17b			52Va				

	L	B	Lc	Lb	R	Lc^1	M	R^1	H	H^1	La
168	349g	219g	42Vd	17b			52Va				
169	349g	219g	42Ve	17b			52Va				
170	349g	219g	42Ve	17bc	52Ri	40Vb	52Va				
171	349g	219g220a	42Ve	17c			52Va				
172	350a	220a	42Ve	17c	52Ri	40Vb	52Va				
173	350a	220a	42Ve	17c	52Ri	40Vb	52Va				
174	350a	220a	42Ve	17c			52Va				
175	350a	220a	42Ve	17c	52Ri	40Vb	52Vb				
176	350a	220a	42Ve	17c			52Vb				
177	350a	220a	42Ve43Ra	17c			52Vb				
178	350a	220a	43Ra	17c			52Vb				
179	350a	220a	43Ra	17d			52Vb				
180	350a	220a	43Ra	17d			52Vb				
181	350a	220ab	43Rab	17d	51Vh	39Vc	52Vb				270
							51Vfg				
182	350a	220b	43Rb	17e			52Vb				
183	350b	220bc	43Rb	17e	52Rgh	40Va					
184	350b	220c		17e			50Vh		180b		
185	350b	220c		17e	52Ra	39Vc	50Va	16(38)Rc	181b		
186	350b	220c	43Rbc	17e							
187	350b	220c	43Rc	17e							
188	350b	220c	43Rc	17e			50Vg	15(37)Vc			273
189	350b	220cd	43Rc	18a				15(37)Vb			238
190	350c	220d	43Rc	18a		36Ve37Ra					
191	350c	220d	43Rcd	18a		37Ra					f.39 *in marg.*
192	350c	220de	43Rd	18a		37Rb					
193	350c	220e		18a		37Rc	50Rf	15(37)Ra	183a		
194	350cd	220e		18a		37Rd	50Rg		181a		308
195	350d	220e		18a		37Re	50Rf	17(39)Va	182d	431c	
196	350d	220ef	43Rd	18b		37Va	50Vf		179a		
197	350d	220f		18b		37Vb	50RgVa	16(38)Rb	182b	431b	
198	350d	220f	43Rd	18b		37Vb	51Vc	|18|40Vc	182d		214
199	350d	220f	43Rd	18b		37Vc	50Vg	|18|40Va	179ab		213
											215
200	350e	220f	43Re	18b				13(35)Rb *in marg.*			

	L	B	Lc	Lb	R	Lc[1]	M	R[1]	H	H[1]	La
201	350e	220fg	43Re	18b			52Rf				265
202	350e	220g	43Re	18b							
203	350e	220g	43Re	18b							
204	350f	220g	43Re	18c							
205	350f	220g	43ReVa	18c			50Vg				
206	350f	220g	43Va	18c			51Rb		181a		
				13e							
207	350f	220g	43Va	18c			50Rf	15(37)Ra	181a		307
208	350f	220g	43Va	18c			50Vb	12(34)Rb			208
209	350f	220g221a	43Va	18c							
210	350f	221a	43Vab	18cd		36Ve					
211	350g	221a	43Vb	18d							
212	350g	221a	43Vb	18d				14(36)V *in*			
								marg. infer.			
213	350g	221ab	43Vb	18d							
214	350g	221b	43Vc	18d			50Vf				
215	350g	221b	43Vc	18de	51Rd	38Rcd					
216	351a	221b	43Vc	18e	51Re	38Re					
217	351a	221b		18e	51Ref	38Re	51Vef	16(38)Va			299
								|18|40Vc			
218	351a	221b		18e	51Rf	38Re					
219	351a	221bc			51Rf	38ReVa					
220	351a	221c		18e	51Rh	38Vc					
221	351a	221c	43Vc	18e	51Rh	38Vcd	50Vc		182b		247
222	351a	221c	43Vcd	18e			50Vd		182bc		249
											328
223	351a			13e	51Va	38Vd	50Vc	14(36)Rc	182c		252
224	351b	221c		18e	51Rh	38Vc	50Vc	15(37)Vb	182a		246
											327
225	351b	221cd		18e19a	51Va	38Vd	50Vb	13(35)Rab	182c		210
226	351b	221d	43Vd	19a	51Va	38Vd	51Vc	13(35)Va	182d		233
227	351b	221d	43Vd	19a	51Va	38Vd	50Vd	15(37)Vb	182c		255
228	351b	221d		19a	51Vb	38Ve	50Vg	13(35)Vb	183b		207
229	351b	221d		19a	51Vd	39Rc		12(34)Ra			
								15(37)Ra			
230	351b	221d		19a	51Vf	39Re	51Vc	13(35)Ra	178d		206

	L	B	Lc	Lb	R	Lc^1	M	R^1	H	H^1	La
231	351b	221d	43Vd	19a	51Vh	39Vb	51Rb		181a		329
232	351c	221e		19a	51Vg	39Va	50Rg	14(36)Rbc	179b		209
233	351c	221e		19ab	52Ref	40Rd					
234	351c	221e	43Vd	19b	52Rd	40Rab					
235	351c	221e		19b	52Rd	40Rb					
236	351c	221e	43Vde	19b							
237	351c	221e		19b		37Vd	51Ra	[19]41Vc	180c		
				23a							
238	351c	221ef	43Ve	19b							
239	351c	221f	43Ve	19e							
240	351c	221f	43Ve	19b			50Ve	15(37)Va			310
							51Rf				
241	351d	221f	43Ve	19b		37Rc	51Vd	13(35)Vb	179d180a		273
242	351d	221f	43Ve	19b			51Rc	14(36)Vb	181c		325
243	351d	221fg	43Ve44Ra	19c		37Ra					
244	351d	221g		19c		37Rc	51Ra		180c		305
245	351d	221g	44Ra	19c		36Ve					
246	351d	221g	44Ra	19c		37Rc	52Ra	16(38)Vc			263
							52Ref				264
247	351d	221g	44Ra	19c		37Rc	51Vg				279
248	351e	221g	44Ra	19c		37Rc	51Vg				280
249	351e	221g		19c		37Re	51Ve	14(36)Vab	178b		
250	351e	221g222a	44Ra	19cd	51Vh	39Vbc	51Vc	14(36)Vbc	180d		236
251	351e	222a	44Ra	19d			50Vg	16(38)Va	181b		
							51Rc				
252	351e	222a	44Rb	19d	52Rc	40Ra	51Rc	17(39)Vc	181c		
253	351e	222a	44Rb	19d							
254	351e	222a	44Rb								
255	351e	222a	44Rb	19d							
256	351f	222a	44Rb	19d							
257	351f	222a	44Rb	19d							
258	351f	222ab	44Rc	19d							
259	351f	222b	44Rc	20a							
260	351f	222b	44Rc	19e							
				20a							
261	351f	222b	44Rc	19e			51Va				

	L	B	Lc	Lb	R	Lc¹	M	R¹	H	H¹	La
262	351f	222b	44Rc	19e			51Va				
263	351f	222b	44Rcd	19e			51Va				
264	351g	222b	44Rd	19e			51Va				
265	351g	222bc	44Rd	19e			51Vab				
266	351g	222c	44Rd	19e			51Vb				
267	351g	222c	44Rd	19e			51Vb				
268	351g	222c	44Rd	19e			51Vb				
269	351g						51Vb				
270	351g	222c	44Rd	19e			51Vb				
271	351g	222c	44Rd	19e			51Vb				
272	351g	222c	44Rde	20a							
				23b							
273	351g	222c	44Re	20a							
274	351h	222cd	44Re	20b			52Ra	16(38)Vc			262
275	351h	222d	44Re	20b							
276	351h	222d	44Re	20b							
277	351h	222d	44ReVa								
278	351h	222d	44Va	20b	51Vg	39Va					
279	351h	222d	44Va	20b	51Ra	37Ve					
280	351h	222d	44Va	20b	51Rg	38Vb					
281	352a	222e	44Va	20b	51Rgh	38Vb					
282	352a	222e	44Va	20bc	51Vd	39Rc	51Re	15(37)Rbc			228
283	352a	222e	44Va	20c	51Vd	39Rc		15(37)Vb			234
284	352a	222e	44Vb	20a	51Vbc	39Ra					
				20c							
285	352a	222e	44Vb	23b	51Ve	39Rd	51Rb		181a		
286	352a	222e	44Vb	20c	51Ve	39Rd	50Vg		179a		
287	352a	222ef	44Vbc	20c	51Ve	39Rd					
288	352b	222f	44Vc	20c	51Vh	39Vb	51Rc	13(35)Rb	181c		
289	352b	222f	44Vc	20c	52Rb	39Vd					
290	352b	222fg	44Vc	20cd	52Re	40Rcd					
291	352b	222g	44Vd	20d	52Rg	40Re					
292	352b	222g	44Vd	20d	52Rg	40Re					
293	352c	222g	44Vd	20d	52Rg	40Va					
294	352c	222g	44Vd	20d	51Rcd	38Rc				429b	
295	352c	222g	44Vd	20d							

	L	B	Lc	Lb	R	Lc^1	M	R^1	H	H^1	La
296	352c	222g	44Vd	20d							
297	352c	222g	44Ve	20d	52Rf	40Rd				430a	
298	352c	222g223a	44Ve	20de							
299	352d					37Vbc	50Ve	14(36)RcVa	178bc		256
300	352d	223a	44Ve	20e		37Rd					
301	352e	223a	44Ve	20e							
302	352e	223a	44Ve	20e			50Vc		181d182a	430a	
303	352e	223ab	44Ve45Ra	20e							
304	352e	223b	45Ra	20e							
305	352e	223b	45Ra	20e							
306	352e	223b	45Ra	20e23b	51Rb	38Ra					
307	352e	223b	45Ra	20 *in*	51Rd	38Rc					
				marg. infer.							
308	352f	223b	45Ra	20 *in*	52Ri	40Vb					
				marg. infer.							
309	352f	223b	45Rab	20 *in*	52Ri	40Vb					
				marg. infer.							
310	352f	223b		21a		40Vc	51Rbc	17(39)Vc	181c		324
311	352f	223bc		21a	52Rb	39Vde	51Rab	14(36)Va	178d		
312	352f	223c		21a	52Rd	40Rb					
313	352f	223c		21a	52Rde	40Rbc					
314	352f	223c		20a	51Vg	39Va	51Rd	15(37)Rb	180b	430d	220
						40Vc	52Ra				261
315	352g	223c		21a	51Vg	39Re			179b	431b	
316	352g	223cd		21ab	51Vb	38Ve	50Vb	15(37)Rc	178d		232
317	352g	223d	45Rb	21b						431b	
318	352g	223d	45Rb	21b							
319	352g	223d	45Rb	21b							
320	352h	223de	45Rbc	21b							
321	352h	223e	45Rc	21b							
322	352h	223e	45Rc	20a							
323	352h	223e	45Rc	21c							
324	352h	223e	45Rc	21c							
325	352h	223ef	45Rcd	21c		36Vb	50Vd				253
326	352h *in*										
	marg. infer.										

	L	B	Lc	Lb	R	Lc¹	M	R¹	H	H¹	La
327				13e		36Rc			182d	430b	
328				20b		39Ra	52Rb	14(36)Rb	183c		278
329				20b							
330				21a			51Rg	[18]40Ra			221
331				21bc							
332				23a			50Vh				
333				23b			50Va	15(37)Rc			229
334				23b	52Rab	39Vd	51Vf				
335				23b			51Vg				282
336						36Rc					
337						36Rc					
338						36Rc					
339						36Rcd					
340						36Rd			182d	430c	
341						36Rd					
342						36Rd					
343						36Rd					
344						36Rd					
345						36Rde					
346						36Re					
347						36Re					
348						36Re					
349						36Vb					
350						37Rb					
351						37Va					
352					51Ra	37Vd					
353					51Ra	37Ve	51Rb				
354						38Ra					
355					51Rc	38Rb					
356					51Re	38Re					
357					51Vb	38Ve	51Ra	[19]41Vc	178d		
358					51Vf	39Re	50Va		183a		230
359						39Va	52Ra	14(36)Ra			277
360					52Rc	39Ve	51Rc	15(37)Vc	181cd		217
361					52Rd	40Rb					
362					52Rf	40Rd	50Va	16(38)Rc	181bc	429d	

	L	B	Lc	Lb	R	Lc[1]	M	R[1]	H	H[1]	La
363					52Rf	40Re	52Rh				
364					52Rg	40Re					
365					52Rh	40Va					
366					52Ri	40Vb					
367					52Ri	40Vb					
368							50Vd	16(38)RcVa			251
369							50Ve				235
370							50Ve				
371							51Rc				
372							51Rd	17(39)Vab			
373							51Rd	17(39)Vb			
374							51Rd				
375							51Re				
376							51Rg	13(35)Vc			272
377							51Rg				
378							51Rg	13(35)Vc			211
								14(36)Ra			
379							51Rgh				
380							51Rh	[19]41Rb			281
381							51Vc				237
382							51Vd			430d	239
383							51Ve				
384							51Ve				218
385							51Vf	[19]41Rb			303
386							51Vf				
387							51Vf				
388							52Rb				
389							52Rb	[19]41Rab			
390							52Rbc				312
391							52Rb	[18]40Vb			313
392							52Rc	[18]40Vbc			314
393							52Rc	[18]40Vbc			276
											315-321
394							52Rcd	[19]41Vab			298
395							52Re				302
396							52Re	[18]40Rb			

	L	B	Lc	Lb	R	Lc^1	M	R^1	H	H^1	La
397							52Rf				266
398							52Rfg	[19]41Rbc			260
399							52Rh				300
400							52Rh				
401							52Rh				292
402								11(33)Va			
403								15(37)R *in marg. super.*			
404								[18]40Rb			291
405								20(42)Rb			
406								20(42)Rb			
407									178d179a		
408										430b	
409										430 *in marg. infer.*	
410										430d431a	
411										431c	
412										431c	
413										431c	
414										431c	
415											269
416			163a								1
417			163a								
418			163a								2
419			163a								3
420			163a								4
421			163a								5
422			163a								6
423			163a								7
424			163a								9
425			163a								8
426			163a								10
427			163a								
428			163a								11
429			163a								12
430			163a								13

	L	B	Lc	Lb	R	Lc¹	M	R¹	H	H¹	La
431			163a								14
432			163a								15
433			163ab								16
434			163b								17
435			163b								18
436			163b								19
437			163b								20
438			163b								21, 71.
439			163b								22
440			163b								23
441			163b								24
442			163b								25
443			163b								26
444			163b								27
445			163b								
446			163b								28
447			163b								29
448			163b								30
449			163b								31
450			163b								
451			163b								
452			163b								
453			163b								
454			163b								
455			163c								32
456			163c								33
457			163c								34
458			163c								35
459			163c								36
460			163c								37
461			163c								
462			163c								38
463			163c								39
464			163c								40
465			163c								41
466			163c								42

	L	B	Lc	Lb	R	Lc¹	M	R¹	H	H¹	La
467			163c								43
468			163c								44
469			163c								45
470			163c								
471			163c								
472			163c								
473			163c								46
474			163c								
475			163c								47
476			163c								48
477			163c								49
478			163cd								50
479			163d								51,90
480			163d								52
481			163d								53
482			163d								54
483			163d								55
484			163d								56
485			163d								57
486			163d								
487			163d								58
488			163d								59
489			163d								60
490			163d								
491			163d								61
492			163d								62
493			163d								63
494			163d								64
495			163d								65
496			163d								66
497			163d								67
498			163de								68
499			163e								69
500			163e								
501			163e								70
502			163e								72

	L	B	Lc	Lb	R	Lc^1	M	R^1	H	H^1	La
503			163e								
504			163e								
505			163e								73
506			163e								
507			163e								74
508			163e								75
509			163e								76
510			163e								77
511			163e								
512			163e								78
513			163e								79
514			163e								80
515			163e								81
516			163e								82
517			163e								83
518			163e								84
519			163e								85
520			163e								86
521			163e								87
522			163f								88
523			163f								89
524			163f								91
525			163f								92
526			163f								93
527			163f								94
528			163f								95
529			163f								
530			163f								96
531			163f								97
532			163f								98
533			163f								
534			163f								
535			163f								99
536			163f								100
537			163f								101
538			163f								102

	L	B	Lc	Lb	R	Lc[1]	M	R[1]	H	H[1]	La
539			163f								103
540			163f								
541			163f								104
542			163f								
543			163f								105
544			163f								
545			163f								106,107
546			163f								108
547			163g								109
548			163g								110
549			163g								111
550			163g								112
551			163g								113
552			163g								114
553			163g								115
554			163g								116
555			163g								117
556			163g								118
557			163g								119
558			163g								120
559			163g								
560			163g								121
561			163g								122
562			163g								123
563			163g								124
564			163g								125
565			163g								126
566			163g								128
567			163g								127
568			163h								129
569			163h								
570			163h								130
571			163h								131
572			163h								132
573			163h								
574			163h								133

	L	B	Lc	Lb	R	Lc^1	M	R^1	H	H^1	La
575			163h								134
576			163h								
577			163h								135
578			163h								
579			163h								
580			163h								136
581			163h								137
582			163h								138
583			163h								139
584			163h								
585			163h								140
586			163h								
587			163h								141
588			163h								142
589			163h								143
590			163h								144
591			163h								145
592			163h								
593			164a								146
594			164a								147
595			164a								148
596			164a								149
597			164a								151
598			164a								150
599			164a								152,153.
600			164a								
601			164a								154
602			164a								155
603			164a								156
604			164a								157
605			164a								158
606			164a								159
607			164a								160
608			164a								161
609			164a								
610			164a								

	L	B	Lc	Lb	R	Lc[1]	M	R[1]	H	H[1]	La
611			164a								
612			164a								162
613			164ab								
614			164b								163
615			164b								164
616			164b								165
617			164b								166
618			164b								
619			164b								
620			164b		•	•					167
621			164b		•	•					168
622			164b								169
623											170
624			164b								171
625			164b								172
626			164b								173
627			164b								174
628			164b								175
629			164b								176
630			164b								177
631			164b								178
632			164b								179
633			164b								180
634			164b								181
635			164c								182
636			164c								
637			164c								183
638			164c								184
639			164c								185
640			164c								186
641			164c								187
642			164c								188
643			164c								189
644			164c								190
645			164c								
646			164c								191

[illegible] FéinSheiceáil 3M

[illegible] chustaiméara: Byrne, Timothy
[illegible] an chustaiméir: 03477819

[illegible] Corpus genealogiarum sanctorum
[illegible] /
[illegible] 800270756
[illegible] dlite: 27/06/2007 22:00

[illegible] na míreanna: 1
[illegible]/05/2007 09:25

[illegible] maith agat as Córas [illegible] FéinSheiceáil 3M a
[illegible]

	L	B	Lc	Lb	R	Lc^1	M	R^1	H	H^1	La
647			164c								192
648			164c								193
649			164c								194
650			164c								195
651			164c								196
652			164c								197
653			164cd								198
654			164d								
655			164d								199
656			164d								199,200
657			164d								201
658			164d								202
659			164d								203
660			164d								204
661			164d								205
662	*(see note)*	229f-233a	49Va-51Rb								
663	353a	223f	45Rd	21cd			52Vb				
664	353a	223f	45Rd	21d	52Rf	40Rd	52Vb				
665	353a	223g224a	45Rde	21d			52Vb52Ra				
666	353a	224a	45ReVa	21d							
667	353a	224a	45Va	22a							
668	353a	224ab	45Vab	22a							
669	353b	224b	45Vb	22a							
670	353bcd	224b225a	45Vb46Rc	20a	•52Ri(=	•40Vbc(=					
				22a23a	•670.72)	•670.72)					
671	353d	225a	35Vcd	23a			53Ra				
		215bc									
672			35Vd36Ra								
673	353 *in*										
	marg. infer.										
674	354a	214a		13a		35Ra	50Rc	11(33)RcVa	177c		
675		214ab		13a		35Rab	50Rabc	11(33)Rabc	177bc		
676		214c				35Rc					
677		214c				35Rd					
678	354a	214cd				35Rd	50Rd				
679		214d				35Rde					

	L	B	Lc	Lb	R	Lc^1	M	R^1	H	H^1	La
680		214d				35Re					
681		214d				35Re					
682	354b	214d				35Re	50Rd				
683	354b	214d215a				35Re	50Rd				
684	354b	215a				35Va	50Rd				
685	354b	215a				35Va	50Re				
686	354b	215b				35Va	50Re				
687		215b				35Vb					
688		215b				35Vb					
689		215c				35Vbc	51Vbcd				237
690	354c	225abc	46RcVa	20a 21cd 23a		36Vab (=690.8.9 12.14.16.17)	50Vde(=M^1) 51Vd(=M^1) (=690.8.10. 16) 53Rab	[19]41Ra (=690.8.10. 16)	183a (=690.16)		254,257-9 (=690.10)
691	354c	225c	46Vb	23a			53Rb				
692 (cf. 722)	354d	225c	46Vb	23a							
693 (cf. 722)	354e						53Rb				
694	354e						53Rb				
695	354e						53Rb				
696	354e						53Rb				
697	354e						53Rb				
698	354e						53Rb				
699	354 *below cols*. a-d						53Va				
700	354 *below cols*. a-d						53Va				
701	354 *below cols*. de										
702	354 *below cols*. de						53RbVa				

	L	B	Lc	Lb	R	Lc¹	M	R¹	H	H¹	La
703	354e						51Vh(g)				283-287 (=3,4,5,7,)
704	365 d-g										
705	365g366d										
706	366de										
707	366e368g	225d229b			92a94d	47Ra49Rb					
708	368g369c	229bf			94dg	49Rbe					
709	369cf										
710	369fg										
711	370a										
712	370cd										
713	370cde										
714	370e										
715	371a										
716	371ab										
717	371b										
718	371cd										
719	371c										
720	371cb						53Vb				
721	371d										
722 (cf. 692, 693)	372a373b	212a214a				34Ra35Ra	54Vab55Vb				268(= 4-6)
723	374c										
724	374c										
725	365 *in marg. inf.*										
726	366 *in marg. sup.*										
727	366, 369 *in marg. inf.*						53Va				
728	367 *in marg. sup.*										
729	367 *in marg. inf.*										

	L	B	Lc	Lb	R	Lc¹	M	R¹	H	H¹	La
730	367 *in marg. inf.*										
731	368 *in marg. sup.*										
732	368 *in marg. inf.*										
733	369 *in marg. sup.*										
734	369 *in marg. inf.*						53Va				
735	373 *in marg. inf.*										
736					51Vh	39Vb					
737							53Va				
738							53Vab				

CORPUS GENEALOGIARUM SANCTORUM HIBERNIAE

RECENSIO MAIOR

1 [a]Patraic m.[a] Calpraind[b] m. Ḟótaide[c] m. Odisi [d]m. Cornuith[d] m. Leoburid[e] m. Ota [f]m. Muric m. Oirc[fg] [h]m. Leo[h] m. Maximi[i] m. Cencreti[j] m. Philisti[k] m. Ferini[l] m. [m]Britini[n] — [opq]a quo[q] Bretnaig[p], [r]*no*[m] Briṭi filii[s] Alani [t]qui primus de semine Iafeth in Europam uenit[ort] — [u]m. Ḟergusa Lethdeirg m. Nemid [v]m. Agno*main* m. Phaim[w] m. Thait m. |Sera|[x] m. Sru m. Esru m. Braimind[y] m. Fatecht[z] m. Magoth[aa] m. Iafeth m. Noe.[uvbb]

[a—a]Patricius filius Lb. [b]c *added above line* B, Alpruind Lb(MH[1]). [c]Odaige B(Lb), Fotaig M. [d—d]m Cormaic B, m. Corniuil Lb, m. Conuith M, *om.* H[1]. [e]Libairn B, Liberiud Lb(Lc[1]R[1]), Leobuird M, Aibuird H[1], *add* m. Mercuit Lb(R[1]). [f—f]*reversed* LbR[1]HH[1]. [g]Oiric B(LbH), Orit R[1]H[1]. [h—h]*om.* H[1]. [i]Malasi H[1]. [j]Eincreiti B(LbLc[1]R[1]), *add* m. Eirisi B(LbR[1]). [k]Peliste Lb, Phoilisde M, Fresi H[1]. [l]Farine Lb, Peirine M. [m—m]*om.* H[1]. [n]Britain BLb, Britainia M, Brite H[1]. [o—o]*om.* Lc[1]. [p—p]*added above line* L, *in text* BLbMR[1]H, a quo Breatain M. [q—q]o tait R[1](H). [r—r]*in marg.* L, *in smaller script* M, *om.* BLbLc[1]R[1]H. [s]m. H[1]. [t—t]is he dodechaid ar tus do sil Iafeth a nEoraip H[1]. [u—u]*om.* R[1]H, m. Ibad m. Magóg m. Iafeth m. Noe H[1]. [v—v]*om.* BLc[1]. [w]Paimp M. [x]*blank with* Sera *in marg.* L, Ṡera Lb(M). [y]Pramint Lb. [z](Ḟ)aithechta Lb(M). [aa]Magoc Lb. [bb]*add* m. Lamiach (m. Mathusalem) LbM(H[1]).

1.1 *Add* BLbMR[1].
[a]Coinceas *no*[a] Cochmas[b] ingen Ochmais[c] [d]a mathair do Frangcaibh[de] 7[f] siur do Martain hí[g].

[a—a]*om.* LbMR[1]. [b]*add* uero Lb. [c]Ochmuisi Lb, Ochinis R[1], *add* im̄. ainm M(R[1]). [d—d]do Frangcuib mathair Patraic Lb. [e]*add* di Cochmais R[1]. [f].i. R[1]. [g]isidhein R[1], *add* iar ḟir Lb.

1.2 (a) *Add* L 353d, M 53Ra.
Do macaib Israel[a] im*murgu* [b]co fír[b] do Patraic. Acht dia roesroíded[c] maicne Israel[a] o Thit 7 o Uespasian[d] fo chethair aird[e] in domain fo daere i ndigail fola Crist, is and doriacht[f] a bunud co Bretnu[g]. Is ar bunad Patraic do maccaib Israel[a] dorat Dia tigernus basti 7 cretmi i nhErinn 7 innarbba demna[h].

[a]Israithel M. [b—b]*om.* M. [c]raheasraineadh M. [d]Uepsian M. [e]airde M. [f]dorocht M. [g]Bretnaib M. [h]demun dosum eisde M.

(b) *Add* BLbM50RdR[1].
Do macaib Israel[a] iar fir do Padraig. Acht dia raossrainti[b] meic Israel[c] o Tit[d] 7 o Uespisen[e] mo[f] ceithri[g] ardibh[h] an domain [i]a nn|d|aire[i] a ndigail fola Crist, is andsin[j] adoracht[k] [l]a bunad sun[lm] co Breatnu[n].

[a]Israth̄ M, *add* tra Lb. [b]rohesretea Lb, roasraintca M(R[1]). [c]Israith̄ M. [d]Thait M(R[1]). [e]*or read* Uesper*i*sen B, Uespian Lb, *add* in di Consul Roman*ach* Lb. [f]ḟo LbMR[1]. [g]ceathar M(R[1]). [h]aird LbR[1], airrde M. [i—i]*om.* Lb, anaeir M. [j]ann Lb. [k]doriacht Lb, dorad M, dosiacht R[1]. [l-l]bunad Patraic Lb, a bunadhas R[1]. [m]sum M. [n]Breatnaibh R[1].

Conad[o] [p]ar a bunad sun[q] do beithi[r] a mBreatnaibh [s]a nn|d|aire[ps] adbearar [t]Breatnaigh dibh[t]; [uv]7 se[w] dosil[v] creidim a nErinn 7 doindarbadh[x] deaman[y] eisti[u].

[o]corob M. [p—p]aire sin Lb. [q]sum MR[l]. [r]beith MR[l]. [s—s]anaeirseach M, *add* aseadh R[l]. [t—t]Bretnach de Lb(MR[l]), *add* ar a taidecht a ṅdaire innte Lb. [u—u]*follows* 1.4. Lb. [v—v]is iaram rosil Lb. [w]ase M(R[l]). [x]roindarb Lb(MR[l]). [y]demnu Lb, de(a)main M(R[l]).

1.3 (a) *Add* L 353d, M 53Ra.
Oenḟiacaịl im*murgu* la Patraiç in tan luid a Cruachan et la epscop oc[a] Achud Ḟobair roḟacbad[b] ind ḟiacail sin, .i. fer há[c], ut Patricius dixit:

A ḟir á[a],
  facus mennutan[d] i mbá,
nocotḟacca[e] cosindiu
  o tú i mbiu, a ḟir á.

Ón aidchi condranac frim,
  atberim fiad[f] Rig na rend[g],
ni dechaid feoil tarut sís,
  ní thanic góu [h]anís dart' chend[h].

In Fiada find fil for nim,
co n-ecnu, co n-airmitin,
  domícc fo bathis báin bil,
  nomléic fo bathis oenḟir. A[i].

[a]*om.* M. [b]rofagaib M. [c]hua M. [d]mc̄nutan M. [e]nochodfiaca M. [f]fri M. [g]rann M. [h—h]tar ded M. [i]a ḟir M.

(b) *Add* BLbM(50Rd)R[l].
[a]In fiacail[a] robai[b] 'na[c] chind in tan tanic co[d] Cruac|h|ain[e], [f]ara crine[g] conasfaracaib[h] a nAchad Abhair[fi] .i. ag[j] Espoc Seanaigh. [kl]Fer ainm[l] na fiacla sin[k] ut dixit Patricius[m].

[a—a]7 ae(i)nfiacail (M)R[l], *add* di*no* Lb. [b]boi Lb, dobai MR[l]. [c]ina Lb. [d]ho Lb, a M. [e]*add* hOigle Lb. [f—f]*reversed* Lb. [g]*add* 7 arsaide som Lb. [h]forfacaib hi Lb, conasfar(g)aib (M)R[l]. [i]Ḟabair LbM. [j]*om.* M. [k—k]*om.* Lb. [l—l]Fear a a hainm MR[l]. [m]*add* Ón aidche roḟasais lium, aderim re rig na rend, ni thanic gó tort anís, ni dechaid feoil sis ath' cend Lb.

1.4 *Add* LbM(51Vh)R[l]|19|41RcVa.
Succait tra[a] ainm baitse[b] Patraic. Cotraige *immurgu* a ainm a[c] ṅdoire; [d]inand on 7 fer noḟognad do cethrar i n-oenfecht[d]. Mogonius[e]a ainm[f] oca[g] ḟoglaimm. Patricius[h] a ainm la[i] Romanchu[j]. [k]Ut dixit[k]:

Succait a[l] ainm baiste[m] iar[n] mbuaid,
Cotraige a ṅdoire dimbuain[o],
  Patricius[p] i lLetha luind[q],
  Magonius[r] 'ca[s] ḟogluimm.

[a]*om.* MR[l]. [b]baisdig M(R[l]). [c]ac M. [d—d]*om.* MR[l]. [e]Mogo(i)mius (M)R[l]. [f]*add* di*no* M(R[l] *after*[e]). [g]ag M. [h]Patricsius M, 7 Patricius R[l]. [i]ag M(R[l]). [j]Romanchaibh R[l], *add* quo(?)(qui) sedet*ur* (sedet) latus reigis (regis) .i. fer lethlama rig M(R[l]). [k—k]is de sin roraigid (in rann) (M)R[l]. [l]*om.* M. [m]co baistidh R[l](*with mark of elision under* co). [n]ar M, co R[l]. [o]dimbuaid MR[l]. [p]Mogoimius M(R[l]). [q]luim MR[l]. [r]robe a ainm MR[l]. [s]ag M, iga R[l].

1.5 *Add* Lc[1].
Tri cetaine Patric; a gen, a bathais, a bas.

1.6 *Add* R[1] (*see note*).
Don lín bliadan o gein Crist co teachtain Naemh Patraic a nErinn .i. cuic bliadna ar cetri ced bliadan[a]. O bas Naemh Patr|aic| co bas Bri|g|di .i. tri fichit bliadan. O geinemain Coluim Cilli co bas Naemh Bri|g|di cetri bliadna.
Tuc Patraic da laim fein gradha do deichnubar ar ḟichit 7 do tri ced easpac, 7 tuc [b]grada do[b] cuic mili sacart, 7 seacht ced |e|aclas robeandach, 7 ní uil uimir ar a gradhaibh o sin amach, 7 tri fir deg ar ḟichit do taithbeodaidh o bas.
Don lin bliadan o geinemain Crist co bas Patraic .i. tri bliadna deg ar cetri fichit 7 cetri ced, 7 is and ba marb Naem Patraic a Sabhall Patraic a n|D|un Da Leatglas, 7 do troisc Naem Patraic da*ichet* la 7 da*ichet* aidhchi ar Cruachan Oidhli ar gradh Gaedeal do cur deaman a hErinn amach. Is eadh ba slan do Patraic se bliadna deg ar fichit ar ced.
Tri haisceada do hiar Naem Patraic ar Dia re n-eg do; .i. in cedna aiscidh dibh indas co m|b|eith aithrighi creitmeach oghdha ag |g|ach aen fo leith do Gaedhelaibh re n-eg doibh, 7 in dara haiscidh dibh na gebhdais anmargaig Erinn ar Gaedhealaibh co brath. In treas aiscidh dibh nach beradh Gaedhel secht bliadna re mbrath. Is ime do iar sum sin ar daigh Anticcrist, uair secht bliadna re mbrath tic Anticcrist: finit.

[c]O genair Crist airemait
.cccc. for caemnochait,
teora b|*liadna*| fair iar sin
co bas Patraic primapstail[c].

[a]*bis*. MS. [b—b]*add* grassa do MS. [c—c]*added at foot of* 12(34)R; *added further in a smaller hand* fichi bliadain ar *cet* d'eis Patraicc rogenair Brenaind m. Findloga.

2 Brigit ingen Dubthaig m. Demri[a] m. Bresail [b]m. Dein[b] m. Conlaida[c] m. Airt Chirp[d] m. Corpre Niad[e] m. Cormaic[f] m. Oengusa Mind[g] m. Echach Find Fuath[h] Airt[i] m. Ḟeidlimid Rec*tada*[j] [k]m. Tuathail Tectmair [l]m. Ḟiachach Findfolaid [m]m. Feradaig Find Fechtnaich m. Cremthaind Niad Naire m. Lugdach R*iab nDerg* m. na tri Find Emna m. Echach Feidlig m. Find m. Fintain m. Rogen Ruaid m. Essamna Emna m. Blathechta m. Labrada L[n]. m. Enna Aignig m. Oengusa Turbig[klm].

[a]Deinmri Lc[1], Dreimhne R[1], Dernuri La. [b—b]*om*. MR[1]. [c]Conlai Lb(MR[1]), Condliga La. [d]Chuirp LbM(R[1]). [e]*om*. H. [f]*add* Mair La. [g]*om*. LbHLa. [h].h. La. [i]*add* ag Aengus m. Echach Finn comraigius cairdius Brighdi fri Corc*ar* Tri 7 fri Fothartaib La. [j]Rechtmuir M(R[1]La). [k—k]*om*. Lc[1]MR[1]H. [l—l]*om*. La. [m—m]*om*. Lb. [n]*so in the manuscript*.

2.1 *Add* LbR[1].
Broicsech[a] ingen Daillbronaig, [b].i. siur Chuimmne[b], do Dal Conchobair a descert [c]Muige Breg[c] [b]mathair Brigte[b].

[a]*add* ainm mathar Bhrigide R[1]. [b—b]*om*. R[1]. [c—c]*no* neg R[1](*above line*).

2.2 *Add* Lc[l].
Tri hochta Brigde; .i. a gen i n-ochtmad uathaid, a cailli i n-ochtmad deg, a bas i n-ochtmad fiched.

3 Fintan [a]Cluana[b] Eidnech[a] m. Gabrein[c] m. Corcrain[d] m. Echdach m. Bresail[e] [f]ut supra[f].

[a—a]*in marg.* L, *in text* RLc[l], *added in small hand* H. [b].i. Ceneil H. [c]Garbain Lc[l]. [d]Corcain H. [e]*add* m. Dein RLc[l]H, *add further* m. Condlaida m. Meic Airt Chirp m. Coirpre Niad m. Cormaic m. Oengusa R(Lc[l]), *add further* m. Echach F*ind Fuath* n*Airt* m. Feidlimid R*echtada* Lc[l]. [f—f]*om.* RLc[l]H.

4 Sarnat ingen Echach m. Baeth m. Nainnida m. Ḟeic m. Ieir m. Cathbath.
Di Ḟothartaib, i mBerriuch.

5 Mochua[a] [b]Tigi Mochua[ab] m. Lonain [c]m. Ṡenaig m. Oengusa[c] [d]m. Lugna[e] m. Bregduilb[f] m. Airt Chirp [g]m.|...|[dgh].

[a]Mochuta Lc. [b—b]*om.* RLc[l]MR[l]H. [c—c]*om.* BLcLb. [d—d]*om.* H. [e]Luna B, Lina Lc. [f]Brecdruilb Lc. [g—g]*om.* MR[l]. [h]*blank* L, Niadh BLc, Coirpre Niad LbR(Lc[l]), *add* m. Cormaic m. Aengusa m. Ethach F*ind Fuath* n*Airt* B(LcRLc[l]), *add* amail ata remaind Lb.

6 Findbarr [a]Insi Domle[ab] m. Aeda m. Dallain m. Liathain[c] m. Briuin[d] m. Eogain[e] m. Airt Chirp[f] [g]m. Corpre Niad[gh].

[a—a]*om.* H. [b]Tleimni M. [c]Cliathain B. [d]Brain B, Brain Deirg Lc. [e]*add* (m.) Bricc (M)H. [f]Chuirp LbM(H). [g—g]*om.* BLcMH. [h]*add* m. Cormaic m. Aengusa Lb.

7 Finan m. Fergnai m. Cobthaig m. Muredaig m. Lasre[a] m. Dare m. Ercain m. Dein [b]ut supra[b].
[c]I [d]Tig Airthir i n*Uib* Ercain[cd].

[a]Meic Laisre Lb. [b—b]*above line* L, *om.* BLcLbRLc[l]. [c—c]*in text after* Finan BLcLb, *om.* RLc[l]. [d—d]Tír *Ua* nEarca B(Lc), Tír *Ua* ṅDega no *Ua* ṅDercain Lb.

8 [ab]Colum Cille[b] m. Feidlimid[c] m. Fergusa[d] m. Conaill Gulban m. Neil Noigiallaig [e]m. Echach Mugmedoin[f] m. Muredaig Tirig[g] m. Ḟiachach[h] Sroptine m. Corpre Liphechair m. Cormaic Ul*fota*[i] m. Airt Oenḟir m. Cuind Cetchathaig [j]m. Ḟeidlimid Rechtada[ej].

[a]*preceded by* Do noemhaib Cland Nell and so sis fodechtsa feb atfiadur H[l]. [b—b]*added above line* .i. Crimtan R[l]. [c]Feidlimthe R[l](H). [d]*add* ceinnḟoda B(*in late hand*)(LbMR[l]H[l]). [e—e]*om.* BLbLc[l]MR[l]H. [f]*add* sund condrecat H[l]. [g]*add* oc tobuch dia thir H[l]. [h]Fiachruch H[l]. [i]Ulatai H[l]. [j—j]*om.* H[l].

8.1 *Add* Lc[l].
Tri cengcaidis Coluim Cille; a gen, a bathis, a bas.

9 [a]Epscop[b] Aed[c] m. Bricc [d]m. Cormaic[a] m. Crimthaind[d] m. Ḟiachach[e] m. Neill Noigiallaig[f] [g]ut supra[g].

[a—a]Aed easpoc m. Cormuic Bricc MR[l]. [b]*om.* H. [c]Aeda BLbLc[l]. [d—d]*om.* H. [e]Fiacrach MH. [f]*add* i Cill Iain Mair Lc[l](*see note*). [g—g]*om.* BLbLc[l]MR[l]H.

9.1 *Add* M.
Is e Aed m. Cormaic Bricc dothathbeogaig Tadg m. Conchobair rig Connacht.

9.2 *Add* R[1] *in marg. sup.*

Fichi bliadan is tri *cet*,
do bliannaibh ni himmerbreth,
cen boegul cen tragud tric
soegul Aeda meic Cormaic.

9.3 *Add* R[1] *in marg. sin.*
Eithne m*athair* Aedha epscoip.

10 Lomman Locha[a] Uair[b] m. Erannain[c] m. Ceispir m. Lathim[d] [e]m. Ḟergusa[e] m. Conaill Gulban[f] [g]m. Neill Noigiallaig[g].

[a]Lacha Lc[l]. [b]Fuair B. [c]Eirinain B, Ernain LbLc[l]. [d]Flaithim BLb. [e—e]*om.* Lb. [f]*om.* Lc[l]. [g—g]*om.* B.

11 Ruanach [a]m. Maain[ab] m. Muredaig[c] m. Neill[d].

[a—a]*om.* BLcLbLa, *in marg.* M. [b]Muain M. [c]*add* m. Eogain BLcLbMLa. [d]*add* Naegiallaig LcLbMLa.

12 Colman[a] m. Luadain[b] m. Aeda Luind[c] m. Mane m. Ḟergusa m. Conaill Cremthainne m. Neill Noigiallaig[d].

[a]*add above line* .i. ho Laind meic Luachain Lb. [b]Lugai B, Lugada Lc, Luachain Lb. [c]Alaind Lc. [d]*add* m. Echach Muidmedoin Lc.

13 Reotaide[a] m. Failbe [b]m. Aedain[b] m. Faeláin m. Tentide m. Luigdech m. Enne Boguine m. Conaill[c] Gulban [d]m. Neill Noigiallaig[d].
Is e coṅgaib[e] [f]Grellaig Maige Tlachtga[f].

[a]Rodaighe B(LcLb), *add* ⁊ Manchán dí Lb. [b—b]*om.* BLcLb. [c]Congaill Lc. [d—d]*om.* B. [e]congab BLcLb. [f—f]Glend Lugmaide Tlacht(g)a(i) BLc(Lb).

14 [a]Molugada[b] m. Lainneain[c] m. Fintain m. Lugdach m. Ennae Boguine m. Conaill Gulban [d]m. Neill[de].

[a]*see note.* [b]Mulaga B(LcLb). [c]Luinnoin B(LcLb). [d—d]*om.* B. [e]*add* Noigiallaig Lc.

15 Lochan[a] m. Cathail m. Cobthaig[b] m. Ennai m. Ailella m. Nathí[c] m. Ḟiachrach [d]m. Echach Mugmedoin[d].

[a]*add* m. Ailella Lc. [b]Taidg B. [c]Dathi Lc. [d—d]*om.* LcLb.

16 Ernain[a] Toraige[b] [c]m. Colmain[c] m. Mainain[d] m. Muredaig m. Eogain m. Neill Noigiallaig[e].

[a]Ernan BLbLc[l], Enna M. [b].i. Toraige H(*in marg.*) [c—c]*om.* M. [d]Muain B, Moain Lb, Main M, Maian H, *add* a quo Ceinel Main M. [e]*om.* M.

17 Mael Rubae[a] m. Elganaig[b] m. Gairb m. Oirballaig[c] m. Con Bairend m. Cremthaind m. Binnig[d] m. Eogain m. Neill Noigiallaig[e].

[a]Rubi H. [b]Calganaig B, Eoganaig MR[l]H. [c]Forballaig BLb, Ollarbaig Lc[l]. [d]Echach Bindig BLb. [e]*om.* R[l].

18 Femmi[a] ingen Cairell m. Lasre[b] m. Dallain m. Eogain m. Neill Noigiallaig[c].

[a]Femin Lb. [b]Meic Laisre Lb. [c]*add* m. Echach Mugmedoin Lc.

19 [a]Daig cerd[b] — [c]7 Femmi soror eius[c] — m. Cairill m. Lasre Luind m. Dallain m. Eogain [d]m. Néill[d].

[a]*see note to* 14. [b]Cernd B. [c—c]*above line* L, *om.* BLcLb. [d—d]*om.* BLc.

20 Muru [a]Othna Móre[a] m. Ḟeradaig m. Ronain m. Eogain Merchruim[b] m. Muredaig [c]m. Eogain m. Neill Noigiallaig[c].

[a—a]*om.* MR[l]HLb. [b]*om.* MR[l]Lb, Mércrium H. [c—c]*om.* LbMH.

21.1 Bec m. [a]De Druad[a] m. Gnoe[b] m. Lugdach[c] [d]m. Dallain m. Bresail m. Mane[de] [f]m. Neil Noigiallaig[g].

2 *Nó*[h]: Bec m. [i]De Druad[i] [j]m. Noe[j] m. Conaill[k] Echlúaith m. Lugdach[l] Mind [j]di Mumain[fj].

[a—a]De (Druada) (BLc)MLa. [b]Nae M, *add* m. Mair MLa. [c]Luig(d)ech B(Lc). [d—d]*in top margin in different hand* La. [e]*add* Móir a quo *Ui* Maine la Conachta MLa. [f—f]*om.* MLa. [g]*om.* B, *add* m. Echach M*ugmedoin* Lc. [h]*om.* BLc. [i—i]d.d. B, Dé Dédruad Lc. [j—j]*om.* BLc. [k]Oilella B. [l]Luighech B.

22 Ninnid[a] Lamidan[b] m. Echach[c] m. Aeda m. Loegaire m. Neill Noigiallaig[d].
[e]Siur[f] dó Cerc[g] ingen Echach[eh].

[a]Ninded Lb(H[l]). [b]Lighan B, .i. Lamidan H(*above line*), *om.* Lc. [c]Echduch H[l]. [d]*om.* H, *add* m. Echach Mugmedoin m. Muiredaig Tirigh m. Fiachruch Srobtine m. Cairpri Liphechair m. Cormaic Ulatai m. Airt Oenfir m. Cuind Cetcathaig H[l]. [e—e]*om.* HH[l]. [f]7 siur Lb. [g]Eirc B(LcLb). [h]*add* m. Aeda Lb.

23 Ninnid[a] apstal[b] m. Fergusa [c]m. Cóimeicc[d] m. Enna[c] m. Neill Noigiallaig.

[a]Ninded Lb. [b]Espoc BLcLb. *See note.* [c—c]*om.* B. [d]Cemoic Lc, Coemoc Lb.

24 Cronan[a] m. Oengusa [b]m. Cormaic m. Ṡenaig[bc] m. Nathí[d] [e]m. Ḟiachrach [f]m. Echach Mugmedoin[ef].

[a]*preceded by* do noemaib Cland Cuinn arcena annossa H[l]. [b—b]*om.* B. [c]*add* m. Cuind m. Bre(a)sail Lc[l](MM[l])R[l]H[l]. [d]Dathi MM[l]R[l]H[l]. [e—e]*om.* Lc[l]. [f—f]*om.* LbMM[l]R[l].

25 Beirech[a] [b]Cluana Cairpde[bc] m. [d]Amargin[e] m. Nemaind[df] m. Fintain m. Máil[g] m. Dobtha[h] m. Oengusa m. Erca Deirg[i] m. Briain [j]m. Echach Mugmedoin[j].

[a]Brec(c)an B(Lc), Berach Lb, Beraig H[l]. [b—b]*om.* MR[l]H[l]. [c]Cairptheach Lc, *add* a ṅdíthrub Cenéil Dóbthai Lb. [d—d]*reversed* H[l]. [e]Neamargein M(R[l]H[l]). [f]Nemnad M(R[l]), Nemnaill H[l]. [g]Meic Mail H[l]. [h]Dofa B(Lc). [i]*added twice above line* Lb. [j—j]*om.* MR[l].

26 Baethin[a] m. Cuanach — [b].i. eter cuanaib[c] [d]rucad é[bd] — [e]m. Cein m. Enna Ḟind[e] m. Neill Noigiallaig.

[a]Blaithin B. [b—b]*above line* LLb, *in text* B, *om.* H[l]. [c]cuanac B, chuanu Lb. [d—d]conructha Lb. [e—e]m. Oengusa m. Erca H[l].

27 Barrḟind[a] m. Muredaig m. Echdach m. Conaill Gulban[b] m. Neill Noigiallaig.

[a]Barann B, Bairrfann Lc, Barrenn R[l]La, *add above line* .i. a nDruim Chuilind hi Tír Cell Lb. [b]*om.* MR[l]La.

28 Epscop Mane m. Echin[a] [b]m. Eogain[b] m. Neill[c].

[a]Enda BLcLb. [b—b]*bis* R[l]. [c]*add* Noigiallaig BLcLbR[l].

29 Aedán[a] [b]Cille More[bc] m. Oengusa[d] m. Echin[e] m. Eogain [f]m. Neill[f].

[a]Aeda Lc. [b—b](o) Chill Aedain (Lb)Lc. [c]*om.* B. [d]Fergusa BLcLb. [e]Fechin Lb. [f—f]*om.* B.

30 Epscop Fiachra[a] [b]m. Fergusa[b] m. Eogain [c]m. Neill[cd].

[a]Ficha(i) M(M[l]), Fiachna(i) R[l]R[l]|18|40RbLa(La[l]). [b—b]*om.* MR[l]La[l]. [c—c]*om.* M. [d]*add* m. Echach Mugmedoin La.

31 Runach[a] m. Muredaig m. Eogain m. Neill[b].

[a]Ruanach M. [b]*add* Noigiallaig M.

32 Beccan[a] [b]Tigi Conaill[b] m. Lugdach[c] m. Tuatain[d] m. Aeda [e]m. Fergusa[ef].

[a]Becca Lc, Brac(c)an (M[l])R[l]R[l]|18|40c, Brecan La. [b—b]*om.* MM[l]R[l]R[l]|18|40RcLa. [c]Luighdeach R[l]. [d]Tuathail BLc. [e—e]*om.* R[l]|18|40Rc. [f]*add* m. Eogain M, *add* m. Eogain m. Neill (Noigiallaig) B(LcLbM[l]R[l])R[l]|18|40RcLa (*with* m. Eogain *twice*).

33 Colman epscop[a] m. Ronain[b] [c]m. Tuatain[c] m. Aeda m. Fergusa[d].

[a]*add* Cilli Colmain Lc, *add* Aille MR[l](La). [b]Ruadain BLcLb, *illeg.* La. [c—c]*om.* B, m. Tuathain Lb, m. Madadain (m. Eogain) MR[l](La). [d]*add* m. Eogain m. Neill Noigiallaig BLc(LbM)R[l](La *see note*).

34 Epscop Brecain[a] m. hUbain[b] m. Tuatain[c].

[a]Bracain RMR[l]. [b]Ubbain Lb, Uhan R[l], Dubain La. [c]Tuathain Lb, Tutain Lc[l], Tuantan R[l]La, *add* m. Aeda m. Fergusa (m. Eogain m. Neill Noigiallaig) B(LcLb)R[l]La.

35 Epscop Cormac[a] m. Echdach m. Ellaind[b] m. Eogain m. Neil[c] Noigiallaig[d].

[a]*preceded by* Eog *with marks of deletion* B. [b]Illaind BLcLb. [c]Neill (Noigiallaig) BLc(Lb)RLc[l]. [d]*om.* BLc, *add* m. Echach R.

36 Dochualén[a] m. Guaire m. Coluim[b] m. Crimthaind[c] m. Binnig m. Eogain[d].

[a]Dacualein B(LbLc[l]). [b]Colmain B. [c]Cre(a)mthainn R(Lc[l]). [d]*add* m. Neill (Noigiallaig) (B)LbR(Lc[l]).

37 [a]Ernaine[b] [c]Dromma *no*[c] Cluana Railgech [d]m. Eogain et[a] Sciri ingen Eogain[d] [e]m. Canannain[f] m. Ailella[e] m. Ḟergusa [g]Caechain[h] m. Echach Mugmedoin[gi].

[a—a]*om.* R51VhLc[l]39VcMR[l]. [b]E(i)rnin (B)Lb. [c—c]*om.* BLbRLc[l]. [d—d]7 Scire cland Eogain Lb. [e—e]*om.* R51VhLc[l]38Vc. [f]Cannan R[l]. [g—g]*om.* Lb. [h]*om.* RLc[l]. [i]*add* m. Muiredaig Tirig Lc[l], *add no* ingen Feideilmid m. Ailella m. Fergusa R51Vh(Lc[l]39Vc).

38 Crone ingen Diarmata m. Garbain m. Branduib m. Meilge m. Enna Boguine m. Conaill Gulban m. Neill Noigiallaig[a].

[a]*om.* R.

39 Dari[a] — [b].i. Sódelb[bc] — ingen Chathair [d]m. Lugdach[de] m. Ṡétna[f] m. Amalgada[g] m. Ḟiach*rach*[h] m. Echach[i] Mugmedoin.

[a]Darii R. [b—b]*added above line* L, in text BLbRLc, *om.* MR[l]R[l]|18|40VcLa. [c]Hoódeilb Lb. [d—d]*om.* RLc[l]. [e]Luigdech B. [f]Senda B. [g]Amalgaidh BLbR[l]|18|40Vc, Amalga Lc[l]. [h]Fiachrae R. [i]Echdach R.

40 Damoṅgóc[a] ailithir[b] m. Sárain m. Tigernaig m. Muredaig m. Eogain m. Neill[c].

[a]Damonoc Lb, *add* Thoraide Lc[l]. [b]Ailitri Lc, .i. Ailithir H(*above line*). [c]*add* Noigiallaig BLcLc[l]H.

41 Colman m. Luachain [a]m. Leda[b] m. Maine m. Ḟergusa m. Conaill Cremthainne m. Neill Noigiallaig[a].

[a—a]*om.* BLc. *See note.* [b]Laeda RLc[l].

42 Enan[a] [b]Dromma Rathe[bc] m. Eirne[d] m. [e]Cael Chrúaid[e] m. Aeda Slane[f] [g]m. Diarmata [h]m. Ḟergus[a][i] Cerbeoil[j] [k]m. Conail Cremthainne [l]m. Neill.[ghklm]

[a]m. Enan Lc. *Jee note to* 41. [b—b]om. MR[l]R[l]|18|40VaHLa. [c]Raiti(ne) (B)Lc, Raithne Lb, R. R, Ruaid Lc[l], *add* a nIathar Mide Lb. [d]Erna Lc, Ernin LbR[l]R[l]|18|40VaHLa, Eirine R(Lc[l]M). [e-e]Cael R, Caeil Lc[l](MR[l]HLa), Tail R[l]|18|40Va. [f]m. S(l)aine M(R[l])R[l]|18|40VaHLa, *add* m. Airt Chuirp m. Fir Chorp m. Laig m. Cormaic Gailing m. Taidg m. Cein m. Oilella Olaim M(*in smaller hand between columns*) (R[l]R[l]|18|40VaLa), m. Airt Chirb m. Nath Chorb H. [g-g]*om.* MR[l]R[l]|18|40VaHLa. [h—h]*om.* Lc. [i]*om.* R. [j]Cerbaill R, *om.* Lc[l]. [k—k]*om.* BLb. [l—l]*om.* R. [m]*add* Noigiallaig Lc[l].

43 Aedgein[a] — [b].i.[c] Bothi[b] — m. Lugair[d] m. Ernin[e] m. Cail m. Aeda Slane[f].

[a]Aithgen M. [b—b].i. Boit(h)c(h)e B(Lc), *om.* M. [c]*om.* Lc[l]. [d]Laegaire BLc. [e]Erine Lc[l](M). [f]*om.* M, *add* m. Diarmata m. Fergusa Cerrbeoil Lc[l].

44 Epscop Oengusa m. Ailella m. Eogain m. Neil[a] Noigiallaig[b].

[a]Neill BLcLbMR[l]. [b]*om.* LcLbMR[l].

45 Fortchern m. Feidlimid[a] m. Loegaire [b]m. Neill[b].

[a]Feidlim(th)e B(Lc). [b—b]*om.* Lc.

46 Crumthir Sinill[a] m. Tigernain[b] m. Ailella m. Eogain[c].

[a]Sinell Lb. [b]Tiger(r)naigh BLcLb(M). [c]*add* m. Neill (Naegiallaig) BLcLb(MR[l]).

47 Darfraech[a] ingen[b] Echach m. Crimthaind m. Feic m. [c]Dega Duirn[c] m. Cairpre Daim Argit m. Rochada m. Colla Focrí[d] [e]m. Echach Domlen m. Cairpre Liphechair[e].

[a]Dearbfraech Lc [b]mac BLc. [c—c]Deduirnn B. [d]Focrích BLb, Dacrich Lc. [e-e]*om.* BLcLb.

48 [a]Ronán Find[b] m. Sarain Sini[c] m. Colgan Cumai[c] m. Tuathail[d] m. Feidlimthi[e] [f]m. Ḟechini[f] [g]m. Fiachrach[g] m. Colla Focrí[h].

[a]*preceded by* Do clainn na Colla Lb. [b]*om.* H, *add* Cille Lainde R[l]La. [c]*om.* BLbLc[l]MR[l]HLa. [d]Thathail M, *add* m. Cruindbeoil Lb. [e]Feidlime B, Ḟédlimid Lb(M), *add with deletion marks* Rachtmair R[l]. [f—f]*om.* LbMR[l]HLa. [g—g]*om.* B, *add* Cassa(i)n R[l](La). [h]Focrich BLbMHLa, Focriaidh R[l], *add* m. Echach Doimplén Lb.

49 Colman — [a].i. Muccaid[a] [b]o Ard Bó[b] — [c]m. Aeda m. Guare[c] m. Amalgada[d] m. Muredaig m. Cairthind[e] m. Eirc[f] m. Echach m. Colla Uais [g]m. Echach Domlen[g].

[a—a]*added above line* L, *om.* BLbLc[l]MR[l]H. [b—b]Arda Bó BLc[l], *om.* MR[l]H. [c—c]*reversed* H. [d]Amalgaidh BLb(R[l]), Amalgda H. [e]Cartainn B(Lb). [f]Ceirc R[l]. [g—g]*om.* BLbLc[l]MR[l]H.

50 [a]Mael Doid[a] m. Fingin m Aeda [b]m. Ḟiachrach [c]m. Fiachach[bc] m. Eogain m. Briuin[d] m. Muredaig m. Imchada[e] m. Colla Focrí[f].

[a—a]Moeldoig Lb(M). [b—b]*reversed* Lc[l]. [c—c]*om.* BLc. [d]Broin M. [e]Indchada M. [f]Focrich BLbMH, *add* m. Echach Doimlen Lc[l].

51 Constans[a] anchorita[b] m. Fualascaig m. [c]Mael Aithgein[c] m. Forannáin[d] m. Totain[e] m. Amalgaid[f] [g]m. Niad m. Conaill m. Fergusa m. Muccada[h] m.Aeda Guaire m. Amalgada[gi] [j]m. Muredaig[j] m. Carthind[k] m. Eir[c][l] [m]m.Colla Uais.
[n]Is é fil [o]i nEoinis[o] for Loch Eirne[mnp].

[a]Consdan̄ B(Lc), Cuano R(Lc[l]M). [b]*om.* BLcLbRLc[l]M. [c—c]Mailaichin B. [d]*add* m. Moel hUidir m. Baetain R(Lc[l]M). [e]Tuatain Lb, Thuathain R(Lc[l])M. [f]Amalga(da) (RM)Lc[l]. [g—g]*om.* RLc[l]M. [h]Murcada BLcLb. [i]Amalgaidh BLc. [j—j]*om.* Lc[l]M. [k]Cairthind Lc[l](M). [l]E(i)rc(c) BLc(LbR)Lc[l](M), *add* m. Echach (Munremair) BLcLbR(Lc[l]). [m—m]*om.* RLc[l]M. [n—n]*om.* Lc. [o—o]a ninis BLb. [p]nErni Lb.

52 Guaire Mór[a] m. Colmain m. Ḟuachtaide[b] m. Ḟergusa m. Loegaire m. Fiachach[c] Tort m. Colla Uais[d].
Is e fil i nAchud Dubthaig [e]i mMaig Lí[e]. For brú na[f] Banna [e]Ichtair atát na[g] dá Guaire[eh].

[a].i. Mor Lb(*above line*). [b]Ful*ach*taidi Lc, Fuachtaite Lb. [c]Fiachra Lb. [d]*add* m. Echach Doimlen Lc. [e—e]*om.* Lb. [f]*om.* Lb. [g]in BLc. [h]*add* .i. Guairi Beg ⁊ Guaire Mor Lc.

53 Guaire[a] Bec m. Lasre m. Fergusa m. Loegaire[b].

[a]Et Guairi Lb. [b]*add* m. Fiachach Tort (a Muig Lii don dá Guairi sin) BLc(Lb).

54 Maignend[a] et Tua et Cobthach et Libren cetri meic[b] Aeda m. Colgan m. Tuathail Chrundbeóil m. Feidlimti[c] m. Ḟiachrach[d] m. Colla Focrí[e].

[a]Maidhnind B. [b]*added above line* Lb. [c]Feidlimid B(Lb). [d]*add* Cas(s)an (BLb)Lc. [e]Focrich BLb, Dacrich Lc.

55 Furudrán et Baetán[a] da[b] mac [c]Maenain m.[c] Colgan[d].

[a]Baithine M(M[l]La). [b]*added above line* M. [c—c]*om.* BLcLbMM[l]La. [d]*add* m. Cruind m. Ḟeig m. Feidlimid m. Fiachrach Cassan m. Colla Focrich B(LcLbMM[l]La), *add further* m. Echach Doimlen (m. Cairpri Lifechair m. Cormaic Ulfota m. Airt Enfir m. Cuind Cetcathaig) M[l](La).

56 [a]Daman Scí[a](?) m. Daimine[b] m. [c]Cairpre Daim Argit[c] m. Echach [d]m. Crimthainn[d] m. Feicc m. Dega Duirn m. Rochada[e] m. Colla Focrí[b].

[a—a]Damandscein B(LcLb). [b]*add* elit L(*below line*), Doimenn B, Do(i)meni Lc(Lb). [c—c]Caid B. [d—d]*om.* Lc. [e]Rocha Lc. [b]Focrich B, Dacrich Lb.

57 Adnach[a] m. Erchoil[b] m. Ḟergusa m. Cormaic m. Dochartaig [c]m. Ḟiachrach[c] m. Eirc m. Colla Óis[d].
Is é congab Lettir[e] Dallain.

[a]Annac B(Lc). [b]Eirc m. Oilella B(Lc)Lb. [c—c]*om.* BLcLb. [d]Uais BLcLb. [e]Litir BLc.

58 [a]Dechoin Áed[a] m. Mane m. Loegaire m. Cairthind[b] m. Eirc[c].
Is é fil i Cúil Mane[d].

[a—a]Decoimet BLcLb. [b]Carthaind BLcLb. [c]*add* m. Echach m. Colla Focri(ch) (B)Lc, m. Echach m. Collai Uais Lb. [d]*add* i Lurg Lc.

59 Baeglech[a] ailithir m. Faeldobair[b] m. Cummine[c] m. Lochine m. Thotain[d] [e]ut supra[e].

[a]Boeglaech Lb. [b]Dob̄ B, Dobre Lc. [c]Cumain(e) (B)Lc. [d]Dotain B, Tuatain Lb, *add* m. Amalgaidh (m. Niad m. Conaill ⁊rl) B(LcLb), *add further* m. Fergusa m. Murchada m. Aeda m. Guari m. Amalgada m. Muredaig m. Cartaind m. Eircc m. Echach m. Colla Uais Lb. [e—e]*om.* BLcLb.

60 Colman m. Eogain [a]m. Guaire[a] m. Forgo[b] m. Carthind[c] m. Eirc[d] [e]ut supra[e].

[a—a]*om.* MR[l]H. [b]Colgo Forgo *with marks of deletion under* Colgo B. [c]Cairthind RLc[l](MR[l])H. [d]Ceirc R[l], *add* m. Echach m. Colla (Focri) B(Lc), m. Echach m. Colla Uais LbM(*in smaller hand*)(R[l]), m. Echdach m. Clothchon R(Lc[l]). [e—e]*om.* BLcLbRLc[l]MR[l]H.

61.1 Aithgne[a] Bothi[b] Domnaig — [c].i. coic Patric[c] — m. Ail[d] m. Massine[e] m. Fergusa m. Duach m. Bresail m. Colla Mind[f].

2 [gh]Uel ita[h]: Aithgein 7 Crumthir Cenannán [i]da mac Ail et Curchach[j] a siúr.[gi]

[a]Aithne Lc, Aithgen LbLc[l], *add* .i. Cormac Lb. [b]Boto B. [c—c]*om.* BLcLbRLc[l]. [d]Cail Lb. [e]Maisi B(LcLb). [f]Mend B. [g—g]*om.* Lb. [h—h]*om.* BLc. [i—i] 7 Curcach .i. triur clainni Ail m. Maissi (m. Fergusa sin) B(Lc). [j]*add* ingen Ail R.

62 Darcairthend[a] ingen[b] Ennae m. Trenai [c]m. Cairthind[cd] m. Eirc[e] [f]m. Colla Uais[f].

[a]Darcaraind B, Dercharthaind Lb. [b]*om.* B. [c—c]*om.* Lb. [d]Carthaind B(R). [e]*add* m. Echach Lb. [f—f]*om.* R, *added later* Lc[l].

63 Moedóc[a] Ferna[b] m. Setnai m. Eirc[c] m. Ḟeradaig[d] m. Amalgada[e] m. Muridaig m. Cairthind[f] m. Colla Uais[g].

[a]Maegoc Lc. [b].i. Ferna H(*above line*), *om.* BLcLb. [c]E(i)ricc (R[l])La. [d]*add* m. Fiachrach RLc[l]MR[l]HLa. [e]Amalgaidh BLcR[l], Amalga Lc[l]. [f]Carthaind BLcLbLa, Cointaind R[l], *add* m. Eircc m. Echach Lb(M). [g]*add* m. Echach Domlen RLc[l].

64 Fiachraig[a] m. Colmain m. Eogain m. Baetain[b] m. Ailella [c]m. Suibne m. Maele[d] Duin m. Ḟínain m. Ailella[c] m. Muredaig Mer[e] m. Imchada m. Colla Focrí[f].

[a]Fiachra BLcLb, Fiachraich RLc[l]. [b]Aedain B. [c—c]*om.* BLc, *through haplography.* [d]Mael R(Lc[l]). [e]*reading doubtful,* Meic(h) (B)Lc, Meith Lb, *om.* RLc[l]. [f]Focrich BLb, *add* m. Echach R.

65 Fland Febla m. Scandlain m. Fingin m. Aeda B*en*nain m. Fiachach[a] m. Muredaig Mer[b] [c]m. Imchada m. Colla Focri[c].

[a]Fiachrach R. [b]*or read* Me(ith), Meith RLc[l]. [c—c]*om.* RLc[l].

66 Colman Cilli[a] [b]m. Eogain[c] [d]m. Muredaig m. Niallain[e] m. Ḟeidlimid[f] m. Fiachrach Cassain m. Colla Focrí[bd].

[a]*add* Moir B(*see note*), More Lc. [b—b]*om.* B. [c]nEogain Lc[l], *add* m. Baetain m. Ailella 7rl Lc. [d—d]*om.* Lc. [e]*add* m. Feic Lc[l]. [f]Feidel*mid* R.

67 Énna Áirni[a] m. Conaill[b] m. Daimine m. Corpre [c]Daim Argit[c] [d]m. Crimthainn[d].
[ef]Li[g] Logene[fh] soror Enna[ei].

[a]Arand R[l], *om.* H. [b]*add* D(e)irg (Lb)MR[l]La. [c—c]*om.* RLc[l]R[l], *add* m. E(a)chach Lb(MR[l])H. [d—d]*om.* MR[l]H, *add* m. Feic m. Dega (Duirn) m. Rochada m. Colla Focrich (LbRLc[l])MR[l]H, *add further* m. Echach R. [e—e]*in text after* Airni RLc[l], *om.* MR[l]H. [f—f]L(iim)lae? R, Liilae Lc[l]. [g]Le B, 7 Lb. [h]Loicene B(Lb). [i]eius RLc[l].

68 Epscop Co[lm]ain m. Raithini[a](?) m. Corcain m. Airt[b] m. Lugdech Cennfotai[c].

[a]Raitine BLc, Raith(f)ir (R)Lc[l]. [b]Airtf(e)ir B(Lc), Airt(t)e (R)Lc[l]. [c]Cenndruim B(Lc), *om.* RLc[l], *add* m. Enna(e) m. Luigdech (R)Lc[l].

69 Techan[a] — [b]nóeb[c](?) .i. (?) sanctus[bd] — m. |Beraig|[e] m. Senaig m. Nathí[f] m. Daimine[g] m. Cairpre [h]Daim Argit[h].
Hi[g] Tír[i] *Ua* ṅGentich[j].

[a]Tecan B(LcLb). [b—b]*added below line* L, *in text* BLcLb. [c]*om.* BLcLb. [d]neb BLc, sanctus Lb. [e]*illeg.* L, Beraigh BLcLb. [f]Nahi Lb. [g]Doimeni Lb. [h—h]*om.* BLc. [i]tiribh BLc. [j]nGe(i)ndtib (B)Lc, nGennti Lb.

70 Modobba[a] m. Segain[b] m. Fortcheirn[c] m. Mael Ruba [de]m. Dicolla[e] m. Critain[d] [f]m. |...| m. |...|[f].

[a]Moabba Lc. [b]Enain BLcLb. [c]Fortenn B(LcLb). [d—d]*om.* BLc. [e—e]*om.* Lb. [f—f]m. Conaill Gulban B, (m. Enna Boguine) m. Conaill Gulban m. Neill Noigiallaig Lc(Lb).

71 Ronnat[a] ingen [b]Fiachnai m.[b] Aeda m. Libreain m. Daleine[c] [d]m. Ennae m. Loegaire m. Neill[de].

[a]Ronait BLb. [b—b]*om.* B. [c]Daimine B, Dallén Lb, Da(i)lline R(Lc[l]), *add* m. Libir RLc[l]. [d—d]*om.* RLc[l]. [e]*add* Noigiallaig B.

72 Conall m. Fiachra[a] m. Mael[b]|Duin|[c] m. Colmain m. Aeda m. Lib|reain|[d] m. Dal|eine|[e] m. Enna m. |Loegaire|[f] [g]m. Neill Noigiallaig[gh].

[a]Fiach(r)ach (B)Lc, Fiacħ LB, Fiachnae RLc[l]. [b]Maele Lb. [c]*illeg.*L, Duin BLcLbRLc[l]. [d]*partly illeg.* L, Libren BLcLbLc[l], Libeir R. [e]*partly illeg.* L, Daillin B, Dallain Lc, Da(i)llen(e) Lb(RLc[l]). [f]*illeg.* L, Laegaire B(Lc)LbR(Lc[l]). [g—g]*om.* Lc. [h]*om.* BLb.

73 Aed Cael m. Feradaig m. Colmain [a]m. Aeda[a] m. |...|[b].

[a—a]*om.* B. [b]*illeg.* L, Daillein B(LcLb), Dailline RLc[l], *add* m. Enda m. Laegaire m. Neill (Noigiallaig) B(Lc)Lb.

74 Molugad[a] m. Lainneoin m. Ḟintain [b]m. Lugdach[b] m. Ennae Boguine m. Conaill Gulban[c].

[a]Moluca BLc, Molugdach Lb, Molug(d)a (R)Lc[l]. [b—b]*om.* Lc. [c]*add* m. Neill (Noigiallaig) (Lc)Lb(RLc[l]).

75 Se|chnasach|[a] m. |...|[b] m. Aeda[c] m. Lugdech[d].

[a]*partly illeg.* L, Sechnasach BLcRLc[l]. [b]*illeg. but like* Fina L, Fina BLc, Finain RLc[l]. [c]*add* Oll*ain* RLc[l]. [d]Lug(d)ach (B)Lc, *add* m. Laegairi m. Neill Lc.

76 Trea[a] ingen Chairthind[b] m. Eirc[c] [d]m. Echach[d] m. Colla Uais.

[a]Treaa M. [b]Chaerthainn M, Cartaind R[l]. [c]Ceirc R[l]. [d—d]*om.* H.

77 Molua[a] [b]m. Sinill[b] m. Amargin[c] m. Cruttin[d] m. Duach[e] m. Briuin[f] m. Echach Mugmedoin.

[a]*add above line* .i. do hIb h*Er*cda Cein do Lb. [b—b]m. Sincill (*no* m. Sinill) (R[l])H[l], m. Mic Sinill La. [c]Aimirge(i)n Lc(M). [d]*add* m. Eogain Sreim Lb. [e]*add* Galaig LcLb. [f]Bria(i)n (Lb)R[l](H[l]La).

78 Findchú[a] [b]m. Setna[b] m. Abrai[c] m. Branáin[d] m. Dobtha[e] m. Oengusa m. Eirc[f] m. Briuin[g] m. Echach Mugmedoin[h].

[a]*add* o Bri Goband LbM(R[l]H[l]). [b–b]*om.* Lb. [c]Abrain BLc, Gabrai MR[l]H[l]. [d]Abrainain B, Brannain Lc. [e]Dobratha B, Dubtai o tat Cenal Dubtai H[l]. [f]Erca Derc Lc(LbMH[l]). [g]Briain BLcLbMR[l]H[l]. [h]*add* Is hi oenitche notgudim ar mo scarad frisin sas. Nirob iffernach cech duine acht co ramguide fri bas. Findchu dixit in sin Lb, *add* Is do claind Branain etc. H[l] (*see note*).

79 Lurach[a] m. Cuanach[b] m. Daire m. Feidlimid[c] m. Eichein[d] m. Fiachra Tort[e] [f]m. Colla Uais[f].

[a]Laurach Lb, Luarach M. [b]Cunach R. [c]Fedlimthi Lb(MH)La. [d]Echain Lc[l], Fechen La. [e]*om.* RLc[l]. [f–f]*om.* Lc.

80 Tigernán[a] m.[b] Ninnida[c] [d]m. Ainmere[e] m. Aeda[d] m. Cairpre m. Amalgada[f] [gh]m. Muredaig[h] m. Cairthind[i] m. Colla Uais[g].

[a]Tigernach Lb, *add* Oirig Lacha Con Lc[l](La). [b]*om.* BLc. [c]Imchada La. [d–d]*om.* Lc[l]La. [e]Ainmirech Lb. [f]Amalga(id) (BLc[l])Lc, *add* m. Ḟiachrach m. Echach Muidmedoin Lc[l]La. [g–g]*om.* Lc[l]La. [h–h]*om.* Lc. [i]Carthaind BLcLb, *add* m. Eircc m. Echach Lb.

81 Cumman[a] 7 Crón[b] 7 Rignach tri[c] ingena Aeda m. Guaire m. Ḟínain m. Amalgada[d] m. Ḟiachrach[e] m. Bresail m. Mane m. Neill Noigiallaig[f].
[g]Cumman 7 Crón i Cill Ingen[h] Aeda i fail Irchulind i Fothartaib Féa[i] et Rignach i Cill Rignaige i n*Uib* Enechglais[j] 7 i Fothartaib Airbr*ech*[kg].

[a]*add* hoc ante debuit esse scilicet inter alios nepotes Neill L(*in marg.*). [b]Cronan Lb. [c]teora Lb. [d]amalga(id) (B)LcLbLc[l]. [e]Fiachach Lc. [f]*om.* LcR. [g–g]*om.* RLc[l]. [h]ingine Lc. [i]Feada Lc. [j]Enechland B, Enechlais Cualand Lc. [k]Airbri BLc.

82.1 [a]Daig cerd[b] — [c]7 Femmi soror eius[c] — m. Cairill m. Lasre Luind[d] m. Dallain m. Eogain m. Neill Noigiallaig[a].
2 [e]Tri[f] primcherda hErenn[g] .i. Tassach la Patric 7 Conlaed[h] la Brigit 7 Daig la Cíaran[i] [j]7 tri[j] epscuip [k]in sin[ek].

[a–a]*om.* Lc. [b]*om.* MH. [c–c]*added above line* L, *om.* BLcLbMH. [d]*om.* MH. [e–e]*om.* MH. [f]teora Lb. [g]*add* in sin Lb. [h]Conlae B. [i]C*r*i(t)ran B(Lc). [j–j] teora Lb. [k–k]iad Lc, eat beos Lb.

83 Dachonna[a] [b]o Ess Mac nEirc[b] et Lugaid[c] [d]Cluana Loeg[d] et Epscop Cormac tri[e] meic[f] Echach[g] m. Illaind[h] m. Eogain [i]m. Neill Noigiallaig[ij].

[a]Dachon BLcLb. [b–b]*om.* RLc[l], Eassa M, Essa (*with* .i. Mac Eirc *above line*) R[l]. [c]Lug(d)ach BLc(Lb). [d–d]*om.* RLc[l]MR[l]. [e]*om.* B. [f]*om.* R. [g]Echdach R. [h]Ellaind RLc[l]. [i–i]*om.* R. [j]*om.* LcLb.

84 Epscop Dronain[a] [b]i Cill Epscuip Dronain[a] [c]i n*Uib*[c] Maele Ruba[b] m. Fiangalaich m. Fianchon m. Mael Odrain m. Ḟailbe Tibri[d] m. Dimmae m. [e]Colmain m. Aeda Cael[ef] m. Libir[g] m. Dalline m. Enna m. Loegaire [h]m. Neil[hi].

[a]Dranain BLcLb. [b–b]*om.* RLc[l]. [c–c]ingine .h. Lc. [d]Tib*eri* BLb, *om.* LcRLc[l]. [e–e]Colmain Caeil m. Aeda BLc(Lb). [f]*om.* RLc[l]. [g]Lib̄ B, Libeir R. [h–h]*om.* Lc. [i]*add* Noigiallaig RLc[l].

85 Fergil naeb[a] Dergaenaig[b] m. [c]Maele Duin[c] [d]m. Colmain[d] [e]m. Ḟeradaig Find[f] m. Aeda Find m. Colmain[e] [g]m. Aeda[gh].

[a]neb Lc, sanctus Lb(*above line*). [b]Dergenaig BLcLb, *om.* RLc[l]. [c—c]Maain B. [d—d]*om.* B. [e—e]*om.* Lb. [f]*above line* L, *om.* BLcLbRLc[l]. [g—g]*om.* B. [h]Aeda Coel R(Lc[l]), *add* ⁊rl Lc, m. Librein m. Dallein (m. Enda m. Laegaire m. Nell) (Lb)RLc[l].

86.1 Mael Dub m. Aeda Findleith[a] m. Neill Kalle [b]m. Aeda Ordnide [...][bc]. [d]Dicitur: Cara m'anmasa Maeldub,
nocon e frith ar baegul,
acht a chulchi's a blae lín
ni rothecht dont ṡaegul.

Doberim teist ar Maeldub,
ar ulc fri demun ṅdaerdub,
co mberad cuil ina crub,
na fil do chul i mMaeldub[d].

2 [e]*Nó*[f]: Fintan ⁊[g] Mael Dub o Laind[h] Mael Duib eter[i] Ros na Rig [j]⁊ Boind[ej].

[a]Find BLb, *add* i Cluain Moir Leith BLc. [b—b]*om.* B. [c]*illeg.* L, om. Lc, m. Nell Frassaig Lb. [d—d]*in lower margin* L, om. BLcLb. [e—e]*in left margin* L, *in text before* Mael Dub BLc, *om.* Lb. [f]*om.* BLc. [g]*om.* B. [h]Laitin B, Leitir hi Lc. [i]ic Lc. [j—j]*om.* BLc.

87 Epscop Colman [a]i Cluain Iain Móir[a] m. Fortchernd m. Dicolla[b] m. Critain[c] m. Airmedaig m. Senaig m. Aedloga[d] m. Oschon m. Miannaig m. Lugdach m. Imchada m. Mechair m. Ḟidchuire m.[e] Echdach m. Ennae Munchain m. Rosa Rigḟota m. Ḟiachrach[f] Suidgi[g] m. Ḟeidlimid Rechtada[h].

[a—a]*above line* L, *attached to preceding pedigree* Lc[l](*see note*), *om.* BLb. [b]Holla B. [c]Crimthain B(Lb). [d]Aedalog B. [e].i. B. [f]Fiachach Lc[l]. [g]Find B. [h]Rechtmair Lb.

88.1 [a]Epscop Aed [b]m. Muredaig m. Fortcheirnd m. Dicolla[c] [d]ut supra[bd], Epscop Manchín [e]i Cill Iain Bic[e], Epscop Diarmata, Epscop Tairchill[f], Epscop Faebarchon, Epscop Cainne[g]; [h]secht[i] meic Muredaig m. Fortcheirn [j]m. Maele Ruba[j] m. Dicolla[ah].

2 [b]Secht n-ingena dna[k] Muredaig[l] i [m]Cill Iain, et Eithne ingen Iain[n] i nOchtur Aird[m], i Cill Chúile[bo].

[a—a]*om.* Lc [b—b]*om.* Lc[l]. [c]Dicollaig B, *add* m. Crimthainn m. Airmedaig m. Ṡenaig .i. hi Cill Ian Bic iat araen Lb. [d—d]*om.* BLb. [e—e]hi Cill Manchin Lb, *om.* Lc[l]. [f]Dairchell Lb. [g]Coinne Lb, *add* Epscop Mac Laisre i Cill Iain Bic Lc[l]. [h—h]*precedes* Epscop Aed Lc[l]. [i].ui. Lb. [j—j]*om.* LbLc[l]. [k]*om.* LcLb. [l]*add* m. Fortchirn m. Dicholla Lb. [m—m]Cill Cuimni ingene Iain i nUachtarda B, Cill Ḟinan ⁊ Cuimni ingen Finan i nUachtarda i Cill Ḟinan ⁊ Lc. [n]Muiredaig Lb. [o]Cuilen BLc, *add* ⁊ in sechtmad epscop .i. Epscop Colmain Lb.

9 Berchan[a] m. Aeda m. Echdach m. Fidchuire[b] [c]m. Cathchon m. Ossain[cd] m. Oengusa m. Eogain Bric m. Airt Chirb[e] m. Fiachach Suidgi.
I nhUib Luachain i[f] n*Uib* Brigti isna[g] Desib Muman[h]; i nDruim Luachain.

[a]Beachan BLc, Beccan Lb. [b]Idcuire B. [c]—[c]m *Cath*doaissin B. [d]Osrain Lb. [e]Chuirp Lc(Lb). [f]7 (a) BLc(Lb). [g]and isna Lc, a Lb. [h]*add* .i. Lb.

0 Colgu[a] [b]Cilli[c] Colgan ic Áth Cluana Medraige — 7 [d]Ḟaeliu soror eius[bd] — [e]m. Aeda[e] [f]m. Lugdach[f] m. Nathí[g] [h]m. Fiach*ach*[i] m. Echach Mugmedoin[hj].

[a]Colgan B(Lc). [b]—[b]*om.* Lc[l]Lc[l]39RaR[l]H[l]. [c]Cluana Lc. [d]—[d]Fael 7 Sorar tri BLc, Fael .i. Sorar (*above line*) clann Lb. [e]—[e]*written twice* BLcLb, *add* Draighnig R[l]. [f]—[f]m. Eogain m. Echach Lc[l]39RaH[l], m. Eoghain Aidhne m. Eachach R[l]. [g]Uait(t)i B(Lc), Dathi Lc[l]39RaR[l]H[l]. [h]—[h]*om.* Lec[l]39Ra. [i]Ḟiachrach (Foltnathigh) LcLbH[l](R[l]). [j]*add* m. Muiredaig Tirig Lc.

1.1 [a]Forannan Domnaig[b] Móir [c]Maigi[d] Femin[c] m. Rónáin m. Ḟiachnai m. Fintain m. Lasre[e] m. Cainnig m. Ernbraind m. Niad[f] m. [g]Brain Ḟind[g] m. Eogain m.[h] Airt Chirp[i] [j]m. Mess Chuirp[j] m. Mes Cegra[k] [l]m. [m]Mesa Fora[m] [n]m. Conuschain Bretnaig[no] m. Condrach[p] [q]Cathbuadaig[r] m. Rigrúaid[q] m. Fiachach Suidgi [s]m. Feidlimid Rechtada[ast].

2 [u]Tri ingena Cainnig m. Ernbraind[v] m. Niad [w]m. Eogain[w] m. [x]Brain Find[x] m. Eogain et cetera[luy].

[a]—[a]*om.* H. [b]Droma B. [c]—[c]*om.* RLc[l]. [d]ige *above line* Lb. [e]Meic Laisre Lb. [f]Niadbrain Lb. [g]—[g]Briain RLc[l]. [h]*om.* B. [i]Chuirp Lb(RLc[l]). [j]—[j]*om.* BLb. [k]Gedra(i) B(Lb). [l]—[l]*om.* Lb. [m]—[m]Meisiforci B. [n]—[n]m. Cainbrethaig RLc[l]. [o]Bre*t*aich B. [p]Condraigh B, *add* m. Cairpre RLc[l]. [q]—[q]*om.* RLc[l]. [r]m. Cathbaigh B. [s]—[s]*om.* BR. [t]*add* m. Tuathail T*echtmair* m. Fearadaig F*ind Fechtnaig* Lc[l]. [u]—[u]*in marg. with marks of ref.* L, *entered separately* B(*see note*)RLc[l]. [v]nbad B, Fernbrain(d) (RLc[l])H. [w]—[w]*om.* RLc[l]H. [x]—[x]Briuin RLc[l]H. [y]m. Bricc m. Airtt Choirp m. Cairpre (Rigrond H) m. Fiachach (Suidgi RLc[l]) m. Feidelmid Rechtada R(Lc[l]H).

2.1 Senan Achaid Cael m. Ernine m. Triain[a] m. Duind Duaig[b] m. Echdach m. Niad Brain m. Briain[c] Ḟind m. Eogain[d] [e]ut supra[e].

2 [f]Cerc[g] soror eius[fh]. [i]Cerc[j] 7 Becrall[k] a dí[e] siair i nAchud Liss[i].

[a]Trien BLc, Trein Lb. [b]Duad BLc, *om.* LbRLc[l]. [c]Bra*nn* B, Brain LcLb. [d]Ain BLc, *add* m. Airt Chirb m. Miscratidsin (Misgadra) (m. Mesin Fuirg m. Mesin Forgill m. Conais Cainbretaig m. Condrai m. Cathbad m. Rossa Rigruaid m. Fiachach Suige m. Fedlimthe Rechtmair) BLc(Lb), m. Airtt Chirp m. Mes Chuirp m. Mes Gegra R(Lc[l]). [e]—[e]*om.* BLcLbRLc[l]. [f]—[f]*above* Senan L, *in text after* Chail Lb, *om.* BLcRLc[l]. [g]7 h*E*rcc Lb. [h]Ṡenain Lb. [i]—[i]*in marg. with marks of ref.* L, *in text* RLc[l], *om.* BLcLb. [j]et Cercc (Serc) R(Lc[l]). [k]*or* Becrab(?) L, Becrall RLc[l]. [l]da Lc[l].

93 Mite[a] ingen Chind Ḟaelad m. Cormaic [b]m. Conchobuir[b] m. Conaill[c] [d]m. Oengusa m. Airt Chirp[e] [f]m. Carpre Rigruaid[fg] m. Ḟiachach [h]Suidgi[i] [j]m. Feidlimid Rechtada[dhjk].

[a]*add* ⁊ Finai (.i. Guirbe ala nainnm di *above line*) mathair Ḟlaind Ḟinai m. Ossai dá Lb, Ite La250. [b–b]*om.* La250. [c]*add* a quo hUi Conaill Gabra La250La309. [d–d]*om.* La250. [e]Chuirp Lb(Lc[1])M(R[1]HLa309). [f–f]*om.* Lb. [g]*om.* LcLc[1], Rig. MR[1](H), Rigeda La309. [h–h]*om.* La309. [i]*om.* MR[1]. [j–j]*om.* BLc. [k]Rechtmair Lb, *om.* R[1].

94 Mobriccu [a]Belaig Ḟeile[ab] m. Sílain m. Dubthaig m. Fergnai[c] m. Muredaig m. Sinill Chossaig[d] m. Bregain[e] Brígaich[f] m. Oengusa Aslethain[g] m. Eogain Bricc m. Fiachach Suidgi [h]m. Feidlimid Rechtada[hi].

[a–a]*om.* RLc[1]. [b]Felaigh B. [c]Fergusa B. [d]Sirchosaig Lc, *om.* RLc[1]. [e]Breacan B(LcLb). [f]*om.* LbRLc[1]. [g]*om.* RLc[1]. [h–h]*om.* BLcLb. [i]*om.* R.

95 Epscop Mac Cairthind[a] m. Cainnig m. Feidlimthi[b] m. Echach m.[c] Clothchon m. Airida[d] m. Mailida[e] [f]m. Bresail[f] m. Briuin[g].

[a]Cartainn B(LbMHLa), *add* Chlochair MLa. [b]Feidlimig M. [c]*om.* HLa. [d]Caireda Lb, Arda M. [e]Maelaeda M. [f–f]*om.* Lb, *add* Bric Lc[1]. [g]Briain BLa, Buain M, *add in later hand* m. Echach Mugmedóin B.

96.1 Ibar[a] epscop m. Lugna m. Cuirc m. Cuirbb[b] m. Corpre [c]m. Neill m. Echach[d], [e]a quo *Ui* Echach[e], m. Sin[c] m. Roṡin [f]m. Triir[g] [h]m. Rotriir[h] [i]m. Airnil[j] m. Maine m. Forgo m. Ḟeradaig m. Ailella Erand[k] m. Ḟiachach [l]Fir Mara[l] [m]m. Oengus|a| Turbig[imn].

2 [o]Uel [pq]ita: Epscop Ibar m. Lugna m. Cuirc m. Cuirb m. Cairpre m. Neill[q] m. Echach[p], a quo *Ui* Echach, m. Lugdach m. Rosa[r] m. Imchada m. Feidlimid m. Cais m. Fiachach Araide[fos].

[a]hIubar Lb. [b]Corb B(Lb). [c–c]*om.* B. [d]Echdach R. [e–e]*om.* RLc[1], *add* Ulad Lb. [f–f]*om.* Lc[1]. [g]Tr(e)in B(Lb). [h–h]*om.* B, m. Rothrein Lb. [i–i]*om.* Lb. [j]Arnail B. [k]*om.* BR. [l–l]*om.* R. [m–m]*om.* B. [n]*om.* R, *add* m. Echdach m. Fir Cetharraith m. Fir Raith m. Fir Anaruith m. Fir Almaich m. Laebchuiri m. Ailella Casfiaclaig m. Condlaid m. hIrero m. Meilge m. Cobthaich Caelbreg m. Ugaine Mair R. [o–o]*om.* R. [p–p]*om.* B. [q–q]*om.* Lb. [r]Rosin Lb. [s]Aradaig B, *add* m. Oengusa Goibnend Lb.

97 Comgall[a] Bennchair[b] m. Setnai [cd]m. Echach[c] m. Broen[de] m. Forgo m. Ernaine m. Crimthaind[f] m. Echdach[g] m. Lugdach [h]m. Rosa[i] [jk]m. Imchada[hk] m. Ḟeidlimid[l] m. Caiss m. Ḟiachach Araide[jm].

[a]*add above line* do noemaib Ulad annso sis H[1]. [b]*om.* H[1]. [c–c]*om.* H. [d–d]*reversed* Lc[1]. [e]Brain BLc, Briuin LbH, Briain H[1]. [f]Cremthaind H(H[1]). [g]Echach HH[1]. [h–h]*om.* H. [i]Sos*us* B, [j–j]*om.* BLc. [k–k]*om.* Lb. [l]Fedlemthe H(H[1]). [m]*add* otat Dal nAraide m. Feargusa Gailinni m. Tibraite Tirig m. Mail m. Muiredaig m. Cathbud m. Alcada m. Cuind Cothaid(?) m. Finchoda m. Muiredaig m. Finnamnais m. Iriuil Glunmair m. Conaill Cernaig m. Amairgein m. Caiss m. Finnachtai m. Cairpp m. Cing m. Rossa m. Rudraigi m. Sithride m. Duib m. Fomoir m. Airgetmair H[1].

98.1 Moninni — [a]qui Darerca[b] prius dicebatur[ca] — ingen[d] Mochta m. Lilchain[e] [f]m. Lugdach m. Conaill m. Echdach m. Cruind[fg] [h]m. Lugdach[i] [jk]ut supra.

2 Uel ita[hk]: Moninni ingen[d] Lilaig[l] m. Lugdach m. Nellini[m] m. Murchertaig m. Muredaig m. Eogain m. Neill[jn].

[a]—[a]*above line* L, *attached to* 97 BLc, *om.* LbLc[l]M. [b]Darrera BLc. [c]dicipatur BLc. [d]m. B. [e]Liccain Lb, Lilaich M. [f]—[f]*om.* M. [g]Cruid B, *add* Ba Drai (m. Echach Cobai) Lc(Lb). [h]—[h]*om.* Lc. [i]*add* m. Rosa m. Imchada m. Feidlimid m. Cais (m. Fiacha Araide) (Lc[l])M. [j]—[j]*om.* Lc[l]M. [k]—[k]*om.* BLb. [l]Lilagai B(Lc). [m]Neillene BLc. [n]*add* Noigiallaig LcLb.

99 Mocholmoc [a]Dromma Moir[a] m. Conrathain[b] m. Corcrain[c] m. Lugdach[d] m. Rosa[e] [f]m. Imchada [g]ut supra[fg].

[a]—[a]*om.* MR[l]HLa. [b]Thain BLc, Crimthain Lb, Conraith M, *add* m. Caerthainn M(R[l]La). [c]Corc(c)ain (M)R[l]H. [d]Luigdeach MR[l]. [e]*add* m. Fedlimti m. Caiss m. Fiachach Araige Lb, *add* Ruaid La. [f]—[f]*om.* LbMR[l]HLa. [g]—[g]*om.* BLc.

100 Buaidbeo m. Lugdach[a] m. Liathchon m. Ḟiachach Araide.

[a]Luigdech Lc.

101 Ternoc m. Ciarain[a] m. Sarain m. Coelbad m. Cruind B*a Drui* [b]m. Echach m. Lugdach ut supra[b].

[a]Ciarog B(LcLb). [b]—[b]*om.* BLcLb.

102 Catan m. Matain m. Braccain m. Caelbaid m. Cruind Ba D*rui.*

103 Fulartach[a] m. Bricc m. Scandail m. Baetain m. Echach m. Conlai[b] m. Caelbad[c].
[d]Is e fil i nDisiurt Ḟulartaig i n*Uib* Falge[d].

[a]Fualartach BLcLb. [b]C*o*lla Lc. [c]Caellaidh B, *add* m. Cruind (B*a Drui*) B(Lc)Lb. [d]—[d]*om.* BLcLb.

104 Epscop Carpre m. Decill m. [N]adslúaig[a] m. Caelbad[b].

[a]N *om.* L. [b]Caelbaid BLcM(M[l]), *add* m. Cruind B*a Drui* (m. Eachach Coba) LcLb(MM[l]).

105 Trian m[a]. Deid[b] m. Luctai m. Findchada m. Ḟeidlimthe[c] m. Ṡogain Salbude[d] m. Ḟiachrach[e] Araide.

[a]*ingen* B. [b]Dedi Lb. [c]Ḟeidlimid Lc. [d]*om.* BLcLb. [e]Fiachach Lc.

106 Murdebur[a] [b]7 Forannán da[b] mac Cuanain[c] m. Meic[d] Thire [e]m. Diarmata m. Ḟind m. Luctai[ef].

[a]Muṅdebur Lb[l]. [b]—[b]*om.* Lb[l]M. [c]Cuana B, Cunain M. [d]Mic B, *om.* M. [e]—[e]*om.* Lb[l]M. [f]Ḟolachtaig Lb, *add* m. Findchada m. Feidlimid (m. Caiss m. Fiachach Araide) BLc(Lb).

107.1 [a]Declan [b]Arde Móri[bc] m. Ernbraind[d].

2 *Nó* [ae]: Declan[f] m. Rosa[g] m.[h] Náir m. Fiạchai[i] m. Conaill m.[j] Mechain[k] m. Oengusa[j] m. Coṛmaic[l] m. Airt Oenḟir[m].
[n]7 Colman Airthir Ḟemin germanus Declain[n].

[a—a]*om.* LcLbMLa. [b—b]*om.* H. [c]Maire R. [d]Erccbrain (Erc) m. Niad m. Briain m. Eogain (Eogain Bricc) m. Airtt Choirp RLc[l](H), *add further* m. Cairpre N*iad* m. Cormaic RLc[l]. [e]a(i)liter R(Lc[l]). [f]*add* o Aird Moir Lb, *add* 7 Conall Airthir Ḟemin da RLc[l]. [g]Imrossa RLc[l](M)H(La). [h]*om.* M. [i]Fiachai*ch* RLc[l]H, Fiachain MLa. [j]*om.* La. [k]Meachair BLc. Mecon a quo Dal Meccon Lb, Mechon M(H), Meiccon m. Ceallaig La. [l]*add* Ulḟota(i) (Lb)M(H)[i]. [m]*added in later hand* H, *om.* LcLbRLc[l]MLa, *add* m. Cuind (Cétcathaig) (LcLb)R(Lc[l]MHLa). [n—n]cf. *above* RLc[l], *om.* MHLa.

108 Fergus [a]7 Muṛidach[b] Brucạch[c] et Mochommoc tri[ad] [ef]mẹic Ennai[f] m. Cormaic[e] m. Ḟergusa Cẹndfotai[g] [h]m. Crimthaind[i] m. Ḟeic m. Dega Duirn[j] m. Rochada [k]m. Ḟiachach Araide[hk].

[a—a]*om.* M. [b]*add* 7 Lc[l]. [c]Brugach RLc[l]. [d].iiii. RLc[l]. [e—e]*om.* Lc. [f—f]*om.* BLb. [g]*om.* RLc[l]. [h—h]*om.* M. [i]Cremthainn Lb. [j]*om.* B. [k—k]m. Colla Dacrich (m. Echach) Lb(R)Lc[l].

109 Comman[a] [b]Rois Chommain[b] m. Faelchon[c] m. Dretleain [d]m. Condla[d] m. Domangin[e] m. Imchada[f] m. Nair m. Erca[g] m. Soguin[h] Salbude[i] m. [j]Ḟiachach[k] Araide[j].

[a]Caman R[l]. [b—b]*om.* MR[l]. [c]Fealcon B. [d—d]*om.* MR[l]. [e]Doma(i)rgein (M)R[l]. [f]Ḟin(n)chada (M)R[l]. [g]Cerca M, *add* m. Tibraide M(R[l]). [h]Soegein R[l]. [i]*om.* BLbMR[l]. [j—j]Conaill Cerrnaig M, Conaill Cremtaind R[l]. [k]Fiacha Lc[l].

110 Cairech Dergain 7 [a]Ness Ernaig*thech*[b] et Cur|c|ach[ac] et Duṭhrach|t|[d] cethri ingena[e] [f]Ennai m.[f] Cormaic m. Ḟergusa Cendḟotai[g] [h]m. Crimthaind[h] [i]ut supra[i].

[a—a]*reversed* Lb. [b]Irritaicthe B, Aurnaigtech Lb, Ernanaig Lc[l]. [c]C(a)urcach B(Lb), Caurca*ch* R, Caurcan Lc[l]. [d]D(a)urach B(Lb), Duthracht RLc[l]. [e]*add* Cormaic m. R. [f—f]*om.* Lc[l]. [g]*om.* RLc[l]. [h—h]*om.* Lb. [i—i]m. Ḟeicc m. Dega Duirn m. Rochada m. Colla Focrich Lb, *om.* RLc[l].

111 Brigit ingen Aeda m. Echach m. Colla[a] m. Coelbad[b] m. Cruind [c]Ba Drui[c].

[a]Conla(i) B(Lb). [b]Caelbaidh BLc[l]. [c—c]*om.* R.

112 Fainche[a] ingen Bledine m. Lugdech[b] m. Echdach m. Carpre m. Ninnida[c] m. Cruind [d]Ba Drui[d].

[a]Fuinche Lb. [b]Lugach B. [c]*add* m. Coelbad(a) R(Lc[l]). [d—d]*om.* R.

113 Fainche[a] ingen Oengusa m. Critain[b] m. Echdach[c] [d]m. Colla [e]ut supra[de].

[a]Fuinche B. [b]Crimthain B. [c]Eathach B(Lc[l]). [d—d]*om.* B. [e—e]*om.* RLc[l].

114 Fergus m. Oengusa m. Critain m. Echdach m. Colla[a].

[a]*add* m. Coelbad m. Cruind R(Lc[l]).

115.1 [a]Braccan[b] m. Sarain m. C|o|elbad[c] m. [d]Cruind Ba Drui[d].

2 [e]Uel ita[af]: Breccan m. Saráin [g]m. Aeda[g] m. Dichoin[h] m. Trichim[ei].

[a—a]*om.* M. [b]Breacan B(LbRLc[1]H). [c]Caelbaidh B(LbRLc[1]H). [d—d]Cruind m. Ech(d)ach m. Lugdach (R)H. [e—e]*om.* H. [f]*om.* BLb. [g—g]*om.* BLb. [h]Dichon BLbRLc[1]M. [i]Trechim Lb.

116.1 [ab]Molua [c]Cluana Ferta[c] m. Carthaig m. Daigre m. [d]Cuirc Ocha[d] m. Ḟergusa Foga[e] m. [f]Cruind Ba Drui[f].

2 [g]Uel ita[bh]: Molua[i] m. Carthaig[j] m. Fualascaig m. Colmain m. Ennai[k] m. Themnen[l] m. Comgain[m].

3 [no]Uel ita[ap]: Molua[oq] [r]m. Carthaig[r] m. Daigri m. Erca[s] m. Imchada m. Lama[t] Feola[u] m. Clithaire[v] m. Focha[w] m. Dubthaig Duind[gnx].

[a—a]*om.* Lc. [b—b]*om.* MM[1]R[1]. [c—c]*om.* RLc[1]HLa. [d—d]Urchocho B, Aurchodai Lb. [e]*om.* H, *add* m. Frechuir (Fraechair, Froecair) RLa(Lc[1]H). [f—f]Cruind m. (m.) Echdach (R)Lc[1]HLa. [g—g]*om.* RLc[1]HLa. [h]*om.* BLb. [i]*add* Chluana Feartta M. [j]Carrtaind B. [k]mEana M[1]. [l]Teimhenen B, Theimin M[1]. [m]*add* m. Ioh̄ (Iohon) m. Carrthaig M(M[1]R[1]). *See note.* [n—n]*om.* MM[1]. [o—o]miohne Lb, *om.* R[1]. *See note.* [p]*om.* B. [q]*add* Cluana Ferta Lc. [r-r]Cr̄ B, m. Fualascaig Lc, *add* sund condricc 7 Mundai m. Tulchain Lb. [s]Erc BLc. [t]Laime BLcLb. [u]Fola B. [v]Cliat(h)aire B(LbR[1]). [w]Ocha R[1]. [x]*om.* Lc, *add* Cochmais(Coic) a (ainm) mathair Molua 7 do sil Luigdech Laga m. Moga Nuagad do Molua. (Mothemneoc .i. coic Molua Cluana Fearta) M[1](R[1]).

117 Molasse[a] apstal[b] m. Nadfraich m. Barrai*n*[c] [d]m. Conbrain[de] m. Dualsen[f] m. Dega m. Cruind[g] [h]Ba Drui [i]ut supra[hi].

[a]*add* Inse Mu(i)re(a)daig R(Lc[1]), *add above line* D(e) Eoganacht Chaisil annso (M)La. [b]aps̄ *in* L, *om.* BLbRLc[1]MR[1]HLa. [c]Barraig B, Branain R[1]La, Barrai*n*? R. *See note.* [d—d]*om.* La. [e]Conbin B, con *above line* R[1]. [f]Duilsen B, Tuailsin Lb(MR[1]HLa). [g]Cruinn m. Echdach m. Lugdach (m. Rosa m. Imchada m. Fedlimid m. Cais m. Fiachach) (R)MH, Cruind m. Eachach m. Luighdeach m. Breasail m. Aengusa m. Nafraich R[1](La). [h—h]*om.* RMR[1]HLa. [i—i]*om.* BLbLc[1].

118 Oengus [a]m. Oengoba[ab] m. Oebleain [c]m. Fidrui[c] m. Diarmata m. Ainmere[d] — [e]Nannan et Tigernan dá mac Nindida m. Ainmere[e] — m. Cellair[f] m. Oengusa m. Nadslúaig m. Coelbad[g] [h]m. Cruind[i] [j]Ba Drui[hj].

[a—a]*om.* H. [b]Ongobha BLb, Nuengoband Lc[1], Ingobunn M(R[1]La), Oengoband H 183b. [c—c]*om.* Lc, m. Fidhrui *no* BLb (*see note*), m. Fi*n*druí H183b. [d]Ainmirech Lb, Aimre M. [e—e]*in right marg. with mark of ref. to* Ainmere L, *om.* BLcLbRLc[1]MR[1]HH183bLa. *See note.* [f]Celboir M, Celtair R[1], Celtchair La. [g]Caelbhaidh BLc(R[1]), Caebad Lc[1], Aidilbad M. [h—h]*om.* B. [i]Cruind m. Echdach m. Lugdach RLc[1], Aruinn M. [j—j]*om.* RLc[1]MR[1]HH183bLa.

119 Glun[ṡ]alach[a] [b]Slebi Fuait[b] m. Costomail[c] [d]m. Echḍach[d] m. Luind[e] m. Lugdach[f] m. Rosa m. Imchada m. Feidlimid[g] m. Ḟiachach Araide[h].

[a]Glunsalach BLbRLc[1]M, *add* .i. Concobair Lc[1](*see note*). [b—b]*om.* RLc[1]. [c]Castamail Lb. [d—d]*om.* Lc[1]. [e]Floind Lb. [f]Luigdeach M. [g]Feidelmid R, *add* m. Cais(s) B(Lb)Lc[1] (*see note*). [h]*om.* R.

120 Conall m. Aeda m. Ṡaráin m. Maine [a]m. Ḟothaid m. Conaill[a] m. Echdach[b] m. Cruind Ba Drui.
Is e con̄gaib[c] Cluain Dallain i nDál Echach i fail Chuain[d] [e]Snama Ech[e].

[a—a]*om.* Lb. [b]Caelbaidh BLc(Lb). [c]congabh i B(Lc). [d]*om.* BLcLb. [e—e]Snamach BLcLb.

121 Moluoc m. Luctai m. Findchada [a]m. Feidlimthe[a] m. [b]Sogain Salbude[b].

[a—a]*om.* BLcLb. [b—b]Sodhain m. Fiathach Arade B(LcLbM).

122 Finnian[a] Cluana Eraird[b] [c]m. Findloga[c] m. Fintain m. Conchraid[d] m. Dairchella[e] m. Senaig m. Diarmata m. Aeda m. Ḟergusa m. Ailella Duib[f] m. Celtchair[g] [h]m. Cuthechair[h] [ij]m. Ḟotaid m. Ḟir Filed[k] [l]m. Rosa m. Rudraige[j] [m]ut ante in genelogia Conaill Cernaig[ilm].

[a]Finden BLb(Lc[l]H)La, Fin*n*la [= Fin*n*ia?] M, Findan R[l]. [b]Iraird B(LbLc[l]R[l])MH(La). [c—c]*om.* LbMR[l]HLa, m. hIrloga Lc[l]. [d]Conraig La. [e]Dairchoello M, Daircelle R[l], Taircella La. [f]Tulduib Lc[l](M), *om.* R[l]HLa. [g]Ce(a)ltair (B)La. [h—h]m. Uidechair B(LbLc[l]M), *om.* R[l]La. [i—i]*om.* Lb. [j—j]*om.* B. [k]*add* m. Glais (Caiss) Lc[l]H(R[l]La), m. Glais m. Nuagad Airgidlaim M. [l—l]*om.* M. [m—m]*corrupted* B, *om.* Lc[l]R[l]HLa.

123.1 [a]Cainnech[b] m. Lugthig[c] m. Lugdach[d] m.[e] Daland[f] [g]m. Echdach[h] m.[i] Ḟidchuiri[j] m. Ḟergusa m. Rosa[k] [lm]m. Imchada m. Fiachu m. Cais m. Isis m. Airirich[n] m. Condlai m. Corpre m. Orb m. Fael m. Corpre Auloim m. Ḟergusa[m] m. Rosa[o] m. Rudraige.

2 [pq]Uel aliter[aq]. Cainnech m. Leintich m. Lugdech[r] m. Eda[s] Alaind[gt] [u]m. Ḟidchuiri[v] [w]m. Altae[w] [x]m. Ogamuin m. Fidchuri m. Delmnae[y] [z]et cetera sicut in genelogia Brendini[lpuxz].

[a—a]*om.* Lc[l]. *See note.* [b]*add* (o) Achaid Bó m. Aedha (Alai[n]d) M(R[l]), m. Aeda La. [c]Lutaig B, Luith(e)ich (MR[l])H(La). [d]Lugdech Lb(MR[l]). [e]*om.* Lb. [f]Talaind Lb(H), Dal(l)ain (M)R[l]. [i—g]*hl* , LbH. [h]Echach M(R[l]La). [i]*om.* La. [j]Fi*n*dcuire B. [k]Roisi B, Roig MR[l], Róith La. [l—l]*om.* MH. [m—m]*om.* R[l]. [n]Cairirech B. [o]Roisi B. [p—p]*in right marg.* L, *om.* R[l]. [q—q]*om.* B. [r]Lugdach Lc[l]. [s]Aeda BLc[l]. [t]Allain B, *add* m. Echach m. Fidcuri m. Fergusa m. Rosa Lc[l]. [u—u]*om.* Lc[l]. [v]Findcuri B, hItcħ Lb, Ithacair H. [w—w]*om.* B. [x—x]*om.* H. [y]Dellman B, *add* m. Eoin m. Usalaig m. Astomain m. Mogai (.i. Ciar *above line*) Toeth m. Ḟergusa m. Roich Lb. [z—z]*corrupt in* B, *om.* Lb.

124 Brenaind[a] Birra[b] m. Nemainn m. Duib Dechoin m. Scellain — [c]Darnisa[d] et Sinech et [e]Crón *no*[ef] Críta[g] tri[h] ingena Ernáin m. Coluim Ruaid[i] m. Nemaind m. [j]Dub Dechoin[j] m. Scellain[k] et cetera[cl] — [m]m. Nastair[n] m.[mo] Taphail m. Branchon[p] [q]m. Airmora[r] m. Achir[s] m. Imchada m. Dubthaig m. Rosa[t] m. Imchada[u] [v]ut supra[qv].

[a]*add above line* Ban R[l]. [b]*om.* H. [c—c]*in marg. with marks of ref. to* Scellain L, *separate* BLb, *om.* Lc[l]H. [d]Dairius(s)a (B)Lb. [e—e]*om.* Lb. [f]*om.* B. [g]Criddai Lb. [h]teora Lb. [i]*om.* BLb. [j—j]Da(th)chon B(Lb). *See note.* [k]Seallain B, *add* sund condric ⁊ Brenaind Birra Lb. [l]*om.* BLb. [m—m]*om.* R[l]. *See note.* [n]Nassair B. [o]m. m. Lb. [p]*add* m. Diarmata et cetera H. [q—q]*om.* H. [r]Fir Morda B(Lb). [s]Cathair Lb(Lc[l]R[l]). [t]Roise B. [u]Ḟindchada LbR[l], *add* m. Echach(Fiachach) m. Caiss m. Ḟisis m. Airerraig(Airich) m. Conla m. Airt m. Coirpre m. Coirp(Oirb) m. Thail(Fael) m. Chuirp (m. Cairpre) Auluim m. Fergusa m. Roich(Rosa) Rodanai Lb(Lc[l]R[l]). [v—v]*om.* BLbLc[l]R[l].

125.1 Ciaran[a] [b]Cluana M*ac* Nois[b] m. Beodain[c] m. Bolggain[d] [e]m. Linnida[e] m. Cuirc [fg]m. Daaed[g] [h]m. Cunnida[fi] [j]m. Cais m. Fraech[k] m. Causcraid [l]m. Messin [m]Sued[n] m.[m] Suiled[lo] m. Ercada[p] m. Mechoin[q] m. Ṇechta[r] m. [s]Aeda[t] m. Coirbb[s] m. Aeda[u] Gnoe m.[v] Fer[w] Gae Lethain[x] m. Ḟeidlimid[y] m. Medrui m. Ḟollomain[z] [aa]m. [bb]Cuirc Dothi[bb] m. Fergusa [ccdd]m. Rosa[ee] [ff]m. Rudraige[aaddff].

2 Don tṡechtmad aicmi do[gg] Latharnaib[hh] Molt dó[ii]. Robaí[jj] [kk]ar tús [ll]a athair[kkll] [mm]i ndaere i mBretnaib[mmnn]. Tanic [oo]iar tain[oo] i[pp] nhErinn [qq]co Cenel Conaill; a ssuide[qqrr] ar imgabail[ss] císa truim[tt] [uuvv]co *Con*nac*ta*[vv], co rogenair[ww] Ciaran ic[xx] Ráith Chrimthaind i mMaig Aé[uu]. Beonaed[yy] saer[zz] [aaa]nomen patris eius[aaa]. Darerca[bbb] [ccc]nomen matris eiusdem[hjcccccddd].

[a]*preceded by* Do noemaib Sil Fergusa fodeathtso H[l]. [b—b]Cluana Mucc Nois Lb, Cluana Mucrais Lc[l], *om.* R[l]HH[l]. [c]hedain B, Boetain (*no* Beoan *above line*) Lb, Beonaid Lc[l]H[l], Baetain MR[l]|19|41Vc, Beoid H. [d]Olcain H. [e—e]*om.* H. [f—f]*reversed* MR[l]|19|41Vc. [g—g]m. Daid B, m. Daig Lb, m. Deda Lc[l], m. Da(i)thi M(R[l]|19|41Vc), m. Cunneim? H(R[l]). [h—h]*om.* R[l]. [i]Chuidida M, *add* m. Feic m. Mail m. Carthaig m. Láre m. Larini m. Cultri m. Glunig m. Coirpri m. Loga m. Medle m. Duib m. Lugnai m. Fedleimthe m. Echach m. Bresail Bain m. Dega m. Reo Soirche m. Reo Doirche m. Tigernmais m. Follaig m. Foebair m. Iorel Fatha m. hErimon m. Miled Espain m. Bili m. Bregaind H. [j—j]*om.* H. [k]Frai B, Na(d)fraich (M)R[l]|19|41Vc. [l—l]*reversed* Lc[l]H[l]. [m—m]*om.* B. [n]Niud Lb(MR[l]|19|41Vc). [o]Mesin Suileth Lb(Lc[l]MR[l]|19|41Vc). [p]Ercci m. Eircc Lb, Eirc(ce) (M)R[l]|19|41Vc. [q]Necoin B, Meiccon Lb. [r]Nechtain LbMR[l]|19|41Vc. [s—s]Aeda Cuirb Lb, Athchuirb .i. Aed ainm eile dó MR[l]|19|41Vc. [t]Aeda m. Aedha B. [u]*add* .i. *above line* L, *add* m. B. [v].i. Lb(*above line*), *om.* MR[l]|19|41Vc. [w]Fergusa Lc[l], Fer in M. [x]*add* m. Ailella Baschain m. Conairi m. Moga Lama *no* Lc[l]. [y]Aithblethe Lb, *add* frisi a nabairthi Aithmillti M(R[l]|19|41Vc). [z]Ollamna B(Lc[l]), Follain H[l]. [aa—aa]*om.* MR[l]|19|41Vc. [bb—bb]Cuircoithi B, Doethe m. Cuircc Lb, Cuirc m. Dothi Lc[l](H[l]), *add* m. Ceir H[l]. [cc—cc]*om.* Lc[l]. [dd—dd]*om.* B. [ee]Roich Lb, *add* Ruaid H[l]. [ff—ff]*om.* Lb. [gg]o MR[l]|19|41Vc. [hh]Lat(h)a(i)rna B(R[l]|19|41Vc)H[l], Latraind M. [ii]*add* Chiaran Lb, *om.* MR[l]|19|41VcH[l]. [jj]boi sium Lb, ar bae H[l]. [kk—kk]*om.* MR[l]|19|41Vc. [ll—ll]*in marg. with ref. mark* L, *om.* BLbH[l]. [mm—mm]*reversed* BLb. [nn]Breagaib 7 a mBreatnaib M. [oo—oo]iarum Lb, iar sin H[l]. [pp]co LbMR[l]|19|41VcH[l]. [qq—qq]*om.* Lb. [rr]sidein M(R[l]|19|41Vc). [ss]ingabhail R[l]|19|41VcH[l]. [tt]truimgaibh B, *om.* H[l]. [uu—uu]*om.* Lb. [vv—vv]*om.* B, co Con(d)achtaib M(R[l]|19|41VcH[l]). [ww]rafuagair B. [xx]a MR[l]|19|41VcH[l]. [yy]Beonat B, Beoan Lb, Beonaind H[l]. [zz]saí B, *om.* MR[l]|19|41Vc. [aaa—aaa]a athair Lb, ainm (a) athar (M)R[l]|19|41Vc(H[l]). [bbb]Curcach ingen Chirann M(R[l]|19|41Vc). [ccc—ccc]a mathair LbMR[l]|19|41Vc, ainm a mathar H[l], *add* qui de est(?) in aria M(R[l]|19|41Vc). [ddd]*add* ut dixit Ciaran (Is dosin ro|r|aidead): Darerccai mo mathairsi, nir bandscal docht(olc), ba Beoan(Beonaid) an saer m'athairsi, do Latharnaib Molt Lb(*in marg.*)(H[l]).

126 Mochuta[a] [b]Lis[c] Moir[b] m. Finaill[d] m. [e]Noe[f] Náir[eg] m. Firb[h] [i]m. Ambrit[j] m. Imchada [kl]m. hEbric[l] m. Mencon[m] [n]m. Aulaim m. Meschon[o] m. Sula[p]

[a]Carthach .i. Mochutu RLc[l]39Ve, Ca(r)rthach (M)La. [b—b]*om.* LbLc[l]MM[l]R[l]LaLa[l]. [c]Leasa B. [d]Fingein Lb, Finain RLc[l]39Ve, Finn M(La), Findenn M[l](R[l]La[l]). [e—e]Naenuair B. [f]ngnoae M[l](R[l]La[l]), *add* m. Cellain(Collain) m. Ṡaigleand LbRLc[l]39VeM(M[l]R[l]La[l]), m. Cellain m. Feic m. Sailgeann La. [g]*only in* L and B. [h]Cirbb R(Lc[l]39Ve), *add* a quo Uí Ḟirb Lb, dia taid hUa Ḟirp M(La). [i—i]*om.* MLa. [j]Amráidh B. [k—k]ut supra RLc[l]39Ve. [l—l]*om.* M[l]R[l]La[l]. [m]Mochon Lb(M[l])R[l](La[l]), Meccon Lc[l], *add* Finmaich(Finmaith) ingen (Finguine m.) Ḟinntain m. Aeda Loga m. Nathi mathair Mochuta M[l](R[l]La[l]). [n—n]*om.* M[l]R[l]La[l]. [o]Mesi Con Lb(Lc[l]). [p]Tala Lb.

m. Moga Airt[q] m. Corpsen[r] Moir[s] [t]m. Echadoin m. Ennae [u]Uais m. Eochamain[u] m. Ḟidchuire m. Telmne m. Eoinne m. Lainne m. Tulsaig m. Demmoin m. Moga Tuatha[v] qui et Ciar [w]m. ...[w] m. Ḟergusa m. Rosa[iknt].

[q]*add above line* .i. Ciar Lb. [r]Oirbsen B(Lb)Lc[l]. [s]*om.* Lc[l], *add* a quo Ciarraige B. [t—t]*om.* BLb. [u—u]*om.* Lc[l]. [v]Taeth Lc[l]. [w—w]*sic with* ∸ *in marg.* L, *om.* Lc[l].

127.1 Brenaind[a] apstal[b] m. Findloga[c] m. Olchon[d] [e]m. Altai[f] [g]m. Ogamain m. Ḟidchuiri[h] m. Delmnai[i] [j]m. Ennae[k] m. Fualascaig[l] m. Astamain[m] m. [n]Mogaed[o], [pq]qui dicitur[nr] Ciar[sp], m. Fergusa [t]m. Rosa[jqu].
[vw]Do Chiarraige Luachra[x], do Altraige[y] [z]Cind Bera[z] 7 do Chorcu Duibni[v].

2 [aa]Uel aliter[bb]: Brenaind m. Findloga[c] m. Olchon[cc] m. Gossa m. Gabli m. Ecni[dd] m. Altae [ee]m. Ogamain et cetera[gtwaaeeff].

[a]Broenfind Lb. [b]*written* ap̄s L(*see note*), espoc BLcM, *om.* LbLc[l]R[l]HH[l]. [c]Find Lc. [d]Elchon Lc[l]. [e—e]*om.* R[l]. *See note.* [f]Ailti m. Ailti H, *add* m. Erbsen [...]r m. (i)achna m. Alta H[l]. [g—g]et cetera Lc. [h]Fi*n*dcuri H. [i]Debh B, Telmne Lc[l], Delbna (*with* m *above* e) H[l]. [j—j]*om.* B. [k]Eoin Lb(H), Einde Lc[l]. [l]Ausalaig Lb(H), Ulroch H[l]. [m]Castoi(m)tin H[l]. [n—n]*om.* Lc[l]. [o]Mogai Toeth Lb(MH), Mugdach Mind H[l]. [p—p]*om.* H[l]. [q—q]*om.* Lb. [r]uocatur H. [s]Ciarraide M. [t—t]*om.* Lc[l]. [u]Roig M, *add* m. Fomoir m. Rudraid m. Sithmirthe m. Duib m. Fomoir m. Argatmair m. Sirlaimh m. Coirpri m. Ollama Fótla m. Fiachach Finnsgothaig m. Airt m. Ebir m. Ír m. Miled Espaine H[l]. [v—v]*after* 2 Lb. [w—w]*om.* HH[l]. [x]*add* do .i. Lb. [y]Altragaib B. [z—z]randai (*above line*) Berai Lb. [aa—aa]*in marg.* L, *om.* BLc. [bb]*om.* LbM. [cc]Findchada LbR[l]. [dd]E(i)cni Lb(M), Ethne R[l], *add* m. Taland m. Ithachair R[l]. [ee—ee]amal ata romaind Lb. [ff]m. Fidhchuire m. Dealbnai m. Eorai m. Uasalaigh m. Astamain m. Mogha Daeth m. Feargusa m. Rossa Ruaidh m. Rudhraighe R[l].

128 Duilech[a] m. Malaig[b] m. Sinill m. Nadfraich m. Ḟiachnai[c] m. Allai m. Conmail[d] Glais[e] m. Ḟergusa m. Rosa[f].

[a]*add* Clochair RLc[l]. [b]Ama[l]gadai Lb. [c]Fiacrach BLb. [d]Co(m)mail (R)Lc[l]. [e]*om.* RLc[l]. [f]Roig Lb, m*eic* Rossa R.

129 [a]Mobaí[b] dna[c] m. Sinill m. Nadfraich[d]. Malán[e] dna[c] m. Sinill et Curnan[f] m. Sinill et Cronan m. Sinill et Maniu[g] m. Sinill[a].

[a—a]*different arrangement* LbRLc[l]. [b]Mobhaedan B(Lb), Mobi Lc[l]. [c]*om.* BLb. [d]*add* m. Fiathach (m.) Allae (m. Conmail Glais m. Fergusa m. Roig) B(Lb), *add* m. Fiachrach RLc[l]. [e]Malach RLc[l]. [f]Cu*n*ran B, Caurnan LbRLc[l], *add* 7 Boetan Lb. [g]*om.* Lb.

130 Epscop Erc[a] Sláne[b] m. Dega m.[c] Branchon[d] m. Airmora[e] m. Cathḟir[f] [g]m. Imchada [h]m. Dubthaig[i] [j]m. Rosa[k] m. Findchada m. Echach[l] m. Cais m. Isis m. Airig[m] m. Carpre m. Fail m. Carpre Uloim[n] m. Ḟergusa[j] m. Rosa[gho].

[a]Searc B, Eirce M(R[l]). [b]*om.* Lc[l]. [c]*om.* B. [d]Branchor RLc[l]39Rb(M), Brachon(d) R[l](H). [e]Firmora BLb, Aurmora RLc[l]39Rb. [f]*add* sund condricc 7 Brenaind Birrai Lb. [g—g]*om.* Lb. [h—h]ut supra Lc[l]. [i]Dubtaige R[l]H, *add* m. Luigdech m. Cais(s) (M)R[l]. [j—j]*om.* MR[l]. [k]Roisi B. [l]Fechu H. [m]Airirich m. Condlai m. Airt H. [n]*om.* H. [o]Roig H, *add* m. Rudraige (m. Sithr*ide*) (RR[l])Lc[l]39Rb M, *add* Easpoc Eogain Ard na Sretha 7 Easpoc Erca Slaine da mac Deaga (m. Branchon iat 7 braithre dano do Brenainn Birri sin) M(R[l]. Cf. La 274).

131 Coeman [a]Santlethan Ardni[a] m. Thalain m. Dubthaig m. Rosai [b]m.[c] Imchada[d] m. Echach — [ef]*no* Fiachach[f] — m. Cais [g]m. Isis[beg].

[a—a]a nArd Leatha(n) B(LcLb), *om.* MH. [b—b]*om.* MH. [c]*om.* B. [d]Findchada Lb. [e—e]*om.* B, m. Cruind B*a Drui* Lc. [f—f]*above line* L, *om.* Lb. [g—g]condric ⁊ Brenaind Birrai Lb.

132.1 Baetán Cluana Andobair[a] m. Sinill m. Nadfraich [b]ut supra[b]

2 Sin im*murgu*[c] ingen Neill [b]m. Mechair[b] de Chorco Bascind, [d]de *Uib* Conaire[d] Lemme Con Culaind, [e]a mathair[e]. I[f] cóiced bliadain flatha[g] Faelain m. Colmain ríg Lagen dolluid co[h] Lag*niu*[i] ⁊ congab [j]Indsi Fualae[j] la hÚ Falge[k] ar tús. Isin .clxxxii.[l] bliadain post Patricii aduentum ad Hiberniam fundauit ecclesiam suam .i.[c] Cluain Andobair ⁊ .xuii.[m] annis in[c] ea habitauit.

[a]ndob BLc. [b—b]*om.* BLc. [c]*om.* BLc. [d—d]*om.* Lc. [e—e]mathair .u. mac Sinill Lc. [f]isin BLc. [g]flaithusa BLc. [h]a B, i Lc. [i]Laigh B. [j—j]inni is fael-(faelan) B(Lc). [k]*om.* B. [l].clxxxxii. B. [m].xuiii. BLc.

133 Epscop Eithern[a] m. Laithbe [b]m. [c]Mes Nube[c] m. Mugdorn[d] Duib. De Ultaib. Is é coṅgab Domnach Mór Meic Laithbe[be].

[a]Sethern(n) (B)Lc, (Ei)treann a nDomnach Mor M. [b—b]do Mugdornnaib M. [c—c]Menube BLcLb. [d]Mundoirn Lc. [e]*add* Finit Slicht Libair Glinni Da Lach sin. Slicht Liubair na Fuachongbala and so bodeasta Lc. *See note.*

134 Ciar m. Ambrit[a] m. Imchada m. Mochon[b] [c]m. Saulim m. Eschon[d] m. Saulo m. [e]Moga Airt[ce] [f]qui ⁊ Ciar[f]. Is é fil i nAchud hÍ la Aes Tiri.

[a]A(i)mbricc B(Lc). [b]*add above line* .i. do Chiarraige dó Lb. [c—c]*om.* Lb. [d]Oschon Lc. [e—e]Moairt B, *add* m. Oirbsen Mar B(Lc). [f—f]*after* Tiri BLc (*see note*), *om.* Lb.

135 Ailbe [a]Imlecha Ibair[ab] m. Olcain[c], [d].i.[e] Naiss[d], m. Arra[f] [g]m. Dala[g] m. Laidḟir[h]m. Imrosa[i] m. Ḟir Thlachtga [j]m. Celtchair m. Cuthechair[j] [k]ut ante[k].

[a—a]*om.* RLc[l]H. [b]*om.* Lc, .i. Iubair Lb (*above line*). [c](h)Olchon BLc(Lb). [d—d]*above line* L, *om.* LbRLc[l]H. [e]m. Lc. [f]Carra BLc. [g—g]*om.* BLc. [h]*add above line* .i. Ara Lb. [i]*add* Nithai Lb. [j—j]m. Fergusa m. Roig Lb. [k—k]*om.* BLcLbH, m. Fothaid m. Fir Filed m. Glais m. Rossa (m.) Rudraige R(Lc[l]).

136.1 Finnian[a] Maige Bile m. Coirpre m. Ailella m. Trichim[b] m. Ḟeicc [c]m. Findchada[c] m. Bresail m. Sirchada m. Ḟiatach Find [d]a quo Dál Fiatach[d].

2 [e]Secht meic Trichim[f]; Laegaire ic Dún[g], Ailill i mMaig Bile[g], Dichú ic Sabull[gh], Durthech[i] ic Oendruim[g], Eogan i Cill Chlethi[g], [jk]Niall i Cill Chlethi[k], Rus[l] ic Dun Da Lethglas[ej].

[a]Finden BLc(R[l]H), Findia (.i. nech do find dia) Lb (*above line*), Findbarr Lc[l]. [b]Cricim R[l]. [c—c]*om.* Lb, m. Imchada R[l]H. [d—d]*om.* R[l]H. [e—e]*om.* LcR[l]H. [f]Trechim m. Ḟeicc Lb. [g]*add* ⁊ BLb. [h]*add* ise rochreit do Patraic Lb. [i]Durthecht B(LbLc[l]). [j—j]*reversed* Lc[l]. [k—k]*om.* BLb. [l]Ross LbLc[l].

137 Felic [a]Find deochain[a] m. Beocraide [b]m. Cunnida — [c]*no* Cunna[bcd]— m. Daathim[e] — [f]*no* Daithid[f] — m. Cais m. Fraich m. Causcraid[g].

[a—a]*om.* H[1]. [b—b]m. Cuind LcLb. [c—c]*added above line* L, *om.* H[1]. [d]Cuinn B. [e]Daith H[1]. [f—f]*added above line* L, *om.* BLcLbH[1]. [g]*add* do Chonmacnib Lb.

138 Comman[a] m. Ainmerẹch m. Bruịdge.
[bc]Do Dál Araide[c], do Ṡil Ṡogain Ṡalbude[bd].

[a]Conman M. [b—b]*om.* MH. [c—c]*om.* Lb. [d]*add* m. Ḟiathach Araide B(LcLb).

139.1 Fachtna — [a].i.[b] Rois m. Erca ar[c] brú Locha [d]Febail *no*[d] Echach[ac] — m. Bronaig m. Corpre Charamail[f] m. Ailella Abrain[g] m. Ḟiatach Find[h] m. Dare m. Ḟorgo m. Feidlimid Find[f] m. Uamonchind m. Corrain m. Caiss m. Argatmair m. Ṡirlaim [i]m. Ḟind [j]m. Blatha[j] [k]m. Labrada[k] m. Carpre m. Olloman Fotla [lm]m. Ḟiachach [n]m. Ṡetnai m. Airt m. Ebrig m. Ebir Duind m. Ir m. Miled Espain[m].

2 [o]Congend[p] 7 Náre di ingin Brónaig[ilno].

[a—a]*om.* Lc[1]. [b]ic Lc, ho Lb. [c]for Lb. [d—d]*om.* Lb. [e]hEthnach Lc. [f]*om.* LbLc[1]. [g]m. Abrain Lb, *om.* Lc[1]. [h]*om.* Lc[1]. [i—i]*om.* B. [j—j]*om.* Lc, m. Bratha Lb, m. Latha Lc[1]. [k—k]*om.* Lb. [l—l]*om.* Lc. [m—m]*om.* Lc[1]. [n—n]*om.* Lb. [o—o]*inserted after* Fachtna Lc[1]. [p]Conchend Lc[1].

140 Mael Celtair[a] m. Ronain m. Echdach m. Muredaig [b]m. Forgo[b] m. Dallain m. Lugdach m. Oengusa[c] m. Fergusa Dubdetaig [d]m. Imchada m. Ḟinchatha m. Ogamain[e] m. Ḟiachach [fg]Fir Umai[g] [h]m. Dáire m. Dluthaig m. Deitsin m. Echdach m. Ṡin m. Roṡin m. Trir m. Rotrír m. Airnil m. Mane m. Ḟorgo m. Ḟeradaig m. Ailella m. Ḟiachach Fir Mara m. Oengusa Turbig ut ante[dfh].

[a]Cealcair Lc, Cedair Lb. [b—b]*om.* BLcLb. [c]*add* Find BLcLb. [d—d]*om.* Lb. [e]Ugamain Lc. [f]*om.* B. [g—g].F. Lc. [h—h]*om.* Lc.

141 Dochumma m. Aedain[a] m. Echdach m. Muredaig[b] [c]m. Forgo [d]ut supra[cd],
[e]7 Cobthach Cael mac rig Airgiall, it e coṅgabat[f] Druim[g] Bó[eh].

[a]Aeda Lc. [b]*add* Muinderg BLcLb. [c—c]*om.* Lb. [d—d]*om.* BLc. [e—e]*between columns with marks of reference* L. [f]congab BLcLb. [g]a nDruim BLc, hi nDun Lb. [h]*add* insin Lb.

142 Diarmait [ab]Disirt Diarmata[b] m. Fergaile[ac] m. Aeda Roin m. Becce Bairche [de]m. Blaithmaic[e] m. Mail[f] Choba m. [gh]Duib Thuinni[h] m. Ḟiachnai[g] m. Demmain m. Cairill[i] m. Muredaig Mundeirg [j]m. Forgo [k]ut ante[djk].

[a—a]*om.* Lc[1]40VcMH. [b—b]*om.* Lc[1]M[1]. [c]Fergusa M[1]. [d—d]*om.* Lc[1]40VcMH. [e—e]*bis* B. [f]Maile B. [g—g]*reversed* Lb. [h—h]*om.* M[1]. [i]*add* as e docreid do Patraic M[1]. [j—j]*om.* BLcLbLc[1]. [k—k]m. Dallain m. Dubthaig m. Luigdeach m. Aengusa Finn m. Ḟergusa Duibdetaig .i. is e dogab Eirinn dar lamaib Chormuic uí Chuinn (ni th[ar] a lamhaib dogab uair fa gilla og Cormac an tan sin) M[1] (*between columns in smaller hand*).

143 Molasse Lethglinni[a] m. Cairill Chruaid[b] m. Muredaig[c] [d]m. Ḟorgo[de].

[a]*om.* Lc[l]H. [b](m.) Cruind (B)Lb, *om.* Lc[l]Lc[1]40VcMH. [c]*add* (m.) Muindeirg BLb(Lc[l])Lc[1]40VcMH. [d—d]*om.* Lc[1]40VcMH. [e]*add* m. Dallain m. Dubthaig m. Miannaig Lb, *add* m. Dallain m. Lugdach Lc[l].

144 Oenu *ua* Loigsi[a] m. Beraig m. Domongairt[b] m. Bairr m. Cairthind[c] m. Cormaic m. Coluim m. Lugnai[d] m. Eogain [e]m. Guaire m. Eirc[e] m. Bacain m. Lugdach Loigsi[f] [g]m. Loigsig Cendmóir[g] [h]m. Conaill Cernaig[hi].

[a]Laísi B, Laisre Lc. [b]*blank line follows* L. [c]Carthaind BLb. [d]Lug *no* Lūa B, Luna Lc, Laugna Lb. [e—e]*reversed* B. [f]Laigsíd B, Laisich Lc. [g—g]*om.* Lc. [h—h]*om.* B. [i]*add* Is e in tOenu sin tra ba comorbai Cluana Mucc Nois i ndiaid Ciarain Lb.

145 Senach 7 Colman da mac Comgaill m. Luaigne [a]m. Eogain[a] m. Guaire m. Eirc m. Milige m. Intait[b] m. Lugdach [c]Loigse [d]m. Conaill Cernaig[cd].
It[e] é[f] congaib Tulach mac[g] ṅComgaill[h] 7 Druim Toga.

[a—a]*om.* BLcLb. [b]Intaird B(Lc). [c—c]*om.* BLc. [d—d]*om.* Lb. [e]is Lb. [f]eat Lb. [g]*om.* Lc. [h]*corrected by scribe from* ṅDomnaill L, Comgaill BLcLb.

146 Caillén[a] [b]i Fidnachaib[c] Maige Réin[b] m. Niatach[d] m. Dubain m. Fraech[e] m. Cuscraid[f] [g]ut ante[g].

[a]Cail(l)in (BLcLb)H[l]. [b—b]*om* H[l]. [c]Finacadh B, Fidnacha Lc. [d]*written* Matach L, Niadh BLc. [e]Raith H[l]. [f]*add* m. Indir Lc, *add* m. Meic Cecht Lb. [g—g]*om.* BLcLbH[l].

147 Coeman[a] m. Tacae[b] m. Baeth[c] m. Baethgil[d] [e]m. Cind Glais[ef] m. Celtchair[g] m. Cuthechair[h] [i]ut ante[i].

[a]Coman Lc. [b]i *very faint* L, Taicae BLc, Taicce M, Taccai Lb. [c]Blaithmaic Lc. [d]Beithgil M. [e—e]*om.* BLc. [f].i. Glas (*above line*) Lb, *in marg. no* m. Cinglaind m. Rossa m. Rudraige M. [g]Clithchuir M. [h]Uithechair BLb(M), *add* m. Ḟir Filed m. Glais Lb. [i—i]*om.* BLcLbM.

148 Crumthir Dathi[a] m. Conamla[b] [c]m. Congalaig[c] [d]m. Dungalaig[de] m. Dúnchada [f]m. Neoil[g] [h]m. Eoil[hi] m. Fidchuire [j]ut ante in genealogia Brenaind[fj].

[a]Nathi B. [b]Caemla B, Coemloga Lb. [c—c]*om.* Lc. [d—d]*om.* M. [e]Dungail BLb. [f—f]*illeg.* H[l]. [g]Neill M. [h—h]*om.* M. [i]Eoin BLcLb. [j—j]ut in Bre(n)ainn B(Lc), et cetera Lb, *om.* M.

149 Crumthir [a]Fraech[b] [c]Cluana[ad] Conmaicne[c] m. Carthaig[e] m. Nethe[f] m. Onchon m. Findloga m. Findir m. Causcraid[g].

[a—a]*om.* Lc. [b]*add* frisinabur Croicheraech H[l]. [c—c]*om.* LbH[l]. [d]*no* B. [e]Crartaig H[l]. [f]Neidhe B(LcLb). [g]Cumscraid B, *add* m. Cecht m. Eirc m. Ercdais m. Meic Cecht m. Usni Finn m. Berri m. Doilbthe m. Lugdach m. Oirbsen Moir m. Duib m. Mag Ruaidh m. Nerta m. Fornerta m. Ecindin m. Segda m. Raidni m. Alta m. Ogomain m. Dolbri m. Duibcride m. Eoin m. Cetguinig m. Esamain m. Mochta m. Moga Doith m. Conmaic m. Fergusa H[l].

150 Iarlathi m. Trena m. Feic m. Imcha|da|[a] m. Bresail m. Sirchada m. Fiatach[b] Find.

[a]Imcha L, Imchada(i) BLc(Lb)RLc[l]R[l]HLa, Idchada M. [b]Fiachach Lc, Fiachrach R[l]La.

151 [ab]Tri[c] ingena[bd] Comgaill[e], .i. Boga 7 Lasre et Colma[af], m.[g] Ḟiangalaig[h] m. Dimmain[i] m. Nuatulain[j] m. Mutulain[k] m. Cantalain m. Ḟiangalaig [l]m. Niad Cendmóir[lm] m. Buain a quo Dál ṁBuain.

[a—a]*part between commas first* RLc[l]. [b—b]*added later* R. [c]teorai Lb. [d]meic Lc. [e]Colman B, *om.* RLc[l] [f]Colman BLcLb, Colina (*or* Colma)R, Coli*na* Lc[l]. [g]*om.* Lc[l]. [h]Fingalaig B(Lc). [i]Dima B(LcLb). [j]Nuathula BLc(Lb), Ruathulain Lc[l]. [k]Nuathulain BLc(Lb). [l—l]*om.* BLcLb. [m]*om.* RLc[l].

152 Dobiu[a] m. Comgaill m. Eirc m. Araide m. Coluimb m. Cainnig[b] m. Buain[c].

[a]Dabiu (b *above line*)Lc[l]. [b]Angid Lb. [c]*add* a quo Dal Buain RLc[l].

153 Colman m. Lugna m. Caiss m. Rectadba[a] m. Cainnig[b] m. Buain[c].

[a]Rechtadu Lb, Rechtada RLc[l]. [b]Angid Lb. [c]*add* a quo Dal Buain RLc[l].

154 Tiu m. Fínain[a] m. Cassain[b] m. Ḟergusa m. Niad Cendmóir[c] m. Buain[d].

[a]Fergusa (*no* Finain *above line*) Lb. [b]Caiss Lb. [c]*om.* RLc[l]. [d]add *et cetera* Lb, a quo Dal Buain RLc[l].

155 Munnu[a] — [b]cuius soror Dígi[b] — m. Tulchain[c] [d]m. Trena m. Dega[de] [f]m. Dubthaig[f] [g]m. Maain[gh] [ij]m. Cuirc[j] m. [k]Fiacha Riatai[ikl].

[a]*add* Tige M*unnu* RLc[l], *above line* Findtan ainnm Munna M, *above line* de genealogia Mundu m. Deglain Dese R[l]. [b—b]*above line* L, *om.* BLbRLc[l]MR[l]La. [c]Taulchain LbR, Telchain La, Degláin R[l]. [d—d]*reversed* LbMR[l]La. [e]Deagha Moir odaid (a quo) Ua Deagha R[l](La). [f—f]*om.*RLc[l]. [g—g]*om.* B. [h]*add above line* no B|aain| L, Bain Lb, Baain MR[l]La, *add* m. Ḟedlimid Rechtadai m. Carthaig sund condricc 7 Molua Lb, m. Roeidi m. Feidelmthe Rechtada m. Tuathail Techtmair (m. Feradaig m. Crimthaind m. Nia Nair m. na tri Find m. Echach Feidlig) (R)Lc[l]. [i—i]*om.* LbRLc[l]. [j—j]*om.* MR[l]La. [k—k]Fiachraide La. [l]Rida B, Reide M, Araidhe R[l], *add* m. Feidlimig Rechtmair *no* m. Carrthaig m. Oililla m. Imchada m. Lama Feola m. Cliathaire m. Fiachach m. Dubthaig Duind M, m. Feidhlímte m. Cormaic m. Feidhlimte m. Cathairtaig m. Daighre m. Erca m. Imcadha m. Lamha Feola m. Liathaire(Cathair) m. Focha m. Dubthaigh Duind R[l](La).

156 Baethine m. Finnach[a] m. Echdach m. Bairr m. Cairthind[b] — [c]qui et Sárbile[d] dicitur[c] — m. Cormaic[e] m. Lugnae m. Eogain m. Guare m. Eirc[f] [g]ut ante in genealogia Óenu[g].

[a]Findaig Lb, Fintain Lc[l]. [b]Carthaind BLb. [c—c]*om.* RLc[l]. [d]Saerbili B. [e]Coluim(m) (R)Lc[l]. [f]*add* m. Baccan m. Lugdach Laigsi m. Laigsig Cendm*oir* Lb, m. Lugdach m. Conaill m. Amargin R(Lc[l]). [g-g]*om.* LbRLc[l].

157.1 [a]Fursu[b] m. Fintain m. Findloga m. Degrota[c] m. Luachain m. Laga[d] Leth*anglais*[e] m. Conaill [f] [g]Anglonnaig m. Feic m. Rosa m. Ḟactna m. Ṡenchada [h]m. [i]Ailella[h] m. Cestaig[i] m. Rudraige[j].
[k]Gelges ingen Aeda Find[l] mathair Fursu[k].

2 [m]Uel ita[n]: Fursu[o] m. F*intain* m. F*indloga*[p] m. Conaill m. Luachain m. Lugdach[q] Laga m. [r]Eogain [s]Moir qui et[r] Mog Nuadat[gms].

[a]*the pedigrees are in reverse order in* RLc[l]. [b]*add* Craibdech Lb(R[l]La). Cf. *below* RLc[l]. [c]Degroga RLc[l]R[l]La. [d]Logo B(LbR[l]). [e]L*eth*ed B, Leith (*above line*) Lb, *om.* RLc[l]R[l]La. [f]*add* m. Eachach (M.) R[l](La). [g—g]*om.* R[l]La. [h—h]*om.* B. [i—i]Oilella Cestadaig Lb. [j]*add* m. Ṡithri Lb(R). [k—k]*om.* RLc[l]. [l]*om.* Lb. [m—m]*between col.s* L, *om.* B. [n]*om.* LbRLc[l]. [o]*add* Craibthech RLc[l]. Cf. *above* LbR[l]La. [p]*add* m. Find Ardi (a quo Conaille Muirtheimni *above line*)Lb. [q]*om.* RLc[l]. [r—r]*om.* Lb. [s—s]*om.* RLc[l].

158 Colmán Mulind[a] m. Conaill m. Conchobuir [b]m. Cais[b] m. Comgain m. Conaill m. Laga[c] Lethanglais[d].

[a]Molind B. [b—b]Chaiss *above line* Lb. [c]Loga(i) B(Lb). [d]*om.* RLc[l], *add* m. Conaill Anglonnaig Lb. *See note to* 159.

159 Epscop [a]Mac Erca[a] m. Fraechain[b] [c]i[d] nDomnuch Mor Maige Coba[c], [e]Coelan[f] m. Luachain[eg], Epscop Luachan m. Duachain[h]. [i]Duachan 7 Luachan 7 Fráechan, [j]tri derbrathir in[k] sin, .i.[jk] tri meic[l] Roire m. Laga[m] m. Conaill[n] [o]et cetera ut supra[iop].

[a—a]Ercca m. Ercca RLc[l]. [b]Fregain M, *add* m. Rori m. Logai Lethanglais m. Conaill Lb, m. Meic Laige R(Lc[l]). [c—c]*above line* L, *see note* BLb, *om.* LcRLc[l]. [d]o Lb. [e—e]*om.* Lb. [f]Colman BLcM. [g]hUachain RLc[l]. [h]*add* m. Rori m. Logai Lethanglais m. Conaill Anglonnaig Lb. [i—i]*om.* Lb. [j—j]*om.* RLc[l]. [k]*om.* BLc. [l]*add* Rosa no B, Rosalaich Lc. [m]Loga BLc, Laige R(Lc[l]), Lugda M. [n]*add* Anglonnaig B(Lc), m. Dedaid m. Sin m. Roṡin (m. Ernaile) R(Lc[l]). [o—o]*om.* BRLc[l]. [p]*om.* Lc.

160.1 Fintan m. Echdach 7 Colman — .i. Colum Roisc[a] Gil Glandai, fil[b] oc Snam Luthair[c] 7 oc Midísiul — et Nannid[d] Cilli Tommae[e] et Lugaid Tiri Da Chraeb et Muridach Cilli [f]Alaid — [g].i. nomen fontis[g] — i n*Uib*[h] Amalgada[fi]. Cóic meic [j]Echach in[b] sin[jk].

2 Aglend ingen Lenin[l] mathair Ḟintain 7 [mn]Coluim 7[n] Lugada[mo]. Ligach Bregmuinech[p] imm*urgu*[q] mathair Nannida[r] 7 Muridaich.

[a]Ruis(s) BLc(Lb)M. [b]*om.* Lb. [c]Luchair Lb. [d]Nan̄ B, Nand Lc, Nanand Lb. [e]Toimmia M. [f—f]*corrupt and illeg.* M. [g—g]*in marg.* L, .i. norponis Lb̄(*after* Amalgaid), *om.* BLcM. [h]tir B. [i]Amalgaid BLcLb. [j—j]*reversed* LcLb. [k]*add* m. Aeda m. Laegaire m. Neill (Noigiallaig) B(Lc)Lb. [l]*add* .i. siur Colmain (Cluana hUamai *above line*) Lb. [m—m]*reversed* BLc. [n—n]*om.* Lb. [o]Luig(d)ech B(Lb), *illeg.* M. [p]Bregmuighech B. [q]*om.* BLcLb, *illeg.* M. [r]Naindeadh B, Nindich Lc, Naindig Lb.

161 Cronan *ua* hElmine[a] i [b]nDisiurt Atha[b] m.[c] Mugnai[d], i Cind Chlair[e], i Fid Eoin[f], et Bríg Mór i Sendomnuch Feda Eoin[g].

[a]hEiline B(LcLb). [b—b]nDisirta B, nDisḟeart ita Lc. [c]Macc Lb. [d]Lugdach (*no* Lugnai *above line*) M. [e]Chlari Lb. [f]*add* ata Lb. [g]*add* bhos Lb.

162 Derinnill Chetharchichech[a] — [b].i. mathair Murodra[b] — mathair Domangairt m. Echach[c] m. Muredaig Mundeirg 7 mathair Ailleain 7 Aedain — [d]cuius filius est[d] Mochumma Dromma Bo — et Cilleain Achaid i lLeith Chathail ar[e] ur Trága[f] Dromma.

[a]Cethircidech LbM, *add* .i. Lb. [b—b]*in marg.* L, *om.* BLcLbM. [c]Ech Lc. [d—d]7 B. [e]for Lb. [f]*add* Du(i)ne B(Lb).

163 Mael Uma[a] m. Baetain m. Murchertaig[b] qui fuit filius Ercae qui fuit filia[c] Loairn[d].

[a]Rube Lc. [b]M*urō* B, Muron Lc, Mugroin Lb, Snch̄ M. [c]Flann B(LcLb). [d]Lodarn B(M).

164 Trí meic Cendḟotai m. Détchain m. Niad .i. Clethe 7 Coimri[a] et Brandub.
It e[b] congabat[c] na trí Ross[d] .i. Ros Clethe 7 Ros Coimre[e] 7 Ros ṁBranduib[f], et Cairpre m. Feidlimid i Fothirbi[g] Móir 'na fail.

[a]Comrae M. [b]eat Lb. [c]congabhsad B(LcLb). [d]Rois BLcLb(M). [e]Comaire *no* Coimre B. [f]Maenduibh B, Aenduib Lc. [g]Fothartaibh *no* Fotairbe B.

165 Cúach ingen Coelbad[a] [b]m. Coluim[c] m. Blait[b] de *Uib* Ellaig[d] *Ua* ṁBairchi Maige Ailbe mathair tri mac ṅDunlaing .i. Illand[e], Ailill[e], Eochaid.
Is [f]de asberar tri[f] lemmend Cuache[g] i ṅGabuir. Co ruc mac cecha fectusa[h] dona maccaib[i] remraite et[j] co tarta tri dúne di dara[k] n-esi .i. Magen Garbain[l], 7 Achad[m] Dairig[n], et Tilach *Ua* ṁBlait. Et[j] adropartsi[o] na tri dúni sin[p] dia brathair .i. do Choeman[q] Ṡantlethan.

[a]Chaelbaid Lc(LbM). [b—b]*om.* Lc. [c]Colmain Lb. [d]Cuaigh BLc. [e]*add* 7 BLcM. [f—f]di ata Lb. [g]Chluichi M. [h]fechta BLcLb. [i]macu Lb. [j]*om.* Lb. [k]da Lb. [l]*om.* B, Gabair LcLb. [m]Achada B. [n]Dairit Lc(LbM). [o]adubairtsi B, dobertsi Lc. [p]*om.* M. [q]Caem BLc(Lb).

166 Teora nóeb[a] im*murgu*[b] *Ua* Loscain[c], do ṡíl Ḟergusa Loscain[d] m.[e] Cathair[f] .i. Cerc[g] *Ua* Loscain [h]i Cnoittiu[h] et Finnia[i] hi Tilaig Madair[j] et Rignach i Cill Rignaige i Fothartaib.

[a]noemu Lb. [b]*om.* LbM. [c]Luascain(e) B(Lc), *add* .i. Lb. [d]Luascain Lc. [e].i. B. [f]*add* Mair Lb(M). [g]Searc Lc, *add above line* .i. mac Larine Lb, cf. *next note.* [h—h]icoitill .i. Lairíne BLc, icotill Lb, cf. *previous note and* 168[b—b]. [i]Finan BLb, Fintan Lc. [j]Magair BLcLbM.

167 Colum ingen Luagni[a] m. Eobrain[b] m. Condath m. Luigdech m. Daigre[c].

[a]Luigne BLcLb, Lugnai M. [b]Meic Cobrain B. [c]Daig BLcLb *which run on* 168.

168.1 Domma[a] — [b].i. mac Lairne[b] — Dromma [c]Dóthe[d]; de *Uib* Neill a athair[ce]; a mathair do Ḟeraib Breg .i. de Ḟothartaib[f] Mac Decill[g]. Is é[h] coṅgab Disert[i] nEnnae iar tect[j] do Enna dar muir[k].

2 Berchan[l] m. Dimma m. Aeda Cróin béus[m] i nDruim Dothe.

[a]*om.* BLc. [b—b]*in marg. with marks of ref.* L, *attached to* 166[g,h—h] BLcLb, *follows* Dóthe M. [c—c]Ua ṅDeuthi air Lb. [d]*om.* BLc. [e]*add* 7 LcM. [f]Ḟothartu Lb. [g]nDe(i)cill Lb(M). [h]i Lb. [i]*om.* Lb. [j]tiacht BLc, tocht Lb, tiachtain M. [k]*add* anair Lb. [l]Brec(c)an B(LcLb). [m]*om.* LcLb.

169 Secht n-epscuip ⁊ *secht* n-ingena i[a] Carnmaig[b] et Mochonoc[c] Cilli Mucraissi.

[a]*om.* BLc. [b]Cairinnmuig B. [c]Mochnocc M.

170 Diucaill[a] ⁊ Colman da mac Credach[b] m. Diarmata[c].
[d]It é coṅgabat[de] Cluain Trelec, [f]et Crita ingen Senȧig ic Russ Torc[fg].

[a]Duchaill BLc. [b]Cre(a)tach (BLc)RLc[l], Rethi Lb, Chreich M. [c]Airmeda Lb, Dermata RLc[l]. [d—d](h)i (R)Lc[l]. [e]congabsat B(Lc)LbM. [f—f]*om.* RLc[l]. [g]Toirchi B(LcLb) M.

171 [Ail]finus ailither ⁊ Mochonoc ⁊ Mochasoc[a] ⁊ Anfegen[b] cum [c]suis omnibus[c] i Tig na Commairge i Maig Itha isin tuascirt.

[a]Mochosog M. [b]Infeigean M. [c—c]sr̄ omnibus BLb, sroinibus Lc.

172 Cellan ⁊ Garban da mac Nisi ⁊ [a]a ndí sier[a] .i.[b] Lasar ⁊ Columba[c] et Conlaed[d] Craibdech i[e] Findchore[f].

[a—a]aimsir BLcLb. [b]*om.* R. [c]Columb BLb, Colu(i)m R(Lc[l])M. [d]Conlae B. [e]ic Lc[l]. [f]Finncoraigh B(LcLb).

173 Brigit [a]⁊ Cumman[ab] ingen Dallbrónaig et Diarmait et Oengus ⁊ Epscop Eogain.
[c]De Ḟothartaib dóib. It[d] é[e] sin[f] filet[cg] i nAchud Togarta i crích Ua ṅDuach Maige[h] Argetrois.

[a—a]*om.* BLcLb. [b]Commain M. [c—c]*om.* RLc[l]. [d]is BLc. [e]iad M. [f]*om.* Lb. [g]fil BLcLb. [h]*om.* Lc.

174 Cromm[a] ⁊ Cumman[b] dí[c] ingin[d] [e]Cronain[f] — [g]*no*[e] Guaire[g] — et Conall m. Cronain[f] i Cill Libir[h] ⁊ i Cill Ingen[d] ṅGuaire.

[a]Cruimni B(LcLb), Guairi M(*see note*). [b]Coman BLb, Comanna Lc, Cumain M. [c]da mac BLc, da Lb, de M. [d]ingine Lc. [e—e]*om.* Lc. [f]Chroinin M. [g—g]*in marg. with mark of ref.* L, *om.* Lb. *See note to* [a]. [h]I(u)bair BLc(Lb).

175 Crumthir Munnu ⁊[a] Crumthir Mechair ⁊[a] Crumthir ṁBecain[b] ic Rus Achaid Liac.

[a]*om.* Lc. [b]Becan B(LcLb).

176 Ultan ⁊ Mael Dub et Ingena[a] Brenaind i nOenmaig[b].

[a]I*ngen* B. [b]maenmag Lc(M).

177 Crumthir Lugnaith[a], [b]dalta Patric ⁊ mac a[c] ṡethar[b], in sechtmad mac in Baird ic Nuthḟeraib[d].

[a]Lugna(i) BLc(Lb). [b—b]*above line* Lb. [c]*om.* BLc. [d]natfertaibh B(Lc), fertaib Lb.

178 Tír[a] Fecc for Loch Mesca; is and rohalt[b] Sanc[c] Brigit, .i. Fecc mac[d] Detig[e] ⁊ Odran[f] et Mechar mac Odrain. Dorat[g] Duí[h] Galach[i] Teṅga

[a]ic Tir Lc, Tire Lb. [b]h *shown as mark of lenition* L, roalt B, ronalt LcM, roail Lb. [c]sns̄ B, sanct LcLb. [d]*om.* B. [e]Deideig B, Deaeig Lc(Lb), Deithid M. [f]Dordan BLc, Ogran M. [g]*add* tra Lb. [h]Duach BLcLbM. [i]*om.* LcM, *add no* B.

Umai m. Ḟergusa m. Muredaig[j] [k]m. Briuin[k] orbba doib[l] o'tá Snám[m] Tíri Feicc co Sail Dea[n].

[j]*add* Mail m. Eogain Sreim (m. Duach Galaig m. Briain m. Echach Muigmedoin) (Lc)Lb. [k—k]*om.* B. [l]*add* .i. Lb. [m]*in marg. with mark of reference* L, *om.* M. [n]Deaga M.

179 Teora ingena[a] Mane m. Cerbaill .i. Dermór et Cumman et Ethne, et Colman Find et Crumthir Duban. In cuiciur sin i nAiriur[b] Boinne.

[a]ingen BLcM. [b]Oirfer B, Orbir Lb, *add* na Lc.

180 Attracht ingen Tigernaig i Cill Saile [a]i Crích Conaill[a].

[a—a]*om.* BLcLb.

181 [ab]Noeb[c] Dál Mes[d] Corb [e]in so[be]:

1 Coemgen [f]m. Coemloga[g]; Coemoc soror eius[fh].
2 Epscop Eogain Aird[i] Sratha[j].
3 Lochan 7 Enna[k] [l]i Cill[l] Manach [m]Escrach [no]i n*Uib*[o] Dunchada[mn].
4 Moṡenoc[p] Mugnai.
5 Mochoemi[q] Tíri Da Glas.
6 Coeman Enaig Thruim[r] [st]et a da[tu] brathair .i.[v] Murdebur[w] 7 Corconutan[asx].

[a—a]*om.* RLc[l]. *See note.* [b—b]*in marg.* L, Fergus Laebderg m. Fothaig m. Eochach Laimdeirg m. Meisin Corb m. Con Corp as uada rochinsead(rogenset) na naim seo .i. M[l](La). [c]do noemu Lb. [d]Me(is)sin BLcLb(M). [e—e]*om.* BLc, *add* sis M. [f—f]Glinne Da Lacha M[l](La). [g]Loga(i) BLc(Lb). [h]*om.* B. [i]Arda (na) LcLb(M[l]), Airde M. [j](na) Sre(a)tha M(M[l]). [k]Sedna M. [l—l]o chill M[l], cilli na La. [m—m]*om.* M[l]La [n—n]*om.* M. [o—o]*in* B, .ī. Lc, ingen Lb. [p]Mothenoc Lc. [q]Mochomhe M[l], Muchonna La. [r]Druim BLc. [s—s]*om.* M[l]La. [t—t]aed a Lc. [u]di Lb.
[v]7 B, *om.* Lc. [w]Muirrdemun M. [x]Corcnadain BLc(Lb).

7 Epscop Etchian[a] [b]m. Mane Eicis[b] [c]m. Ḟergusa — [d].i. Laebdeirg[cd] — [e]o[f] Chluain Fata Baetain[g] Aba[h].
8 Epscop Nathi [i]m. Senaig[i] [j]m. Ḟergusa Laebdeirg[j] i Cúil[k] Fothirbi[l].
9 [m]Moacru[n] m. Senain[o].
10 Conlaed[p] Craibdech epscop [q]Cilli Dara[mq].
11 [r]Petran[s] ó Chill [t]Lainni[r].
12 [u]Biclend[t] [v]*no* Bicliu[v] Uscidi o Raith Biclend[eu].

[a]Etcen B(LcLbRLc[l]M[l]La), *add* .i. M[l]. [b—b]7 Mac inn Ecis La. [c—c]*om.* M[l]La. [d—d]*in marg. with mark of reference* L, *in text without* .i. BLcLbM, Lam*deirg* RLc[l]. [e—e]*om.* RLc[l]. [f]i M[l]La. [g]Baithin BLc, 7 Boithin Lb, 7 Baedan La. [h]Eabha MM[l], Oba La. [i—i]*om.* Lb. [j—j]*added between columns* M[l], *om.* La. [k]Cluain M[l]. [l]*add* a nUlltaib (7rl) (M[l])La. [m—m]*om.* M[l]La. [n]Mohocrai Lb. [o]Se(a)naig (B)LcLb. [p]Coindli BLc. [q—q]Cillid B. [r—r]*placed before* 7 M[l]La. [s]Patran Lc. [t—t]Laidibhiclenn B(Lc). [u—u]*om.* M[l]La. [v—v]*added above line* L, *om.* BLcLb, *only* Bicliu M.

13 [a]Epscop Aedain m. Mane m. Ḟergusa [b]Laebdeirg.
14 [c]Becnat ingen Cholmain m. Eda[d] i[e] Cill Becnatan [f]7[g] i Tír Choicir[f].
15 Coimell 7 Trenan[h] [i]Drui i nImgan[i].
16 Cillini m. Dermata i nUachtur[j] Achaid.
17 Lumsech[k] 7 Fedelm[l] i Cill Lum̄sigi[abcm].

[a—a]*om.* M[l]La. [b—b]*om.* RLc[l]. [c—c]*separate in* L, *run on* BLcLbM. [d]Aeda BLcLbM. [e]o M. [f—f]*om.* Lb. [g]*om.* BLc. [h]Trena an B. [i—i]Duin Imgain M. [j]Usai*r* ur Lc. [k]Laimsech Lb. [l]Feidl̄ B, Felim Lb. [m]Laimside BLc(Lb).

182.1 Muccin — Mucinne[a] — m. Moche m. Barrind[b] m. Ḟindchada m. Dega m. Droide[c] m. Buain m. Loegaire Birn Buadaig m. Oengusa Osrithi[d].

2 [e]Dicnait[f] ingen Gabrin[g], derbsiur Fintain Cluana Eidnech, mathair Muccín[e].

[a]*above line* L, Maigni M, *om.* BLcLb. [b]Branaind BLcLb. [c]Drogai Lc, Drodai Lb, Droigida M. [d]Oisergi m. Cremthainn Lb. [e—e]*follows* Osrithi *along foot of page* L, *om.* BLcLb. [f]Muccnait M. [g]Gabrain M.

183 Mael Anfaid [a]Cilli[b] Mael Anfaid[a] [c]m. Anfothaig[c] m. Garbain m. Crunmael m. Comgaill m. Lachtchair[d] m. Dungaile m. Murgaile m. Brain m. Maele Duin m. Ḟechine m. Ṡenaig m. Nathi m. Trichim[e] m. Crechtaire[f] m. [g]Eirc Buadaig[g].

[a—a]*om.* RLc[l]. [b](h)i Cill BLc(Lb). [c—c]m. Anfagaidh B(Lc), *om.* Lb. [d]Lasair B, Lachtair LcLb. [e]Trechim Lb. [f]Rechtaire Lb. [g—g]Erbuainne B(Lc), Eircc m. Conchind m. Drodai m. Buain m. Loegaire Birnd B*uadaig* Lb.

184 Dabeoc[a] [b]Glinni[c] Gerg[bd] m. Luanin[e] m. Dibroga m. Thola m. Dorblusa[f] m. Dichon m. Trichim[g].

[a]Dabeoog B. [b—b]*om.* H. [c]o Glind Lb. [d]Derg BLb. [e]Luanind H. [f]Diblínsi B, Doirplosa MH. [g]Trechim m. Feic m. Imchada Lb.

185 Samthand [a]Cluana Brónaig[ab] ingen Díaráin[c] m. Ḟerdomain[d] m. Dichon m. Trichim[e].

[a—a].i. *no* Cen̄ Bronaig H (*above line*). [b]Bronach B. [c]Di(a)marain B(Lb), Diarnain Lc[l], Dimmar M(R[l]), Diamrain H. [d]Ferdomnaig BLb, Ferdomna*n* M(R[l]H). [e]Trechim Lb, Crithim M, Cruitin R[l].

186 Adhuar[a] m. Nechim[b] m. Forbaird[c] m. Aeda m. Lugdach m. Bairr m. Cairthind[d] [e]ut ante in genealogia Óenu[e].

[a]Adur B. [b]Echim? Lb. [c]Forbrain BLcLb. [d]Carthaind B, Carthaind m. Cormaic m. Choluim m. Lugnai m. Eogain m. Guaire m. Eircc m. Baccain m. Lugdach Laigsi m. Laigsig Cendmair m. Conaill Cernaig Lb. [e—e]*corrupt.* BLc, *om.* Lb.

187 [a]Colman et[a] Senach da[b] mac Lugna m. Eogain m. Guaire m. Eirc m. Bacain[c] [d]ut ante in eadem genealogia Oenu[d].
It é filet[e] i Tilaig M*ac*[f] Comgaill 7 i nDruim[g] Thogae[h] .i.[i] isind Uachoṅgbail.

[a—a]*om.* Lb. [b]*om.* BLb. [c]Bacanut B, Bacunt Lc, Baccain m. Lugdach L*aigsi* Lb. [d—d]*om.* BLcLb. [e]fil BLc. [f]mec Lb. [g]Druimnib (*or read* Druimmb) Lc. [h]Togaidhe B. [i]7 Lb.

188 Manchan[a] Léith[b] m. Sillain[c] [d]m. Conaill m. Luachain m. Laga[e] m. Conaill Anglonnaig m. Ḟeic m. Rosa[f].
[g]Mella mater eius[dg].

[a]Monchan B. [b]*om.* R[l]La. [c]Sinill *no* Silain B(Lc), *add* m. Threaduirn m. Lugdach Lagha m. Moga Nuaghad (m. Mogha Neid m. Deirg m. Deirgtineadh o taid Clanda Deirgtinedh) M(R[l]La). [d—d]*om.* MR[l]La. [e]Loga BLcLb. [f]*add* m. Fachtna (m. Ṡenchada) BLc(Lb). [g—g]*om.* B, 2 mr̄ Lc, ē m̄r̄ Lb.

189 Scuthine Slebe Mairge[a] m. Setnai[b] m.[c] Trebthaig[d] m. Dala[e] m. Laidḟir[f] [g]ut ante in genealogia[h] Ailbi[gi].

[a]Margai Lb. [b]Senna B, Setnaig R[l]. [c]*om.* R[l]La. [d]Cobthaich Lc. [e]Dula BLc, Daula Lb. [f]Latir arai Chon Corp m. Immrosa Nitha m. Ḟir Thlachtga m. Fergusa m. Roig Lb, Ladir Arad R[l]. [g—g]*om.* LbR[l]La. [h]*om.* BLc. [i]Ailbhi B, Failbe Lc.

190 Martan[a] epscop m. [b]Dunain Deirg[bc] [d]m. Mael Ḟinniad[e] m. Ercbrai[n][f] m. Beochaill[g] m. Condelgaig m. Onchon m. Mael Ḟithrig m. Fechin m. Rois[h] m. Colmain m. Caelchon[i] m. Loairn[j] m. Ruaid m. Cuirc[k] m. Lugdech[l] Mind[m] [n]m. Cormaic Cais[c] m. Ailella Óluim[d].
[o]I[p] Cúil Breccain[q] i n*Uib* Falge atá Martan .i.[r] i Tuaith[s] Da Maige[no].

[a]*add above line* Mumnenses sancti L. [b—b]Dunadaig 7rl Lc. [c]*om.* Lc[l]. [d—d]*om.* Lc. [e]Finain BLb. [f]Ercbrae B, Ercbrain LbLcLc[l]. [g]Eocaill B. [h]m. Roisi B, Roṡin Lb. [i]Faelchon B, *add in marg. infer.* Coelchu m. Loairn m. Ruaid, ua Cormaic Caiss co nglanbuaid, primgiall Ḟer Muman amach, o'tat aicme Ruiss Temrach Lb. [j]Logairnd B. [k]m. Cais B, Caiss m. Conaill Echluaith Lb. [l]Lugdach Lc[l]. [m]Mind m. Oengusa Tirig Lb, *om.* Lc[l]. [n—n]*om.* Lb. [o—o]*om.* Lc[l]. [p].i. B, .i. hi Lc. [q]Bracain BLc. [r]*om.* BLc. [s]Tuaig B.

191.1 Colman[a] — [.i.] [b]m. Darane[bc] — m. Oengusa m. Nadfraich m. Cuirc m.[d] Luigdech [e]Find[f] m. Ailella Flainn Bic [g]m. Ailella Flainn Móir[g] m. Ḟiachach Mullethain [h]m. Eogain m. Ailella Óluim[e].

2 Is aire[i] asberarsum[j] mac Darane[k] .i. Sant[l] ingen Ges[m] a mathair et ba combritsi[n] et rochunnig[o] fora[p] siair co roainmnigthe in mac uathi. Ar ni bae mac lee[q]. Et dobert[r] a siur anísin[s]. Roalt[t] iarum Darane[u] mac a sethar [v]conid de asberar[vw] Colman mac Darane[hx].

[a]*add above line* .i. mathair Lc. [b—b]*om.* Lc[l]. [c]Dairine BLcLb. [d]*om.* B. [e—e]*om.* BLcLa. [f]*om.* LbLc[l]. [g—g]*om.* LbLc[l]. [h—h]*om.* LbLc[l]. [i]ead B [j]adberarsom BLc. [k]Da(i)rine (B)Lc(La). [l]Snact BLc, Sangc La. [m]Ge(a)sa (B)Lc, Aengusa La. [n]haimritside Lc. [o]dochuindigh B(Lc). [p]for B, ara Lc. [q]lei uodein Lc. [r]robert BLa. [s]*add* di Lc. [t]7 ronalt Lc. [u]Dair(f)ine (B)Lc. [v—v]daige iarum adhbar B. [w]adberar Lc. [x]Dairine (desom) B(Lc).

192 [a]Mac Doborchu[ab] m. Onchon m. Dibechain m. Mailáin m. [c]Con cen Mathair[c] m. Nainnini[d] m. Nannida[e] m. Aedain — [f]cuius frater Crónan Sapiens[f] — m. Ḟergusa Tregbotha[g] m. Blait m. Ḟeidlimid[h] — [fi]qui 7[i] Ailill Lamneg dicitur[fj] — m. Breoda[k] m. [l]Echach Glunig[lm].

[a—a]Dobharchu Lc[l]. *See note.* [b]Doborchon B(LcLb). [c—c]*precedes* Dibechan Lc, *conachn mathar*e Lc[l]. [d]Aennedai Lb. [e]Nindeada Lc(Lc[l]), Naenined Lb. [f—f]*om.* Lc[l]. [g]Dergbotha BLcLb, *om.* Lc[l]. [h]Fedlimthi Lb. [i—i]m. BLcLb. [j]*om.* Lb. [k]Brada Lc, Breda Lb. [l—l]Echach m. Dairi Barraig m. Cathair Moir Lc[l]. [m]Lug̃ B.

193 Fínan Lobur[a] m. Conaill m. Echach[b] m. Thaidc m. Céin m. Ailella[c] Óluim.

[a]Labar M. [b]Echdach H. [c]Oilla M.

194 Ultan [a]m. Bruidgi[a] m. Ernaine[b] m. Garbain[c] m. Senaig [d]m. Muredaig m. Thalgluind[e] m. Brocain m. Cormaic[f] m. Thaidg m. Cein[g] [h]m. Ailella Oluim[dh].

[a—a]*om.* MHLa. [b]Eranine M, Eraine La. [c]Gabrain La. [d—d]⁊rł M. [e]Tailgliund B. [f]*add* Gaileng La. [g]*added later*(?) a Caisil Lc[l]. [h—h]*om.* HLa. *See note to* 200.

195 Ciannan[a] m. Setnai[b] m. [c]Trena — [d]*no* Drona[cd] — m. Thigernaig m. Ḟindchain[e] m. [f]Ḟeic m. Imchada[fg] m. Condlai m. Thaidg[h] m. Cein [i]m. Ailella[i].

[a]Cian Bithbeo H[l]. [b]Senna B. [c—c]Drona(i) B(Lb), Threna Lc[l], Tronai MR[l]HH[l]. [d—d]*above line* L. [e]Findchaim B(Lb)H(H[l]). [f—f]*reversed* MR[l]HH[l]. [g]Findchada Lc[l]M(R[l]) HH[l], *add* U(al)laig (BLb)Lc[l]. [h]Taic Lc[l]. [i—i]*om.* BH, *add* Auluim Lb(Lc[l]MR[l])H[l].

196 Cumman ingen Ailleain[a] m. Aeda[b] m. Baetain m. Echach m. Briain[c] m. Enna m. Cathbad[d] m. Echach Gunnata[e] m. Ḟeic m. Imchada [f]ut ante[f].

[a]Aileallain B. [b]Aeda m. Taidg B. [c]Brain Lc[l]. [d]Cathbada Lc. [e]Gunnat LbMH, *om.* Lc[l]. [f—f]m. Bresail m. Sirchadha m. Fiatach Finn (a quo Dal Fiatach) B(Lc)Lb, *om.* Lc[l]MH.

197 Luadrind[a] ingen [bc]Cholmain m. Ḟalbe[c] m. Ḟindlatha m. Dala[d] [e]m. Drona m. Suail[ef] m. Eoin[g] m. Idgaire[h] m. Airt Chirp[i] [j]m. Ḟir Da Choire[jk] m. Laithig[l] m. Cormaic Galeṅg m. Taidc m. Cein [m]m. Ailella[bm].

[a]Luaithreng H[l], *add* Cille Luathrind Lb, *add above line in later hand* G.L. anso sios H. [b—b]*mostly illeg.* H[l]. [c—c]Ḟailmi (*with* b *above* m) m. Oilbi (M)R[l]. [d](h)Ail (B)Lb. [e—e]*om.* BLb. [f]Sauil MR[l]. [g]Eoinne Lc[l], Cein R[l]. [h]Gaire B, Ḟidchuri Lb, Midgaire Lc[l], Fidgaire MR[l]. [i]Chuirp MR[l](H). [j—j]*om.* MR[l]. [k]Cho(i)rp (Lc[l])H. [l]Lathaigh BLb, Laithigu MR[l], *add no* m. Dalai m. Eoin Ḟidchuire m. Airt Chuirp m. Lui a quo Luigne Lb. [m—m]*om.* B, *add* Aulaim Lb(Lc[l]MR[l]HH[l]).

198 Liadain[a] ingen[b] Diarmata m. Duach m. Cairthind[c] Móir[d] m. Blait [e]m. Cais[e] [f]m. Thail[f] [g]m. Conaill Echluaith [h]m. Lugdach Mind ut supra[gh].

[a]Litain Lc, Liadaine Lb. [b]m B. [c]Carthainn B(LcLbMR[l]La). [d]*om.* Lc[l]. [e—e]*om.* H. [f—f]*om.* BLcLbLc[l]M, m. Tail a quo (Dail) Caiss (R[l])La. [g—g]*om.* R[l]HLa. [h—h]*om.* BLcLbLc[l]M.

199 Beccan [a]Cluana Aird[ab] m. Murchada m. Muredaig m. Diarmata m. Eogain[c] m. Ailella Uluim.

[a—a]*om.* MR[l]HLaLa[l]. [b]Iraird BLc. [c]*add* Moir B, m. Ailella Fland Bic m. Fiachach Fir Da Liac m. Ailella Fland Mair m. Fiachach Muilleatain m. Eoghain Moir R[l](LaLa[l]).

200 Odrán magister[a], [b]i lLettrachaib[c], i n*Uib*[d] Daigri, et Medran[e] Saigri[f] dá[b] mac Meic Craith m. Throchaill[g] m. Essamain Daigre[h] [i]m. Nuadat [j]Nemnich.
A[k] Caille Cind Ḟebrat[ijl].

[a].i. magistir R[l]. [b—b]*om.* R[l]. [c]Laitrib BLc, lLathrachu Odrain Lb. [d](l)leth (B)Lc(Lb). [e]Medraigi B(LcLb). [f]o Ṡaigir Lb. [g]Rochaill R[l]. [h]m. Daigre Lb(R[l]), *add* m. Beil(?) m. Mundigh m. Forait R[l]. [i—i]*om.* R[l]. [j—j]*om.* Lb. [k]i BLc. [l]Abrat Lc.

201 [a]Berchan [b]profeta 7[b] episcopus 7 poeta[c] m. Muridaig̣ — [d]qui 7 Mịcan[d] — m. Dega Dimmasaig[e] m. Anbchellaig[f] m. Ḟerchair m. Ḟeradaig m. Colmain m. Baetain m. Echach m. [g]Loairn m. Eirc Móir[g] m. Echach Munremuir [h]m. Oengusa Fir m. Ḟeidlimid Asliṅgthig m. Oengusa Budnig m. Senchormaic ṃ. Cruithluthi m. Find Fecci — [i].i. Ramand[i] — m. Achir Chirr m. Ḟiachrac̣h — [i].i. Antoit[i] — m. Cathmail m. Echach Riata, qui 7 Carpre Rigḟota a quo Dál Riata, m. Conaire Chaem m. Lugdach Find, qui 7 Ollsuthach *no* Olldotig, m. Corpre Chromchind — [i].i. a smech fora brunnib[i] — m. Dare Dornmair m. Cairpre Findmoir ṃ. Conaire Moir m. Etersc̣eoil m. Eogain m. Ailella m. Ḍedaid m. Ṡin m. Roṡin m. Morga m. Ḟeradaig m. Ailella Erand m. Ḟiachach Fir Mara m. Oengusa Turbig[ah].

[a—a]Berchan m. Micain m. Dega do Chruithnib do M(La). [b—b]profans LcLb. [c]*add* (qui) 7 Bercan (BLc)Lb. [d—d]*above line* L, *om.* BLcLb. [e]m. Díma B(LcLb). [f]Aubecell B(Lb), Anbell Lc. [g—g]Loairn Mair m. Erc B(LcLb). [h—h]*om.* BLcLb. [i—i]*added above line* L.

202 Manchíne Lumnig m. Setna[a] m. Cais [b]m. Thail[b] [c]ut ante[c].

[a]Sei*na* B, Senia Lc. [b—b]*om.* Lb. [c—c]*om.* B, m. Conaill Echluaith (m. Luigdech Mind) Lc(Lb).

203 Epscop Mac Lasre m. Conaill Echluaith m. Lugdech[a] Mind[b].

[a]Lugach Lc. [b]Mind m. Oengusa Tirig Lb.

204 Feidelm[a] et Ronnat dí[b] ingin Rónain m. Oengusa Uill m. Urchlosaig[c] m. Ailgile m. Tairdelbaig m. Caidleni[d] m. Conaill Echluaith [e]m. Echach Balldeirg m. Cairthind m. Blait ut supra[e].

[a]Feidlim(id) B(Lc), Felim Lb. [b]da BLcLb. [c]Aurchlosaig Lb. [d]Caillene B, Odlain m. Aeda Lb. [e—e]om. BLb, m. Lugdach Mind Lc.

205 Molaṅga[a] Saṅgil m. Finain m. Echach m. Ailgile[b] m. Tairdelbaig[c] [d]ut ante[d].

[a]Molag(a) Lc(Lb). [b]Algil Lb. [c]Saerdhelbaig B. [d—d]*om.* BLcLbM.

206 Coeman Brec [a]o Rus Ech[a] — m. Nisi[b] — m. Nemadain[c] m. Eirc Móir[d] m. Echach[e].

[a—a]o Ruisech B, *om.* Lb[l]MH, *add.* a Mide Lb. [b]Meic Nisi Lc. [c]Nemadadan Lb[l]. [d]*om.* LbLb[l]MH. [e]*add* Mundramair B(LcLbLb[l]MH), 7 mac mathar don Choeman sin Mac Rustaing Lb.

207 Tola Craidbech[a] m. Dunchada m. Ernaine[b] m. Garbain[c] [d]m. Ṡenaig m. Muredaig [e]m. Thalgluind[e] m. Brocain[f] m. [g]Cormaic[h] m. Taidc[g] m. Cein[di].

[a]Craibtheach BLc(Lb), *om.* MR[1]HLa, *add* ho Disiurt Tola i nOes iar Ḟorcus Lb. [b]Ernbrain(e) (BLc)Lb. [c]Gabhrain R[1]La. [d—d]*om.* H. [e—e]*om.* BLcLb. [f]Bracain R[1]. [g—g]*reversed* Lb. [h]Cormaic Gailing M(R[1]La). [i]Cen m. Ailella Oluim Lc(LbMR[1]).

208 Ruadan [a]Lothra apstal[ab] m. Fergusa Birn[c] [d]m. Ęchdach[d] m. [e]Duib Dein[e] m. Dáre Cerba [fg]m. Duach Duind[g] m. Mane Munchain[f] [h]m. Ailella Flainn Bic [i]ut ante[hi].

[a—a]*reversed* BLb. [b]ap̄s L(*above line*) (*see note*), esp̄c B(Lb), .i. ep Lc, *om.* MR[1]La. [c]*om.* BLcLb. [d—d]*om.* Lc. [e—e]Duibhdera BLc, De(a)ra Duib LbM(R[1]), Drenna Duib La. [f—f]*om.* LbMR[1]. [g—g]*om.* BLcLa. [h—h]m. Eogain Moir BLc. [i—i]m. Fiachach Muillethain m. Eogain m. Oilella Auluim (m. Eogain Moir do chosain Eiri re Conn Cedchathach) Lb(M), m. Fiachach Fer Da Liach m. Ailella Flannmoir m. Fiachach Muillethain m. Eogain Moir m. Ailella Oluim La, m. Fiachach Muilleathan — .i. da mac Fiachaig .i. Ailill Flann Mor ⁊ Ailill Flann Bec — m. Eoghain Moir m. Ailella Oluim — xix. m*eic* Ailella Al*uim* crinais a cland *acht* triair .i. Eogan Mor ⁊ Chian ⁊ Cormac — m. Mogha Nuaghat — .i. da mac Mug Nuadat .i. Ailill Aulom ⁊ Lugaid Lagha — m. Mogha Neit m. Deirg m. Deirgtine m. Enna Muncain m. Loith Moir m. Nafemis m. Eachach Fir Ḟuirmi m. Duach Dalta Deadhadh m. Cairpri Luisc Leithet m. Luighdeach Luaighne m. Ḟindad Mair m. Niadh Seaghamair m. Adhamair Flighais Foltcaim m. Ḟir Chorb m. Mogha Corb m. Cobtaigh Caim m. Rachtada Righdeirg m. Eachach m. Luighdeach m. Airt m. Ailella Find m. Eachach Uarceas m. Duach Find m. Ennda Airt m. Luighdeach Iarduind m. Duach Find m. Setna Indaradh m. Breis Righ m. Airt Imligh m. Felim Ollfindnachta m. Rachtada Rotha m. Roain Righeirledh m. Failbhe Erchoraigh m. Caiss Cétcoingnidh m. Aildergoid m. Muinemhoin m. Caiss Clothaigh m. Anurda m. Glais m. Rossa m. Roteachta m. Nuadhat Deglaim m. Eachach Faebhardirg Glais m. Conmail m. Eimir Ḟind — cethra meic Emir Ḟind. Aer, Orba, Feron, Fergna — m. Milead Easspáine — .i. secht meic Miled .i. Dond Colptha, Amargeng, Ir, Eber, hErimon, hErech Febria, ⁊ Arennac osar na claine sin — m. Bile m. Breoghain — .i. .x. meic Bregoin*n*. Brego, Bile, Blad, Cualo, Cuailge, Fuat, Murthemne, Eblo, Nar, Ith — m. Bratha m. Dethatha m. Arcadha m. Alloit m. Nuadat m. Nenuaill m. Eimhir Find m. Aighne m. Eimir Gluinfind m. Lamhḟind |m. Eteoir(?) *above line*| m. Agnoín m. Tait m. Ogamain m. Bogamain m. Eimir Scuit m. Sru m. Eassru m. Gaedil Glais m. Nuil m. Feiniusa Forsaig m. Bathaith m. Ibath m. Gomir m. Maghoith m. Iafeth m. Nae m. Lamhḟiach m. Mathasaleam m. Eneoig m. Ireith m. Malaleith m. Caineain m. Ein|o|sa m. Seith m. Adaim m. De thalamhuide cre lathair nDe) Rawl.[1] (*text between dashes is added above line in MS and is mostly in different hand*), *add further in marg. sup.* |...| ⁊ ua Ailella ana*r*ta*r* Eoganachta Caisil r̄l. Eochaidh fidhach Fidhindte daghuad daghadearse m. Daire caem Ceirba os laech leirg na lear, *in marg. infer.* Tri meic hErimoin .i. Muimne, Lugne, Lagne.

209 Secht meic Oengusa m. Aeda m. Eirc m. Echach Munremuir [a]m. Oengusa Fír[a] [b]ut ante in genealogia Berchain[b] .i. Mothrianóc[c] Ruscaig[d], Itharnaisc[e] Cloenta, Eoganan[f] Leccaig, Mochulli Dresnada[g], Mothairean[h] Tilcha[i] Fortcheirn[j], Troscan[k] Arda Breccain[l], Agatan ar[m] ur Ethni[n].

[o]Inde dixit Colum Cille:

Secht meic aille Oengusa[p] etcetera[oq].

[a—a]*om.* BLcLb. [b—b](7) Uann ingen Brecan (a mathair) B(Lc). [c]Mothrinoc Lb. [d]*om.* Lb. [e]Ithar Lc. [f]Eogan BLcLb. [g]Resnada BLc(Lb). [h]Modairen BLcLb. [i]Tulcha BLcLb. [j]Fortchi BLcLb. [k]Trioscan BLc, Taur*us*can Lb. [l]B. BLc, Bo Lb. [m]for Lb. [n]Theith*us* B, Ethi*us* Lc. [o—o]*om.* Lb. [p]*om.* B. [q]gasraid do rer De, fa fortail a ferta son, a crabad nir cle Lc.

210 [a]hUriu[b] epscop[a] m. Cuain m. Lugdach[c] m. Ḟintain m. Mechair m. Conaire m. Deicce m. Imchada m. Cuirb m. Lugdach[c] m. Ailella[d] Baschain m. Conaire[e].

[a—a]*reversed* Lb [b]hUiredu B(LcLb). *See note.* [c]Lui(g)dech B(LcLb). [d]*add* m. Oengusa m. Coirpre Lb. [e]*add* Chóeim Lb, Moir Lc[l], m. Moga Lama Lc.

211 Finan Cam [a]Cind Ettig[a] — [b]Becnat nomen matris eius[b] — m. Moenaig m. Ardda m. Fidaig[c] m. Corcain[d] m. Nudin[e] m. Irchuind m. Cormaic[f] m. Corpre Músc m. Conaire[g] Chaem[h].

[a—a]Cind E(tt)ich m. Ceinetigh BLc(Lb). [b—b]*in top marg.* L, *om.* BLcLb. [c]Fidhi B. [d]Corcrain BLcLb. [e]Muinde BLc. [f]*add* Ḟind m. Cuirc Duibh(ne) B(LcLb). [g]*add* m. Moga Lama Lb. [h]*om.* BLcLb.

212 Lactain[a] [b]Achaid Úir[bc] m. Tarbín[d] [e]m. Nuachair m. Carthind[f] m. Cainnig[g] m. Cairpre Músc[eh].

[a]Lachtnan Lc. [b—b]*om.* R[l]. [c]Aur Lb. [d]Torbire Lb(BLc), Torbine R[l]. [e—e]m. Nathi m. Maelain m. Scelain m. Casceni m. Olcaín m. Carthinnd m. Cainnig m. Nocori m. Neill m. Nathri m. Eatrai m. Cuirp m. Duibi m. Liacind m. N(ad)su(rd) R[l]. [f]Cairthaind Lc. [g]Conchind Lb. [h]*add* m. Conaire Lb.

213.1 Fintan Find — [a].i.[b] Dromma Inġ[ac] — m. Eogain m. Cattain[d] m. Ḟergusa m. Ḟindchada m. Ḟeic m. Findchaín[e] [f]m. Conlai[f] m. Taidc m. Céin[g].

2 Uel ita[b]: Fintan m. Eogain [h]m. Catain[h] m. Aedain m. Colmain m. Ḟergusa m. Conchobuir m. Mail Mata[i] m. Muredaig m. Eogain m. Durthech[j] m. Cairpre Luisc m. Loich Moir m. Mafemis[k]. [h]Require in genealogia Ailella Uluim[h].

[a—a]*above line* L, *in text* BLcLb. [b]*om.* BLcLb. [c]Aing B, *om.* Lc. [d]*Chath*ain B, Chaain Lc. [e]Findcaim (m.) Uallaig B(Lc)Lb. [f—f]*om.* Lc. [g]*add* m. Ailella Oluim Lc(Lb). [h—h]*om.* BLcLb. [i]Umai Lb. [j]Dur*ach*ta B, Durrth*acht* Lc(Lb). [k]Nadfebis Lb.

214 Epscop [a]Beoaed o Ard[a] Charna m. Olcain[b] m. Commain[c] [d]m.[e] Maithne[d] m. Triuin[f] m. Liuin[g] m. Lugdach[h] m. Con[i].

[a—a]Beoaeda (Beoid) Arda Lc(M). [b]Olchon LcM. [c]Cuimain M. [d—d]*om.* Lb, m. Maithine M. [e]*om.* B. [f]Thruine M. [g]Luain BLcLb, Luin M. [h]Luigdech BM. [i]Meic Con LcM.

215.1 [ab]Colmán m. Lénin m. Gannchon m. Donola m. Conamla m. Colgan m. Crundmael m. Ailt m. Oengusa Carraig m. Moga Nuadat [c]m. Dergthene[bc].

2 Secht [d]n-ingena Lénine[d]; Aiglend, Machain[e], Luiden[f], Druiden[g], Lucell, Rimthech, Brigit[h]. Et[i] óga[j] in[k] sin uile[l] [m]cenmotha Aiglend a[n] hoenur[mo].

[a]2 *precedes* 1 RLc[l]. [b—b]*om.* Lc. [c—c]*om.* BLbLc[l], *add* m. Duach Find R. [d—d]*ingen* Aileinin B, *add* .i. LcLbRLc[l]. [e]Macha Lb. [f]Luaiden Lc. [g]Drucen Lc. [h]Bruig̃ Lc. [i]*om.* BLcLbRLc[l]. [j]eog̃ B. [k]*om.* LcRLc[l]. [l]*om.* B. [m—m]excepta prima RLc[l]. [n]*om.* B, na Lc. [o]*add* uair ba hi sin mathair Cholmain fessin Lb.

216 Finan Dromma[a] [b]Abrat m. Garbain m. Amalgada[c] m. Enna[d] [e]a quo *Ui* Ennae[bef].

[a]o Dhruimm Lb. [b—b]Neoit m. Aeda m. Echach m. Aengusa m. Muiredaig Mail Lc. *See note.* [c]Amalgaid BLc[l]. [d]Einne RLc[l], *add* m. Oilella m. Natfraich m. Cuirc m. Luigdech Lb. [e—e]*om.* Lb. [f]E(i)nne (R)Lc[l].

217 Molaca[a] m. Duib [D]ligid[b] m. [c]Duib Dechoin[c] m.[d] Duib Chuilli[e] m. Lactnai[f] m. Colla m. Causcraid m. Fir[g] Chulchi[h] m. Buain[i] m. Moga Ruith[j].

[a]Molacha La. [b]lidi B, Dligid LbRLc[l](M)R[l]R[l]|18|40Vc(La). [c—c]Eogain M, Deochain R[l]La, Oeochain R[l]|18|40Vc. [d]*large* m. B. [e]Thuilchi M, Chuile R[l]R[l]|18|40VcLa. [f]Lactnan B, Luchta(i) M(R[l])R[l]|18|40VcLa. [g]Fil M. [h]Cuile BLb, Ailche MR[l]R[l]|18|40VcLa. [i]Briain La. [j]*add* m. Ḟergusa (m. Roig) (Lb)Lc[l], a quo Fir Muigi (m. Fergusa) (MR[l]La)R[l]|18|40Vc.

218 Mochulli m. Diculli[a] m. Commain m. Dega m. Baide[b] m. Colla [c]m. Causcraid[c].

[a]Diucaill RLc[l]. [b]Buide Lb, Baede R(Lc[l]). [c—c]*om.*B, *add* m. Fir Chuile m. Buain m. Mogai Ruith Lb.

219 Cuanu m. Cailchin m. Dimmain m. Findbairr m. Findloga m. Deche[a] m. Con Filed m. Causcraid.

[a]Deic(c)e B(R)Lc[l].

220 Breccan[a] m. Eirc m. Coluim m. Sabarnaig[b] m. Imgáin[c] m. Taidc m. Céin[d] [e]m. Ailella[e].

[a]Brac(c)an B(Lb), *add* m. Cinnbarca R(Lc[l]). [b]Sab̄araig B. [c]Imdain m. Findcada (Uallaig) m. Conla B(Lb). [d]*add* a Caisel R. [e—e]*om.* B, *add* Oluim Lb(RLc[l]).

221 Silan[a] epscop [b]m. Falbe[b] m. Laidcind[c] m. Ḟiachach[d] m. Scellain m. Eirc[e] Bic[f] m. Eogain m. Conaill Cloen m. Gerain[g] m. Duach m. [h]Nioth[i] m. Con[hj] [k]m. Lugdech[kl].

[a]Sillan H. [b—b]m. Oche H, *om.* La. [c]Laigind B. [d]Fiachrach MHLa. [e]Ir(cc) (M)H. [f].i. Bic Lb(*above line*). [g]Gabrain La. [h—h]*reversed* La. [i]Inoth B, Meicnia(d) (LbM)La, Niadchon RLc[l]. [j]Meic Con LcLbRLc[l]M. [k—k]*om.* Lb, *add* m. Daire M. [l]Lugdach H.

222 Factna [a]m. Moenaig — Moṅgaich[ab] — m. Cairill m. Ḟiachnai m. Rossa m. Eirc[c] m. Trenae m. Duach [d]m. Niad[de] [f]m. Con[g] [hi]m. Maic niad[fi] m. Lugdech[j] Loigdi[hk].

[a—a]m. Mongaig m. Maenaig BLc(Lb)La[l], m. Mongaig m. Inceanaig M, m. Mongach .i. m. Moenaig H, Mongach, .i. mong mór robi fair, m. Maenaig La. [b]*in marg. with ref. mark to* Moenaig L. [c]Mac E(i)rc (M)HLa[l]. [d—d]*om.* La. [e]Meicniot B(LbH). [f—f]*om.* M. [g]Meic Con BLcLb. [h—h]*om.* Lb. [i—i]*om.* LcLa. [j]Lugdach HLa[l]. [k]*om.* BLcHLa, Laigde a Rus Aeiliter M(*in smaller hand*).

223 Colmán ailithir[a] m. Grillini[b] m. [c]Aeda m. Ṡani[c].
[d][Is uad ainmnigter] Ros [Oi]lithir[d].

[a]Ailithi Lc[l]. [b]Girill(in) M(R[l]La). [c—c]Aeda S(l)aine (M)R[l]La, Diarmada m. Fergusa Ceirbeoil m. Conaill Cremthainne m. Nell Naígiallaig Lb, *add* m. *followed by blank* R[1]. [d—d]*in marg. and mostly illeg.* L, *text within brackets from* Lb(MR[l]HLa), *om.* RLc[l].

224 Mothemnioc[a] m. Corbbain[b] m. Lugada[c] [d]m. Teimen[d] [e]m. Themniain[ef] m. [g]Senaig m. Cerddain m. Cerdda Bice[gh] [i]m. Cerddraige[i] m. Tigernaig m. Ailella Uluim[j].

[a]Motheineoc Lb, *add above line* .i. Temnen La[l]. [b]Ce(a)rbain (B)Lb, Cobhrain R[l]La, Cordain H. [c]Luighech B(Lb), Lugeda R[l]HLa(La[l]). [d—d]*om.* MH. [e—e]*om.* R[l]La. [f]Teimin Big B. [g—g]*om.* B. [h]Bic LbLc[l]MR[l]. [i—i]*add* a quo Tulcha Gossai Lb, *om.* RLc[l]. [j]*om.* Lc[l]La.

225 Cronán[a] m. Odrain m. [b]Domangin — [c]*no* Amargin[bc] — m. Phuirg[d] m. Olchon m. Amraith[e] m. [f]hOeluirg — [c].i. Deirg[fc] — m. Eirc[g] m. Abarnaig[h] m. Finnchain[i] m. Ḟeic m. [j]Imchada — [c]*no* Findchada[jc] — [k]m. Condlai m. Taidg m. Cein[kl].

[a]*add* Rosa Cré La, Roscraensis abbas R[l](*in late hand*). [b—b]Amairghein B(LbH), Domungein R(Lc[l]), Doma(i)rgein (MR[l])La. [c—c]*added above line* L. [d]Puirg B, Ḟuirg Lb(R[l]H), Phurig RLc[l], Ruicc M, Fuiric La. [e]Imraith La. [f—f]hOelurg Derg B, Elerig Deirg m. Imchadai Lb, Oeluirig m. Deirg R(Lc[l]), hOeluirig M, Caeluirig R[l], .h.Luirg Deirg H, Eoluirg La. [g]Serc B, Irc(c) (MR[l])H. [h]Sabarnd (*with stroke over* arnd) B, Sabarnaig Lb, Aban(n)aig MR[l](HLa). [i]Findchaim B(Lb)MR[l]HLa. [j—j]Findchada (Uallaig) B(LbH), Findchada m. Ulaig RLc[l], Imchada Uallaig MR[l]La. [k—k]*om.* B. [l]*add* m. Oilella Oluim (m. Eogain) Lb(R)Lc[l]MR[l]HLa.

226 Dimma[a] Dub m. Oengusa [b]m. [c]Cairthind[bd] [e]m. Find[ef] [g]m. Blait [h]m. [i]Caiss [j]ut supra[eghij].

[a]*in marg.* se meic Combraite .i. Dima Dubh, Dima Becc, Dima Odur, Gobban, Breccan, Baetan R[l] (*see note*). [b—b]*om.* Lc[l]. [c—c]Carthaind Find Lb(H). [d]Carthainn BMLa. [e—e]*om.* MR[l]La. [f]Ḟindi Lc. [g—g]*om.* Lb. [h—h]*om.* H. [i—i]Tailc(Tail) (m.) Cais B(Lc). [j—j]m. Conaill (Echluaith) m. Luigdech m. Oengusa Tirich(*om.*) R(Lc[l]).

227 Cormac [a]*Ua* Liathain[a] m.[b] Dimmai[c] m. Commain m. Condmaig m. Congaile[d] m. Corpre m.[e] Sinnaig[f] m. Echdach Liathain, [g]a quo *Ui* Liathain, [h]m. Dare Cerba [ij]m. Mane Munchain[j] m. Ailella Flainn Bic[ghi].

[a—a]*om.* MR[l]HLa. [b]*bis* H. [c]Immai R[l]. [d]Congail BLcLb. [e]*om.* Lb. [f]Sinaig RLc[l]H. [g—g]*om.* RLc[l]. [h—h]*om.* MR[l]HLa. [i—i]*om.* B. [j—j]*om.* LcLb.

228 Senan[a] [b]Insi Cathaig[b] m. Eirggind[c] m. Dubthaig m. Decce m. Imchada[d] m. Cuirb[e].

[a]*added in lower marg.* tri meic Errgind .i. Cael 7 Liath 7 Senan R[l]. [b—b]*om.* R[l]HLa. [c]Geirgind B(LbRLc[l]MR[l]HLa). [d]Indcadha R[l]La. [e]Coirpri MR[l], *add* m. Luigdech m. Oilella m. Oengusai m. Coirpre Baschain m. Conaire m. Moga Lama Lb.

229 Benian[a] — [b] salmchetlaid Patric[b] — [c]m. Sescniain[cd].
[e]Do[f] Chiannacht[g] Glinni Gaimin, do[h] Síl Taidc m. Cein[i] dó[ej].

[a]Beneo(i)n B(Lb), Benaen Lc[l], *add* .i. LbR[l]. [b—b]*above line* Lb, *follows* Sescniain RLc[l], *om.* R[l]15(37)Ra. [c—c]*om.* R[l]. [d]*add* m. Cerbaill m. Aengusa m. Nafraich m. Cuirc m. Luighdeach m. Ailella Fland Bic m. Ailella Fland Moir m. Fiacha Muillethain m. Eoghain Moir m. Ailella Oluim R[l]15(37)Ra. [e—e]*om.* R[l]15(37)Ra, *reverse order* Lb. [f]a Lb. [g]Chiandacta(ib) BLb(Lc[l]). [h]*add* .i. do R[l]. [i]*add* m. Ailella Aulaimm (m. Moga Nuadat) R(Lc[l]), a Caisiul R[l]. [j]*om.* BRLc[l]R[l].

230 Flannan[a] [b]7 [c]Aedan Cluana[c] Domail [d]i nAlmain[d] da[b] mac Tairdelbaig m. Caidleni[e] m. Conaill Echluaith [f]ut supra[f].

[a]*add* Cille Dalua m. Tairdelbaig R, Cilli Dallan Lc[l], Mór MR[l]. [b—b]*om.* MR[l]HLa. [c—c]*om.* B. [d—d]*om.* RLc[l]. [e]Caitlein B, Cathail LbR[l], Atrein R(Lc[l]MHLa), *add* m. Aedai m. Conaill m. Echach Balldeirg (*om.* RLc[l]) (neach dobaist Patraic R[l]) m. Carthaind Find(*om.* RLc[l]HLa) m. Blaid(*om.* R) m. Caiss(Cormaic Caiss H, Tail R[l]La) Lb(RLc[l]MR[l]H), *add further* m. Cormaicc R. [f—f]m. Luigdech (Mind MR[l]H) m. Oengusa Tirich m. Fir Chorbb (*om.* M) R(MR[l]HLa), *add further* m. Mogha Corb m. Cormaic Cais (o fuil Dail Cais) m. Ailella Oluim (m. Moga Nuaghat) (R[l])La, *om.* BLbLc[l].

231 [a]Buti[b] Manistrech[ac] m. Brónaig m. Balair m. Cais m. Niad[d] m. Airmedaig[e] m. Findchain[f] m. Ḟéic[g] [h]m. Imchada[i] m. Conlai m. Taidc m. Cein[hj].

[a—a]Baidemain (a)istreach B(Lc). [b]Buide .i. beo M. [c].i. Manisdrech Lb(*above line)*, *om.* RLc[l]MHLa. [d]Naid Lc[l]. [e]*add* m. Fergusa RLc[l]MHLa. [f]Findchaim BLc(Lb)Lc[l], Cain M. [g]Fothaig La. [h—h]*om.* MHLa. [i]Ḟindchada Uallaig Lb. [j]*add* m. Oilella Oluim (Buti .i. beo *no* buti .i. teni ut dicitur bót fo Bregu, unde dicitur butelach .i. hignis magnus) (Lb)RLc[l].

232 Cummini[a] Fota[b] m. Fiachra[c] m. Ḟiachrach[d] — [e].i.[f] Garrini[e] — m. Duach Iarlathi[g] m. Mani[h] m. Corpre[i] [j]m. Cuirc[j] m. Lugdech[k] [l]m. Ailella [m]Flainn Bic[lmn].

[a]Cumain(e) BM(La). [b]*om.* H. [c]Fiac̄ B, Fiachna(i) (Lb)RLc[l](H)La, *illeg.* M. [d]Fiachra R[l]. [e—e]*below line* L, *in text* BLbR[l], *om.* RLc[l]HLa, .i. *only, due to tear in page* M. [f]*om.* BLbR[l]. [g]*om.* RLc[l]MH. [h]*add* Muncain R[l]. [i]*add* Luachra R[l]. [j—j]*om.* R[l]La. [k]Lugdach R(La)H, *add* m. Ailella Deirg R[l]La. [l—l]*om.* BH. [m—m]Oluim m. Eogain Moir M. [n]*add* m. Ailella Flainn Móir (m. Fiacha Muillethain m. Eoghain Moir m. Ailella Oluim) R(R[l]La).

233 Comgan [a]Gl*inne*[b] Usen[a] m. Diarmata m. Dega[c] m. Themne m. Fir Chorb m. Moga Corb m. Cormaic Cais[d] [e]m. Ailella Uluim[e].

[a—a]*om.* RLc[l]. [b]o Glind Lb. [c]Aeda *no* Dega B. [d]*om.* R. [e—e]*om.* B.

234 Epscop Forcitail i Cill Tidill m. Tail m. Dega[a] m. Cuirc m. Luigdech[b].

[a]*add* .i. Conaill B, m. Conaill (.i. Corcc) Lc(Lb). [b]Lugdach m. Oilella Flainn Bic Lb, Lugdach m. Bairr m. Cairthind m. Cormaicc m. Coluimb m. Meic Lugnae m. Eogain m. Guaire m. Eircc m. Bacain m. Conaill Cernaig et cetera R(Lc[l]).

235 Fathlind[a] m. Aeda Damain[b] m. Crimthaind m. Cobthaig m. Duach Iarlathi[b] m. Mani[c] Maithni[d] m. Carpre m. Cuirc m. Lugdech.

[a]Faithlenn R(Lc[l]Lb). [b]*om.* B, *above line* Lb. [c]*om.* RLc[l]. [d]*om.* BLb.

236 Gobban[a] Find[b] m. Lugdach[c] m. Dallain m. Cairpre Chael[d] m. Echach Liathain m. Dare Cerba [e]m. Mane Munchain[e]

[a]*add* o Cill Goban Lc. [b]*om.* Lc. [c]Lugna Lc, Luigdech Lb. [d].i. Coel Lb(*above line*). [e—e]*om.* BLc, m. Oilella Flann Bic Lb.

237 Colman[a] [b]Imrama[c] Othna[bd] m. Fergnai[e] [f]m. Olchon[fg] m. Echach Munremuir[h] [i]m. Oengusa Fír m. Feidlimid Aslingthe ut supra in genealogia Berchain[i].

[a]Coman BLb. [b—b]*om.* Lb[l]. [c]*om.* BLb. [d]*above line* L, m. Etra B, Ethrai Lb, *om.* MR[l]H. [e]Ḟergusa m. Fergna B, Ḟergusa (*no* Fergna *in marg.*) M, *add* m. Aeda Lc[l]MR[l]HLb[l]. [f—f]*om.* B. [g]*add* m. Ailella R[l]. [h]Muidmedoin Lb[l](MR[l]). [i—i]*om.* LbLb[l]Lc[l]MR[l]H.

238 Mac Táil Cilli Culind[a] et Caelan[b] Cilli Clethi[c] [d]da mac[d] Echdach m. Derggain m. Coluimb[e] m. Cronain m. Oengusa m. Nadfraich [f]m. Cuirc[g] m. Lugdech[fh].

[a]Cuillind Lb. [b]Colman BLcLb. [c]Clethidai Lb. [d—d].i. cland Lb. [e]Coluimbe Lc. [f—f]*om.* BLc. [g]Conaill Cuirc Lb. [h]*add* m. Oilella Flainn Bic Lb.

239 Berchan[a] — [b]⁊ a thrí sethracha, [c][.i. B]rig[c] ⁊ Copp[d] ⁊ Lasar [e][...ll] Dara ⁊ i Cill Ingen Nemnann[be] — m.[f] Nemnann[g] m. Aeda m. Eirc m. Echach Muinremuir[h] m. Oengusa[i] Fir[h].

[a]Bre(a)can (B)Lc. [b—b]*in marg. with ref. mark* L, *in text* BLcLb. [c—c]*bracketed letters lost through fracture of margin* L, .i. Brig BLcLb. [d]Corb B. [e—e]*om.* BLcLb. [f]clann Lb. [g]Nemain(d) (B)LcLb. [h]*om.* BLcLb. [i]*add* m. Nadfraich (m. Cuirc m. Lugdach) BLc(Lb).

240 Dalbach [a]Cule[b] *Collainge*[ac] m. Branduib m. Ṡirṡlataig[d] m. Ḟergnai m. Donnain[e] m. Dimmai[f] [g]m. Bresail[g] [h]m. Tassaig[h] m. Echach Liathain[i] [j]a quo *Ui* Liathain[j].

[a—a]*om.* M. [b]Cilli BLc. [c]C. BLc, Collainge Lb, Collai|n|g M[l](R[l])La. [d]Sirluadhaide B(Lb), Ḟirluagaidi Lc, Sirlaitha(igh) (R[l])La. [e]Dunain M. [f]Dimmain M[l]. [g—g]*om.* Lb. [h—h]m. (Oilella) Taisig BLc(Lb), *om.* MM[l]R[l]La. [i]Leith M, *add* m. Daire(Maine R[l]) Cerbai (m. Ailella Flainn Bic) Lb(M[l]R[l]La), *add further* m. Fiachach Fir Da Liach m. Eogain (Moir) m. Oilella Oluim (R[l])La, *add further* no as o Eochaig Liathan m. Daire Cearba *ua* daid *Ui* Cearba(Cirb) i mBreagaib M[l](R[l])La. [j—j]*om.* BLcLbMM[l]R[l]La.

241 [a]Colum apstal[b] [c]Tiri Da Glas[c] [d]m. Nannida[d] [e]m. Nastair[ef] m. Crimthaind Bic[g] m. Echach m. Oengusa m. Crimth*ann*áin[h] Móir[i] m. Cathair[j] Moir.

[a]*add* Lagnenses sancti L(*above line*). [b]ap̄s L (*see note*), epscop BLc, *om.* LbLc[l]MR[l]HLa. [c—c].i. Tire H. [d—d]m. Crimtain m. Ninde(a)da M(R[l])La, m. Nindeada Lc(LbH), *om.* Lc[l]. [e—e]*added later* R[l]. [f]Nasdai*n* B(Lc), Nadstair Lc[l], Na(s)sair M(R[l])La. [g]*om.* BLcLbMR[l]HLa. [h]*or read* Crimthainn Áin?, Crimthain B(Lc)Lb(M)R[l](HLa). [i]*added with other pen* L, *om.* BLcLbLc[l]MR[l]H. [j]Cartainn B.

242.1 Momedoc[a] [b]Feda Duin[b] — [cd]Aed proprium nomen[d] — et Colman Culi[e] dá[c] [f]mac Midgnai[fg] m. Nannida[h].

2 [i]Conchend[j] a siúr[i].

[a]Momaedhoc B(LbM), Mocholmoc Lc, Maedhog R[l]. [b—b].i. Feda Duin La(*above line*), *om.* H. [c—c]*om.* MR[l]HLa. *Cf. below* Lb. [d—d]*added with other pen* L, *om.* BLcLbMR[l]HLa. [e]Cilli B, Chilli Colmoc Lc. [f—f]*om.* Lc. [g]*om.* B, Midnai M, *add* m. Meti Lb(MR[l]H)La. [h]Nindeda m. Uaineda BLc, Nindedai m. Nastair m. Crimthain (m. Cathair Máir) (Lb)MR[l]HLa, *add* Colmán Cúile m. Midgnai .i. brathair Momoedoc Feda Duin Lb. [i—i]*om.* MR[l]HLa. [j]⁊ Concenn B(LcLb).

243.1 Secht meic Lugada[a]; Lasran[b], Boetan[c], Garban[d], Baethin[e], Senchan[f], Ruadan[g], Cronan [h]qui 7[h] Mochua [i]Cluana Dolcain.

2 [jk]Cronan di*diu*[ik] m. Lugada m. Nathi m. Dolbaig m. Setnai m. Conandla[l] m. Oengusa m. Alella Cethig m. Cathair Moir[jm].

[a]Lugada (m. Nahi m. Dolbaig m. Setnai m. Connlai m. Oengusa m. Oilella Cetaig m. Cathair Mair) .i. Lc(Lb). [b]Laisren Inbir M*en*a Lc[l]. [c]Bochtan(g) (BLc)Lb, *add* Ruba Baedan Lc[l]. [d]*add* Cluana Senbo Lc[l]. [e]*add* Inse Breslen Lc[l]. [f]Seanch B, *add* Dubaid Lc[l]. [g]*add* Ratha Lc[l]. [h—h]*om.* BLcLb. [i—i]*om.* Lc[l]. [j—j]*om.* Lb. [k—k]Cronaind B, Cronan Lc. [l]Co(n)nla (B)Lc. [m]*om.* BLc[l].

244 [a]Tigernach epscop[ab] [c]Cluana Eois[c] m. Corpre m. [d]Fergnai — [e]*no* [Fer]gusa[ae] — m. Ennai m. [f]Labain — [e]*no* Labrada[ef] — m. Brioin[g] m. Echach m. Dáre Barraig m. Cathair Moir[h].

[a—a]*reversed* MHLa. [b]*om.* Lc[l]. [c—c]*om.* MHLa. [d—d]Fergusa BLbMHLa, Ḟergnae Lc[l]. [e—e]*added above line* L. [f—f]Laebain BLb, Labrada Lc[l], Labain MHLa. [g]Brain BLb(M), Briain Lc[l], Briuin HLa. [h]*add illeg. note in marg.* M, Darfraich(?) ainm a mathar La.

245 Epscop Aed[a] m. Brocain [b]m. Cormaic[b] m. Diarmata m. [c]Echach [d]Gunich[c] [e]m. Oengusa[d] m. Eirce[f] m. Breccain m. Feicc[e] m. Dare Barraig m. Cathair Moir.

[a]Oeda Lc(Lb), *add* m. Mael Odrain Lc[l]. [b—b]*om.* Lc [c—c]Echguinig Lc. [d—d]*om.* Lc[l]. [e—e]*om.* BLcLb. [f]Erc Lc[l].

246 [a]Dí[b] ingin[a] Ailella[c] — .i. Mugain[d] 7 Fedelm[e] [f]i Cill Ingen[g] Ailella[f] — [h]m. Dunlaińg[i] m. Enniai[j] Niad m. Bresail Belaig m. Ḟiachach[k] Bacceda m. Cathair Moir[hl].

[a—a]ingena LbMR[l]La. [b]da BLcLc[l], na da MM[l]R[l]. [c]*add* m. Dunlaing (rig Laigen) Lb(MM[l]R[l]), rig Laigen La, *add further* 7 asiad dochreid do Patraic ag Dun Nais, 7 da mac in rig Dhunlaing .i. Ailill 7 Illann M(R[l]La). [d]Mumain Lb, *add* is uaithi Ceall Mughaine i nUib No in Tuadhmumain R[l](La). [e]Feidlim BMM[l], Felim Lb, Feidlimti R[l]La. [f—f]*om.* Lc[l]MM[l]R[l]La. [g]ingine Lc. [h—h]*om.* LbM. [i]Dunlaingi La. [j]Enda BLcLc[l](M[l]R[l]La). [k]Fiatac .i. La. [l]*add* m. Feidhlime m. Cormaic m. Cairbri R[l].

247 [a]Dí[b] ingin[a] Chormaic m. Ailella [c]m. Dunlai[n]g[c]: Ethni 7 Darcárthend[d] [e]i Tilaig[ef].

[a—a]ingena MLa. [b]da LcLb. [c—c]*om.* MLa, *add* .i. BLcMLa, m. Enda(i) Niad (Lb)Lc[l]. [d]Daire Cartann B, Derchartaind Lb(M), Darceirtend La. [e—e]*om.* Lb. [f]Tulaig (O Felmeda) B(Lc)Lc[l], Tulaig meic Ḟeilmida (Feidlimthi) M(La).

248 [a]Dí[b] ingin[a] Charpre[c] m. Cormaic [d]m. Ailella [e][m. Dunlaing][e] m. Enna Niad[df]: Cumman[g] 7 Sodelb [h]i Cill[h] Nais[i].

[a—a]ingena LbMLa. [b]da BLc. [c]*om.* Lc[l], *add* dino M(La). [d—d]*om.* MLa. [e—e]*om.* LLb, m. Dunlaing BLcLc[l]. [f]*add* m. Bresail Belaig m. Fiachach Aicceda m. Cathair Mair Lb, *add also* .i. LbMLa. [g]Cumain BLb, Cuimni M, Cuine *no* Cumne La. [h—h]*om.* B. [i]Neis(s)i (M)La, *add* mathair Seigin 7 Brigi La.

249 Molliṅg[a] Lua*chra*[b] m. Faelain[c] m. Ḟeradaig [d]m. Eirc[d] m. Fiachnai[e] m. [f]Oengusa, [g]*no* Eogain[fg], m. Dega m. Labrada m. Bresail Belaig[h] [i]m. Fiachach Bacceda[j] m. Cathair Moir[i].

[a]Molind Taircell do Ciaraidhe Luachra (.i. Tairchell ainm baisde Moling 7 Nemnaid do Ciaraigi Luacra a mathair) R[l] (*above line*), *add* 7 Dairchell ainm Moling prius Lb(*see note*). [b]a (l)Luachair B(M *above line*), Luacħ Lb, Luacair H, *om.* Lc[l]. [c]Fail B, Failind Lb(H). [d—d]*om.* B. [e]Fiacħ B, Fiacrach LbMR[l]H. [f—f]Eogain BLbMR[l]H, Oengusa Lc[l]. [g—g]*above line* L. [h](.i. Brecc) a quo Osraige Lb(*above line*), Bric(c) MR[l](H), *om.* Lc[l], *add* is ann condreagaid (fri) Clannaib Catair (M)R[l]. [i—i]*om.* BLbMR[l]H. [j]*om.* Lc[l].

250 C̣oemgen[a] m. Coemloga ṃ. Coemḟeda [b]m. Crinḟeda[b] m. Cuirbb[c] m. Ḟergusa Laebdeirg[d] [ef]m. Ḟothaid[f] m. Echach Lamdeirg m. Messin[g] Corbb[h] [i]m. Con Corbb[j].
[k]Cento vicesimo anno etatis suae quieuit[eik].

[a]*add* Glinde Da Lacha LbRLc[l]M. [b—b]m. Crin(d)eda B(Lc), m. Crimḟeda RLc[l], *om.* LbMR[l]HLa. [c]Cuirc H. [d]Lamdeirg RLc[l], Fortamail MR[l]La, *om.* H. [e—e]*om.* Lc. [f—f]*om.* MR[l]La. [g]Misin Lc[l], Meise R[l](HLa). [h]*add* m. Coirpri M, m. Concubhair Abradruaidh (*misplaced* La) m. Find Fileadh m. Rossa Ruaidh m. Feargusa Fairge m. Nuadhat Neacht m. Setnai Sithbaic m. Luighdeach Luaith(Luath.r.) m. Breasail Bric m. Fiachach Foibric m. Ailella Glass m. Muiredaigh Foglais m. Nuadat R[l](La). [i—i]*om.* BR[l]HLa. [j]*add* m. Mogai Corp Lb(*cf. note to* 249[a]), (m. Find Ḟiled) m. Conchobair Abratruaid RLc[l](M). [k—k]*om.* LbRLc[l]M.

251 Epscop[a] Eogain [b]Aird[c] Sratha[bd] [e]m. Cainnig — [f]*no* m. Epscuip Erc[ef] — [g]m. Cuirbb ut ante[g].

[a]*om.* M[l]R[l]H. [b—b]*om.* H. [c]Arda BLcLbMR[l], Airde M[l]. [d]Sr*eth* B, Sre(a)th M[l](R[l]). [e—e]m. Epscuip Eirc (Sláine) B(LbM), 7 Epscop Mac Eircc Lc, m. Ca(e)innig (M[l])R[l]H. [f—f]*above line* L. [g—g]*om.* BLc, (m. Dega m. Branchon (Brocain M) m. Fir Mora m. Aich*ir*(?) m. Imchada m. Dubthaig m. Findchada m. Echach m. Caiss m. Isiss m. Oirig m. Airt ṃ. Coirpre m. Cuirp Auluim m. Fergusa m. Roich Lb(M), m. Coirpri(Cuirc H) m. Ḟergusa m. Fothaig m. Eathach m. Meisin Corb M[l](R[l]H).

252 Conlaed — [a].i. cunnail aed[a] — Craibdech[b] m. Cormaic m. Oengusa [c]m. Echach[c] m. Setnai [d]m. Deimre[d] m. Echach Lamdeirg[e] [f]m. Messin[g] Corb [h]m. Con Corbb[fh].

[a—a]*above line* L, *om.* other mss. [b]Ce(a)rd Lb(M)R[l], .i. Cerd H(*in small hand*). [c—c]*om.* Lc[l]. [d—d]*om.* BLc, m. Emri (Enre M) m. Fothaid LbMR[l](H *see note*). [e]*om.* RLc[l]MR[l]H. [f—f]*om.* Lc. [g]Mescon R[l], Mes H. [h—h]*om.* BLbRLc[l]MR[l]H.

253 Craeb 7 [a]Lasar[b] et Find[a] tri[c] ingena[d] [ef]Meic Ieir[f] m. Nair[e] m. Fothaid m. Echach Lamdeirg[g].

[a—a]*reversed* Lb. [b]Laisair LcLb. [c]teora Lb. [d].ı̄ B. [e—e]Eircc m. Iair Lb. [f—f]her B(*see note*), Ieir Lc. [g]Lamdoit Lb, *add* m. Mesin Corb B(Lb).

254 Epscop Nathí m. Ṣenaig m. [a]Ḟergusa m. Laebderg[a] m. Echach Lamdóit m. Ẹimre m. Ḟothaid m. Echach Lamdeirg[b].
I Cúil[c] Ḟothirbi[d].

[a—a]Fergusa Laimdeirg BLc. [b]*add* m. Mesin Corb B. [c]Cill BLc. [d]Fothoirbi B(Lc).

255 Findbarr Cilli Adgair[a] m. Aeda m. Connois[b] m. Foramain[c] m. Oescain[d] m. Ḟothaid[e].

[a](h)Adhamair BLc(Lb). [b]Conindais BLc. [c]Foramain BLc, Forandain Lb. [d]Oschaein Lb. [e]*add* m. Echach Lamdoit m. Mesin Corp Lb.

256 Dagan [a]Inbir Doele[a] — [b].i. nomen amnis[b] — m. Colmadan[c] m. Conaill m. Énain m. Sinill m. Conaill m. Cathir[d] m. Airmora[e] m. Nastair m. Ḟothaid m. Echach Lamdeirg m. Messin Corb [f]m. Con Corb[f].

[a—a]*ingen* Berdaili BLc, *add* a nIb Cendselaig Lb. [b—b]*above line* L, *om.* BLcLb. [c]Colmadain BLc, Colmain Lb. [d]*Cath*air B, Iair Lc. [e]Airmorda B, Aramorai Lb. [f—f]*om.* BLcLb.

257 Ingena[a] Báeth m. Setnai m. Ḟedlimid m. Echdach m. Rosa Falge m. Cathair Moir.

[a]ingen BLcLb.

258 [a]Tri meic[a] Conaill [b]m. Airmora[b] m. Nastair[c].
It e [d]filet i[d] Cill[e] Garraisce.

[a—a]teora hingena meic Lb. [b—b]iar*m*mordha B. [c]*add* m. Fothaid m. Echach m. Mesin Corp Lb. [d—d]congabsat Lb. [e]*add* Maign̄ Lc(*see note*).

259 Eochu Cluana Rétach[a] 7 Magister Cilli Mag*istrech*[b] [c]da mac[c] Cathain m. Nathí m. Echach Gunich m. Dare Barraig m. Cathair Moir.

[a]Ratha(ch) (BLc)Lb. [b]Maig̃ B, Maignend Lc, Magist*r*ech Lb. [c—c]*written as if separate entry* BLc.

260 Brigit 7 Temair[a] 7 Sogaes[b] tri ingena[c] [d]Meic Dara[d] m. Ḟergusa [e]m. Ennae Niad, et[f] Iustan[eg] 7 Fintan da mac Ḟergusa i[h] Senchill.

[a]Temr̄ B. [b]Sogest B, Sogeas Lc. [c]*ingen* B. [d—d]Dair B, Dari Lc, Dara Lb. [e—e]an BLc(*see note*). [f]*om.* Lb. [g]Ustan Lb. [h]o Lb.

261 Berchan m. Dimmae Duind m. Aeda[a] Croin m. Mael Anfaid m. Mael Umai m. Colmain m. Corpre m. Ailella m. Dunlaiṅge[b] m. Ennae Niad[c].
I[d] nDruim [e]Dothe atá[e] in Berchan sa[f].

[a]*om.* Lb. [b]Dunlaing BLc. [c]*add* m. Bresail Belaig m. Fiachach (B)aicceda m. Cathair Mair Lb(M). [d]ho Lb. [e—e]Dotheda BLc(Lb). [f]sin BLcLbM.

262 Berchan[a] m. Dimmae m. Ḟergnai m. Ḟergusa [b]m. Aeda[b] m. Amalgada[c] m. Mane Máil[d] [e]qui fuit germanus[f] Cathair[g] Moir.
I nDomnuch Ṡinchill i n*Uib* Máil [h]atá in Berchan[i] sa[eh].

[a]Brecan BLc. [b—b]*om.* Lb. [c]Amalga(idh) (B)Lc. [d]*add* m. Feidlimig Firurglais M. [e—e]*in smaller, largely illegible hand* M. [f]*add* eius Lb. [g]m. Cathair BLc. [h—h]*om.* Lb. [i]Brecan B.

263 Berchan m. Decill[a] m. Caitt m. Ḟothaid m. Echach Lamdeirg m. Messin Corb.
[b]I Senchill i n*Uib* [c]Briuin Cualand[bc].

[a]Deichill M. [b—b]*in smaller hand* M. [c—c]mBriuin Gualand B, *add* (ata) in Berchan sin Lb(M).

264 Berchan m. Declain do ṡil Daimine Daim Argait.
[a]I nInis Rocha for Loch Erne[ab].

[a—a]*in smaller hand* M. [b]*add* (ata) in Berchan sin Lb(M).

265 Berchan m. Maín[a] do ṡíl Luigdech[b] Loigde[c].
[d]I[e] ṅGlind Berchain[df].

[a]Maine Lb. [b]Lugdach LcLb. [c]Laide BLc, *add* do Lb. [d—d]*in smaller hand* M. [e]ho Lb. [f]*add* (ata) in (Berchan) sin Lb(M).

266 Berchan m. Beoaid Barrḟind de [a]Chorco Thrí[a] [b].i. Mobí Glasi Nóenden[c] i nnGall*aib*[bd].

[a—a]Corco(a)rtri (B)LcM, Chorcḟirthri Lb. [b—b]*in smaller hand and almost entirely illegible* M. [c]Naindidhen B, Noiden Lb. [d]nGail BLc, nGaileng Lb, *add* in Berchan sin Lb.

267 Berchan m. Ultain m. Aedgein[a] m. Colmain m. Ṡilain.
[b]I[c] Cluain Cai[d] atá[be].

[a]Aegegen Lc. [b—b]*in smaller hand and mostly illegible* M. [c]o Lb. [d]Cain BLcLb, [...] fota M. [e]in sin Lb, *om.* Lc, *add* (...) sin B(M).

268 Berchan m. Fidne [ab]i Cill Fidne[b], i[c] Cluain Caín i nDelbna Ethra[ad].

[a—a]*in smaller hand* M. [b—b]*om.* Lb. [c]o Lb. [d]*add* in ([Ber]can) sin Lb(M), *add in lower marg. with mark of ref.* no Ethra ainm lathach 7 is ria atberthea Laith Da Bend inde dicitur Delbna Ethra L.

269 Berchan m. Aeda; [a]ante scripsimus inter sanctos na nDesi[a].

[a—a]*in smaller hand* M.

270 Berchan Cluana Sasta[a].

[a]Sosda M.

271 Berchan m. Nemnand[a].
[b]Quos ante scripsimus non quod isti omnes sint Lagnenses sed quia quidam eorum[b].

[a]Nemaind BLcLb. [b—b]*refers to* 261-71. *Latin slightly corrupted in* BLcLbM.

272.1 Colman[a] m. Ainmerech m. Bruidge[b] m. Nadbuidb [c]m. Illadan [d]m. Dunlaiṅge[e].

2 Et[d] Brandub abb Cilli Dara m. Fiachrach[f] m. Muridaig m. Bruidge[g] m. Nadbuidb.
I[h] rRus Branduib[ci].

[a]Coman Lb[l]. [b]Bruige B, Bruide Lc. [c—c]*om.* Lb[l]. [d—d]*om.* Lb(*see note*). [e]Dungaile BLc. [f]Fiachra Lb. [g]Bruidi B(Lc). [h]o Lb. [i]Brand i Tir *Ua* nAmalga Lc.

273 Crundmael m. Ronain m. Coluim[a] m. Cormaic Cam[ṡ]róin[b] m. Nathí m. Crimthaind m. Enne Chenselaig.
I[c] [d]Cluain Aird[d].

[a]Colmain Lc. [b]Camsroin BLcLb(*above line*). [c]7 i Lb. [d—d]Cluain Iraird B, Cluairaird Lc, *add* do Lb.

274.1 [a]Segine Gabuil[b] m. Senaig[c] [d]m. Nathí m. Cormaic[d]

2 Et[ae] Falbe[f] m. Echach Clithair[g] [h]m. Coluim[h] m. Cormaic[i].
[jk]It e failet[k] i[l] rRaith Bilig[jm].

[a—a]*om.* R[l]La. [b]Gabail BLc(Lb), *om.* M. [c]Senaig Gamna .i. Goibnen M. [d—d]m. Coluim m. Cormuic m. Nathi m. Crimthainn m. Enna Cheindsealaig M. [e]m. BLcLb (*see note*), *om.* M. [f]*add* m. Cenandain R[l]. [g]Clichair Lc, Clith MR[l], Cliach La. [h—h]*om.* MR[l]La, *add* m. Coluimbi Lc. [i]*add* m. Nathi m. Crimthainn m. Enna Cheinnselaig M(R[l]La). [j—j]*om.* R[l]La. [k—k]*om.* LcLb, Seigin ⁊ Failbi it e congabsad M. [l]o Lb. [m]*add* do Lb.

275 Finnacta Findchorad m. Colgan m. Bresail m. Ḟiachrach m. Crundmael m. Ronain m. Coluim[a] m. Cormaic Cam|ṡ|roin[b].

[a]*add* a quo Síl Coluim Lb. [b]*om.* BLc, Camṡron Lb, *add* m. Nahii m. Crimthainn m. Enda Chennselaig Lb.

276 [a]Ronán epscop[a] m. Aeda m. Senaig m. Cairthind[b] Muaich[c] m. Etarscela m. Oengusa Ailchi[d] m. Ḟergusa Forcraid m. Tuathail Tigich[e] m. Mane Máil[f] [g]a quo *Ui* Máil[g].
I[h] Raith Ronáin i n*Uib* Cellaig Cualand.

[a—a]*reversed* Lb, *add* m. Cormaic Lc. [b]Carthaind BLcLb. [c]*om.* BLcLb. [d]Aichli BLc. [e]Tige B, Tigid Lc, Tiag̃ Lb. [f]*add* m. Cathair Mair Lb. [g—g]*om.* LcLb. [h]*om.* B, (.i.) o Lc(Lb).

277 Aduar[a] m. Echcind[b] m. Aeda Caemchind m. Máil m. Droido[c] m. Buain m. Loegaire Birn Buadaig m. Oengusa Osrethi[d] [e]m. Crimthaind Móir m. Iair m. Ṡetnai m. Ailella m. Lugdach m. Labrada m. Carthaig m. Nuadat m. Condlai m. Bresail *Bricc*[e].

[a]Adur BLc. [b]Etħc*inn* B, Ecħ Lc. [c]Groigídha B, Droda Lc. [d]Osraidi B. [e—e]*om.* BLc.

278 Oengus — [a].i. Muccín[a] — Lamidan[b] m. Barrfind m. Findchada m. Dega[c] [d]m. Dreda[d] m. Buain[e].

[a—a]*above line with mark of ref. to* Oengus L, .i. mucaid (*above line*) BLc(Lb), .i. Muccin m. Moch(a)e *in text after* Lamidan R(Lc[l]). [b]*add* m. Flainneda B(Lc). [c]Deda B, Aeda Lc. [d—d]*om.* BLc, m. Dro(e)da Lb(R), Dreoda Lc[l]. [e]*add* m. Laegaire B. (m. Oengusa Osfrithi) BLc(RLc[l]), *add further* m. Ieir R.

279 Comgall [ab]oc Boith[b] Chonais[a] et Cele Crist da mac Echach m. Cormaic m. Eogain[c].

[a—a]*above line* L, *in text* RLc[l], *in text after* Cele Crist BLcLB. [b—b]Boithi LcR(Lc[l]). [c]*add* m. Neill (Noigiallaig) R(Lc[l]).

280 Epscop Sinill m. Aeda [a]m. Scandail[a] m. Scanlain m. Thimchiuin[b] m. Ronain m. Oengusa[c] [d]m. Crimthainn[d].

[a—a]*om.* BLcLb. [b]Tiumchai B, Thimcha(in) (Lc)Lb, Timchuin RLc[l]. [c]*add* Osraige BLb. [d—d]*om* BLcLb.

281 Epscop Erc m. Fergna m. Elchada[a] m. Allaid[b] m. Bresail m. Muridaig m. Crimthaind.

[a]Aelcada RBLc. [b]Alldaid RLc[l].

282 Senṡinchell[a] m. Cenḟinnain[b] m. Macha[c] m. Cruaich m. Dulge m. Imchada[d] m. Brolaig m. Lugdach[e] m. Labrada[f] m. Cormaic m. [g]Con Corbb[g].

[a](Sen)sinell (BLc)Lb, Sinchell Cilli Aichid RLc[l], Dasincheall (.i. Sincheall) (M)R[l]La. [b]Cenannain R(Lc[l]MR[l]La). [c]Imchadai Lb, Maichae M. [d]*add* m. Condlaida R(Lc[l]MR[l]La). *See note.* [e]Bre(a)sail (R[l])La. [f]*add* (m. Trena) m. Imchada (RLc[l])MR[l]La. *See note.* [g—g]Concubhair R[l]La.

283 Sinchell[a] — [b].i. Ocṡinchell[b] — m. Corcain[c] m. Eirc m. Cruaich[d].

[a]Sinell Lb, *add* m. Cormaic BLc, Calbus RLc[l], Mael da*no* R[l], Maedan La. [b—b]*in marg.* L, Icsenchill Lc(*in text*), *om.* BLbRLc[l]R[l]La. [c]Corcrain Lb. [d]Ruaich BLcR[l]La, *add* m. Duilge m. Imchada Lb(RLc[l]*bis*)R[l](La), *add further* .i. ho Chill Ṡinill do Lb.

284.1 Secht meic [a]Nesain[b]: Diucaill[a], Muridach [cd]qui ⁊[d] Cronan — [e].i. Craibdech .d.[ce] — Cairell[f], Fland[g] et hi quattuor in Eṅga[h] sunt. Nessi[i] uero ⁊ Nessluga[j] in Insula sunt[k]. Beoan [l]i Fid[l] Chulend.

2 Beoan di*diu*[m] m. Nessain m. Eirc m. Aeda m. Colmain[n] [o]m. Ailella[o] m. Dunlaiṅge[p] [q]ut ante[q].

[a—a]Ne(a)chtain m. Duach Daill (.i.) B(Lc). [b]*add* .i. Lb. [c—c]*om.* RLc[l]. [d—d]*om.* Lc. [e—e]*in marg.* L, *in text* (*without* .d.) BLb, *om.* Lc. [f]*om.* BLc. [g]*om.* Lb. [h]Ena BLc. [i]Soesi BLcLb, Nis(s)i (R)Lc[l]. [j]Nesluaga BLcLb, Neslug RLc[l]. [k]*om.* RLc[l]. [l—l]Feda RLc[l]. [m]*om.* BLcLbRLc[l]. [n]Coluim Lb, *add* m. Cairpre (m. Cormaic) R(Lc[l]). [o—o]*bis* Lc. [p]Dunlaiṅg BLcLbRLc[l]. [q—q]m. Ennae (Niad) R(Lc[l]).

285 Aed [a]Cluana Mór[a] m. Eogain m. Bruidgi[b] m. Nadbuidb m. Illaind[c] m. Dunlaiṅg[d] [e]m. Ennae Niad[ef].

[a—a]*om.* LbMH. [b]Bruigi B(MH), Brui(g)de Lc(Lb), Buidgi RLc[l]. [c]Oilella B(Lc), Illadoin Lb(MH). [d]Dunlainge H. [e—e]*om.* LbMH. [f]*add* m. Bresail m. Fiachach m. Cathair R, m. Bresail B*elaig* Lc[l].

286 Fiac Slebti[a] m. Ercada[b] m. Ḟeic m. Dare Barraig[c] m. Cathair[d] Moir[c].

[a]Slebe(.i. Droma Gablai *above line*) Lb, Cilli Sleibe M(*see note*), *om.* H. [b]Erca BLc. [c]*om.* RLc[l]. [d]*add* m. Feidelmid R(Lc[l]).

287.1 Abban Maige Arnaide[a] [b]⁊ Cilli Abbain[b] m. Lagnig[c] m. Cainnig m. Labrada[d] m. Cormaic m. Con Corbb.

2 [e]Et[f] Daman et Miaca[g] [h]fratres eius[h], [i].i. i F[id Mor] .i. i Cl[uain] F[at]a[i], et[f] Senach et Líthgein et Duban et Tomdenach i[j] [k]Rus Glassi[k]; [l]septem[m] fratres sunt.

3 [no]Mella nomen matris eorum, soror S*ancti* Coemgin[lo].

[a]Arn̄ R, Arnan Lc[l]. [b—b]*om.* RLc[l]. [c]Luigind BLc, Lug̅ Lb. [d]*add* m. Imchada RLc[l]. [e—e]*om.* RLc[l]. [f]*om.* Lc. [g]Muac B, Miach Lc. [h—h]*between columns with mark of ref.* L, *om.* BLcLb. [i—i]*in marg. and largely illeg.* L, *in text* BLcLb; a Fidh Mor .i. a Cluain Fada B(Lc), Fedai Moir ⁊ hi Cluain Fota Lb. [j]ic Lc, o Lb. [k—k]rreglaiss B. [l—l]*om.* B. [m]⁊ septim Lb. [n—n]*om.* Lb. [o—o]*om.* Lc.

287.4 Secht ṁbliadna delb|gla|na[p] déc,
i[q] fulliud[r] armi[s] tri chét.
[t]|saegul Abb|ain[t] delbda duind,
airet[u] robui i coluind[en].

[p]*illeg. in part* L, delbglana BLc. [q]*om.* BLc. [r]fuiled BLc [s]armithi B, *add* 7 B(Lc). [t—t]*partly illeg.* L, saeghal Aban B(Lc). [u]in airet B(Lc).

288 Ciaran Saigri[a] m. Luaigne[b] m. Ruanaind[c] Duach[d] m. Conaill m. Corpre Niad[e] m. Buain [f]m. Dimbuain[f] m. Echach Lamdóit[g] [h]m. Amalgada[i] m. Loegaire Birn Buadaig m. Oengusa Osrethi[hj].

[a]*om.* H. [b]Luigne BLcLbM. [c]Ru(a)maind (BLc)RLc[1]MH, Ruman Lb, Ruimind R[1]. [d]*om.* MR[1]H. [e]*om.* RLc[1]MR[1]H. [f—f]*om.* BLcLbMR[1]H. [g]Leithtriuin RLc[1]. [h—h]*om.* BLcLb. [i]Amagada R, Amalga Lc[1]. [j]*add* m. Crimthaind m. Iair m. ṡetna m. Ailella m. Lugdach m. Labrada m. Carthaig(Caertaind R[1]) m. Nuagad m. Connlai m. Breasail Bricc M(*between columns in smaller hand*)(R[1]), *add further* sund conrecaid Ossraighi agus Laighin. (Da macc Bresail Bricc, Flaithri 7 Lugaid Lothfind, Cenel Flathri Osraige, Cenel Lugaid Lothfind Lagein) R[1](*in lower marg.*).

289 Fiachna[a] Find [b]ó Chill Ingen[c] Fiachna[bd] m. Cobthaig m. Aeda Aird[e] m. Dimma Duib[f] m. Ḟergnai.
De *Uib* Máil.

[a]Fiacħ B, Fiacha Lc(Lb). [b—b]*om.* RLc[1]. [c]*om.* Lc. [d]Fiacħ BLb, Ḟiachach Lc. [e]*om.* RLc[1], *above line* Lb. [f]*om.* RLc[1].

290.1 Cammine[a] [b]Insi Celtra[b] m. Dimmae m. Ḟergusa m. Ailella m. Nathí m. Crimthaind m. Ennae[c] Chendselaig[d].

2 [e]Uel ita[ef]: Cammine m. Colmain m. Comarbaig m. Insain m. Aine[g] m. Ambrit[h] m. Mochon m. Saulim[i] m. Eschon[j] m. Saulo[k] m. Moga Airt qui 7 Ciar[l] [m]dicitur.

3 [n]Uel ita[mn]: Cammine m. Dimmae m. Ḟeidlimid[o] m. Crimthaind m. Scandlain m. Aeda Find[p] m. Ḟergnae m. Ḟergusa[q] m. Eogain Sreim [r]m. Duach Galaig m. Briuin[s] [t]m. Echach Mugmedoin[rt].

[a]Caemin Lc. [b—b]*add above line* for Loch Deirgdeirc Lb. [c]*add* m. Labrada m. Bressail m. Fiachach m. Cathair R. [d]*om.* R. [e—e]a(i)liter R(Lc[1]). [f]*om.* BLcLb. [g]Maine Lb. [h]*add* m. Imchada RLc[1]. [i]Saluluim B, Masaulim Lb. [j]Mese Chon R(Lc[1]). [k]Saumain BLc, Asamain Lb. [l]Ciara Lc[1]. [m—m]*om.* Lc. [n—n]*om.* Lb. [o]Feidelmid R. [p]*above line* Lb. [q]*add* m. Muiredaig Mail BLcLb. [r—r]*om.* RLc[1]. [s]Br(i)ain B(LcLb). [t—t]*om.* Lc.

291 Moṡenoc[a] Mugna[b] m. Senchain m. Sinill m. Conaill m. Ḟothaid m. Echach [c]Lamdeirg[d] ut ante in genealogia Coemgin[c].

[a]Mothenoc LcLc[1]. [b]m. Mugnae RLc[1]. [c—c]m. Messin Corb m. Con Corbb R(Lc[1]). [d]Lamdoit Lb.

292 Fiachra Goll[a] [b]o Chluain[b] Ferta m. Dáire [c]m. Fergusa m. Ennai m. Labrada[d] [e]m. Brain[ef] m. Echach Guinig[g] m. Dare[c] Barraig[g] m. Cathair Moir[g].

[a]*above line* L, *om.* RLc[1]. [b—b]Cluana RLc[1]. [c—c]*om.* BLc. [d]Labrain Lb. [e—e]*om.* Lb. [f]Briain RLc[1]. [g]*om.* RLc[1].

293 Diarmait — [ab].i.[c] Modimmócc[b] Glindi[d] Usen[a] — m. Siabairr[e] m. Dallain [f]m. Erca m. Breccain[fg] m. Ḟeic m. Dare Barraig[h] m. Cathair Moir[h].

[a—a]*above line* LLb, *in text* BLc. [b—b]*om.* RLc[l]. [c]*om.* B. [d]lindi B. [e]Sibarr BLc. [f—f]*om.* BLc. [g]Braccain Lb. [h]*om.* R.

294 Sinchi ingen Annuda m. Dálaiṅg[a] m. Ḟidchellaig[b] m. Oengus|a|[c] Osrethe[d] [e]m. Crimthaind[e].

[a]Dalaig(h) (B)LcLb. [b]fiach̄ (ell) (BLb)Lc. [c]Aengusa BLc(LbR)Lc[l]. [d]Osraighe B, Osergi Lb, *om.* RLc[l]. [e—e]*om.* LcLb.

295 [a]Epscop Lugach[ab] [c]i Cúil Bennchair[c] m. Lugdach[d] m. Luchtai[e] m. Anrodain[f] [g]m. Maeli[h] Tuili m. Aedloga[i] m. Daurthecht[j] m. Ṡenaig m. Retaig[k] m. Ḟerbba[g] m. Imchada m. Ambrit[l] m. Mochon m. Saulim[m] m. Meschon[n] [g]m. Etechta[go] m. Saulo[p] m. Moga[q] Airt[r], [s]qui ⁊ Ciar[t] [u]dicitur[s], m. Ḟergusa m. Rosa[uv].

[a—a]*reversed* Lb. [b]Lugdach Lc, Lug̅ Lb, Lugaid H[l]. [c—c]*above line* L, *in text* BLcLb, *om.* H[l]. [d]Lugach BLc, Lugeach H[l]. [e]Lugna *no* Lugda H[l]. [f]Aedrae H[l]. [g—g]*om.* H[l]. [h]Moil Lb. [i]Aeda Loga BLb. [j]Durrtacht BLc. [k]Readaig B, Regaig Lc, Rethi Lb. [l]Eibric H[l]. [m]Masaulaim Lb, Ulain H[l]. [n]Mesi Con BLcLb(H[l]). [o]Echada BLc, Ech̄ Lb. [p](Ma)saulaim BLc(Lb), Sula H[l]. [q]Mo B. [r]*add* m. Oforbsen m. Eochodon m. Aithiti m. Ochamoin m. Fidmuri m. Deilbe m. Eonne m. Laimne m. Ulsaig m. Domoin m. Moga Tuath m. Ceir otat Ciar*aide*(?) H[l]. [s—s]qui dicitur Ciaraide H[l](*after* Sula). [t]Cara B. [u—u]*om.* BLcLb. [v]Rossa Ruaid m. Rudraide H[l].

296 Chaelḟind ingen Chael m. Ḟindchada m. [a]Lugdach m. Luchta[ab].

[a—a]Loga m. Luchta m. Lugach Lc(*see note*). [b]*add* m. Anrudain m. Moili Tuile Lb.

297 Iarlathi[a] m. Loga m. Dana m. Moduirn[b] m. Dubain[c] m. Ḟraech[d] [e]m. Causcraid [f]immecomraicet Conmacni[ef].

[a]m. laithi Lc(*see note*). [b]*Meic* Auirn B(LcLb), Mugurnd H[l]. [c]*add* otát Cenal Dubain H[l]. [d]Raith Lc, Fiachrach Lc[l]. [e—e]*om.* BLc. [f—f]do Chonmacnib Lb, *om.* RLc[l]H[l].

298.1 Lugna[a] m. Moenaig m. Fiachna m. Rosa m. Eirc m. Trena m. Duach m. Maicniath[b] m. Con[c] m. Lugdech[d].

2 Hí sunt fratres eius[e] .i. Epscop Brandub, Causan[f], Fachtna, Molua, Lochan i nUíb Echach, Cailchin[g], Manchin Cula[h] Cassin.

[a]*see note.* [b](m.) Mot(B)Lc. [c]Meic Con BLcLb. [d]Lug(e)ach (B)Lc. [e]om. Lc. [f]Cuasan BLb(*see note*), Cuasach Lc. [g]Cail(l)in BLc(Lb). [h]Cuala (⁊) BLc(Lb). *See note.*

299 Senan [a]Lathraig Briuin[a] m. Fintain Srenedo[b] m. Glinnir m. Cuirc m. Cureda[c] m. Fiacca[d] m. Máil[e] [f]m. Carthaig m. Laire m. Larine m. Cuiltri m. Cluinig[g] m. Immite m. Corpre Immete[h] m. Lugo [i]m. Liṅgo[i] —

[a—a]*om.* Lc[l]MR[l]HLa. [b]m. Srenedo Lc[l]H, m. (F)irennatha M(R[l]La). [c]Cairitan M, Carittha R[l](La). [d]Fiacha(i) (M)H(La), Fiachna R[l]. [e]*add* m. Laegaire MR[l](La). [f—f]*om.* MR[l]La. [g]Glunig H. [h]*om.* Lc[l]H. [i—i]*om.* Lc[l].

[j]*no* Mogo[j] — m. Mede[k] m. Duib m. Ruibrig[l] m. Duib [m]m. Tressaig[m] m. Lugnai m. Mata m. Ḟeidlimthi m. Saille m. Clothrad m. Cothail[n] m. Roe[o] m. Carthaig m. Clithraim[p] m. Maireda [q]m. Caireda m. Bresail m. Almone m. Moethcelt[r] m. Rohiel m. Cermata m. hIrieil[s] m. Dega m. Reo Sorcha m. Reo Dorcha m. Maireda [m]m. Amais[m] m. Ṡingite m. Inbuithe m. Tigernmais m. Ḟallaig[t] m. Ethriel m. Iareoil[u] m. hErimoin[fqv].

[j]—[j]*above line* L, *om.* Lc[l]H. [k]Me(i)dle (Lc[l])H. [l]Rubraig Lc[l]. [m]—[m]*om.* H. [n]Clothail Lc[l]H. [o]*add* m. Mail H. [p]*add* m. E(o)chach Lc[l](H). [q]—[q]ut supra in genealogia Murgene Lc[l]. [r]Moithgilt H. [s]hIorel H. [t]Follaig H. [u]*add* Fatha H. [v]*add* m. Miled Espane H.

300 [a]Liban — [b].i. Murgen[ab] — [c]ingen Echach m. Maireda[c] [d]m. Caireda[d] [e]ut supra[e].

[a]—[a]Liban ⁊ Muirgenach (.i. gein in mara *above line*) BLc(Lb), Muirgen .i. Liban Lc[l]. [b]—[b]*above line* L. [c]—[c]*om.* BLcLb. [d]—[d].i. Cland Chaireda Lb. [e]—[e](m. Breasail m. Almoine m. Meucelt (Moethgelt Lc[l]) m. Reohiel m. Cearmada m. Iriel m. Deaa (Dega Lc[l](LcLb)) m. Reo m.(*om.* Lc[l]) Sorcha m. Reo Dorcha) m. Maireda m. Amais m. Singeide m. Inbothaigh m. Tigernmais m. Follaig m. Eithreoil B(Lc)LbLc[l], *further* (m. Ireoil Fatha m. Eremoin) m. Miled Espáne Lb(Lc[l]).

301.1 Moboe[a] Fota i[b] nAiriud[c] Moboe[d] m. Senaig Fírepertaig[e].

2 Et Fraechnat[f] soror eius.

[a]Moi BLc, Mobíi Lb. [b]o Lb. [c]nair BLc, Daire Lb. [d]Mobíi Lb. [e]m. Firep(er)taigh B(LcLb). [f]Frecnat Lb.

302 Mac hÍ — [a].i. Colmán[a] [b].i. Conna[b] — m. Amargin[c] [d]m. Sarain[d] m. Liadglassi[e] m. Duib[f] m. Andgain[g] m. Ferbba[h].
[i]Is[j] é fil i nAchud[k] hÍ [l]la Áes Tiri[il].

[a]—[a].i. Colm(a)et (B)Lc, *om.* H. [b]—[b]*above line* L, in text BLc, *om.* Lb, m. Conna MHH[l]. [c]Aimirge(i)n Lc(M). [d]—[d]*om.* M. [e]Liadla(i)si (B)Lb, Liadnaisi Lc, Liadg(l)airi (M)H. [f]Duibni M(H[l]), Duibe H. [g]Angai B(Lc)Lb. [h]*add* o fuilet U Ferba, m. Imchada m. Eibric m. Mochoc m. Aulaim m. Meseschon m. Saula qui dicitur Ciara m. Moga Airt m. Fuirbsen Mór m. Eochadain m. Aitri m. Ochamoin m. Fidmuire m. Deilmbne m. Eoinne m. Laime m. Ulsaighi m. Domoin m. Moga Tuath m. Cer, a quo Ciarraide, m. Fergusa m. Rossa m. Rudraide H[l]. [i]—[i]*above* Mac hÍ L, *in text after* .i. Conna BLc, *after* Ferbba Lb, *om.* MHH[l]. [j]⁊ is Lc. [k]Acha B. [l]—[l]Laestire B(Lc). *See note.*

303 Faindith[a] ingen Marcáin m. Carthaig m. Domungin m. Ḟindchon m. Mellrach[b] m. Faelain m. Dorbbo m. Failgine[c] m. Connad m. Lugdech[d] m. Daigri[e].

[a]*written* Famdith L. [b]Mellraig Lb. [c]Ailgene B, Ḟoelgeni (*with* e *above* g) Lb. [d]Lugdach Lb. [e]Daire BLcLb.

304 [a]Cuan ⁊ Colman et [b]Bec Bile[b] et Connadil[ac] cethri meic Ṡilain m. Aedlugo[d] m. Findchon m. Mellrach[e].

[a]—[a]*rearranged* Lb. [b]—[b]Becanbile Lc, Becile Lb. [c]Conn na(n)dil B(Lc). [d]Aeda Loga BLcLb. [e]Maelach BLc(Lb).

305 Factna i Cill Tomma[a] et Gabrán[b] et Eoil tri meic Dubthaig m. Lugair m. Lugdech[c] m. Ruaid m. Rosa[d] m. Marthened[e] m. Congail[f] [g]Chlaringnig[h] m. Ailella[g] Anglonnaig m. Oengusa Umaill. Di Chonnactaib[i].

[a]Toae Lc. [b]Garban BLcLb. [c]Lugdach Lc. [d]Roisi BLcLb. [e]Martenet Lc. [f]Conaill Lc. [g—g]*om.* Lc. [h]Carn B, Chlaraig Lb. [i]*add* in sin Lb.

306 Fethgna[a] Figlech[b] [c]m. Nechtain[c] m. Mael Bile m. Amargin[d] m. Ninne[e] m. Loegaire m. Cellaig m. Cathbath[f] m. Echdach.

[a]Fethna BLc, *add above line* .i. comorba Patraic Lb[l]. [b]Feidleach Lc, *om.* Lb[l]RLc[l]. [c—c]*in marg. sup. with ref. mark* Lb[l]. [d]Aimirgen LcLc[l]. [e]Ninneda Lb. [f]Cathbaig B.

307 Land[a] ingen Becce[b] m. Cuanach.

[a]Lenn B(LcLb). [b]Beicc Lb.

308 Martra m. Tinni oc Senbrug Dromma Snechta[a].

[a]Snecht B.

309 Cuanu[a] m. Duanamail[b] i Cill Cula Balldeirg[c].

[a]*add* m. Dunadaig Lc[l]. [b]Dunamail BLcLbRLc[l]. [c]Derg BLc.

310 Mac Liac — [ab][.i.][c] Dicaill[bd] — Dromma Glais[ae] m. Cernaig[f] m. Aeda m. Guaire Gaíth[g] m. Amalgada[h] m. Muccada[i] Ruaid[j].

[a—a]do Cill Dromglais B, .i. Diucaill Glais H(*above line in small hand*). [b—b]*above line* Lb, *om.* MR[l]La. [c]*om.* L, .i. LbLc[l]. [d]Diucaill Lb. [e]Glaissi LbM. [f]Cerndaig R[l]. [g]*om.* Lc[l]MR[l]HLa. [h]Amalgaid BLb, Amalga Lc[l]. [i]Murchada BLbR[l]. [j]*add* m. Colla Uaiss Lc[l](MR[l]HLa).

311 Colman Elo m. Beodgna[a] m. Moctae[b] m. Cunnida[c] [de]m. Oengusa[e] m. Fiaclae[f] m. Mail [g]m. Carthaig m. Laire m. Lugdach m. Larine [h]ut ante in gen[ealogia] Senain[dghi].

[a]Beognai B(Lb)RLc[l](MR[l])H. [b]Bochtai M. [c]Cainnai M(R[l]). [d—d]*om.* MR[l]. [e—e]*om.* H. [f]Fiacle BLb, Fiacchae RLc[l], Fiacha H. [g—g]*om.* H. [h—h]*Latin corrupt* BLb, m. Loga m. Cuiltre m. Cermata m. Cluana(i) m. Condla(e) m. Ailella m. Cairpre (R)Lc[l]. [i]*add* .i. o Laind Cholmain Elai do .i. Ela ainmm mna boi isin baile prius. Is uaithe ainmnichther Land Ela Lb(M *in lower margin in small hand;* R[l] *after* Cuinna).

312 Feidlimid[a] m. Crimthaind m. Duib Da Chrích m. Colmain m. Ṡechnasaig m. Ḟingin m. Aeda[b] m. Crimthaind[c].

[a]Feidelmid R. [b]*add above line* Duib Lb. [c]*add* m. Fedlimid m. Oengusa m. Natfraich m. Cuircc m. Luigdech Lb.

313.1 Sec[h]t meic Dubtain[a] .i.[b] Comman, Comran[c], Dochonna[d], Fergna, Pilipp, Lurint[e], Manchin[f].

2 [gh]Manchin di*diu* m[h]. Dubtain[g] m[i]. Ruin[j] m. Tithumain[k] m. Rouithen m. Gurthigirn m. Clothnoscain m. Peleithir[l] m. Britain a quo Bretnaig.

[a]Gutan B, Duthain Lb. [b]*om.* RLc[l]. [c]Corman BLb. [d]Docona B, Docconu Lb, Dochoma R(Lc[l]). [e]Laurint RLc[l]. [f]*add* .i. Lb. [g—g]*om.* Lb. [h—h]*secht* (meic) (R)Lc[l]. [i]m. m. B. [j]Ruain BLb. [k]Titcumain B. [l]Pleit*ir* B.

314 [a]Barri[b] [c]et[a] Modichu[cd] m. Amairgin[e] [f]m. Duib Dubni[fg] [h]m. Airt[i] m. Carthind[j] m. Flaind[hk] [l]m. Ninnida[l] [m]m. Echach[n] m. Corpre[m] Ardchind[o] m. Echach[p].

[a—a]*om.* M[l]La[l]. [b]Barra(i) B(Lb), *add* .i. Corcaige Lb (*above line*), Corcaidi Lc[l]40Vc(M). [c—c]*om.* Lc[l]40VcMR[l]HH[l]La. [d]Modhia (?) B Modigu Lb, *add* da BLbRLc[l]. [e]Aimirg(e)in Lc[l](MM[l]), Amergen Lc[l]40Vc. [f—f]*om.* RLc[l]M[l]H[l]La[l]. [g]Debhne B. [h—h]*om.* BLb. [i]*add* Chuirb M. [j]Caerthainn MM[l](R[l]), Cearthinde H[l]. [k]Laind Lc[l]40VcH[l]. [l—l]m. (F)indeda (Lc[l]40Vc)MR[l]La, m. Nidneda H, *om.* H[l]. [m—m]*bis* Lc[l]. [n]*add* Fergaig H[l]. [o]*om.* RLc[l]R[l]La, *add* m. Briain BLbLc[l]40VcM(M[l])R[l]HH[l]LaLa[l]. [p]*add* Mugmedoin BLbRLc[l]Lc[l]40VcMM[l]R[l]H[l]LaLa[l], *add further* brathair do Barra Modigo .i. naem do naemaib Lulchaich M[l](La[l]).

315 Fechine Fabair[a] m. Cailcharna[b] [cd]m. Cillini[d] m. Grillini[c] — [e]*no* Cillini[e] — m. Cail m. Aeda m. Saini[f] m. Airt Chirb[g] [h]m. Niad[i] Corb[hj].

[a]Fobair R, *om.* HH[l]. [b]Cailcharin H. [c—c]*om.* H[l]. [d—d]*om.* RLc[l]H. [e—e]*above line* L, *om.* BLbRLc[l]HH[l]. [f]*illeg.* H[l]. [g]m. Coirp H[l]. [h—h]m. Coirpre N*iad* R(Lc[l]), m. Fir Coirp H[l]. [i]Nad H. [j]*add* m. Cormaicc (m. Aengusa m. Echach Find F*uath* n*Airt*) R(Lc[l]), m. Laidigh m. Cormaic Gaileing o tat Galenga(?) o tat Ceneol Conamla m. Taidg m. Cein m. Ailella Olaim m. Muga Nuadut H[l].

316 Mael Ruain Tamḷachta[a] m. Colmain m. Ṡenain m. Agnidi[b] m. Moctai m. Cunnida m. Ḟiacca[c] m. Mail[d].

[a]*om.* MR[l]HLa. [b]Agnuidi La. [c]Fiach*ach* BLb, Fiacha(i) Lc[l]M(R[l])HLa. [d]*add* m. Laegaire MR[l]La.

317 Mobí Chlarinech[a] apstal[b] m. Beónaid[c] m. Bresail m. Ailgil[d] m. Idnai[e] m[f]. Athrai[g] m. Lugnai — [hi].i.[j] tri hog[i] — m. Bregduilb[k] m. Airt Chirp m. Corpre Niad[h].
[l]De Ḟothartaib[l].

[a]*above* Mobí L, Clairnech B. [b]Epscop BLcLb (*after* Mobí), *om.* H[l]. *See note.* [c]Beognaig Lb, Beoan H[l]. [d]Ailigil m. Selbaig H[l]. [e]Inda(i) (B)Lc(Lb). [f]*om.* H[l]. [g]Aithri BLc, *add* m. Nia Moir H[l]. [h—h]fri rate Fer Tri .i. Gait m. Oengusa Gai Ailb m. Echuch Finn m. Fedlimid Rechtmair m. Tuathail Techtmair m. Fiachruch Finnalaid m. Feraduig Fechtnaig m. Cremtaind Niad Náir m. Lugduch Riab nDerg m. na tri Finn Emna m. Echach Fedlig ocus ci atbera nech combud mac do Fir Tri Idna Athra ni fír son eter ór nae meic robatur oc Fir Tri ocus ni mac dib sin Idna Athra ó nach mud eter H[l]. [i—i]*above line* LLb, *in text* BLc. [j]*om.* BLcLb. [k]Bredu(i)lb B(Lc). [l—l]*om.* H[l], *add* do Lb.

318.1 Telli[a] m. Segáin m. Colgan m. Thuathail m. Crundbeóil m. Feidlimid m. Fiachrach Cassain m. Colla Focrí[b].

2 [c]Et Bebil soror eius qui est i lLaind Rónáin Ḟind.

3 Et Sodelb nomen matris eorum qui est i Tig Thelli.

4 Fratres Telli filii Moenain m. Segáin.

5 Ideo Telli dicitur quia stratum eius fuit in tellure[c].

[a]*add* o Thig Thelli Lb. [b]Focrich BLb. [c—c]*om.* BLcLb.

319 Mac Culind — [a]Cunnid prọprium nomen[a] — m. Cathmọga m. C̣athbath[b] m. Cattáin[c] m. Ḟergossa m. Ḟindchada m. [d]Ḟéic [e]m. Ḟindcháin[de] m. Imchada Ulaig[f] m. Condlai m. Taidc m. Céin m. Ailella Óluim.

[a—a]*above line* L, *om.* BLcLb. [b]Cathbadha BLc(Lb). [c]Cathain BLcLb. [d—d]Findchaim m. Feig B(Lb). [e—e]*om.* Lc. [f]Uallaig BLcLb.

320.1 Findchu Bri[a] Gobann m. Setna[b] m. Abrai[c] m. Branain[d] m. Dobtha m. Oengusa m. Eirc[e] m. Briuin[f] m. Echach Mugmedoin.

2 [g]*Uel* ita[h]: Findchu m. [i]Find m. Loga[i] m. Findbairr m. Ail m. Masside[j] m. Fergusa m. Duach m. Bres[ail][k] m. Colla[l] [m]m. Carpre Lifechair[gm].

[a]o Bri BLcLb. [b]Senda BLc. [c]Abraidh B. [d]Brain BLc(Lb). [e]Erc(c)a(i) Lc(Lb), *add* Deirg BLcLb. [f]Briain BLcLb. [g—g]*in marg.* L, *in text* BLcLb. [h]A(i)liter (B)Lb. [i—i]Findloga Lc. [j]Mes(s)ide BLc(Lb). [k]*partly illeg.* L, Bresail BLcLb. [l]*add* Mend BLc(Lb *above line*). [m—m]*om.* BLcLb.

321 Lugaid m. Oengusa m. Nadfraich [a]m. Cuirc[b] m. Lugdech m. Ailella Flainn Bic.
[c]Cuius reliquiae sunt[ac] i[d] nDruim Inasclainn[e].

[a—a]*om.* BLc. [b]Conaill Cuirc(*above line*) Lb. [c—c]*om.* Lb. [d]ho Lb. [e]Ḟindasclaind B, *add* do Lb.

322 Banbán m. Dondgaile m. Dondgalaich m. Aurchlosaig[a] m. Ḟir Ṡin m. Corbbain[b] m. Etnui[c] m. Duib Dunig m. Aṅgain[d].

[a]Urclosaigh BLc. [b]Cobrain B. [c]Enda B(Lc)Lb. [d]Argain B, *add* m. Fiachach Suigde Lc.

323 Mochonna ẹt Eltine et Colum tri meic [a]Ḟlannain [b]m. Cobdenaig m. Colmain m. Ḟlannain[b] m. Branduib [c]m.[a] Etarsceli[cd] m. Nathi m. Oengusa Builg.

[a—a]*om.* Lc. [b—b]*om.* BLb. [c—c]*om.* Lb. [d]Etersceoil B(Lc).

324 Colman Craibdẹch[a] m. Sechnasaig [b]m. Ḟingin[b] m. [c]Aeda Duib[c] m. Crimthaind m. Ḟeidlimid m. Oengusa [b]m. Nadfraich[b].

[a]m. Craibtheach Lc, in Chrabuid Lb. [b—b]*om.* Lb. [c—c]Adra m. Duibh BLc.

325.1 Ṛonan[a] m. Beraig m. Critain m. Ercloga[b] m. Ernini[c] [d]m. Ureni[e] m. Ṡechnasaig m. [f]Coluim[d] m. Culae[fg] m. Muridaig m. Loegaire m. Neill Noigiallaig[h].
[ij]Is e coṅgab Druim Inasclainn[j].

2 Siur[k] dó Cairech Cluana Bairend[l]. Cairech Dergain iṅgen Beraig m. Critain[im].

[a]*add* Find M. [b]Ercolaoga La. [c]Ernaine Lc, Ernaide MLa. [d—d]*om.* BLc. [e]Ureiri M. [f—f]Coluim Chuile M, Colmain Cuile La. [g]Cuille BLcLb. [h]*om.* La. [i—i]*om.* Lc[l]MLa. [j—j]*om.* Lb. [k]Sur BLc, ⁊ siur Lb. [l]Ba(i)rind B(Lc), *add* .i. BLcLb. [m]*add* m. Erclogai Lb.

326 Ba mín, ḃa már mac Alpraind,
  craeb fína fo mes,
ni fail nad íccad, rofess,
  acht co rrisad a less.

Secht coicait sruithepscop
  ronorddain in cád,
im trichait cet crumthirech n-og
  forsra furim grad.

Tri chet abgitrech roscrib,
  ba bil lith a lám;
secht cét cell conacaib
  dosnacaib do bar[a].

[a]*or read* lar.

ADDITIONS FROM THE OTHER MANUSCRIPTS

327 Boithin m. Brenaind[a] m. Fergusa Cendfota[b] m. Conaill Gulban[c] m. [d]Neill Naegiallaig[d].

[a]Branaind H[l]. [b]*om.* Lc[l]HH[l]. [c]*om.* HH[l]. [d—d]Nellaig H[l].

328 Diarmait[a] m. Lugna[b] [c]m. Lug*dach*[cd] m. Findbarr m. Fraich[e] m. Cath-con [f]m. Oengusa[g] m. Nahii[h] m. Fiac[h]rach [i]m. Echach Mugmedoin[fi].

[a]*add* Inse Clothrand Lc[l](MR[l]La). [b]*bis with marks of elision* R[l]. [c—c]*om.* M. [d]Lugach Lc[l]R[l]H, Lugdhach La. [e]Raei*n or read* Raei*ch* Lc[l], Raich R[l], Rein H. [f—f]*om.* H. [g]Beccon Lc[l], *add* m. Eogain m. Aililla Inbanna m. Eogain Bel m. Ceallaig m. Oililla Moltt M(R[l]La). [h]Dathi MR[l]La. [i—i]*om.* Lc[l]M.

329 Fland m. Fairchellaig m. Ḟidnaig m. Foelan m. Ronain m. Colmain m. Dubthaig m. Eoin m. Mugdhuirn m. Thorna Eces do Chiarraige Luachrai.

330.1 Cumain[a] Cadan [b]m. Crundchon[b] m. Rumain[c] m. Echach Bailldeirg[d] m. Carthaind Find[e] m. Bloit[f] m. Caiss[g].
[h]⁊[i] Enach[j] Duib[k] for[l] bru Ṡinda[m] a chell.

2 Is[n] and beos[i] doberrtha[o] fuiltt[p] rig Dal Caiss iar ngabail giall Chaisil[q] [r]doib et cetera[hr].

[a]Cuimine R[l]La. [b—b]*om.* La. [c]Rumainn M, Ruamhaind R[l], Ramainn La, *add* m. Echach m. Conaill Echluaith m. Conaill Eaclaig m. Conaill La. [d]*add* m. Conaill Eachluaith R[l](*with marks of elision*). [e]*above line* Lb, *in text* MR[l], *om.* La. [f]*add* a quo hUi Blait La. [g]Tail La, *add* (m. Conaill Echluaith) m. Luigdech Minn m. Aengusa Tir:g (MLa)R[l], *add further* m. Fir Corp m. Mogha Corp m. Cormaic Caiss m. Ailella Oluim (m. Mogha Nuagat a quo Leth Mogha) R[l](La). [h—h]*between columns in small hand* M. [i]*om.* MR[l]La. [j]aenach R[l]. [k]nDuib MR[l]. [l]ar MR[l]La. [m]na Sinda MR[l]La. [n]⁊ as M(R[l]La). [o]dogerrtha M(R[l]La). [p]folt R[l], a ḟuilt La. [q]*add* na rig MR[l]La. [r—r]*om.* MR[l]La.

331.1 Tri noeim isin oenbaile .i. a nUcht Mama. Colman ainmm cech noeim 7 Lugaid athair cech Colmain .i.

2 Colman m. Luigdech m. Loegaire m. Neill Naigiallaig.

3 Colman m. Luigdech m. Aengusa m. Natfraich m. Cuirc m. Luigdech.

4 Colman m. Luigdech m. Conaill m. Briain m. Echach Muidmedoin.

332 Mochuda[a] m. Luigdech[b] m. Nahii[c] m. Collai m. Aengusa m. Oilella Cethig m. Cathair Mair.

[a]Mochutta M. [b]Lugada M. [c]Nathi M.

333 Ciaran m. Branduib[a] m. Bresail m. Briuin[b] m. Ḟianbotha[c] m. Nastair m. Dimain.

[a]Brannaim M(R[l]La). [b]Briain MR[l]La. [c]Findbotha M.

334 Fergna[a] m. Finntain m. Beochraide m. Cuindeda[b] m. Caiss m. Fraich m. Causcraid.

[a]add (.i.) m. ind Filed (a quo Ceall meic in Filed) RLc[l](M *in small hand above line*). [b]*add* m. Dathim RLc[l], m. Dad M.

335.1 Coelchu[a] [b]Cluana Cuasa[b] m. Coil m. Condlai[c] do Chiarraige hAei[d].

2 Mongind Cluana Cain 7 Rebrad[e] a[f] di[g] ṡiair 7 Ciuin[h] ainm a mathar.

[a]Calchu La. [b—b]*om.* MLa. [c]Connlada do Ceinel Conlada MLa. [d]*om.* M, he La. [e]Rabra(dh) (M)La. [f]in M. [g]da MLa. [h]Cumne La.

336 Laisren m. Feradaig m. Nindeda m. Fergusa m. Conaill Gulban m. Nell Naegiallaig.

337 Seigine m. Fiachna m. Feradaig m. Nindeada m. Fergusa m. Conaill m. Neill.

338 Cumine m. Arnaine m. Fiachna m. Feradaig m. Nindeada m. Feradaig [*recte* Fergusa].

339 Failbi m. Pipain m. Amalgada m. Duach m. Nindeada m. Fergusa m. Conaill Gulban m. Neill Naegiallaig.

340 Adamnan m. Ronan m. Tindi [ab]m. Aeda[a] m. Coluim[b] m. Setna m. Fergusa m. Conaill m. Neill Naegiallaig[c].

[a—a]*om.* H[l]. [b—b]*om.* H. [c]*add* Ronait ainm a mathur H[l].

341 Dunchad m. Cind Ḟaelad m. Mail Choba m. Aeda m. Ainmirech m. Setna m. Fergusa.

342 Dorbaine Fota m. Altaine m. Meic Laisre m. Cronain m. Loairn m. Fergusa m. Conaill.

343 Faelchu m. Dorbain m. Tindi m. Fergusa m. Libir m. Nathi [a]m. Nathi[a] m. Conaill Gulban m. Neill Naegiallaig.

[a—a]*dittographical error?*

344 Cilline Droichtech m. Dicholla m. Cilline m. Amalgada m. Feradaig m. Feici m. Cerbaill m. Conaill Cremthainne m. Neill Naegiallaig.

345 Slebine m. Congaile m. Duib Duin m. Slebine m. Seigine m. Cronain m. Loairn m. Fergusa m. Conaill.

346 Flann m. Maili Duin m. Snedgaile m. Airnelaig m. Maili Duin m. Cind Ḟaelad m. Gairb m. Ronain m. Lugdach m. Setna m. Fergusa.

347 Mael Brigdi m. Tornain m. Mail Caich m. Baethechtra m. Dichubnius(?) m. Congaili m. Failbe m. Ḟaelain m. Aedain m. Gentig m. Lugdach m. Boguni m. Conaill Gulban m. Neill Naegiallaig.

348 Dubthach m. Dubain m. Mael Uidir m. Fergusa m. Baethechtra m. Congaile.

349 Colman m. Echach m. Ailella m. Guairi m. Lugdach m. Laegairi m. Neill Naegiallaig.

350 Loman Lacha Gili m. Dallan m. Bresail m. Maine m. Domnaill m. Echach m. Fiachach m. Cairpre Lifechair m. Cormaic m. Airt m. Cuind Cetchathaig.

351 Cuanda m. Miduirnn m. Duib Ratha m. Enda m. Neill Naegiallaig.

352 Epscop Mac Lasre m. hUbain m. Thuatain m. Aeda.

353 Fergna m. Anmerech m. Ailella m. Cairthinn[a] m. hEircc m. [b]Echdach m. Clothchon[bc].

[a]Caerthainn M. [b—b]*between columns in small hand* M. [c]Colla Uais M.

354 Athracht ingen t[S]áráin m. Caelbaidi m. Cruind Ba Draide m. Echach Coba.

355 Fainiu 7 Lugai*n di* i*ngin* Nadfraich.

356 Barrḟind Metine m. Muredaig m. Domnaill m. Laegaire m. Echach Cais[a] a quo hUi Echach Muman.

[a]*om.* Lc[l].

357 Mac Nisi[a] Condere[b] m. Faibrig[c] m. Eircce[d] m. Fiaccae[e] m. Mail [f]m. Droido[f].

[a]Meissi M. [b]*om.* MR[l]H. [c]Fabraig MR[l], Forib H. [d]Eirc(c) (M)R[l]H, *add* m. Olo m. Lucte(?) H. [e]Fiacha(e) (Lc[l])MR[l]H. [f—f]m. Drodo Lc[l], *om.* MR[l]H.

358 Domungairt[a] m. Echdach m. Muiredaig [b]m. Forgo[b] m. Dallain[c] [d]m. Lugdach m. Oengusa m. Imchada m. Fergusa Dubdetaig [e]m. Imchada m. Finnchada m. Ogamuin m. Fiachach m. Daire m. Dluthaich m. Deitsine m. Echdach m. Sin m. Roṡin[de].

[a]Domananngort Lc[l]. [b—b]*bis* La. [c]*add* m. Dubthaig MHLa. [d—d]*om.* MHLa. [e-e]*om.* Lc[l].

359 Molaissi Echrois[a] m. Deglain[b] m. Dega m. Trena[c] m. Fiachrach[d] Ḟir Roeada[e] m. Feidlimid[f] Rect*ada*[g] [h]m. Tuathail Techtmair[h].

[a]Indsi Muridaig M(La), *om.* R[l]. [b]*punctum under* i Lc[l]. [c]*add* m. Dubthaig m. Baa MR[l]La. [d]*add* m. *with marks of elision* R[l]. [e]Raeidid M. [f]Feidhlimte R[l](La). [g]Rechtmair M(R[l])La. [h—h]*om.* MR[l].

360 Crummaine[a] Leccna[b] m. Cormaicc m. Baetain[c] m. hEircc m. Fiachach[d] m. Muiredaig m. Taidc m. Cein [e]m. Ailella Auluim[e].

[a]Cumaine M. [b]*om.* H. [c]Baithin M, Boethine R[l], Baethbine La. [d]Eathach M, Fiachrach R[l]La. [e—e]*om.* MH.

361 Mochromma Dissertа*ch*[a] m. Rigain m. Insain m. Aine m. Ambrit m. Imchada.

[a]Disertan Lc[l].

362 M[o]choemoc Leith[a] m. Beoain[b] m. Mellain [c]m. Nessain[c] m. hEircc m. Cuinnida[d] [e]m. Finnchain[f] m. Cuscraid[e].

[a]Leithi MR[l], *om.* HH[l]. [b]Becain(?) H. [c—c]*om.* MR[l]. [d]Cairida M(R[l]HH[l]). [e—e]*om.* MR[l]H, *added below line* H[l]. [f]Findchaim Lc[l], Caein H[l].

363 Ultan m. Cronain[a] m. Fintain m. Findloga m. Conaill [m.][b] Conchobair[c].

[a]Ronain M. [b]*om.* R(*see note*). [c]*attached to following pedigree*(119) Lc[l], *add* Collo ingen D(i)mai m. Mind do Gailingaib a mathair Ulltain 7 (dl)igid Ulltan comroinn do fagbail oc (C)laeinn Cormuic Gailing M.

364 Secht meic Draigin[a]; Euthech, Anmere, Mac Chiair, Drucan, Finan, Faelan, Mechar.

[a]*see note.*

365 Segine Sochla et Colman et Mac Lasre tri meic Cronain m. Loairn m. Fergusa m. Conaill[a] m. Neill Noigiallaig [b]m. Echach[b].

[a]*add* Gulban Lc[l]. [b—b]*om.* Lc[l].

366 Colman[a], Guaire 7 Mael Dub m. Ultain hic Beluch Buaidge hic Dun Bile[b].

[a]*add* 7 Lc[l]. [b]Baile Lc[l].

367.1 Crothu ingen Briuin 7 Dechoin Cormac 7 Gobban m. Cormaic 7 Aed m. Cremthaind 7 Conmac m. Cremthaind hi Cill Crui[a].

2 [b]Crunmael m. Ronain i Cill Crui[ab].

[a]Criu Lc[l]. [b—b]*see note.*

368 Aedan[a] m. Colmain m. Aililla m. Conaill m. Feicc m. Bresail m. Feidlimthe m. Fiacrach Cassan m. Collo Focrich[b] [c]m. Eochach Doimlein m. Cairpri Lifechair[cd].

[a]Caedín La. *See note.* [b]Focriaidh R[1]. [c—c]*om.* R[1]. [d]*add* m. Cormaic Ulḟota m. Airt Enḟir m. Cuind Cetchathaigh La.

369 Baedan[a] .i. Mobeoc[b] m*ac*ua Lada[c] o Chluain Abannabair[d] i nUaib Muiridaig.

[a]Baethan La. [b]Maboe La. [c]*see note.* [d]Abannair La.

370 Findlud 7 Findtanna m. Dimmain m. Ḟingein m. Demain m. Caeirill m. Muiridaig Muinddeirg.

371 Tri meic Duib m. Urgnuill m. Cais Ruba m. Conaill m. Losnada Lathar nGle m. Rossa m. Rudraide.

372 Mochua Balla m. Becain m. Baeirr m. Nathi m. Lugdach m. Thalann m. Ithchair m. Alta.
[a]Ic Lugaig chomraigius 7 Caeinneach[a].

[a—a]*om.* R[1].

373 Cormac m. Cuilinnain m. Sealbaig[a] m. Duib[b] Da Crich m. Colmain m. Ṡechnasaig m. Ḟingein m. Aeda m. Crimthainn m. Feidlimthe[c] m. Aengusa m. Nadfraich m. Cuircc m. Luigdeach[d] [e]m. Oilella Flainn Big[e].

[a]*add* m. Ailgine R[1]. [b]*om.* R[1]. [c]Feidlimid R[1]. [d]Lugdach R[1]. [e—e]*om.* R[1].

374 Lai[s]ren m. Colmain m. Luchttai m. Findchada m. Feidlimti m. Sogain m. Fiach*ach* Araide.

375 Scath ingen Tigerrnaig m. Baetloga m. Baethlatraind [m.]? Floinn m. Caelchon m. Oirtcirrn m. Conaill Oirisi m. Briain m. Echach Muigmedoin.

376 Colman[a] Mor[b] m. Duach m. Ainmirech[c] m. Conaill m. Eogain[d] m. Echach Bricc[b] m. Nathi[e] m. Fiacrach m. Eochach Muigmedoin[f].

[a]Calman R[1]. [b]*om.* La. [c]Ainmreach R[1]. [d]*add* Aidhne R[1]La. [e]Dathi La. [f]*add* m. Muiredaigh Tirigh m. Fiachaigh Sroibtine m. Coirpri Lifechair m. Cormaic Ulḟata m. Airt Aenḟir m. Cuind Cetcathaigh R[1](La).

377 Cuan i nUaib Berrchon m. Odrain m. Ronain m. Coirpri m. Fiacrach Find m. Breasail m. Maine Mair m. Eochach Fir Da Giall m. Domnaill m. Imchada m. Collo Fochriaid.

378 Bracan Airne[a] m. Eochach Bailldeirc m. Carthaind Find[b] m. Blaeid m. Caiss[c] m. Conaill Echluaith m. Luigdech Mind[d] m. Aengusa Tirig m. Fir Chorp m. Moda[e] Corp m. Cormaic Cais m. Oilella Oluim.

[a]Airnde R[1]. [b]*om.* La. [c]Tail R[1], Tail Cais a quo Dail Cais La, *add* m. Crimthaind La. [d]*illeg.* R[1]. [e]Mogha R[1]La.

379.1 Aelchu, cui nomen Pupu Airne, m. Faelchair m. Edalaig[a].

2 Et ba ri Osraigi [b]in Faelachair sin[b]. Is[c] uada Sil Faelachair[d] la hOsraige[e].

3 Ime[f] doberar[g] do Pupa .i. Papa o rogab apdaine na[h] Romo dar eisi Gridoir[i], 7 forḟacaibsum a apdaine 7 doluig[j] d'iarraig[k] a maigistreach tairis[h] [l]co hiarthur Eorpu 7 co hArainn na naem[l]. Conad hi in tres roilic aingil Airrni raeilig[m] Phupa m. Faelechair m. Etalaig[a].

[a]Fadalaigh La. [b—b]Fáelchar m. Fadalaig La. [c]et is La. [d]Faelchair La. [e]hOsraigib La. [f]7 is ime La. [g]atberar La. [h]*om.* La. [i]*add* Roma La. [j]dochuaid La. [k]a ndiaigh taisi La. [l—l]co hAraind iarthair Eorpa La. [m]*add* teglaig La.

380.1 Brig ingen Chobtaig m. Crimthaind m. Enna Ceindsealaig mathair[a] Seigin .i.[b] mac[c] Seigine[d] et Easpoic Aedain et Aeda m. Ainimrech rig Eirind.

2 [e]Amail rochan Dallan Forgaill:

Colum Cilli,
  Aedh co feraib Eiri[n]d ime,
Loingsech Breag mban,
  Adamnan hua Tinne.

Tathmet Semgein 7 Sleibin,
  batar amrai,
fagaib d'aentuaith, madh dia feisir,
  seisir samlaigh[e].

[a]m. R[1]La. [b]*om.* R[1]La. [c]mathair R[1]La. [d]*om.* La. [e—e]*om.* R[1]La.

381.1 [a]Cairnech[b]; do Breatnaib Corrn do. Is[c] imi sin[b] aderar[d] Cairrneach[e] fris.

2 .i.[a] Cairrneach m. Luitheich m. Luigdeach[f] m. Thalunn[g] m. Ithachair m. Altta[h].
Is amlaig sin innisis Gilla Caemain a Stairib na mBreatan[i].

[a—a]*follows* 2 La. [b]*om.* La. [c]7 is La. [d]atberar La. [e]Cornech La. [f]Lugdach La. [g]Dalann La. [h]Ata Lc. [i]mBretnach La.

382 Comgoll m. Cairill m. Luigdeach[a] m. Ainnida[b] [c]m. Cirbairt m. Connla[c] m. Cuind Cetchathaig.

[a]Lugdach H[1]La. [b]Anniuda H[1], Aindiudha La. [c—c]m. Lugdach m. Cressin H[1].

383.1 Fidmuine, .i. *Ua* Suanaig, m. Fidbadaig m. Conndealgaig m. Comain m. Ṡuanaig m. Bruigde m. Brenainn m. Echach Bricc m. Nathi m. Ḟiacrach.

2 Fidmuine 7 Fidairle da macc Ḟidbadaig m. Coinnealgaig.

383.3 hUa Suanaig, ni huarach
im saerig ic neirge neimech,
hEiriu ard, amre ha ethe,
iss ed a chleithe cleirech.

384 Brenainn 7 Domaingein uil[a] a Tuaim Muscraide 7 Faichlech Chluana Tuaiscirt 7 Faelan Chilli Tulach cethra meic Ḟindloga m. [b]Olchon m. Alttai m. Ogamain m. Fibchuire m. Dealmnai m. Ennai m. Ḟualascaig m. Axamain m. Moga Taeth m. Fergussa[b].
Do Chiarraide Luacra doib[c].

[a]fuil La. [b—b]*om.* La. [c]sin La.

385 Sarnatt[a] ingen Aeda Gabalḟata m. Ṡenaig Chind Gamna m. Eogain Aigne[b] m. Eochach Bricc[c] m. Nathi[d] m. Fiacrach.

[a]Sernait La. [b]A(i)dne (R[l])La(*with* e *above* d). [c]*om.* R[l]La. [d]Dathi R[l]La.

386 Ailind ingen Eogain Aidhne m. Echach Bricc m. Dathi m. Ḟiacrach.

387 Dairi Barrach m. Cathair as uada rochinsead na naim seo .i. Tigerrnach Cluana hEois 7 Fiacc 7 Fiacra et Mac Tail Cilli Cuilinn 7 Mac Cuill a Manainn 7 Fiachra Goll 7 Eimin a lLeith.

388 Caeirill m. Currnain m. Threna m. Finnchada m. Nair m. Earcca m. Tipraide m. Sogain m. Conaill Cearrnaig.

389 Eadamair[a] ingen Eogain m. Thail m. Ainnli m. Cairida m. Finnchaim[b] m. Cuscraid m. [c]Meic Echt[c].

[a]Adhamair R[l]. [b]Finnchadaim *with elision marks under* ad M. [c—c]Cecht R[l].

390 Maine[a] easpog m. Caechain m. Eircc m. Rossa m. Ailella m. Echach Muigmedoin.

[a]*preceded by* De geinil*chaib* (Genealogia na) naem Ua(*om.*) nOilella (annso sis) M(La).

391 Mainchin m. Cail m. Ceanannain m. Aengusa m. Ḟergusa m. Oilella m. Echach Muigmedoin.

392 Imraitech [a]i nImliuch[a] m. Dunchada m. Tipraide m. Mail[b] Duin m. Ealgaigh m. Nathi m. Ḟiacrach.
Ar at iad da mac Ealgaig m. Nathi .i. Cobthach 7 Mael Duin.

[a—a]Imliuc(h)a R[l](La). [b]Maile R[l].

393 [a]Do[b] geinilach mac[c] Caelbaig[d] di*no*; iss ed[e] do Chlaeinn Oililla m. Echach Muigmedoin iat .i.[af].

1 Senach m. Cail m. Ceanannain[g] m. Aengusa m. Ḟergusa m. Oililla[h] m. Echach Muigmedoin[i].

[a—a]separate entry R[l]. [b]*om.* R[l]La. [c]*om.* La. [d]Coelbadh R[l]. [e](.i.) is R[l](La). [f]*om.* R[l]. [g]Cennain La 276. [h]Allan La 315. [i]*added later* agus is da derbrathir da chele Seanach 7 Mancin Luimnig R[l].

393.2 [j]Finnoll m. Cail m. Ceanannain[k] m. Aengusa m. Ḟergusa m. Aililla[l].

3 Drenon[m] m. Cail m. Ceanannain.

4 Colman m. Cail m. Ceanannain.

5 Feradach m. Cail m. Ceanannain.

6 Aed Finn[c] m. Cail m. Ceanannain[n].

7 Fedbor[o] m. Cail m. Ceanannain.

8 7 at iad sin fuil a Cluain[p] Aird a Ciarraige Airtig[q] [r]7 a nImliuch Gailing la Luigniu[jr].

[j—j]*om.* R^{l}. [k]Cennain La. [l]Allan La315, *add* m. Eathach Muigedmeoin La 276, 315. [m]Dremon La. [n]Ceannain La. [o]Febor La. [p]nDruim La. [q]*add* no Cluain Aird La. [r—r]*om.* La.

394.1 Faithlech m. Finnloga [a]Chluana Tuaiscirt[a]: [b]is don Ḟaithlech sin[b] do-slecht[c] Fergus[d] m. Raigillaig dar eis mBrenainn, 7 is ag[e] Faithlech forḟagaib[f] Brenaind a manchu .i. Sil Aeda m. Eachach Tirmcharna. Doig ae Aed m. Echach tug Eanach Duin [g]ina laim sin[g] do Dia 7 do Brenainn, 7 slechtais fein do Brenainn [h]et tug a mancu do[h] .i. Uata m. Aeda 7 Curnan m. Aeda athair Mael Ruain. Is*ed*[i] sin[j] forḟuair[k] Sil Churnnain do beith ra Brenainn. Cid tra acht slechtais Fergus mar adrubrumar do Ḟaichleach 7 lenais a mac he .i. Muiridach Muil-lethan[j] 7 leansad[l] a sil in Muiridaig sin co haimsir Muirgiusa Moir m. Tomoltaig. Conad o[m] sin amach dolensad[n] Sil nIndrachtaig[o] do Chiarain cona chomarbaib[p].

2 Sosead[q] di*no* [r]Sil Currnain 7[r] Sil Conchobair m. Muiridaig for[s] Brenainn doridissi 7 Sil Cheallaig m. Raigillaig 7 Sil Currnain m. Aeda[t] 7 Sil Eachach Tirmcharrna cenmotha[u] Sil nIndrachtaig [vw]7 cid[w] iadsaidein ataid[x] cinedaig dib nach benad[y] ra Ciaran.

3 Clann[z] Taidg 7 Murthuile ra Brenainn benaid o aimsir Thipraite m. Thaidg alle, 7 ba hairdrig Conacht uile in Tipraide sin.

4 Sil Fothaig di*no* ra hEspoc Sachall[aa] 7 ra Padraicc beanad.

5 Clann Murchada di*no* fri(?)[bb] Choman[cc] beanatt o aimsir Finnachta m. Gleitnichain[dd] alle.

[a—a]*added between columns* M, *om.* R^{l}La. [b—b]dearbrathair do Brenaind m. Ḟindlogha he 7 is do Faithleach R^{l}(La). [c]roslecht R^{l}. [d]*add* Mor R^{l}. [e]*om.* R^{l}. [f]roḟac La. [g—g]i nalmsaine R^{l}(La). [h—h]7 a micc R^{l}(La). [i]7 ise(adh) (R^{l})La. [j]*om.* La. [k]rofurail La. [l]leanaid R^{l}. [m]as La. [n]role(a)nsat (R^{l})La. [o]Muircertaigh R^{l}. [p]comarabaib R^{l}. [q]saeseat R^{l}(La). [r—r]*om.* R^{l}La. [s]fri La. [t]*add* .i. Sil Mail Ruain R^{l}(La). [u]uile aginnochta R^{l}, fuile ganmota La. [v—v]*om.* R^{l}. [w—w]*om.* La. [x]7 ataid La. [y]benann La. [z].i. Clann La. [aa]Sochill La. [bb]re La. [cc]Cumain La. [dd]Glethechain La.

394.6 Sil Chonnmuig[ee] re Patraicc beansad[ff] cip innus robeansad.

7 Clann Choscraid 7 Murchada m. Moenaig is la Brenaind iat [gg]re Faichlech[vgg].

[ee]*add* dano La. [ff]benait La. [gg—gg]riam Brenaind re Faithlech 7 roim Faithlech La(*with some subpunctuation*).

395 Easpoc Fergusa m. Colmain[a] m. Diarmuta m. Feargusa Ceirrbeoil m. Conaill Chremthainn m. Neill Naegiallaig.

[a]*add* Bic La.

396 Dachonna[a] m. Tigerrnaig m. Aengusa[b] m. Conaill Gulban m. Neill Naegiallaig.

[a]*no* Daconda R[1](*see note*). [b]*add* m. Fergusa R[1].

397 [a]Crimthan ainm baisdig Choluim Chille et[a] Eithni ingen Dimai m. Nai do Chorbraide Ḟanud [b]a mathair[b] .i. do Cheinel Coirpri m. Filed m. Eichin[c] o Buais, 7 Deirbḟinn[d] Dualḟada[e] ainm eile d'Eithni. Et Eogan sosar[f] brathair Choluim Chille. Cuimne 7 Minchloth 7 Sinech a tri deirbṡeatracha; .i. Cuimne mathair mac nDecill .i.[g] Moerrnocc[h] et Caiscne. Minchloth[i] mathair mac Enain; aen dib sidein[j] Colman. 7 Sinech mathair m*a*c Coichinn.

[a—a]*om.* La. [b—b]mathair Coluim Cilli La. [c]Ethen La. [h]Deibfind La. [e]Bélfota La. [f]fos La. [g]7 La. [h]Monernoc La. [i]*add* imorro La. [j]side La.

398.1 [a]Athracht[b] ingen Thalain m. Dubthaig m. Rossa m. Imchada — sunn[c] chomraigius 7 Comgoll Bennchair — m. Ḟeidlimthe [d]m. Caiss[d] m. Ḟiachach Araide o taid Dal nAiraide[a].

2 [e]Derbrathair Attracht[ef] .i.[g] Coeman m. Talain o ta[h](?) Ard (C)aemain i nUaib[i] Cinnsilaig [j](7 as ... roscuir)[j] flaithius[k] Connacht (im) Chloinn Chinn Faelad m. Colgun dia tuc gialla Luigne[l] uad [m]7 dia (chloind) co n(derrnad)[m] [n]slige ndroichid[n] dar Ḷoch Teiced[o] Rathmogadh.

[a—a]*om.* La. [b]Athrachta R[1]. [c]ic mac sin R[1]. [d—d]*bis with marks of elision* R[1]. [e—e]*see note*. [f]d'Athrachta R[1](La). [g]*om.* R[1]La. [h]tait R[1], ta La. [i]yb La. [j—j]isi docuir R[1](La). [k]*first written* failte *with marks of elision* R[1]. [l]Laigen La. [m—m]7dia nernda R[1](La). [n—n]sluaigheadh R[1], sligid La. [o]Deicheat R[1], Techet .i. Drochet La.

399 Finnachta Luimnig i nUaib Ceindsealaig ata a cheall, et as e aeṇnaem[a] Sil Muiridaig in Finnachta si(n), 7 doḟagaib[b] rige *Connacht* dia deoin fein[c] ar grad De. In[d] tres mac do Thomoltach he 7 is do sin[c] doraiged[e]:

Findachta m. Tomoltaig,
co n-ilar[f] a daghmaine,
[g]rorecc rige Conacht[g] caem
ar tocht do[h] thaib Ḟarmaile[i].

[j]Rob e med a fognoma do Dhia co roibe neamh dia braithrib occa do

[a]bus naem La. [b]rofacaib La. [c]*om.* La. [d]7 an La. [e]doraid in rand La. [f]n-imat La. [g—g]roreccsat Condachta La. [h]co La. [i]Formaile La. [j—j]*om.* La.

chind a mogsaine[j] .i. do chloinn Tomoltaig m. Murgaile[k] o taid Sil Muiridaig.
[j]Ad mora a ferta 7 a[d] diaisnissi a bailiudha. As i talmuntaib 7 (ar) ḟlathus a tabair [...] reic do ar [...] 7 ar daera a [...] ar saer[...] a tig De[j]. A nUaib Deaga Mora ata a cea(ll) .i. Luimnech Ḟinnacta.

[k]*add* m. Inrachtaig m.(?) Murethaig La.

400 Mac Finn o Chill Chian(a)in m. Clucheacair m. Diarmuta m. Conamla m. Congalaig m. Dungalaig o taid Clann Dungalaigh m. Dunchada m. Ḟidchaire o taid *Ui* Ḟid(chaire).

401 [a]Etain Tu(ama Noa) ar bru Builli [.i.][a] Edain(d) i*ngen* Lig(in)[b] [c]o (taid)[c] Sil (Ligin)[d].

[a—a]*om.* La. [b]Ligine La. [c—c]dia La. [d]Ligine ar slicht Duach Dalaig m. Briain La.

402 Da absdal dec Indsi Fail.

Da Finden, da Colman caidh,
Caindeach, Ciaran, Comgall cain,
da Brenainn, Ruadan co lí,
Ninned[a], Mo Bi, Mac Na[d]fraith .i. Molaisi Diamindsi[b]

[a]d *with a subscript?* [b]*sic. for* Daimindsi.

403 Cíar Ascad ingen Cholla m. Diccolla[a] m. Nathí m. Maelain m. Scelain m. Cascine m. Olcaín m. Carthainn m. Cainnig.

[a]*first* c *added above line* R[1].

404 Epscop Eoghain m. Cormaic[a] m. Neill[b].

[a]*add* m. Cairpri La. [b]*add* N*oigiallaig* La.

405 Epscop Maeláin m. Daire m. Eachach m. Aeng*us* m. Lomáin.

406 Brandamh Tighe nEathach m. Eachach m. Ainmreach[a] m. Aengusa m. Lomáin.

[a]ain *added above line* R[1].

407 Domnall *Ua* hEnne m. Murcada m. Muirgiusa m. Ennai m. Conaill m. Debtaig m. Ansin m. Mathgamna m. Conaill m. Eochach m. Tairdelbaig.

408 Moenaccan m. Duib Dá Dos m. Sennaig m. Setna (F)ergus[a].

[a]*see note.*

409 Cuan Atha Eascruch m. Ferg(usa) m. [...] m. [...] m. [...] m. [...] m. Nell[a] Noegiallaig.

[a]*written* Noell *with mark of elision under* o.

410.1 Is do Claind Branain m. Dubthae in m[...] Conch(enn) o Chill Achai(d 7) Cruimter [...](ofa)[...] 7 Findchua Bri G*obann* 7 Rairri o Tuaim Sruthra 7 Failbi Find [...] 7 Dochua oc Cill Eo 7 Fintan.

2 (M)echen Cael ingen Canand m. Branain m. Dobtha m. Oengusa.

3 Methen Find ingean Branain m. Dubtha m. Oengusa.

4 Mes Raeda ingean Branain m. Dubtha m. Oengusa.

411 Colman m. B[...] m. Innill m. Bronaig m. Doigri m. Diarmata m. (Luchta) m. Lugna Fir Tri.

412 Crumthir Finnbar[a] m. Bresail m. Ailgil m. Selbaig m. Idna Athra m. Nia Moir m. Fir Tri.

[a]*written* Finbarb *with mark of elision under second* b.

413 Cruimthir Sarain m. Bronaig m. Doigri m. Diarmata.

414 Furudran [a]m. Coirpri Cruim[a] m. Cremtaind m. Echach m. Oengusa m. Nadfraich.

[a—a]*written* Coir m. Pri Cruim.

415 Epscop Ibair, do Ulltaib do .i. do Ṡil Mudorn*n* Duib dia'tat Mudorna. Epscop Ibair m. Lugnan 7 [a] ba Sas[a] ainm a mathar 7 dona Desib di, 7 renanus altum .i. moruasal a ainm fein, Epscop Ibair.

[a—a]*see note.*

RECENSIO MINOR

416 Patraic mac Alpraind[a] [b]ar slicht Britain meic Feargosa Leithdeirg[bc].

[a]*add* m. Fótaide La. [b—b]7 aderait aroili gomad do ṡil Fergusa Leithdeirg do Patraic La. [c]*add* Atberait foirenn comadh do macaib Israhel do Patraic iar fir, 7 comadh ar gaél fola Crist dothiucfadh Patraic a nEirind do dichur druagh 7 demon, 7 ara bunad do beith do Bretnaib atbertha Bretnach fris. Sucait ainm baisti Patraic; Cotraidhe a ainm ac daíre; Magonius a ainm oc foghlaim; Patricius a ainm ac Romanchaib. Cochmais ingen Ochmais ainm a mathar, 7 bean do Frangcaib hí, 7 siur do Martain hí La.

417 Seanan m. Fintain, .i. naem do macaib M*air*eada, ar slicht Tigernmais m. Follaig.

418 Colam Cilli m. Feidlimid[a] [b]m. Feargusa[b] [c]m. Conaill Gulban[c].

[a]Feidlimthi La. [b—b]*om.* La. [c—c]ar slicht Conaill Gulban m. Neill Naigiallaig La.

419 Comgall Beannchair m. Setna ar slicht Cais m. Fiachach[a] Araide [b]de Ultaib[b].

[a]Etach La. [b—b]*om.* La.

420 Cumain[a] ingen [b]Failbe ar slicht Echach Gundat[b] m. Ḟeig.

[a]Comain La. [b—b]Ailella Áne m. Echach Gunatha La.

421 Feichin m. Caelcharna[a] ar slicht Taidc m. Cein [b]de Mumain[b].

[a]Ilcharna La. [b—b]*om.* La.

422 Ciaran m. Beodain[a] ar slicht [b]Reo Deoirchi m.[b] Thigernmais m. Ḟollaich[c].

[a]Baedain La. [b—b]*partly illeg.* La. [c]*add* no atberait aroili comad do ṡlicht Fergusa m. Rosa do La.

423 Finden Muigi Bili m. Cairpri ar slicht Sirchada m. Fiatach Find [a]a quo Dal Fiatach .i. Ulaid[a].

[a—a]*om.* La.

424 [a]Aitchean Dairi[a] m. Aengusa m. Nadfraich.

[a—a]Aidcendairi La.

425 Maedoc m. Setna ar slicht Eachach m. Colla Uais.

426 Dallan m. Colla ar slicht Echach[a] m. Colla Uais.

[a]*add* m. Carthaind La.

427 Brigit ingen Dubthaig ar slicht Aengusa Mind m. Echach Find Fuath nAirt.

428 Brenaind Birra[a] ar slicht Cuirp m. Fergusa m. Rosa.

[a]Birre La, *add* m. Nemainn La.

429 Buite m. Bronaig ar slicht Taidc m. Cein.

430 Bearach[a] m. Nemergein[b] ar slicht Earca Deirg m. Briain[c].

[a]Brec La. [b]Amergin La. [c]*add* m. Echach Muidemoin La.

431 Baithin m. Cuanach ar slicht Enna m. Conaill Gulban[a] m. Neill[b].

[a]*om.* La. [b]*add* Naighiallaig La.

432 Beccan m. Murchada ar slicht Eogain m. Aililla Uluim[a].

[a]Óluim La.

433 Barrḟind m. Muireadaig[a] m. Eachach[a] m. Conaill Gulban[b].

[a—a]ar slicht La. [b]*add* m. Neill Naighiallaig La.

434 Earnan[a] Indsi Cain ar slicht Fergusa m. Conaill Gulban[b].

[a]Ernín La. [b]*om.* La, *add* m. Neill La.

435 Nindid m. Eachach[a] [b]ar slicht[b] Laegairi m. Nell.

[a]*add* m. Aeda La. [b—b]m. La.

436 Ailbi m. Olchain[a] ar slicht [b]Ḟir Tlachtga m. Fergusa *no*[b] Fear Tlachtda m. Celtchair[c] m. Uitheochair.

[a]Olchon La. [b—b]*om.* La. [c]Celtair La.

437 Molaisi Leithglindi ar slicht [a]Muireadaig Muindeirg[a].

[a—a]Fiatach Find a quo Dail Fiatach La.

438 Samthand Cluana Bronaig ingen Diamrain[a] [b]ar slicht[b].

[a]Dimarain LaLa[l], *add* m. Dichon La[l]. [b—b]*om.* La, *add* Sirchatha m. Fiatach Find La[l].

439 Mochaemog m. Beoain ar slicht Fraich m. Cuscraid[a].

[a]Cumscraig La.

440 Conla m. Cormaic ar slicht Echach m. Mesin Corb [a]de Laignaib[a].

[a—a]*om.* La.

441 Aed m. Bric [a]ar slicht Fiacha[a] m. Neill Noigiallaig[b].

[a—a]m. Fiachach La. [b]*om.* La.

442 [a]Caillin m. Niathach[a] ar slicht Fraich m. Cuscraid[b].

[a—a]Cáilín Nithaig La. [b]Cumscraig La.

443 Cruimthir Fraich[a] m. Cairrthaich[b] ar slicht [c]Ireil m. Conaill Cernaig[c].

[a]Fraechan La. [b]Carraig La. [c—c]Moga m. Conmaige m. Fergusa La.

444 Sciri ingen Eogain [a]ar slicht Feargusa m. Echach Muidmeadoin[a].

[a—a]m. Canann m. Ailella C*et*aigh m. Cathair Mhoir La(*see note*).

445 Mochuta m. Luigdech ar slicht Aililla C*et*aig m. Cathair Mair.

446 Mobi Clairineach m. Comgaill ar slicht Eachach m.[a] Maireada.

[a]*om.* La.

447 Finan Lobar m. Conaill ar slicht Cein m. Ailella Uluim.

448 Benen[a] m. Sescnen[b] ar slicht [c]Taidc m. Cein[c].

[a]Beneoin La. [b]Sescnin La. [c—c]Aengusa m. Na|dfraich| La.

449 Tola m. Dunchada ar slicht Chairpri m. Fiachach[a] Suidi.

[a]Fiacha La.

450 Seanan Indsi Cathaig m. Ceirrcind ar slicht Imchada m. Cairpri Baschain.

451 Cumain Fota m. Fiach*na* ar slicht Cairpre m. Cuirc m. Luigdech.

452 Dari — .i. Sodealb — ingen Chathair ar slicht Enna m. Amalga.

453 Bec m. De ar slicht Imchada m. Colla Focrich.

454 Colman Ela m. Beodna ar slicht Echach m. Aeda.

455 Cianan m. Troain[a] ar slicht Taidc m. Cein [b]m. Ailella Uluim[b].

[a]Trogaine La. [b—b]*om.* La.

456 Crumaine m. Cormaic ar slicht Taidc m. Cein.

457 Colmán[a] m. Nindeada ar slicht Crimthaind[b] m. Cathair.

[a]Colum La. [b]Crithmain La.

458 Caemgen m. Caemloga [a]ar slicht[a] Eachach Laimderg m. Meisin[b] Corb.

[a—a]m. La. [b]Mesi La.

459 Cuana m. Cailcine[a] ar slicht Moga Ruith m. Fergosa.

[a]Ilchein La.

460 Cruimtir[a] Dathi m. Caemloga [b]ar slicht Eoin[b] m. Idcuire[c].

[a]*add* m. La. [b—b]ion La. [c]Fidchuiri La.

461 Ciaran Sai[g]re m. Luigne ar slicht Oengusa Osraide.

462 Caerech[a] ingen Conaill Deirg [b]ar slicht Chairpre[b] Dam Argaid.

[a]Cairech La. [b—b]demain m. La.

463 Cuanna[a] m. Miduirn ar slicht Enna m. Neill[b].

[a]Cuanan La. [b]*add* N*oigiallaig* La.

464 Cairill m. Cairnan[a] ar slicht Sodain m. Conaill Cernaich.

[a]Carnain La.

465 Cuimen[a] ingen Aillen[b] ar slicht Ḟeic m. Imchada.

[a]Cumai La. [b]*add* m. Aeda La.

466 Ciaran Belaich Duin m. Cairthaind ar slicht Sodain m. Ḟiachach Araide.

467 Coman m. Faelchon ar slicht Sodain chednai[a].

[a]fos La.

468 Colman Imrama m. Fergnai[a] ar slicht Echach m. Colla Uais, [b]do Ḟearaib Li[b].

[a]Fergusa La. [b—b]*om.* La.

469 Deada[a] m. Cairill ar slicht Dallain m. [b]Eogan m. Nell[b].

[a]Dega La. [b—b]Eógain Bhric m. Airt Cuirb La(*see note*).

470 Deglan m. Eirc ar slicht Bric m. Art Chuirp.

471 Flandan m. Tairrdelbaig ar slicht Cais m. Conaill Echl*uaith*.

472 Iarlaithi m. Loga ar slicht Fraich m. Cuscraid.

473 Breccan m. M*ai*ccaim[a] do Chruithneachaib[b].

[a]Caí La. [b]*add* do La.

474 Enan Droma Raitine m. Muain.

475 Molaisi Daimindsi m. Nadfraich[a] [b]ar slicht Chais[b] m. Ḟiachach Aride.

[a]Natf*r*a La. [b—b]*om.* La.

476 Damaedoc thAilithre[a] ar slicht Muiredaich m. Eogain[b].

[a]Ailithre La. [b]*add* m. Neill La.

477 Fiacc[a] m. Earchada[b] ar slicht Dairi Barraig m. Cathair Moir.

[a]Fiach La. [b]Fercada La.

478 Becca[n][a] m. Murchada ar slicht Eogain m. Aililla Oluim.

[a]Becan La.

479 Mael Ruba[a] m. Eoganaid[b] ar slicht Echach[c] Bindich m. Eogain[d].

[a]Rubrain La[l]. [b]Eoghain La. [c]*om.* LaLa[l]. [d]*add* m. Neill LaLa[l].

480 Mael Doid m. Fingin[a] ar slicht Imchada m. Colla Focrich.

[a]Finain La.

481 Colman m. Guairi ar slicht Eachach m. Colla Uais.

482 Colman m. Eogain ar slicht Echach m. Colla Uais.

483 Deglan Imrois m. Nair [a]ar slicht[a] Oengusa Find[b] m. Cormaic[c] [d]m. Airt m.[d] Cuind *Cetcathaig*.

[a—a]m. La. [b]*om.* La. [c]*add* Ulat La. [d—d]*ua* La.

484 Barra[a] Corcaide ar slicht Chairpri m. Briain m. Eachach Muidmedoin.

[a]Barre La.

485 Epscop Mac Cairthaind[a] ar slicht Breasail m. Briuin[b].

[a]Carthaind La. [b]Bruin La.

486 Ailbe m. Colcan ar slicht Imrosa m. Ḟir Tlachtda m. Celtchair m. Uith*echair*.

487 Ronan Find m. Sarain ar slicht Ḟiachrach Casain m. Colla Da[a] Crich.

[a]Fo La.

488 Cairnech[a] m. Sarain a brathair.

[a]*om.* La.

489 Tri hingena Chaindig[a] m. Niad ar slicht Art Chuirb m. Fiachach[b] S*uigde*.

[a]Caindi La. [b]Fiacha La.

490 Epscop Findchad m. Sednai ar slicht Erc[a] Deirg m. Briain.

[a]r *added below line* Lc.

491 Murchan[a] — .i. Muru — m. [b]Airmedaich ar slicht Muireadaich m. Eogain[b].

[a]Murchud La. [b—b]Cairida m. Ronain m. Aedain m. Néill La.

492 Caeman Breac m.[a] Nisi Mair[b] ar slicht Erc m. Echach Munreamair.

[a].i. Mac La. [b]*om.* La.

493 Brenaind m. Findloga ar slicht Moga Doid[a] m. Fargusa [b]m. Roich[b].

[a]*add* m. Conmaic La. [b—b]*om.* La.

494 Feargna[a] m. Fintain ar slicht Fraich m. Cuscraig[b].

[a]Fergus La. [b]Cumscraig La.

495 Fintan Cluana Eignech m. in Gaibrein ar slicht Chairpri[a] Niad m. Cormaic m. Aengusa.

[a]*om.* La.

496 Epscop Ibair m. Lu*na*[a] ar slicht Moduirn Duib o[b] tait Mudorna *no* is do Clandaib Deadad[c].

[a]Lughna La. [b]dia La. [c]*add* do La.

497 Epscop Ethreann[a] a nDomnach Mor m. Lafebe[b] do Mudornnaib do[c].

[a]Ethren La. [b]Lefebe La. [c]fos La.

498 Maedoc Cluana Moir[a] m. Eogain[b] m. Bruide.

[a]Moiri La. [b]Aedain La.

499 Condla m. Cormaic ar slicht Eachach Laebdeirg[a] m. Mesin[b] Corp do Laignib.

[a]Laimdeirg La. [b]Meisi La.

500 Athracht ingen Ṡarain ar slicht Cruind Ba Draide.

501 Dabeooc[a] m. Luainind[b] ar slicht Sirchada m. Fiatach Find [c]a quo Dal Fiatach[c].

[a]Dabeadhoc La. [b]Luadund La. [c—c]*om.* La.

502 Feidlimid m. Deda[a] [b]ar slicht[b] Taidc m. Cein m. Aililla[c].

[a]Aeda La. [b—b]m. La. [c]*add* Oluim La.

503 Colman m. Duach ar slicht Eachach m. Dathi.

504 Ruadan Lothra ar slicht Dairi Chearba.

505 Tigernach Cluana Eois[a] m. Cairpri ar slicht Dairi Barraic [b]m. Cathair[b].

[a]hEdais La. [b—b]*om.* La.

506 Comgall m. Setna ar slicht Cais m. Fiachach Araide.

507 Conall Cosdamail m. Findchada ar slicht Ireil[a] Glunmair[b].

[a]Ireoil La. [b]*add* m. Conaill Chernaigh La.

508 Dub Duin Atha Lunga m. Fergusa ar slicht Feic m. Imchada.

509 Epscop Aed[a] m. Cormaic Bricc ar slicht Ḟiachach[b] m. Neill.

[a]Aeda La. [b]Fiachrach La.

510 Etain ingen Eogain Bel m. Duach Galaig[a] [b]m. Briain[b].

[a]Dalaigh La. [b—b]*om.* La.

511 Epscop Maine m. d'Eichen m. Eogain m. Neill.

512 Enan m. Ernin[a] ar slicht Art Chuirb [b]m. Cormaic[b].

[a]Eirnim La. [b—b]*see note* La.

513 Eaxpr̄(?)[a] Earc[b] m. Deada ar slicht Corb Uluim m. Fergusa[c].

[a]*For* epscop, *see note* LcLa. [b]m. Eirc La. [c]*add* m. Roith La.

514 Epscop Beoith m. Ulchain ar slicht Liuin[a] m. Luigdech m. Con [b]m. Luigdeach[b].

[a]Linin La. [b—b]*om.* La.

515 Fintan m. Setna ar slicht Earca[a] Deirg m. Briain[b].

[a]Eirc La. [b]*add* m. Echach M*uigmedoin* La.

516 Finden m. Fintain ar slicht Oilella m. Cealtchair[a].

[a]Celtair m. Uithechuir La.

517 Fin|d|bar|r|[a] m. Aeda ar slicht Art Chirb[b] m. Ḟiachach[c] *Suigde*.

[a]Findbarr La. [b]Cuirb La. [c]Fiacha La.

518 Fachtna[a] m. Maenaig ar slicht Maicniad[b] m. Con.

[a]na *written twice and without deletion marks* Lc. [b]m. Nia La.

519 Furadran 7[a] Baedan *da* m. Chollain ar slicht Ḟiachrach Casan m. Colla[b].

[a]m. La. [b]*add* Fochrich La.

520 Epscop Eog*an* m. Epscuip Eirc[a] ar slicht Corb[b] Uluim m. Ḟeargosa[c].

[a]Eirce La. [b]Cuirb La. [c]*add* m. Róith La.

521 Fiac m. Fearchair[a] ar slicht Dairi Barraig[b] m. Cathair[c].

[a]Eirce La. [b]Baire La. [c]*add* Moir La.

522 Mochua[a] m. Lonain ar slicht Art Chuirp [b]m. Cairpri[b].

[a]Muchua La. [b—b]*precedes* ar slicht La.

523 Monindi ingen Mochta ar slicht Chais m. Ḟiachach Araide.

524 Manchan m. Failbi ar slicht Bogaine[a] m. Conaill Gulban.

[a]Bogai*n* La.

525 Redade[a] [b]7 Cunter 7 Rigan[b] 7 Mianach ceithri[c] m. Ḟailbi m. Aeda[d] ar slicht Bogaine m. Conaill[e].

[a]Redada La. [b—b]7 Cruntur *sic. leg.* Cruimther? Rigan La. [c]tri La. [d]Aedain La. [e]*add* Gulban La.

526 Tola m. Dunchada[a] ar slicht Cormaic m. Thaidc m. Cein [b]de M*um*ain[b].

[a]Murchada (*no* Duncadha *above line*) La. [b—b]*om.* La.

527 Trega[a] ingen Chairthaind[b] [c]ar slicht[c] Echach m. Colla Uais, [d]de Lurc[d].

[a]Trea La. [b]Carthaind La. [c—c]m. La. [d—d]*om.* La.

528 Ultan m. Ernain[a] ar slicht Echach m. Colla Uais.

[a]Cernain La.

529 Furrsu Chraibtheach ar slicht Loga Laga m. Moga Nuad*at*.

530 Luaithreand ingen Colmain ar slicht[a] Taidc m. Cein.

[a]*add* Cormaic m. La.

531 Mothenoc[a] m. Sinill ar slicht Echach m. Meisi Corb.

[a]Maeuenog La.

532 Cruimthir Sinill m. Tigern*aig* [a]ar slicht[a] Eogain m. Neill.

[a—a]m. La.

533 Diarmaid Indsi Clothlann m. Lugna ar slicht Dathi m. F*iachrach*.

534 Ronan m. Bearaig ar slicht Laegairi m. Neill Noigiallaig.

535 Colman m. Luachan ar slicht[a] Diarmada m. Cerbaill.

[a]*add* Maine m. La.

536 Dachuilin[a] m. Guairi[b] ar slicht Bindich [c]m. Eogain[c].

[a]Dacuilin *or read* Dacuilm La. [b]Cuire La. [c—c]*om.* La.

537 Domangort[a] m. Eachach m. Muireadaich Muindeirg.

[a]Damangort La.

538 Enna Toraidi m. Colmain ar slicht Muireadaich[a] m. Neill N*oigiallaig*[b].

[a]*add* m. Eogain La. [b]*om.* La.

539 Garban epscop m. Aengusa ar slicht Chonaill Creamthaind[a].

[a]*add* m. Neill La.

540 hIarlaithi m. Trena ar slicht Sirchada m. Ḟiatach Find.

541 Lurach[a] ar slicht Ḟiachach[b] Tort m. Colla Uais.

[a]*add* m. Cuanach La. [b]Fiacrach La.

542 Molua m. Sinill ar slicht Duach Galaich m. Briain.

543 Runach[a] m. Muireadaich m. Eogain m. Neill Noigiallaig[b].

[a]Ruanach La. [b]*om.* La.

544 Oengus m. Ingoband ar slicht Nadsluaig m. Cae[l]baid m. *Cruinn*.

545 [a]Na tri *Ui* Ṡuanaich[a], Fidmaine[b] [a]7 Fidairli 7 Fidgus[a] ar slicht Lifeochair m. Dathi[c] m. F*iachrach*[d].

[a—a]*om.* La. [b]*add* m. Fidbaig La. [c]Nathi La. [d]*add* Fidairle 7 Fidbus da mac ele Fidbadaig et Foramla ingen Dima Duib mathair na hUa Suanaigh La.

546 Mundu[a] m. Tulchain ar slicht [b]Fiachach Araidi[b] m. Feidlimid[c] Rechtmair.

[a]Onrum La. [b—b]Firgi La. [c]Fedlimthi La.

547 Moling a Luachair ar slicht Labrada m. Bresail B*elaig*.

548 Bearchan m. Deglain ar slicht Rochada m. Colla Da[a] Chrich.

[a]fo La.

549 Bearchan m. Bochan[a] ar slicht [b]Aengusa m.[b] Echach Find Fuath nAirt.

[a]Bocain La. [b—b]*om.* La.

550 Feichin Fabair m. Grilline[a] ar slicht Oengusa m. Echach[b].

[a]Grillein La. [b]*add* Find Fuath nAirt La.

551 Bearchan Mor m. Aeda ar slicht Ḟiachach[a] Suidi[b].

[a]Fiacha La. [b]*add* m. R. La.

552 Epscop Aed[a] ar slicht Ḟiachach[b] Suide beos[c].

[a]Aeda La. [b]Fiacha La. [c]*om.* La.

553 Gridair[a] Beloir[b] m. Gormaltaich ar slicht Chuirc Duibindi[c] m. Cairpri Musc.

[a]Grighoir La. [b]Roma La. [c]Duibne La.

554 Mochelloc m. Aiblean ar slicht Chuirc Duibinde[a].

[a]Duibne La, *add* fos La.

555 Odran m. Menchra[a] ar slicht Conairi Moir.

[a]Maencha La.

556 Bearchan Cluana Sosta m. Muireadaich ar slicht Chairpre Rigḟota m. *Conaire*[a].

[a]*add* Moir La.

557 Muru m. Fearadaig ar slicht Fiatach Finn[a].

[a]*add* a quo Dail Fiatach La.

558 Epscop Eitchen[a] m. Maine ar slicht Mesin[b] Corb.

[a]Echen La. [b]Meisi La.

559 Epscop Eogain m. Eircc ar slicht Mesin Corb.

560 Bearchan m. Deaga ⁊ Mosenoc[a] m. Senchan ar slicht Mesin[b] Corb m. Con Cuirp[c].

[a]Mutheaoc La. [b]Mesi La. [c]Corb La.

561 Dalbach m. Bronaig ar slicht Eachach[a] Liathain[b].

[a]*om.* La. [b]*add* a quo Ui Liathain La.

562 Bearchan m. Dima ar slicht Enna Niad m. Breasail Belaich.

563 Maedoc Cluana Moir m. Eogain ar slicht Cathair Moir[a].

[a]*add* fos La.

564 Mac Nisi m. Faebraide[a] ar slicht Echach m.[b] M*uireda*.

[a]Feradaig La. [b]*om.* La.

565 Mael Ruain Tamlachta m. Colmain [a]ar slicht[a] Eachach m.[b] Muireada.

[a—a]m. La. [b]*om.* La.

566 Colman m. Lugna[a] ar slicht Echach m.[b] Muireada.

[a]Luana La. [b]*om.* La.

567 Martain m. Dumain ar slicht [a]Aililla Oluim[a].

[a—a]Moga Corb m. Cormaic Caiss La.

568 Aedan m. Tairrdelbaig[a] ar slicht Cormaic Cais.

[a]Toirbelaig La.

569 Enne Airne ar slicht Rochada m. Colla Da Chrich.

570 Cronan m. Odran ar slicht Taidc m. Cein.

571 Liadan[a] ingen Diarmada ar slicht Cais m. Conaill Eachluaith.

[a]Lidan La.

572 Comgall m. Aililla ar slicht Conla[a] Ruaid[b] m. Cuind *Cetcathaig*.

[a]*added in marg.* Lc. [b]*om.* La.

573 Garban epscop m. Aengosa ar slicht Conaill Creamth*ainne* m. Neill.

574 [a]Silan epscop[a] m. Failbe ar slicht Duach m. Meic[b] Con[c].

[a—a]Epscop Sarain La. [b]*om.* La. [c]*add* m. Macnia La.

575 Epscop Fiachach[a] m. Fergusa m. Eogain m. Neill

[a]Fiatach La.

576 Epscop Earc Slaine m. Deaga ar slicht Chais m. Rosa Ruaid.

577 Manchan m. Sinill ar slicht Luigdeach Laga m. Moga N*uadat*.

578 Beccan m. Murchada ar slicht Eogain m. Aililla Flann Bic.

579 Mael Doid m. Fingin ar slicht Imchada m. Colla Da Chrich.

580 Mochuda m. Lugada ar slicht Aililla Ce*t*aich m. Cathair Moir.

581 Molaisi Echrois[a] m. Deglain ar slicht [b]Fiachrach Raeda[b] m. Ḟeidlim[c] Rechtmair.

[a]*om.* La. [b—b]Ḟirrige La. [c]Fedhlim*id* La.

582 Colman m. Eogain [a]ar slicht[a] Echach m. Colla Uais.

[a—a]m. La.

583 Cuana m. Fualascaig ar slicht Eachach cetnai[a].

[a]m. Colla Uais La.

584 Caeman Breac ar slicht Eirc m. Eachach Munramair.

585 Feargna m. Ainmireach ar slicht Echach m. Colla Uais.

586 Findbarr m. Aeda ar slicht Bricc m. Art Chuirp.

587 Eogan Arda Sreath[a] m. Caindig[b] ar slicht Echach m. Mesin[c] Corb.

[a]Sratha La. [b]Enda La. [c]Mesi La.

588 Crumaine[a] m. Cormaic ar slicht Taidc m. Cein.

[a]Crumain La.

589 Cronan m. Aengusa [a]ar slicht[a] Breasail m. Dathi[b].

[a—a]m. La. [b]*add* m. Fiachrach La.

590 Moluac[a] m. Luchta ar slicht Conaill Cernaig.

[a]Moluoc La.

591 Laisren m. Colmain ar slicht Conaill Cernaig.

592 Caemgin Glindi Da Lacha m. Caemloga ar slicht Echach Laimdeirg m. Mesin Corb.

593 Mugain[a] ingen Dunlaing m. Enna Niad; is uaithi[b] Cell Mugaine[c] a Tuadmumain.

[a]Mugaine La. [b]*add* ata La. [c]*add* a nIb No La.

594 Colco m. Aeda ar slicht Eachach m. Dathi m. Fiachrach.

595 Aedamair[a] ingen Eogain ar slicht Findchaim m. Cuscraid[b].

[a]Amuir La. [b]Cumscraig La.

596 Maine[a] epscop[b] ar slicht Aililla m. Eachach Muidmedoin.

[a]Aine La. [b]*add* m. Ecain La.

597 Mainchin m. Cail ar slicht Ailella m. Echach Muidmedoin.

598 Senach m. Cail ar slicht Aililla[a].

[a]*add* m. Echach M*uigmedoin* La.

599 Fidgoll m. Cail[a] 7 Dreannan[b] m. Cail 7 Colman m. Cail 7 Fearadach m. Cail[c] [d]ar slicht Aililla uile doib[d].

[a]*add* mar in cetna La. [b]Drenon La. [c]*add* 7 Faebur m. Cail La. [d–d]*om.* La.

600 Brecan (m.) Airne ar slicht Cais m. Conaill Eachluaith.

601 Cuana Achaid Bernchon[a] m. Odran ar slicht Imchada m. Colla Da[b] Crich.

[a]Bertchon La. [b]Fo La.

602 Sarnad ingen Aeda Gabalḟada ar slicht [a]Echach m.[a] Nathi[b].

[a–a]*om.* La. [b]Dathi m. Fiachrach La.

603 Cumain Cadain m. Crundchon ar slicht Chais m. Conaill Echluaith.

604 Epscop Fergusa m. Colman Bic m. Diarmada.

605 Dachonna m. Tigernaich ar slicht Fergusa m.[a] Conaill Gulban.

[a]*above line*; *scribe first wrote* ar slicht *which he then deleted.*

606 Mac Tail Chilli Cuilind ar slicht Dairi Barraig m. Cathair[a].

[a]*add* Moir La.

607 Caindeach m. Aeda ar slicht Ḟidc*uir*i m. [a]Doilbri do sil[a] Fergosa m. [b]Rosa Ruaid[b].

[a–a]*om.* La. [b–b]Roith La.

608 Modichu m. Aimirgin ar slicht [a]Cairpri Airdchind[a] m. Briain m. Echach Muidmedoin.

[a–a]Airdchind .i. Cairbri La.

609 Findachta m. Tomaltaich m. Murgaili m. Indrechtaich m. Muireadaich Muillethain rig Conacht, 7 se arna naemad, 7 is uada ita Baile Ḟindachta, 7 is [e] thuc dimblad ar rignaib Conacht trena mirbail.

610 Edain ingen Luigni ar slicht Duach Galaig m. Briain.

611 Tigernan Oirig Locha Con ar slicht Amalgaid m. Fiach*rach*.

612 Colman m. Aengusa m. Nadfraich, .i. Colman m. Dairi[a].

[a]Dairine La.

613 Ciaran m. Beoain ar slicht Reo Doirchi m. Thigermais m. Ḟollaig.

614 Ceithri meic Cailcharna .i. Fechin 7 Murchon[a] 7 [b]Diarmaid 7 *Con*aille[bc] .i. a nDruim na nAingeal [d]ar slicht Taidc m. Cein[d].

[a]Murchad La. [b—b]*reversed* La. [c]aille La. [d—d]*om.* La.

615 Lurach m. Cuanach ar slicht Fiachra[a] Tort m. Colla Uais.

[a]Fiachrach La.

616 Runach[a] m. Muireadaig [b]ar slicht[b] Eogain m. Neill.

[a]Ruanach La. [b—b]m. La.

617 Aedan m. Colman ar slicht Ḟiachra Casan m. Colla Da Crich.

[a]Fo La.

618 Seacht n-ingena Dallbronaich do Dal Chonchobair lasna Desib Muman.

619 Mac Liag ar slicht Mucada Ruaid m. Colla Uais.

620 Loman[a] m. Earnain[b] ar slicht Ḟeargusa m. Conaill Gulban

[a]*corrected beneath line from* Lonan Lc, Lonan La. [b]Earamain La.

621 Conall m.[a] Maine Cail ar slicht[b] Bogaine m. Conaill Gulban.

[a]*added above line* Lc. [b]*add* Cathair m. La.

622 Croine[a] ingen Diarmada ar slicht[b] [c]Bogaine chedna[c].

[a]Corone La. [b]*add* Melge m. La. [c—c]Bogaine m. Conaill m. Neill La.

623 [a]Finan m. Pibain ar slicht Fergusa m. Conaill Gulban[a].

[a—a]*only in* La.

624 Caithleand[a] m. Aeda Damain ar slicht Chuirc m. Lui[g]d*ech*.

[a]Cathlenn La.

625 Eithne ingen Dima[a] ar slicht Dairi Barraich m. Cathair[b].

[a]*add* m. Nae La. [b]*add* Moir La.

626 Condachtach m. Mael Odrain[a] ar slicht Oengusa m. Conaill Gulban.

[a]Dogair La.

627 Dachonda[a] ar slicht Illaind m. Eogain m. Neill.

[a]*add* Essa La.

628 Epscop Cormac m. Eachach ar slicht [a]an Illaind chedna[a].

[a—a]Illaind m. Eogain m. Neill La.

629 Damongoc m. Sarain ar slicht Muireadaich m. Eogain.

630 Cainder ingen [a]Eogain — [b]*no* Feidlimid[ab] — ar slicht Dallain m. Eogain[c].

[a—a]Feidlimti La. [b—b]*above line* Lc. [c]*add* m. Neill La.

631 Condad[a] 7 Odba[b] da ingin Cholmain ar slicht Laegaire[c] m. Neill Noigiallaig[d].

[a]Conda La. [b]Obda La. [c]Enna m. Laegairi La. [d]*om.* La.

632 Rignach 7 Cuman[a] 7 Troain[b] *tri* hingena Aeda ar slicht Maine m. Neill.

[a]Coman La. [b]Treaan La; *read* Crón.

633 Eochaid m. Aililla, .i. Dallan Forgaill, ar slicht Colla Uais.

634 Aithgrind m. Dail ar slicht Colla M*in*d[a] [b]a Mudorn[b].

[a]Mbenn La. [b—b]*om.* La.

635 Cruimthir Ciara[n][a] m. Dail ar slicht Colla M*in*d[b].

[a]Ciana La. [b]Mbend La.

636 Curcach in[gen] Dail ar slicht Colla Meand m. Eachach Doimlen.

637 Meadran m. Meancra ar slicht Conaire Chaim[a].

[a]*om.* La.

638 Brid 7 Corb 7 Lasair 7 Lemain ar slicht Cairpre Rigota[a].

[a]Rigḟota m. Conairi La.

639 Findlod[a] m. Dimain do Dail Fiatach Find[b].

[a]Findlug La. [b]*om.* La.

640 Aengus m. Muici, re n-abar in[a] Muicin, ar slicht Conla m. Bresail Bric o buil*et*[b] Osraide.

[a]*om.* La. [b]fuilit La.

641 Epscop Eichen[a] m. Maine ar slicht Breasail Bricc.

[a]Eitchen La.

642 Seacht meic Luguda .i. Garban 7[a] Baedan 7[a] Laisrend[b] 7[a] Senchada[c] 7 Ruadan[d] 7 Cronan, .i.[e] Mochua, ar slicht Ailill*a* Cetaich m. Cathair Mair.

[a]*om.* La. [b]Lasrean La, *add* Baedan La. [c]Senchan La. [d]Ruadna La. [e]*add* ainm baisti La.

643 Modimoc[a] Glindi Uisen ar slicht Cathair Moir.

[a]Modimo La.

644 Goll Cluana Ferta ar slicht Cathair Moir cetna[a].

[a]*om.* La.

645 Maedog Cluana Moir m. Eogain ar slicht Cathair fos.

646 Naoile[a] m. Aengusa ar slicht Cuirc m. [b]Aengusa *no*[b] Luigdeach.

[a]Naaili La. [b—b]*om.* La.

647 Fraechnad ingen Dimain ar slicht Moda[a] Cuirp m. Cormaic Cais[b].

[a]Moga La. [b]*add* m. Ailella Oluim La.

648 Beneoil m. Sesnain[a] ar slicht Oililla Olaim.

[a]Sesgnain *with deletion mark under* g? La.

649 Oengos [m.][a] Oiblean m. Nadfraich[b] ar slicht Chaelbaid m. C*ru*i*nn*[c].

[a]m. La. [b]Fidra La. [c]*add* Badraige La.

650 Mac Liag Thiri[a] Da Glas [b]ar slicht Chearnaich m. Colla Uais[b].

[a]*om.* La. [b—b]m. Cernaig ar slicht Colla Uais La.

651 Eithni ingen Dima m. Nai [a]di Corbraide Ḟanad[a] mathair Colaim Chilli [b]m. Feidlimid[b].

[a—a]*om.* La. [b—b]*om.* La.

652 Rim ingen Ḟiachna [a]m. Fiachrach[a] Gairine m. Duach Iarlaithi m. Maine m. Cairbre m. Cuirc m. Luigdeach mathair Chumain[b] m. Ḟiachna 7 Comdain[c] 7 Crimthaind Chualand m. Aeda Cirr rig Laigen 7 Chuana m. Cailchine,[d] .i. laech Liathmaine, 7 Breacan Dairindsi.

[a—a]*om.* La. [b]*add* Fota La. [c]*add* m. Da Cerda 7 Guairi m. Colmain La. [d]Cairchene La.

653 Seacht meic[a] Dubthaig *ui* Lugair .i. Ecsin, Fear Corb, Comgall, Treana, Gabran[b], Fachtna[c], Eor[d].

[a]*above line* Lc. [b]Gobran La. [c]Fiachna La. [d]Eeir La.

654 Sucaid ainm baisdi Padraic, Codraidi a ainm a ndairsine, Mogom*ius* a ainm aca foglaim, Patricius a ainm ac Romanchaib.

655 Aengus ainm baisdi [a]Meic Nisi[a].

[a—a]Monissi La (*see note*).

656 Ingena Cormaic m. Aililla [a].i. Eithni 7 Sochar Caerthann[a] a Tulaid m. Ḟeilmeda[b].

[a—a]deitine et Dearcaerrtaind La. [b]Fedlimthi La.

57 Dachuailen[a] ainm[b] Dachuiliuin[c] 7 is inand esen 7 Cuan[d] Atha Eascrach[e] la Conachta[f].

[a]Dachua Aileoin La. [b]*add* baisti La. [c]Daculin La. [d]Cuanu La. [e]Escra La. [f]Connachtaib La.

58 Dima ainm baisdi Muru m. Deaga, [a].i. Muru[a] Eathna Moiri[b].

[a—a]*om.* La. [b]*first* i *below line* Lc.

59 Aed ainm baisdi in da Maedoc .i. [a]Maedoc Ferna Moiri[b] 7 Maedoc Cluana[ac].

[a—a]*reversed* La. [b]Moir La. [c]*add* Moiri La.

60 Fintan ainm baisde Munnu m. Tulchain

61 Crimthand ainm baisde Colaim Chilli 7 Eog*an* [a]a brathair[a].
[b]Finit dona naemaib[b].

[a—a]Eogan fos brathair Coluim Cilli La. [b—b]*om.* La (*see note*).

RECENSIO METRICA

62.1 [a]Naoimhsenchus naomh Insi Fail
d'eolchaib as toiscc a thóccbhail,
bunadh[b] gach naoim danab[c] dluigh
a[d] breith go a[e] dheala nduthaigh.

2 Ereamon, Iór, Eimher caidh[f],
tri meic Miledh [g]co morgrain[g],
uatha naoim Ealcca[h] romtha,
acht siol Luicchdech mic Íotha.

3 Milidh is Lucchaidh dona[i],
da ua Breocchain mec Bratha,
acht as e Lucchaidh ro leth
an cethramadh ard oireach.

4 Naoimh Ua cCuinn is na nDeisi,
Fotharta is Laighin leisi,
is cland Dedhadh archena[j],
is meic Eachach Muiredha.

5 Naoimh cloinne Eiriomoin soin
ni ticc eolach 'na n-acchaidh,
as naoim naomhtha re a riomh tra
[k]sliocht sain[k] Lughdech mic Iotha.

[a]*preceded by prose introduction* Brux. (= *Ir.texts* 3(1931), 40-1). [b]sloinde(a)d B(Lc). [c]darab B. [d]do B. [e]*om.* BLc. [f]ail BLc. [g—g]a hEaspain B. [h]Egla B. [i]re la B(Lc). [j]arnela B. [k—k]do sil BLc.

662.6 Naoim cloinne Rucchraidhe ruaid,
siol Ír [l]oirdirc co morbuaidh[l],
o Eimher mac Miledh uill
naoimh sil Oilella Oluim.

7 As iad sin cethrar gan feall
or geinsett[m] ardnaoimh Erend;
sloinnfetsa sin mar nach saobh
sloinnte uaisle na n-ardnaom[n].

8 Patraicc mac Calpruinn[o], ar tus,
mic Fodaidhe[p], as caomhrús[q],
mic Odis mic Cornil[r] aird
mic Liber mic Meirc morgaircc

9 Mic Oda[s] mic Oric[t] moill
[u]mic Muiricc mic Oirc luathloind
mic Leo mic Maxim aird
mic Otraig uallaigh iomgaircc

10 Mic Eris mic Pelist luinn[u]
mic Ferine[v] na bferglond
mic Briotain[w] Mail, [x]maith fir[x],
mic Fercchusa mic Neimhidh.

11 [y]Do siol an[y] Neimhidh sin tra
Cruithnigh is Brethnaigh Cluada[z],
senathair Gailian nar gann,
Fer mBolcc is Tuath De Danann.

12 [aa]As da shiol Patraicc[aa], ro fes,
dlecchar dhín a shaóirshenchus[bb];
gen gob[cc] do shiol mac[dd] Miledh ngle[ee],
leis do naomadh ar naoimne[ff].

[l—l]m. Miled co mbuaidh B(Lc). [m]cindset B. [n]*add* n(aem.s.e.n) (B)Lc. [o]Alpruind B(Lc); *later corrected to* Calpruind B. [p]Podaidi B. [q]a *added under the line after* caomh *in* Brux., caemar*us* Lc. [r]Cormuic B, Gormuith Lc. [s]Ada BLc. [t]Mu(i)ric(h) B(Lc). [u—u]m. Oiric m. Leo luathluind m. Macsím m. Otraidh aird m. Eris uallaich imgairg m. Feilisti na laech lond B(Lc). [v]Feren*uis* B, hErinis Lc. [w]Britisa B(Lc). [x—x]don muig BLc. [y—y]is do sil BLc. [z]buada Brux., Cluada BLc. [aa—aa]do sil Patraic sin B. [bb]dindsenchas BLc. [cc]go B(Lc). [dd]*om.* B. [ee]de B. [ff]naoimine Brux., *add* N(aem) (B)Lc.

[a]Sliocht Conaili Gulban Mic Neill[a]

662.13 Colaim Cille criche Cuind
mac Feidlimid, ós gach druing,
mic Ferguis an gnioma gaircc
mic Conaill Gulban glanaird[b].

14 Baoithin mac Brenainn don roinn
mic Fergussa mic Conuill;
clann da derbrathar malle
Baoithin is Colaim Cille.

15 Adhamnan[c] mac Ronain rain
mic Tinne mic Aedha ain
mic Colmain mic Sedna uill
mic Fergussa mic Conuill.

16 Dúnchad mor mac Cinn Faoladh
mic Maol Copa gan claonadh;
Maol Copa fa dercc a drech
mac Aedha mic Ainmireach.

17 Seigin, Colman is Laisre,
tri mic Ronain cen taise
mic Loairn ernbasa [d]an fuinn[d]
mic Ferccusa mic Conuill.

18 Laisren mac Feradaicch finn,
Seighin mac Fiachra barrfinn,
[e]Comman caemh[e] mac Ernain ain
ocus [f]Ailbe mac Ronain[f].
Naoim Sil [g]Luigdech os gach druing
ua[g] Fergusa mic Conuill.

19 Loman [h]Locha hUair[h] ealaicch[i],
mac sein uasal [j]Airemhain,
do shiol Flaithim let on lainn[j],
mic Fercchusa mic Conuill.

20 Faolchu mac [k]Dobrain a hÍ,
naemh uasal do siol [l]Dathí;
Dathi[l], ba rathmar a reim[k],
mac Conuill Gulban airmgeir[m].

21 Bairrfiond o Neill, naemda a rath,
mac Muiredaicch mic Eachach;
Eochaid mac Conuill[n] chliaraigh
mic Nell nertmair Noigiallaigh.

a—a *add* Brux. b BLc *insert* 28 *here*. c Adaman B, a Adamnan Lc. d—d finn B(Lc). e—e Cuma(i)n fe(i)n (B)Lc. f—f Failbe m. Pipain B. g—g Ninde(a)da . . . meic (B)Lc h—h Lacha Fuair BLc. i indnaigh B, arsin Lc. j—j Eranain m. Cespir m. Laithim luind B. k—k Dorbain co cail, m. Tinni m. Fergusain, m. Libir m. Nathi teind B. l—l Nathi, Nathi Lc. m glanseing B, m. Nell Lc. n Congail Lc.

662.22 Fland mac Maoile Duin co mbaidh
is Adlann mac Eiccneachain,
da naomh gan crobaidh re cath
do siol Ronain mic Lucchdach[o].

23 Conall mor mac Maine Chaoil,
Caolmaine mac do Chathaoir;
Cathaoir, ba coimseach ngoile,
an sechtmadh[p] mac Boghaine.

24 Croine chraibdech, rucc acca[q],
ingen dercach Diermada,
do siol Meilge, ba mor muirn,
mic Boghaine mic Conuill.

25 Fionán mac Pipain Ratha
mic Amalgadha an atha
mic Duach mic Fir an Ghosa
mic Ninnidh mic Fercchussae.

26 [r]Rodaighe is Manchán gan cain
dá mhac Failbe mic Faolain;
Modoftha mac Enain uill
mic Boghaine mic Conuill[r].

27 [s]Connachtach craibdech, na ceil,
fa mac sein do Maol Dhroigin
do siol Aengusa uallaicch
mic Conuill [t]co ccaommbuadaib[st].

28 [u]Odhran Ía an chrabaidh chruaidh
mac Aingheine co morbuaidh
mic Boghaine an gaisccidh géir
mic Conuill Gulban glainfeil[uv].

29 [w]Molucchach mac Luindeoin[w] lain
is Maol Bricchde mac Tornain,
do siol Luicchdheach [x]iad go mbaidh
's Malachias an p[r]iomfháidh[x].

30 [a]Aitchett an Coimdhe do shior
naoimh sleachta Conaill dár ndíon,
o Cholaim na ngniomradh n-ard
gusan Maol ro char Bernard[a].

| [a—a]*add* Brux.| [o]Luigdech Lc. [p]seacht B. [q]ega B(Lc). [r—r]Manchan m. Failbe co mbloidh, do sil Aimgeni uasail, Aingen co slog mairisloind, m. Bogune m. Conaill B(Lc). [s—s]*precedes* 26 BLc. [t—t]caim chathbuadhaigh B, co cathbuadaib Lc. [u—u]*follows* 13 BLc. [v]m. Neill B. [w—w]Molug(u)a m. Lonain (B)Lc. [x—x]na blaigi, m. sen luigneach (buidnech Lc) Boghuine B(Lc). Brux's *originally similar reading was changed by Cúchoigríche Ó Cléirigh.*

[a]Enda Mac Néill[a]

662.31 Nindidh mac Ferguis co rath,
et Baoithin mac Cuanach
mic Aenghois[b] mic Enda fel,
sósar cloinne [c]nair nertNeill[c].

32 [a]Cuanna mac Miodhuirn amuicch,
co ngaibh Muigh Lacha i mBrecchaibh,
do siol Enda fel gan oil,
mac sein Neill nair mic Eochaid[a].

[a—a]*add* Brux. [b]Condmaig B(Lc). [c—c]nertmair Neill B.

[a]Sliocht Éocchain Mic Neill[a]

33 Dachonna is Lucchaidh go rath,
epscop Corbmac mac Eachdach,
tri mic enathar [b]go mbail[b]
do síol Iollaind mic Eocchain.

34 Cele Crist mac Eachach Cais
is Comgall Boithe Conais,
da derbrathair [c]dar dual gail[c]
do siol Chorbmaic meic Eogain.

35 Dachuailen mac Guaire gloin,
[d]Máel Ruba[d] mac Ealganaicch[e],
[f]combraithre oile iad soin[f]
do siol Binnigh mic Eogain.

36 Epscop Maine[g] mac Eichin
mac Eoghuin, dedla an deithbir[h],
Aedhan mac Ferrcchusa[i] gloin
mic Eichin fós mic Eogain.

37 [a]Bécan caomh mac Lucchdach lain,
Colmán espoc mac Ruadhain,
is epscop Brecain co mblaidh
do ṡiol Ferghais mic Eocchain[a].

38 Epscop Fiachna, fial a blaidh,
mac Fergussa[j] mic Eocchain,
Ruanach[k] mac Muiredaig moill
mic Eocchain mic Nell nertgloinn[l].

[a—a]*add* Brux. [b—b]gan ail B(Lc). [c—c]sin gan ail B(Lc). [d—d]is Mael Ruba B. [e]Elgaid B. [f—f](da der)brathair ele sin B(Lc). [g]*added between columns* Lc. [h]degfir B. [i]Acngusa BLc. [j]Aengusa B. [k]Ruach BLc. [l]nertmuill B.

662.39 [a]Mura mac Feradaig feil
mic Ronain rain don rigfreimh
mic Muiredaicch fa mor gail
mic Eocchain mic Nell nertmair[a].

40 [m]Domnocc naom[m] mac Sarain sain
mic Ticchernn mic Muiredaicch;
Earnan[n] mac Colmain chnedaicch
mic Moain[o] mic Muiredhaicch.

41 Sinell mac Ticchernaigh[p] trein,
mac d'Oilill[q] mac Eocchain feil,
is epscop Aengusa iar soin
mac Oilill uais[r] mic Eocchain.

42 Fionntan, Maeldubh fa maith mein,
[s]bád mic sein[s] Aeda Finnleith,
do siol Muirchertaigh[t] don muicch
mic Muiredhaicch mic Eocchain.

43 Féme ingen Chairill chain
is Daigh [u]deigcherd a brathair[u],
da bfiarfaighter can doib soin,
do siol Dallain mic Eocchain.

44 Naoimh Eocchain is Conuill chaoimh
ailim-si iad ar entaoiph;
a nguidhe as caomna ar gach [v]cair
an cuire niamdha naomhsoin[v].

[[a—a]*add* Brux.] [m—m]Damongoc BLc. [n]Endai*n* B. [o]Ronain BLc. [p]Tigernain BLc. [q]AilΓ B. [r]fos BLc. [s—s]mic siden BLc. [t]Muircherta B. [u—u]a derbrathair B. [v—v]cain, na cuiri naemdha naemain BLc *add* N(aem) (B)Lc.

[a]Sliocht Laeghaire Mic Neill[a]

45 Beoan, Ossan[b], Cassan coir[c]
ocus Ricchell [d]gan eccoir[d],
clann[e] Athracht[f] mic Aedha ain,
mic sein[g] Liubair mic Dallain.

46 Cainder inghen Faolain ain
mic Liubair fos mic Dallain;
Condath[h] ocus Odhba án,
da ingen sin do Cholman.

[a—a]*add* Brux. [b]Assan BLc. [c]triur B. [d—d]a nderbsiur B, nirb ecoir Lc. [e]*om.* B. [f]Artraig B(Lc). [g]se(i)g B(Lc). [h]Condnat B.

662.47 [i]Colman mac Enda enghaicch[i]
mic Laegaire [j]a laechTemraigh[j]
[k]mic Néll Noigiallaigh nertmair,
saoirghiallaigh, feil, oirbertaigh[k].

48 Iolladan mac Eachdach uir
is Feirgil[l] mac Maoile Duin,
epscop Ronain, dreimne tor,
mac Fiangalaicch mic Fianchon[m].
[n]Do siol an Énda chedna
mic Laegaire laoichdedla[n].

49 Conall mac Fiachna [o]fa dhail[o]
is Aedh Caol[p] mac Feradaicch,
do siol Enda [q]go ngne ngloin,
a scela as me do meabhraigh[q].

50 Aodh Mor mac Fercchois ier soin
ocus Oedh Becc a brathair,
Lasair a siur gan caire,
ua d'Feilim[r] mac Laogaire.

51 Foirtchern mac Fedlimid fos
mic Laogaire go laochnos,
Laocchaire neimchreidmech nar,
[s]as uadh[s] Caoinne[t] ingen Berrsáin.

52 Diarmaid, Copthach dom chaomna,
da mac Baedain mic Aedhae;
Aedh mac Guaire na gaile
mic Lucchach[u] mic Laocchaire.

53 [a]Colman Ruis Glanda gan cair
's Muiredhach[v] Cille hAlaicch;
Lucchaid Tire Da Chraobh dna
is Nanand Cille Toma.

54 Fionntan firnaem, fer co rath,
coicc mic oirecchda Eachach,
meic Oilill co comhland cruaidh,
siol Laocchaire go laochbuaidh[a].

55 [w]Comaigh ingen Eachach aird,
Colman, a brathair gan maircc,
mac Ailella mic Guaire
mic Lucchach na laochuaille[w].

[a—a]*add* Brux.] [i—i]m. Enna roclechtad cell B. [j—j]m. laechNell B. [k—k]*om*. B. [l]Fergal BLc. [m]Fiadhcon B(Lc). [n—n]*om. in Ir. texts* 3(1931) 48, *om*. B. [o—o]tiar thair B. [p]Caech Lc. [q—q]don edain, ni crin gega a ngenelaigh B. [r](d)de(i)lim B(Lc). [s—s]ua do B. [t]Candi B(Lc). [u]Luigdeach B. [v]Muiredhhach Brux. [w—w]*follows* 56 B.

662.56 Fuinche Garb[x], nach canad cam,
ingion chraibdhech do Chriomthann,
mac Guaire fós na [y]ngal ngrinn,
fa[z] mac do Lucchaidh[aa] lainbinn[aa].

57 [bb]Earc, nachar chlaon[bb] re cionaidh,
deirbsiur Nindidh Laimiodain
mic Eachach [cc]mic Aeda ain[cc]
mic Laecchaire [dd]go laochbaidh[dd].

58 [ee]Caireach Cluana Boirenn bind[ff]
ingean Beraigh mic Chriomhthainn,
do siol Luicchdeach an lassair,
Sccannlach inghen tSechnasaigh[ee].

59 Ronan mac Beraigh malle,
Mael Tuile mac Nochaire
[jj]is Liadain chaomh co ngloine,
do siol lanmaith Laocchaire[jj].

60 [hh]Colam Toma fa glan gle
ocus Colam caom Cuile,
do siol Laecchaire nar faemh
proicept ergna na n-ardnaom[hh].

61 [ii]Naoimh cloinne Laocchaire luinn
mic Neill mic Eachach aluinn,
a nglor rem guide gan len,
[jj]a n-uile[jj] ogh is firen[ii].

[x]garg BLc. [y—y]gaili, m. Lugdach m. Laeghairi B (*which is followed by* 55). [z]om. Lc. [aa—aa]Laegaire Lc. [bb—bb]Serc nar cuibdig B(Lc). [cc—cc]ain m. Aeda B. [dd—dd]lanaebdha B. [ee—ee]Cairec caem ingen Berraig, Scannlach ingen Muiredhaich, do sil Laegairi moir em (co leir), na da oig nairrem (na da firrem) B(Lc). [ff]*add* no buirr Brux. [gg—gg]do sil Luigdeach ba maith men, m. Laegairi m. laechNell B(Lc). [hh—hh]*add* Brux. [ii—ii]*om.* B. [jj—jj]na nuili Lc.

[a]Sliocht Conuill Chremthainne[a]

62 Garban epscob, lith gan ail,
mac Aengussa mic Ardgail
mic Conuill Chremthainn chliaraigh
mic Nell nertmair[b] Naoighiall[aigh].

63 Colman mac Luachain imne
mic Aedha Luaith mic Maine
mic Fercchusa gan gainne
mic Conuill chaoim Chremthainne.

[a—a]*add* Brux. [b]ne(a)mt(h)ruim B(Lc).

662.64 Aodh geal mac [c]Lucchdach alle,
Colmán o Ros Oilithre[c],
do siol Aeda Slaine sluinn
mic Diarmata mic Cerbuill.

[c—c]Lugaid moir min, 7 Enan m. Ernin BLc.

[a]Fiachu Mac Neill[a]

65 Epscop Aeda mac Bric bind
[b]mic Corbmaic caoim[c] mic Cremthainn[b]
mic Fiachra[d] feil [e]an fiadaigh[e],
mac sein[f] Neill Naoigiallaigh.

[a—a]*add* Brux; *first written* Fiacra: Fiachach potius *added in another hand*. [b—b]m. do Cormac Cremthainn B. [c]moir Lc. [d]Fiachach B. [e—e]miadaich B. [f]side(n) B(Lc).

[a]Maine Mac Neill[a]

66 Righnach is Cumman[b] is Croin,
tri hingena Aeda moir,
do siol Maine moir miadhaigh,
mac ele Nell Naoigiallaigh[c].

67 [d]Craobsenchus cia[d] ar nach diamair
naem cloinne Neill Naoigiallaigh,
[e]muna saobh an sliocht[e] [f]ro can[f],
ferta na naom dom naomadh[g].

[a—a]*add* Brux. [b]Coman Lc. [c]BLc *add* 90 *here*. [d—d]Craebcobinsce B. [e—e]men saer a sleachta B, ni saeb a slechta Lc. [f—f]re seal Lc. [g]*add* N(aem. s.c.) (B)Lc.

[a]Fergus Mac Eachach Moighmedhoin[a]

68 Scire chaidh[b] is Corcair chaomh[c],
da ingin Eocchain araon
mic Ferguis, [d]go rath degsoidh[d],
mic Eachach maith Muidmedhoin.

69 Ernan [e]Droma Relec rain
mac Eachach mic Eocchain ain[e]
[f]mic Oilella feil gan oil[f]
[g]mic Fercchusa is mic Eochain[g].

[a—a]*add* Brux. [b]*om.* BLc. [c]cet caem BLc. [d—d]in remraith oil B(Lc). [e—e]Cluana Reilgeach lain, m. Eogain m. Canannain B. [f—f]m. Ailill m. Fergais ain (uill) B(Lc). [g—g]m. Echach maith Maidmedhain B, m. Echach mogda in morgluind Lc.

[a]Fiachra Mac Eachach Muighmedhoin[a]

662.70 [bc]Mac Duach[c], fa diles d'Ib Cuinn,
mac Ainmire mic Conuill
mic Eoghain mic Eachach uill[d]
mic Dathi, [e]fa cruaidh comluinn[e].

71 [f]Diermuid Insi Clothrand chaoimh
mac Lugna uallaigh fiorchaoin
mic Lucchdach mic Fionnbarr feil
mic Fraich[g] mic Cathchon chlaidreidh.

72 Cathchu mac Beccchon badhaicch,
co[h] ngasraidh saoir sogradaicch,
mic Dathi mic Fiachrach[i] uill,
an ri da n-iarrta urraim[fj].

73 Collca mac Aedha[k] an gossa
is Cronan mac Aengossa,
do siol Dathi mic Fiachrach[l]
don dis [m]niamdha naoimbriathrach[m].

74 [f]Colcca is Aedh as[n] Sosar shencc,
tri meic Aeda na n-oirpell;
ba mac don Aedh Aodh eile,
slat nachar foem oirbire,

75 Mic Lucchdach mic Dathi[o] finn
mic Fiachra an gotha glebinn,
an flaith nir methach miodoil,
mic Eachach maith Muidmedoin[f].

76 Daire ingen Chathaoir cháeimh
mic Luicchdech[p] mic Sedna saeir
mic Amalgaidh ruanaidh reidh
mic Fiachra[q] uallaigh airmgeir.

77 [f]Na tri Úa Suanaig suilbir,
Cummin caemh re hathchuingidh,
drem caomhnár nar chláon gotha,
Aedhan saor i Seanbotha.

78 Triallach is Derbiledh bind
do chloinn Fiachra mar airmhim,
[r]as do siol Dathi an fuilt chlaoin
na hogha ocus na hardnaoimh[fr].

[a—a]*add* Brux. [b]B *interpolates* 80, 79 *here*. [c—c]*add in marg*. .i. Colman Lc. [d]*cain* B. [e—e]m. Fiacrach B. [f—f]*om*. B. [g]Raei*n* (or read Raei*ch*?) Lc. [h]don Lc. [i]Ḟiachra Lc. [j]morraim Lc. [k]Fir B. [l]Fiachraidh BLc. [m—m]oga oigbriathr*aig* B, naemda naembrathraig Lc. [n]s *added above line* Brux. [o]Uaiti Lc. [p]Lugdach BLc. [q]Fiacraidh B, Fiach̄ Lc. [r—r]ar slicht Dathi na sreb saer, do bi re head na ard-naem N. Lc, *add in upper marg*. Tigernan Lacha Con cain, m. Nindig m. Cairpre clain, m. Amalgaid m. Fiachra, don Gamanraid glancliachda Lc.

[a]Brian Mac Eachach Moighmedhoin[a]

662.79 [b]Barra[c] ocus Modíchu dil,
da mac uaisle Aimirgin,
do siol Cairpre mic Briain moir,
[d]ropa brathair Neill.nertchoir[d].

80 [e]Molua mac Sinill 'na thír
mic Aimirgin mic Ernin
mic Duach mic Briain buidnigh bil
[f]mic an Mhuidmedoin moirmir[bef].

81 [a]Berach o Chluain Chairpthi chruinn
mac Aimirgin mic Nemnaind
mic Fionntain feil mic Mail mais
mic Doftha is mic Aengais.

82 Fionnchú naem mac Sedna slain
mic Abra is mic Branáin
mic Doftha mic Aenghais feil
mic Erca Deircc don deigfreimh.

83 Maoldubh mac Amalgaidh uill
mic Fothadh is mic Conuill;
Conall mac Briain an miodhoil[g]
mic Eachach mir Muidmedoin[a].

84 Naoimh cloinne Eachach[h] toir tiar,
ailim-si iad ar enrian,
cubaidh doibh soinnmhe [i]re sáoi[i],
[j]ar [k]nid doinnmhe[k] na degnaeimh. N[j].

a—a*add* Brux. b—b*placed after* 69, *with* 80 *before* 79 B. cBairra B, Bairri Lc. d—dm. sen Echach Muigmedhoin B, m. Echach maith Muidmedoin Lc. e—e*om*. Lc. f—fm. Echach mogha mormir B. g*add* no an fledhoil Brux. h*om*. B. i—irosaib BLc. j—jor ní do macni na deadhnaim.N. B. k—kni doindmi Lc.

[a]Sil Na cColla[a]

85 Berchan[b] mac [c]Decclain mic Feicc[c]
mic Decchad Duirn [d]co ndeigmeid[d]
mic Rochadha[e] riogda rain
mic Colla Fo[f] Chrich comlain.

86 [a]Teccan mac Beraigh gan beim,
Damnad Sceine mac Daimhein,
do siol Rochaidh reidh don muigh
mic Colla Fo Chrich cobsaidh[a].

a—a*add* Brux. bBrecan Lc. c—cTelcha(i)n m. Be(i)c B(Lc). d—dfear gan breg B. eCrochadha B. fda Lc.

662.87 Ronan mac Sarain ier soin
mic Colgan [g]mic trenTuathail[g]
mic Felim [h]mic Eichin uill[h]
[i]mic Feicc mic Colla chlethchuirr[i].

88 Becan is Cairnech[j] gan cradh
da derbrathair do Ronan;
mathair an trir occhda uill
Be Bona ingen Louirn[k].

89 Loman mac Dallain amne
mic Bresail moir mic Maine
mic Domnaill mic Iomchaid aird
mic Colla Da[l] Chrioch chathgaircc.

90 [m]Becc [n]mac De mic Gnoe mic Mair[n]
mic Luicchdeach luind mic Dallain
mic Bresail mic Maine Moir
[o]o'ttád Uí Maine an mhiodhoil[m o].

91 Maicchneann ocus Tua tren,
Cobthach araén is Libren,
do siol Colla Fo Chrich chais
ceithre mic Aedha ernbais[p].

92 Baedan is Furadhran fial
da mac [q]Colgan gan dimiadh[q],
do siol Colla Fo[r] Chrich chruaidh
don dis naemhda co nertbuaidh.

93 [a]Telle mac Seicchin sluacchaig
mic Colccan mic caemhThuathail,
mac derbrathar e gan cradh
d'Furadran is do Baodan[a].

94 Maol Doid mac Fingin an aicch
ocus Fiachra mac Colmain,
do siol Colla Da[s] Chrioch choir[t]
do reir eolach[u] ni heccóir.

95 Muiredach, Fercchus [v]fa hócc[v],
Brucchach ocus Mochaemócc,
ceithre mic Edna romthá
do siol an Cholla chedna.

|[a—a]*add* Brux.| [g—g]is m. Tuathail B. [h—h]Echen gan go B. [i—i]m. Fiacrach ism. Collo B. [j]Caireach B. [k]Lauirn Lc. [l]mo B. [m—m]*placed after* 66 BLc. [n—n]deag m. Danai m. Nair B(Lc). [o—o]m. Nell ba rig da nert loiḡ B, m. Neill Naigiallaig nertchoir Lc. [p]ardmais B. [q—q](Ma)enan co mormiad (B)Lc. [r]mo B, da Lc. [s]fa B, fo Lc. [t]doib B. [u]*om.* B(*with addition above line in later hand*). [v—v]cofog B, fanot Lc.

662.96 [a]Do chloinn an Edna gan ail
Durach nar thadhaill cionaidh,
is Curcach chaemh nar choirteach
ocus Ness an urnaigtheach[a].

97 [w]Derfhraeich [x]ingen Eachach uíll,
[y]Enda Airdne[y] mac Conuill,
Flann Feabla[z] mac Scandlain chain
[aa]do síol Cholla co ccathgail[aa].

98 [a]Constans mac Fulasccaig feil,
Adhnach mac Eirc nar aiccmeil,
do siol Cholla Uais gan cair,
rob' airdri ar Erinn iathgloin[a].

99 Guaire Mor mac Colmáin chrin
is Guaire Becc [bb]mac Laisrin[bb],
da naom nar throma 'na ttoigh
do siol Cholla Uais adhboil[cc].

100 [a]Baeghlach ailithir imne,
Dechoimed[dd] caemh mac Mainc,
Dercharthainn ingen Enda,
do siol Cholla airmdedlae[a].

101 Colman mac Aodha in nArd Bo,
Maedocc mac Sedna ni go,
da naemh sin do chlos co caidh
do siol [ee]an Cholla chomlain[ee].

102 Mac Liacc is Modichu dil
da mac Cernuicch cuirp chnisghil,
[ff]is Colman mac Eocchain gloin[ff]
do siol Cholla[gg] Uais adhbail[hh].

103 Lurach mac Cuanach 'na chill
ocus Trea ingen Carthind[ii],
o Cholla Uais do fedar,
as uadha do geinettar.

104 Ticchernach[jj] mac Nindidh naoi,
Conamail mac Failbe faoi,
da naom sin dochuas[kk] do chach
o Cholla Uais gan anbfath.

|[a—a]*add* Brux.| [w—w]*precedes* 96 BLc. [x]Dearbraich B(Lc). [y—y]7 Eanna BLc. [z]Faebla B. [aa—aa]7 Colman m. Eogain BLc. [bb—bb]liargin B, m. Lairin Lc. [cc]angbaidh B. [dd]*corrected in marg. to* Deochain Aedh Brux. [ee—ee]Colla Uais imlain B, m. Colla imlain Lc. [ff—ff]da naem sin do clos gan chair B(Lc). [gg]*om.* B. [hh]uasail B. [ii]Cremthainn B. [jj]Tigernan BLc. [kk]adcuas BLc.

662.105 [ll]Eochaid mac Colla[ll] os cech druing,
dar chomainm Dallan Forguill,
mic Eirc mic Muiredaig min
mic Colla Uais [mm]gan fairbrigh[mm].

106 Aithgen, cruimther Ciaran caoin,
Curcach a siur ingen Daoil,
Colla Mend cruaid na goile
uaidh[nn] an triar tend[oo] tocchaide.

107 Naoim Ua cCuinn cuiret[pp] rem les,
ro fodhlas iad(h) co dileas
les m'anma slicche[qq] nach saobh
[rr]sirrett formna[rr] na ffiornaemh. Noeimh.

[ll—ll]Eocho m. Alla B(Lc). [mm—mm]fa hairdrig B(Lc) [nn](is) uada (B)Lc. [oo]*om.* B. [pp]cuiri B(Lc). [qq]a sligi B. [rr—rr]finne fagla B(Lc).

[a]Sil Eachach Finn Fuath nAirt[a]

108 Bricchitt ingen Dupthaigh duinn
mic Dreimhre[b] mic Bresail buirr
mic Dein mic Connla mic Airt
mic Cairpri Niadh mic Corbmaic,

109 Mic Aengois moir, miadh ngart,
mic Eachach Finn Fuath le hArt
mic Feidlimidh Rechtmair rain
mic Thuathail Techtmair thiucchái r.

110 Fionntain Cluana hEidhniuch uill
mac Gairb[c] mic Corcráin chlethchuirr[d],
[e]acc Bresal mac Aenghois tricc[f]
comraices [g]se re[g] Bricchitt[e].

111 [h]Mobi Clairenach gan chain,
darb' ainm Berchan mac Beoain[h],
acc Art Cirb a ccairdes riamh,
ocus Bricchit ar einrian.

112 [i]Decclan Airde Moir amuicch,
Colman mac Eirc a brathair[i],
comraiccit re Bricchit mbain
acc Art Cirb, nochan eccoir.

113 [a]Aedhan mac Lucchair malle
is Enan Droma Raithe
is Feichin Fabair co mbla,
do siol[j] an Airt Chirb chedna[a].

[a—a]*add* Brux. [b]Emri B, Dremne Lc. [c]Garbain B. [d]cuirr B. [e—e]m. Eachach m. Breasail bain, m. Den m. Condlai comlain B. [f]tic Lc. [g—g]7 Lc. [h—h]Brecan m. Bocain brigaig, bratair Mobi Clarinig B(Lc). [i—i]Feichin Fabhair m. Cillin, Declan m. Erc naribin BLc. [j]*corrected from* sioll Brux.

662.114 Fiondbarr mac Aedha [k]gan ail[k],
[l]ocus Bairrfionn a brathair,
Mochua mac Lonain gloin,
d'aoinfreim is ingen Dubthaigh[l].

115 [a]Epscop Díma mac Senaicch,
Fionan mac Fergna fledhaicch,
do siol Eachach uathmair Finn
brathair do Chonn mac Feilim[a].

116 Sarnad ingen Eachach uill
mic Baoith mic Ninnedha[m] luinn,
do siol Eachach Finn Fuath nAirt,
or geinsett[n] ardnaoimh Fothairt.

[a—a]*add* Brux. [k—k]na ndam BLc. [l—l]is Mocua m. Lonan, ic Art Cirp condrecaid fos, re Brigit nach beg bladnos BLc. [m]Deadha B. [n]gen B.

[a]Sil Fiacha Suighde[a]

117 Mide ingen Chind Faoladh,
Brec mac Siollain[b] nar saobhadh,
do siol Fiacha Suigdhe soin,
brathair do Chonn is d'Eochaid.

118 [a]Senan mac Ernéne ain
is Earc a siur gan miobaidh,
do shiol Rossa Ruaidh alle,
robadh mac d'Fiacha Suigde[a].

119 Berchan caemh[c] mac Aedha ain
is Forandan mac Ronain,
[d]do siol Fiacha chedna chain
mic Feidlimidh reidh Rechtmair[d].

120 Epscop [e]Aedh, epscop Tinne[e],
epscop Tairchell gan time,
epscop Diarmada gan on
ocus epscop Faobarchon,

121 Epscop Mainchin, an seisedh
derbrathair doibh [f]ro feisedh[f],
[g]cia nach cluined ní ón dreim,
mic Muiredhaicch mic Foirtcheirn[g].

122 Brathair a n-athar gan feall
epscob Colman mac[h] Foirtchern[i],
do siol Fiacha Suighde soin,
or[j] naemhadh drem do noemaibh.

[a—a]*add* Brux. [b]Silain BLc. [c]mor BLc. [d—d]Lc *adds in marg. sup. an illegible note beginning* Mac Nissi (?). [e—e]Aedha m. Tinni B. [f—f]rus fesedh BLc. [g—g]cia nach luinedair co tenn, o Muiredach m. Fortrend B(Lc). [h]*om.* B. [i]Fortrend B(Lc). [j]car BLc.

662.123 Naoimh na nDeisi is naoim Fothart[k],
naoimh cloinne Cuinn co rogart[l],
[m]do síol[m] tri mbrathar mbuan mbalc[n]
Fiachaidh, Conn, Eochaid Fothart[o].

[k]Fothard BLc. [l]rogarg BLc. [m—m]sil sin BLc. [n]mblac B. [o]Fuathnart BLc, *add* co saera m'anam ar claen co robam mar gach deagnaem. Naem. B.

[a]Sil Conaire[a]

124 Naoimh cloinne Dedhad andes[b]
at[c] nesa doibh iar[d] ccairdes,
mar dogeinsett gan caire
[e]o Chairpre mac Conaire[e].

125 Grecchoir[f] Roma fa mor aoibh
mac Ormolta[g] mic Conlaoidh
mic Arda mic Dathi[h] thailc
mic Cuirc mic Cuinn mic Corbmaic,

126 Mic[i] Cuirc Duibne[j] na ndal
mic Coirpri Muscc na mordal[k]
do siol tocchaidhe co ttréoir
Conaire mic Eidirsceoil.

127 Mocheallocc mac Oiblein aird
Insi Labrainne landgaircc,
coindricc is Gregoir[f], gart ngle,
acc Corc Duibne mac Cairpre.

128 Lachtnín[l] mac Cairpri [m]iar tain[m]
[n]is Fionan[n] Camm[o] mac Maonaigh,
do siol Chairpri Musc [p]co mbla[p],
mic Conaire mic Moccha.

129 [a]Senan Insi Cathaigh chain
mac Geirrginn is mac Dubtaigh
mic Dece mic Iomchaid aird
mic Cuirb mic Luicchdech lonngaircc,

130 Mic Oilella mic Aengais saoir
mic Coirpre beoda Bascaoin,
mac do Ṡharaid ingen Chuinn
is do Chonaire an morgloinn[a].

[a—a]*add* Brux. [b]gan ches B, co des Lc. [c]as B. [d]sen BLc. [e—e]o macaib caim Conairi B. [f]Gridair BLc. [g]Gormolta B. [h]Nathi BLc. [i]mac B. [j]Duibindi BLc. [k]mordam B. [l]Lachtnan B. [m—m]ar soin B. [n—n]*added above line* Lc. [o]caem BLc. [p—p]romtha BLc.

662.131 Odhran [q]ba maicchistir[q] maith
ocus Medran mac Mioncraith[r],
da brathair tocchaidhe toir[s],
do siol Chonaire cheolaicch[t].

132 [a]Senach mac Coirill gan cradh,
d'aoinfreimh e ocus Odhran
is Éolangan co ngloine,
senoire sil cConoire.

133 Ciar Esccat, Gobnat co mbloidh
ocus Sciath ingen Meachair,
na tri naomhogha as iad soin
do shiol Chonaire chobsaidh[a].

134 Berchan Cluana Sosta[u] saoir
mac Muiredhaicch co moraoibh[v],
o Chairpre Rigfoda[w] [x]an[y] ral
o bfuilit oiricch Alban[x].

135 Brigh [z]is Corb[z], Lassair, Leamain,
Sedna, Berchan mac Nemain[aa],
do siol Loairn, ricch Alban,
mic Erca na mormarccadh.

136 [bb]Colman Insi meic Erca
brathair Loairn [cc]co bferta[bb][cc],
acc Earc mac Eachach co n-agh
[dd]coindreccus ocus[ee] Berchan[dd].

137 Colman Iomrama fein fo
mac Ferccna gan iomarghó,
do Dal Riada na ngniom n-ain
do siol Chonaire chomláin.

138 [a]Caemhan Breac mac Nissi nair
combrathair craibdheach Colmain,
dá ionnúa iad gan meabail
do siol Eachach Muinremair[a].

139 [ff]Naoimh cloinde Conaire chaoimh
do airmes uile d'entaoibh,
a nguidhe ni claon an chiall,
an[gg] uile naomh ar enrian[ff].

|[a]—[a]*add* Brux.| [q]—[q]*reversed* BLc. [r]Mencraith BLc. [s]ar sin B. [t]cuanaich B. [u]Sesta B. [v]morblaid B. [w]rigad BLc. [x]—[x]co mblaid or geinset ardnaem Alban B. [y]com Lc. [z]—[z]ispoc B, iscop Lc. [aa]Nemail BLc. [bb]—[bb]Caeman brathair Loairn lain, m. Erc m. Echach co mbaid B. [cc]—[cc]m. Erca Lc. [dd]—[dd]coinaiges sene Berchan B. [ee]se re Lc. [ff]—[ff]*added after* 149 Lc, *om.* B. [gg]na Lc.

[a]Dal bFiatach[a]

662.140 Finden Maighe Bile bain
mac Coirpre uallaigh iomnáir[b],
[c]don tslocch pá[c] coimferrdha i[d] ccath,
do Dhal oirecchdha[e] Fiatach.

141 [a]Se mic Trichimh mic Feicc Find,
Eocchan, Laecchaire is Oilill,
Ross, Durthacht, Dichu gan len,
combraithre iad do Finden[a].

142 Damhangort[f] mac Eachach uill,
Iarlaithe mac Trena thruim,
dias ciallach [g]nachar thraicc treoin[g]
do Dail fFiatach na fireoin[h].

143 Do Dal bFiatach luaiter linn
[i]Molaisi mór[i] mac Cairill;
do Dal bFiatach fos fadhail[j]
Munna mor mac Feradaigh.

144 Diarmaid mac Fergail fa faidh,
Fiondlucch[k], Fionntain mac Diomain,
do Dail fFiatach iad malle,
tredha ciallach co n-ainmne[l].

145 [a]Maol Cedair mac Ronain rain
is Dachumma mac Aedain,
do siol Aengois Finn doib soin
mic Fercchus(a) Duibdedaicch[a].

146 [m]Cummain ingen Aillen gloin,
Fachtna firen mac Bronoicch,
o Ros mac Earca gan brath,
do Dal firbrethach Fiatach[m].

147 Samthann Cluana Bronaicch bain
ingen duthrachtach[n] Diamrain[o]
mic Ferdomain an óil[p] mir
mic Diochon moir mic Trichim.

148 Dabeoocc Glinne Geircc[q] trá
mac[r] Luainim mic Dibroga
mic Tola[s] mic Dorblais[t] dil
mic Díchon fos mic Trichim.

[a–a]*add* Brux. [b]imlain BLc. [c–c]dan daim is B. [d]*added above line* B, *om.* Lc. [e]aireadga B, oired Lc. [f]Domangort BLc. [g–g]nar craidh re cin B. [h]primfir B. [i–i]Damalaisi B(Lc). [j]fagaib B. [k]*followed by a hole cut in the page* Brux. [l]na(i)ne (B)Lc. [m–m]Do Dal Fiatach armotha, Fachtna Rois o M. Erca, Epscop Ibair m. Lugna, do sil Deadhadh dedurna B(Lc). [n]duthrachtaig B. [o]Di(ar)rain B(Lc); *with* di *above line* B. [p]oili B. [q]Glearg B. [r]mic Brux. [s]Dala B, Thala Lc. [t]Dirblois B(Lc).

662.149 Naoim sin Dail fFiatach gan feall,
Corc Duibne is Corcc[u] Baisceann,
[v]is Dal Riada[w] co rathaibh,
Fiacha[x] as é a senathair[vy].

[u]Corco BLc. [v—v]o Chonairi nocho claen, ni donaidi gach degnaem. N. B. [w]Iatach Lc. [x]Dedad Lc. [y]139 *placed here* Lc.

[a]Laicchin[a]

150 Naoimh Laicchen o Labraidh lan,
'na ndiaicch so as ord a n-iomradh,
mar do siolsat[b], línibh lá,
o Lucchaid is o Chonnla.

151 Lucchaid is Connla gan cradh
da mac do Breasal Brecnar,
Osraighe o Chonnla na ccnedh,
Lucchaid senathair Laicchen.

152 Ciaran Saicchre an [c]asdair,
ced naomh diobh ro chreidesdair,
mac Luccne ba lomda gail
do siol Connla mic Bresail[c].

153 [d]Aengus mac Mucaidh ba min,
dana[e] hainm [f]aniu Mainchin[f],
do siol Chonnla [g]co ngloine
or chin forccla[g] Osraighe[d].

154 [a]Maol Anfaid mac Gabrain gloin
congaibh i cCill Mael Anfaidh,
is rob abb Dairinsi dna,
do siol Nuadat mic Connla[a].

155 Caeimgin mac Caemhlogha [h]gan cair,
Caemhan Enaigh a brathair,
is epscop Eitchen gan oil,
do siol Mesin Chorb chobsaidh[h].

156 Epscop Eocchain, luaiter libh,
[i]o Ard Sratha co sruithiph[i],
do siol Mesin Chorp gan crad,
d'eiccsip as ord a n-iomradh.

[a—a]*add* Brux. [b]silad BLc. [c—c]craidi glain, do cret ar tus do Laig*in*, m. Luigne m. Rumaind Duach, m. Conaill m. Cairpre cruach B, *add* m. Buain m. Dimbuain co mblaid, m. Echach m. Amalgaidh, m. Laegairi Birn Buadhaid, m. Aengusa ilbuadhaich B. [d—d]*om.* B. [e]danad Lc. [f—f]annud Munchin Lc. [g—g]cen chairi, do criochorba Lc. [h—h]amne, Epscop Echin m. Maine, do sil Mesin Corb cen chair, iarmo Lug*dach* m. Bresail B(Lc). [i—i]m. Erc ⁊ m. Caindigh BLc.

662.157 Condlaedh[j] caom[k] fo cerd co mbloidh
mac Corbmaic, epscop uasoil,
do síol Mesin Chuirb [l]chermna,
mac sein Con Chorb choimhferrda[l].

158 [a]Craob ocus Lassair is Fionn,
ingena Eirc na moirdiond,
do siol Mesin Chuirb gan cair
d'espucc Nahí mac Senaich.

159 Dacchan Inber Daoile duibh
's Fionnbarr o Chill Adhamuir,
do siol an Meisin Chuirb chaoimh
na sruithe ocus na saornaoimh[a].

160 Berchan mac Deccill[m] na ndamh
is Mosenocc[n] mac Senchain,
do siol Mesin Chuirb chedna,
brathair Niadh Chuirb chorpdedla.

161 [o]Niadh Corb mac Con Chorb bleidigh,
uaidh Cathaoir mac Feidlimidh,
daighfer or sioladh ni saobh[o]
riograidh Laicchen na n-ardnaem[p].

162 Colum[q] Tire Da Glas gloin
mac Ninnedha[r] co nertbloidh;
Mo[s] Maodhocc Feda Duin daoibh,
do siol Chriomtainn mic Chathaoir.

163 [a]Colum Cuile fa caomh rod
roba brathair do Maodhocc,
is Coinchend a shiur ba bind
do shiol Chathaoir mic Felim.

164 Sinill mac Corcrain ón chill
is Sinill sen mac Cindfinn,
coindreccaid ag Cruach dar linn
do shiol Chathaoir mic Felim.

165 Abban Muicche hArnduicch uill
is Cille hAbbain áluinn,
Daman, Duban is Senach,
Lithghen, Miach is Toimhdenach[a].

|[a—a]*add* Brux.| [j]Conlatha B, Condla Lc. [k]*om.* B. [l—l]can chair, damsa is ord da indisin B(Lc). [m]Dega BLc. [n]Motenoc BLc. [o—o]Do sil Niadad Cuirp cairid, m. Cathair m. Feidlimid, uad sen ro siladh ni saebh B(Lc). [p]*add.* N. BLc. [q]C *written large* B. [r]Muiredhaigh B(Lc). [s](i)s Mo B(Lc).

662.166 [a]Secht mic Luigind co n-ana
mic Caindigh mic Labradha
mic Corbmaic mic Con Chorb chaoimh
do siol chomramhach Chathaoir[a].

167 Secht mic Lugadha gan len
Garban, Baedan is Laisren,
Boithin[t], Senchan[u], Ruadan rán
ocus an seachtmad, Cronan.

168 Mochua ainm ele dó soin,
do Chronan uasal eccnaigh,
do siol Oilella chedaicch
mic Cathaoir co ccaeimgeccaibh[v].

169 [a]Fiacc Slebe mac Earcaid ain
mic Feicc oile co nertbhaigh
mic Daire Barraigh fa bind
mic Cathaoir Moir mic Felim[a].

170 Ticchernach mac Cairpre on chrois,
epscop caidh Cluana hEoois,
[w]nochar chrion [x]a chaidhe on chraoibh[wx],
do siol Daire[y] mic Cathaoir.

171 Diermuid mac Siabhra, [z]as e sin[z]
Modhioma[aa] Glinne hUissin,
is Goll Cluana Ferta caoin[bb]
do siol Daire[y] mic Cathaoir.

172 Molincc mac Failen gan feall,
darb ainm tocchaide Tairchealla,
ua Dedhadh iathgloin co n-aoib
do siol Fiachach mic Cathaoir.

173 [a]Felim is Mughain co muirn,
cland Oilella mic Dunluing,
Eithne is Derchairthinn trá,
cland Corbmaic mic Oilella.

174 Sodealb is Cummain ro chraitt
do chloinn Choirpre mic Corbmaic,
na se bannaema bad caoin
do siol Fiachach mic Cathaoir[a].

|[a—a]*add* Brux.| [t]Baedan BLc. [u]Senchad Lc. [v]caemchetaib Lc [w—w]neach na roibi nai misaib Lc. [x—x]caidhi in da craib B. [y]Laire B. [z—z]na sleg BLc. [aa]is Modim B, Modimmoc Lc. [bb]faid B, fain Lc.

662.175 [cc]Berchan mac Dioma ba daigh
do siol Enda Niad nertmair
mic Bresail Bélaig co n-aoiph
mic Fiachach Baic mic Cathaóir[cc].

176 [a]Bricchit ocus Soighes saor
is Temhair nar char míotaóm,
do siol Enda Niadh amuicch
mic Breasail buada Belaicch[a].

177 Caimin[dd] mac[ee] Dioma iar ndeadhail
do siol Eachach[ff] Ceinnsealaicch
mic Labraid mic Bresail [gg]bind
ua Cathaoir Uallaigh imgrind[gg].

178 [a]Finachta mac Colccan ain
is Crunnmaol coemh mac Ronain,
Seighin Gabail mac Senaicch,
do siol Enda Cheindsealaigh[a].

179 Maodhócc án[ee] mac Eocchain [hh]gloin
congaibh Cluain Moir go miorbuil[hh],
[is] Beoan mac [ii]Eirc chaoin
do siol chomramhach Cathaoir[ii].

180 Berchan mac Dioma dona[jj],
Ronan epscop mac Aedha,
do siol Maine [kk]Mail nar fill[kk]
brathair Cathaoir mic Felim[ll].

181 Naoim Laicchen sin siol Labraidh,
[mm]gurab dion iad[mm] dom anmain,
a ccrabhadh ba cath nar chle[nn],
[oo]bad rathmar[pp] is bad roighne[oo][qq].

|[a—a]*add* Brux.| [cc—cc]*preceded by* 225 BLc. [dd]Caemain Lc. [ee]*om.* BLc. [ff]Enna B. [gg—gg]baid, m. Fiachach baic m. Cathair B. [hh—hh]airi, Cluana Mor na mirbuili B(Lc). [ii—ii]Eri araen, do sil Cathair na cednaem. Naem B(Lc). [jj]romtha BLc. [kk—kk]móir nar mill B. [ll]Feidhlim BLc. [mm—mm]corba din .c. B. [nn]claen B. [oo—oo]dula fa rath na ndegnaem.N. B. [pp]rath Lc. [qq]*add* N. Lc.

[a]Siol Eachach Mic Muiredhaigh[a]

182 [b]Senan Laithricch Briuin[b] gan brath
mac Fionntain do siol Eachach,
Eochaidh mac Muiredaicch mais,
craobh ar leith chum[c] ticchernais.

[a—a]*added in later hand* Brux. [b—b]Enna labraich traig B. [c]co B.

662.183 [d]Epscop[e] Mac Cairthinn[d] [f]ba caidh[f],
Mael Ruain[g] Tamlachta mac Colmain,
is acc Fiachra an oil gan cradh
comraicces se[h] re Senan[i].

184 Colman Eala on Laind [j]gan cradh[j]
mac [k]Beoghna is[k] mic Mochta,
combrathair dhó Mac Nisi,
eolaicch acca indisi.

185 Mobi mac[l] Comgaill [m]go n-acch[m]
ocus mac Lughna, Colman,
da iondua iad ar dheala
[n]do siol Eachach[n] Muireadh[a].

186 Colman, Lasar, [o]Bogha uas druincc[o],
[p]teora hingena[p] Comgaill,
do Dail mBuain [q]iad archena[q],
do siol Eachach Muireadha.

187 Naoim sil Eremhoin nar fill
ro fodhlas iad[r] co hinnill,
tenn mo dechtadh[s] [t]doib gan tass[t]
acc nertadh[u] a[v] naoimhsenchass. NOEMHSEANCHUSS.

[d—d]Mac Nisi m. Faebraidh BLc. [e].i. Aedh *added above line* Brux. [f—f]faid B, ain Lc. [g]Ruanain B. [h]*om.* B. [i]Seanchan Lc. [j—j]rola B. [k—k]Boguine B(Lc). [l]m.m. B. [m—m]can crad B, co n-ad Lc. [n—n]doilebh̄ B. [o—o]Bogar binn B(Lc). [p—p]is teora *ingen* BLc. [q—q]inbir ena B(Lc). [r]daib *above line* B. [s]teachtad B. [t—t]mar ba des BLc. [u]ad *added above line* B. [v]na Lc.

[a]Sil Ir Mic Miled[a]

188 Findén[b] [c]cáidh mac Fionntain feil[c],
oide naémh Eirenn eissein,
do siol Oilella Tealduib[d]
mic Cealtchair[e] mic Uitheachair[f].

189 [a]Caemhan mac Tacca 'ga thigh
mic Baith ocus mic Baithgil,
do shiol Chealtchair 'ga mbui an luin,
[g]fer rob athlamh a n-iomguin[ag].

[a—a]*add* Brux. [b]Fintan B. [c—c]m. Finnlogha fen B(Lc). [d]Tech(t)mair toir B(Lc); Temair *in* B *before correction.* [e]Celtair B. [f]Cuitheochair BLc; Celtcair *in marg.* Brux. [g—g]m. Cealtcair m. Uithecair *before correction* Brux. (Cf. 188d).

[a]Sil Fergusa Mic Rosa[a]

662.190 Mochuarocc [b]nachar char crodh[b],
Ailbe Imleach mac Olchon,
do siol Fir Thlachtga trén dóibh[c]
[d]mic Fercchusa mic fionnRoigh[d].

191 [a]Scuithin Slebe Maircce amuicch
mac Setna is mic Trebthuicch,
do siol Ḟir Thlachtgha malle
do Scuithin ocus d'Ailbe[a].

192 Epscop Erc mac Deccha um dail,
[e]Brenainn Biorra mac Nemain[e],
do siol Chairbre[f] Uluim doibh
mic Fercchussa [g]mic morRoicch[g].

193 [a]Caemhan o Ard Lethain leir
mac[h] Taláin aobda airmgeir,
do shiol Dubthaigh os gach druing
'ga ccomraicsiomh fri Brenainn.

194 Deruisi, Sinech, Criadha,
tri hógha nar ainiardha,
clann Earnain mic Colmain chain
do siol diograisech Dubthaigh[a].

195 Brenainn mac Fionnloga[i] [j]os druing[j]
is Mochuda mac Fionndaill,
dias naemda go ngne ngossa
do siol Chéir mic Fercchusa.

196 Mochuille mac Dichuill dil,
Molacca mac Duibh Dlighidh,
is[k] Caollaind co cceill ngosa
[...][l] mic Ferghossa.

197 Ciaran mac Beoain co n-aoib,
risa n-abar[m] Mac an tSaoir,
eolaigh ro tuicc mar ata
do siol Chuirc mic Fergusa.

198 Caindech mac Luighticch[n] Lemna
[o]mic Lucchaidh alaind Emhna,
do shiol[o] Fercchus[a] mic Roigh
or geinsett naoimh co nertchóir.

a—a*add* Brux. b—bnach coir da(ch) rad B(Lc). cduibh *before correction* Brux, tair B, do Lc. d—dm. Celt*chair* m. Cuitheochair B, m. Celtchair ni himargo Lc. e—eBrenaith Bairra m. Memain B. fCuirbre *before correction* Brux. g—gmoir m. Roig BLc. hmic Brux. i*om.* B. j—jfind BLc. kiss *before correction* Brux. l*blank in* Brux., ar slicht Cer B, do cloind Cer Lc. mmabar B. nLugdaich B, Lugaid Lc. o—odo sil imchail oigh Emna, mac sen B(Lc).

62.199 Iarlaithe [p]mac Loccha[p] lain[q]
is Mochoemhocc mac Beoain,
da naem gan formad abus
o Chonmac ba mac[r] d'Fergus.

200 Caillin mac Mochta nir mer
is Ferccna[s] mac ind filedh,
do siol Chonmhaic gan chaire
mic Fercchais ua Rudruide.

[200[b]] [a][t]Felic deochain roba daigh
is cruimther Fraoch mac Carthaigh,
do siol Chonmaic chaoim na ccath
mac do Meidb ingen Eachach[t].

201 Malan is Curnan gan cradh,
Cronan caomh ocus Baedan,
ceithre mic Sinill iad soin
mic Nadfraich is mic Fiachaid,

202 Mic Alla mic Conmaic glais
mic Fergusa reidh rendmais;
Duilech mac Amalgaidh áin,
mic Sinill chedna chomlain[a].

[a—a *add* Brux.] p—p *above line* Lc. [q]imlain BLc. [r]mach Brux. [s]*corrected from* Ferccus Brux. t—t *added in marg. in hand which wrote notes* Brux.

[a]Sil Laoighsigh Mic Conuill[a]

203 Senach[b] sen ocus Colman,
da mac Comgaill fa comlan,
do siol Laoigsicch[c], lathar ndil,
mic Conuill mic Aimirgin.

204 [a]Oenda ua Laoigsi na lend
mac[d] Beraicch bailc na mbéimend,
Baoithin mac Fiondaigh 'ga thigh,
do siol Luccach mic Laoigsicch[a].

a—a *add* Brux. [b]Senchan BLc. [c]Lugaid B, Lugach Lc. [d]mic Brux.

[a]Sil Iareil Mic Conuill[a]

205 Comgall Bennchair[b] mac Sedna
ar ar[c] cheist uaman ecca,
[d]ba firén ar[d] nach frith faill,
do siol Ireil mic Conuill.

a—a *add* Brux. [b]Bendch B. [c]nar BLc. d—d firrem [Ulad] BLc.

662.206 [a]Ulltan Aird Brecain co mblaidh
mac[e] Ronain is mac[e] Fionntain,
do siol Ireil glunmair gloin
mic Conaill chomhnairt chubaidh[a].

207 Molaise Daimhin[se][f] de
mac[g] Nadfraoich co ffaobraighe[h],
[i]do siol Ireil feil co mbla[i]
's Moninne ingen Mochta[j].

208 Ternocc mac Ciarocc[k] co rath
ocus Buaidhbeo[l] mac Eachach,
[m]Commán ua Bruighde gan col[m],
ocus Comman mac Faolchon.

209 [a]Bricchit ingen Aedha féil
is Fuinche ingen Bleidhein,
Breacan mac Sarain slain
is Mocholmocc mac Corcrain.

210 Trian mac Deide, fer uas dreim,
epscop Cairpre mac Deccill,
do siol Ireil glondaigh gloin
mic Conaill chopsaid Chernoicch[a].

211 Da mac Cuanain[n], dingnaib dal,
Muirdebair[o] is Farannan;
Moluocc mac Luchta lain[p]
ocus Cathan mac Mandtain[q].

212 Aengus mac Aengobann gloin,
Glunshalach mac Costamail[r],
[s]Conall mac Aeda na ndail
as e congaibh Cluain Dallain[s].

213 Epscop Iubair mac Lughna
[t]mic Cuirc mic Duirb[t] deghhurghna
mic Cairpre mic Neill gloingle
do síol Fiacha[u] Aruidhe.

[[a—a]*add* Brux.] [e]mic Brux. [f]Daimindsi B(Lc). [g]mic Brux, *bis* B. [h]fae *above line* B. [i—i]Cruimthir Fraech m. Cortaich caimh B(Lc). [j]Eachach no Mochta Brux., Luc(c)ain (B)Lc. [k]Ciair B, Iaeir Lc. [l]Beobeo B. [m—m]Epscop Mac Carthaind con col B(Lc). [n]Cuainin BLc. [o]Muirdelbair Brux., Muirdebur B(Lc). [p]imlain B, imlaim Lc. [q]Madain BLc. [r]Astamail BLc. [s—s]do sil Ire(i)l Glunmair ghil, m. Conaill m. Aimirgin B(Lc). [t—t]m. Erc m. Cuirb B(Lc). [u]Fiachach B.

662.214 [v]Athracht ingen tSarain trein
mic Caelbaid mic Cruinn co cceill,
dathglan [w]an gniomh a guide[w],
do siol rathmar Rudhruide[vx].

215 Fursa[y] [z]Craibdeach fa fer caidh
is Manchan Liath mac Sioláin,
epscop Luachain co ngloine,
do siol riocchda Rudraighe[z].

216 [a]Colman mac Luachain nar luind
is Colman Muilind mac Conuill,
eapscop Mac Erca co ccill,
do siol Sencha mic Oilill.

217 Naoim cloinne Rudhraighe reidh,
siol Ír oirdirc go ndeigreimh,
guid lem co narbam claon,
an cuire craibhdheach caomnaomh. N[a].

|[a—a]*add* Brux.| [v—v]*om.* B. [w—w]a gnim re guidi Lc. [x]*add* Naim sil Irel uili sin, m. Conaill m. Aimirgin, flaitheas anma do gach aen, maitheas edma na n-ardnaem. Naem B(Lc). [y]*written large* B, *begins new section* Lc. [z—z]m. Fintain cuirp chaim, do sil Lugdach Laga in laich, mac sen Eogain Taidhlig tend, brathair Aililla Ul*oim* B(Lc).

[a]Sil Eimir

218 Colman[b] mac Leinine lain
is Motheimneocc mac Cerbain,
do siol da brathar iad soin,
Oilill Olom is Lucchoidh[a].

219 Becan mac [c]Cula an[c] chuil chais,
Ruadhan Lothra mac Fergais,
do siol Eocchain Moir [d]os druing
mic Saidbe is Oilill Oluim[d].

220 Naili mac Aengois na n-each,
[e]ua do Chorc mor mac[e] Luigdeach
mic Oilella an ga lethain
mic Fiacha[f] móir Muillethain.

221 [a]As do chloinn Aengusa uill
Lucchaid o Druim Inescclainn,
Faelan, Colman gan bine
diarbo buime Dairine.

[a—a]*add* Brux. [b]*here and at the beginning of 225* Brux. *has an asterisk.* [c—c]Culan BLc. [d—d]re la, m. Ailella m. Moga BLc. [e—e]uadh do cuir mor m.m. B. [f]Fiach(ach) (B)Lc.

662.222 Corpmac ua Liathain co rath
is Gobban Fionn mac Lucchach,
do siol Daire Cherba chain
mic Oilill Flannbicc buadaicch.

223 Cummin Foda, fa fer caidh,
's Faithlenn mac Aedha Damhain,
do siol Cuirc mic Luigdech doib,
fa mac Oilella an tsaorsloicch.

224 Colman o Chill Chleiticch find
is Mac Tail Cille Cuilind,
da mac Eachach, fa dercc dreach,
do siol Chuirc lain mic Luighdeach[a].

225 [g]Dalbach mac Bronaicch co mbloidh
Cuile[h] Colluincce cedaicch,
do siol Eachach[i] Leith co n-ácch[j]
or geinsettar Úi[k] Liathain[g].

226 [a]Epscop Foircedail gan oil,
Colman an Chrabhaidh chredhail,
do shiol Chuirc chalma na ccrech
ropad mac laochda Luigdech.

227 Fionan Droma hAbrad gloin
mac[l] Garbain mic Amhalgaidh,
do sliocht Chuirc mic Luigdech leir
mic Oilill Flannbicc buainreidh[a].

228 Martain mac Dunain[m] gan liudh
ocus Fraochnat a deirbsiur,
do siol Mogh[n] Cuirb, [o]maith drema[o],
mic Luicchdech mic Oilealla.

229 Aedhan, Flannan co menmain,
da mac tocchtha Toirrdelbaicch,
do siol Chorbmaic Chais [p]fa bind
roba mac oirrderc dh'Oilill[p].

230 [a]Mainchin Luimnicch co mbuga,
Liadain ingen Diermada
is epscop Mac Laisre lat,
triur naem ro chin o Chorbmac.

| [a—a]*add* Brux.| [g—g]*placed before* 175 BLc. [h]Cu(a)la (B)Lc. [i]Enna Lc. [j]nad Lc. [k]U B. [l]mic Brux. [m]Dumain BLc. [n]Moga *before correction* Brux., Moga BLc. [o—o]roba BLc. [p—p]c(h)ena, mac sen Saidbi is Ailella B(Lc).

662.231 Feidlim ocus Racchnait ran
da ingin iad do Ronan,
Molacca Saingil on tuaith,
do siol Chonaill fel Eachluaith.

232 Dioma mac Aenghuis gan on,
Cummaoin Cadain mac Crunnchon,
do sliocht Cháirthinn Finn mic Bloid
mic Táil mic Conuill eachgroid[a].

233 Cianan[q] mac Setna immalle
is Ulltan mac dergBruigde[r],
ó Chianan[s] mac Oilella uill[t]
mic Mogha[u] Nuadat nertgluinn[v].

234 [w]Cronan mac Odhrain[w] ba caidh
is Luaithrend ingen Cholmain,
do chloinn[x] Taidcc mic Cein Chaisil
mic Oilella ardmaisicch.

235 Tola mac Dunchadha duinn,
Fionan Lobar mac Conuill,
do[y] sliocht[x] Taidcc mic Cein chedna
mic Oilella airmdedla.

236 Sescnen athair Beneoin binn,
Cathmogh athair Mic Cuilind,
[z]do shiol Chein chomnairt doib soin
is do Buite mac Bronoicch[z].

237 Fionntain Droma hIng co mbloidh
[aa]is Bracan mac Eirc uasail[aa],
do sliocht[bb] Taidcc mic Cein [cc]co n-aoibh
na fireoin is na fiornaoimh[cc].

[q]Ciana BLc. [r]Bruidne BLc. [s]Cian Lc. [t]in oil B. [u]*om.* B. [v]nertmoir B. [w—w]Cruman m. Cormaic BLc. [x]ṡil B. [y]ar Lc. [z—z]Buidhi m. Bronaich buan bla, do ṡil Cein m. Ailella B(Lc). [aa—aa]Eogan athair an uasail B(Lc). [bb]ṡil BLc. [cc—cc]nar clai, m. Ailella co rognai B(Lc).

[a]Sil Lucchdech Mic Ithe[a]

238[b] [c]Fachtna is Lucchna na ndamh,
epscop Branduibh is Cassan,
Molua, Cailchine gan meath
is Lochán i nUibh Eachach,

[a—a]*add* Brux. [b]*the scribe enumerates the final five entries* 236-40. [c—c]*not in* BLc *as such, which lead off this section with the first couplet of* 240.

662.239[b] Mainchin Cula Cais dona,
naomchlann Maonaigh mic Fiachna,
do siol Luicchdech mic Con chaoimh,
mac do Maicniadh co moraoiph[c].

240[b] Epscop Beoaid[d] Aird Charna,
Olcan a athair amhra,
[e]Siollan epscop mac Failbe,
do siol Lucchdech co láindaingne[e].

241[b] Naoimh cloinne Luicchdech saoir soin[f],
[g]d'eis airimh naomh mac nGolaimh,
ro tuirmes an cethrar caoin
or geinsettar ar n-ardnaoimh.

242[b] Gach naomh dar airmes ann sin
guidhed lem gusan cCoimdidh,
go rísem an siothflaith saor,
sósadh soinmeach na bfíornaomh. Noemhshenchus[g].

[d]Beoaich Lc. [e—e]*forms part of following quatrain in* BLc, *which read here:* m. Main m. Boith m. liunLog, m. Triun m. Lugdach m. Con B(Lc), *add* Fachtna m. Maenaigh male, Silan epscop m. Failbe, do sil Dairi m. Trena, m. Lugdach m. Con cena B(Lc). [f]soir B. [g—g]ro fodlas caemclann Golaim, nocho nuair senchaidh saer acht ceathrar o buil deghnaem. Naemsenca̅. Mise are faesam na fine, na naim uaisli aingli ainglighi, ma gach gnim romcar co claen, gurab din damh gach deghnaem. Naemh. s.e.a.ncasnaem B(Lc *which has first quatrain only*). B's *final quatrain is the first quatrain of a poem elsewhere ascribed to* Mac Craith Mac an Ghabhann (*see* Introduction, *note* 79).

MISCELLANEOUS ITEMS

663.1 [a]Crumthir[b] Mechair 7 Mursan[c] i Cill Crui[ad].

2 Colman m*accua* Miadchon[e] i[f] nDomnuch Ḟemin.

3 Epscop[g] Etchiain[h] m. Mane i[f] Tig Dochua[i] m. Nemain.

4 Fidnat[j] ic[f] Rus m. Ceit[k] i Cruachán[l] Ceneoil Ucha[m].

5 Colum Drummḟota[n] [o]ingen[p] Aeda a[q] Drummut[or] Gesilli[s] i Cill Chalma[t] [o]i mMaig Lifi[o].

6 Darerca 7 [u]Clothach i[f] nDisiurt[u] Meic Cailli.

[a—a]*in preceding column* Lb. [b]thir *above line* M. [c]s *above line* M. [d]Chrai annsin M. [e]Nua(d)chon (BLb)Lc, Midchon M. [f]o Lb. [g]7 epscop Lb. [h]Etce(i)n (B)Lc, Cein Lb, Eichian M. [i]Dachua(i) Lc(Lb)M. [j]Findchadh BLcLb, Fignat M. [k]E(i)rc(c) BLc(Lb). [l]Crua̅ī BLc. [m]Aucha Lb. [n]Droma Foda (7) B(Lc)Lb. [o—o]*om.* Lb. [p]ingena Lc. [q]*om.* B, o M. [r]Druimad B, nDruim Ḟoda Lc. [s]*written as if name of saint* BLc(*with construe mark*)Lb. [t]Colman BLc(Lb), Chalmta M. [u—u]Clotcinisirt B, Cloth i nDisert Lc.

563.7 Ingena[v] Conaill i [w]Cennaib Ech[w] i mMide.

8 Trean[x] ingen M*eic* Leat[y] i[f] Cluain Gamna.

9 Minchuin[z] ic[aa] Tig Minchuni[bb] i nAsul[cc].

10 Bicsech i[f] Cill Bicsigi i mMidi.

11 Ultan 7 Eltini i[f] Cluain Dabcha i Fid Eoin.

12 Ronsech ingen Charpre i Tír Ḟolaiṅg[dd] [ee]ic Glasloch[ee].

13 Beccan[ff] 7 Colán[gg] 7 Cocán[hh] tri meic Colmain m. Dermata i[ii] Fothirb[jj] Sinill.

[v]ingen BLcLb. [w—w]hibecħ B, Cenelaib Echach Lc. [x]Triean M. [y]L(a)ed B(Lc), Leit Lb. [z]Micu(i)n B(Lc), Muccin Lb. [aa]i BLc, o LbM. [bb]Micuin BLc, Muccin Lb. [cc]Aisiul M. [dd]Folaigh BLcLb. [ee—ee]iglasloch B(LcLbM). [ff]Beachán BLc. [gg]Colgan B(LcLb). [hh]*add* insin Lb. [ii]for Lc. [jj]Fo(i)trib (B)LcLb, Fothartaib M.

64 Secht meic Restituit[a] de Longbardaib[b]: Sechnall epscop[c], Nectain epscop[d], Dabonna[e] sac*art*[f], Mogornan[g] sacart[f], Darioc[h] epscop, Auxilinus[i] epscop, Lugnaith[j] sac*art*[f].

[a]Reiscituit B(Lc), Resciuit Lb, Rechtituid Lc[1]. [b]Loungbarruibh BLc, Longbardu Lb, Longbardaib M. [c]*add here and after other entries* 7 Lb. [d]*om.* BLcLb. [e]Dabunna M. [f]Sanc B. [g]Mo(m)gonran (B)Lc, Mogurnan Lb, Modoirnan M. [h]Daróic(h) BLc(Lb), Darigoc Lc[1]. [i]Ausaille RLc[1], Mochu M. [j]Lugna Lc[1].

65 Nonbur Síl Chonaire[a].

1 Senach m. Cairill[b]; Eolaṅg[c] i[d] nAthbi Bolg i mMuscraige Mittini[e]; Odran i[d] lLettrachaib[f] i mMuscraige Tire. Trí senore Sil Conaire sin[g].

2 [h]Ceir Ascad[h] — [i].i. nomen campi[i] — i[j] Cill Ceiri[k]; Gobnat[l] i[dm] mBairniuch[n] i cocrich Muscraigi Mittini 7 Eoganacht Locha Lein; Sciath ingen Mechair ic[o] Firt Scethi[p] i mMuscraigi Aeda. Trí óga Síl Chonaire sin[g]

3 Lachtain[q] Achaid Uir[r] o Belaig Ḟebrat[s] i Sleib Chain; Finán[t] Cam Cind Ettig i cocrich Éle 7 Fer Cell; Senan Insi Cathaig. Trí caindle Síl Chonaire sin[g].

[a]*add* .i. LbM. [b]7 *added here and passim* Lb. [c]Olangan M. [d]o Lb. [e]Tire Mitain B(Lc). [f]lLatrachaibh BLc(Lb), *add* Odrain Lb. [g]in sin Lb. [h—h]C(e)rescad (BLc)Lb. [i—i]*in marg.* L, *om.* BLcLbM. [j]o LbM. [k]Chiarascad M. [l]*add* in chaillech gobger Lb. [m]*add* cill i B. [n]Buirnech Lb, mBerrnuch M. [o]i Lb. [p]Sceith BLcLbM. [q]Lachtnan Lc. [r]Aur Lb, *add* 7 i nAes Chind Chuille i nOsraigu Lb. [s](F)abrat (B)LcLb. [t]Find B.

665.4 [a]Inde[b] dicitur[a]:

Nonbur[c] Síl Chonaire
o nach[d] [e]berar ní i ndeolaid[e],
[f]tri caindle, tri senore[g],
tri oga[f] foclait[h] eolaig.

5 It é[i] na trí senore[g]
cantais fri[j] Crist a comrad;
Senach[k] mac Cairill cen chrad[l],
Eolangán[m] 7 Odran.

6 It é na tri callecha
nochardais Crist cen dechair;
Ciar Ascad[n], Gobnat [o]co mblaid[o],
7 Sciath ingen Mechair.

[a—a]*in marg.* L, *in text* M, *om.* BLcLb. [b]unde M. [c]*add* do BLcLb. [d]na Lb. [e—e]bera mind eolaigh BLcLb. [f—f]*arranged differently* M. [g]se(a)noraig (B)Lc. [h]coiclid BLc(Lb). [i]iad Lc. [j]re BLcLb. [k]tri Senach (*with mark of deletion under* tri) B. [l]grad B. [m]Eolganan Lc. [n]Asgnaidh B(Lc), Uscach Lb. [o—o]co*m*lbaid Lb.

7 [a]Trí caindle Sil Chonaire[a]
[b]saerthar os[b] Mumain[c] medan;
Lactain[d] find forglidi[e] án[f],
Fínan Cam[g] 7 Senán.

8 [h]Senan[i] i[j] Sleib[k] Lumnig [l]na lec[l],
Lactain[m] o Belaig Ebrat[n],
rigan[o] na rand, rád[p] cen chlith,
7 Finan Cam[q] Cind Ettig[h].

9 Inund a recht[r] ic[s] Ríg nel[t],
inund a cert 's a cenel,
inund oentu[u] fodasgaib[v]
i nnim 7 i talmain. N[w].

[a—a]hit e na tri coindle sin Lb. [b—b]saersad sin BLc(Lb). [c]Mudain B. [d]Lachtnin BLc, *add* in BLcLb. [e]forbaili(g) B(Lc). [f]*om.* BLcLb. [g]Caem BLc. [h—h]*om.* Lc. [i]Seasan B. [j]*om.* BLbM. [k]Slibi B. [l—l]nachlag BLb. [m]Lactnin B. [n]Abhrad B(Lb). [o]o rig Lb. [p]fath BLb. [q]caem B. [r]racht BM. [s]*con* Lc. [t]nell BM, reil Lc. [u]aentaig M. [v]rodasgeibh BLc(Lb). [w]nonbhur BM, 7rl Lb.

666.1 Secht meic Tarbin[a] [b]in so sis[bc] .i. Silán[d] ic[e] Áth na Cell ar[f] brú Aba Móri; Sinill Caelan[g] ic[e] Áth na Cell[h]; Senán Líath i[e] Cill Senain[i]; Trian[j] i[e] nDomnuch Mór[k] Muscraige Mittine [l]dib linaib[lm]; Mochoba[n] Lis[o] Moir; Crochan[p] i[e] Cill Crochain[q] i cocrich Laigsi 7 Ossairgi; Lactain[r] [s]i nAchud[s] Úr i nAes Cind Chaille[t] [u]i nOss*airgi*[u].

2 Secht n-ingena Tarbin[v]: Corcsech[w], Ceirsech[x], Cronsech[y], Sodelb, Cellsech ic[e] Áth na Cell[z].

[a]Cairbri B, Tairbi Lc, Thorbire m. Nuach*air* Lb. [b—b]*om.* LcLb. [c]*om.* B. [d]Sinill Lc. [e]o Lb. [f]for Lb. [g]Ce(a)llan (B)LcLb(*with punctum between it and* Sinell). [h]Ceallan Lc. [i]tSenain BLb, *add* Leith Lb. [j]Tri BLc. [k]*add* a BLc. [l—l]*om.* Lb. [m]lintib Lc. [n]Mocuda B(Lc), *add* o Lb. [o]Leasa B. [p]Crocho BLc(Lb). [q]Crochi B. [r]Lachtnan Lc. [s—s]Echach B, Achaid LcLb. [t]Cilli BLc. [u—u]*om.* BLc, i nOsraigib beos Lb. [v]Tairbri B(Lc), Torbiri Lb. [w]Corfeasach B, Coireasach Lc, Coirsech Lb, *add* 7 BLc(*which adds same to following entries*). [x]Cair(p)easach (B)Lc. [y]*om.* Lb. [z]*add* 7 Lc, 7rl Lb.

667 Molasse 7 Mochumma[a] 7 Colum Crom[b] 7 Ronan 7 Darlugdach[c] [d]i lLemdruim[d]; Sac*art*[e] Colum *ua* Crimthaind[f]; Molassi Lemdromma[g].

[a]Mochaem BLc, Mochoma Lb. [b]Cron BLcLb. [c]Darluḡ B, Darlugaid Lc, Darluigdech Lb. [d—d]*om.* BLc. [e]Se(a)ch (B)Lc. [f]*add* 7 Lb. [g]Lamdroma BLc, *add* beos Lb.

668 Fecht oén[a] da tánic Semplán[b] sacart[c] Tiri Da Glas co Tír Crónin[d] do [e]Licc na Sinnach[e] [f]ri toscib[f]. Is and baí Dirmaid[g] oc glanad urdrochit[h] a thaigi [i]7 a[ij] luasat[k] ’na laim. [l]Luid iarum a chú[l] fona clerchib [m]co roletrad[m] in sacart. Rabual[n] in sacart in coin [o]iar sin[o]. Robual[p] iṁ[q] Dirmaid[g] [r]in sacart[r] dint[s] ṡluasait co robris menistir Coluim robui[t] fora[u] muin. Dolluid iarum[v] Lactain[q] comarba Coluim do acru in gnima sin co flaith *Ua* ṅDróna .i. co Ruiden[w] m. Lainnen[x]. Co tartsat[y] *Ui*[z] Dróna secht cumala o Dirmaid[g] do muintir[aa] Choluim 7 do Lactain 7[q] dorat[bb] Lactain[cc] na[dd] secht cumala sin[ee] do airchinniuch[ff] Lemdromma[gg] .i. do[q] Uamnach[hh].

[a]náen BLc, *om.* Lb. [b]Te(a)mplan (B)Lc. [c]Se(a)ch B(Lc). [d]Cruimin BLc. [e—e]Lignaire BLc(Lb). [f—f]fria dethbirius Lb. [g]Diarmaid BLc(Lb). [h]úirdre(a)nach a ndorus B(Lc), aurdreich a ndorus Lb. [i—i]cona Lb. [j]*om.* BLc. [k]sluasat B(LcLb). [l—l]laige qu B, laigis cu Lc, 7 laidig cu Lb. [m—m]cor leadair B(LcLb). [n]bualaig B(Lb), buailis Lc. [o—o]iarum Lb. [p]buailidh BLc, buailis Lb. [q]*om.* BLcLb. [r—r]esen B(LcLb). [s]dia Lb. [t]boi Lb. [u]ara BLc. [v]tra Lb, *add* íar sin B, lesin Lc. [w]Raigen Lc. [x]Laimen BLc, Lairen Lb. [y]dardra B, tartsadur Lc. [z]hua B. [aa]murt*ir* B. [bb]dorata tra Lb. [cc]Lachtnan Lc, *om.* Lb. [dd]*bis* Lc. [ee]le(i)s (B)Lc, sin lais Lb. [ff]o(i)rind(e)acht B(Lc). [gg]Lamdroma BLc. [hh]*ua* Uamnach B(Lc), Uamnachan a ainm sium. et cetera. Lb.

669.1 [a]Da mac Gabrin[b], .i. Maelan [c]7 Melán[c], ic[d] Tuaim [e]Da Ḟiach[ae].

2 Crumthir Lappain[f] i[g] Cluain[h] Medoin.

[a—a]*om.* Lc [b]Gabra(i)n B(Lb). [c—c]*om.* Lb. [d]a B, o Lb. [e—e]dfiach B, *add* 7 Lb. [f]Labain B, Laeban Lc, Lafan Lb. [g]o Lb. [h]Cill BLc.

669.3 [c]Epscop Santain[i] [j]et[c] epscop Sanctain[jk] et epscop Lethnain[l] tri meic Cantoin[m] ríg Bretan. [c]It é filet i Cill Epscuip Santain[cn].

[i]Sechtain BLc. [j—j]*om.* LcLb. [k]*om.* B. [l]*punctum under first* n? L, Letain B(LcLb), *add* 7 Mádocc Oilithir Lb. [m]Caind(e)oin B(Lc). [p]Techtain BLc.

670 [a]Brigitae sanctae subiectae erant omnes hae uirgines sanctae[b] quarum [c]loca et nomina enumerabimus.

1 Cainer ingen[ac] Chruthechain[d] i[e] Cill Chulind i Cairpre.

2 Cainer ingen Airmind[f] [g]i[h] Cluain[g] Corind.

3 Indú Már[i] 7 [j]Indú Bec[j] dí[k] ingin Breccáin m. Brénaind i[h] Cill [l]Da Indend[l].

4 Bríg ingen Ḟergusa i[h] Cill Brígi[m].

5 Cetheora[n] ingena Fergnai m. Ḟergusa i[h] lLethráith[o] .i.[p] Delbnat[q] et[r] Cainer, Deimlir[s] 7 Fuin[che?].

6 Fainder cuicir[r] [t]i[u] Cluain[v] Brónaig[tw].

[a—a]*om.* B, *see note* Lb. [b]et sac̄ Lc. [c—c]*om.* LcLb. [d]Crutanach BLcLb. [e]oi B, o LcLb. [f]Airmedaigh BLc, Amrind Lb. [g—g]*om.* BLc. [h]o Lb. [i]*om.* BLcLb. [j—j]Indu*m*ach Lc, Induibech Lb. [k]da BLcLb. [l—l]Daindein BLc, Daninde Lb. [m]Brigde Lc. [n]Ce(i)tri (BLc)Lb, *add above line no* .u. Lb. [o]lLe(i)ting (B)Lc, Letrach Lb. [p]7 (in) B(Lc). [q]De(a)lbna B(Lc). [r]*om.* Lb. [s]7 Deinde (i)mlir (B)Lc, Derlir Lb. [t—t]*om.* B. [u]7 hi Lb. [v]Cill Lc. [w]*add* beos Lb.

7 Necht ingen Chommain i mBruig Broc.

8 Fedbair ic[a] Boith Roichnig.

9 Ingena[b] Choluim 7 Ingena[b] Bresail i[a] Cill Chalaid 7 i[a] Caill[c] Lugmind.

10 Curchass[d] ic[e] Tig[f] Curchaissi.

11 Lassar i[a] Cill Lasra[g] i[h] n*Uib* Bresail. Is inti roloisc[i] Brigit in ṅgarmuin oc funi ind[j] loég.

12 Corpach ingen Ḟiachnai[k] m. Nui[l] i[a] Cill Corpaigi[m].

[a]o Lb. [b]ingen BLcLb. [c]Cill BLcLb. [d]Curcaisi Lc. [e]i BLc, o Lb. [f]cill Lc. [g]Lasair BLc, Lasrach Lb. [h]ingen Lb. [i]roloisce(a)dh (B)Lc. [j]*om.* BLc. [k]Fiach̄ BLcLb. [l]Nuig BLc, Noei Lb. [m]Corbaigh BLc.

13 Cron [a]Muni Taplain[a] i[b] nInis Crone for Loch Andind[c].

14 Findnat[d] i[e] rRus m. Ceit[f].

[a—a]Muind Tiaplan B(Lc). [b]*om.* BLc, o Lb. [c]Cro(i)ne (B)Lc. [d]Findat BLc, Findtud Lb. [e]o Lb. [f]Cerrceit B, Eircc *no* Ceitt Lc.

70.15 Find ingen Mantain[g] i[e] Tracht Findi[h].

16 Aibind ingen Mani[i] i[e] Cluain[j] Draignigi.

17 Failtem*ail*[k] ingen[l] Mael Echdach[l] ic[m] Telaig Ḟunechda[n].

18 Lút[o] ⁊ Crumthir[p] Lugaeth ic[m] Tig[q] Lúta[r] i [s]Fotartaib Maraib[s].

[g]Matain BLcLb. [h]*om.* B, Find LcLb. [i]Man*uis* BLc, Manuis Lb. [j]Cill BLc, [k]Failti Find BLcLb. [l-l]Maillech̄ B, Maelechr̄ Lc, Moeltšechnaill Lb. [m]i BLc, o Lb. [n]Ḟuinech̄ B, .h. nEchach Lc, Ḟuinche Lb. [o]Luaith BLc, Luit Lb. [p]*add* ⁊ Lb. [q]Thelaig Lb. [r]Lug̃ B, Lugach Lc, Lugdai Lb. [s—s]Ḟothartu Mára Lb.

19 Crumsech ⁊ Créd[a] ic[b] Raith Gairni[c] ⁊[d] i[e] nEtargabuil [f]⁊ i[f] Fordruim.

20 Ronsech ic[g] Tig [h]Maile Achaid[h].

21 Ciar ingen Duib Rea i[i] nAiriud[j].

22 [k]Bicell ⁊ Bicsech[k] i[i] nImliuch[l] na Lega[m].

23 Columb ingen Beraig i[i] nImliuch Már.

24 [no]Ingena Cetain[o] i[i] Cluain Ech[np].

[a]Creda LcLb. [b]*om.* B, i Lc, o Lb. [c]*Or read* Gaisni L, Gairm B(*with stroke over* g)LcLb. [d]*om.* Lb. [e]ingen Lc, an Lb. [f—f]*om.* BLc, o Lb. [g]a B(Lc), o Lb. [h—h]Mailechlaind BLc, Moelšechnaill Lb. [i]o Lb. [j]Ard BLc, dairiud Lb(*with punctum over* d). [k—k]*reversed* BLcLb. [l]*added above line* .i. uime a ḟliuch Lb. [m]Laega Lc. [n—n]*follows* 25 Lb. [o—o]Ingeadain B(LcLb). [p]Ech̄ BLcLb.

25 [a]Ingena[b] Fiachnai[c] ic[d] Tuaim Neill[a].

26 Caibell[e] ingen Aeda Bairr[f] i[d] Cill Lusca.

27 Trea[g] ingen Meic[h] Cairthind[i] i[d] nAird Trea[j].

28 Cethri[k] ingena Meic Iair .i. Derbinill ⁊ Derinill et Coel ⁊ Comgell.

29 Caimell ingen[l] Dermata i[d] nDisiurt [m]Brigte i[d] Cill Suird[mn].

30 Tri[o] ingena Ernin[p] m. Coluim Ruit[q] .i. Darnisa[r] ⁊ Sinech ⁊ Crón. A mbrathair[s] i nEnuch[t] Dirmaige[u].

[a—a]*precedes* 24 *and written as if beginning of new section* Lb. [b]ingen BLcLb. [c]Fiach̄ BLcLb. [d]o Lb. [e]*om.* B, Coemell Lb. [f]Abarr BLc. [g]Treada B. [h]*om.* BLcLb [i]Carthaind BLcLb. [j]Tre(a)da (B)Lc. [k]*om.* Lb. [l]i B. [m—m]*separate entry* Lb. [n]Sust BLcLb. [o]Tr Lc, teora Lb. [p]Ernain Lc. [q]Ru(a)id B(Lb), *om.* Lc. [r]Dairn(a)isi BLc(Lb). [s]mbadar BLc(Lb). *See note.* [t]nAenach BLc(Lb). [u]D(a)urmaige BLc(Lb).

670.31 Brunsech ingen Chrimthaind i[a] mMaig Threga[b].

32 Ciar 7 Midan da[c] ingin Cerain[d] 7 Finnech[e] ingen Ṡenaig[f] Ḟind. Do[g] Chen*iul* Chormaic dóib uile. It e[h] congabat[i] Ros Iarṅglais.

33 Scoth[j] 7 Meṅgan[k], [l]inund athair 7[l] mathair leo 7[m] do Dál Messin Corp dóib. It e sin[n] fil[o] i Cellaib Maigi Uachtarchaib[p] 7 Ictarchaib[q] 7[n] i Cluain Moescnae[r].

34 Dochatti[s] [t]i[a] nAchud[t] Chorcaigi.

35 [u]Brig[v] ingen Amalgada[w] 7 Cillini 7 Cellan i nAchud Aeda[u].

[a]o Lb. [b]Threaa Lb. [c]di Lb. [d]Caerain BLc(Lb). [e]Findaith B, Finda(i)ch (Lc)Lb. [f]Stcn̄ B, Tenaig Lc. [g]o BLcLb. [h]eat Lb. [i]congabsad Blc(Lb). [j]Scot(t) BLc(Lb). *Written as if beginning of new section* Lb. [k]Mongan BLc, Mongu Lb. [l—l]clann oenathar 7 inann Lb. [m]*om.* Lb. [n]*om.* BLcLb. [o]filed B(LcLb). [p]Fuachtardaibh BLc, hUachtair Lb. [q]Ichtair Lb. [r]Muisgne B(LcLb). [s]Docaidi B(LcLb). [t—t]anach B. [u—u]*entered separately* Lb. [v]Brigid BLc. [w]Amalga(id) B(Lc).

36 [a]Cainer[b] [c]de *Uib* Dega[c] cetmunter Nannida[d] m. Dermata[e] et Bronach et Senán m. Becain et Luan 7[f] a dí[g] ingin .i.[g] Curchach 7 Mita [h]i Cill Ingen Luain 7[h] i Cill Bronche iar cetgabail[a]. Segine m.[i] Cerain[j] 7 Elltine m*athair*[k] Ronain m. Cenannain. Et Gnathnat 7 Dicuill[l] m. Ronain iar ṅgabail[m] tan*aisi*[n]. Dí[o] ingin Eltini[p] 7[n] Crumthir ṅDelgini[q] 7 Mac Onchon d*na*[r] beus [s]ina tresgabail[s]. [t]Mac Onchon [u]in suí[u] i[v] rRaith Scothban[t].

[a—a]*entered separately* Lb. [b]Caimer BLc(Lb). [c—c]ingen Deagada B. [d]Nahindeda BLc, Nindedai Lb. [e]Dre(a)main (B)LcLb. [f]ed(a) Lc(Lb). [g]*om.* BLcLb. [h—h]ingen Luanait BLc. [i]ingen m. BLc. [j]Cearain Lc, Cerrain Lb. [k]mac BLcLb. [l]Dicolł B, Dicholl Lc. [m]ngail BLcLb. [n]*om.* BLcLb. [o]da BLcLb. [p]E(i)lltire (BLc)Lb. [q]Gluntann B(LcLb). [r]da BLcLb. [s—s]mairtscabas BLc, inathresc Lb. [t—t]*precedes* dí ingin Eltini BLcLb. [u—u]annsin B(Lc), *om.* Lb. [v]o Lb.

37 Pol 7 Deineth[a] 7 Martan[b] epscop Tamlachtan[c] ic[d] Domnuch [e]Mor i Febib[e].

38 Cron ingen Aeda 7 Emini[f] m. Altini[g] i[h] nDomnuch Mor [i]Sanct Brigti[i].

39 Aed m. Fortchirn[j] et Corpre m. Binnig[k] et[l] Pol 7 Deneth[m] i[n] nInis Beoaed[o].

40 Neman 7 [p]Bia i Cill[p] Bia.

41 Ness 7 Mac Carthind[q] i[h] Cill Nesse et Garban m. Erennaig inti beus.

42 Gentine 7 Segine na[r] da chrumthir sin[s] i[h] Tír Guare.

[a]Dineth Lb. [b]*add* 7 BLcLb. [c]Tamlachta BLc(Lb). [d]a BLc, o Lb. [e—e](ei)ibib (B)Lc, Ḟebe Lb. [f]Eim BLc. [g]Eiltine Lc. [h]o Lb. [i—i]Sannocht Briga B(LcLb); *written as separate entry* Lc. [j]Fe(i)rtcind (B)Lc. [k]ḃithB, B*er*aig LcLb. [l]*om.* Lc. [m]De(i)ne (B)Lc, Denethan Lb. [n]*om.* Lc, o Lb. [o]Medbedaid Lc. [p—p]Buachail(l) (BLc)Lb. [q]Ca(i)rthaind B(Lc)Lb. [r]in BLc. [s]*om.* Lb.

670.43 Eltini [a]m Meic[a] Mailain i[b] Senchui[c]. Lochini[d] m. Illain[e] [f]7 Ness beus[f] i[b] Senchui[g].

44 Baethboth[h] m. Cronain[i] i[b] rRuba Ṡenaig.

45 Conlaed 7 secht n-epscuip 7 secht sacairt 7 secht n-ingena[j] óga [k]i nDind Ḟlatha[k] Geneoil[l] Lugair.

46 Melan[m] 7 Fairchellán[n] i[b] Cill Condala[o].

47 Findech 7 Ciar 7 Mida[p] tri[q] ingena Ciarain, brathair side[r] Senaig Ḟind, 7 Mosegu[s] 7 Ḟintain 7 Affraic ingen Cumlachtaig[t] 7 Cummain[u] ingen Cummini[u] i[b] Cluain Fota .i. i[v] n*Uib* Culinn[w].

48 Cummini[u] m. Fothlain m. Beccain m. Ḟergusa i[x] [y]nDerc Daim[y] 7 Becc m. [z]Duib Duili[z] m. Garbain m. Ḟintain i[b] Craebaig[aa] 7 i [bb]nDerc Doim[bb].

[a—a]ua Lb. [b]o Lb. [c]Sencaid B, Senachad Lc. [d]Loithin B. [e]Gillain BLc, Illaind Lb. [f—f]7 Nesbus B(Lc)Lb. [g]Senchaid B, Senachaid Lc, *add* beos Lb. [h]Boeth 7 Both Lb. [i]Ronain Lc. [j]*om.* Lc. [k—k]inandlatha BLc. [l]Cene(oi)l B(LcLb). [m]Maelan BLcLb. [n]Fairchellach Lc. [o]*add* 7 BLc. [p]Mide Lc, Mita Lb. [q]teora Lb. [r]sen BLcLb. [s]Mosedo B, Mosseoda Lc. [t]Cum(l)aclaigh (BLc)Lb. [u]Cumaine BLcLb. [v]ingen Lb. [w]Cualł B, Cualan*n* Lc, Chuallaig Lb. [x]m*eic* BLcLb. [y—y]Derc(d)aib (B)Lc. [z—z]Duib Guile B(Lc). [aa]Crebaigh BLc, Rebaid Lb. [bb—bb]Ercdaim Lb.

49 Nemnat i[a] Cluain Mór Lugnad[b].

50 Berchan m. Nemnaill[c] 7[d] Brig 7 Coip[e] 7 Lassar [f]tri ingena Nemnaill[f] et Broccán 7 Cronan da mac Lochin[g] i[a] Cill Lathraig[h] os thuile.

51 Mugrellóc[i] 7 Mochellóc 7 Maeldub i[a] Cluain Conaire Maelduib.

52 Brig[j] 7 Tigern[k] 7 Duthracht[l] i[a] Cill Muni i mMaig Liphi[m].

53 Sinech[n] 7 Mac Nisi[o] 7 Eithni[p] i[a] Cill Roiss.

54 [q]Finán 7 a dí ṡiair[q] ic[a] Tig Airthir[r]. Finech 7 Mooinis[s] dí[t] ingin Dibechain[u] beus[v] ic[a] Tig Airthir[w].

[a]o Lb. [b]Lugna BLc. [c]Nemain Lb. [d]*add* a tri sethracha .i. Lb. [e]Cois B, Coir Lc, Corp Lb. [f—f]*om.* Lb. [g]Loiccín B. [h]Latraige B(Lc). [i]Mog̅loc B, Mongloc LcLb. [j]Brig̅ B. [k]Diern(d) B(Lc), Digern Lb. [l]Dubtracht BLc. [m]*add* doib Lb. [n]Sinach BLc. [o]I*n*dsi B(Lc). [p]Eidine Lc. [q—q]Findenach 7 aidi siair B(Lc). [r]Ortain B, Dortan Lc. [s]Moinis BLc, Mohonis Lb. [t]da BLcLb. [u]Dobecan BLc. [v]*after* Airthir Lb. [w]Gorthir B.

670.55 Ilet[a] 7 Ernan[b] i[c] mMethus[d] Chaille.

56 Moenóc ic[e] Glais Eille i n*Uib* Ercain.

57 [f]Crit ingen Baetain isinn Ernaidiu.

58 Ronan m. Beraig ic Tig Threbtha.

59 Columb ingen Dulechain i nEnuch Gabrini.

60 Fureman 7 Trostan 7 Aedgein tri meic Fidgein Lega ic Tig Derescain ic Tibprait Sabraille[f].

[a]7 Leit BLc, Lett Lb. [b]Ernain BLc. [c]ic Lc. [d]mMedis Lb. [e]o BLcLb. [f—f]*om.* BLcLb.

61 [a]Crai 7 Ricenn, [b].i. siur Patric[b], i Cill Cai[a].

62 Aed m. Cormaic 7[c] Illand m. Aeda i[d] nImliuch Fornocta[e].

63 Collidan[f] 7 Barri[g] 7 Finan 7 Midnan[h] 7 Manchan 7 teora ingena Ercdaith[i] i[d] Cind Tracta.

64 Senach m. Echin[j] 7 Srafan 7 Sinchell 7 Brutiuc[k], [l].i.[m] epscop[n] 7 aite Coemgin[lo], 7 Epscop Mac Cairthind[p] 7 Conlaed 7 Brigit i[d] Cuil Chorra.

65 Mac Nisi dna[q] i[d] Findchoraid.

66 Cumman[r] 7 Ronnat[s] [t]ic[d] Tig[t] Acronain[u].

[a—a]*om.* BLcLb. [b—b]*added above line* L. [c]*om.* Lc. [d]o Lb. [e]Fornocht BLcLb. [f]Coillidan BLc, Colladan Lb. [g]Barra(ig) (BLc)Lb. [h](F)indan BLc(Lb). [i]Ercbraich BLc(Lb). [j]Feigin B(Lc). [k]Bruiduc B(LcLb). [l—l]*added above line* L, *in text* BLcLb. [m](in) cuic (B)Lc, in .iiii. Lb. [n]*add* in sin Lb. [o]caem BLc(Lb). [p]Carthaind BLcLb. [q]*om.* BLcLb. [r]Coman BLcLb. [s]Ronan LcLb. [t—t]*bis* Lc. [u]Crona(i)n (B)Lc(Lb), *add* 7 Lb.

67 Modimmóc rogab Tech Mochua[a] m. Lonain.

68 Cron[b] ingen Ernaine i[c] mMarcaig 7 Ingena[d] Cobthaig et Temoir ingen[e] Ernini[f] i[c] Cluain Salaind.

69 Feidelm[g] 7 Epscop Daurthech[h] i[c] Cill Achaid Draignige[i].

70 Aed m. Ernin[j] 7[k] teora ingena Aeda[l] .i. Añgais[m] 7 Dartinne 7[n] Bronaig[o] i[c] Cill Araid[p].

[a]M*ei*c Cua B, Mucna Lc. [b]Cronan BLc. [c]o Lb. [d].ī. BLc, ingen Lb. [e]an BLc. [f]Ernaine LcLb. [g]Feidľ BLc, Fedelim Lb. [h]Durrthach BLc. [i]Draignine B(Lc). [j]Fernine BLc. [k]*om.* BLc. [l]Ernnine *no* Aeda B(Lc). [m]Anslas BLcLb. [n]*om.* Lb. [o]Bronach Lb. [p]Aird BLcLb.

670.71 Fiachra[q] Caech m. Feidlimid 7 Ennac[r] [s]m. Nemnain[s] [t]i Cill Ennga[u] 7 Epscop Dimma[tv] beus[w].

72 Muninne[x] 7 Lonan 7 Molasse tri meic Dubthaig 7 ingine[y] Cainnig[z] 7[k] Mochommoc[aa] m*accua* Lugair[bb] [cc]i[c] nDind[cc] Ḟlatha Geneoil[dd] Lugair [ee]7 crumthir noeb de muntir Patric [ff]immalle fri[ff] Dubtach[eegg].

[q]Fiacħ BLcLb. [r]Endai Lb. [s—s](m.)7 Edmnaind (B)Lc, m. Emnaind Lb. [t—t]7 Epscop Dimbae o Chill Endgai Lb. [u]Anga BLc. [v]Diambe B. [w]*om.* BLcLb. [x]Nannine R, Naindi Nae Lc[l]. [y].ī. BLcLc[l], ingen Lb. [z]Choinde BLc. [aa]Mocaemo BLc(Lb). [bb]*add* 7 Perigrinus ailither 7 Dubtach R(Lc[l]). [cc—cc]anin BLc. [dd]Cene(oi)l BLc(LbRLc[l]). [ee—ee]moale la Patric R(Lc[l]). [ff—ff]Mailere BLc(*as if name of saint*), aroen re Lb. [gg]*add* m*accua* Lugair Lb.

73 Martar ingen[a] Ḟiachrach[b] m. Muridaig m. Illadain[c] m. Dunlaiṅge[d] .i.[e] Bríg 7 Mugain[f] 7 Sarnat[g] 7[e] Brig aile [h]7 Sarnait[h] dí[i] ingin Grellain[j] m. Gaillin[k] i[l] Cill Bairnig[m].

74 [n]Nathfraech sacart 7 ara Brigti i Cíll Cula Dumai.

75 Sodelb ingen Chuanain ic Tig Cendorcha.

76 Affrica ingen Chumlachtaig 7 Adán *ua* ind Eicis i nImliuch Tuascirt[n].

77 Laignech 7 Fondil[o] i[l] Cill Ḟeirbe[p].

78 Bríg ic[q] Tig Brige[r]. Is lé tomlachtá[s] na bae[t] fo thrí i[u] n-oenló [v]dona epscopaib[v], 7 is lé topacht[w] in lathi ṁbuana[x] dia mbuannmech[y] fon tír archena.

[a].i. BLc. [b]Fiacħ B, Fiacha Lc. [c]Illadai B. [d]Dunlaing LcLb. [e]*om.* Lb. [f]Mumain Lc. [g]Ornaid(e) (B)Lc, Ornatt Lb. [h—h]7 Ciannad Lc, *om.* B. [i]da BLcLb. [j]Ḡlain(e) (B)Lc, Gerlán Lb. [k]Cailline BLc. [l]o Lb. [m]Bairrfinde B, Barraind Lc, Birend Lb. [n—n]*om.* BLcLb. [o]Foendil Lb. [p]Erbi B(Lc). [q]a B, i Lc, o Lb. [r]Brigde Lb, *add* 7 BLc. [s]doblitha B, dobligthea Lc(Lb). [t]baid B. [u]asin B, san Lc, isin Lb. [v—v]don epscop BLcLb. [w]tobach BLc(*bis*)Lb. [x]a mbuana BLc, buanai Lb. [y]munananindech BLc, mbuanninech Lb.

79 Bíte 7 Brigit dí[a] ingin Ḟiachnae[b] i[c] rRátha[d] Brigti i Crích *Ua* Cormaic, [e].i.[f] *Ua* Loisc[eg].

80 Docholmoc[h] m. Fergusa 7 Sárnat i[c] Cill Tuascirt[i] [j].i. Tiri[j].

81 Conach 7 Lucennan 7 Colmán Mór m. Fergusa i[c] nArd Chonaig.

82 Petrán[k] i[c] nDomnuch Eochaille[l] et Duthracht[m] 7 Temair[n].

83 Lassar 7 Cummain dí[a] ingin Cholmain m. Ḟiachnai[o] i[c] Cluain Cain[p].

84 [j]Conóc m. Concertaig et Sodelb ingen Marcain i nDumu Ríg[j].

[a]da BLcLb. [b]Fiacrach B, Fiacħ LcLb. [c]o Lb. [d]Raith BLcLb. [e—e]*in marg.* L, *in text* BLcLb. [f]7 BLcLb. [g]Loscain Lb. [h]Dacolmoc BLcLb. [i]Tircc Lb. [j—j]*om.* BLcLb. [k]Petra Lc, Patran Lḅ. [l]Eocoimilli B. [m]Dubtracht BLc, Daurthacht Lb. [n]*add* 7 Lc. [o]Fiacħ BLb, Ḟiachrach Lc. [p]*add* dóib Lb.

670.85 [a]Muscellóc ⁊ Lochan ⁊ Lasar i nDercni.

86 [b]Epscop Domungin ⁊ Epscop Nathí, — [c].i. duo fratres[c] — is é dobered grada for cler*chib* ⁊ call*echaib* la Brigit, et Epscop Senach ⁊ Mogobbóc m*accua* Láimi is é congab Lethglend post. Et Brigit[d] Mór siur do Epscop Domungin. Di Mumain dóib. Et Mobí Berchán et Mobí Brócan filet i Sruib. It e sin uile congabat Sruthair ṅGuaire[a].

87 [b]Ingena[e] Trena ⁊ ingena[e] Meic Rithe[f] .i. [Boi*n*]g[g] ⁊ [h]Tigern i[i] rRus Chonaill.

88 Epscop[h] Dimmae m. Senaig de Ḟothartaib[j] ic[k] Tig Dimmae.

[a—a]*om.* BLcLb. [b].m. *in marg.* L. [c—c]*added above line* L. [d]*or read* Bríg? L. [e]Ingen BLc. [f]Re(i)thi (BLc)Lb. [g]*or read* Líg L, Boing BLc, Bung Lb. [h—h]Tiger(n)*us* ⁊ Conall epscop B(Lc). [i]o Lb. [j]Ḟothartu Lb. [k]i BLc, o Lb.

671 Is[a] iat so[b] in cethrur ar fichet batar[c] i n-urd la[d] Patric .i.[d].

1 Sechnall a[e] epscop.

2 Mochta[f] a ṡacart.

3 [g]Epscop Erc[g] a brithem.

4 Epscop Mac Cairthind[h] a trenḟer.

5 Benen[i] a ṡalmchetlaid[j].

6 Coeman Cilli Riatai[k] a maccoem.

7 Sinell Cille Aires[l] a[d] astiri.

8 Athgin Bothi[m] Domnaig a choic.

9 Crumthir Mescan[n] o Domnuch [o]Mescan[p] a chirbsiri.

10 Crumthir ṁBescnai[q] o[r] Domnuch[o] Dula[s] a ṡacart[t] mése.

[a]ba Lb. [b]*add* tra Lb. [c]dobadar B^l. [d]*om.* B. [e]*om.* BLb. [f]*om.* Lb, *add* Lugmad BLc. [g—g]*add in marg. infer.* Epscop Ercc (.i. brethem Patric) cech ni concertad ba cert, cech oen b*er*ess cert fodreith bendacht Epscoip Eircc fair Lb(*above line*). [h]Carthaind BB^lLcLbM. [i]*add* m. Sescnen B^lLc. [j]salmchellaig B. [k]Ruada B, Ruaid Lb, Raite M. [l]hAirisi B, hArais Lb. [m]Bithe B. [n]Meschon M. [o—o]*om.* BLb. [p]Measc B^l, Meschon M. [q]inbescainnai B^l, Mescnai M. [r]a B^l. [s]Daula Lb. [t]sanc B^l.

11 [a]A thrí[b] gobaind[c] [d]o Domnuch Arnoin[de] ⁊ Loibán[f] ⁊ Fortchern[g].

12 A trí cerdda[h] Essiu ⁊ Biti[i] ⁊ Tassach[j].

[a—a]*entries arranged differently* Lb. [b]dí Lb. [c]*add* (.i.) Mac Cecht B^l(Lc). [d-d]*om.* Lb. [e].ŀ m *above* n L, Armoin(d) (B)M, Anoin B^l. [f]Laban B, Loib B^l. [g]Fercern B, *add* i Raith Semni B^lLc. [h]*add* .i. BLc. [i]Bithe BLb. [j]Tosach B, Tasan B^lLc.

671.13 A tri drunecha[k] Lupait[l] 7 Erc[m] ingen[n] Dáre 7 Crumthiris[a].

14 Odrán[o] i[p] nDisiurt Odrain [q]i n*Uib* Falgi[q] a ara[r].

15 [s]Crumthir Catan[t], [u].i.[v] o Thamlachtain Ardda[uw], 7 Crumthir Brocan[x] a da[yo] ḟoss[sz].

16 Crumthir Manach [aa]a ḟer[aa] denma[bb] connaid.

17 Roddan a buachaill.

[k]danacha B, *add* .i. Lc. [l]Lipaid M. [m]Arcc M. [n]7 B. [o]Odrad B^l. [p]o B^lLcLb. [q—q]*om.* B^lLc. [r]gilli arad B^l(Lc), ara carpait Lb. [s—s]*after* 10 B^lLc. [t]Cadain Lc, Caadhan M. [u—u]*above line* L, *in text* B^lLcM(*after* Brocan), *om.* BLb. [v]*om.* B^lLcLb. [w]*om.* M. [x]Brocco M. [y]di Lb. [z]*add* messi B^l(Lc). [aa—aa]ar B. [bb]*om.* BLb.

672 Conad do chuimnedad na n-anmand sin 7 aesa uird Phatraic adbert Flann.

1
Munter Phadraic na paiter
drem 'ca roibi roLaiden,
aichnid dam, ni cuird chranda,
a n-uird is a n-a[n]manna.

2
Ge da[g]ne tolach am' thig,
a Chlothna meic Mail Enaig,
mo sa munt*er* sa, ni brég
do Deochain mac Britniet.

3
Mar ata i nArd Macha
nochon [f]ine anbflatha
ni du dimes bar slog sin,
terc uaib dileas .h. Deochain.

4
Da thricha epscop gan [ḟ]ell
d'e(s)pscubaib imin Tailgend,
naemda a n-uird, is fath glic,
deich sacairt ceithri *fich*it.

5
Mac Cailli a epscop can acht
is Mochta ar sin a ṡacart,
Epscop Erc, a breithium bind,
a threnfer Epscop Mac Cairthind

6
Benen a ṡailmcedlaid saer
7 Caeman a maccaem,
Sinell a ḟer beinmi cluic
7 Aithchen a ḟirchuic.

672.7 Cruimthir Mesca can bine
a chara 'sa chirbsiri.
Cruimthir Coluim na bindroind,
sacart mesi meic Calpraind.

8 Cruimthir Brocain nach bi ar dail
7 Cruimthir caem Cethain,
ina meis rolas ac loigi,
Cromdumain a mucaide.

9 A liachtreoir, fa la[n]mor rath,
Colman *ua* findḞiachrach.
a bearrthoir fathach fechtach,
Cruimthir ḟirchain firḟeartach.

10 Cael gilla a chresa scene,
Talan dond a dorrsoire,
Saran saerḟer narb ella,
ba he a daileam deiglenda.

11 Crumthir Lonan fa luirg moir,
Crumthir Lennan a estreoir,
Mac Catha, int erlom inmain,
do derdad a deigimdaig

12 A thri druinecha nach dis,
Lupait, Erca, Cruimthiris,
Odran a ara gan oil,
Rodan in broda a buachail.

13 A thri gobaind, ailli ar dealb,
Mac Cecht, Laeban is Fortchern.
A thri cerda, fa mor rath,
Aissmiti, Tairill, Tasach.

14 A thri sair, ba[a] maith a cond
Caeman, Cruithnech, Luchraid lond,
iad dorigni damliag ar tus
a nErind, ard a n-imthus.

15 A thri dithrebaid din chland,
Donda, Domangort, Digall,
a thri lega osna legaib,
Sechnan, Ogma, Aithemail.

16 Mac Nisi in chrabaid chredail,
taisech caid in chelebail.
Comedaid a lebar lan,
Setna credal mac Corcrain.

[a] ua MS.

672.17 Taisech a theglaig ergna,
Derball fada flaitheamda.
Srafan aesmar solam sen,
taisech a lobar lainmer.

18 Senphadraic sochla slogach,
cend a ṡruithi senorach,
taisech caem corcra a scoili,
Blocda mac [b]meic Ḟodaide[b].

19 Bec mac Maenan a maer s*cuir*,
Ilach eochrair a[c] deochain.
Mican mac Bili brendaig
a ḟer tigi in airdecnaid.

20 Aedan ua Ieccail can on,
Beoaid nobid fa[d] chochol[l],
Fachtna, do thuaith thruim Themra,
fa chuach tholl a thigerna.

21 Rigoc Indsi Bo Findi,
Epscop Enan Englindi,
mac iar maithead ina lathar,
mac sethar ar saerbrathar

22 Molaca, Manell, Monend,
bidis araen ris Tailgend,
Brocan, can malairt da deoin,
ba iad[e] a charaid cen eoin.

23 Taman a chruitin ciuil,
[f]ar *cuir*[f] iasc*ur*i imchiuin.
Fiac ba he a bard cen bine.
Sechnall garg a glanḟile.

24 Sen(n)an a brathair co mblad.
Martain brathair a mathar.
Calprai(i)n[n], a athair glan gle,
mac Otai meic Otise.

25 Brocan scribnig a scoile.
Cruimthir Lugna a luamairi.
nochon e ni nach canta,
7 Mac hI a ḟirdalta.

[b—b]*see note.* [c]u MS. [d]ba MS. [e]chiad MS. [f—f]*see note.*

672.26 Blidrend a chirmairi coir.
Moab mac Asra a choin[n]leoir.
   Cruimthir Manach, fa mor rath,
   a f̊er coir re condudach.

27 Gornias in sacart robaist.
German a oidi gan aisc.
   Morbaith a buime molta.
   Nia mac Cuill a chomalta.

28 Cosmos, a mathair co mbloid,
ingen Ochmais do Ḟrangcaib.
   Maith ben rochind ar gloine
   co ruc seser saerchloinde.

29 Maith fer dar ba muinter mor,
da dard a bachall gan bron,
   flaithi ca cluinter na cluic,
   maith muinter muinter Padraic. M.

30 An impidi sin le Fland,
co ria fochraic[g] can imrall.
   Co *m*(m)[b]e iter ḟlaithib nime
   ac maithib na muintere.
m.u.i.n.t.e.r.

[g]fochuaic MS.

673 Saegul Mochaemóc Leith
nocho chelat tuir na tréith
   da secht ṁbliadan cethri cét
   ni iarmar ní immarbr[éc][a].

[a][ ] *illeg.*

BIBLICAL AND CLASSICAL GENEALOGIES

674 Maire[a] ingen[b] Iochim m. Ioseph m. Eli [c]m. Elizar[c] m. Mathatha[d] m. Leue m. Melchi m. Iohannae[e] m. Ioseph m. Mathiae [f]m. Amos[f] m. Nauum[g] m. Esle[h] m. Nage m. Maath m. Mathathiae[i] m. Simei[j] m. Ioseph[k] m. Iuda m. Iohanna m. Ressa m. Zorobab̄[l] m. Salathiel m. Nerei[m] m. Melchi[n] m. Addi m. Cossam m. Elimadam m. hEr m. Iesu[o]

[a]Muiri B(Lc^{l})MR^{l}, Maria Lb. *added above* Genealogia matris domini nostri Iesu Christi B(Lc^{l}), Cuidid ainm Muiri ar dus ut dicitur(?) R^{l}. [b]filia Lb. [c–c]*om.* LbMR^{l}H. [d]Mathan Lb, Nathan MR^{l}H. [e]Iamne BLc^{l}. [f–f]*om.* BLc^{l}. [g]*first* u *added above* L. [h]Eili R^{l}. [i]Mathiae Lb. [j]Simez BLc^{l}, Iesimei R^{l}, Szmei H. [k]Iosdech M(R^{l}), Iosedeth H. [l]*in marg.* Zorobabel L, Sorbobel B(Lc^{l}), Zorobel Lb, Zorobabel M(R^{l}H), *add above* † Orobabel M. [m]Heli Lb. [n]Mechi BLc^{l}. [o]*add* m. Elizar Lb(MR^{l}H).

m. Soryn[p] m. Mathia[q] m. Leui m. Semeon m. Iuda m. Ioseth[r] m. Iona m. Eliachim [s]m. Melcha[st] m. Menna m. Mathiae[u] m. Mathan[v] [w]m. Salomon[w] m. Dauid [x]m. Iese[x].

[p]Sorim BLc[1], Iorim LbM(R[1])H. [q]Mathat Lb(MR[1]). [r]Iosep(h) (B)Lc[1](LbMR[1]H). [s—s]*om.* Lc[1]. [t]Melia MR[1]H. [u]Mathathia MR[1]. [v]Nahan BLc[1], Nathan LbMR[1]H. [w—w]*om.* BLc[1]LbMR[1]H. [x—x]*om.* R[1], m. Ioase M, *add* m. Obeth (7rl) BLc[1](Lb).

675 [a]Ioseph custos Mairi[ab] m. Iacob m. Mathan m. Elizar m. Eliud m. Iachim[c] m. Sadoch[d] [e]m. Eliacim[e] m. Obeth m. Zorrbo*bel*[f] m. Salahel m. Oechomae[g] m. Iotas[h] m. Amon m. Mannases m. Ezecias[i] [j]m. Achar[k] m. Iacham[l] m. Amaisia[jm] m. Ioais[n] m. Iosapath[o] m. Assa m. Abiam m. Robuam m. Salamon [p]m. Dauidh[p] m. Iasse m. Obeth m. Booz m. Salamon m. Nason m. Aminadab m. Aram m. Esrom m. Fares[q] m. Iudae[r] m. Iacob m. Isac m. Abratham m. Tharae m. Nachor [p]m. Seruch[ps] m. Ragau[t] m. Failleach m. Ebir m. Sale [u]m. Cainain[u] m. Arafaxat m. Semh m. Nae m. Lamiach m. Mathasalem[v].

[a—a]Cristus filius Ios*eph* .i. custos Marie, ernastaid togaide sium mathar in Choimded Lb, Christus m. Ioseph MH, Ioseph .i. custos Muire R[1] *add in marg. sup.* Triar dotroisg in corgus coir, Muiri i|ngen| Iac|i|m sen(oir) |...|(?) 7 in orslat ele crit og m naingim(?) R[1]. [b]Mairiae Lc. [c]A(i)chim Lb(M)R[1]H. [d]*add* m. Azur Lb(*above line*)(M)R[1]H. [e—e]*above line* Lb. [f]Zorrobobel Lc[1](R[1]H), Zorobel Lb, Sorbabel M. [g]Iochoniae Lc[1]Lb(R[1]H), Iochonias M. [h]Iohas Lc[1], Ossias Lb, Iosias M(R[1]H). [i]Aczcchae Lb, Oistecias M, Eschiae R[1]. [j—j]*om.* M. [k]Achaz Lc[1]LbH, Ascher R[1]. [l]Iotham Lc[1]LbR[1], Iothas H, *add* m. (As)sariae Lb(R[1]). [m]Ozias H. [n]Ioramh MH, *add* m. Achaz m. Ioram Lb(R[1]). [o]Iostabath Lc[1]. [p—p]*om.* R[1]. [q]Paires Lc[1]. [r]Iudas LbMR[1]H. [s]Saruch MH. [t]Reu LbMR[1]H. [u—u]*om.* LbMR[1]H. [v]*add* m. Enoch m. Iareth m. Malalel m. Cainen m. Enos m. Seth m. Adaim Lc[1](LbMR[1]H), *add further* qui fuit dī Lc[1], m. De Bi LbMR[1]H.

676 Nin m. Peil m. Ploic[a] m. Piris m. Agamail m. Poronesis[b] m. Gomuilis[c] m. Pletis[d] m. Ristis m. Oistis m. Amailis m. Fonais m. Tristis m. Assuir m. Sem m. Nae m. Laimiach.

[a]Ploisc Lc[1](*with* s *above line*). [b]Phronessis Lc[1]. [c]Comuilis Lc[1]. [d]Fletis Lc[1].

677 Alaxander m. Pilip Luisc m. Aminice m. Alaxandair m. Pilip m. Pildis m. Pherergi[a] m. Tranayc[b] m. Poloris m. Argonic m. Franoris[c] m. Fergis m. Heiren[d] m. Hislyc m. Eliprasis[e] m. Plaguis m. Frenesis m. Agitoiris[f] m. Arconis m. Argoilis m. Teipsis[g] m. Trorou m. Caiminis m. Ioinis m. Iauan m. Iafeth m. Nae m. Laimiach [h]m. Mathasal*em*[h].

[a]Perargi Lc[1]. [b]Taranayc Lc[1], *add* m. Athroyc m. Phloiyc Lc[1]. [c]Franonis Lc[1]. [d]Ern Lc[1]. [e]*add* m. Heresis Lc[1]. [f]Agitolis Lc[1]. [g]Typis Lc[1]. [h—h]*om.* Lc[1].

678 Samuel m. Elcanna m. Ierotham[a] m. hEliuth [b]m. Thou[b] m. Suub[c] m. Elchanna m. Assur m. Chore m. Amminadab m. Gaad m. Leui m. Iacob m. Isaac[d].

[a]Herotam B, Hirerotham Lc[1]. [b—b]*om.* B. [c]Supe(i)frat(a)icda (B)Lc[1]. [d]*add* m. Abra(t)ham (B)Lc[1].

679 Agmem[n]on[a] m. Aitir m. Pilip[b] m. Tantail m. Mercoir[c] m. Ioib m. S[ad]uird[d] m. Pic m. Peil m. Treis m. Trois[e] m. Mesrom m. Cain[f] m. Nae [g]m. Laimiach[g].

[a]Aigmemnon Lc[l]. [b]Pelaip Lc[l]. [c]M*ei*ccoir B, M*er*cuir Lc[l]. [d]Saduirn Lc[l]. [e]Troist Lc[l]. [f]Caim Lc[l]. [g—g]*om.* Lc[l].

680 Sinachiribh[a] m. Asarodan m. Zergom m. Salmanaz[b] m. Teglad Fallazar[c] m. Pul. Ipse[c] Pul rex Asiriorum qui primum tribum Ruben et Gad transtulit in Asiros.

[a]Sinachirp Lc[l]. [b]Salamnazar Lc[l]. [c]Fallnastair Lc[l]. [d]spise B, ipse Lc.

681 Ballastair[a] m. Labasairdech m. Meocusser[b] m. Ebill[c] Moradach m. Nabgadon m. Merech[d] [e]Baladon[f] m. Baladon[e].

[a]*or read* Ballastais B, Ballastair Lc[l]. [b]Neochusser Lc[l]. [c]Euil Lc[l]. [d]Marech Lc[l]. [e—e]*separate pedigree* Lc[l](*see note*).

682 Saul[a] m. Ciss m. Abel[b] m. Seóir [c]m. Bechóir[c] [d]m. Aphia[d] m. hUiri [e]m. Emeni[e].

[a]Sabul B. [b]Ebir B. [c—c]*om.* M. [d—d]*om.* BLc[l]. [e—e]⁊ B, *om.* Lc[l], Eimin *with* profeta *of* 683 *added* M.

683 Hestras profeta[a] m. Seleu[b] m. Azariae[c] m. Celchae m. Sellum m. Saduc m. Achitob m. Amariae[d] m. Erarath[e] m. Azariae[f] [g]m. Oziae[gh] m. Bocci m. Abisius m. Finees m. Elizar[i] m. Aaron m. Ambra.

[a]*om.* BLc[l], *attached to* Emeni *of* 682 M. [b]Silui B. [c]Airiea M. [d]*add* m. Astra B(Lc[l]). [e]Mererath BLc[l]. [f]Zairoe B, Zariae Lc[l]. [g—g]*om.* M. [h]hOstoe B(Lc[l]). [i]Aaz B, Elisdar Lc[l].

684 [a]Emán cantator[a], [b]⁊ frater eius stabat a dextris[b], m. Iohel m. Samuel[c] m. Elcanna[d].

[a—a]Eincantadar B. [b—b]*added at end* BLc[l]. *See below.* [c]*add* Anna nomen matris eius BLc[l]. [d]Alcanna M, *add* m. hIroboam m. Ebel m. Thau m. Saup m. Elcanna m. Maath m. Amassia m. Elchanda m. Iohel m. Zariae m. Saphoniae m. Taath m. Assir m. Abiasaph m. Core m. Isar m. Cad m. Israel et frater eius Asaph astabat a dextris eius B(Lc[l]).

685 Asaph m. Barachiae m. Sunima[a] m. Michael [b]m. Basre[c] m. Melchiae[b] m. Athanae m. Azariae[d] m. Adia m. Ethom[e] m. Semei m. Eth m. [f]Gerson m. Leui[f].
Frater eius [g]stabat a sinistris[g].

[a]Summae B, Sumina Lc[l]. [b—b]*bis* B. [c]Bairi B(Lc[l]). [d]Starae BLc[l]. [e]*add* m. Zamma BLc[l]. [f—f]Gersom Leui ⁊ B(Lc[l]). [g—g]astabat ad sinistram eius BLc[l].

686 Ethan m. Chusi m. Abdi m. Maloch m. Iasabiae m. Amasiae m. Elchiae m. Amassabi[a] m. Bonini[b] m. Sonmer[c] m. Moori m. Musae[d] m. Merari m. Leui [e]et cetera[e].

[a]Amasa(z) (B)Lc[l]. [b]Bonni Lc[l]. [c]Sommer Lc[l]. [d]Muisse BLc[l]. [e—e]*om.* BLc[l].

687 Lamiach Bigamas m. Matasael[a] m. Manuel[b] m. Hirad m. Enoch m. Cain m. Adaim.

[a]Mathusael Lc[l]. [b]Manuhel Lc[l].

688 Moisi [a]m. Amra[a] m. Caid m. Leue m. Iacob m. Isac m. Abraham m. Thare m. Nachor ut supra.

[a—a]*om.* Lc[l].

689.1 Britus m. Siluin[a] m. Ascain m. Aenias[b] m. Anacisen m. Capen m. Asaraci[c] m. Trois[d] m. Erectonii m. Dardain m. Iouis[e] [f]m. Saduirn [g]m. Peli[g] m. Pulloris[h] m. Ohionis[fi] m. Trois[j] m. Esram[k] m. Cain[l] filii[m] [n]maledicti ridentis p*at*rem .i.[n] Nae[o].

2 [p]⁊ aliter Britus[p] m. [q]Isicionis m. Alain[q] m. Etheoin[r] [s]m. Ton[t] m. Bainb[u] m. Semionis [v]m. Mairii[v] m. Iacathi[w] [x]m. Aurthachi[sx] m. Ooth m. Abyr[y] m. Sru[z] m. Esru[aa] m. Baath[bb] m. Iobeth m. Ianaind[cc] m. Iath*fed* m. Nae[dd].

3 [ee]Britanus[ff] aliter m. Feargusa[gg] m. Neimid m. Agnon m. Kaim[hh] m. Taid m. Sera m. Zru[ii] m. Bramin m. Fathecht m. Magoth[jj] m. Iathfed m. Nae m. Laimiach.

4 No Britinus[ff] filius Alaii[kk] qui primus de seimine Iathfen[ll] in Eoropam uenit. Alii dicunt combad do macaib Israel do Padraic. Dia rohinsat[mm] Meic Israel la Tit ⁊ la Uaespoc[nn] i ndigail fola Crist, is ann doriacht bunadh Padraig co hErind[ee].

[a]Selbin Lc[l], Silui La. [b]Aeneae Lc[l], Aeiniassa M. [c]Asairgi m. Ile M(La). [d]*add* a quo Troianna MLa. [e]Ioib MLa. [f—f]*added in small hand* M. [g—g]*om.* MLa. [h]Polloir M(La). [i]Ophionis Lc[l], Apion M(La). [j]Treis M, Tses La(*with punctum under first* s). [k]Me(a)sra(i)m Lc[l](M)La. [l]Caim Lc[l]MLa. [m]m. MLa. [n—n]*om.* MLa. [o]*add* mad iar naroili im̄, is Britan Mael m. Ḟergusa Leitdirg seinathair na mBreatan, amal asbert in duine eolach: Britan Mael mac na flatha, saer in slichtradh dar sretha, mac in Leithdeirg a lechtmuir, otait Breatnaig in beatha M(La). [p—p]Britus aliter Lc[l], Brittus MLa. [q—q]Isacon m. Alainius M, Hisicon [m] Alaini La. [r]Ethoir Lc[l], Feithiuir m. Agamoin M(La). [s—s]*leaf either cut away or illeg.* La. [t]Toi Lc[l](M). [u]B[...]db M. [v—v]*om.* M. [w]Iathecht M. [x—x]*om.* M. [y]Aibir M. [z]Raa MLa. [aa]Sra La. [bb]Sru(u) M(La). [cc]Ioau M, Ioan no m. Ionan La. [dd]*add* Is amlaid sin im̄ adfiadaid sdaire Roman seanchus Breatan M(La). [ee—ee]*om.* MLa. [ff]Britus Lc[l]. [gg]*add* Lethdeirg Lc[l]. [hh]Paim Lc[l]. [ii]Sru m. Esru Lc[l]. [jj]Magoc Lc[l]. [kk]Alani Lc[l]. [ll]Iafed Lc[l]. [mm]rohinraid Lc[l]. [nn]Uesber Lc[l].

MISCELLANEOUS ITEMS

690 [a]De gen*er*ibus sanctorum Clainde[b] Lugdach[ac].

1 Aed m. Guaire m. Lugdach[d] m. Loegaire .i. [e]oc Gabuil[e] Mucraigi[f] oc[g] Lochaib Erni[h].

2 Fainche[i] Garb ingen[j] Chrimthaind[k] m. Guaire m. Lugdach[l] m. Loegaire i[m] rRus Airthir[n] ic Lochaib[o] Erni.

3 Comaig[p] ingen Echach[q] m. Ailella m. Guaire m. Lugdach[d] m. Loegaire ic[m] Snám Luthair[r] [s]i n-oenchill[s] 7 a[t] brathair, .i.[u] Colman m. Echach, for Lochaib[v] Erne[w]. Is é dna fil [x]i mMidiṡiul[x].
Aglend[y] im̄[z] ingen Lenin[aa] a mmathair.

[a—a]*added above* LM, *added after* 1 *with corruption of Latin* BLcLb. [b]Cluain Lb. [c]Luigde(a)ch BLb(M). [d]Luigdeach M. [e—e]oc(h)ail(l) BLc(Lb). [f]Muscraidi BLc(LbM). [g]hi Lb. [h]Ernni*us* BLc. [i]Fui*n*e B, Fuin(d)che (Lc)Lb. [j]mac BLc. [k]Chremthainn M. [l]Luigde(a)ch B(M). [m]o Lb. [n]Arthair B. [o]Loch BLb. [p]Coma Lb. [q]Eochaigh M. [r]Luchair Lb. [s—s]*om.* M. [t]*om.* BLc. [u]*om.* Lc. [v]Loch BLcLb. [w]Erneib Lc. [x—x]ainigisel B(Lc), oc Miisel Lb. [y]Ai*n*dli Lc. [z]dí Lc, *om.* Lb. [aa]*add* .i. siur Cholmain fessin Lb.

4 Ruman[a] m. Colmain in fili[b] [c]dia 'tá[c] Sil [d]Rumain i nAth[d] Truim. Tri[e] filid[f] in domain .i. Homer[g] o Grecuib 7 Fergil o Latinnaib et Ruman o Gaedelaib[h].
Secht meic Rumain: Subne[i] epscop[j], Cendfaelad epscop, Rudgius[k] et[l] Muridach[m], Cellach[mn], Conall[m], Cairpre.
Fuinecht[o] ingen Maele[p] Fithrich[q] m. Dimma m. Colmain mathair Cormaic 7 Baethgalaich[r] 7 Rumain; trí meic Colmain *ui* Subni .i. Corp*re*[s] [*or read* Corp*mac*] epscop m. Colmain [t]dia n-epert[t] Oengus *ua* Oibleain:

[u]Dlomthus cach[u] co ollmuir
féil [v]Chormaic[w] co *n*glanbuil[vx],

[y]Baethallach[z] m. Colmain[y].

5 Cairech Cluana[aa] Bairend siur Ronain m. Beraig et cetera ut ante.

6 Cainne[bb] ingen Brosain m. Muredaig ic[cc] Tig Cainne lasna[dd] Desi[ee] Breg.

[a]Ruma Lc. [b]filed Lb. [c—c]otatt Lb. [d—d]Ruminath B. [e]teora Lb. [f]fileda BLc. [g]Emhar B(Lc), (h)Eber (Lb)M. [h]Goedelu Lb. [i].i. Uib(n)e (BLb)Lc. [j]*add* 7 Lb. [k]Ruidius epscop M. [l]*om.* Lb. [m]*add* 7 BLc. [n]*om.* Lc. [o]Finnecht M. [p]Moel Lb. [q]Fichre BLc. [r]Baethalaig BLc. [s]Corp̄ B, Cairp̄ Lc(Lb), Coirp*r*i M. *See note.* [t—t]ut dixit Lb. [u—u]dlom tassach Lb, dlom*us* cach BLc(M). [v—v]*added in marg.* M. [w]Corc̄ B. [x]*n*glanbuilida*ch*? M, *add* 7rł Lb. [y—y]*om.* Lb. [z]Baethgalach B. [aa]i Cluain BLc. [bb]*bis* Lc. [cc]o Lb. [dd]hi Lb. [ee]De(i)sib (B)LcLb(M).

690.7 Scandlach[a] ingen Sechnasaig m. [b]Coluim Cuile[b] m. Muredaig m. Loegaire m. Neil[c] i[d] nArd Scandlaig[e] i Cen*iu*l[f] Ardgair[g].

8 Cainer[h] ingen Chaelain[i] m. Libir[j] m. Daillini[k] m. Loegaire[l].

9 [m]Aed Mór m. Fergusa m. Ḟeidlimid m. Loegari[l] et[n] Aed Bec a brathair [o]i[p] nAth Truim[moq].

10 Coinet[r] ingen Cholmain m. Aeda [s]m. Libir[s] et Odba[t] ingen Cholmain[u] et Ricell[v] ingen Attract[w] m. Aeda m. Libir[x] — siur do[y] Chassan m. Attract[z] — [aa]et Ronnat ingen [bb]Ḟiachna m. Aeda[bb] [cc]m. Libir[cc] i Cluain Cuirc i mMaig Locha sin[aa].

[a]Scandlaech Lb. [b]Clochuile B, Colchuile Lc. [c]*add* Naigiallaig LcLb. [d]o Lb. [e]Scandlaige Lb. [f]Ceƚ B, *om.* Lc. [g]Ardgail Lb. [h]Caeimḟer M. [i]Cholmain M[l], *add* m. Aeda M[l]R[l]La. [j]Li(u)bair BLcLb(MR[l])La, Librein Lc[l]. [k]Doillen Lb, Dallain M, *add* m. Enna Lc[l]. [l]*add* m. Neill Naegiallaig Lc[l]. [m—m]*arranged differently* Lc[l]. [n]*om.* Lc. [o—o]*om.* LcLc[l]. [p]ag M. [q]*add* atat Lb. [r]Co(i)ned BLc(Lb), Coimed M, Coenet R[l]. [s—s]m. Libair BLcLbM, *om.* M[l]R[l]La. [t]O(b)ba (M[l]R[l])La. [u]*add* m. Aeda M[l]R[l]La. [v]Riagail R[l]. [w]Athrachta R[l]. [x]Li(u)bair BLcLbM(M[l])R[l]La, *add* m. Endai m. Loegaire m. Neill Naegiallaig .i. Lb, m. Daillne m. Ennai M[l](R[l]La). [y]*om.* Lb. [z]Cat(t)racht B(Lc). [aa—aa]*om.* M. [bb—bb]*reversed* B, *add* derbratair d'Athro*cht* La. [cc—cc]m. Libren Lc, m. Libair .i. Lb, *om.* M[l]R[l].

11 Lasar ingen Ḟergusa a siur i Cluain Lagen i Crich Loegaire[a] Breg.

12 Illadan[b] m.[c] Echdach[d] m. Aeda m. Daimine m. Ennae m. Loegaire m. Neil[e] [f]i[g] rRaith Liphiten[h] la[i] Firu[j] Cell [k]i mMide[fk].

13 [l]Beoan m. Attract[m] [n]et Ossan[o] m. Attract[ln] i[g] rRaith Ossain 7[p] i[g] rRaith Attrach[q] ri[r] Ath Truim aníar.

14 Mael Tuile m. Nochure m. Ḟoractair[s] m. Mael Derir m. Tuammine m. Baetain[t] m. Muredaig m. Loegaire m. Neill[u]

15 Colum Cule 7 Colum Tommae[v] [w]da mac[w] Muridaig m. Loegaire m. Neill[x].

[a]Laeghe BLc(Lb). [b](7) Liadan (B)Lc, Liagaine Lb. [c]*ingen* Lb. [d]Ech B. [e]*add* Naigiallaig (m. Echach Muidmedoin) Lb(Lc[l]). [f—f]*om.* Lc[l]. [g]o Lb. [h]Lifen Lb. [i]hi Lb. [j]Fer(a)ib (B)Lc, Tir Lb. [k—k]*om.* Lb. [l—l]*arranged differently* Lb. [m]Athrachta BLc. [n—n]*om.* B. [o]Casan M. [p]*om.* B. [q]Athracht(ai) (B)LcLbM. [r]fri(a) (B)LcLb. [s]Forachtaig Lb. [t]Baethain M. [u]*add* Naigiallaig BLcLbLc[l]. [v]Trom(f)ada (B)Lc. [w—w]cland Lb. [x]*add* Naigiallaig LcLb.

16 Garban[a] epscop m. Oengusa m. Ardgail[b] m. Conaill Cremthainne m. Neill[c].

17 Cerc[d] ingen Echach[e] m. Loegaire[f] [g]i[h] Tig na hErḟoclaige[i] i mMugdornaib[gj].

[a]Gabran M[l]R[l]. [b]Ardail Lc. [c]*add* Naigiallaig BLcLbLc[l]M[l]R[l]HLa. [d]Cer BLc, Searc Lc[l]. [e]*add* m. Aeda Lc[l]. [f]Laegda m. Aire Lb, *add* m. Neill Naegiallaig Lc[l]. [g—g]*om.* Lc[l]. [h]o Lb. [i]Foclaige B(LcLb). [j]Murndaib B.

690.18 Diarmait m. Baeth m. Aeda m. Loegaire [k]m. Neill[k] ic[h] Airiud[l] [m]Sinnaig, [n]*no* Senaig[mn], ic[o] Lochaib[p] Erne et a brathair[q] Cobthach mac Baeth i[h] nAchud Maic[r] i Crích Loegaire.

[k—k]*om.* BLcLb. [l]Araid BLc, Ard Lb. [m—m]Senaigh B(Lc)Lb, Sinaig M. [n—n]*added below* L. [o]ar Lc. [p]Loch BLcLb. [q]*add* .i. Lb. [r]Baith B, Etaich Lc, Inaich (*or read* Maich) Lb.

691 Ethne — [a]ic[b] Ros Tiprat[ac] — ingen Dimmae m. Noe m. Fechin[d] m. Corpre filed[e] m. Ailella Máir m. Breccain[f] m. Feic m. Dare Barraich m. Cathair M*oir*.
Derbḟind Belḟota[g] ainm aile di[h].

[a—a]*added above line* L, *in text* M, *after* Cathair Moir BLcLb. [b]o Lb. [c]Tipraite M, *add* 7 Lb. [d]E(i)chin Lb(M). [e]fileda B. [f]Brac(c)ain BLc(LbM). [g]Beladh BLc. [h]*add* ba hisin beos mathair Colaim Cille Lb.

692 Secht n-ingena Dalbrónaig etc. *See note.* Cf. 722.4-13.

693 Clann Darerca etc. *See note.* Cf. 722.16.

694 Lomman Atha Truim m. Dallain m. Bresail m. Mane m. Domnaill m. Colla Mind m. Echach Domlen.

695 Tri meic Angain m. Retacha[a]: Mac Rethi 7 Cairnán[b], Colman i Cill Etargabla i Fid [Manach][c].

[a]Ratach .i. M. [b]Cairrnen M, *add* 7 M. [c]*illeg.* L, Manach M.

696 Allabair 7 Dessabair 7 [a]Lessabair[b] 7 Midabair[a] i Cill Arad [c]ic Raith Lid[...][c].

[a—a]*reversed* M. [b]Lasabair M. [c—c]a crich Aradh M.

697.1 De chomlib Dáil Chaiss do mMobae .i. Baethanan[a] m. Sinill.

2 Iamnat im̄. ingen Ṡinill mathair Émin Ruis Glais.

3
Sin ingen Néill, niamda a dath,
ba máthair don Baeth buadach.
Mochaemra[b] ingen Neill náir
mathair cháemalaind Chronáin.

4
[c]A Iamnat ingen Ṡinill
meic Nadfraeích [...] atberim,
ragaid do mac éc innocht,
bia cen abb is cen epscop[c].

[a]Baethan M. [b]Mochaerath M. [c—c]*in marg infer. with* cecinit *added above* L, *om.* M.

698 Scandlach sétig[a] Aeda Róin rig *Ua* Falgi bert ingin do Aed Róin, .i. Crednat a ainm, 7 dobert a mmathair dia hingin a rath[b] conid Crednat ingen Aeda Roin congab Ráth[c] Scanlaigi [d]i Termun[d] Brigti.

[a]seidchi M. [b]rathan M. [c]ratha M. [d—d]eidir mun M.

699.1 Trea[a] ropo maith in ben,
ingen Ronáin rig Lagen,
cona caemcheil gnathaig cain,
máthair Baithin maic Finnaig[b].

2 Finnach foglaid robaí i ṅgait
isin sciaich forsin[c] tiprait,
dia tánic d'indlat a lám
Trea rindbalc ingen Ronain.

3 O roderc in foglaid féig
for ingin Ronain roréil,
rosní[d] ní dia thoil a cuirp
forin gas[e] ṁbilair ṁblathguirt.

4 Rochaith inn ingen in ṅgas
forsa [mbai][f] int adbar amnas,
suairc in saerchéim asa gleo
[g]dia racompred[g] Baethin bithbeo.

[a]Treaa M. [b]Indaig M. [c]osin M. [d]rossnig M. [e]gois M. [f]*illeg.* L, mbai M. [g—g]dia*r*cho*m*be*r*t M.

700.1 Cros Chammin, dar m'irlabra,
do bennachad mo laide,
meic Colmain meic Comarbaig
meic Insain is meic Aine.

2 *No*[a] Cammin caem, inar caṅgnim[b],
mac Dimmae de roLagnib,
a Fothartaib[c] Fea fuarustair,
is ass, iar fír, dia athair.

3 *No*[a] Camin Insi Celtra cain
mac Dimmae meic Feidlimid,
meic Ḟlaind, luchair lathairṅglain[d],
d'Uib[e] Briuin Ratha a Connactaib.

[a]*om.* M. [b]caingnib M. [c][...]a*r*t M. [d]latharngle M. [e]duaib M.

701 Colum Cille cecinit.

1 Secht meic áille Oengusa
lotar co íath ṅhErenn,
Mothrianoc is Itharnaisc,
Eoganán aille remend.

2 Mothrianoc i rRuscachaib,
la *U* Falge rofaemad,
Cend Leccaig im Eoganan,
Itharnaisc án i Cloenad.

3 In cethrur forḟacabsat,
luidset dar farge fostán,
Torannán is Agatan,
Muchulli an is Troscan.

4 Troscan tren tarrasair
i nArd Breccain co mbinni,
Torannan in tairbertach
os toraib Tulcha tinni.

5 Mochuille in Dresnatha
Fothart Fea, feidm n-ualle,
Agatan 'na disiurtan
ar bru na Ethni uaire.

6 Uais itge condrancatar
forind Ardríg find fethal,
combad oenláe a n-estechtsum
'na cure comlan cethrar.

7 I pridnoin Iuin etamuin
luidset a bethaid brethglain
di deoin Meic Dé datharail
'na curi comlan cethrair.

8 Ind lecc fora tancatar
dar tríathmuir trethnaig,
Agatan a sosarsum
rosfuc a crandcor cethruir.

9 Na manistri fuaratar
i nde[r]natar a ferta,
is la *U* Neill Noigiallaich
co rrath in Spirta sechta. S.

702.1 Brathir Fursu, cóir a rad,
Mochoe[a], nach [b]daimend acrad[b],
Epscop Mac Erca glan gne
o[c] Domnuch Mor in Maige[d].

2 Colman[e] Mulind[f], mór a rath,
[g]domunim o ranoemad[g]
Colman Comraire co llí,
Manchan [h][do] Liath [lige][h].

3 Ba hísin a siur uile,
Damnat[i], beoda[j] in dune,
et ba langart la[k] nech
Damnat chonnalb Chonaillech.

4 Ba d'Uíb[l] Laga[m] na llend
in sesiur[n] dorurmisem[o],
7 Damnat ní gó dam
cona sessiur derbbrathar. B[p].

5 Ingen[q] Milcon[r], miad cen on,
a mmathair a mmorfessiur,
is Milcon, miad cen raind,
ropo mug maith Mac Albraind[s]. B.

[a]*glossed* .i. o Oendruim i lLeith Chathail (Chliathain) L(M). [b—b]damann acrad M. [c]a M. [d]*glossed* .i. M*ag* Co|ba|L. [e]*glossed* .i. o Daire Chaechain i nDal Riatae (ata) L(M). [f]Cuilind M. [g—g]a nDomnach Mor donaemad M. [h—h]*partly illeg.* L, doliathad lige M. [i]*glossed* .i. Tigi D*amnatan* i Sl*eib* Betha L(M). [j]fa beoda M. [k]le M. [l]dub M. [m]*glossed* .i. i Conaillib L(M). [n]*add* sin M. [o]doruirbsim M(*with* b *above line*). [p]*om.* M. [q]*glossed* Bronach nomen eius L. [r]*glossed* de Dal Araide L. [s]Alpraind M.

ALIASES OF THE SAINTS

703.1 Crimthand ainm Coluim Cille.

2 Oengus ainm Meic Nisi Condere[a].

3 Cunnid ainm[b] Meic Culind Lusca[c].

4 Carthach ainm[b] Mochutu Lis[d] Moir.

5 Moeca ainm Fechin Fabuir[c].

6 Gnia ainm Muru Othna M*oire*.

7 Dachua[e] ainm[b] Dachualen[f].

[a]Condeirgi M. [b]*add* baisti La. [c]*om.* La. [d]Lesa La. [e]*add* Aileoin La. [f]Dachuilind M, in da Chailin 7 comad esidein Cuan Atha Escrach la Condachta La.

703.8 Darerca ainm Moninni [g]Cilli Slebe[g].

9 Carthach ainm Cummini.

10 Crónán [ainm][h] Mochua meic Lugdach[i].

11 Cunnid ainm Coluim meic Crimthainn.

12 Tairchell ainm Molling.

13 Fer Da Chrích ainm Meic Cairthind[j].

14 Aed ainm Mael Doid M*u*c*nama*[k].

15 Colman[l] ainm Meic Lenin.

16 Aed ainm Moedoc[m] Ferna[n].

17 Lasren[o] ainm Molassi.

18 Finnbarr[p] ainm Finnen Maige Bili.

19 Eog[q][an ainm] Mic [Olchon][q].

20 Diarmait [q][ainm Modimoc][q].

21 Sa[q][nntlethan ainm Chaemain][q].

22 [r]Oengus ainm Meic Nisi náir,
Crimthand ainm Coluim comlain,
Col*um* mac Crimthaind, deilm n̄dil,
is dó ba comainm Cunnid[r].

[g—g]*above line* L, *om.* M. [h]*om.* L, ainm M. [i]Luigdeach M. [j]Carthaind .c. M. [k]mc̄.c. M. [l]Colum M. [m]*add above line* da *and beneath* .i. Maedoc M. [n]*add in marg.* Moire .i. Maedoc m. Nairetlainde 7 Maedoc Chluana Moir M. [o]Lasair M. [p]Barren M. [q—q]*illeg.* L, *reading between brackets from* M. [r—r]*added below cols.* a-d L, *om.* M, *add* Succaid ainm baisdig Patraic ... *etc.* MR[l](see 1.4), *add further,* Finntan ainm Munna m. Thulchain. Is do rob ainm Maedoc M(*at foot of previous column*).

704 Nomina episcoporum Hibernensium incipiunt.

1 E Patricius
E Patricius Ruis Delae
E Patricius hostiarius
E Secundinus, .i. Sechnall
5 E Benignus
E Tassach
E Bron
E Tigernach
E Eugen bis
10 E Mac Nisi
E Mochta
E Buti
E Ciannan
E Ibar
15 E Beoaed
[E] Corpre bis
[E] Cerbbán
E Iserninus
E Cathar
20 E Cethech
E hErcc quinquies
E Ailbe
E Declan
E Carthach
25 E Senan
E Moínend bis
E Mac Cuilind
E Iarlaithe
E Aed
30 [E] Illand bis
E Mél
[E] Melchu
E Ictar
E Murithach
35 E Loarnach bis
E Sachell
E Cormaide quater
E Martan bis
E Acher
40 E Diu
E Midan
E Idan
E Cillini
E Dind
45 E Eitchaín
E Aildan
E Mac Uamae
E Aidgein
E Muadan
50 E Fraichan
E Talan
E Mac Rithe bis
E Rón
E Mellan bis
55 E Grellán
E Odrán bis
E Blaan
E Ailill bis
E Conall bis
60 E Conlae
[E] Lugbae
E Aidbe
E Dimmae
E Nathfráich
65 E Cloathach
E Olcan bis
E Lonan
E Segan
E Senan bis
70 E Feidlimid bis
E Griguir
E Conaire
E Dauid bis
E Fiachra
75 E Daniel
E Follomuin
E Senach
E Beone
E Dron
80 E Cairill Garb m. Aeda
E Indlene
E Coblath
E Helene
E Colum ter
85 E Ainmiri bis
E Fictair
E Étail
E Fiachra bis
E Dimma
90 E Barrand
E Ercaed
E Mac Ercca bis
E Comgellán bis
E Brenaind
95 E Benen

704. E Luccat
E Beogen bis
E Breccan
E Fiachna
100 E Banban bis
E Mac Ríme
E Uidrine
E Findbarr bis
E Colman ter
105 E Nectan
E hErnin
E Moninn
E Donnan
E Guasacht
110 E Moinis
E Nem
E Failbe
E Nathí bis
E Fintan
115 E Eogan Aird Sratha
E Domongart i lLoin
E Sabarnach
E Rochad
E Columb
120 E Bulggeni
E Beothin
E Mochonóc
E Garban
E Oengus m. Conaill
125 E Oengus m. Aeda Roin
E Oengus i Sraith Epscoip Oengusa
E Oengus Cluana Éicni
E Oengus Derci Daim
E Diarmait i Cluain Iraird
130 E Diarmait i rRaith Diarmata
E Diarmait i nDomnuch Mór
E Diarmait i Sraith Melgi
E Diarmait i Cill Achaid Goan
E Diarmait i nImliuch
135 E Diarmait i rRaith Chairill
E Diarmait i Carraic Bretan
E Diarmait i nAchud Chaíl
E Diarmait Glinni Uisen
E Nem i nDruim Berthach
140 E Nem i nDomnuch Neman
E Nem i Findloch
E Neman i Cein Murthemni
E Ném i nEdiunn Mór
E Nem i nEdonn Bic
145 E Sinchell
[E] Aedan
E Bec Fine
E Senan
[E] Mac Cainnae
150 E Fircran
[E] Conenach
E Ruadan
E Mac Rithe
E Mac Cairthind
155 E hEithern i nDomnuch Mór Mugdorn
E Duran
[E] Cérin
E hUnniuc
[E] Molling
160 E Comgaidi
E Corban
[E] Lomb
E Indas
[E] Mórin
165 E Mac Táil
[E] Fiac
E Lugech
[E] Commán
E Brandub
170 E Nannid
[E] Manchin
E Mellan
E Exorcist
[E] Santlár
175 E Dimma
[E] Santán
E Brenan
E Tabarn
[E] Daurthach
180 E Conchend

04. [E] Luachan
E Sillan bis
[E] Dagan
E Berchan i Cluain Sasta
185 E Gemman i nDomnuch Mór
E Gemman
E Baetán
[E] Berchan Senchilli
E Altechon
190 E Ernach
[E] Mochellóc
[E] Beoan
[E] Sarán
E Anfudan
195 E Fergna
[E] Cillini
E Rifín
[E] Fithal
E Fer Fugill
200 E Dallán
[E] Tigernach
E Mornedoc Feda Duin
E Colman septies
E Senchan
205 [E] Cummine
E Dairchill
E Molibba
E Emine
[E] German
210 E Bobai
[E] Doimthechan
E Morioc
E Líber Find
E Fintan
215 E Mocholmóc
E Mochommóc
E Aed
E Findech
E Suibne
220 E Tarnoe
E Gubbi
E Barrán
E Barrchu
E Beoan
225 E Colman quater
E Nessan
E Comgell
E Lochen .i. Locha Indin
E Duach
230 E Mac Caille
E Conlaed
E Aithmetan
E Teltoc
E Berach
235 [E] Loegaire
E Loemin
[E] Duthaig
E Nemnan
E Coman
240 E Cuinne
E Findlug
E Factna
E Caíte
[E] Iustan
245 E Mínu
[E] Fergus
E Munnu
E Midan
E Illand
250 E Enan
E Id
E Enii
E Finnech
E Connad
255 E Guaire
E Aedgein
E Gribuir
E Muadan
E Fraechan
260 E Bechan
E Loppan
E Gillan
E Dai
E Conla
265 E Concraid
E Mac Aidain
E Cathub
E Douch
E Dego
270 E Senchan
E Cathchan
E Findchan
E Etan
E Cairnne
275 E Cairell
E Lugidan
E Saran

704. E Critan
E Setna
280 E Santan decies
E Mantan decies
E Broccan
E Eíthne
E Aed bis
285 E Mac Cuill
E Achell
E Enne
E Enna
[E] Aildan
290 E Aibden
E Carthach
E Cobtach
Finit de Episcopis.

705 Incipit de sacerdotibus

1 S Finnian Cluana Iraird Maccua Tellduib sacerdos ⁊ magister
S Ciaran m. in t[S]áeir
S Brenaind Birra
S Brenaind M*accua* Alta
5 S Colum Tiri Da Glas
S Colum Cille
S Comgall Bennchair
S Cainnech M*accua* Daland
S Molassi Daminsi
10 S Mobí Clarenech
S Enne Airne
S Molua m. Oche
S Nessan Corcaige
S Colman Ela
15 S Cormac *Ua* Liathain
S Oenu M*accua* Laigsi
S Molasse m. Declain
S Sinchell sosar
S Fintan Cluana Eidnech
20 S Coemgen Glinne Da Locha
S Munnu m. Tulchain
S Magnend Cilli Magnend
S Mobae M*accua* Alta
S Fintan Cluana Cain
25 S Fintan Dromma Ińg
S Fintan Methuis Móir
S Fintan Cilli Lacha
S Fintan Dromma Lethluim
S Fintan Corthi Bic
30 S Fintan i Tulchaib
S Fintan Insi Liac
S Fintan Cilli Achid
S Fintan Cilli Ruaid
S Fintan Tuamma Carech
35 S Fintan Cula Micain
S Fintan i nAirenuch
S Cainnech sexies
S Diarmait sexies
S Colman sexies
40 S Coeman sexies
S Aed sexies
S Odran sexies
S Tunni
S Enne bis
45 S Laed
[S] Libran
S Lucenn
S Lucell
S Lugan ter
50 S Lasru
S Lonan ter
S Lothech
S Luigne
S Lugan bis
55 S Liathan bis
S Licce
S Beone
S Bicge
S Becgan bis
60 S Broccine
S Barrḟind
S Bicgne
S Brocan
S Beoan
65 S Berach
S Biucru
S Aithmet

S Ailan
[S] Ailither bis
70 S Aedbe
S Altine
S Aedan
S Aelbe
[S] Colbe
75 S Cantan
S Corcan
S Catan
S Cathach
S Cronan
80 S Coinne
S Cummine
S Crunmael
S Anfadan
S Cuaran
85 S Conchraid
S Comman
S Cormac
S Cruadeni
S Colggu
90 S Crederc
S Cilli
[S] Cana
S Conain
S Cairnan
95 S Cathaer
S Ciaran
S Cobthach
S Critan
S Coemgeni
100 S Condoc
S Conlóc
S Caillidi
S Ciaru
S Cathar
105 S Cathach
S Cellach
S Mac Loga
S Dai
[S] Dimma
110 S Donnan
S Diblini
S Demman
S Dicull
S Drochdene
115 S Daithnau
S Dergadan
S Duban
S Dechnan
S Diun
120 [S] Daigre
S Enan
S Eolach
[S] Ernine
S Finán
125 S Faelan bis
S Fonascach
S Fiacc
S Flannan
S Fiachna
130 S Fidrue
S Failchu
S Findchan
S Fiachra
S Fuacgan
135 S Fergus
S Gaini
S Gentini
S Guaire
S Grellan
140 S Glaisne
S Iustan
S hOillan
S Ercbe
S hErc
145 [S] Ibar
S Murgen
S Mochaeme
S Monois
S Menn Bairend
150 S Moinne
S Dubad
S Scandal
S Saran
S Nathí
155 S Critan
S Mell
[S] Gaibreni
S Dahenach
S Declán
160 S Riced
[S] Muridach
S Loarnach
S Eugen bis
S Setan
165 [S] Cair

705. S Lochan
S Condla
S Baiscne
S Sodamna
170 S Beolaig
S Nem
[S] Maedor
S Tinnu
S Dergan
175 S Pite
[S] Colum bis
S Meltan
S Garban
S Senchan
180 S Feidlimid
S Molappóc
S Maene
S Sinell
S Riced
185 S Lugba
S Rigla
[S] Eoan
S Saigru
S Finnach
190 S Sinnach
S Nessan
S Ailbe
S Mogemóc
S Eochaid
195 S Amargenn
S Tispir
[S] Sín
S Liber bis
S Cruthnechan
200 S Cruitin
[S] Dua
S Corcc
S Blocc
S Fergg
205 [S] Cliaman
S Cailan
[S] Cuanán
S Cilline
[S] Cathal
210 S Dichu
[S] Condla bis
S Cascend
[S] Olcan
S Astar
215 [S] Iust
S Santan
[S] Lugaed
S Ronan
[S] Daigre
220 S Beoaed
[S] Carthach
S Conamail
[S] Lochan
S Froechan
225 S Cendḟota
S Eochaid
S Rechtaire
S Dumassu
S Comgaide
230 S Maitan
[S] Fota
S hErmech
[S] Sigi
S Trianoc
235 S Oísine
[S] Munnu
S Findech bis
[S] Beoane
S Dianach
240 [S] Regol
S Senach
[S] Bron
S Fin bis
[S] Sarán
245 S Cillan
[S] Setne
S Mac Luga
[S] Conán
S Tigernach
250 [S] Congus
S Cuinne
[S] Berach
S Luguran
S Euganan
255 S Muadan
[S] Ross
S Adomnan
S Comgell
[S] Ficht
260 S Dallan
[S] Coel
S Tempur
[S] Lasrán

705. S Mac hUda
265 [S] Loṅg
S Subne
[S] Rotan
S Cobban
[S] Fige
270 S Manchan
[S] Brigán
S Brandub
[S] Conben
S Domthechan
275 [S] Conla
S Sillan
[S] Finnech

706 Incipit de Diaconibus

1 Dechoin Nessan
D Stephan
D Mantan
D hAilchi
5 [D] Lugair
D Cellach
[D] Iustan
D Dubthach
D Talán
10 [D] hErc
D Fintan bis
[D] Iucan
D Massan
[D] Nem
15 D Ieir
[D] Sechan
D Grellan
[D] Columb
D Aedgen
20 [D] Lugnei
D Maccan
[D] Orcan
D Sétna
[D] Mél
25 D Findchan
D Conne
[D] Baite
D Aedo
[D] Ossan bis
30 D Moisi
[D] Fergus
D Beoaed
[D] Aed
D Bolg
35 [D] Amalgaid
D Nathí
[D] Brócan
D Luchan
[D] Elche
40 D Froechan
D Dubthach
D Senach bis
[D] Tinne
D Cassan
45 [D] Mac hÍ
D Daigre
[D] Daiae
D Eoaet
[D] Lenine
50 D Leaed
[D] Ciaran
D Coilbe
[D] Liber
D Iohain
55 [D] Saran
D hUargnaid
D Runce
[D] Coimlug
D Cate
60 [D] Ruadan
D Nesba
[D] Cainnech
D Dergan
[D] Cairell
65 D Fiachrach
D Lugaid
[D] Colman
D Cronán
[D] Finnech
70 Decoin a Tig na nDechoin la Ultu
D Lithchin
[D] Erc
D Bernach
[D] Cámmine
75 D Comman
[D] Colman

707 Comainmnigud noem hErenn so sis

1 Aedan Irluachra
Aedan *Ua* ṅGarrchon
Aedan m. Oengusa
Aedan Inorois
5 Aedan m. Declain *no* Mellain
Aedan m. Barrḟind
Aedan m. Carthaig
Aedan m. Blaain
Aedan m. Congnaid
10 Aedan Liss Moir
Aedan Echaird
Aedan Cluana Dartada
Aedan Cluana Tarb
Aedan Tulcha Lathim
15 Aedan Daire ṁBruchais
Aedan laech
Aed Ferna
Aed m. Bricc
Aed *Ua* Dunlaing
20 Aed Dromma Senaig
Aed Foibreni
Aed Bec
Aed Mor
Aed Cluana Cáin
25 Aed m. Colgan
Aed m. Gormain
Dá Aed Culi Caitt
Aed Slebti
Aed Dromma Cairill
30 Aed Tigi m. Bricc
Aed m. Mursan
Aed Cilli Derci Daim
Da Aed Atha Truim
D[a] Aed Cluana Domai[l]
35 Brenaind Birra
Brenaind m. ua Alta
Brenaind m. Cronain
Brenaind Libir
Brenaind m. Nathí
40 Brenaind m. Muinfathe
Brenaind m. Tire
Brenaind m. Garbain
Brenaind m. Dimmae
Brenaind m. Fiachrach
45 Brenaind Etarcluana
Brenaind Dromma Liac
Brenaind Dromma Liss
Brenaind Tigi Oissín
Brenaind Roiss Chaim
50 Brenaind Aird Eo
Brenaind Aird Goan
Barrḟind m. Aeda
Barrḟind Metine
Barrḟind *Ua* Neill
55 Barrḟind m. Cormaic
Barrḟind Rois Drochit
Barrḟind Cind Tuirc
Barrḟind Cilli m. Lugni ⁊ Ailill
Breccan .i. Craibdech
60 Breccan m. Echach
Breccan Cind Bairche
Breccan m. Tuathail
Breccan Achaid Chaitt
Breccan Maige Ochtair
65 Breccan Echdromma
Breccan Feili
Breccan m. Saráin
Breccan dalta Finniain

Title/om. R, so sis/ and so(sis)(B)Lc^{l}. 4 Inorois/ ind Rois RBLc^{l}. R *has* similiter *in marg. opposite this entry.* 5 m. Declain/ *om.* RBLc^{l}. 9 Congnaid/ Congnaich B. 10 Echaird/ Echairid RBLc^{l}. 14 Tulcha/ Tilcha RLc^{l}. 15 ṁBruchais/ Bruchas R, Bruacha(i)s B(Lc^{l}). 16 *Add.* xvi. sunt RBLc^{l}. 18 Similiter *opposite* R. 19 *Followed by* 28 RBLc^{l}. 20 *Followed by* 29 RBLc^{l}. 21 *Followed by* 30 RBLc^{l}. 24 *Followed by* 31 RBLc^{l}. 25 *Followed by* 32 RBLc^{l}. 26 m. Gormain/Cormain RB(Lc^{l}) *Followed by* 33 RBLc^{l}. 27 Aed Cuili Caitt *bis* RLc^{l}. 33 Aed Atha Truimm *bis* RLc^{l}. 34 Aed Cluana Domail *bis* RLc^{l}. *Add* .xxi. sunt RBLc^{l}. 36 Similiter *opposite* R, m. ua/ m. Lc^{l}. 40 m./ *om.* BLc^{l}, Muinfathe/ Muinfote RB(Lc^{l}). 50 Aird/ Ard(d)a (R)BLc^{l}. 51 Goan/ Gain B.*Add* .xuii. sunt RBLc^{l}. 58 ⁊ Ailill/ B. ocus Ailill RBLc^{l}. *Add* .uiii. sunt RBLc^{l}. 59 .i. Craibdech/Breccan Craibdech R(BLc^{l}). 61 Bairche/Bairc(c)i (R)BLc^{l}. 67 m./ *om.* RBLc^{l}. 68 Finniain/ Finnia R(BLc^{l}).

707. Breccine Tigi m. Berchain
7 Brecnat
70 Brocan Toirc Roiss
Brocan Cloen
Brocan Escrach
Brocan scribnid
Brocan Cluana Immorchair
75 Colum Cille
Colum m. Crimthainn
Colum m. Riagail
Colum m. *ua* Airte
Colum m. Angle
80 Colum Achaid Domongairt
Colum Locha Suide
Colum Cairech
Colum Ratha
Colum Locha Cré
85 Colum epscop la Ultu
Colum epscop i Tethbai
Colum epscop la *U* Fidgeinte
Colum Coel
Colum croxere
90 Colum m. Aeda [...]
Colum m. Blaain
Colum epscop i nAchud Co[...]
Colum m. Faelgusa 7 C[...]
Colman Alo
95 Colman m. Lenin
Colman Cilli Ruaid
Colman m. Darane
Colman *Ua* Liathain
Colman *Ua* Fiachrach
100 Colman Lator
Colman Bán
Colman Bec
Colman Tigi Molling
Colman Duibculind
105 Colman crumthir
Colman m. Cobthaig
Colman m. Fiachra
Colman Achaid Liac
Colman Etargabla
110 Colman Cetharlethan
Colman Salach
Colman Dub
Colman m. Flannain la Laigni
Colman m. Flannain la Connacht*u*
115 Colman Darinsi Móri
Colman Ardinsi Móri
Colman m. Cairill
Colman coic
Colman Cerr i Cluain Ruiss for brú Locha Dergdeirc, is e ernes a n-itge d[...]
120 Colman Baldub
Colman Oenchossid
Colman m. Cuansi
Colman Amlabar
Colman Claren(en)ech
125 Colman Cluana Draignigi
Colman Cluana Tibrinni
Colman Cluana Cáin
Colman Culi F[...]
Colman Culi Tacrai
130 Colman Culi Enechdach
Colman m. *ua* Guali
Colman Dromma Moir
Colman Baeth

69 m. Berchain 7 Brecnat/ (Breccan m. Berchain), Breccan ocus Brecnat (R)BLc[1]. *Add* .xiiii. (sunt) (RB)Lc[1]. 70-74 *om.* RBLc[1]. 75 Cille/Cilli m. Feidelmid R(BLc[1]). 77 Riagail/Riagaill RBLc[1]. 80 Achaid Domongairt/Achaid, Colum Domanguirt RBLc[1]. 82 Cairech/Airech B. 90 [...]/Claen R(BLc[1]). 92 Co[...]/ Chrom(m)a(i)n (R)BLc[1]. *Add* Colum et Croinse(a)ch R(B)Lc[1]. 93 7 C[...]/ Colum 7 G[...]nuais (?) R, Colum 7 Genuair BLc[1]. *Add* .xxii. sunt RBLc[1]. 95 Lenin/Lenine RBLc[1]. 101 *om.* RBLc[1]. 107 Fiachra/Fiachna R(B)Lc[1]. 113 Flannain/ Scan(d)lain B(Lc[1]),la Laigni/ la Laigniu R(*above line*)BLc[1]. 114 la Connachtu/ *above line* R, la Condach Lc[1] 116 *om.*B, Ardinsi/ Aird(d)i (R)Lc[1]. 119 i Cluain ... d[...]/ *om.* RBLc[1]. 120 Baldub/ Balldub RBLc[1]. *Add* Colman Catlug RBLc[1]. 122 Cuansi/ An(n)se B(Lc[1]). 128 F[...]/ Fotil RBLc[1]. 130 Enechdach/ Ainechdach R(B)Lc[1].

707. Colman Lainne
Colman in Disirt
Colman Lici
Colman m. Ennae
Colman Fiachnae
Colman Betherbe
Colman Segene
Colman Sendomnaig
Colman Ratha Domnaig
Colman Dromma Sala[...]
Colman Ratha Crúi
Colman m. Muadain
Colman m. Fraechain
Colman Imrama i nOthain
Colman Imrama i nAraind
Colman hAuach
Colman Ailche
Colman m. Artrach
Colman m. *ua* Fortgech
Gobníne
Colman Gaila
Colman Cluana Conachaid
Colman Ailech Fịnne
Colman Achaid Flesge
Colman Cluana Daigri
Colman Cluana Moir
Colman Tennchilli
Colman Fáne
Colman Dobai
Colman Dromma Iairn
Colman m. *ua* Dulduil
Colman m. Ailella
Colman *ua* Derchella
Colman m. Torraig
Colman m. Beccain
Colman m. Locge
Colman m. Tuammáin
Colman m. Cassain
Colman Gall
Colman Dromma Senglassi
Colman Enaig Dubain
Colman *ua* Dommain
Colman m. Indréthe
Colman m. Mantain
Colman Cilli m. Duach
Colman Cuae
Colman m. Brenaind
Colman m. Domongairt
Colman Insi Braigle
Colman m. *ua* Chuind
Colman m. Cammain
Colman Goll
Colman Lomm
Colman m. Dallain
Colman Aithchimbid
Colman m. Lucgáin
Colman m. Maele
Immorchair
Colman m. Máil
Colman Deorad
Colman Inbir Dúin
Colman Dúin Bó
Colman Rois Laíg
Colman Cromglinni
Colman Finnech
Colman Leccaig
Colman m. Odrain
Colman Saraín
Colman m. Máinaig
Colman Alaire
Colman m. Nucgein
Colman Achaid Ichtair
Colman Cond
Colman m. Inbricc

135 *bis* RLc^{l}. 138 Fiachnae/ m. Fiachna(e) (R)BLc^{l}. 139 Betherbe/Becherbe RBLc^{l}. 140 Segene/ Se(i)gine R(B)Lc^{l}. 141-2 *Reversed* RBLc^{l}. 143 Sala[...]/ Salaig RLc^{l}, Senaich B. 145 m. Muadain/ (m.) Nuadain B(Lc^{l}). 146 *om.* BLc^{l}. 147 Othain/Othain (m̄)Bic (R)BLc^{l}. 149 hAuach/Uamach RBLc^{l}. 150 Ailche/ Aichli Lc^{l}. 151 m. Artrach/ M*um*an RBLc^{l}. 152 Gobníne/Colman Goibnine RBLc^{l}. 160 Fáne/Faille *no* Fane R(B). 163 Dulduil/ Tullduib R(BLc^{l}). 166 *Add* Colman m. Breccain R(B)Lc^{l}. 167 Beccain/Breccain Lc^{l}. 170 Cassain/Caisin B. 172-3 *Reversed* RBLc^{l}. 175 Indréthe/ Indretne? R(B), Inreithi Lc^{l}. 177 *om.* RBLc^{l} 178 Cuae/ Oue B. 185 *After* 189 RBLc^{l}, Lomm/ Lonn RB(Lc^{l}). 190 m./ *om.* B. 193 Dúin/Duine RBLc^{l}. 194 Rois/Crois B. 196 Finnech/Fiinne(a)ch R(B), Fuineach Lc^{l}. 199 Saráin/ m. Sarain B. 205 Inbricc/ Inbraicc Lc^{l}. *Add* Colman Nuceine R, C. Muic(c)ene B(Lc^{l}).

707. Colman m. Dubthaig
Colman Maigi Eo
Colman Cacin
Colman Stiallain
210 Colman Cluana hÍ
Colman Dairi Darsanna
Colman Inbir Bice
Colman m. Bindbairr
Colman Cutlach
215 Colman Glassi
Colman m. Baetain
Colman Ard Rethi
Colman m. Cathbath
Colman *ua* Dallain
220 Colman *ua* Lonain
Colman m. Ennae
Colman m. Beoadan
Colman m. Findchan
Colman m. Ainmerech
225 Colman Oengusa
Colman Diarmata
Colman Mulind
Colman Erni
Colman m. Senain
230 Colman Librain
Colman Coemchon
Colman m. Fergusa
Colman m. *ua* Coirtged
Colman m. Senaig
235 Colman m. Cairill
Colman m. Libir
Colman m. Geráin
Colman m. Aedgein
Colman m. Aeda
240 Colman m. Breccain
Colman m. Fergnae
Colman m. Fergusain
Colman *ua* Findig
Colman Taige m. Cireni
245 Colman m. Critain
Colman Lobor
Colman Demmain
Colman m. Conaill
Colman m. Grellain
250 Colman m. Carthaig
Colman m. Echdach
Colman Cluana Tarb
Colman Tigi Eocain
Colman Crón
255 Colman Cule Inbir
Colman m. Eologo
Colman Britt i ṅGailinni
Colman Lemchailli
Colman Claraig
260 Colman Crimchailli
Colman m. Maitnán
Colman Leathchailli
Colman Bine
Colman Fine
265 Colman Cilli Giallain, ar Colman nomen eius prius fuit
Colman Calath
Colman Banbán
Colman Cossalach
Colman m. Airerdain
270 Colman Etarcluana
Colman epscop
Colman Fote
Colman persan
Colman Fochlaid
275 Colman m. Dáin
Colman m. Aeda
Colman Craibdech
Colman m. Nemain
Colman m. Mael Duib
280 Colman m. Fintain
Colman m. Lucinni

209 Stiallain/ Staillain B. 211 Darsanna/ Colman Tharsanna RBLc^{l}. 213 Bindbairr/ Finnbairr R(BLc^{l}). 217 Ard/Aird(d) (R)BLc^{l}. 219 ua/ m. BLc^{l}. 225 Oengusa/ m. Aengusa Lc^{l}. 228-9 *Reversed* RBLc^{l}. 228 Erni/ Ernine RBLc^{l}. 232-3 *Reversed* RBLc^{l}. 241 Fergnae/Fergusa B. 244. Cireni/Cirere R(B)Lc^{l}. 247 Demmain/Demnan B. 250 *Add* Colman m. Flannain. Colman Lenine RBLc^{l}. 251-2 Reversed RBLc^{l} 255 Inbir/nb*ir* B. 261 Maitnán/Maitnain RBLc^{l}. 265 ar … fuit/ *om.* RBLc^{l}. *Add* Colman m. Duach RBLc^{l}. 266 Calath/ Alath RBLc^{l}. 267 Banbán/Banbain RBLc^{l}. 269 m. Airerdain/ (A)urar(d)dain (R)BLc^{l}. 272-3 *Reversed* RBLc^{l}. 274 *Add* Colman Fote. Colman m. Nemain RBLc^{l}. 275 Dáin/ Ca(i)rd(d)ain (R)BLc^{l}. 278 *After* 274 RBLc^{l}. 281 Lucinni/ Luccin R(Lc^{l}), Luccim B.

707. Colman m. Derggain i Cluain Torc ar bru Banna i n*Uib* Echach
Colman Sinill
Colman Lére
285 Colman m. Brain
Colman Comrithi
Colman Tigi Mocholmóc
Colman Lagen
Colman Aingleain
290 Colman m. Luachain
Colman m. Fraichain
Colman Uachtair Aird
Colman m. Commain
Colman Mór de Chonnachtaib
295 Colman Rúscaig
Colman Declain
Colman m. *ua* Caiss
Colman Rois Branduib
Colman Bec i Cluanaib
300 Colman bliugere Brigti
Colman cairchaire Brigti
Colman Bec Culi Cairech
Colman m. *ua* Bairddeni
Colman m. Cronain
305 Colman Mecneche
Colman Cluana Bruchaise
Colman Insi Bó Finni
Colman Glinni Delmuic
Colman Rois
310 Colman m. Libir
Colman m. Falbe
Colman m. Brais
Colman m. Adachtain
Colman m. Findnig
315 Colman m. Erenaig
Colman m. Fote
Colman m. Critáin
Colman m. Damnatan
Colman Linni Duachail
320 Colman Linni Dusegu
Colman Cilli Bruchis
Comgall Bennchair
Comgall Bothi Conais
Comgall m. *ua* Chéin
325 Comgall Cluana Crema
Comgall Tilcha Conadan
Comgall Cilli Ciche
Comgall dalta Findbairr
Comgall dalta Tigernaig
330 Comgall coic Ciarain
Da Chomgall Ratha Sithbi
Comgall m. Aeda
Cainnech m. *ua* Dalann
Cainnech m. *ua* Buachalla
335 Cainnech Drumḟota
Cainnech Irruiṣ *Ua* Micain
Ciaran m. int Ṡaer i Cluain m. Nois
Ciaran m. Lagne 7 Carthach i Saigir
Ciaran m. Tulchain
340 Ciaran m. Carthind
Ciaran m. Eirc
Ciaran ind Aird
Ciaran m. Branduib
Ciaran m. Fintain
345 Ciaran Lettrach
Ciaran Tiprat m. Nénnae.
Ciaran Echdromma
Ciaran Cilli Ciarain
Ciaran Rois Torc
350 Ciaran Dirchaill
Ciaran Iarthair Maige
Ciaran Faidche

282 Derggain/ Tregain B, i Cluain ... Echach/ *om.* RBLc[1]. 283 Sinill/ m. Sinill RBLc[1]. 284 Lére/ m. Leire R(BLc[1]). 290 m./*om.* Lc[1]. 292 Aird/ *om.* RBLc[1]. 298 Rois/ Crois Lc[1]. 302 Bec/*om.* RBLc[1]. 305 Mecneche/ Meccnaige R(BLc[1]). *Add* Colman m. Mail Duib R(BLc[1]). 309 Rois/ Noiss RB, m. Nois Lc. 310 *After* 314 RBLc[1]. 311 *Add* 321 R(BLc[1]). 314 Findnig/Finnich RB(Lc[1]). 316-8 m./ *om.* RBLc[1]. 321 *After* 311 RBLc[1]. *Add* .cc.x.7 uiii. RBLc[1]. 325 Crema/ Trena RBLc[1]. 326 Tilcha/ T(a)ulcha (R)BLc[1]. 329 *Om.* RBLc[1]. 332 *Om.* RBLc[1]. *Add.* ix. sunt RBLc[1] 336 Ua/*om.* RBLc[1]. *Add* .iiii. sunt RBLc[1]. 337 i ... Nois/*om.* RBLc[1]. 338 m. Lagne, i Saigir/ *om.* RBLc[1]. 344 Fintain/ Finain RBLc[1]. 345 Lettrach/m. Letreach B. 346 m. Nénnae/Ennae RBLc[1]. 350 Dirchaill/Dirchailli RBLc[1].

707. Ciaran Tulche Airdde
Ciaran Aird hEó
355 Ciaran Cluana Eidnech 7
Inglonnan 7 Breccan
7 Clethnat
Da Chiaran Dromma Iairn
Ciaran m. Senaig
Ciaran Aerecuil
Ciaran Enaig Dúin
360 Enne Airne
Enne Cilli na Manach
Enne Cilli Casil
Enne i Cill Énne
Enne Gor Craibdech
365 Enan Rois Móir
Enan Dromma Móir
Enan Bec
Enan m. Muadain
Enan m. Gemmain
370 Enan Glinni Faidli
Enan i nAichdanaib
Enan Mór. Et Aidán
Finnian m. *ua* Thelluib
Finnian m. Corpre
375 Finnio Gilldae
Finnio Sen
Finnio Óac
Findbarr Corcaige m.
Aeda
Findbarr Cilli Adgair
380 Findbarr Cilli Cuṅge
Findbarr Cluana Loscthi
Findbarr Cilli na Retaire
7 Briccine
Findbarr m. Buidi
Findbarr m. *ua* Fiatach
385 Fintan Cluana Eidnech
Fintan Maeldub
Fintan m. Tulchain
Fintan Duin Blesce
Fintan Cluana Laíg
390 Fintan m. Gaillini
Fintan m. Briton
Fintan m. Ciarain
Fintan m. Decill
Fintan m. Taicthig
395 Fintan m. Setnai
Fintan m. Luimb
Fintan m. *ua* Milbai
Fintan Cór
Fintan Fernae
400 Fintan Lemchailli
Fintan *ua* Bresail
Fintan m. Coppain
Fintan m. Massain
Fintan Ron
405 Fintan Imlecha Bic
Fintan Achaid Ailbe
Fintan Achaid Draignige
Fintan Tigi Samain
Fintan m. Berchain
410 Fintan Maige Bolg
Fintan i nOentreib
Fintan Lagen
Fintan Enaig Aeda
Fintan Bolgṡalach
415 Fintan Rátha Moinnóc
Fintan Crochdromma

353-4 Ciaran Tulchi Airdde hEo R(BLc^{l}). 355 Cluana/Cille B, 7 Inglonnan/ Ciaran 7 Inglonnan R(B)Lc^{l}, 7 Breccan/ Ciaran 7 Brec(c)an (R)B(Lc^{l}), 7 Clethnat/ Ciaran 7 Clethnat R(BLc^{l}). 356 *Add* Ciaran m. Cumascaich B. 359 *Add* .xxui. sunt RBLc^{l}. *Add further* Dirbilead Inse Ceite i nnIrrus Domnand. Dirbilead ingen Bric. .ii. sunt Lc^{l}. 360 Enna/ Enne RLc^{l}. 363 i Cill/ Cilli RBLc^{l}. 364 *Add* .u. sunt RBLc^{l}. 368 Muadain/Nuadain Lc^{l}. 369 Gemmain/ Genimain B. 371 nAichdanaib/ niachdanuibh B. 372 *Add* .ix. sunt RBLc^{l}. 373 Finnian/Finnia R(BLc^{l}), Thelluib/Tellduib RBLc^{l}. 377 *Add* .u. sunt RBLc^{l}. 378 m. Aeda/ Findbarr m. Aedo RB(Lc^{l}). Lc^{l} *also adds* 381 *here.* 379 Adgair/Adair BLc^{l}. 381 Cluana/Cille B. 382 7 Briccine/Findbarr 7 Bric(c)ine (R)BLc^{l}. 384 *Add* .ix. sunt RBLc^{l}. 385 Cluana Eidnech/ m. Echdach RBLc^{l}. 387 Tulchain/Taulchain R. 391 Briton/Britchon Lc^{l}. 396 Luimb/ Luinib BLc^{l}. 398 Cór/ Corach RBLc^{l}. 399-400 *Reversed* RBLc^{l}. 399 *Add* Fintan Ferche RBLc^{l}. 403 m./ *om.* B, Massain/ Mesain Lc^{l}. 411 Fintanan Oentreibi R(BLc^{l}). 414 Bolgṡalach/ Blocsala(i)ch B(Lc^{l}).

707. Findchú ó Brí Gobann
Findchú m. Eogain
Findlug Duin Blesce
420 Findlug m. Dallain
Findlug m. Cammain
Findlug m. Libir
Findlug m. *ua* Chuind
Findlug m. Aeda
425 Findlug Enaig Liac
Findlug m. Declain
Findlug m. Senchain
Findlug m. Mael Duib
Findlug m. *ua* Chéin
430 Findlug m. Beraich
Findlug m. Gabrain
Findlug Borr
Findlug m. Fiachra
Findlug Tigi m. Luimb
435 Findlug Bron
Findlug m. Oengusa
Findlug m. Brenaind
Findlug m. Gorbain
Findlug m. Corb
440 Findlug m. Gobae
Fínan Camm
Fínan Lobor
Fínan m. Coche
Fínan Cluana Caichne
445 Fínan Ferdál
Fínan m. Colmain
Fínan Daire Chalgaig
Fínan Murbuilg
Fínan m. Eogain
450 Fínan ferdaigis Munnu
Fínan Enaig Luaigne
Lonan Treoiti
Lonan m. Tulchain
Lonan Garaid
455 Lonan m. Luimb
Lonan Cilli Gollre
Lonan m. Nemain
Lonan Tulche
Lonan Craibdech
460 Lonan m. *ua* Magen
Lonan m. Lasrain
Lonan Dron m. Oengusa
Liber Lethdubi ⁊ Muchian
Liber Clochair
465 Liber Uachtair Aird
Liber Cuile Móre
Liber i Caiemnain
Liber Domnaig Libir
Liber i Telaig
470 Liber i rRaith Libir
Liber i rRaith Gairb ⁊
Diucaill
Liber Senchoe
Liber i nInbiur Latharnai
⁊ Segan
Liber Tamlachta
475 Liber Find
Liber Temen
Libran Martartaige
Lochan Dromma Laigde

417 Findchú/ F*intan* Indchua R(B)Lc[1], ó Brí Gobann/ *om.* RBLc[1]. *Add* F*intan* Indlug RBLc[1]. 418 Findchú/F*intan* RBLc[1]. 419-40 Findlug/F*intan* RBLc[1]. 419 Duin Blesce/ m. Gobbain RBLc[1]. 423 *Add* 434 RBLc[1]. 429 ua Chéin/ huichein R. 430 Beraich/ Berach R. 431 m./ *om.* RB. 433 m./*om.* B, Fiachra/Fiachna RB, Fiacħ Lc[1]. 434 *After* 423 RBLc[1]. 436 *After* 432 B, m./ *om.* Lc[1]. 437 m./ *om* RB. 438 Gorbain/ Cobrain RBLc[1]. 439 m./ m. ua RBLc[1]. *Add* F. m. ua Chae RBLc[1]. 440 m./ *om.* RBLc[1]. *Add* F.Cluana Cain. F.Dromma Ing. F.Methuis Máir. F. Cilli Airthir. F.Cilli Locha. F.Dromma Lethluimm. F.Coirthi Bic. F.i. Taulchaib. F. Indsi Liac. F.Cilli hAchid. F.Cilli Ruaid. F. Dromma Cairech. F. Cula Miccain. F.Airenaich. .lxxiii. sunt R(BLc[1]). *See note.* 450 Munnu/ .i. Mundu R(*above line*) (B)Lc[1]. 451 *Add* .xi. (sunt) (R)B(Lc[1]). 452 Treoiti/ Treoit RBLc[1]. 453 Tulchain/Taulchain R, Telcain Lc[1]. 456 Gollrc/Golre RBLc[1]. 458 Tulche/Taulch(a)e RB(Lc[1]). 460 Magen/ Maigni RBLc[1] 461 Lasrain/ Laisren Lc[1]. 462 *Add* .xi. sunt RBLc[1]. 463 ⁊ Muchian/ Liber ⁊ Mochian RBLc[1]. 466 Cuile/ Cille RBLc[1]. 471 ⁊ Diucaill/ Liber ⁊ Diucaill R(BLc[1]). 473 i nInbiur/Inbir RBLc[1], ⁊ Segan/ Liber ⁊ Segan RBLc[1]. 477 Martartaige/ Martar dl̄ge B. *Add* .xuiii. sunt RBLc[1]. 478-82 Lochan/Lu(i)ccin R(BLc[1]).

707. Lochan Dromma Garmna
480 Lochan Dromma Laigse
Lochan Damdaedromma 7 Daimde
Lochan Tige m. Luimb
Lucan 7 Odran
Mochua m. Lugada
485 Mochua m. Caele
Mochua Cháin
Mochua m. Cuinnini
Mochua Chairem
Mochua m. Fintain
490 Mochua m. Mael Duib
Mochua Bile
Mochua Eolaiṅg
Mochua Cháil
Mochua m. Nemain
495 Mochua Corciche
Mochua m. Mellain
Mochua m. Garbain
Mochua m. Daigri
Mochua m. Indissi
500 Mochua Beone
Mochua Atha Escrach
Mochua m. Lugbi
Mochua m. *ua* Manche
Mochua m. Lonain
505 Mochua m. Oíchlain
Mochua m. Eogain
Mochua m. Odrain
Mochua m. Cuanach
Mochua m. *ua* Chuind
510 Mochua Gat
Mochua m. *ua* Loppae
Mochua Catt
Mochua Luachra
Mochua m. Lugair
515 Mochua Tomma Grene
Mochua Airbi
Mochua Glaissi
Mochua Cóisech
Mochua Cáel
520 Mochua m. Nisse
Mochua m. *ua* Choraig
Mochua m. Caemloga
Mochua m. Bennain
Mochua m. Baitain
525 Mochua m. Muadain
Mochua Ratha Moch[...]
Mochua Cluana Cáin
Mochua m. Brenaind
Mochua Balla
530 Mochua Conachaid
Mochua m. Loṅgthi
Mochua Aileni
Mochua Eono
Mochua Indaigi
535 Mochua Amlabar
Mochua m. Find
Mochua Allrín
Mochua Chruad
Mochua Cronbec
540 Mochua m. *ua* Laigdi
Mochua chlam
Mochua m. Tecain
Molua m. Oche
Molua Tigi Molua
545 Molua m. *ua* Gaili
Molua Mór
Molua Bec

479 *Add* Dromma Arathair RBLc[l]. 480 *om.* B, Laigse/Laicsich Lc[l]. 481 Damdaedromma 7 Daimde/ Dromma Damdai. Luiccin et Daimde R(B)Lc[l]. 482 m./ *om.* RBLc[l]. 483 Lucan/ Lucall RB(Lc[l]). *Add.* .uiii. sunt RBLc[l]. 484 *Preceded by* Mochua (Balla) RB(Lc[l]). *See note.* 485 Caele/ Cailli Lc[l]. 486-7 *Reversed* RBLc[l]. 487 Cuinnini/ Cuimmine R(BLc[l]). 497 m./*om.* R. 499 m./ *om.* RBLc[l], Indissi/Innse B. 506 m./ *om.* B. 507 m. *om.* Lc[l]. 508 Cuanach/ Cuanan Lc[l]. 510 Gat/ Got(t) B(Lc[l]). 512 Catt/ Ca(i)ttene (R)BLc[l]. 514 m./*om.* RBLc[l]. 516 Airbi/ Airbri R(BLc[l]). 518 *Om.* B, Cóisech/ Cois(s)e (R)Lc[l]. 523 m. *om.* Lc[l] 526 Ratha/ m. Rotha Lc[l], Moch[...]/ *om.* RBLc[l]. 527 *Om.* RBLc[l]. 529 Balla/ Crannan Lc[l]. *See note.* 533 Eono/Eond BLc[l]. 534 Indaigi/m. Indaigi RBLc[l]. 536 m. / *om.* RBLc[l]. 537 Allrín/ Albul B. 538 Chruad/ Cruadchain RLc[l], Cruachan B. 540 Laigdi/ Laigid Lc[l]. 542 Tecain/ Tetain B. *Add* .lix. (sunt) R(BLc[l]). 543 Molua (Laga). Molua m. Ocha RB(Lc[l]).

707. Molua Dairi
Molua rétaire
Molua m. Sechnasaig
Molua m. Coluimb
Molua m. Clarenig
Molua m. Cummeni
Molua m. Blae
Molua Guirt Chonaig
Molua Obaid
Molua m. Diblini
Molua Achaid Uidir
Molua Corpre
Molua Craibdech
Molua Ratha Mo[lua]
Molua m. Fintain
Molua Lobor
Molua m. Scillini
Molua m. Baird
Molua chlam
Molua m. Laindain
Molua Damrai
Molua Baldub
Molua coic
Molua Menn
Molua Daire Eidnig
Molua Dromma Crithaig
Molua [...]ach
Molua [...]
Molua [...]
Molua Dromma Inasclainn
Molua Cammachaid
Molua Drochta
Molasse m. Nadfraich
Molasse m. *ua* Imda
Molasse m. *ua* Dartada
Molasse m. Lugdech
Molasse m. Lugair
Molasse m. Lugada
Molasse m. hErnedi
Molasse m. Fiachrach
Molasse m. Echdach
Molasse m. Decill
Molasse m. *ua* Naratha
Molasse m. Declain
Molasse m. Branduib
Molasse m. Rimida
Molasse m. Suibni
Molasse Lemdroma
Molasse Crotta
Molasse m. *ua* Nechtai
Molasse m. Dimmain
Molasse m. Fermetho
Molasse m. Brenaind
Molasse m. Milchon
Molasse m. Feradaig
Molasse m. Marcín
Molasse m. Sarin
Molasse m. Findchain
Molasse m. Erini
Molasse m. Colmain
Molasse m. Eogain
Molasse m. *ua* Cáte
Molasse m. *ua* Caisrige
Molasse m. Beoaeda
Molasse m. *ua* Chonna
Molasse m. Aedgein
Molasse m. Croibi
Molasse m. Rimide
Molasse Tigi Munnu
Molasse hIae
Molasse m. Senain
Molasse Tigi Lasre

550 m. / *om.* B. 552 m. / *om.* RBLc^{l} 553 Cummeni/ Cuimmin R(BLc^{l}). 554 Blae/Balae Lc^{l}. 557 m. / *om.* RBLc^{l}. 559 Corpre/ Cairpreach B(Lc^{l}) 561 Mo[lua]/ *om.* RBLc^{l}. 564 m. / *om.* BLc^{l}. 572 Eidnig/ Eicnich Lc^{l}. 574 [...]ach/ m. Lugdach R(B)Lc^{l}. 575 [...]/ Mo(i)thla (R)BLc^{l}. 576 [...]/ Chroibe R(B)Lc^{l}. 579 Drochta/ Drochait RB(Lc^{l}). *Add* .xxxuiii. (sunt) R(B)Lc^{l}. 580 *Add.* .i. Molaisse Inse Muiredaich Lc^{l}. 587, 588 m. / *om.* Lc^{l} 589 *om.* BLc^{l}. 590 Naratha/ Nathrae R(B)Lc^{l}. 591 Molasse/Mollaise Echrais Lc^{l}. 593 Rimida/ Luimcada B. 595 Lemdromma/m. Lemdroma B. 599 m. Fermetho/(m.) Fen(n)eda R(Lc^{l}), Beneda B. 601 Milchon/ Milain RBLc^{l}. 604 Sarin/ Sarain RBLc^{l}. 610 Caisrige/ Casraige R(Lc^{l}), Carraigi B. 612 m. *om* RBLc^{l}. 614 m./ *om.* RBLc^{l}. 615 m. Rimide/ Rimid RBLc^{l}. 618 m./ *om.* Lc^{l}. 619 Lasre/ Glasreain R(BLc^{l}). *See note.*

707. 620 Molasse Cluana Locha
Molasse Tiri da Glass
Molasse Aird Ḟuthe
Moṡamoc Dublinne
Moṡamoc Gall
625 Moṡamoc Bothaire
Mochonoc Gailinne
Mochonoc Insi Fail
Mochonoc ailithir
Mochonoc Maigni
630 Mochonoc Dubthaire
Mochonoc Uamach
Mochuanoc Glinni Da Locha
Mogoroc Dergne
Mogoroc Sruthra
635 Mogoroc Mucrois
Mogoroc i lLaind Lére
Mobeóc Micrend
Mobeóc Brenaind
Mobeóc m. *ua* Cati
640 Mobeóc Tarcochae
Mobeóc m. Dallchoca
Mobeóc m. Brónaig
Mobeóc m. Nessain
Mobeóc m. Cairlain
645 Mobeóc m. Eirc
Mobeóc m. Cassain
Mochummae m. Aedain
Mochummae m. *ua* Gaili
Mochummae Rotan
650 Mochummae m. Sarán
Mochummae m. Sulain
Mochummae m. Branduib
Mochummae Dromma Snectai
Mochummae Lainni Dochummae
655 Mochummae m. Cairrain
Mochummae Fotae
Mochummae Tigi Mocumma
Mochummae Bolgain
Mochummae Find
660 Mochummae m. Aedain
Mochummae Clarenech
Mochummae m. Critain
Mochummae m. Dallain
Mochummae Dromma Medoin
665 Mochummae m. Guaire
Mochummae m. Credail
Mochummae Daire Ardda
Mochummae Riagol
Mochummae Setnai
670 Mochummae Disertan
Mochummae Cherr
Mochummae Chadain
Mochummae Chuarain
Mochummae m. Gulbain
675 Mochummae Chonóc
Mochummae m. *ua* Chein
Mochummae m. Aradain
Mochummae Cluana Mór
Mochonna Daire
680 Mochonna Ratha
Mochonna m. Brenaind
Mochonna m. Erscenain
Mochonna m. Libir
Mochonna m. Cairill
685 Mochonna m. Lugain
Mochonna m. Lusmaige
Mochonna m. Coluim
Mochonna m. Critain
Mochonna Erene
690 Mochonna Bec

621 Tiri/Tre R. 622 *Add* .xliiii. R, .xliii. (sunt) (B)Lc^{l}. 623 Mosamoc. Mosamoc Duiblinne R. 625 Bothaire/ Bothi Cummair R(BLc^{l}). *Add.* iii. sunt RBLc^{l}. 631 Uamach/ hUm(i)ach R(BLc^{l}). 632 Mochonoc Mochuaroc. Mochonoc Glinne Da Locha R(BLc^{l}). *Add* .uiii. sunt RBLc^{l}. 634 Sruthra/ Srutha R. 636 *Add* .iiii. sunt RBLc^{l}. 637 Micrend/ Imcrend B(Lc^{l}). 638 Brenaind/ m.Brenaind R. 643, 644 m. *om.* B. 646 *Add.* .x. sunt RBLc^{l}. 651 m./ *om.* RBLc^{l}. 654 Dochummae/ *om.* RBLc^{l}. 655 m. Cairrain/ Cairnain RBLc^{l}. 665 m./*om.* B. 666 m./ *om.* RBLc^{l}. 668 Riagal/ Riagla RBLc^{l}. Add Mochumma hEoin RBLc^{l}. 670 Disertan/ Dis(f)ertach RB(Lc^{l}). 677 m./ *om.* BLc^{l}. 678 *Add* .xxxiii. (sunt) R(B)Lc^{l}. 680 Ratha/ Ratha Mochonna RBLc^{l}. *Add* Mochonna Tigi Mochonna R(B)Lc^{l}. 681 m./ *om.* Lc^{l}. 682 m./ *om.* BLc^{l}. 686 m./ *om.* B. 688 m. *om.* Lc^{l}. 689 Erene/ Erine RLc^{l}, Erere B.

707. Mochonna m. Airide
Mochonna Cuairne
Mochonna m. Aedgein
Mochonna m. Fintanain
695 Mochonna Insi Fail
Mochonna coic
Mochonna Insi Patric
Mochonna Dromma Torraig
Mochonna m. Eirc
700 Mochonna m. Cairetain
Mochonna Atha Dalrach
Mochonna Essae
Mochonna chreisen
Mochonna Thulach
705 Mochonna Insi Caimme
Mochonna Collmaige
Mocholla m. Aeda
Mocholla m. Fintain
Mocholla Lugair
710 Mocholla Brenaind
Mocholla cairchaire Munnu
Mocholla m. Bánain
Mocholla m. Baitain
Mocholla m. Oengusa
715 Mocholla m. Diarmata
Mocholla m. Cuind
Mocholla Tigi Mocholmóc
Mocholla Rímeda
Mocholla Daire
720 Mochoemoc Leith
Mochoemoc m. Cuanach
Mochoemoc m. Ainmerech
Mochoemoc m. Dimmain
Mochoemoc Brecc i rRus Ech
725 Mochoemoc m. Libir
Mochoemoc m. Airdne
Mochoemoc m. Toccae
Mochoemoc Imlecha Lúain
Mochoemoc Cilli Dirmaige
730 Mochoemoc Ṡantlethi
Mochoemoc Maigi Nemnata
Mochoemoc Enaig Truim
Mochoemoc Tigi Mael Duib
Mochoemoc Cluana Bruchaisi
735 Mochoemoc Roiss Cuae
Mochoemoc Tailcha Tuamma
Mochoemoc Ratha Ruadain
Mochoemoc m. Eirc
Mochoemoc Cruthnechan
740 Mochoemoc Bennchuir
Moṡenoc Mugnai
Moṡenoc Beithech
Moṡenoc m. Lugair
Moṡenoc Britt
745 Moṡenoc Insi Airdde
Moṡenoc Insi Cathaig
Moṡenoc m. Duimle
Moṡenoc Insi Da Chairech
Moṡenoc m. Baiti
750 Moṡenoc Insi Lim
Moṡenoc m. Brónaig
Moṡenoc m. Cáte
Moṡenoc dalta Brenaind
Moṡenoc Loairn
755 Moṡenoc Setnai
Moṡenoc *ua* Guaire
Moṡenoc m. Decill
Moṡenoc Ḟintain

691 m./ *om.* Lc^1, Airide/ Araide RLc^1, Caraidhi B. 692-3 *Reversed* RBLc^1. 692 m./ *om.* Lc^1. 693 m./*om.* RBLc^1. 700 m. Cairetain/ Eireitain B. 705-6 Mochonna Inse Caimme Colmaige R(B)Lc^1. *Add* .xxix. (sunt) RB(Lc^1). 709 Lugair/ m. Lugair RBLc^1. 711 Munnu/ .i. Munno B(Lc^1 *above line*), Munnu R (*above line*). 717 Mocholmóc/ Mochol*la* RB(Lc^1?). 718 Rímeda/ m. Rimc(a)da R(B)Lc^1. 719 *Add* .xiii. sunt RBLc^1. 720 Leith/Leith Moir RBLc^1. 721 Cuanach/ Cuana*in* Lc^1; 722 m. *om.* Lc^1. 729 Dirmaige/ Draignigi RB(Lc^1). 731 Nemnata/ M*en*nota R(Lc^1), m. Nota B. 737 Ruadain/ Ruaidin B. 740 *Add* .xxi. sunt RBLc^1. 747 m./ *om.* Lc^1. 752 *om.* RBLc^1. 754 Loairn/ m. Loairn B. 755 Setnai/ m. Setnae R(B). 758 Ḟintain/ m. Fintain RBLc^1.

707. Moṡenoc *ua* Sailinni
760 Moṡenoc m. *ua* Gairb
Moṡenoc m. *ua* Mind
Moṡenoc m. Midnain
Moernoc aircsirend
Moernoc m. Lerech
765 Moernoc Airid
Moernoc m. Cruissin
Moernoc m. Cuarain
Moernoc m. Lugni
Moernoc m. Ḟeradaig
770 Moernoc Sapór
Moernoc clam
Moernoc Cluana Da Ochra
Moernoc Tamlacta
Moernoc i nEnoch
775 Moernoc i Taíbaib i nAichle
Moernoc coic Ciarain
Moernoc goba Patric
Moernoc hó Ard
Moernoc m. Bledini
780 Moernoc Casceni
Moernoc hi Toraig
Moernoc Crimchailli
Moernoc Findchain
Moernoc Escrach
785 Manchan Leith
Manchan Moithla
Manchan Achaid Tairb
Manchan Escrach
Manchan Cilli Airdi
790 Manchan Cilli Manach
Manchan m. Eirc
Manchan Airdde Trichime
Moboe m. *ua* Aldae
Moboe m. Cuanach
795 Moboe m. Indach
Moboe m. Lugadach
Moboe m. Brenaind
Moboe m. Senaig
Moboe Colli
800 Moboe m. Muridaig
Moboe m. Aedloga
Moboe ho Leth
Moboe ó Bendchur
Mochellóc m. Oíblen
805 Mochellóc Tigi Mocholoc
Mochellóc Dubthaire
Mochellóc Disirt Cind Tracht
Mochellóc Sruthrae
Mochellóc Disirt Mochellóc
810 Mogobboc m. *ua* Laíme
Mogobboc Find
Mogobboc m. *ua* Chein
Mogobboc i Cill Magnend
Mogobboc m. *ua* Ruain
815 Mogobboc artifex
Mogobboc dalta Coluim
Mogobboc Liathdromma
Mogobboc m. Naisc ⁊ Fergus
Modichu Lilchaig
820 Modichu m. Culdubain
Modichu Cluana Brain
Modichu coic Magnend
Modichu *ua* Medóin
Modichu Ernaide
825 Mochritoc Aireni
Mochritoc coic Finnio
Mochritoc m. Cailig
Mochritoc m. Maeli Cosni

759 Sailinni/ Saillni RBLc^{l}. 760, 761 m. *om.* RB. 762 *Add* (Mosenoc) .xxi. sunt (R)BLc^{l}. 764 Lerech/ Laireach B. 765 Airid/ Airid Sinnaig R(BLc^{l}). 773 Tamlacta/Tamlachta Nango RBLc^{l}. 774 Enoch/ Aenuch B. 776-7 *Reversed* B. 782 Crimchailli/ m.Crimchailli B. 783 Findchain/ m. Findchain R(B)Lc^{l}. 784 Escrach/ Eascrach B., *add* .xxii. (sunt) R(BLc^{l}). 790 *Om.* B, Manach/ na Manach RLc^{l}. 791 *Om.* RBLc^{l}. 792 Trichime/ Trichme R, Crithme B, Trichine Lc^{l}. *Add* .uii. sunt RBLc^{l}. 795 Indach/ Indnach R, M̄ach B. 803 *Add* .xi. sunt RBLc^{l}. 805 Mocholoc/ Mochelloc RBLc^{l}. 806 Dubthaire/ m. Dubthaire B. 807 Cind/Finn B. 808 Sruthrae/ Sruthra Guaire R(B)Lc^{l}. 809 *Add* .ui. sunt (R)BLc^{l} 812-3 *Reversed* RBLc^{l}. 818 ⁊ Fergus/ Mogobboc ⁊ Fergus RBLc^{l}. *Add* .x. RBLc^{l}. 822 Magnend/ Mednenn B. 824 *Add* .ui. (sunt) RB(Lc^{l}). 828 m. Maeli Cosni/ Mailchroin Lc^{l}.

Mochritoc Craibaige
830 Mochritoc Dromma Móir
Mochritoc m. Comgain
Mochritoc Tigi Mocritóc
Mochritoc Rúscaig
Mochritoc Dromma Ruis
835 Mochritoc m. Beoain
Mochritoc Inse Ulad
Mochritoc i nAchud Reot
Mochritoc Etargabla
Mochritoc Findglassi ⁊ Mochuae
840 Mochoe Glinni Da Locha
Mochoe Noendromma
Mochoe m. Oengusa
Mochoe m. Ruadain
Mochoe Cilli Cleithe
845 Mochoe Cilli Lochmainge
Mochoe Muade Uachtair
Mochoe Enaig Senmail
Mael Ruain Tamlacta
Mael Anfaid Darinsi
850 Mael Dithreib
Mael Curaig
Mael Dub i Tig Mail
Mael Dub m. Fáelain
Mael Doborchon
855 Mael Odor m. Crummaine
Mael Tuile m. Diain
Mael Deid Lis Móir
Mael Gaimrid i nAraind
Mael Corgais
860 Mael Anbis i nGlind Da Locha
Mael Coisne i Cluain Eoin
Mael Coisne m. Dall
Mael Rubai .i. Aporcrosan
Mael Muthir
865 Mael Doid
Mael Membra Fingin
Mael Tuli i Cluain Ached
Mael Ochtraig i nAchud Bó
Mael Tachuir
870 Mael Doborchon m. Cellaig
Mael Aithgen
Mael Dub i Cluain Guill
Mael Odran m. Caiss
Maelan ⁊ Gessan ailithir
875 Mael Bec
Mael Coba
Mael Mine
Mael Chethar
Mael Dub Bec
880 Mael Duin
Mael Dub Cind Eich
Molóce m. *ua* Noise
Moloce m. Colmain Find
Moloce m. Duib Dligid
885 Moloce Tigi Molaca i n*Uib* Cellaig Cualand
Morióc m. *ua* Laigde
Morioc i rRoss Bronaig
Morioc i ṅGlind Da Locha
Mošinu m. *ua* Lugair
890 Mošinu m. *ua* Mind
Mošinu Imlecha Cassain
Mošinu Glinne Munaire
Mošinu m. Cathair

832 Tigi Mocritóc/ Thigi Modichō Lc^{l}. 833 Rúscaig/ Tigi Ruscaich B. 837 i nAchud Reot/ Achaid Reoit R(BLc^{l}). 839 ⁊ Mochuae/ Mochritoc ⁊ Mochuae RBLc^{l}. *Add* .xui. (sunt) R(B)Lc^{l}. 841 Noendromma/ Noidromma R(BLc^{l}). 843 m./ *om.* RBLc^{l}. 845 Lochmainge/ Lochmaige R(BLc^{l}). 846 Muade Uachtair/ hUachtair Muaide R(BLc^{l}). 847 *Add* .uiii. (sunt) RB(Lc^{l}). 848 *Preceded by* Na Mail (ann)so B(Lc^{l}), Tamlacta/ Tamlachtan RBLc^{l}. 858 i nAraind *added to* Mael Corgais (859) RBLc^{l}. 860 *Add* Mael Coisne hIrruiss R(B)Lc^{l}. 862 m./ in mac RBLc^{l}. 863 Rubai/ Ruibe B, .i./ *om.* RBLc^{l}, Aporcrosan/ Aporcronsam B. 869 Tachuir/ Tathchuir R. 870 Doborchon/ Dorchon RB(Lc^{l}), Cellaig/ Cellain B. 872 i Cluain/ Cluana RBLc^{l}. 873 *After* 881 RBLc^{l}. *Add* Mael Odran ⁊ Donnan RBLc^{l}. 874 Ailithir *after* Maelan RBLc^{l}. 875 *Bis* RLc^{l}. 877 *Add* Mael Bec B. 879 *Add* Mael Dub m. Aeda RBLc^{l}. 880 *Om.* RBLc^{l}. 881 *Add* Mael Dub m. Cais .xxxuiii. (sunt) RB(Lc^{l}). 885 Molaca/ Molaigi B, i nUib ... Cualand/ *om.* RBLc^{l}. *Add* .iiii. sunt RBLc^{l}. 888 i nGlind/ Glindi RBLc^{l}. *Add* .iii. sunt RBLc^{l}. 890 Mind/ Muind RBLc^{l}. 893 *Add* .u. (sunt) RB(Lc^{l}).

Indech i Tig na nDechoin
895 Indem i nDruim Lethan
Odran m. Cairill
Odran ara Patric
Odran magister
Odran i nAirthiur hUten
900 Odran Airlithe
Odran crumthir
Odran Cluana Crandche
Odran m. *ua* Araide
Odran m. Senaig
905 Odran m. Beodan
Odran m. Critain
Odran m. Bronaig
Odran Roiss Chaimm
Odran brathair Chiarain
910 Oidrine m. *ua* Buachalla
7 Fechine
Odran Conodor Lis Moir
Ronan m. in Ruáid
Ronan Find m. Sárain
Ronan Magdúin
915 Ronan Rechrainne
Ronan Tigi Rónain
Ronan clam
Ronan m. Fergusa
Ronan m. Mael Uidir
920 Ronan Lethrois
Setna Echdromma
Setna m. Daill
Setna m. Branduib
Setna m. Findchain
925 Setna Dromma m. *ua* Blai
Setna epscop
Setna Darane
Setna Rois Iatharnai
Setna Cáin
930 Setna *ua* Guaire
Setna Uamae
Setna m. Critain
Tua m. *ua* Roda
Tua Odrain
935 Tua i Cluain Cran*um*
Tond i nEnuch
Tigernach Cluana Eois
Tigernach Blattine
Tigernach m. Echdach
940 Tigernach Cilli Móire
Tigernach Ratha Cere
Tigernach i Fraechaib
Ardda
Ultan Ardda Brecain m.
Conchobair
Ultan m. Araide
945 Ultan m. [*ua*] Aignich
Ultan Tigi Tultóc brathair
Fursu
Ultan Cerr
Ultan ministir

895 *Add* .ii. RBLc[l]. 897 ara/arda B. 899 i nAirthiur/ Airthir RB(Lc[l]). 900 Airlithe/ Oilithre Lc[l]. 902 Crandche/ Crandcha Lc[l]. 909 brathair/ frater RBLc[l]. 910 ua/*om.* RBLc[l], 7 Fechine/ Odran 7 Fechine RBLc[l] 911 *Add* .xuii. RBLc[l]. *Add further* Patraic m. Calpuirn. Patraic Ruis Dela. Patraic Aisdire. .iii. R(BLc[l]). 912 *Preceded by* Ronan (Find) m. Beraich RB(Lc[l]), in/ *om.* B. 915 Rechrainne/ Rechrann RB(Lc[l]). 920 *Add* .x. sunt RBLc[l]. 922 Daill/Dall RBLc[l]. 925 m. ua/ m. RLc[l], *om.* B. 927 *Add* Setna m. Trena R(B)Lc[l]. 928 Iatharnai/ Latharnae RB(Lc[l]). 932 *Add* .xiii. sunt RBLc[l]. 933 .m./*om.* RBLc[l], Roda/ Roida RBLc[l]. 935 i ... Cranum/ Cluana Crainn R(BLc[l]). 936 Tua Odur i nEnuch R(BLc[l]). *Add* .iiii. sunt RBLc[l]. 941 Cere/ Cre B. *Add* Tigernach Daire Meille. Tigernach et Anfiss R(BLc[l]). 942 i Fraechaib/ 7 Fraechan B, Ardda/ *om.* RBLc[l]. *Add* .uiii. sunt RBLc[l]. 943 Ardda Brecain/ *om.* RBLc[l], m./m. ua RBLc[l]. 946 brathair Fursu/ Ultain frater Fursu RBLc[l]. 948 *Add* .uii. sunt RBLc[l].

708 Comanmand naebúag hErenn in so sís

1 Brigit ingen Dubthaig
Brigit ingen Domma
Brigit ingen Manach
Brigit ingen Moenan
5 Brigit ingen Ennae
Brigit ingen Chollae

Title/ Do ogaib in so (sis) RB(Lc[l]). 2 Domma/ Dimae Lc[l].

708. Brigit Uachtair Aird
Brigit Insi Brigti
Brigit i Fich Mane
Brigit Ratha Brigti fri Currech .i. ingen Muridaig ⁊ Aidammair
Bríg[it] Senbotha ⁊ Fidnat i Tig Fidnatan
Brig[it] ingen Aedo
Brig[it] Maige Chungu
Brig i ndEirnaide
Brig Tigi Bríge
Brig ingen Scandail
Brig ingen Fiachnai
Brig ingen Ennae
Brig Cilli Bríge
Brig ingen Chochlaig ⁊ Rím ⁊ Dercairthend
Brig ingen Cholgan ⁊ Duthracht
Brig Lainni Brigi
Da Bríg Ratha Forge ⁊ Cuansech
Brig ingen Chusseda
Cairell Chraibdech
Cairell Achaid
Cairell Cilli Cairill
Cairell Tigi Coisli
Cairell Cilli Aird i Crich Ross
Cairell ingen Amen
Cairell ingen Áne
Cumman ingen Ailella
Cumman ingen Dimmain
Cumman Tigi Cumne
Cumman ingen Ḟergusa
Cumman ingen Chianain
Cumman ingen Daí
Cumman ingen Baí
Cumman ingen Critain
Cumman ingen Ronain
Cumman ingen Baitain *ui* Buáin
Cumman Derg
Cumman ingen Ṡenain
Cumman ingen Chollae
Cumman ingen ḣErc
Cumman ingen Ḟintain
Cumman ingen Lucain
Cumman ingen Feidlimid ⁊ Ulaith
Crone ingen Ercain.
Crone ingen Caitti
Crone Galmai
Crone Methais Baile
Crone ingen Ṡetnae
Crone ingen Aeda
Crone ingen Ḟiachna
Crone ingen Ultain
Crone Cilli Crone soror Patricii
Crone Cind Tracta
Crone Goirt Airchinni
Crone Disirt Mairge
Crone Tairhibru
Crone Insi Móre
Crone Disirt Dommae
Crone Cilli Airdde
Crone ingen Garbain ⁊ Copad
Columb Craibdech
Columb Drumḟota
Columb ingen Fiachna
Columb i ndErnedi

9-10 *Bis* B. 10 fri ... Muiridaig/ *om.* RBLc[1], ⁊ Aidammair/ Brigit ⁊ Aidamair RBLc[1]. 11-13 Brig/ Brigit RBLc[1]. 11 ⁊ Fidnat/ Brigit ⁊ Fiadnat RBLc[1], i Tig Fidnatan/ *om.* RBLc[1]. 13 Chungu/ Luinge R(BLc[1]). *Add* .xu. sunt RBLc[1]. 14 Brigit ingen Deimidi B, Brig ingen Dernine Lc[1]. 20-21 Brig ingen Cochlaig ⁊ Rim. Brig ingen Cholgan ⁊ Dercairthind. Brig ⁊ Duthracht R(BLc[1]). 23 Da Bríg/ Brig .ii. Brig R(B)Lc[1], ⁊ Cuansech/ Brig ⁊ Cuansech R(B)Lc[1]. 24 *Add* .xiii. RBLc[1]. 25 *Add* Cairell Cechce R(B)Lc[1]. 27 Cairill/Cairilli RBLc[1]. 29 Cilli/Giŧ B, i Crich Ross/ *om.* RBLc[1]. *Add* Cairell Cilli Cairille R(BLc[1]). 30 Amen/ Ainen RBLc[1]. 31 ingen/ *om.* RBLc[1]. *Add* .ix. sunt RBLc[1]. 32 Ailella/ Ailleain RBLc[1]. 38 Baí/ Bain RBLc[1]. 41 ingen/ *om.* Lc[1], uí Buain/ *om.* RBLc[1]. 42 Derg/ ingen Deirg R(BLc[1]). 48 ⁊ Ulaith/ Cumman ⁊ Ulad RBLc[1]. *Add* Cumman Tigi Cumne RBLc[1]. *Add further* .xix. sunt RBLc[1]. 49-65 Crone/ Cron RBLc[1]. 57 soror/ siur RBLc[1] 59 *om.* Lc[1]. 65 ⁊ Copad/ Cron ⁊ Copad RBLc[1]. *Add* .xuiii. RBLc[1]. 67 Drumḟota/ Droma Fota B. 69 i ndErnedi/ Merdigi B.

708.70 Columb ingen Femme
Columb ingen Nadšluaig
Columb Cluana Mugna
Columb ingen Ennae
Columb ingen Aeda
75 Columb Caite
Columb Lemchailli
Columb ingen Baitain
Columb ingen Oengusa
Columb ingen Ainmerech
80 Columb ingen Libir 7 Finsech
Columb Cluana Locha
Columb ingen Nadfraichain 7 Rothine
Columb ingen Senaig
Columb ingen Brain
85 Columb Dromma Culind
Columb Cilli Columbae
Columb ingen Comgaill
Columb Dub
Columb ingen Lugni
90 Columb Cilli Mithine
Columb Topair Thuammae
Columb ingen Altbi
Columb ingen Critain
Columb ingen Maet
95 Columb ingen Crimthaind
Ernain Cilli Abbáin
Ernain Dromma Aildae
Ernain Cluana Ciarain
Ernain Tigi Coscle
100 Ernain Cundlig
Ernain Craibdech
Ernain Cilli Loairn
Ernain Cilli Mudi
Ernain Cilli Bice
105 Ernain Cilli Móre
Ernain Cilli Ernine
Eithne ingen Ultain
Eithne ingen Dáire
Eithne ingen Chaiti
110 Eithne ingen Loegaire
Eithne ingen Santain
Eithne ingen Ḟiachrach
Eighne ingen Laíg
Eithne mathair Coluim Cille
115 Eithne 7 Mell i nDaire Melle
Fainche ingen Brenaind
Fainche ingen Luachain
Fainche ingen Demmain
Fainche ingen Bledini
120 Fainche Tigi Fainche
Fainche Cuilligi
Fainche Troscad
Fainche Garb
Fainche ingen Caemaire
125 Fainche ingen Diammain 7 Sinche
Fainche ingen Loairn
Fainche Ṭigi m. Nessain
Feidelm Find
Feidelm Lathraig .i. Uair
130 Feidelm ingen Aeda
Feidelm ingen Crimthaind
Feidelm 7 Mugain 7 Eithne tri ingena Ailella
Rignach ingen Aeda m. Echdach
Rignach Domnaig Rignaige
135 Rignach Cilli Rignaige
Rignach Tulchi Aird
Rignach Dromma Culind
Rignach Tigi Luimb 7 Echdach
Sinech Cruachain

70 Femme/ (F)e(i)mine (B)Lc^{l}. 72 Mugna/ Muguna RLc^{l}. 75 Caite/ ingen Chaitte R(B)Lc^{l}. 80 7 Finsech/ Colum 7 Findse(a)ch R(B)Lc^{l}. 82 7 Rothine/ Colum 7 Roithine R(B)Lc^{l}. 94 Maet/ Niad RBLc^{l}. 95 *Add* .xxxii. (sunt) RB(Lc^{l}). 96-105 Ernain/ Ernan RBLc^{l}. 97 Aildae/ Aelad B. 99 Tige/ Cille BLc^{l}. 104 Bici/ Buidi B. 106 Cilli/ *om*. BLc^{l}. *Add* .xi. (sunt) B(Lc^{l}). 108 ingen Dáire/ i nDaire R(BLc^{l}). 115 *Add* .ix. (sunt) R(?)B(Lc^{l}). 123 *Add* hic Loch Eirne R(BLc^{l}). 125 7 Sinche/ Fainche 7 Sinche RBLc^{l}. *Add* Fainche Cille Fainche R(BLc^{l}). 127 Nessain/ Mesain B. *Add*. .xiii. sunt R(BLc^{l}). 129 .i. Uair/(h)Uair (R)BLc^{l}. 132 Feidelm 7 Mugain i Cill Ingen Ailella. (Feidelm 7 Eithne) (RLc^{l})B. *Add* .ui. (sunt) (RLc^{l}) B. 134 Rignach Domnaig/ i nDomnuch R(BLc^{l}). 136 Tulchi/ Taulcha R, Cilli B. 138 Luimb/ Luimbe R(B)Lc^{l}, 7 Echdach/ Rignach 7 Echtach RB(Lc^{l}). *Add* .ui. sunt RBLc^{l}. 139 Cruachain/ Cruachain Maige Abna R(BLc^{l}).

140 Sinech Dromma Airthir
Sinech Tigi Sinchi
Sinech i ndErnaide ⁊ Cuacras
Sinech Ichtair Methais
Sinech ingen Taibline
145 Sinech soror Coluim
Sinech Airdi Cróne
Sinech soror Bíti
Sinech Derg
Sinech ingen *ui* Buain
150 Sinech Cluana Bairnig

142 ⁊ Cuacras/ Sinech ⁊ Cuacras RBLc^{1}. 145, 147 soror/ siur RBLc^{1}. 148-50 Sinech Derg hui Buain Cille Bairnich R(B)Lc^{1}. *Add* .xi. RBLc^{1} *Add further* finit amen finit. Hii omnes sancti inuoco in auxilium meum (per in)tercession(em Sanctae) Mariae sanctarum ⁊ (sanctorum) quarum ⁊ quorum Deus nomina |...| uit ⁊ quos presciuit (⁊ per)distinauit confirmis fieri imaginis filii sui in uitam aeternam in Xp̄o Ihū Amen R(BLc^{1} *which omit* |...| uit *and spell* presciuit *as* prescibit).

709 Macrad noeb hErenn in so sís.

1 Meic Aeda
Meic Nessain
Meic Dallain
Meic Lugni
5 Meic Eoain
Meic Demmáin
Meic Ainmerech
Meic Daigri
Meic Dicu
10 Meic Attracht
Meic Sorain
Meic Nair
Meic Dairenn
Meic Lonain
15 Meic Midgnu
Meic Declain
Meic Caila
Meic Aida
Meic Coila
20 Meic Draigin
Meic Eoainn
Meic Aidgein
Meic Ḟintain
Meic Grelláin
25 Meic Lugair
Meic Massan
Meic Lugedan
Meic Lonain
Meic Dimmae
30 Meic Aedgenain
Meic Loce
Meic Midnan
Meic Coila
Meic Dubain
35 Meic Fintain
Meic Licce
Meic Brenaind
Meic Miannach
Meic Móinaig
40 Meic Móinain
Meic Beodan
Meic Coilain
Meic Nessain
Meic Fraichain
45 Meic Findcháil
Meic Cammain
Meic Dimmae
Meic Phil
Meic Dubthaig
50 Meic Gosso
Meic Locae
Meic Barrḟindain
Meic Sinaig
Meic Cairill
55 Meic Senchain
Meic Rotain
Meic Muadain
Meic Ḟerchair
Meic Lugain
60 Meic Ercain
Meic Comgain
Meic Caimmin
Meic Runce
Meic Ḟlannain
65 Meic Ercbi
Meic Ḟindbairr
Meic Daimraidi
Meic Miṅgthi
Meic Micain
70 Meic Mainne

709. Meic Tulchain
Meic Scellain
Meic Torain
Meic Ḟind
75 Meic Ḟergussan
Meic Maele
Meic Dubgoband
Meic Mantan
Meic Trianach
80 Meic Lugni
Meic Brocain
Meic Beadri
Meic Aithmeit
Meic Triallach
85 Meic Dulgin
Meic Berchain
Meic Ḟergnaid
Meic Artrach
Meic Ḟerruis
90 Meic Ainmerech
Meic Brogairb
Meic Dimmain
Meic Finnaig
Meic Colpain
95 Meic Aidain
Meic Beccain
Meic Minain
Meic Mellain
Meic Náir
100 Meic Blait
Meic Conlaed
Meic Baird
Meic Comgain
Meic Glasschon
105 Meic Dechet
Meic Decell
Meic Berrain
Meic Deaín
Meic Nechadain
110 Meic Gaillini
Meic Curitan
Meic Berrchon
Meic Iarlathi
Meic Braimene
115 Meic Aindlend
Meic Cellachain
Meic Connaid
Meic Crommaid
Meic Odrain
120 Meic Ailella
Meic Róneni
Meic Tipraite
Meic Eirmine
Meic Finnio
125 Meic Ġuntrae
Meic Ḟactnai
Meic Mincon
Meic Lucain
Meic Cetene
130 Meic Fir Fene
Meic Bachrae
Meic Maine
Meic Derggain
Meic Luachain
135 Meic Doromail
Meic Comgaill
Meic Oengusa
Meic Cainnig
Meic Gerrain
140 Meic Sarain
Meic Mommain
Meic Giallain
Meic Collain
Meic Bairreni
145 Meic Scandail
Meic Coímain
Meic Rúnain
Meic Mantain
Meic Cannain
150 Meic Coirtchend
Meic Scanláin
Meic Ergnaid
Meic Gossa
Meic Cailig
155 Meic Crimthaind
Meic Ḟergnae
Meic Demmain
Meic Fidais
Meic Fingin
160 Meic Sideoin
Meic Rumain
Meic Ḟergusa
Meic Rubcain
Meic Ṡetnai
165 Meic Eogain
Meic Oengusa
Meic Lasrain
Meic Lasrenn

709. Meic Laithbi
170 Meic Dercodib
Meic Diarmata
Meic Lugair
Meic Lugadan
Meic Dubthaig
175 Meic Rosnado
Meic Sindchain
Meic Cainnichain
Meic Liac
Meic Bresleain
180 Meic Dáiri
Meic Reṅgain
Meic Cairill
Meic Ningein
Meic Libir
185 Meic Donnáin
Meic Cannsa
Meic Murchon
Meic Damain
Meic Mellain
190 Meic Oiblain
Meic Oblain
Meic Barreni
Meic Granadan
Meic Beccan
195 Meic Trichim
Meic Muridaig
Meic hErcc
Meic Dremoin
Meic Liathain
200 Meic Garbain
Meic Uinnsend
Meic Sinill
Meic Mannain
Meic Lasre
205 Meic Mallain
Meic Pipain
Meic Sillain
Meic Rigain
Meic Maisse
210 Meic Ercnaisc

710 Oenmeic hErenn in so sís.

1 Mac Corpre
Mac Nise
Mac Cuill
Mac Táil
5 Mac Caille
Mac Laisre
Mac Lasrend
Mac Luimb
Mac Moínaig
10 Mac Artrach
Mac Lugair
Mac Lugain
Mac Barrain
Mac Muadain
15 Mac Echdach
Mac Ercbi
Mac Daigri
Mac Beraig
Mac Critain
20 Mac Lenin
Mac Sarain
Mac Flaind
Mac Dommain
Mac Donnain
25 Mac Ruadain
Mac Scandlaich
Mac Fintain
Mac Aidgin
Mac Brenaind
30 Mac Enain
Mac Senain
Mac Mennain
Mac Oṅgnaid
Mac Damain
35 Mac Comgain
Mac Cellain
Mac Oibleain
Mac Decill
Mac Lasráin
40 Mac Ríme
Mac na Cerdda
Mac in Goband
Mac int Ṡaer
Mac Colocae
45 Mac Talairg
Mac Cregain
Mac hErc
Mac Massain

710. Mac Albanaig
50 Mac Cecht Gobae
Mac Rustaig
Mac Tinne
Mac Murchon
Mac Bauber
55 Mac Findchain
Mac Nissi Cilli Bruane
Mac Nissi Cluana
Mac Failchon
Mac Cairthind
60 Mac Uacleni
Mac Sinetho
Mac Dochai
Mac Lasrain
Mac Conchaith
65 Mac Miannach
Mac Spirto
Mac Cluim
Mac Bricc
Mac Conne
70 Mac Mael Udir
Mac Glasse
Mac Caimse
Mac Uachline
Mac Loegaire
75 Mac Mótu
Mac Nissi Rois Draignigi
Mac Dara
Mac Dubain
Mac *ui* Cloistig
80 Mac Coirtched
Mac Conriss
Mac Commain

711 Ingenrada noeb hErenn in so sis.

1 Ingena Pilip
Ingena Cainnig
Ingena Manchain
Ingena Fiaich
5 Ingena Nathe
Ingena Cuacain
Ingena Cainne
Ingena Talmanig(?)
Ingena Colmain
10 Ingena Caimill
Ingena Aidain
Ingena Lugach
Ingena Senaig
Ingena Lasrain
15 Ingena Fothaid
Ingena hUabbain
Ingena Senain
Ingena Coluim
Ingena Cummatan
20 Ingena Barrain
Ingena Comgain
Ingena Eṅgain
Ingena Fiadot
Ingena Eltine
25 Ingena Fuilcc
Ingena Lucain
Ingena Neillini
Ingena Diarmata i Cluain Sasta Berchain
Ingena Colgan
30 Ingena Aildain
Ingena Bain
Ingena Coinne
Ingena Eitcheain
Ingena Crunmael
35 Ingena Becadain
Ingena Fergusa
Ingena Dimmain
Ingena Cathlaiṅge
Ingena Critain
40 Ingena Luthaig
Ingena Findchada
Ingena Fi[...]
Ingena [...]
Ingena [...]
45 Ingena [...]
Ingena [...]
Ingena Berchain
Ingena [...]tain i Cúil [...]mat
Ingena Olcain i Cuil Fota
50 Ingena Cillini
Ingena N[...]
Ingena Sin[...]

711. Ingena Meic Nadbuidb(?)
Ingena Ainmerech
55 Ingena Derg
Ingena [...]gin
Ingena Cronain
Ingena [...]
Ingena [...]
60 Ingena [...]
Ingena Gnoe
Ingena Brócain
Ingena Sinchill
Ingena Nadfraich
65 Ingena Caila
Ingena Daigri
Ingena Branchind
Ingena Beoaeda
Ingena Eoainmain
70 Ingena Erclaingi
Ingena Santain
Ingena Nadfraich
Ingena Findchain
Ingena Locain
75 Ingena Glassain
Ingena Comgill
Ingena Erccain
Ingena Eogain
Ingena Fergnai
80 Ingena Colbain
Ingena Conaill
Ingena Dochu
Ingena Triallaich
Ingena Domungin
85 Ingena Trianach
Ingena Cairthind
Ingena Aeda Budi .i. Cummain 7 Crón 7 Rignach Cilli Rignaigi .i.o Chill ingen Aeda i fail Irchulind i Fothartaib Fea.
Ingena Setnai
Ingena Dubthaig
90 Ingena Cathchon
Ingena Airchoil
Ingena Bresail
Ingena Becce
Ingena Rethe
95 Ingena Ultain
Ingena Demain
Ingena Meic Lasre
Ingena Grellain
Ingena Midgin
100 Ingena Baíth
Ingena Murithaig
Ingena Nemnand
Ingena Nemand
Ingena Irnath
105 Ingena Loarnaig
Ingena Aith[...]
Ingena Coilan
Ingena Cobthaig.

712 Híc[a] incipiunt sancti qui erant bini unius moris

1 Iohannes[a] Baptiza	Epscop Ibar.
2 Petrus apostolus	Patricius.
3 Paulus apostolus	Finnian Cluana I*raird.*
4 Andreas apostolus	Colum Cilli
5 Iacobus apostolus	Finnian Maigi Bile.
6 Iohannes apostolus	Ciaran Cluana Mac Nois.
7 Pilippus apostolus	Cainnech.

[a]*preceded by construe mark* L

712.8	Bartholomeus apostolus	Brendinus Senior.
9	Tomas apostolus	Brenainn Cluana Ferta.
10	Mattheus apostolus	Colum Tiri Da Glas.
11	Iacobus apostolus	Comgall Bennchoir.
12	Simon apostolus	Molassi Daminsi.
13	Tatheus apostolus	Sinchellus Iunior[a].
14	Mathias apostolus	Ruadanus Lothra.
15	Maria[a]	Brigita[a].
16	Martinus	Epscop hErcc Slaine.
17	Paulus heremita	Coemgen Glinne D*a Locha*
18	Antonius monachus	Fechini Fobair.
19	Augustinus Sapiens	Lonṅgarad.
20	Ambrosius [H]i*m*mno*dicus*[b]	Mac ind Eicis.
21	Iob patientiae	Munnu m. Tilcain.
22	Ieronimus Sapiens	Manchan Leith.
23	Clemens papa	Ciaran Saigri.
24	Grigorius Moralium	Cummini Fota.
25	Ciprianus Kartaginensis	Mochutu Lis Moir.
26	Laurentius diaconus	Dechoin Nessain.
27	Beda Sapiens 7 monachus	Buti m. Bronaig.
28	Ilarius episcopus 7 Sapiens	Sechnall epscop.
29	Cornelius papa	Moedoc Ferna.
30	Siluester papa	Adomnan epscop.

[a]*preceded by construe mark* L. [b]imm̊ L. *Stokes* (*Lis.Lives* 298) *suggests* hymnodicus (cf. *Fél.* 110).

712.31	Bonifatius papa	Molassi.
32	Paucomius monachus	Garald m*onachus*
33	Pastor monachus	Cammine monachus.
34	Benedictus caput monachorum totius Europae	Fintan Cluana Eidnig caput monachorum totius Hiberniae.
35	Augustinus episcopus Aṅglorum	Barre episcopus Muma|n 7 Con|nacht.

713 [a]Lucht oentad Mael Ruain in so[a] .i. Mael Ruain Tamlachta.

1 Mael Tuile m. Noechuire.

2 Mael Anfaid Darinse Máre.

3 Fland Find m. Fairchellaig i nDaire na Fland.

4 Fland m. Duib Thuinne i nDaire na Flann.

5 Flannán m. Tairdelbaig i Cill Dalua.

6 Mael Dithrub .i. anchorita Tíri Da Glass.

7 Dimman Arad.

8 Dalbach Cule Coll*ainge*.

9 Feidlimid m. Crimthainn.

10 Diarmait in Dísirt.

11 Eochaid epscop Tamlacta.

12 Oengus *ua* Óibleáin.

13 7 nosfiurad in ballán dia rochan Cormac m. Culennain: Ballan barrglas et cetera.

14 [b]Cormac m. Culennain cecinit.

Mael Rúain, Mael Tuile, im gním ṅgle,
Mael Anfaid na Darinse,
na tri Flaind, Mael Dithreib dil,
Dimman, Dalbach, Feidlimid.

[a—a]*added above* .i. iar Patric 7 iarsna da apstal déc Insi Fail L.

713.15 Diarmait, Eochaid, ard a scél,
7 Oengus *ua* Oiblén,
lucht na *h*oentad[c] sin uile
im Mael Rúain, im Mael Tuile, Mael Ruain[b].

[b–b]*added below col.* e L. [c]h *indicated by mark of lenition* L.

714 Ba hamra inti Adomnán. Ba mor serce 'mo Dia 7 'mo chobnesom. Is lais rotarclamtha in mórmartra nóeb i n-oenscrín 7 is i in scrín sin dorat Cillini Droichthech mac Dichlocha dochum hErenn do denam síd 7 attaig Ceneoil Conaill 7 Eogain. Is é in so lín na martra ut Adomnanus cecinit.

1 A maccucain i[s] sruith in tiag[a]
nodgaibi fort muin;
méti 'mo ṡnadud rígu,
eter íru 7 muir.

2 Fail and soscela in Meic Máir
Maire míni mó cach ṁbuaid;
asain duit la gelbáin ṅgrein[b]
lebrán [...][c] Eoin uaig.

3 Fail and sanctum sanctorum
assin chórum mór;
fail and a crund irdarc(?)[d] n-úag
fris raairlecht Pól.

4 Fail and iar sain, sochla fiss
doformaig ar less,
étach rofig Maire mass
7 robói fria cnes.

5 Fail and étach Meic ind Ríg
assa cés for cach n-óen;
fail and, iss amru cach ṁbríg,
a ḟuil ḟir assa thoeb.

6 Fail and saerchriss Senphóil,
a díthreib co mbuaid,
foḟuair Antón, inmain cléir,
issind úaim úair.

7 Fail and forbratt Martan máir,
noco chóir a cheal,
dia tubairt in ṁbréit don chlum,
ba foa doluid fora cheal.

[a]*glossed* .i. in scrin MS. [b]*last letter doubtful* MS. [c]*about three letters illeg.* MS.
[d]*facs.* irdairc.

714.8 Fail and .á., fiacail Patric nóeb,
assin Mache buadaig báin;
fail and fiacail slunti baird
Declain deoda ónd Aird Máir.

9 Fail and folt Maire ingini,
is cóir cen a chel;
fail fesléne sanct Brigte
assa ludai for nem.

10 Fail and fessléni Choluim
Cille, clú co mbail;
fail and laído dergeni
Brénaind buadach forin muir.

11 Fail and mullach Mochutu,
condagab Les Már;
fail and mullach Mochoe,
lam' Choemóc co ngrád.

12 Fail and almu Donnáin nóeb,
rombaí fora glún;
fail and gúalu Coluim
meic Crimthainn cúib.

13 Fail and int anart robói
secht m̄bliadna, buán ré,
im chorp ard issetnai iá,
ba huag fri Dia cechtar de.

14 Fail and cassleni Senaig
7 Senain sluind,
cochlan ulla Molua,
asna fua Fínain Chaimm.

15 Fail and cassal Chainnig credail
as rocet mór salm;
so dodúsaig, is scél derb,
in mórfessiur marb.

16 Fail and cassal Ennae Airne
ó'tá Araind rogiall,
lais congabsat an̄gil uaíg
[ ][e]

[e]*one line omitted in* MS.

14.17 Nóeb doruirmius, rígda an dám,
romsnadat sech demna drong;
'com churp 7 m'anmain,
om chind codam bond.

18 Ciped cruth 'mo saedrat
Scuitt scel n-amra n-aitt[f],
sruith ind aithne duit,
ba huág, ba hidan, a maicc. A.

[f]*facs.* uaitt.

15 [. . . . . .] inso.

Luid epscop [...]lle do th[a]bairt [...] a hifurn. Bói a [...] oc cathugud fri demna on trath co araile. Co tuc mathair [...]. Et bui epscop Moinenn ac comet a chuirp seom colleic. Dorala iarum a spirut docum a chuirp 7 b[a] scith 7 focheird osnaid. Imchommarc epscop Moinenn [iar] suidiu a n-asbert fris. 'In [n]-aigther éc, a Brenaind', ar epscop Moinenn. 'Agur em', ar Brenaind. 'Bás derb. Amser inderb. Deirge carat. Gnus écrat. Techt anaichnid. Tir ingnad. Conar dorcha. Drub cen tathchor. Fubtad feirge. Bubthad mbiasta. Glend n-uathmar nad roisc doene recat ass lán di theini 7 biastaib. Drochet clóen anbsaid dar sodain meni chongbat do daggnima. Rí airchend ar do chind. Breth anairchend la saide. Ascid do (c)oibsen. Coscrad do delba. Attreb nane. Othrus, [a]no turus[a], fota. Frescisiu bratha. Ernaide essergi. Essergi ainm [...] rithe. Imadag. A'.

'Is cos[n]aide chena ind flaith nemda fobíth is écsamail frisin flaith n-irchraidi 7 issiside cartait na ríg talmaide. Dallaidside amal cheo, marbaid amal chotlud, athcummaid amal rinne, timdibid amal faebair, loscid amal tenid, bádid amal muir, sluicid amal chuithe, fordiuclannaid amal beist. Ni hinund sin 7 flaith forcomat ind naeb 7 ind fíreoin. Is [b]láith ligda ara irglaine, is argit gel ara gelbane, is tinne óir ara rathmaire, is ord grene ara etrochtaigi, is lí ṡula ara sáeraille, is oenach ar oebinni, is mellca ara rebaigi, is flaith ar inmaire, is cruit ar cheolbhinne. Mochin riofa ind flaith sin ainm i fil Dia fodesin, rí mór caín cáid cumachtach tren noemglan firian feig forsaid trocar dearcach dilgidach sen óc ecnaid armitnech oebda uasal innocbaid cunnail cobsaid connerclech trócar treoda tidnaicthech, cen tossach, cen ḟorcend. Róisam roattrebam a ḟlaith ind ríg sain in secula seculorum. Ammen.

[a]—[a]*above line* L.

16.1 Brenaind m. Findloga m. Elchon m. Altai de Chiarraigi Luachra do Alltraige Chaille; i n-oenamsir la Oengus m. Nadfraich rig Muman rogenair.

2 Is í a mathair atchonairc i fís, andar lé, tinne de ór de thárniud 'na hucht 7 a dá cich do lassad fora bruini.

716.3 Atchuaid Findlug in fís sin dia anmcharait .i. do Epscop Erc m. Ogamuin m. Fidaig. Et atbertside co ngenfed gein amra ón mnaí atchonnairc in fís.

4 Atchonnairc dna Epscop Erc, indair leis, níam theined dar crích Altraige, ⁊ ba lán do anglib ó nim co lár. Luid Epscop Erc do thig Ḟindloga iarnabarach, ⁊ coṅgab in mac ina ucht, et focheird a ḟoesam ⁊ a oentaid fris.

5 Is í ind sin aidchi immustarla Bec m. De in fáid i tig Meic Arddae m. Fidaig, ríg Ciarraige Luachra. Immuscomarcar in rí: 'Cid atchí dún innocht, a Bic'.
'Atchiu co ṅgenedar do rí etrut aniar ⁊ muir'. 'Ni ḟetamar ém', ar Macc Arda, 'síl saer notlessad ríge forn etruind ⁊ muir'.
Atbert Bec: 'mac berair innocht do Ḟindlug, bod é do rí do gres'.

6 Dotháet immurgu bróen dian do thopur Iordanen co rothinsan fair i ndenus a baiste. Conid de asrubradsom Brendinus .i. broen dian di anuas *no* i ndenus a baisti.

717 Donnan Ega

Ega nomen fontis i nAldasain, [a].i. carrac eter Gallgaedelu ⁊ Cend Tiri ina camair immuich[a], i Cattaib i tuaisciurt Alban. Et ibi Donnanus cum sua familia martirium subiit. Quod sic contigit quaedam mulier diues illic habitabat ante Donnanum; ⁊ illic pascebantur pecora eius. Haec ergo propter inuidiam quam circa illos habebat quibusdam latronibus persuasit ut interficerent Donnanum cum suis. Sed cum illi latrones illuc uenissent, inuenerunt eos in oratorio psalmodiam cantantes; ⁊ ibi nec potuerant eosdem interficere. Dixit autem Donnanus discipulis suis: 'Eamus in refectorium ut hi possint interficere nos; ubi uiuere carnaliter solebamus; quia quandiu simus ubi Deo satisegimus placere, mori non possumus; ubi uero carni benefecimus carnis dispendium soluemus'. Sic igitur in refectorio suo in nocte Paschae occisi sunt. Quinquaginta quattuor autem numero passi sunt simul cum ipso Donnano.

[a—a]*added above line.*

718.1 Sarbili ainm Moninni prius o tustidib. Darerca o baithiss. Moninne ond ḟilid (...). Is de atá dui .i. fili balb rathroisc aicce ar co tissed a erlabra dó. Et iss ed toesech rolabair .i. nin, nin. Unde dicebatur Moninne, ⁊ Ninníne Éices ainm in ḟiled. *No* iss ed atbertis na caillecha óca mo ninna ria, ⁊ inde Monannec ⁊ Moninne dicitur.

2 Moninne caid arcanam,
breo cen barand tuaid bruidind,
fo néib gréne doscaraim,
fo baraind i Sleib Chulind.

18.3 Rochacht ar Crist a colaind,
nistarall trist domunim,
mad rogab crabud grinni
Moninne Slebe Culind.

4 O gabais cris foa colaind,
iss e seo fiss domunim,
ni thormalt sáith *no* ṡéire
Moninne Slébe Culind.

5 Noí fichit bliadan, ba lla,
iar rím riagla cen timme,
cen baes, cen bet, cen baegul,
ba hé saegul Moninne. M.

6 Patraic robathas cailli
Conaille flatha finne,
fo miad masse class cunnail,
aisse munait Moninne.

7 Ba hóg, ba hór gle glanna,
ba mind óir, ba slóg singe,
ba gaire gúr cach clainne,
ba múr mainne Moninne. M.

8 Hi pridnoin nọebad aille,
nirbo léim lium i llinne,
fosrogab dor[...] rige
dochum nime Moninne. M.

19 Cinti crábuid 7 gnathaigthe scoile Sinchil[l] so sis.

Crábud cen scís. Umla cen ḟodord. Étgud cen ḟorcraid. Aíni cen elniud. Ailithri cen impúd. Bíthecht fri bésaib. Bennachad prainne. Praind cen ḟuidell. Feidli fri foglaim. Frithalim tráth. Tír frecor nime. Nertad cech oen. Nefní dont ṡaegul. Santugud offrind. Eitsecht fri uaslib. Adrad do genus. Gabail ic fannaib. Foisitiu menic. Michatu cuirp. Cátu anman. Oenucht fri écin. Éscas co galaraib. Crossigell co toe. Tróige do thinnius. Scrutan screptra. Aisnis ḟorcitail. Onóir do ṡenaib. Saere i sollomnaib. Cumri cantana. Comet cairdessa. Mnaa do imgabail. Aduath do airscelaib. Miscais do raidsechaib. Cen rochtain ar rochomrad. Cen anoentaid oentaige. Cen escas d'acallaim chobnesam. Isle dia magistir. A mmagister a mmog. In comdiu a tigerna.

20 Lon Garad cosfind. I tuasciurt Ossairge o Disiurt Garad, [a]i mMaig Garad[a], i n*Uib* Fairchellain, [b]7 o Chill Gabra i Sleib Mairge[b]. Is ed atberar[c] co torchratar tiaga libair hErenn 7 a soscelai 7 a llibuir

[a—a]*above line* L, *in text after* Fairchellain M. [b—b]*om.* M.

foglamma dia n-aidlenaib i n-aidchi éitsechta Luin Garad[d] amal nothuctis nach ticfad co bráth nech mar Lon ṅGarad.
Unde[e]:

Atbath Lon Garad;
ro[g]ab[f] don
is dith legind 7 scol
[Indsi][g] hEr*enn* dar da hor.

[c]adberaid M. [d]nGarad M. [e]*add* dicitur M. [f]*partly illeg.* L, gab M. [g]*illeg.* L, indsi M.

721.1 Epscop Ibar, tri bl*iadna* trichat tri fichit [...][a] uita eius. Lugna nomen patris eius 7 di Ultaib doside 7 do Artraigib da [...]ruth[b]. Bassar im*murgu* nomen matris eius 7 di Désib Breg diside.

2 Cethri meic 7 .iii(i).[b] ingena ic Lugna .i. Ibar epscop, Mobeoc, Coeman Brecc, [c](Mac Lugna)[c]. It é .iiii. ingena .i. Caínech Apad, Mellit Manach, Brondḟind Brecc, Corrtharach Cain.

3 Trí anmand batar for Epscop Ibar .i. Nennán ainm dó .i. nínan ar a lenmaidecht. Columba Cille testante: Nennán nobilissimum principalem episcopum.

4 Ecmacht dna agnomen dó .i. accu mó a acht .i. a chubat. Ar robatar .xu. ina airdi. Eodem testante: abbatem catholicum egregium .i. longissimum.

5 Cognomen im*murgu* dó, Ibar, et ideo impositum est ei. Fecht luid Lugna ina charpat 7 a ben immale riss, .i. Bassar. Sech Raith Cennaig lotar. 'Carpat fo ríg sechnon', ar in druí tall istig.

6 'Tiagar dia ḟis cia fil and', ar in rí .i. Colman m. Némain, et robaist Epscop Ibar eside iar sain. Et roiarfaig in techtaire acus fuair a ḟis conid é Lugna robuí 'sin carpat, 7 iss ed roraid in rí: 'mentax est magus quia non est rex in curru'.

7 Dixit magus: 'interrogate illum', id est Lugnam, 'utrum habet uxorem egram'. Nuntius, poirtans lapidem in manu sua occulte, iuit 7 dixit: 'portaui causam sanitatis uxoris si esset in dolore'.

8 Lugna respondit: 'quid portasti'. Ille respondit: 'cathedram cepae portaui a rege(?)'. Et postea nuntius manum dé [...][a] ut dixit, ita fuit, 7 .xii. unga[...][a] habens in ea. Una ex illis suauit [...][a] magnitudine 7 illam cathedram cepae dedit, [d].i. Lugna[d], uxori sua 7 manducauit eam.

[a]*illeg.* L. [b]*partly illeg.* L. [c—c]*partly illeg. or read* Maclisogeis? L. [d—d]*above line* L.

21.9 Et postea habuit calorem per totum corpus suum et faciem rufam ualde. Et postea parturit filium habentem similem colorem illi arbori que taxus, [d].i. ibar[d], uocatur, 7 ideo infans ille nominatus est Ibar.

10 In mac tan*aise* im*murgu,* Mobeoc, ideo nominatur quia mater eius dixit: 'mo mac beoda ócc so'.

11 A[n][b] tres mac Cóemán .i. cóem 7 án é 7 sacerdos fuit.

12 Quartus autem filius [...][a] episcopus fuit quem nunc dicimus Mac Luṅge quasi Mac Lugna. Et ideo dicebatur Mac Lugna quia pater eius ualde amabat eum pre ceteris.

13 Ut discipuli Mocta dixerunt: 'non uenerunt filii Lugnae .i. Ibar episcopus et(?) Coemanus pontifex, uel sacerdos, et Mac Lugna'. Et Mocta dixit: 'cur tertius filius [...][a] matris propriae nomine'.

14 Discipuli responderunt: 'proprium nomen habet str[...]na[b] noluit [...][a] filium suum iuniorem alii uocari ob amorem quia filii Lugna uocauit'. Et dixit Mocta: 'bud irgna et cetera [...][a] 7 bid ard a inad híc 7 in futuro'.

[a]*illeg.* L. [b]*partly illeg.* L. [c—c]*partly illeg. or read* Maclisogeis? L. [d—d]*above line* L.

ON THE MOTHERS OF THE SAINTS

22.1 [a]Ondbaiuin[b], *no*[a] Gombauin[c], do Bretnaib mathair Patric 7 a choic sethar[d]; [e]*no* Conches *no* Cochmas a ainm[e].

2 Dediu[f] ingen Trena m. Dubthaig *ui*[g] Lugair[h] mathair Ṡenain m. Ḟintain 7 Manchin[i] m. Collain[j] 'sin[k] Chorund 7 Caillín[l] [m]Coluim Cille[n] 7 Feidlimid Cilli Moir Dithruib[n] et Dega m. Cairill 7[m] Femmi[o] [p]ingini Cairill[p] et Diarmata Insi Clothrann. Tricha noeb 7 noebóg[q] do ṡíl Dubthaig *ui*[r] Lugair fo hErind.

3 Fainchi[s] ingen Dallbronaig mathair Conaill 7 Eogain 7 Cairpre tri meic Nemain.

[a—a]*om.* M. [b]Ondbahum B(Lc[l]). [c]Gondb(a)um B(Lc[l]), Gondbathum M. [d]seathrach BLc[l], *add* .i. Lupait 7 Tigris 7 Darerca (7 Liamain) 7 Rícend BLc[l](M). [e—e]alii dicunt; Conchas (Coincheas) ainm a mathar 7 siur do Martain hí; *no* gomad Chochmais ingen Ochmais a mathair B(Lc[l]M). [f]Deidh M. [g]ua M. [h]Lugaigh B. [i]Mai(n)chen B(Lc[l]), Minchein M. [j]Gollain M. [k]isin BLc[l], asin M. [l]Cailein B, Caillein(e) (Lc[l])M. [m—m]*om.* M. [n]*om.* BLc[l]. [o]Feima B, Feidmi M. [p—p]a siur (sethar) B(Lc[l]), *add* a sethar M. [q]tricha ogh BLc[l]M. [r]meic B, hua M. [s]Fuinchi M.

4 Secht n-ingena [a]Dalbrónaig do Dál Chonchobair asna[b] Desib Breg[c] [d]in so[ad].

[a—a]la Dallbronach de quibus dicitur BLc[l](M). [b]lasna Lc46Vb, i Lb. [c]Muman La. [d—d].i. Lb, *om.* La.

Brocsech[e], Sanct Broc, Cumman[f], Caimell,
Fannchi[g], Findbarr[h], Feidelm[i],
[j]secht n-ingena sain adrímem[k],
do[l] Dallbronuch adfédem[j].
Rogenatar[m] nóeb 7 nóeboga imda[n] ón morfessiur sa[o] tra[p].

722.5 [q]Rogenair[r] chetus[s] Brigit[t] o Brócsig[q].

[e]Broiseach B, *add* 7 La. [f]Coman La. [g]Fuinch(e) (Lc46Vb)Lb(M). [h]*bis* La. [i]Feidil Lc46Vb, Felim Lb, Feidl(e)im M(La). [j—j]*om.* Lc46VbLb. [k]ade(i)rim B(Lc[l]). [l]*om.* BLc[l]MLa. [m]*add* imorro La. [n]herimda BLc[l](Lc46VbM), ile Lb, *om.* La. [o]sin Lc46VbLbM. [p]*om.* BLc[l]Lc46VbLbMLa, *after* rogenetar Lb. [q—q]Brocsech tra mathair Brighti La(*preceding* rogenetar). [r]dogenair Lc[l], roge(i)n Lc46Vb(Lb). [s]cetamus BLb(Lc[l]M). [t]Brigach B. [u]Brosich B.

6 [a]Oen[b] aile dib[c] Cumman[a]. Dosrala[d] do[e] acallaim Patric[f] 7 si thorrach fora céttorrches [g]co tarat[g] Patric crois[h] dia[i] bachaill[j] [k]dara[l] broinn. Et[km] is í[n] gein boí[o] ina broinn [p]in tan sin[pq] [r]Epscop Mane[r] 7 robaé[s] in chross sin [t]ina etun[tu] céin[v] [w]ropo beo[wx]. Et atbert[y] Patric[z] icá sénad[aa] co ngenfitis nóeb 7 noebóga imda uadi[bb]. [cc]Conid iar[dd] sin genatar[ee] uadi morfesiur ar dib fictib do noebaib acht[ff] Tuathal Maelgarb [gg]a oenur[gg] et Ailill m. Mochta[cchh].

[a—a]oen dna dona caillechaib so La, *om. except for* Cumain B[l]. [b]ingean M. [c].i. BLc[l], dib .i. Lb, di M. [d]dorala (side) BLc[l](Lb)MLa. [e]*om.* B. [f]*add* co tuilam (tuilain, tuilen) 7 cnai olla findi lee B(Lc[l]M). [g—g]dorad B[l]Lc46Vb, c*on*astard Lb, co tard MLa. [h]*above line* Lc[l]. [i]da BB[l]Lc46Vb, don La. [j]*add* Ísu La. [k—k]*om.* B[l] [l]di fora Lc46Vb. [m]*om.* Lc46Vb. [n]e BB[l]Lc[l]Lc46VbLbMLa. [o]roboí La. [p—p].i. La. [q]*above line* Lb, *add* .i. BB[l]Lc[l]Lc46VbLbM. [r—r]*reversed* La. [s]robhi B[l], roba Lc46Vb, boi Lb. [t—t]*om.* B[l]. [u]enech Lb. [v]an fad B[l], in gen Lc46Vb, agein M. [w—w]robai beo BB[l]Lc46Vb(La), ba beo he Lb. [x]B[l]Lc46VbLb *break off here. See note.* [y]asbert BLc[l]. [z]fria BLc[l], *om.* M. [aa]signumug M. [bb]*add* 7 comad lir finda na cnae findi na aingil for toradh a bronn B(Lc[l]M). [cc—cc]conid de atberar Maine Crosach de 7 atbert Patraic fria co ngenfitis noim 7 noemogha uathi La. [dd]ar BLc[l]. [ee]rogeinedar B(Lc[l]M). [ff]*written with large* a L, 7 BM, ocus Lc[l]. [gg—gg]*om.* BLc[l]M. [hh]*add* ar nídad naemsidhe B(Lc[l]M).

7 Is uadi ém[a] rogenair Moninne Slebe Culind et da mac Comgaill[b] i mMaig Coraind[c] et Epscop Mane Echenaig i Tír *Ua* nAilella et Epscop Roin[d] i Cill Epscuip Roin[d] i Cairpre[e] Móir [f]et Muridach [gh]i Cill[h] Alaid [i]i Tir[i] *Ua*[j] nAmalgada[fgk].

[a]*om.* BLc[l]M. [b]Conaill BLc[l], Oililla M. [c]Conaill B. [d]Broin B(*with* b *above line*). [e]crich Cairbri B. [f—f]*follows* Ailella *above* BLc[l]M. [g—g]*reversed* B. [h—h]Cilli Lc[l]M. [i—i]Thiri M. [j]*om.* B. [k]nAmalgaid BLc[l].

8 Et Cammini[a] Insi Celtra [b]et Senan Insi Cathaig et Riaguil Muccinsi la Dal Cais[bc] et Senan[d] Lathraig Briuin[e] et Eirne[f] Cluana Rai[l]gech[g] i mMide et secht n-epscuip Cluana[h] Emain[i] ar brú[j] Sinna.

[a]Caemgein B. [b—b]*entries reversed* BLc[l]M. [c]*add* dibh lin(a)ibh B(Lc[l]M). [d]Senach M. [e]Bruin Lc[l]. [f]Eirnin M. [g]Railge(a)ch (BLc[l])M. [h]*om.* B. [i]hEabain M. [j]*add* na BLc[l]

22.9 Et Loeban[a] 7 Fortchern [b]i nOidim[b] [c]i Ceru[c] i Partraigi[d] et Grellan Craibige[e] i n-airthiur[f] Maige Luirg et Sciri o Chill Sciri et Corcair [g]Chet di[g] ingin Eogain et secht[h] n-ingena Cathbath[i] i Cill Chomlach[j] i mMaig Luirg et Lomman Locha Gille[k] eter Chairpre 7 Brefni et Midu Midbrisi m. Factna ic Sligig[l].

[a]Laebach B. [b—b]*om.* B, andoaim M. [c—c]ig*eru* B, *om.* Lc[l], *add* 7 M. [d]Partrai B, Partraidi Chera Lc[l]. [e]Craibhi BLc[l], Craibdige M. [f]iarthar B. [g—g]Ceti BLc[l], Chend da M. [h]*om.* BLc[l], tri M. [i]Cathbaig M. [j]Chomlaich M. [k]Gili BM. [l]Slige(a)ch (B)Lc[l].

10 Et Mell[a] Chraibdech ic Beluch Gabrain 7[b] ic Daire Melle et Osnat o Criched[c] i ṅGlind Dallain i Cairpre Mór[d] et Dabríg Cluana[e] Lochain et Darfiled[f] Indsi Cethig[g] i nIrrus Domnand et secht n-ingena Caechain i Tir *Ua* Fiachrach Adni et Miadaine[h] Ratha Arad et Brig Cochlach a Crích[i] Cairpri et Tuathal Maelgarb [j] rí hErenn[j] et Ailill m. Mochta [j]brathair Dommai[j].

[a]*or read* Inell L, Indeall M. [b]*om.* B. [c]cridech M. [d]*add* Droma Cliabh BLc[l]M. [e]Cluacha B. [f]Dirbhileadh BLc[l](M). [g]Geidh M. [h]Miadain M. [i]*om.* BLc[l]M. [j—j]*om.* BM. [j—j]quia brathair Moninde B(Lc[l]), da brathair Moninde M.

11 Et condrancatar[a] imacall*aim* uile [b]in buiden[b] seo i Carn Tracta[c] Eothaile 7 doringset[d] oentaid[e] [f]et asbertatar[f]: 'nech[g] conscerad[h] [i][j]i talmain[j] a n-oentaid[i] na[k] ricfa[l] a anim nem, et na[m] biad a athgabal[n] i talmain[o], et in carn sa in rachomraicsem[p], co tí muir dar Róe[q] *Ua* Fiachrach [r]na ticfad[r] tairis'. Et asbert[s] Epscop Mane.

Nech[t] conscera oentaid ár noeb[u],
sech bid clóen[v] bid mer,
ni aittrebba talmain tind[w],
ni ria[x] [y]a anim for nem[y].

[a]*add* in B. [b—b]na naim BLc[l]M. [c]Traga Lc[l]. [d]dognised Lc[l]. [e]a n-aentaigh ann B(Lc[l]M). [f—f]7 rofagadar trena mirbailib M. [g]aneach B. [h]noscerad BLc[l]M. [i—i]*reversed* BLc[l]. [j—j]i talamh BLc[l], *om.* M. [k]nach M. [l]ricfadh B(Lc[l]M). [m]no Lc[l]. [n]chomarpa M. [o]talamh BLc[l]. [p]rachomrachomraicsem (= *uncorrected dittography*)L, caemnacair B, comrancamar Lc[l], rochomraigsium M, *add* ar siat B(Lc[l]M). [q]Re BLc[l]. [r—r]ni targa BLc[l], narthi M. [s]*add* a sindsear .i. B(Lc[l]M). [t]*om.* BLc[l]M. [u]Ne(a)m (B)Lc[l]. [v]*add* 7 BLc[l]. [w]tend (7) (B)Lc[l]. [x]ricfa BLc[l], roichfi M. [y—y]amenn B.

12 [a]Feidelm ingen Dallbronaig mathair Ite Cl*uana*[b] Dedad[a].

[a—a]*om.* BLc[l]. [b]*or read* Cl*ainne*? L, Chluana M.

13 [a]Sanct Bróc ingen Dalbronaig 7 Fedbair[b] ingen Dalbronaig [c]i mBothaib Ech[c] Roichnig. [d]Cul Ugaine[d] ainm a cille i mMaig Luigne[a].

[a—a]*om.* BLc[l]. [b]Feadbhor M. [c—c]*om.* M. [d—d]a Cuil Iugaine M.

14 Bassar[a] do Désib Breg mathair clainni Lugna .i. Epscop Ibar 7 Mobeoc 7 Coeman Brecc 7 Mac Luṅga[b] .iiii.[c] filii[d] Lugna[e].

[a]Lasair BLc[l]M. [b]Luingi BLc[l], Luigni M. [c]ceithri M. [d]meic BLc[l], fili M. [e]*add* (sin) 7 (BLc[l])M.

Caínech[f] Abbad immurgu[g] 7 Mellit[h] Moínech[i] 7 Brondḟind Brec 7 Cortharach[j] Cain[k] .iiii.[l] ingena Lugna[m].

[f]Caindech BLc[l], Caeinneach M. [g]*om.* BLc[l]M. [h]Meallait M. [i]Maenach BLc[l], Mainiuch M. [j]Cartharach B, Corcrach M. [k]Caem BLc[l]. [l]ceithri BM. [m]Lugdach Lc[l], *add* (and)sin B(Lc[l]M).

722.15 Lupait siur Patric [a]mathair[b] M*ac*chú Baird [ac]; Sechnall, Nectain, Dabonna, Mogornan[d], Darióc[e], Ausaille[f], Crumthir Lugnath[g].

[a—a].uii. Findbairr B. [b]*add* .uii. Lc[l]M. [c]in Baird Lc[l], *add* .i. BLc[l]M. [d]Mogornach B, Modorrnan M. [e]Darigoc Lc[l]. [f]Ausaill M. [g]Lugna B.

16 [a]Darerca siur Patric mathair cóic n-epscop ṅdéc 7 da óg[ab]; Epscop Mél[c], Epscop Melcon[d], Epscop Munis[e], Rioc[f] Insi Bó Finni, Crummaine Lecna[g], Midnu, Mogenóc[h], [i]Lomman Atha Truim, Luran Duanaire[i] [jk]o Daire Lurain[k] et[j] Loorn[l] o Chill Chunnu andís[m], Ciaran, Carantot, Epscop Coluimb, Brenaind Fine[n], Epscop Mac[o] Caille, Brocan [p]7 Broccaid[pq].
Eiche[r] 7 Lallóc[s] o Ṡenlus iar[t] ṁBadbgnu[u] na di chaillig.

[a—a]Clann Darerca .xui. episcopi et duae uirgines *as heading in* L[l]M[l]. [b]*add* .i. BLc[l]M. [c]Mael BLc[l], *add* 7 *here* (BLc[l]) *and passim* M. [d]Melcho L[l]M[l]B(Lc[l]M). [e]*add* tres filii Cnois L[l]M[l]. [f]Rigoc Lc[l]. [g]*om.* L[l]M[l]BLcM. [h]Modenocc M. [i—i]*reversed* M[l]. [j—j]*om.* L[l]M[l]. [k—k]*om.* BLc[l]. [l]Loaen B, Lorainn M, Luran M[l]. [m]ndisert B. [n].i. Fini (*added above line*) L[l], ind M[l]. [o]*added above line* B. [p—p]*om.* L[l]M[l]. [q]Brocait B, Brochaidh M. [r]Eith(n)i M(M[l]). [s]Iallóc L[l], Illand M[l]. [t]*om.* M. [u]mBadnai M.

17 [a]Uanḟind ingen Ḟindbairr[a] mathair Mobí Chlarinig.

[a—a]hUanfindbarr B.

18 [a]Mella[b] mathair Chainnig sac*airt*[c] 7 Tigernaig Daire Melli[a].

[a—a]*see note.* [b]Me(a)ll BLc[l](M). [c]*om.* BLc[l]M.

19 Coemell [a]ingen Chenḟinnain[b] m. Cesi m. Lugdach[ac] mathair Choemgin 7 Chaemain [d]Ṡantlethain[e] o[df] Airdni[g] et Nadchaemi[h] Tiri Da Glas et Coemoice[i].

[a—a]*om.* BLc[l]. [b]Cheindḟindain M. [c]Luigdeach M. [d—d]*om.* BLc[l]. [e]Thannleathain M. [f]*om.* M. [g]Airne BLc[l]. [h]Netcaimi B(Lc[l]M). [i]Caimeilli o Chill Caimilli B(Lc[l]M).

20 [a]Minchloth [b]derbḟiur do Chóemiill[b] mathair Choluim[c] m. Crimthainn[a].

[a—a]*see note.* [b—b]ingen Cenandain m. Céisi m. Lugdach m. Labrada m. Aengusa m. Nadfraich (B)Lc[l]M[l]. [c]Colma(i)n B(M[l]).

21 Ronnat ingen Ṡegini m. Duach m. Barrḟinnain do Chen*iu*l Ennae m. Neill mathair Adomnain m. Ronain.

22 Sin ingen Neill m. Mechair di Chorco Bascinn, de *Uib* Conaire Léime Con Culainn, mathair chóic mac Sinill .i. Moboe[a] m*accua* Alla, is é congab Cluain Da Andobar, 7 Malach[b] 7 Caurnán[c] 7 Crónan.

[a]Mobhi qui dicitur BLc[l]M. [b]Malan BLc[l]M. [c]Cur(r)nan BLc[l](M).

722.23 Ethni ingen Dimma m. Noe qui ⁊ Derḟind Belḟota[a] de Chorpraigi[b] Fanat mathair Choluim Cille.

[a]Belada Lc[l]. [b]Forbraidhi B.

24 Cumman siur Coluim Cille[a] mathair da mac Decill .i. Moernoc[b] ⁊ Cassine[c].

[a]Chill M. [b]Maernoc B. [c]Caisene BLc[l].

25 Minchloth mathair mac Némain[a] [b].i. Cholmain ⁊ Chobrain[b].

[a]nEnain BLc[l]. [b—b]quorum unus Colum (Colman) dicitur BLc[l], quorum .i. Cholmain ⁊ Gobrain un*us* Colman dicitur M.

26 Sinech[a] mathair Chéin.

[a]Sinach M.

27 Derinill Chetharchichech[a] mathair Domungairt m. Echach et Ailleain [b]et Aedain[c] et Muru Othna et Mochumma Dromma Bó[b] et Chilleain Achaid Chail i lLeith Chathail ar brú[d] [e]Traga Duni[e] Dromma.

[a]ce(a)tha(i)rcoiced (B)Lc[l]. [b—b]*om.* B. [c]*add* ⁊ Mochuma M. [d]ur BLc[l]M. [e—e]Tragda B.

28 Erc[a] ingen Loairn[b] [c]m. Eirc[c] rig Alban mathair Mael Umai m. Baetain.

[a]Earg B. [b]Logairrn M. [c—c]*om.* BLc[l]M.

29 Pompa ingen Loairn[a] [b]m. Eirc[b] mathair Charnig ⁊ Breccain m. Ṡárain et Ronain[c] m. Ṡarain.

[a]Logairrn*n* M. [b—b]*om.* BLc[l]M. [c]*add* Ḟind BLc[l](M).

30 Colla[a] ingen Dimma Mind[b] de Galengaib mathair Ultain m. Ronain.

[a]Collo M. [b]*om.* M.

31 Aglend[a] ingen Lénin[b] mathair Ḟintain ⁊ Choluim[c] — [de].i. Cholmain Midísil[e] — ⁊ Lugada[d].

[a]Ailgenn B(Lc), Aiglind M. [b]Lei*n* B. [c]Cholmain M. [d—d]*om.* M. [e—e]*om.* BLc[l].

32 Ligach[a] Bregmuinech[b] mathair [c]Nainneda[d] et Muridaig[c].

[a]Ligan BLc[l]. [b]Bregmuine M. [c—c]*om.* Lc[l]. *See note.* [c]Nindeada B, Nainnid M.

33 [a]Gelgeis ingen Aeda Find mathair[a] Fursu[b] Chraibdig[c].

[a—a]*om.* Lc[l]. *See note to* 32. [b]Ursa M. [c]Craibthi B, Craibdigi M.

34 Iamnat [a]ingen Ṡinill[a] mathair Emin Báin Uissenaig[b] de Chorco Soilcind[c] Cruaich; iss e fil[d] ic Rus Gl*assi*.

[a—a]*om.* BLc[l]. [b].h. Ṡenaig M. [c]Thoillginn M. [d]d*us* fil M.

722.35 Maithgemm[a] ingen Aedain m. Gabrain rig Alban mathair[b] Molassi m. Cairill. [c]Is é congab Lethglend[c]. Unde[d]:

Molasse lassar[e] di[f] thenid
cona chlassaib tomaid[g],
abb Ráthchille[h], rí int ṡenaid,
mac Maithgemme Monaid.

[a]Maithgnem B, Maithgin M. [b]*add* rig *with deletion marks* B. [c—c]*om.* BLc[l]. [d]ut dicitur BLc[l]M. [e]*om. but space left* B. [f]*om.* Lc[l]. [g]comaid BLc[l](M). [h]*add* 7 BLc[l].

36 Bochra mathair tri mac Fidl*imid*[a] .i. Laidcend et Cainnech et Aed Chobran.

[a]mBochra BLc[l], Feideilm M.

37 Guas 7 Feidelm[a] dí[b] ingin Mani m. Neill. Et[c] is sí ind Ḟeidelm[a] sin mathair Munnu m. Tulchain.

[a]Feidlim M. [b]da BLc[l]M. [c]*om.* M.

38 Brócsech[a] mathair Mael Ruain Tamlachta[b].

[a]Broiseach B. [b]Tamlachtan M.

39 Nem Luagne[a] mathair Ḟintain Dromma Ing[b].

[a]Laignen M. [b]Aing B.

40 Lassar mathair Ḟinneain[a] epscoip.

[a]Ḟindtain M.

41 Brig mathair Chomgaill sacairt.

42 Derfraích[a] ingen Echach[b] m. Crimthainn[c] [d]ríg Airgiall[d] mathair Tigernaig m. Cairpre [e]Cluana Eois[e].

[a]Darfraich B(Lc[l]). [b]Aedha *no* Echach B. [c]*add* m. Feg m. Degha Duirn m. Cairpri Daimargaid B(Lc[l]M). [d—d]*om.* BLc[l]M. [e—e]in epscoip BLc[l]M.

43 Mugain[a] mathair Brenaind sacairt[b].

[a]Mumain B. [b]*om.*B.

44 Cael mathair Ruadain sacairt.

45 Sochlo[a] mathair Ḟechin.

[a]Sochla BLc[l]M.

46 Eithni mathair Aeda epscoip[a].

[a]in epscoip B, eipin M.

47 Sochlo mathair Molua [a]m. Ocha[a].

[a—a](m. Fotha) .i. Lugaidi sac*airt* BLc[l](M).

22.48 Ness mathair Choemain sacairt.

49 Feidelm[a] mathair Chunnida[b] epscoip, [c].i. M*ei*c Culinn Lusca[c].

[a]Feidlim M. [b]Chruindida Lc[l]. [c—c]*added above line* L, *in text* BLc[l]M.

50 Suaibsech mathair Mael Rubai [a]m. Elgonaig[a].

[a—a]Maelgonaich B.

51 Nemnat[a] Chiarraigech[b] mathair Molliṅg Luacra.

[a]Nemnann B. [b]Chiarraide M.

52 Necht mathair Míti ingen[a] Chindḟaelad.

[a]ingine M.

53 A Fina[a] ingen Chindḟaelad mathair Ḟlaind[b] Ḟina m. Ossu[c].
B Aliter[d]. Fina ingen Cholmain[e] m. [f]Ninnida mathair[f] Baétain m. Murchertaig [g]m. Muridaig[g] mathair Flaind[b] Ḟina ríg Saxan.

[a]*corrected from* Faela *to* Fina B. [b]Loind Lc[l]. [c]Gosa B(M). [d]*om.* M. [e]*add* Rime BLc[l]. [f—f]*om.* BLc[l]. [g—g]*om.* B, *add* 7 M.

54 Lassar mathair Cholmain m. Luachain.

55 Caemnat do Dál Buachalla do Ultaib mathair Baethini m. Cuanach.

56 Tailech[a] mathair Ḟinnia M*accua* Thell*duib*[b].

[a]Taidlech M. [b]*or read* Tell*aig*? L, Te(a)llduibh BLc[l](M).

57 Darerca mathair Chiarain m. Beonaid[a].

[a]Beoain B.

58 Cness ingen Chomchaidi di Dal Cheithinn[a] mathair Meic [b]Nisi Chondere[b].

[a]Cethern B(Lc[l]M). [b—b]Missi m. Conairi B.

59 Sant mathair Ailbi Imlecha[a] et Cholmain m. Oengusa qui dicitur[b] Mac Darane[c].
Is de im*murgu*[d] asberarsom[e] Mac Darane[f] .i. Sant [g]ingen Gési[g] a mathair 7 ba comrit[h] hí[i]. Ba hamrit im*murgu*[d] Daráne[c] et rochunnig[j] fora siair a mac ar[k] altram[l] co raainmnigthe[m] uadi, ar robatar[n] meic lee, et dobert a siur [o]di anísin[o]. Roail[p] Darane[c] mac a sethar conid de asberarsom[q] Colman m. Darane[r] [s]7 Colman m. Santi[s], ut dicitur[t]:

[a]*om.* BLc[l], Imlech M. [b]*om.* Lc[l]. [c]Dair(ḟ)ine BLc[l](M), *add* 7 M. [d]*om.* BLc[l]M. [e]adberar BM, *add* Colman BLc[l]M. [f]Dairene BLc[l](M). [g—g]ingengeingeisi M. [h]coiridh M. [i]si BLc[l], side M, *add* 7 BLc[l]M. [j]rochuindigsi BLc[l]. [k]for BLc[l]M. [l]*add* 7 BM. [m]rohainmniged M. [n]ni (ra)badar BLc[l](M). [o—o]inn sin B(Lc[l]), di dō M. [p]roalt(a) iarum BLc[l](M). [q]adberar B, asberar Lc[l]M. [r]Dairine B(M), *add* de BLc[l]. [s—s]*om.* BLc[l]M. [t]*add* Fiachu Muillethan 7 Fiacho Fear Da Liach (sed tamen non probabile est ar Fiacha Muillethan 7 Fiachu Fer Da Liach) duo nomina unius

Darane[f] mathair in ríg,
Colmain meic Darane[u] áin,
ba mac d'Oengus mac Nadfraích
fer[v] fo[w] toṅgdis[x] laich lain[y].

hominis sunt (quamvis) imperiti aliter putant sic fuit Ailill Flann Mór 7 Ailill Flann Beg sed sciendum est Ailill Flann Mór nullam prolem habuit sed Ailill Flann Beg ei proles nominatur. Sic Colman m. Dairene 7 Colman m. Sainte nominatur ut dicitur B(Lc[l]M). [u]Dairíne B(M). [v]in fer M. [w]co Lc[l]. [x]toigidis B. [y]laim BLc[l]M.

722.60 Eithni mathair Maedoc[a] Ferna.

[a]Maedoic M.

61 Cumman mathair Cainire o Chill Chainre[a].

[a]Chaineri B(Lc[l]M).

62 Finmed ingen Ḟingin[a] m. Ḟintain m. Aedloga[b] [c]m. Nathí[c] de h*Uib* Meic Coinne[d] de Chorco Duibni mathair Mochutu [e]Lis Moir[e].

[a]Fináin B. [b]Aeda Logha M. [c—c]*om.* M. [d]Ca(e)indig Lc[l](M). [e—e]*above line* L.

63 Fiamain ingen Diarmata m. Baeth[a] m. Loegaire m. Neill mathair Berchain m. Muridaig [b]m. Dega m. Ainbchellaig[b] o Chluain Sasta[c].

[a]Baich M, *add* m. Aedha BLc[l]. [b—b]*om.* BLc[l]. [c]Sesta B, Sosda M.

64 Bríg ingen Chobthaig m. Crimthaind m. Ennae Chenselaig mathair Ṡegin 7 Epscoip[a] Aedáin 7 Epscoip Etchain[b] et Aeda m. Ainmerech.

[a]*om.* BLc[l]. [b]Eitchen*n* B, Eitchen Lc[l](M).

65 Trea[a] ingen Ronain m. Colmain m. Corpre ingen[b] ríg Lagen mathair Baithini m. Ḟinnaich[c] et a chet[h]ri[d] brathar .i. Baisaich[e] 7[b] Ḟintain et[b] Sligere[f] 7[b] Cummine[g].

[a]Trega M. [b]*om.* B. [c]Ḟin*acht*a B, Ḟiannach M. [d]ceathrar B. [e]Baesach BLc[l], Besrach M. [f]Slegeri B(Lc[l]), Sligri M. [g]Cui*m*me B, Cumaine Lc[l]M.

66 Rím[a] ingen Ḟiachra[b] m. Fiachrach[c] m. Duach Iarlathi mathair Chummin[d] Fota[e] et Chomgain m. Da Cherda et Guaire m. Colmain et Crimthainn Chael m. Aed[a][f] Cirr [g]m. Ṡenaig[g] rig Lagen et Chuanu m. Cailchin[h] et Braccain Darinsi.

[a]Run B. [b]Ḟiachna BLc[l], Ḟiachrach M. [c]Ḟiachach M, *add* Cairini B, Gairine Lc[l]M. [d]Cuimme B, Cumain(e) (Lc[l])M, *add* m. Fiachna BLc[l]M. [e]*om.* BLc[l]M. [f]Aeda BLc[l]M. [g—g]*added above line* L, *om.* BLc[l]M. [h]*add* laech Liathmune Lc[l].

67 Finecht[a] ingen Lochini m. Dimma Chiret[b] o Chill Conaig mathair Mochua m. Lonain.

[a]Fuindecht BLc[l](M). [b]Cirt B, Cirig M.

68 Scandlach mathair Chrednaite[a] ingen Aeda Roin ríg *Ua* Falge.

[a]Cretnathi B(Lc[l]).

22.69 Cullend[a] mathair Cholgan m. Aeda 7 Faelinni[b] a ṡethar i[c] Cill Cholgan ic Ath Cl*uana*[d] Medraigi ut dicitur:

Cuillend mathair Cholgan chain[e],
torcbad[f] i mMaig Uillend ed,
la Failbe, [g]cend[h] casil[g] cuil,
dolluid i Caissel ar cel.

[a]Cuillind M. [b]Ailinde M. [c]o M. [d]*om.* BLc[l], Chluana M. [e]chaem M. [f]togbad B(Lc[l]). [g—g]gan cais(c)e(a)dh (B)Lc[l]. [h]rig M.

70 Fial di Scorbraigi[a] Maigi Lagen mathair Laisren m. Ḟeradaig[b].

[a]Chorbraide M. [b]*add.* m. Nindedha B(Lc[l]M).

71 Bochra mathair tri mac nIrlamain[a] .i. Ḟidlimid[b] 7 Liadnain[c] 7 Dulechain.

[a]nUrlaman B(Lc[l]M). [b]Fi(d)lin (BLc[l])M. [c]Liaidain BLc[l], Lignain M.

72 Caeltigern ingen Chaemloga[a] siúr Chaemgin mathair cethri mac Colmada .i. Dagain Inbir Daele et Moboe 7 Molibba et Ménoc[b] Glinni Faidli[c].

[a]*add* m. Crimeda BLc[l]. [b]Momenoc B(Lc[l]), Moenocc M. [c]Fedhle B(Lc[l]), Ailbi M.

73 Onba[a] di Chonaillib Suilidi mathair Ṡegini[b] m. Ḟiachnai[c] m. Ḟeradaig[d].

[a]Orba M. [b]*om.* M. [c]Fiacrach B. [d]*add* m. Nindedha BLc[l].

74 Fuinecht ingen Maili Fithrig m. Dimmae m. Col*main* mathair Chormaic[a] epscoip [b]i nAth[b] Truim 7 Baethallaich [c]7 Ossain[c] 7 Rumaind.

[a]Cholmain M. [b]Atha M. [c—c]*om.* BLc[l].

75 Liamuin[a] ingen Calpuirn[b] siur Patric mathair Nechtain[c] Cilli Unci 7 qui dicitur Mac Lemna 7 is é atá i Findabair Aba ar brú Bóinni.

[a]Bamuin? B. [b]Calpraind B(Lc[l])M. [c]Meachtain B.

76 Deichter ingen Muridaig Mundeirg [a]ríg Ulad[a] mathair [bc]Matóc[d] [e]7[c] Epscoip Santain[f] [g]m. Samuel[h] Chendisil[beg].

[a—a]*om.* BLc[l]M. [b—b]*reversed* B[l]. [c—c]*om.* BLc[l]Lc35Ra. [d]Madach M, Maedoic M[l], *add* Ailithir B[l](M[l]). [e—e]*om.* M[l]. [f]Sangtain BB[l](Lc35RaM), Scantain Lc[l]. [g—g]*om.* Lc35Ra. [h]Ismel B[l].

77 Cainer[a] Cluana Da Ṡailech mathair *secht* mac Lugada .i. Enan[b] [*sic leg.* Cronan], qui 7[c] Mochua[d] Cluana Dolcáin[e], 7[f] Lasrain[g] 7[f] Baitain[h] 7[f] Garbain, Baithin[i] 7[f] Senchain, Rotdain[j].

[a]Cairer BLc[l]M. [b]Cronan BLc[l]M. [c]*om.* Lc[l] [d]Mochu B. [e]Daolcan BLc[l]M. [f]*om.* BLc[l]M. [g]Lassaran Lc[l]. [h]Baeta B. [i]Bethin Lc[l]. [j]Rod(d)an B(Lc[l])M.

78 Cuimni[a] ingen Cochmaidi[b] mathair Fraichain[c] Dromma Gamna[d].

[a]Cnes(s) B(Lc[l])M. [b]Comchoidi B(Lc[l]M). [c]Raechain B. [d]Dagamna BLc[l].

722.79 Cainech Abbad ingen Lugna mathair Blait m. Laignig .i. Abbain [a]m. Laignig[a].

[a—a]*om.* BLc[l]M.

80 Mella mathair Manchain Leith 7 a da ṡethar .i. Grella 7 Greillsech.

81 Becnat [a]ingen Chéin[a] mathair Ḟinain Chaim.

[a—a]*om.* BLc[l]M.

82 Didnat [a]ingen Mechair[a] mathair Barrḟind[b] Dromma Culinn.

[a—a]*om.* BLc[l]. [b]Bairfindi B.

83 Damrad[a] ingen Ailella Find m. Aeda[b] Róin ríg *Ua* Falge mathair mac[c] ṅDamraid[d] [e]i [f]Míliuc Ḟiaich[f] de quibus dicitur:

Cuan, [g]Conbran, Colman[g], Cass,
Tnuan, Angan[h] amnas,
Mo[becoc?][i] din tir si thair,
secht meic dilsi do Damraid[ej].

[a]Damrat M. [b]*add* Findl B. [c]*add* in BLc[l]M. [d]Damrait B, Damraig M, *add* .i. Colman 7 Cuan 7 Mobeco B(Lc[l]M). [e—e]*om.* BLc[l]. [f—f]Mullach(?) Iach M. [g—g]*reversed* M. [h]*add* fa M. [i]Mobecocc (*with first* c *above line*) M. [j]Damrait M.

84 Soben ingen Dubtain[a] m. Rinni[b] o Dún Bó mathair Reotaide[c] Grellcha.

[a]Dubthaig Lc[l]. [b]Ru*n*e B(Lc[l]), Cruinni M. [c]Rodaid Lc[l], Rodaige M.

85 Aebfind ingen Ainmere m. Ronain ríg na nArdda[a] mathair Ennae[b] Airne [c]m. Conaill 7 Libae[d] i nAraind[c].

[a]hArda BLc[l]M. [b]Eindi M. [c—c]*om.* BLc[l]. [d]Libe M.

86 Subthain[a] ingen Ṡetna siur Chomgaill mathair [b]Mael Rubae[b] [c]m. Elganaig[cd].

[a]Subtan BLc[l], Suibthen M. [b—b]Maeli Ruibhi B. [c—c]*om.* BLc[l]. [d]Ealgnaig M.

87 Saerlaith[a] ingen Chuilebaith[b] m. Baethgaile mathair Mael Brigte m. Thornain.

[a]Sorbfhlaith M. [b]Cuilendebaidh B, Chuileabaig M.

88 Moṅgḟind ingen Chirdubain di Cheniul Chinnend[a] mathair Iarlaithe [b]m. Loga[b] [c]o Thuaim[c] Da Gualann.

[a]Cirenn B(Lc[l]M). [b—b]*om.* BLc[l]. [c—c]Tuama BLc[l]M.

89 Dína ingen ríg Saxan mathair *deich* mac ṁBrachain[a], ríg [b]Bretan, m[b]. Brachameoc[c] di Bretnaib .i. Mogoroc Sruthra, [d].i.[e] Dergne[df], 7[g]

[a]Brac(c)a(i)n B(M). [b—b]*om.* BLc[l]M. [c]Bracineoc? BLc[l], Braithneocc M. [d—d]*added above line* L, *in text* B (*before* Sruthra) Lc[l]M. [e]7 BLc[l]M. [f]Draigne B, Deirgine M. [g]*om.* BLc[l]M.

Mochonoc ailithir[h] o[g] Chill[i] Muccraissi 7 o[j] Gáilinni[k] i nDelbna Ethra[l], [m]Diraid[n] Etardromma, Duban [o]i rRind Dubain[o] Ailithir[mp], Cairinne o[g] Chill[i] Chairinni[q], [r]Cairpre ailithir o[s] Chill Chairpre i Síl Ḟorannáin[r], Iast i Slemnachaib[t] Alban[u], Elloc[v] Cilli Moellóc[w] ic Loch Garman, Paan o[x] Chill[y] Paain i nOssairge[z], Coeman ailithir o[aa] Chill[bb] Cháemain i nGesilli 7 in aliis locis. Et mathair Mobeoc Glinne Gerg[cc], ar ba[dd] mac side[ee] Brachain[ff] m. Brachameoc[gg].

[h]*om.* B, .i. ailithir (*above line*) Lc[l]. [i]Cilli BLc[l]M. [j]i BLc[l]. [k]ngngelenga B. [l]Beathra BLc[l]. [m—m]*entered after* Elloc *below* BLc[l]M. [n]Dinrad? Lc[l], Dirid M. [o—o]*om.* B. [p]*add* i nAes na hImmirgi B(Lc[l]M). [q]Cairin BLc[l]. [r—r]*entered after* Elloc BLc[l]M. [s]i BLc[l](M). [t]Le(a)mnachaib (B)Lc[l]. [u]Cliabh B, *om.* Lc[l]. [v]Alloc M. [w]Mellóc B(Lc[l]M). [x]i B, *om.* Lc[l]M. [y]Cilli Lc[l]M. [z]Osragaibh B(Lc[l]M). [aa]i B, *om.* Lc[l]. [bb]Cilli Lc[l]. [cc]Garg B, Deirg M. [dd]aba B. [ee]sein B(M). [ff]Braccain M. [gg]Bracheoc B, Brachaineoc Lc[l], Braichneocc M, *add* ut dicunt alii BLc[l](M).

22.90 Sinell[a] ingen Chenannain siur[b] senSinchill mathair Maignend[c].

[a]Silend B. [b]deirbsiur BLc[l]M. [c]Maignind M.

91 Eithni ingen Feidlimid [a]m. Tigernaig[a] mathair Chomgain Glinne Usen[b].

[a—a]*om.* BLc[l]. [b]hUisin M.

92 Brónach ingen Milchon [a]m. Buain[a], 'ca mbaé[b] Patric i ndaíre, mathair[c] [d]Mochae Noendromma[d] oc[e] Loch[f] Cuan 7 Colmain[g] Chomraire oc[h] Uisniuch[i] et Colmain Mulind[j] oc[h] Daire Chaechain[k] i nDal Riatai 7 Epscuip Meic Erca[l] o Domnuch Mór Maige Coba 7 Damnatan[m] Slebe Betha[n] 7 Fursu Craibdig in Perona[o].

[a—a]*om.* BLc[l]. [b]mbi M. [c]*om.* B. [d—d]Mochaine Droma M, *add* o Naedruim BLc[l]M. [e]*om.* BLc[l]M. [f]Locha BLc[l](M). [g]*om.* BLc[l]. [h]o BLc[l]. [i]*add* Midhi 7 Manchan o Liath Manchan i nDe(a)lbna Bethra B(Lc[l]). [j]Muilindii? M. [k]Naechain B. [l]Cearcca M. [m]Domnadan B. [n]Bethad BLc[l]M. [o]Parona in Gail(l)ia (BLc[l])M.

93 [a]Clothbeo[b] ingen Conchobair [c]do Dál Chonchobair[c] mathair[d] Diarmata m. Aeda Róin ríg Ulad[ae].

[a—a]*om.* BLc[l]. [b]Clothbeoan M. [c—c]*om.* M. [d]*meic* M. [e]hUa Ḟailge M.

94 Magna siur D*aui*da[a] Cilli Mune mathair Ṡetna m. Essen[b] do Artragib[c] Cliach. Is e congaib Cluain [mBicc][d] eter[e] Chrotta Cliach 7 Sliab Marce[f] [*sic leg.* Muicce]. Is e fil i Cind Ṡale 7 a da brathair .i. Mogobba[g] 7 Moeltioc[h].

[a]Duidi B, Duida Lc[l], Daibith M. [b]Cen B, Sesen Lc[l]. [c]Artruga B(Lc[l]). [d]Big B(Lc[l]), Muc*rann*? M. [e]a M. [f]Muicce B(Lc[l]M), *add* 7 BLc[l]M. [g]Mogabha B. [h]Maelteocc M.

95 Eisten ingen[a] Moche[b] m. Barrind siúr Muccini Magni[c] mathair Ḟalbi[c] m. Conlocae[d] [e]o Disiurt Chind Chlair[e].

[a]*om.* Lc[l]. [b]Mochae Lc[l]M. [c]*om.* BLc[l]. [d]Conloga M. [e—e]*om.* BLc[l].

722.96 Brondḟind Brecc ingen Lugna siur Epscoip Ibair mathair Ṡenaig Gairb o Chill Móir ⁊ Miachu ⁊ Toimtenaig Ruis[a] Glassi et Lithgein Cluana Móir Lithgein[b].

[a]Rosa BLc[l]M. [b]*om.* BLc[l]M.

97 Rignach siur Ḟinniain[a] mathair Phitain[b] [*sic leg.* Fintain?] Fochaillchei[c] ⁊ Mocholmóc[d] Cluana Iraird ⁊ Garbain o Chill Garbain [e]i fail[e] Achaid Aball.

[a]Findein M. [b]Findtain B(Lc[l]M). [c]Fochailligi BLc[l], Ḟochlithe M. [d]Mocalmog B. [e]—[e]asail M.

98 [a]Ethni ingen Choncraid[b] mathair Mochap[c] Cilli[d] Móri ⁊ mathair Aeda epscoip i lLothur Imlich[e] et Cholmain Rechrainni[f] et Athchain[g] Inbir Cholpthai et Ernain[h] Toraigi et na secht[i] Nemann Dromma Lethan, Sceithe[j] ingini Mechair o Ḟirt Sceithi[k] i mMuscraigi[a].

[a]—[a]*om.* BLc[l]. [b]Chonchrainn M. [c]Mocob M. [d]Cill M. [e]Imlech M. [f]Racrainde M. [g]Aithgein M. [h]Eirnin M. [i].iiii. nepscoip *no* M. [j]Sciath M. [k]Sceith M.

99 [a]Medb ingen Garbain m. Brocain[b] m. Garbain m. Dubchertain[c] de *Uib* Saithgil do Chiarraigi Luachra mathair Chailinni i*ngine* Cael m. Findchada m. Lugdach[d] m. Luctai m. Anrodain m. Mael Tuile m. Aithchlecha[e] m. Ferba.
Et mathair Finnatan[f] ⁊ Blathnatan ⁊ Chuirigi[g].
Et mathair Lurichi[h] [i]et Findnatan[i] ⁊ Blaithe[j] ⁊ Caesige[k] et Fednatan[l].
Et mathair Epscuip Lugach[d] m. Lugdach[d] m. Luchtai. Is e fil[m] i Cuil Bennchair ⁊ i rRaith Maige Tuascirt ⁊ ic[n] Túaim Ḟobair[o] i lLuignib[a].

[a]—[a]*om.* BLc[l]. [b]*add* m. Brocain *through dittography*? M. [c]Duibcherrnain M. [d]Luigdeach M. [e]Athchlachtai M. [f]Findtain M. [g]Chuiride M. [h]Luirich M. [i]—[i]*om.* M. [j]Blaithche M. [k]Cheiside M. [l]Adnatain M. [m]*add* a Muig Roichead M. [n]a M. [o]Gabair M.

100 [a]Dustric ingen Truist[b] ríg Bretan Tuascirt mathair Lonain m. Talmaig o Threoit[c]; de qua[d] dicitur:

> [e]Trust, rí int ṡaerinbir[e] on tráig,
> rothecht oeningin imṡláin,
> Dustricc, fri cach sodail sain[f],
> mathair Lonain m. Thalmaig[a][g].

[a]—[a]*om.* BLc[l]. [b]*om.* M. [c]Throich M. [d]qui M. [e]—[e]Dustriucc saer in ben M. [f]sin M. [g]Dalbaig M.

101 [a]Finmaith[b] ingen Charthaig m. Nethi m. Onchon, derbṡiur do Chrumthir Ḟraech, mathair Beraig m. Nemaill[c] m. Nemaṅgin m. Ḟintain et mathair Midambaire[d] náemoige[a].

[a]—[a]*om.* BLc[l]. [b]Finmaich M. [c]Nemainn M. [d]Midamair na M.

102 Coemoc siur Chaemgin mathair Dagain m.[a] Colmada[b] ⁊ Mobae[c] m. Colmada[d] ⁊ Menóc[e] Glinni Faidli[f] ⁊ Ruis Mór[g] Menóc[h] ⁊ Molipa m. Araide [i]de Dál Araide[i].

[a]m*athai*r B. [b]Colmain M. [c]Mobhi B. [d]Coilmida M. [e]Moenoc M. [f]Faibli M. [g]Moir BLc[l]M. [h]*om.* BLc[l], ⁊ Maenocc M. [i]—[i]*om.* BLc[l].

722.103 [a]Ethni ingen Ṡarain m. Cholgan[b], derfiur do Rónán[c], mathair Chritain Chertrannaig do muntir Chomgaill[a].

[a—a]*om.* BLc[l]. [b]Olgan M. [c]Roinin M.

104 A [a]Brig ingen Forannain m. Conaill m. Toctain m. Amalgada, derbṡiur Mael Aithgeain, mathair Luchthigern[b] m. Lugdach[c]. Is e fil i Tuaim Findlocha i Tratraige.
B *No* Bríg ingen Aeda Damáin 7 frater eius Faithlend m.[d] Aeda Damain[ae].

[a—a]*om.* BLc[l]. [b]Luchthaigearrn M. [c]Luigdeach M. [d]ingen M. [e]*add* Finid amen Finid M(*see note*).

Add BLc[l]M.

105 [a]Rignach ingen Cochlain, siur Beoaeda[b] Arda Carna, mathair Colman[ac].

[a—a]B 213b36, Lc 34Vb25, M 55Va38. [b]Beoigh M. [c]*add* m. Echach Lc[l]M.

106 [a]Alma ingen rig Cruithnech mathair Seirb[b] m. Proic[c] rig Canandan[d] Egipti 7 is esin in sruthsenoir congeibh Cuillennros[e] hi Sraith Er*en*n[f] hi Comgellaibh[g] eter Sliabh Nocel[h] 7 Mur nGuidan[ai].

[a—a]B 214a19, Lc 34Vb/35Ra, M 55Vb14. [b]Sealbh M. [c]Poircc M. [d]Canand Lc[l](M). [e]Cluain Imrois M. [f]hIrend Lc[l](M). [g]Comgellgaib Lc[l], Coimcheallaib M. [h]Noithil M. [i]nGiudan Lc[l], nGuidna M.

MISCELLANEOUS ITEMS

723 Ciaran cecinit.

1
An rim[a], a rí richid ráin,
corbom etal risin dáil,
co cloister cech ní atber;
i[s] sanct cech sen, a Dé máir.

2
A Meic Maire, miad cen ón,
a mmo Chomde, co rric nem,
a ruiri na n-aṅgel find,
in n-anfa frim corbom sen.

3
Attchimse mo guide rutt,
ar baig Maire diandit macc;
menbad tacrad latt, a rí,
co ndernaind ní[b] bud maith latt.

4
Maccan berair riana ré
ní fintar feib ara mbé;
asa óete lenta baeís,
a ggáes cach aés bes ni thé.

[a]*followed by erasure of 1 or 2 letters.* [b]*in marg. with marks of ref.*

723.5 Ni horta laeg ria n-aes daim,
ar cach sen as tressiu a chách;
ní orta uan na horc maith,
ni coilte [c]cr[aeb] r[ian]a[c] bláth.

6 Buain guirt riasiu bas abbuig,
is m[...][d] cacaid, a rí rind,
is é in loṅgud riana thráth
blath do choll in tan bas find.

7 Fuiniud i mmedon laa,
ni hord baa rian [...]
matan i n-aidche, in dedoil
riana medon, cia mó col.

8 Cluinti itgi notguidiu
is mo chridiu deroil (d)úir[e],
a Meic mo Dé, cia nomrodba,
is bec mo thorba dond úir.

9 Duitsiu, a meic mo tholtu,
cen cop é sentu dom churp,
ce nambera cen taithlech
noco bia m'aithfer fort.

10 Is fort ṡnádud cach a mbí,
ria ndul am chri, a rí slán,
ic do guide dam cen dichil,
an rimim[f], a rí richid ran. A.

[c—c][ ] *illeg.* [d]*about 2 letters illeg.* [e]*letter before* u *barely visible.* [f]*error for* rim.

724.1 Cethrur ar ḟichet nosfail
im Ḟeidlimid mac Crimthain,
is oenimpide leo ar nim
7 oenitgi i talmain.

2 Dímman Arad, maith in maín,
is Lobrán Uaithne re thaíb,
Mael Tuile, Mael Anfaid án,
Mael Ruain is Eochaid imṡlán.

3 Molliṅg is Chinaed cen cháin,
7 Oengus mac Oebliain,
Diarmait 's int Oengus aile,
Dalbach Cúle Collainge.

724.4 Rectgus 7 Rectgniad réil,
Brocan 7 Epscop Scéiṫh,
Mochonna Daire is ḟerr de,
Feradach is Dub Tíre.

5 Fland mac Fairchellaig rofess,
Fland mac Duib Chonna ra chnes,
Flannan is Mael Dithrub dil,
is Feidlimid mac Crimthain.

6 Mairg duni dothaet riu sain,
do Gallaib dọ Gaedelaib;
cethrur ar fichet ar fecht
do naemaib 'na n-iarmorecht.

7 Noco bia a chomarba i fus;
noco gebthar i flathius;
iss ed dede rotá de
gorta is gairde n-amsire.

8 Nobítís, ni sáeb int ṡreth,
maroen i nDaire Eidnech,
ic denam chrabuid cen gus,
ic crossigill i corgus.

9 Do Daire Eidnech co becht
tecait do denam a fert,
co toraig a techta thair
arin licc i Tamlachtain.

10 Forin licc sin tic do nim
angel de muntir richid,
co tabair dóib ó Christ cet
na hitge 'ma n-oentaiget.

11 Cóir áli riu as cach alt,
ar a náre, ar a noebdacht,
hé Dia fodéin nodossail,
in sessiur sain for chethair. C.

12 Tictis Druim nAbrat ille,
na noeb sin nosailemni,
noathigtis sund co mblaid
na da thrath co bo chethair. C.

MARGINAL ENTRIES IN L.

725 Cairell, Cairin, Comgall cail,
Diarmait, Garban is Lugaid,
Baetan, bág buada co mblaid,
secht n-escuip Cilli [...].

726 Colum Cille [m.] Feidlimthi m. Fergusa. Ferg[...] lasa [...] geill [...] Conall mor m. Neill. Eithni [...] nadbiu in rígan de Chorpraigiu. Mathair [...] co gle (?) ingen Dimma m. Noe.

727.1 Mochen, mochen, a Brenaind,
a breo rochloss co lLetha;
mochen, a chomsid Cluana,
dia fognat[a] buada in betha.

2 Mochen 7 morochen,
a meic Findloga [findais][b],
as rathmar dait cach ṅdoinmis[c],
latt commus Cathrach Gillais.

3 Dochuad co Glend na Leoman,
fúar mór tend sech cech n-erdam,
fota úad ata [mittu (?)
im do][b] thichtu, im do thernam.

4 I tír thall Taprofane,
dianid áge crand gréne,
ic Iordanan co n-úare,
ropsat deoradán Féne.

5 Rofegais fot [in crochda,
ce][b] tech[e] nimtha do sechna,
dar Sliab Sión roscuchtha
do thraigthe luchra lethna.

6 Dar lár slébe da fresdul,
rí gréne glain[f] [g]co san[...][g],
[as tu roan fri][b] apstail,
aithle th'astair iar troscud.

7 I trebaib Grécrogabais,
a[h] bféraib déc dochuadais,
is mór n-insi rofegais
im Insi S[alutoiris].[b]

[a]fognaid M. [b]*sic*. M. [c]nonnais M. [d]neramh M. [e]thogh M. [f]glaeine M.
[g—g]coscor M. [h]tri M.

727.8 [i]Do Róim romilis romuich,
do Thorinis fot ainiuch,
duthaig dait, a rí ruirech,
tuirech ic hÍ is ic Ailiuch.

9 Áillcge deit inda midól
7 failte fri fledol,
tú it luing ó áilén d'aileón,
rom chrideon is mochenon. M.[i]

[i—i]*added in lower margin of* 369 L.

728 Colman mac Nemain. Fainchi ingen Dallbronaig, siur mathar Brigti, setig do Neman. Bai dna Fanchi i n-ambriti co cian co ndoluid co [...] di. Ainis Brigit tredán i n-eclais i Cill Dara co toracht angel 7 co n-epert fria: 'A Sanct Brigit bennach broind do sethar 7 dofussema mac sainemail acci .i. Colman a ainm, 7 rop é do lamsu fora mullach, 7 corop Finnian moccu Tellaig rombaiste 7 rodnaile fri eclais.' Et rothussib Fannchi iar [...] Neman, .i. Conall 7 Eogan 7 Carpre, 7 issin tiprait as robaisted Epscop Ibar robastit na mmeic sin.

729.1 Hú Néill uile ar cúl Coluim,
ni scáth muni.
Iar cúl Finniain Maigi Bili
Ulaid uili.

2 Clanna Connacht ar cúl Chiarain,
cen nach comraind.
Dál nAraide n-uasal n-imrind
iar cúl Comgaill.

3 Betid Lagin iar cul Brigti,
clú co saidbre.
Mumu uili cona toirthi
iar cul Ailbe.

4 Ardnoeb hErenn cona manchaib
iss e a n-ude.
Cach raen rantait a mbith,
iar cul Patric uile.

Breth ind aṅgil and sin eter ardnoebaib hErend.

730 Lugna m. Moenaig m. Fiachna m. Rosa m. Trena m. Duach m. Meicnia m. Meic Con m. [...]. Hi sunt septem illius fratres .i. Epscop Brandub, Causan, Factna, Lugna, Molua, Lochan i nUib Ech[ach], Cailchin, Manchin Cula Cassin [...][a].

[a]*add separately in late hand* Comgall Bennchair, da Comgall Ratha.

731.1 [...]ern cumtaig class,
confoat a n-oentachas.
Ciaran[a], Cainnech is mochen,
Epscop Erc 7 Coemgen

2 Epscop Eogain Aird Sratha,
Brenaind fial [m. Fin]dloga,
Dechoin Nessain, digrais dót,
Iarlathi 7 Mochaemóc.

[a]*add above line* no da Brenaind.

732.1 [...] cen chrinad cotla
i mbaí Mochoe Noendromma;
lucht int ṡámuid i mbaí in suí,
ní tharraid acht a n-innduí

2 [...] chain do M'choe cain
int enan[a] dona nemdaib,
tri hadbaind do barr in chraind,
cóica bliadan cech adbaind.

[a]*add above line* .i. angelus.

733.1 Adomnán rohalt i nhÍ,
mac réil Rónain m. Thinni,
m. Aeda m. Lugada tra,
m. Setna m. Ḟergusa[a].

2 A mathair madchin i crí,
Ronnat ingen Ṡegini.
Segini ind orddain áin,
dagmac Duach m. Barrḟinnain[b].

[a]*add* .i. do Cheniul Lugdach. [b]*add* .i. do Cheniul Ennae.

734 [a]Is é Senbrenainn[a] dorat in chomairli do Cholum Cille, daig batar nóib hErenn i cocud friss iar loscud dia muntir Dromma Liss, ar ndiultud friu. Dia n-epertsom[b]:

Druim Lis,
cell bec for acce Fanat;
o'ndiu immach co tí bráth[c]
mennut násadach namat.

[a—a]Is e sin in Brenainn M. [b]n-eipersium M. [c]in brath M.

Is í immorro in[d] chomairle tuc Brenainn: 'Cuir dar cend[e] in cloich mbic s[eo][f] it ḟiadnaise'. Roscuir[g] post Colum Cille in cloich dar cend[h] ⁊ iss ed bái inti .í.í.i.í.eirg.í. doí[i]. *No* is é Molasse Daminsi tuc in chomairle[j] dó ⁊ quibus huius est.

[d]*om.* M. [e]do cheann M. [f]seo M. [g]rochuir M. [h]a ceann M. [i]do.i. M. [j]*add* sin M.

735 Nem macc ua Birn. Nem tribus nominibus uocabatur .i. Nem ⁊ Púpu ⁊ Cailbe. Nem primum nomen est a parentibus. Pupu apud Scottos, id est Papa; eo quia cathedram Petri petiuit .i. Cailbe .i. Cáel beo, eo quia ho[*min*]es mirabantur eum ui*de*re. Unde Senan Insi Cathaig cecinit.

Abbas almus amabil*is*,
Romae rector docibilis,
Papa pastor probabilis,
Caelbe custos regiminis.

Comarba Petair is Póil
tudchait Cailbe anair o Róim,
Nem macc ua Birn, brathair gle,
dian chomainm Pupu Airne.

MISCELLANEOUS ITEMS FROM THE HAGIOGRAPHICAL PARTS OF RLc[l] AND M.

736 Daire Domth[ig][a] m. Sithbaicc m. [F]ir[a] Fuibde m. Daigmanrai[d][a] m. Cluthunne m. Loga Feidli[g][a] m. Eirchisse m. Fithaisse m. Gosa m. Sir m. Aidne m. Log[a][a] m. Ethamain m. Mail m. Lugd[ech][b] m. hItha[c].

[a]sic. Lc[l]. [b]Lugach Lc[l]. [c]*add* m. Breogain Lc[l].

737.1 Bennacht (t)redian Finnein[a] Fail
for Baedan, for Ḟurudran,
for Diarmuid mor mac Nadcaeir,
for [b]Mocholmocc (leir)[b] lindglaein.

2 Is forna [...]naem co li
rogabsad a Laeinn Leiri[c],
for trib caegaibh [...](eai)ghlan
fuilid a n-uirib talman.

3 Tri chaegad naem d'ḟeraib Cant,
tri chaegait Rom, tri chaegit Francc,
cae(g)a (d)o Breatnaib fo tri,
tri caegait Lugair legnaidi.

[a]*read* finnem? [b—b]*read* Mochoimocc Leith? [c]*followed between columns by* nō rann.

737.4 Forsna sruithib ilar ngrad
eitir theoir i[s] secht dail,
forsna firmanchu maithe
thathaigdis cach aen laithi.

5 For Brigid buanbuadach Nell,
for a n-aide, for Chairel[l],
for Motṡeanoc, gaire gart,
for Mobricco mo bennocht. B*en*acht.

I lLoind Leiri fuilid hi omnes.

738.1 Atad asin cheide chruaid
dafichid deg naem n-aenuaidh,
ni meassa cach fear fe(sach)
na(...) in da Chiaran chaemḟertach.

2 Ataid fri duirrthech atuaig,
im Chaimine co nglanbuaidh,
da fer deg iar sasad noll
dogendais neamh don iffirrnn.

3 Ataid fri duirrthech anes
ochtur eili co nglanchneas,
mad dia toitsid neamh ar lar
robdis tualaing a thogbail

4 A n-idg(i)uile maraen
na fil san cheide clithnaemh,
linne coro buan ar mblad,
a ri na sluag ca taad. Atad asin ceide cruaid.

NOTES

1 (416, 662.8-10). See A. Anscombe, 'The Pedigree of Patrick', *Ériu* 6 (1911) 117-20. The implications of 1 for the dating of the Corpus in its present form are discussed in the Introduction (note 30). Its first four, and only genuine, names occur fully or in part in Patrick's *Confessio,* the early 'Lives' by Muirchú and Tírechán, Fiacc's Hymn and the *Vita Tripartita*. Cf. *Lib.Hymn.*I, 97(gloss); *V.Trip.* 432 (Homily on Patrick); AFM I, 130 ff (in verse form); *GRSH* 37; *Gen. tracts* 51; DF 696b. See also the note to 689 below.

1.1 Omitted in L, this and 1.4-1.6 are included here because they follow 1 in the later MSS. Cf. L. Bieler, *The Patrician Texts in the Book of Armagh* (Dublin, 1979) 66 (Muirchú I 1,1); *V.Trip.* 8,16 (= *B.Phátr.* ll.83, 194), 433 (Homily on Patrick, cf. *Lis. Lives* 1.48); DF 697a; see also 722.1, where a different tradition is also represented.

1.2 Discussed by Anscombe, *loc.cit.* (note 1): (a) forms an addition to the Corpus proper in L and, hence, in M. Cf. *Lis.Lives* ll.39-46; L. Bieler, *Four Latin Lives of St. Patrick* (Dublin, 1971) 50-51 (*Vita Quarta* § I); DF 696d; see also 416 (add La).

1.3 As in 1.2, (a) forms an addition to the Corpus in L and M. In M (b) is introduced by a large initial. In Lb it follows 1.4. Cf. *V.Trip.* 140 (= *B.Phátr.* 86) for the verse, with a different bishop involved.

1.4 Follows 703 in M, 398 in R[1]. Cf. L. Bieler *op.cit.* (note 1.1) 63 (Muirchú, *prol.*), 124 (Tírechán 1,1): *V.Trip.* 16 (= *B.Phátr.* 10), 440 (Homily on Patrick, cf. *Lis.Lives* ll.147-9), *Lib.Hymn.* I, 3 (gloss), 6 (preface); see also 654.

1.5 For the tradition of Patrick's death on a Wednesday, see *V.Trip.* 552 (= Lb 220a 24). Cf. *PRIA* 59C3 (1958) 145, § 8 (Annales Roscreenses) where three *Cetaíne* are attached to Brigit (cf. 2.2). See also Introduction (§23).

1.6 Precedes I in R[1]. The verse is added in the lower margin. Cf. *V.Trip.* 500, ll.12-27 (Extract from Nennius' *Historia Britonum*) (= A.G. Van Hamel, *Lebor Bretnach,* Ir. MSS. Comm., Dublin, |1932| 69-70, §54). The passage is only in the Latin version of the *Historia,* an account in Irish of Patrick's miracles being dismissed by the translator as *'uisce do loch'*. The first paragraph is also taken from Nennius; Van Hamel, p.27, §15.

2 (427, 662.108-9). *Fothairt;* specified as Uí Bresail in Uí Ḟailge in *CGH* 84. Her *hereditas* was *'in duobus campis Nepotum Folgi'* (D. Ó hAodha, *Bethu Brigte* (Dublin, 1978) 2, ll.44-5), that is Tuath Dá Maige, later the deanery of Totmoy, in the dioc. of Kildare. Omitted in BLc, the entry is longest in L, in keeping with the strong Fothairt bias of its general arrangement (Introduction §2). Cf. *CGH* 84; *Fél.* 64; *ZCP* 19 (1932) 119; *Lis.Lives* ll.1152-3; Lb 220(in lower margin); *GRSH* 74; P. C. Bartrum, *Early Welsh Genealogical Tracts* (Cardiff, 1966) 64,71 (the first two generations in Welsh dress). See also K. Meyer, *Hail Brigit* (Dublin, 1912) 18 (§26).

2.1 Cf. 722.4.5, the likely source.

2.2 Cf. *Fél.* 64; *Lis. Lives* 1.1351; *PRIA* 59C3 (1958) 145, §8.

3 (495,662.110). *Fothairt.* Cluain Eidnech was closely connected with the family of Áed mac Crimthainn, author of the arrangement in L (Introduction §2). Cf. *CGH* 84 (=*ZCP* 8 (1911) 301); *Fél.*^{2} 52; Rawl. B 505 194V; *Anal.Bolland.* 46 (1928) 120 §5; *GRSH* 78; DF 718a1. For a different parentage see *Heist VSH* 145. See also *Plummer VSH* 1, lxx; 2,96.

4 (662.116). *Fothairt.* Cf. *CGH* 341 (= L 316b 5), the possible source of 4 which is only in L; *GRSH* 75; DF 718b1.

5 (522, 662.114) *Fothairt.* Cf. *Fél.* 74; *Fél.*^{2}*184* (= *Fél.* 262); *GRSH* 75; DF 718b1; *SG* 146 (where he is attached to Ceinél Eogain). In *Plummer VSH* 2, 184 he is assigned to the Luigne of Connacht.

6 (517, 586, 662.114). *Fothairt.* Cf. *GRSH* 75; DF 718c1; *Fél.*^{2} 115 (where the pedigree belongs to the Déise)(= *Fél.* 166).

7 (662.115). *Fothairt.* Uí Ercáin is the district around Moone, Glashely, Kilrush, and Nurney in south Kildare (*V.Trip.* 188 (= *B.Phátr.* 114); *CGH* 339; 670.53-7 (54 refers again to Fínán and Tech Airthir). Cf. *GRSH* 75.

8 (418, 662.13.14) *Ceinél Conaill.* In Lc[1], representing the Book of Glendalough recension, 8 is followed by the pedigrees of a number of abbots of Iona (Introduction §8). Lb, while generally following the arrangement of L, adds here the pedigree of Baithín, Colum Cille's first successor. Adamnán (*V.Col.* 4[a](Second Preface), appendix) gives the first three generations of the pedigree. Cf. *CGH* 163; *Fél.*[2] 99(= *Fél.* 144); *Lis. Lives* ll.808-9; *T.Hom.* 100. *Scottish Gaelic Studies* 2 (1928) 126, §13; *Lib.Hymn.* 1, 162; Rawl. B 505, 117; *Misc.Hag.Hib.* 102, §7; NLI G 2 (intercalated leaf); B 84b31; *GRSH* 38; DF 697a.

8.1 Cf. NLI G 2, f.3 (an intercalcated leaf copied from the Book of Glendalough, i.e. R; Introduction §21). AI 563 states that 'his first night in Alba was during Pentecost'.

9 (441, 509, 662.65) *Clann Cholmáin* (*Ceinél Fiachach*). The addition (f) belongs to 87, which follows 9 in Lc[1]. Cf. *Plummer VSH* 1, xxvi*n*, 34; *Fél.*[2]168; Rawl. B 505 149V; B 85b (under Ceinél Bóguine); *Anal. Bolland.* 46 (1928) 121; *GRSH* 56; DF 705a; *M.Don.* xli; D. Murphy, *The Annals of Clonmacnoise* (Dublin 1896) 91.

9.1 Cf.DF 705a (drawn from M). Tadc mac Conchubair, king of Connacht, died in 900 (AU 899). Two miracles performed by Áed *post obitum* are included in his *vita* (*Heist VSH* 179, §§43, 44).

9.2 Áed's mother, who belonged to the Múscraige Tíre, is not named in *Heist VSH* 167 (§1).

10 (620, 662.19) *Ceinél Conaill*. Cf. *GRSH* 41; DF 697b.

11 (31, 543, 616, 662.38) *Ceinél Eogain*. The addition (c) is also in 31 (L). Cf. *CGH* 134; *GRSH* 48; DF 701a.

12 (41, 535, 662.63) *Clann Cholmáin*. The medial *d* of the unusual patronymic may be due to a misreading of *ch* in the exemplar, (but cf. Lc 58Re 38, Gilli Luadain). Cf. K. Meyer, *Betha Colmáin Maic Luacháin* (RIA Todd Lect. Ser. 17, Dublin, 1911) 4, §§3, 4; *GRSH* 54 (cf. 103); DF 704a.

13 (524, 525, 662.26) *Ceinél Bóguine*. Compare Lb's addition (a) with 524, 525 below. Cf. *GRSH* 43; DF 700a.

14 (74, 662.29) *Ceinél Bóguine*. 14 and 19 are added in the top margin of L with a mark of reference to 347c. In the derivative versions (B etc) the entries are incorporated together at a point corresponding to L 347e 18. Cf. *GRSH* 42; DF 700b.

15 *Uí Fiachrach*. Cf. *GRSH* 63; DF 711a.

16 (538, 662.40) *Ceinél Eogain* (*Ceinél Moín*). Cf. *GRSH* 46; DF 701a.

17 (479, 662.35) *Ceinél Eogain* (*Ceinél Binnig*). Cf. Lc 55Ra 5 *et seq.*; *GRSH* 47; DF 701b.

18 (82, 662.43) *Ceinél Eogain*. Cf. *GRSH* 46; DF 701a.

19 (82, 469, 662.43) *Ceinél Eogain*. Daig is mistakenly assigned to the Déisse in 469 (La). Cf. *Fél.* 50: *Fél.*[2] 132 (= *Fél.* 186); *GRSH* 45; DF 701a.

20 (491, 557, 662.39) *Ceinél Eogain*. 557 assigns Muru to the Dál Fiatach. Cf. *GRSH* 47; DF 701b.

21 (453, 662.90) 1. *Ceinél Maine*, 2. *Dál Cais*. MLa (e) attach him to the Uí Maine, *GRSH* 69 (Cf. 453 below) to the Airgialla. Cf. 1. *GRSH* 69.1; 2. *CGH* 235; M 32Va 58; DF 738a.

22 (435, 662.57) *Ceinél Lóegaire*. Cf. *GRSH* 52: DF 705c; Lc 62Vd 9 (Serc ingen Echach); B 87a[2].

23 (662.31) *Ceinél Énna*. L (b) reads *aps.* in reference to Nainnid (Láimderc), one of the twelve apostles of Ireland (cf. 117, 127, 208, 241, 317, and 402). Cf. *GRSH* 58; DF 708.

24 (589, 662.73) *Uí Fiachrach*. See note to 328. Cf. *GRSH* 62; DF 711a.

25 (430, 662.81) *Uí Briúin, Ceinél Dobtha*. Preceded in H[1] by a passage on the saints of Ceinél Dobtha (410). Cf. *BNÉ* I, 23; *Fél.*[2] 51 (= *Fél.* 74); Lc 69Va 1-22; Rawl. B 505 191V; *GRSH* 59; DF 710b. See also *Plummer VSH* 1, xxxiii.

26 (431, 662.31) *Ceinél Énna*. Cf. *Fél.*[2] 53 (= *Fél.* 76); B 85b[a]; *GRSH* 58; DF 708.

27 (433, 662.21) *Ceinél Conaill*. Cf. *Fél.*[2] 88 (= *Fél.* 134) where the second pedigree assigns him to Ceinél Fiachach; *BCC* 134; *GRSH* 38; DF 697c.

28 (511, 596?, 662.36) *Ceinél Eichin* (*Ceinél Eogain*). Cf. *GRSH* 47; DF 701c.

29 (662.36) *Ceinél Eichin* (*Ceinél Eogain*). The variant Cell Áedáin (b-b) probably refers to the same place as Cell Mór, Kilmore, co. Monaghan. Cf. *GRSH* 44; DF 701c.

30 (575, 662.38) *Ceinél Eogain*. Cf. *GRSH* 46; DF 701c.

31 See 11.

32 (662.37) *Ceinél Eogain*. The variant Braccán (a) suggests that, as Colgan thought (*GRSH* 44, § 5*n*), we have to do with a doublet of 34. Cf. *Fél.*[2]91; *GRSH* 44; DF 701c.

33 (662.37) *Ceinél Fergusa* (*Ceinél Eogain*). If *Aille*, which MR[1]La add (a), is correct then Lc's *Cille Colmain* may be based on it and, as such, a *vox nihili*. La (d) incorrectly places *m. Eogain* after *Ronain*. Cf. *GRSH* 45; DF 701c.

34 (662.37) *Ceinél Eogain*. Arguably a variant of 32. Cf. *GRSH* 44; DF 701c.

35 (83, 628, 662.33) *Ceinél Eogain*. Cf. *GRSH* 45; DF 702a.

36 (536, 662.35) *Ceinél Binnig* (*Ceinél Eogain*). Cf. B 76b 40; Lc 55Rb 48; *GRSH* 45; DF 702a.

37 (444, 662.68-9) *Síl Fergusa Cháecháin* (cf. *CGH* 132). For a possible explanation of L's variant *Dromma* (c-c) see Introduction §3. I have no other reference to the alternative descent in RLc[1] (i). Cf. *Fél.*[2] 65; *GRSH* 65; DF 711d.

38 (622, 662.24) *Ceinél Bóguine*. Cf. *GRSH* 39; DF 700a.

39 (452, 662.76) *Uí Fiachrach*. Preceded in BLcLb by 14, 19. Cf. *Ir. texts*. 3 (1931) 2; *GRSH* 62; DF 711b.

40 (476 (Damaedoc), 629, 662.40 (Domnocc, Damongoc)) *Ceinél Eogain*. Cf. *ZCP* 8 (1910-12) 296; Lc 54Vb (Damaedoc); B 88e (Modomnoc); *GRSH* 45 (Domhnocc); DF 701b (Damongoc, Damnog).

41 (12, 535, 662.63) *Clann Cholmáin*. A doublet of 12. B and Lc (which adds *m.*) run on 42.

42 (474, 512, 662.64 (BLc).113) *Clann Cholmáin; Luigne* (MR[1]La); *Fothairt* (H). Cáel Cruaid is not among the sons of Áed Sláine in B 79b. Cf. *Fél.*[2] 132 (= *Fél.* 188); *GRSH* 75; DF 704b.

43 (662.64 (Áed Gel).113) *Clann Cholmáin*. Probably a doublet of Aithgne of Both Domnaig (61). Cf. *GRSH* 54, §§1,2; DF 739b.

44 (662.41) *Ceinél Eogain*. Cf. *V.Trip.*156; *GRSH* 44. DF 702a.

45 (662.51) *Ceinél Lóegaire*. Cf. *V. Trip*. 66; *GRSH* 51; DF 706b.

46 (532, 662.41) *Ceinél Eogain*. Cf. *GRSH* 48; DF 702a.

47 (662.97) *Airgialla*. Cairpre Dam Argit is more correctly Darfráech's brother (*CGH* 140 etc.). Cf. 722.42; *GRSH* 70; DF 716a.

48 (487, 662.87) *Airgialla*. Only DF, which used L, otherwise includes *Sini, Cumai* (c). For a discussion of the pedigree see *Éigse* 15 (1974) 176-9. Cf. *Fél.* 72; *Fél.*[2] 89 (= *Fél.* 134); *GRSH* 72; DF 714b.

49 (481, 662.101) *Airgialla*. Cf. *CGH* 141, 144, where he assumes a secular character; *Fél.* 76; Lc 81Rd; *GRSH* 66; DF 714b.

50 (480, 579, 662.94) *Airgialla*. Cf. *GRSH* 71; DF 715a.

51 (583, 662.98) *Airgialla*. A late saint; see AU 777. RLc[1]M's added names (d) do not figure in the secular pedigree of Constans' family (*CGH* 145). Cf. *CGH* 146; Lc 80Vb; *GRSH* 66; DF 713b, bb.

52 (662.99) *Airgialla*. Lb's omission (e-e) is made up in 53. Cf. *GRSH* 67; DF 713b.

53 (662.99) *Airgialla*. Cf. *GRSH* 67; DF 713b.

54 (662.91) *Airgialla*. Cf. *SG* 37; *GRSH* 69, 71, 72; DF 713c.

55 (519, 662.92 (BLc).93) *Airgialla*. Cf. *GRSH* 69, 70; DF 714b.

56 (662.86) *Airgialla*. BLcLb's reading (a-a) suggests that the lengthmark over *Scí* should be read as an *n*-suspension? Cf. *CGH* 140; *BNÉ* 1, 197; *GRSH* 70; DF 714b.

57 (662.98) *Airgialla;* L's *Erchoil* (b) was misread as two names in the derivative texts (BLcLb). Cf. *CGH* 142; *GRSH* 66; DF 713c.

58 (662.100) *Airgialla*. Lb (c) gives the correct descent. Cf. *CGH* 144: *GRSH* 66; DF 712c.

59 (662.100) *Airgialla*. Cf. *CGH* 145; *GRSH* 66; DF 712b.

60 (482, 582, 662.97(BLc).102) *Airgialla*. LbMR[1] (d) give the correct descent. RLc[1] (d) appear to attach him to the Dál nAraide (cf. 95 below). Cf. *CGH* 141 (secular pedigree?), 143, 416 (Lc); *GRSH* 66; DF 713a.

61 (634, 636, 662.106) *Airgialla*. Probably a doublet of Áedgein of Both (43). Lb's *.i. Cormac* (a) is possibly a misreading of *.i. coic Patraic*. Cf. *GRSH* 73, §§1,2; DF 715b.

62 (662.100) *Airgialla*. Cf. *GRSH* 67; DF 713a.

63 (425, 662.101) *Airgialla*. The addition *m. Fiachrach* (d) is correct (cf. *CGH* 141). Cf. *Fél.*[2] 39: (= *Fél.* 54); *BNÉ* 1, 190, 265; *Anal. Bolland.* 46 (1928) 119; Lc 81Rc; *GRSH* 67; DF 714a.

64 (662.94) *Airgialla*. *Mer* (e) seems an error for *Meith* (cf. 65). The first three names are given in L 42c (*comarbada Patraic*) (= *V.Trip*. 542) and *Ériu* 4 (1910) 126. Cf. *Fél.* 70; *GRSH* 70; DF 715a.

65 (662.97) *Airgialla*. RLc[1]'s *Meith* (b) is more correct (cf. 64). Flann's pedigree is ommited in BLcLb due, possibly, to haplography. The first three names occur in L 42c (= *V.Trip.*542). Cf. *GRSH* 71; DF 714b.

66 *Airgialla*. B's *Moir* (a) is written *mo* with *ir* above it and may reflect, corruptly, *m. Eogain*. Lc's version (c) seems to be taken over from Fiachraig's descent (64). Lc[1]'s addition (e) is also in the secular pedigree (*CGH* 183,419). Cf. *GRSH* 70; DF 715a.

67 (569, 662.97) *Airgialla.* La's 240, which is largely illegible, seems to belong here. The addition (e-e) is obviously corrupt and may have read *Li |bae frater et| Logene soror Enna* (cf. 722.85). See *Plummer VSH* 1, lxii, lxiv. Cf. *M.Tall.* 25; Rawl. B 505 90R; *GRSH* 70; DF 714b. In *Anecd.* 3 (1910) 60 he is assigned to the Cianachta.

68 Inserted at the foot of a column and partly illegible, Colmán's pedigree, which is preserved differently in a section on Dál nAraide in B 168a[3], gives him an obscure tribal affiliation.

69 (662.86) *Airgialla.* The lenition of *c* in *Techan* is probably not original. For *Nóeb .i. sanctus* (b-b) L appears to read *nomen sanctus* (*sic*); Cf. *CGH* 114; *GRSH* 72; DF 714b.

70 (662.26) *Déise Breg, Ceinél Bóguine.* Illegible in L, the blank space (f-f) is not filled in from the derivative versions due to their lack of agreement. Modobba's pedigree forms part of a secular genealogy in *CGH* 161. Cf. *GRSH* 42 (Moaba); DF 700d (Modoba).

71 *Ceinél Lóegaire.* Also in 690.10. Fiachna is not one of two sons of Áed listed in *CGH* 166. Cf. *GRSH* 52; DF 705c.

72 (662.49) *Ceinél Lóegaire.* Cf. B 88e; *GRSH* 49; DF 707a.

73 (662.49) *Ceinél Lóegaire.* L's reading at (b) was either *Dailléine* or *Daillíne,* but the correct reading would have been *Libréin* (cf. 72 and *CGH* 166). Cf. *CGH* 166; *GRSH* 49; DF 707a.

74 (14, 662.29), *Ceinél Bóguine.* A doublet of 14.

75 *Ceinél Lóegaire.* The correct reading at (b) was probably *Fínáin.* Cf. *GRSH* 53.

76 (527, 662.103) *Airgialla.* Omitted in the derivative versions, BLcLb, Trea's pedigree is written along the top margin of L. Cf. *GRSH* 68; DF 712c.

77 (542, 662.80) *Uí Briúin.* Preceded in L by *hoc ante,* suggesting misplacement of 77, 78. Lb's addition (a) seems to be correct (*CGH* 425-6). Cf. *GRSH* 60; DF 710d.

78 (320.1.2, 490, 515 (Fintan), 662.82) *Uí Briúin.* Placed here in the left margin, the entry is a doublet of 320.1. Lb's addition (h) is also in *Fél.*[2] 172. In H[1] (h) the pedigree forms part of 410. For other versions see the note to 320.

79 (541, 615, 662.103) *Airgialla.* Cf. *CGH* 417; *GRSH* 67; DF 713a.

80 (611, 662.78 (*add* Lc).104) *Airgialla, Uí Ḟiachrach.* Reference to Tigernán is also incorporated into 118. Lc[1]La's additions (a,f) give him an Uí Ḟiachrach descent. Cf. *GRSH* 68; DF 713a; *Hy Fiach.* 10.

81 (632, 662.66) *Ceinél Maine.* L's note (a) suggests misplacement here. The omission of the second part (e-e) in RLc[1] suggests that this may have been added in L. Cf. *GRSH* 57; DF 703.1.

82.1 (18, 19, 469, 662.43) *Ceinél Eogain.* A doublet of 18, 19. With 82.2 compare DF 701a.

83 (35(Cormac), 627, 628, 662.33) *Ceinél Eogain.* Cf. *GRSH* 45, 46; DF 702a. See also *Brit. Mus. Cat.* 2, 275.

84 (662.48) *Ceinél Lóegaire.* L adds 84, 85 in the left margin, whence they are incorporated into the text of BLcLb. In RLc[1], however, they are already in the text. In Lc 62Vc Dronán forms part of a secular pedigree. Cf. *GRSH* 52, §36 (Rónán); DF 707a.

85 (662.48) *Ceinél Lóegaire.* See note to 84. Cf. *CGH* 166; *GRSH* 51; F 707a.

86 (662.42) *Ceinél Eogain.* Máel Dub is not among the two sons of Áed Findliath named in *CGH* 135. Cf. *GRSH* 47; DF 702b. For the two quatrains see also *Fél.*[2] 158-9. See P. Grosjean in *Anal. Bolland.* 69 (1951) 77-88; 70 (1952) 312-3.

87 (662.122) *Déise.* Lc[1] (a-a) attaches the church to 9 which precedes it in the MS. BLc interpolate 92, 93 here. Cf. Lc 102Rb; *GRSH* 77; DF 718c-719a.

88 (552, 662.120-1) *Déise.* In fact Lc[1] (g) is the only version with seven names. Lb (o) noticed the discrepancy and tried, unsuccessfully (cf. 662.122), to correct it. Cf. *GRSH* 76; DF 718c.

89 (269, 551, 662.119) *Déise.* Cf. *GRSH* 76; DF 719b.

90 (594, 662.73-4) *Uí Ḟiachrach.* In L this entry, which breaks the sequence of Déise saints, is added at the foot of a column. The derivative versions (d-d) took *soror* to be a proper name. R[1]'s addition of Draignech to Áed is confirmed by Adamnán's *V.Col.* (1.17 = 23a). Cf. *GRSH* 61; DF 711c.

91 (489(= 2), 662.119) *Déise.* B's separation of 1 and 2 (u-u) stems from a failure to understand L's marks of reference. Cf. *CGH* 394; *GRSH* 77; DF 719c.

92 (662.118) *Déise.* Misplaced in BLc. Cf. *GRSH* 77; DF 719c.

93 (662.117) *Déise.* Lb's addition (a) is misplaced (cf. *CGH* 135, and 722.52.53 below). La's attachment of Íte to the Uí Chonaill Gabra (c) stems from her position as patron, with Senán, of that area (*Plummer VSH* 2, 118, §8). Cf. *Plummer VSH* 2, 116, §1; *Anal. Bolland.* 46 (1928) 121; *Fél.* 44; Lc 166Vb; *GRSH* 77; DF 720a.

94 (662.117) *Déise*. Cf. *GRSH* 76; DF 719b.

95 (485, 662.183.208) *Dál nAraide*. Cf. *GRSH* 95; DF 728c.

96 (496, 662.146.213) *Uí Echach (Dál nAraide)*. Cf. *CGH* 152 (*Mugdorna*, cf. below 415, 496); *Fél.*[2] 76 (= *Fél.* 118); *GRSH* 100; DF 735c.

97 (419, 506, 662.205) *Dál nAraide*. Cf. *ZCP* 14 (1923) 72; *Anal. Bolland.* 46 (1928) 120; *Fél.* 130; *GRSH* 99, DF 736a.

98 (523, 662.207) 1 (*Dál nAraide*), 2 (*Ceinél Eogain*). Lb separates the two pedigrees. Moninne's *vitae* assign her to Dál nAraide (Uí Echach Ulad), *Heist VSH* 83, §1; M.Esposito, *Conchubrani Vita Sanctae Monennae* (PRIA 28C12 (1910) 208, §2, 244). Cf. *Fél.*[2] 116 (= *Fél.* 166); *GRSH* 47, 101; DF 702b, 735c.

99 (662.209) *Dál nAraide*. Cf. B 168c; *GRSH* 101; DF 735b.

100 (662.208) *Dál nAraide*. Cf. *Fél.*[2] 169 (= *Fél.* 242); *GRSH* 98; DF 735b.

101 (662.208) *Dál nAraide*. Cf. *GRSH* 101; DF 735b.

102 (662.211) *Dál nAraide*. Cf. *GRSH* 99; DF 735b.

103 *Dál nAraide*. Cf. *GRSH* 100; DF 735b.

104 (662.210) *Dál nAraide*. Cf. *V.Trip.* 166; B 168d; *GRSH* 99; DF 735c.

105 (662.210) *Dál nAraide*. Cf. *GRSH* 101; DF 735a.

106 (662.211) *Dál nAraide*. Cf. *GRSH* 100-1; DF 735a.

107 (470, 483, 662.112) 1. *Déise* 2. *Dál Meiccon* (=?). Entered at the foot of a column, this interrupts a Dál nAraide sequence. L's *Ernbraind* (d) is the form given in the secular pedigree of the Déise (*CGH* 253). See note in *Plummer VSH* 1, lx. Cf. *Fél.*[2] 120 (= *Fél.* 170); *B. Deccláín* 6; *Plummer VSH* 2, 35; *GRSH* 74; DF 715c. See also *B.Deccláín* 22 for a statement of his relationship with Colmán, and M. Dillon, C. Mooney, P. de Brún, *Catalogue of Irish Manuscripts in the Franciscan Library Killiney* (Dublin, 1969) 67, §9.

108 (662.95) *Dál nAraide, Airgialla* (RLc[1]). Apparently taking Brucach to be a qualifier of Muiredach, L and its derivatives (except Lb) wrongly give the number of saints as three. For a discussion of one implication of the Airgialla descent (k-k) see *Éigse* 15 (1974) 182. Cf. *GRSH* 69, 71; DF 714e.

109 (467, 662.208) *Dál nAraide*. Grosjean (*Anal. Bolland.* 77 (1959) 174) briefly discusses this pedigree. Cf. *GRSH* 99; DF 736b.

110 (662.96 (with omission of Cairech)) *Dál nAraide, Airgialla* (Lb). For a brief discussion of Cairech Dergán's several pedigrees see *Éigse* 15 (1974) 184. Her attachment to the Airgialla in Lb (i-i) reflects the tradition that she was a sister of Énna Áirne (cf. *Fél.*[2] 50). Cf. *Fél.* 70; *GRSH* 70-2; DF 714e.

111 (662.209) *Dál nAraide*. Cf. *GRSH* 98; DF 732a.

112 (662.209) *Dál nAraide*. RLc[1]'s addition (c) is correct. Cf. M 18Va; *GRSH* 100; DF 732a.

113 *Dál nAraide*. Cf. *GRSH* 100; DF 712c (among Airgialla).

114 *Dál nAraide*. The omission of 114 in BLcLb is no doubt the result of haplography. Cf. *GRSH* 100; DF 712c (among Airgialla).

115 (662.209) 1. *Dál nAraide*, 2. *Dál Fiatach*. The alternative pedigree, 2, follows 1 at the foot of the column in L. Cf. *GRSH* 98 (= 1); DF 723d (= 2), 732a (= 1).

116 1. *Dál nAraide*, 2. ?, 3. *Corco Ocha*. Pedigrees 1 and 3 are in any case closely related (cf. Lc 125Ra[1]; *CGH* 155). The confusion in notes m, o-o was caused by a misreading of *Molua* as *m. Iohne*. The text omitted in M (n-n) is added by R[1] in the top margin of a separate folio (13 (35)). With Lb's addition (r-r) compare 155 (h). Molua is given a different Ciarraige pedigree in *Fél.*[2] 60. See *Plummer VSH* 1, lxxxiii. Cf. *Heist VSH* 131; *Anal. Bolland.* 46 (1928) 121; *ZCP* 14 (1923) 103; *GRSH* 101 (= 1); DF 732a (= 1, 2, 3).

117 (475, 662.207) *Dál nAraide; Eoganachta* (MR[1]La). His usual church is Daiminis but RLc[1]'s Inis Muiredaig is again attached to the saint in the Lc version of the list of homonymous saints Molaisse (707.580). For another reference to Molaisse as *apstal* see *SG* 25. Barrain (c) should perhaps read Barrai*ch* in LR. Cf. *SG* 17 (Eoganachta); *Fél.* 206 (Eoganachta); *GRSH* 100 (Dál nAraide); DF 736a (Dál nAraide), 738c (Eoganachta).

118 (544, 649, 662.212) *Dál nAraide*. BLb's addition of *no* (c-c) derives ultimately from a misinterpretation of L's *cend̄* in the adjacent column (see *Éigse* 18 (1981) 162-4). While the mark of reference (e-e) is to be construed as stated, the Ainmere in question is in fact Ainmere m. Áeda of the Airgialla; see above 80. Cf. *GRSH* 98; DF 732b.

119 (662.212) *Dál nAraide*. Lc[1]'s addition (a) belongs to the previous pedigree (363) where, in the original source, i.e. R, *m.* (= *meic*) is omitted. In the same way, R's *Fiachach* (= *m. Fiachach*) (g) is attached in Lc[1] to the following pedigree (364) and *m. Cais* (g) is added in a later hand; see also *Éigse* 18 (1981) 165-6. Cf. *GRSH* 100; DF 734c.

120 (662.212) *Dál nAraide*. For the alternation *Echdach/Caelbaidh* (b) see also *CGH* 324. Cf. *GRSH* 99; DF 732b.

121 (590, 662.211) *Dál nAraide*. Cf. *GRSH* 101 (with Colgan's critical note).

122 (516, 662.188) *Síl Fergusa*. The *m. Glais* added in Lc[1] etc. (k) is the more usual reading. Cf. *CGH* 116, 321*n*; Lc 131Vc; *ZCP* 8 (1912) 334-5; *Lis.Lives* 75; *Fél.*[2] 182 (= *Fél.* 258) *GRSH* 114; DF 732c.

123 (607, 662.198) 1. *Síl Fergusa*, 2. *Ciarraige*. Lc[1]'s version is a conflated text (a-a and the addition (t)). The reference to Brénainn's pedigree (z-z) is to 127. Cf. *CGH* 279; *Anal. Bolland.* 46 (1928) 121; *GRSH* 107; DF 730c.

124 (428, 662.192-3) *Síl Fergusa*. For the text added in (c-c) see also its possible source (670.30). BLb's *Da(th)chon* (j-j) may be explained by the fact that three deletion marks occur as reference marks under *ui* of *Duib Dechoin* in L. R[1]'s omission (m-m) is possibly due to an illegible or confused exemplar since it also places *Tapaill* before *m. Sgellain*. Cf. *CGH* 279; Lc 131Vc; *ZCP* 8 (1912) 335; *GRSH* 111; DF 729b.

125 (422, 613, 662.197) *Síl Fergusa* (*Latharna Molt*). Lb's *mucc* (b-b) may stem from the belief that Nós of the name was a swineherd (*Onom.* 266). Lc[1]'s alternative descent (x) belongs to the Corco Baiscinn. The pedigree given here is, of course, more specific-ally of the Corco M'druad (cf. *CGH* 254). M's variant *Breagaib* (n-n) may be compared with *i Crich Ua Néill* of *Lis.Lives* 119 (1.4001) and with *in regione Midhi* of *Plummer VSH* I, 200. For the poem added in LbH[1] (ddd) see also Lc 137Rc (*ZCP* 14 (1923) 109), Lc 193Vb; M 18Vb; *Fél.* 202. Cf. 1. *Lis.Lives* 118-9; *Anal. Bolland.* 46 (1928) 122; *Fél.* 204; *GRSH* 109; DF 730a; 2. *Lis.Lives* 119-20; Lc 193Vb.

126 (662.195) *Ciarraige* (*Síl Fergusa*). Lb's *Fingein* (d) may be compared with *Fíg-enius* of Mochuta's *betha* and *Fingenn* of his Latin Life(*BNÉ* 1, 291, *Plummer VSH* 1, 170). The names added to *Noe* (f) belong to the Uí Ḟirb (*CGH* 301-2; cf. *Fél.*[2] 60). For the addition on his mother (m) see also 722.62. Cf. *Fél.*[2] 60 (= *Fél.* 86); *Anal. Bolland.* 46 (1928) 121; *GRSH* 107; DF 729a. See also *Plummer VSH* 1, xlv.

127 (384, 493, 662.195) *Ciarraige* (*Síl Fergusa*). Compare Lb's 'etymological' *Broen-find* (a) with the Lb note to the Calendar of Oengus (*Fél.*[2] 86) and with *BNÉ* 1, 45 (§7), *Lis.Lives* 100-01. Brénainn is one of the twelve Irish apostles (b); cf. 402 below etc. R[1], having omitted much of the text through haplography (e-e), subsequently conflated the variant pedigrees (dd, ff). The first *Fomoir* of H[1]'s addition (u) is due to confusion with the second. Cf. *Fél.*[2] 87 (= *Fél.* 132); *Lis.Lives* 350 (= 716.1); *Anal. Bolland.* 46 (1928) 119; *GRSH* 107; DF 729b.

128 (662.202) *Conmaicne* (*Síl Fergusa*). Cf. *GRSH* 106; DF 733a. See also *Fél.*[2] 169.

129 (132 (Báetán), 662.201 (Báetán)) *Conmaicne* (*Síl Fergusa*). Cf. *GRSH* 105 (with Colgan's note), 113; DF 731a, 733a.

130 (513, 576, 662.156 (BLc).192) *Síl Fergusa*. La omits the pedigree but, with MR[1], includes the addition (o). In Brénainn's Life (*Lis.Lives* 350; cf. *Ériu* 4 (1910) 160) this (?) Erc is provided with a Ciarraige descent. See also Eogan epscop mac Eirc epscuip. Cf. *ZCP* 8 (1912) 335 (332); Lc 131Vc; *GRSH* 111; DF 733a.

131 (662.193) *Síl Fergusa*. Lc (e-e) attaches him to Dál nAraide, as does his sister's pedigree (398.1). Elsewhere (*V.Trip.*108), however, Attracht is assigned to the Gregraige of Loch Teichet in Connacht. Cf. *GRSH* 111; DF 733c, 734b.

132 (129, 662.201) *Síl Fergusa*. Báetán is a doublet of Mobáe (129). This entry is used by J. Carney to buttress his Patrician chronology; see J. Carney, *The Problem of St. Patrick* (Dublin, 1973) 18-20. For Sin see also 722.22.

133 (497) *Ulaid* (*Mugdorna*). As I argue in *Éigse* 18 (1981) 161-76, Lc's reference to its sources (e) is misplaced here; it belongs more properly to Lc 40Vc 36, where its version of the recension in L (Lebor na Nuachongbála) begins. Cf. *CGH* 152; DF 732c.

134 *Ciarraige*. The placing of *qui ⁊ Ciar* after *Tiri* in BLc (f-f) stems from its position in L under *Moga Airt* but below *Is é . . . Tiri*, which is run on to *Moga Airt*. Exactly the same phrase identifies Mac Í's church in 302 (cf. *CGH* 304). Cf. *CGH* 304; *GRSH* 107; DF 732c.

135 (436, 486, 662.190-1) *Síl Fergusa* (*Araid*). Cf. *CGH* 26, 386; *Anal.Bolland.* 46 (1928) 121-2; *Fél.* 206; *GRSH* 110; DF 731b, 736c.

136 (423, 662.140-1) *Dál Fiatach*. BLb's omission (k-k) is due to haplography. In B 166b 13 et seq. the Uí Thrichim are located at Dún Dá Lethglas (Downpatrick). Cf; *CGH* 411; *Fél.* 206; B 166b 33,40; *ZCP* 14 (1923) 56-8; *GRSH* 83; DF 723a.

137 (662.200[b]) *Conmaicne*. Cf. GRSH 106; DF 733b.

138 (272, 662.208) *Dál nAraide, Uí Dúnlainge*. Commán is assigned in 272, and more usually elsewhere, to the Uí Dúnlainge of Laigin. Cf. *CGH* 73; *GRSH* 99; DF 726c.

139 (662.146) *Dál Fiatach*. Cf. *GRSH* 83; DF 737b.

140 (662.145) *Ulaid*. Cf. *GRSH* 84; DF 722c.

141 (662.145) *Ulaid*. Cobthach Cóel is probably identical with Cobthach m. Áeda (54). Cf. Lc 130Rc; *GRSH* 83; DF 722c.

142 (662.144) *Ulaid*. Compare *V.Trip.* 224 with M[1]'s addition (i). M[1]'s other addition (k-k) alludes to the tradition contained in *Cath Crínna* (*SG* 319). Cf. Lc 133Ra; *GRSH* 82; DF 723a.

143 (437, 662.143) *Ulaid*. Cf. *Fél.* 116; *GRSH* 87; DF 722c.

144 (662.204) *Loígse*. *Ua Loígse* should probably read *macc ua* [= moccu Loígse] (cf. *Fél.*[2] 38). Lb's addition (i) is probably based on *Fél.*[2] 38. Cf. *GRSH* 102; DF 731c; *Gen. tracts* 141.

145 (187, 662.203) *Loígse*. A different, but Loígse, descent is also given these saints in 187. BLcLb's reading *Comgaill* (h) seems more correct (cf. *CGH* 90). Cf. *CGH* 90; *GRSH* 102; DF 731cc. See also P. Grosjean in *Anal.Bolland*, 69 (1951) 81-4, and Introduction §2.

146 (442, 662.200) *Conmaicne*. Cf. *B.Fenagh* 4; *GRSH* 105; DF 729c.

147 (662.189) *Ulaid?*. In Lb this is preceded by 148. Cf. *GRSH* 114; DF 733c.

148 (460) *Luigne* (*Síl Fergusa?*). The attachment to Brénainn's pedigree (j-j), i.e. 127, seems incorrect (see *CGH* 439). Cf. *Ir. texts* 3 (1931) 4 (§11); *GRSH* 124; DF 729cc.

149 (443, 662.200[b].207(BLc)) *Conmaicne*. With H[1]'s *Croicheraech* (b) compare *Celtica* 1 (1946) 66, *B.Fenagh* 192n. Cf. *B.Fenagh* 384; *GRSH* 105; DF 729c.

150 (540, 662.142) *Dál Fiatach*. Compare Iarlaithe of the Conmaicne (297). Cf. *V.Trip.* 218-20; *BNÉ* 1, 47-8 (composite pedigree) (= *Lis.Lives* 104); *Acta Sanctorum*, Nov. 9, 186; *GRSH* 15; DF 724.

151 (662.186) *Dál mBuain (Ulaid)*. Cf. *GRSH* 96.

152 (446, 662.185) *Dál mBuain (Ulaid)*. Cf. *GRSH* 96.

153 (566, 662.185) *Dál mBuain (Ulaid)*. Cf. *GRSH* 96.

154 *Dál mBuain (Ulaid)*. Cf. *GRSH* 97.

155 (546) *Corco Roíde, Corco Ocha* (MR[1]La). R[1](a) was probably thinking of Déclán of Ardmore. In their addition (e) R[1]La no doubt had in mind the Uí Dega of Wexford. With Lb's addition (h) compare 116 (r-r). Munnu's *vita* (*Heist VSH* 198, 247; cf. *GRSH* 42) assigns him to the Ceinél Conaill. Cf. *M.Tall* 122; *Fél.* 226; *Anal.Bolland.* 46 (1928) 121; Lc 60Rb; B 82a; *O'Clery* §831.

156 (662.204) *Loígse*. To judge by *CGH* 88 etc., *Sárbile* (c-c) was the more usual reading. The reference to Óenu's pedigree (g-g) is to 144. Cf. *Fél.* 76; *GRSH* 102; DF 734c; *Gen. tracts* 141.

157 (529, 662.215) 1. *Ulaid* (*Conaille Muirtheimne*). 2. *Eoganachta*. Fursu's attachment to Conaille Muirtheimne is repeated in *Fél.*[2] 35. Cf. *GRSH* 104, 125; DF 737c.

158 (662.216) *Ulaid*. Cf. *GRSH* 103; DF 737b.

159 (662.215-6) *Ulaid*. In L this entry straddles two columns. Partly written over it but in the adjacent column is 171 which, in M, precedes 159, the inference being that M, or its source, had direct access to L (Introduction §11). In BLb (c-c) (cf. DF 737b) the reference to the church forms part of 158. Cf. *GRSH* 103-4; DF 737b.

160 (662.54) *Ceinél Lóegaire*. Entries 160-171 of L 349, right column, and 172-182 of L 350, left column, are of a miscellaneous character and appear not to have formed part of the Corpus proper (Introduction §2). For Colum's (Colmán's) full pedigree see 349 below. Lb's omission of Colum (m-m) may have been due to its separate allusion to Colmán of Cloyne (1). 160.2 appears to be taken directly from 722.31.32. Cf. *GRSH* 51-2; DF 707c.

161 See note to 160. With the reading in M (d) compare Áth Mac Lugnai (in R. Thurneysen ed. *Scéla Mucce Meic Dathó* (Med. Mod. Ir. Ser. 6, Dublin, 1935) 19 (§20)), which lay between Fid Gaible, now the r. Feegile, and Drochat Cairpre, now Drehid in the bar. of Carbury, co. Kildare. The *clár* of Cenn Cláir may then refer to Clár Daire Móir (*Onom.* 247) which lay between Dublin and Drochat Cairpre; Fid Eóin is likely to have been the name of a wood in this locality, so rich in its association with

Brigit (cf. 663.11). The same general inference may be drawn from the reference to Cenn Cláir as a limit of Uí Dannbairr of Fotharta Laigen (Lc 97Ra). On the other hand, *B.Brigte* 6, 7 seems to place Fid Eoin in Tethbe.

162 See note to 160. Compare 722.27, the likely source.

163 See note to 160. *Ceinél Eogain*. Lc's *Rube* (a) is no doubt due to confusion with Máel Rubae of Aporcrossan. The misreadings in BLcLb (b) arose from a reading of c̄ as ō in the common source, just as Flann (c) goes back to a mistaken expansion of flā (= filia). The reference to Ercc may apply to Máel Uma rather than Muirchertach (cf. 722.28). In *CGH* 134-5 Máel Umae is described as a *herois/rígféinnid* and is treated as such in the Irish Life of Colmán Ela (*BNÉ* i, 173, §23), which also gives him a different pedigree. Cf. *GRSH* 47.

164 See note to 160. Here the names of the saints appear to be extracted from the church names. For their descent compare *CGH* 96.

165 See note to 160. *Ellaig* (d), misread as *Cuaigh* in the source of BLc, reads *Cellaig* in *CGH* 340 (= L 316a), which appears to be the source of this entry. Cf. *Gen. tracts* 149; *RC* 48 (1931) 220.

166 See note to 160. *Uí Lóscáin*. The addition of (*mac*) *Lairine* in Lb (g) and BLc (h-h) in place of 168 (b-b) is an error in the common source, L's *.i. m. Lairne* being in the margin opposite *Domma* (168). Cf. *CGH* 44, the probable source, which has *Tailech máthair* before *Finnia*.

167 See note to 160. *Ciarraige*. Cf. *CGH* 311.

168 See note to 160.2. *Uí Dúnlainge*. *M's* placing of *mac Lairne* after *Dóthe* (b-b), as in the MS of L (which however has a mark of reference to show its correct place) is another indication of the use of L by M or its source (Introduction §11). See also note to 166. Cf. (in reference to 2) *GRSH* 86; DF 724c.

169 See note to 160. Like 171 below this seems to be an extract from a litany.

170 See note to 160. This entry, with 172, 173, 175, forms an unbroken sequence in R(Lc[1]), which may be the source (Introduction §3). Cf. *Ir. texts* 3 (1931) 81, §6.

171 See note to 160. |*Ail*|*finus* is restored from the reading in the likely source (*Ir.lit.* 64)(= L 373d). There, however, *Mochasoc* reads *Mochasco*.

172 See notes to 160, 170. Cf. *Ir. texts* 3 (1931) 81, §7.

173 See notes to 160, 170. *Fothairt*. Cf. *Ir. texts* 3 (1931) 81, §8.

174 See note to 160. L's mark of reference (g-g) is placed over *Cronain* and under *Cromm*. M (or its source) (a) clearly misread it to refer to the latter.

175 See notes to 160, 170. Cf. *Ir. texts* 3 (1981) 81, §9.

176 See note to 160.

177 See note to 160. BLcLb (d) run on 178. Compare 722.15.

178 See note to 160.

179 See note to 160. Cf. *M.Tall.* 54.

180 See note to 160. Cf. *Gorm.* 154. Since *Gorm.* demonstrably used L as a source for its notes, this may also be the case here.

181 See note to 160. *Dál Meisin Corb*. In RLc[1] (a-a) this tract follows the full pedigree of Cóemgein (250). M[1]LaLb frequently join the names by adding 7. In BLcLb *Escrach* (3) is treated as a personal name. Cf. *CGH* 41 (= L 313a); L 385ab. For 181.1.7.13 see *Fél.* 72.

182 See note to 160. *Osraige*. M's *Maigni* (a) is the correct reading (*M.Tall.* 20). Cf.DF 727 and 278 below.

183 (662.154) *Osraige*. Here the Corpus proper resumes. Cf. *Fél.* 56; *GRSH* 94; DF 727 (*in marg.*).

184 (501, 662.148) *Dál Fiatach*. Cf. *GRSH* 82; DF 723b.

185 (438, 662.147) *Dál Fiatach*. Perhaps, *Díaráin* (c) should be read as *Dimaráin*. Cf. *Fél.* 260. *GRSH* 84; DF 723d. See also *Plummer VSH* 1, lxxxvii.

186 *Loígse*. According to *CGH* 93, which omits the patronymic *m. Nechim*, Áduar was the eponymous ancestor of a segment of the Loígse. The reference to Óenu's pedigree (e-e) is to 144. Cf. *GRSH* 102; DF 734c.

187 *Loígse*. A doublet of 145. B(Lc)'s *Bacanut* (c) shows influence of the Latin (d-d) which is otherwise omitted in their source. Concerning (d-d) see 186.

188 (577, 662.215) *Ulaid, Eoganachta?* (MR[1]La). P.Grosjean, the editor of La, mistakenly added Manchán's pedigree to that of Colum of Terryglass (*Ir.texts* 3, 100 §273). For the notice of his mother see also 722.80 and, for a conflicting version, 722.(92). Cf. *GRSH* 104; DF 737b.

189 (662.191) *Síl Fergusa* (*Araid*). Ail*ell*a (i) should read Ailbe (135). In *CGH* 387 Scuithín is supplied with a different pedigree. Cf. *Fél.*[2] 32; *GRSH* 110; DF 731c.

190 (567, 662.228) *Dál Cais*. Lb's addition (i) is from the *Dindshenchas* poem, *Temair toga na tulach;* see E. Gwynn, *The Metrical Dindshenchas* 1 (Todd Lect. Ser. 8, Dublin, 1903) 24. Cf. NLI G 2 3a; *GRSH* 120; DF 740b.

191 (612, 662.221) *Eoganachta*. The version in La (§39), which Grosjean omitted from his edition (*Ir. texts* 3), is added in the lower margin. It is mostly illegible and somewhat differently arranged. Lc's addition (a) in fact refers to Daráine. Note the unusual agreement between Lb and Lc[1] (f, g-g, h-h) (cf. Introduction §7). With 2 compare 722.59, *Fél.*[2] 121, DF 740b and, for a different version, *Plummer VSH* 2, 65-6. Cf. *CGH* 197; *Fél.*[2] 121 (= *Fél.* 172); *GRSH* 116; DF 740b.

192 *Laigin (Uí Bairrche)*. The fact that Doborchú's alias was Mac Onchon (L 313bb 38) (= *CGH* 47) may have led to the prefixing of *mac* here. Significantly Lc[1] omits it. With the addition (f-f) in L and its derivatives compare *CGH* 49.

193 (447, 662.235) *Cianachta*. Here H enters in the margin some unrelated names. Cf. Lc 222Vd; *GRSH* 123; DF 742a.

194 (528, 662.233) *Cianachta*. Cf. *Fél.* 202; *GRSH* 124; DF 742cc.

195 (455, 662.233) *Cianachta*. Cf. *V.Trip.* 160; *Fél.*[2] 171; B 194b, 195ac; Lc 223Ra; *GRSH* 123; DF 739c.

196 (420, 465, 662.146) *Dál Fiatach*. Cumman's inclusion here may be due to L's *Ḟeic m. Imchada* in 195 (cf. *ut ante* of 196). Cf. *Fél.*[2] 91; M 13V; *GRSH* 82; DF 723b.

197 (530, 662.234) *Cianachta, Luigne* (Lb). Her attachment to the Luigne — which reflects the location of her church — is also expressed in *GRSH* 123. Cf. *Ir. texts* 3 (1931) 5, §11; DF 742b.

198 (571, 662.230) *Dál Cais*. Cf. GRSH 120; DF 738a.

199 (432, 478, 578) *Eoganachta*. BLc's *Iraird* (b) is no doubt due to confusion with the better-known church. Cf. *Ir.texts* 3 (1931) 1, §1; *GRSH* 115; DF 742a.

200 (555, 637, 662.131) *Múscraige Tíre; Síl Conaire*. Omitted in MLaH, this pedigree occurs in the margin of the generally cognate R[1] where its local — i.e. Lorrha — interest probably led to its inclusion. Possibly *A Caille Cinn Ḟebrat* refers to Ailill Ólum of 194 to whom it is run on in L. Cf. Lc 107Rd (= B 145d); *GRSH* 79.

201 (270, 473, 556, 662.134.136) *Cruithne, Dál Riata*. The length and detail of the pedigree in L may be due to the comparatively local dedication at Cluain Sasta (Clonsast), co. Offaly. Some of the glosses also occur in L's version of the descent of the kings of Scotland (*CGH* 328-9). Cf. *GRSH* 80; DF 721b.

202 (662.230) *Dál Cais*. Cf. *CGH* 235; *GRSH* 120; DF 740b.

203 (662.230) *Dál Cais*. *CGH* 235 gives a different descent. Cf. *GRSH* 120; DF 740b.

204 (662.231) *Dál Cais*. Cf. *GRSH* 120,121; DF 740b.

205 (662.231) *Dál Cais*. *Ut ante* (d-d) refers to 204. Cf. *CGH* 239 (= M 29Vb); *GRSH* 120; DF 740b.

206 (492, 584, 662.138) *Dál Riata*. Presumably *Nisi* (gen.) is to be taken as the maternal name of the saint (cf. *GRSH* 81*n*). With Lb's addition (e) compare *Fél.*[2] 145. Cf. *Fél.*[2] 142; *GRSH* 81; DF 722c.

207 (449, 526, 662.235) *Cianachta*. In 449 Tola is assigned to the Déise. Cf. *Fél.* 102 (a variant pedigree), *GRSH* 124, DF 742a.

208 (504, 662.219) *Eoganachta*. Like Brénainn (127) etc., Ruadán was one of the twelve Irish apostles (cf. 402). The space devoted in R[1] to the pedigree accords with the Lothra provenance of the manuscript. In *BNÉ* 1,317 (cf. *Plummer VSH* 2, 240; *Heist VSH* 160) the saint's family is given as Síl (Uí) Duach. *Ut ante* (i-i) probably refers to 191. Cf. *BNÉ* 1, 317; *GRSH* 118; DF 738c.

209 *Dál Riata*. The maternal name given in BLc (b-b) is more likely to reflect a misreading in their source of L's text. L's reference to Berchán (b-b) is to 201. The relationship between 209 and 701, where the poem (o-o) is given in full, is expressed by marks of reference in L. Curiously the text added in Lc (q) is not found at 701. Cf. *GRSH* 80-1; DF 721b. For a discussion of this entry see now D. Ó Cróinín, 'The oldest Irish names for the days of the week', *Ériu* 32 (1981) 95-114; pp. 104-114.

210 *Corco Baiscinn*. If the correct form of the saint's name is *Uidriu* (see *CGH* 380), then L's sharing of *Uriu* with RLc[1] suggests that the Book of Glendalough (R) was L's source here (Introduction §3). Cf. *CGH* 380; *GRSH* 79; DF 721b.

211 (662.128) *Corco Duibne*. With L's addition (b-b) compare 722.81. BLcLb's reading (f) represents the more correct sequence (*CGH* 378-9). Cf. *GRSH* 78; DF 722b.

212 (662.128) *Múscraige*. R[1]'s version (e-e) represents the Múscraige Treithirne (Uí Chuirc) descent (*CGH* 373-4). In Lc 107Rd he is assigned to the Uí Chainnig. See also Introduction §12. Cf. Lc 107Rd (= B 145c); *GRSH* 78; DF 722b.

213 (662.237) 1. *Cianachta*; 2. = ?. L's note (h-h) suggests that he too was at a loss as to the family intended by the second pedigree. Cf. *GRSH* 123; DF 739c.

214 (514, 662.240) *Corco Loígde*. Cf. *Fél.* 92; *GRSH* 127; DF 744b.

215 (662.18) *Síl Luigdech Lága*. With Lb's addition (o) compare 160.(2). Cf. M 32Vab; *GRSH* 125; DF 743c.

216 (662.227) *Eoganachta, Connachta* (Lc). Lc's version (b-b) shows a typical local preference on the part of the scribe (Introduction §6); Druimm Neoit (Drummod) is near Mohill, co. Leitrim. Cf. *GRSH* 59, 117.

217 (662.196) *Fir Maige Féine*. See Introduction §20 (at note 155). Cf. *Ir. texts* 3 (1931) 13; *GRSH* 112; DF 731a.

218 (662.196) *Fir Maige Féine*. See Introduction §20 (at note 155). Cf. *Ir. texts* 3 (1931) 13; *GRSH* 112; DF 731b.

219 (459); *Fir Maige Féine*. See Introduction §20 (at note 155). Cuanu, *al.* Laéch Liathmuine, is sometimes referred to as 'king of Fir Maige Féine' (*Ériu* 19 (1962) 75), whence, perhaps, the omission of the pedigree in Lb, *GRSH* and DF. Cf. *Ir. texts* 3 (1931) 13; *Ériu* 19 (1962) 75.

220 (662.237) *Cianachta*. RLc[1]'s addition (a) would appear to be reflected by Breccán of (?) Cenn Bairche (707.61). *GRSH* 122 separates the two. Cf. DF 742c.

221 (574, 662.238(BLc).240) *Corco Loígde*. In B *e* of *epscop* is written large and Silán is attached to the previous entry. Cf. *CGH* 257 (= M 34Rb, = *Misc.Celt.Soc.* 32): *GRSH* 128; DF 744a.

222 (298, 518, 662.238) *Corco Loígde*. In other sources the paternal name also alternates between Moénach (*CGH* 261) and Mongach (*M.Tall.* 63). In M 34Vb the text reads *Fachtna Mongach m. Maenaigh*. M's reference to Ros Ailithir (k), while applicable also to Fachtna, may derive from an exemplar in which, as in L, Fachtna's pedigree is followed directly by that of Colmán ailithir. Cf. *CGH* 261; M 34Vb; *Fél.*[2] 75 (= 298); *GRSH* 127; DF 744a.

223 (662.64) *Fothairt?, Clann Cholmáin* (Lb). The entry is added in at the foot of the column in L. Cf. *GRSH* 54; DF 704a.

224 (662.218) *Cerdraige Tulcha Gossa*. Cf. *CGH* 219; *GRSH* 126; DF 743b.

225 (570, 662.234) *Cianachta*. Cf. *Anal.Bolland.* 46 (1928) 120; *GRSH* 123; DF 742b. See also *Plummer VSH* 1, lix (note).

226 (662.232) *Dál Cais*. R[1]'s addition (a) does not belong here (see *CGH* 364). Cf. *CGH* 240; *GRSH* 119; DF 738a.

227 (662.222) *Uí Liatháin*. Cf. *GRSH* 115; DF 740a.

228 (450, 662.129) *Corco Baiscinn*. Gerrcenn (c) is the correct paternal name. Cf. *V.Trip.* 206; *Lis.Lives* 54; *Anal. Bolland.* 46 (1928) 120; 66 (1948) 218-9; *Fél.* 86; B 147e; *GRSH* 79; DF 722a.

229 (448, 648, 662.236) *Cianachta, Eoganachta* (R[1]); In Beinén's Irish Life (*Acta Sanctorum*, Novembris, 4, 171) he is given a Cianachta pedigree but is called 'the king of Cashel's son'. Cf. *GRSH* 122; DF 741b.

230 (471, 568, 662.229) *Dál Cais*. Lc[1]'s version of the church name (a) is a misreading of its originai exemplar (R). with R[1]'s addition (e) compare *V.Trip.* 206. Cf. *CGH* 237; *GRSH* 119; DF 738a.

231 (429, 662.236) *Cianachta*. With M (b), Lb (j) compare *Fél.*[2] 180. Cf. Lc 223Ra; *Fél.*[2] 180; (= *Fél.* 256); *GRSH* 122; DF 741b.

232 (451, 662.223) *Eoganachta*. L's *Fiachra* (c) is probably a misreading of the exemplar's *Fiachna* with *n* written like *r* as in R, the possible source (Introduction §3). Cf. *CGH* 226; M 26Va; *Fél.* 242; *GRSH* 116; DF 738b.

233 *Dál Cais*. Cf. *Fél.* 78; M 32Vb (cf. Va); *GRSH* 119; DF 738cc.

234 (662.226) *Eoganachta, Loígse* (RLc[1]). Cf. *GRSH* 117; DF 740b.

235 (624, 662.223) *Eoganachta Locha Léin*. Faithlenn appears to be the correct form of the nominative (*M.Tall.* 68; *CGH* 220). Cf. *CGH* 220; *GRSH* 117; DF 738b.

236 (662.222) *Uí Liatháin*. In Lc's addition (a) the reference is probably to a local church (cf. Kilgobban near Killala, co. Mayo); Lc tends to 'localize' (cf.216). Cf. *CGH* 227 (with a slightly different descent); *GRSH* 117-8; DF 740a.

237 (468, 662.137-8) *Dál Riata*. The reference to Berchán (j-j) is to 201. In 468 he is assigned to the Fir Lí. Cf. *GRSH* 80; DF 722c.

238 (606, 662.224) *Eoganachta*. In 387 (cf. *CGH* 46) Mac Táil is assigned to the Uí Bairrche. Cf. *GRSH* 118; DF 740a.

239 (271, 662.135) *Dál Riata*. With the note on Berchán's sisters (b-b) compare 638 and 670.50. Cf. *GRSH* 80-81; DF 721a.

240 (561, 662.225) *Uí Liatháin*. I have no other reference to the Uí Cherba (Chirb) of Brega (i). Cf. *GRSH* 117; DF 738aa.

241 (457, 662.162) *Uí Chrimthannáin* (*Laigin*). Very naturally, in view of Áed mac Crimthainn's own family ties, the Leinster section begins with two saints of the Uí Chrimthannáin (cf. Introduction §2). Colum was also, of course, patron of Áed's church of Terryglass. He was one of Ireland's apostles (b) (cf. 402 etc.). In his edition of La (*Ir. texts* 3 (1931) 100) Grosjean mistakenly added Manchán's pedigree (188) to that of Colum. Cf. *CGH* 55, 56; *Fél.*[2] 83, 175; DF 724c.

242 (662.162) *Uí Chrimthannáin*. See note to 241. Cf. *CGH* 55; *Fél.*[2] 64, 88 (= *Fél.* 100, 114); *GRSH* 91; DF 727a.

243 (642, 662.167-8) *Laigin*. The first part is closely related to 722.77. See also note to 332. Cf. *CGH* 69; *GRSH* 86, 87, 89, 90, 91; DF 724b, 727ab.

244 (505, 662.170) *Uí Bairrche*. The maternal name added by La (h) should read *Darfraích* (cf.722.42); Grosjean read *Darsrothib*. Cf. *CGH* 48; *Fél.*[2] 72 (= *Fél.* 112); *GRSH* 92; DF 724b.

245 *Uí Bairrche*. Lc[1]'s addition (a) seems more correct (cf. *CGH* 53). Cf. *GRSH* 85; DF 724c.

246 (593, 662.173) *Uí Dúnlainge*. In BLcLb this follows 247. In Lc[1]MM[1]R[1]La the entry is arranged differently. With MR[1]La's further addition (c) compare *V.Trip*. 184. With R[1]La's addition (d) compare 593. In *CGH* 340 BLc add this and the following two entries from a MLa-type exemplar. Cf. *Fél.*[2] 181; *GRSH* 89-90; DF 726c.

247 (656, 662.173) *Uí Dúnlainge*. See note to 246. IN LbLc[1] the entry is arranged differently. Cf. *CGH* 340 (BLc); *GRSH* 87-8; DF 726c.

248 (662.174) *Uí Dúnlainge*. See note to 246. Lc[1] arranges the entry differently. La's addition (i) is obscure but it may stand in some relationship to 722.64.

249 (547, 662.172) *Uí Dega Ua Ceinselaig/Osraige*(Lb). The attachment to Ciarraige Luachra in R[1](a) more properly belongs to Nemnat, the saint's mother (cf.722.51). Lb's addition (a) is mistakenly placed after 250. Cf. W. Stokes, *The Birth and Life of St. Moling* (Paris, 1906) 4; *SG* 153 (= *IT* 4, 1, p.75); *BNÉ* 1, 244; *Anal. Bolland*. 46 (1928) 119; *GRSH* 90; DF 724a. See also *Plummer VSH* 2, 190.

250 (458, 592, 662.155) *Dál Meisin Corb*. For a note on the pedigree see *Éigse* 18 (1981) 175-6. A slightly variant version of the saint's age (k-k) is given in *BNÉ* 1, 166, §44. Cf. *CGH* 41 (B); L 385a; *BNÉ* 1, 125; *Anal. Bolland*. 46 (1928) 119; *GRSH* 86; DF 726b.

251 (520, 559, 587, 662.156) *Dál Meisin Corb, Síl Fergusa* (Lb). This follows 252 in Lb. L's addition (f-f), which is adopted as the better reading by BLb(Lc) and which is also in M, should perhaps be placed after *m. Cuirbb* since the reference is evidently to Epscop Erc. m. Dega. Cf. L 385a; *Fél.*[2] 132 (= *Fél.* 188); *GRSH* 88; DF 725b.

252 (440, 499, 662.157) *Dál Meisin Corb*. In Lb this entry precedes 251. Compare L's etymology (a-a) with *Fél.*[2] 83. H's *m. Fothaid* (d-d) is incorrectly placed after Eochu. Cf. *CGH* 42 (L etc.); L 385a; *Fél.*[2] 83; *GRSH* 86; DF 725a.

253 (662.158) *Dál Meisin Corb*. In B (f-f) *her* is written as if to begin a new entry. Cf.L 385a; *GRSH* 87, 89, 90; DF 725a.

254 (662.158) *Dál Meisin Corb*. Lb omits this. Cf. *CGH* 42 (L etc.); L 385a: *GRSH* 91; DF 726a.

255 (662.159) *Dál Meisin Corb*. To judge by *CGH* 42 *Foramain* (c) should read *Forannain* with Lb. For a note on the pedigree see *JCHAS* 82 (1977) 79. Cf. *CGH* 42; L 385a; *GRSH* 89; DF 726a.

256 (662.159) *Dál Meisin Corb*. With L's gloss (b-b) compare *Fél.*[2] 145. For a comment on the pedigree see *Dinnseanchas* 6 (1975) 83 (and note). Cf. L 385a; *GRSH* 87; DF 726b.

257 *Uí Ḟailge*. The names of the two daughters are given in *M.Tall*. 28 (cf. *Fél.*[2] 65). Compare also *CGH* 57 where the father's pedigree is given. *GRSH* omits. Cf. DF 727c.

258 *Dál Meisin Corb*. With Lb's reading (a-a) compare *CGH* 37 (*teora ingena Eogain m. Conaill conacabsat Cill ṅGarraisc*). Lc's addition (e) was no doubt due to confusion with the following pedigree (b). *GRSH* omits. Cf. L 385a. DF 727c.

259 *Uí Bairrche*. Cf. *CGH* 48; *GRSH* 88; DF 727c.

260 (662.176) *Laigin*. Lb's entry is in two parts on separate pages. Lc's misreading (e-e) is written as if to begin a new entry. Cf. *CGH* 48; *GRSH* 86; DF 727b.

261-271 The section on saints named Berchán is lacking in RLc[1] and was probably first devised by Áed mac Crimthainn who, having listed three Laigin saints of the name (261-3), added the others *non quod isti omnes sint Lagnenses* (see 271). M is probably based on L at this point.

261 (168, 562, 662.175) *Laigin*. In BLcLb the entry follows 262.

262 (662.180) *Uí Máil*. See note to 261. In Lc the entry is accompanied by a mark of reference (~) as if to indicate a new section. In *CGH* 346 this Berchán forms part of a secular pedigree. Cf. *GRSH* 86; DF 724d, 726b.

263 (560, 662.160) *Dál Meisin Corb*. Cf. *CGH* 41; *GRSH* 86; DF 725a.

264 (548, 662.85) *Airgialla*. Cf. *GRSH* 69; DF 716a.

265 *Corco Loígde*. In *Misc. Celt. Soc.* 46 Berchán is given a different descent, but it is not clear if the saint is intended. *GRSH* omits. Cf. DF 749b.

266 (317, 549?, 662.111) *Corco Trí, Fothairt* (317). A doublet of 317 where a much fuller descent is given. *Pace* Lb (d) (cf. *Onom.* 434, 'Gailenga Bicc'), the reference is probably to Fine Gall. See note to 317.

267 *Ciarraige?* Compare Colmán son of Sílán of the Ciarraige (*CGH* 311)? In *GRSH* 76 (cf. *M.Don.* 138) Berchán of Cluain Chaí is attached to the Déise. Significantly, *Gorm.* and *M.Don.* include in the same list Ultán m. Aédgein, Sillán and Colmán; so the pedigree is probably fabricated from the calendar list. *GRSH* omits. Cf. DF 749b.

268 *GRSH* omits. I have no other reference to L's addition (d). Cf. DF 749b.

269 *Déise*. BLcLb omit. The prior entry is 89 above.

270 In 722.63 this Berchán is identified as the son of Muiredach (= 201 above).

271 See 239.

272 *Uí Dúnlainge*. In Lb the two parts of the entry are separated, whence the omission of *et* (d-d). Lc's addition (i) again illustrates its tendency to give local colour to entries (cf. 216, 236); the place in question is not in Tirawley, however. Cf. *CGH* 73; *GRSH* 86-7; DF 726c.

273 (662.178) *Uí Cheinselaig*. In 275 Crunnmáel, a king of Uí Cheinselaig, belongs to the secular part of the pedigree (cf. *CGH* 15). Elsewhere, however, he is also regarded as a saint (367.2, *M.Tall.* 51). Cf. *GRSH* 87; DF 727c.

274 (662.178) *Uí Cheinselaig*. M arranges the entry differently. In L 390b *Gabuil* (b) is attached to *Senaig* (c). BLcLb's *m.* (e) is doubtless due to the fact that their common source failed to notice the change in L from a *meic*-series to *et*. Cf. L 390b: B 136b *GRSH* 92; DF 726c.

275 (662.178) *Uí Cheinselaig*. See note to 273. Cf. L 390b; *GRSH* 89; DF 727c.

276 (662.180) *Uí Máil*. Another 'secular' saint (cf. 273); Rónán's grandson, Fiannamail (†680) became king of Leinster. Rónán's brother, Crimthann, also king of Leinster, is reputed to have been slain by the saint. Cf. *CGH* 76; *GRSH* 91; DF 724d.

277 *Osraige*. Lb omits this entry. Cf. *CGH* 105; *GRSH* 93.

278 (182.1, 640, 662.153) *Osraige*. A doublet of the interpolated entry, 182.1. Cf. *CGH* 103-4; *GRSH* 93, 94; DF 727.

279 (662.34) *Ceinél Eogain*. Cf. *GRSH* 44, 45; DF 702c.

280 *Osraige*. Cf. *GRSH* 94; DF 726c.

281 *Osraige*. In the left margin opposite *Erc* is written .n̄ within a square box. Cf. *GRSH* 93.

282 (662.164) *Laigin* (*Uí Labrada*). If L was using R (see Introduction §3), then its omissions (d, f) could have occurred through haplography. But in *CGH* 35 the same omissions are found. Cf. *CGH* 35; L 383b; *GRSH* 91; DF 725c.

283 (662.164) *Laigin* (*Uí Labrada*). BLc's *m. Cormaic* (a) is probably due to an uncorrected confusion with *Corcain* in the source. How, among the derivative texts, Lc (b-b) arrived at its unique *Icsenchill* I cannot explain. Cf. *CGH* 35 (= *Sen-sinchell* R, *Sinchell* L); *GRSH* 91; DF 725c.

284 (662.179) *Uí Dúnlainge*. The entry is arranged differently in RLc[1]. 1 and 2 are separated in Lb. Cf. L 380a; *GRSH* 86; DF 727c.

285 (498, 563, 645, 662.179) *Uí Dúnlainge*. Cf. *CGH* 73; *GRSH* 85; DF 726c.

286 (477, 521, 662.169) *Uí Bairrche*. Compare Lb's *.i. Droma Gablai* (a) with *V.Trip.* 242. M's *Cilli Sleibe* (a) is doubtless the result of confusion with the pedigree of Moninne of Killeavy which precedes 286 in M. Cf. *CGH* 50 (different descent); *GRSH* 89; DF 724b.

287 (662.165) *Laigin* (*Uí Labrada*). Compare with the quatrain (4), which is written in the lower margin of columns abc in L, the versions in *Fél.*² 63, 160. Different mothers (3) are given the saints in 722.79.96. Cf. *Anal. Bolland.* 46 (1928) 122; *Fél.* 74, 228; L 383b: *GRSH* 85; DF 727. See also *Plummer VSH* 1, xxiii.

288 (461, 662.152) *Osraige.* Beginning with *m. Crimthaind* (j) R¹'s text is in a different hand. In a Cornish *vita* Ciarán is provided with a very different but still Irish pedigree (*Anal. Bolland.* 59 (1941) 262-3; cf. pp.265-7 for Grosjean's discussion of Ciarán's descent). Cf. *Fél.* 88, *Anal. Bolland.* 46 (1928) 121; *GRSH* 93; DF 725b.

289 *Uí Máil.* I have no other reference to the descent of this saint.

290 (662.177) *Uí Cheinselaig, Ciarraige, Uí Briúin.* For a metrical version of this entry see 700.1.2.3. Cf. *CGH* 301 (= 2); *GRSH* 62,63,87; DF 727b.

291 (531, 560, 662.160) *Dál Meisin Corb.* RLc¹'s addition of *m.* (b) is surely an error. The reference to Cóemgen is to 250. Cf. *CGH* 41; L 385a; *GRSH* 90; DF 726a.

292 (644, 662.171) *Uí Bairrche.* BLc's omission (c-c) is haplographical. Cf. *GRSH* 89; DF 724a.

293 (643, 662.171) *Uí Bairrche.* Cf. *GRSH* 88; DF 727b.

294 *Osraige.* Cf. *GRSH* 94; DF 725b.

295 *Ciarraige.* Cf. *GRSH* 108; DF 733c.

296 (662.196?) *Ciarraige.* In Lc *m. Luchta* precedes *m. Loga* but, by use of the letters a, b, the sequence is corrected. For a discussion of the entry see P. Grosjean, 'The pedigree of Saint Caelainn' *The Journal of Celtic Studies* 1 (1950) 193-98. Cf. *GRSH* 107; DF 733c.

297 (472, 662.199) *Conmaicne.* Lc (a) regarded the pedigree as a continuation of 296. See also 150 above. Cf. *GRSH* 106; DF 734b.

298 (662.238) *Corco Loígde.* BLc join *Lugna* (a) to the preceding pedigree. Lb, which inserts ⁊ between the names of the brothers in 2, also writes *Cuasan* (f) as if it were the beginning of a separate entry. In BLcLb Cuala (h) is treated as a personal name. For Fachtna see also 222 above. Compare also 730. Cf. *Fél.*² 75 (= *Fél.* 116); *GRSH* 127, 128; DF 744bbc.

299 (417, 662.182-3) *Slicht Echach m. Maireda* (*Ulaid*). Omitted in BLcLb, this entry is given a special prominence in L through its length, in H through its decorative character from *m. Lugo* onwards, and in the *recensio minor* (417) through its second place after Patrick. In Lc¹ this entry is separated from, but occurs after, 300 (q-q). Cf. *GRSH* 97; DF 728a.

300 *Slicht Echach m. Maireda* (*Ulaid*). In BLcLb this entry forms a continuation of 298; *Muirgenach* (a-a) in the same MSS no doubt reflects L's *Murgen ingen Echach.* Cf. *GRSH* 97; DF 744c.

301 BLcLb's readings (c) are clearly the result of the omission of an abbreviation in their common source. I have no evidence of the family of this saint. *GRSH* omits. Cf. DF 751b.

302 *Ciarraige.* This entry forms a continuation of 301 in BLcLb. In Lc *Laestaire* (l-l) is written as if it were the beginning of a new entry. See also note to 134. *GRSH* omits. Cf. DF 751b.

303 *Ciarraige. CGH* 311, the only other source I have been able to discover for the pedigree, reads *Faimdid.*

304 *Ciarraige.* In LcLb the names are in a different order. Compare *CGH* 311.

305 (653) *Connachta.* B appears to have an erasure between *m.* and *Dubthaig.*

306 In L's list of the successors of Pátraic (cf. Lb¹'s addition (a)), Fethgna († 874 (AU)) is assigned to Clann Echdach (L 42d (= 1.6040)).

307 *Airgialla.* Entries 307-9 are placed in the lower margin of Lb.

308 See note to 307. This entry and 309 are together among the final entries of the RLc¹ recension. Cf. *Ir. texts* 3 (1931) 80.

309 *Ciarraige?.* See notes to 307, 308. Lc¹'s addition (a) is no doubt an uncorrected error for *Dunamail.* Compare the apparently secular Cuanu m. Dúnamail in *CGH* 290. Cf. *Ir. texts* 3 (1931) 80.

310 (619, 650, 662.102) *Airgialla.* Omitted in R, this is one of Lc¹'s independent additions (Introduction §8). Cf. Lc 81Rc; *GRSH* 67; DF 712c.

311 (454, 662.184) *Ulaid.* L's reading (f) appears to be a misreading of *Fiacc(h)a* in its source, here possibly R (Introduction §3). Senán (h-h) is entered under 299 above. With the addition in Lb etc (i) compare *Fél.*² 147. Cf. *Anal. Bolland.* 46 (1928) 121 (with the mistaken inclusion of Niall Naégiallach); *Fel.*² 147; *GRSH* 95; DF 728b.

312 *Eoganachta*. Cf. *CGH* 215; *GRSH* 117; DF 741a.

313 *Bretnaig*. For *Dubtain m. Ruin* see also 722.84. Cf. *Gen. tracts* 51-2.

314 (484, 608, 662.79) *Uí Briúin*. In Lb the sequence is broken here; 322 follows. For some implications of the pedigree see *JCHAS* 82 (1977) 67. Cf. *BNÉ* 1, 11; *Anal. Bolland*. 46 (1928) 121; *GRSH* 59; DF 710a.

315 (421, 550, 614, 662.112 (BLc).113) *Fothairt, Cianachta* (H[1]). In H[1]'s addition (j) *Galenga* (?) comes after *Laidich* in the MS; *o tat Ceneal Conamla* is a gloss. In *GRSH* 54, Féichín is attached to the Clann Cholmáin. Cf. *Fél*. 48; *RC* 12, 321; *GRSH* 54, 75; DF 718c, 739a. See also *Plummer VSH* 1, lxiv (note).

316 (565, 662.183) *Ulaid*. Cf. *Fél*. 166; *GRSH* 97; DF 728b.

317 (266, 549?, 662.111) *Fothairt* (*Corco Trí*). A doublet of 266. Mobí (b) was another of the Irish apostles (cf. 402). Cf. *Fél*.[2] 156; *GRSH* 74; DF 718b.

318 (662.93) *Airgialla*. I have no other reference to the material in 2-5 which is in L only. The *fratres* of 4 refers, however, to Furudrán and Báetán (see 55 above); *m. Segáin* of 4 may therefore belong by right to *Telli*. Cf. *GRSH* 72; DF 714c.

319 (662.236) *Cianachta*. With L (a-a) compare 703.3. Cf. *GRSH* 124; DF 739c.

320 (78, 490, 515, 662.82) 1. *Uí Briúin*. 2. *Airgialla*. Within Uí Briúin, Findchú is attached to the Ceinél Dobtha (see 410.1). L's reading (m-m), which is omitted in the derivative texts, would appear to be mistaken, unless the Airgialla descent is an assumption on the part of BLcLb (l). See also note to 78. Cf. *Lis.Lives* 84; *Fél*.[2] 173; *GRSH* 59, 73; DF 710b, 715b.

321 (662.221) *Eoganachta*. At this point Lb adds 331. Cf. *CGH* 197; *GRSH* 118; DF 740a.

322 *Ciarraige*. See note to 314. Lc's addition (d) is clearly an error but it is followed in *GRSH*. The *Dunig* of *Duib Dunig* is not supported by *CGH* 307. Cf. *CGH* 307; *GRSH* 76; DF 733bb.

323 *Corco Loígde*. Cf. *CGH* 262, the possible source; *Misc. Celt. Soc*. 16 (= M 34Rd 61); *GRSH* 127-8; DF 744b.

324 (662.226) *Eoganachta*. Lb's reading *in Chrabuid* (a) occurs also in *CGH* 215, *GRSH* 116, DF 741a, *RC* 48 (1931) 222.

325 (534, 662.59) *Ceinél Lóegaire*. Colum (m.) Cúla (f-f) is the saint of that name. For a discussion of some implications of this pedigree see *Éigse* 15 (1974) 176-9. See also D. Ó Corráin, in idem ed. *Irish Antiquity* (Cork, 1981) 330. Cf. *Fél*.[2] 169 (= *Fél*. 242); *Anal. Bolland*. 17 (1898) 161; B 88a; *GRSH* 52; DF 706b.

326 Only in L, which, appropriately enough, ends its version of the Corpus proper as it began, with an entry on Patrick. A section of *disjecta membra* follows in L (see below 663 ff). For another version of 326 see *V.Trip*. 550-2 (= Lb 220a).

327 (662.14) *Ceinél Conaill*. In all manuscripts containing it, this entry on Iona's first abbot after Colum Cille occurs immediately after that on Colum Cille himself (8). Cf. *Fél*.[2] 99 (= *Fél*. 144); Rawl. B 505 124V; *Anecd*. 3 (1910) 2; *GRSH* 38; DF 697a.

328 (533, 662.71) *Uí Ḟiachrach*. R does not contain this entry. It must, therefore, have been added to Lc[1], together with 24 above which follows it and which also has a local Uí Ḟiachrach interest. Since MR[1] have these entries in the same order, their source is likely to have been used by Lc[1]. The variant readings in (e) can be accounted for by assuming a form *Raeich* (written *Raeī*) in the exemplar. Cf. *Fél*.[2] 34; *GRSH* 62; DF 711c.

329 *Ciarraige Luachra*. Only in Lb. Cf. *GRSH* 108; DF 737cc.

330 (603, 662.232) *Dál Cais*. Cf. *GRSH* 119; DF 738a.

331 1. *Ceinél Lóegaire*. 2. *Eoganachta*. 3. *Uí Briúin*. In Lb only; see note to 321. Compare *Ir. texts* 3 (1931) 86-7 where the text is edited by Grosjean from Egerton 92 with the Lb text in the form of a footnote. For Colmán (1) compare *GRSH* 51.

332 (445, 580) *Laigin*. Assuming confusion between *Mochuda* and *Mochua*, this is probably in origin the same saint as in 243. A similar confusion occurs in 5 (a) above.

333 *Déise*. Cf. *CGH* 158.

334 (494, 662.200) *Conmaicne*. Cf. *Fél*. 86; *GRSH* 106; DF 733bb.

335 *Ciarraige Aí*. Cf. *GRSH* 107.

336 (662.18) *Ceinél Conaill*. Entries 336-48, comprising, with 8 and 327, a list of abbots of Iona, lead off the RLc[1] recension (Introduction §8). Cf. *GRSH* 41; DF 697c.

337 (662.18) *Ceinél Conaill*. See note to 336. Cf. *GRSH* 43; DF 697c.

338 (662.18) *Ceinél Conaill*. See note to 336. Colgan (*GRSH* 40) identifies him with Cuimíne Find. Cf. *GRSH* 39; DF 698a.

339 (662.18 (B)) *Ceinél Conaill*. See note to 336. Cf. *GRSH* 41; DF 697c.

340 (662.15) *Ceinél Conaill*. See note to 336; but this entry is also in HH[1] where it is near that on Baíthíne m. Brénainn (327 above). Cf. K. Meyer, *Cáin Adamnáin* (Oxford, 1905) 2; *Arch. Hib.* 1 (1912) 365; *Fél.* 210; B 84b; *GRSH* 37; DF 697ab.

341 (662.16) *Ceinél Conaill*. See note to 336. Cf. *Fél.* 136; *GRSH* 40; DF 697b.

342 *Ceinél Conaill*. See note to 336. Cf. *GRSH* 40.

343 (662.20) *Ceinél Conaill*. See note to 336. Cf. *GRSH* 40; DF 698c.

344 *Clann Cholmáin*. See note to 336. Cf. *GRSH* 54.

345 *Ceinél Conaill*. See note to 336. Cf. *GRSH* 43.

346 *Ceinél Conaill* (*Ceinél Lugdach*). See note to 336. Cf. *GRSH* 40; DF 698b.

347 (662.29) *Ceinél Conaill* (*Ceinél Bóguine*). See note to 336. Note the omission of *m. Dichubnius* (?) in 348. Cf. B 85b; *GRSH* 42; DF 698c.

348 *Ceinél Conaill* (*Ceinél Bóguine*). See notes to 336, 347. Cf. *GRSH* 40.

349 (160, 662.53.55) *Ceinél Lóegaire*. Cf. *Anecd.* 3 (1910) 2; *GRSH* 49; DF 706b.

350 (662.89, 694) *Airgialla?* Compare with 694 which is added in LM only and which, as well as giving Lommán a slightly different descent, assigns him to Áth Truim. In 662.89 and elsewhere the saint is attached to the Airgialla. Cf. *Fél.* 68; *GRSH* 71; DF 714bb.

351 (463, 662.32) *Ceinél Énna*. Cf. *Fél.* 114; *Anecd.* 3 (1910) 2; *GRSH* 58; DF 708.

352 *Ceinél Eogain*. The only other source for the pedigree (*GRSH* 47) adds some names, including a different name for the saint's father.

353 (585) *Airgialla*. Cf. Lc 81Rd; *GRSH* 67; DF 712c.

354 (500, 662.214) *Uí Echach Coba*. Cf. *GRSH* 98 (where the saint is confused with the saint of 398); DF 732b.

355 I have no other reference to the descent of these saints.

356 *Uí Echach Muman*. For a discussion of the pedigree's implications see *JCHAS* 82 (1977) 67, 79. Cf. *GRSH* 115.

357 (564, 662.184) *Ulaid*. The addition of *m. Droido* (f-f) in RLc[1], which gives a Loígse character to the pedigree, is probably an error. Cf. *GRSH* 97; DF 728a.

358 (537, 662.142) *Dál Fiatach*. MHLa's addition (c) is the more usual reading (*CGH* 286 etc.). Cf. *Fél.* 116; Lc 130Rc; *GRSH* 83; DF 723e.

359 (581) *Corco Roíde*. The only other place in which Echros is attached to Molaisse is in the Lc version of 707.591. In both instances the scribe, Giolla Íosa Mac Fhirbhisigh, is showing his local interest.

360 (456, 588, 662.234 (BLc)) *Cianachta*. Cf. *GRSH* 123; DF 742c.

361 *Ciarraige*. For the same alternation *Dísertach/Dísertán* see 707.670 where *Mochromma* is given as *Mochummae*. Cf. *CGH* 301; *GRSH* 108.

362 (439, 662.199) *Conmaicne*. Cf. *Anal. Bolland.* 46 (1928) 120; *Fél.* 96; La 9a (see *Celtica* 5 (1960) 71); *GRSH* 106.

363 (662.206) *Dál Conchobair, Dál nAraide*. The omission in R (b) is due to the wish of the scribe to leave space for the large initial beginning the following pedigree. This was misunderstood by Lc[1] which attached *Conchobair* to the following pedigree (c). With M's addition (c) compare 722.30 (cf. B 195a). For Ultán's specific attachment to Dál Conchobair of Brega see *M.Tall.* 68 (cf. *Onom.* 332). Cf. *GRSH* 101; DF 733e, 734a.

364 Lc[1] (a) adds *.i. Fiacha* which, for the same reason as given in 363, belongs to the previous pedigree (119). The saints have a Tír Amalgaid context (*V.Trip.*140, *Ir. texts* 3 (1931) 4, 6).

365 (662.17) *Ceinél Conaill*. Compare 342, 345 above, where Mac Laisre and Séigíne are respectively included in the secular parts of pedigrees. Cf. B 85a; *GRSH* 39, 41, 43; DF 697b.

366 I have no other reference to these saints. Cf. *Ir. texts* 3 (1931) 80.

367 In RLc[1] (b-b) is written as a separate entry. Other than that of Crunnmáel (273) I cannot identify the descent of these saints. Cf. *Ir. texts* 3 (1931) 80.

368 (617) *Airgialla*. Here begin the additions to M etc. One may assume that *Áedán* followed *mc* in La's exemplar, whence *Caedín* (a). Cf. *GRSH* 82 (where Colgan inserts it, by mistake, under Dál Fiatach); DF 716a.

369 La's *Moboe* (b) is the correct reading. *Lada* (c) is an error for *Alla*. See also notes to 129, 132. Cf. *Fél.*[2] 182.

370 (639, 662.144) *Dál Fiatach*. Cf. *GRSH* 83; DF 723a.

371 *Ulaid?*. I have no other reference to these saints.

372 *Ulaid*. Cf. *Lis.Lives* 138; DF 731a.

373 *Eoganachta*. R¹'s addition (a) is more correct. Cf. *CGH* 197, 217.

374 (591) *Dál nAraide*. If, as seems likely, the saint's name is an error for Laisrén, then compare Molaisse m. Colmáin (707.607).

375 *Uí Briúin*. Cf. DF 710f.

376 (503, 662.70) *Uí Ḟiachrach*. Cf. *BNÉ* 1, 312; Lc 71Rb (= *Hy Fiach*. 36); *GRSH* 61; DF 711a.

377 *Airgialla*. Cf. DF 714cc (written *Cran?*).

378 (600) *Dál Cais*. Cf. M 33Ra; Lc 224Vb, 230Rb, *GRSH* 119; DF 738a.

379 Compare 735 and *Fél.*² 102. See also *Plummer VSH* 1, lxiii (note). La's version is also published by Grosjean in *RC* 49 (1932) 183.

380 With 1 compare 722.64, B 136b and L 390b. Another version of 2 is to be found in Laud 615, 135 where it is attributed to Cuimín.

381 For his descent from Bretain Chorn see also *Fél.*² 87. A lengthy account of Cairnech, including a version of this entry from DF 749b, is given in J. H. Todd, *The Irish Version of the Historia Britonum of Nennius* (Ir. Arch. Soc., Dublin, 1848) ci-cxi. The pedigree given here is borrowed from Cainnech (123); for a variant pedigree see 488, 662.88.

382 (572) I cannot identify the descent. For Connla m. Cuinn Chétchathaig see *CGH* 130, where he is mentioned without descendants, not inappropriately in view of the tradition in *Echtra Condla* that he disappeared without trace (*ZCP* 18 (1930) 193ff).

383 (545) *Uí Ḟiachrach*. For another version of both quatrain (3) and pedigree (1) see *Ir. texts* 3 (1931) 3; Cf. *BNÉ* 1, 312; Lc 71Ra (= *Hy Fiach*. 34-6); *GRSH* 62; DF 711b.

384 *Ciarraige Luachra*. For Brénainn see 127 above. Cf. *GRSH* 107; DF 729c.

385 (602) *Uí Ḟiachrach*. Cf. *Ir.texts* 3 (1931) 4; *Hy Fiach*. 54, DF 711b.

386 *Uí Ḟiachrach*. Cf. DF 711b.

387 *Uí Bairrche*. Cf. *CGH* 46; M 11Va (the possible source).

388 (464) *Sogain*. Cf. *GRSH* 99; DF 737a.

389 (595) *Conmaicne*. Cf. *GRSH* 105; DF 729cc.

390 (596) *Uí Ailella*. Cf. *GRSH* 64; DF 712a.

391 (597) *Uí Ailella*. Cf. *GRSH* 64; DF 712a.

392 *Uí Ḟiachrach*. Here both M and La agree in interrupting the Uí Ailella sequence. Cf. DF 711d.

393 (598, 599) *Uí Ailella*. R¹'s addition (i) is mistaken: Mainchín of Limerick is regularly attached to the Dál Cais (202). However, Molua's *vita* (*Plummer VSH* 2, 208) refers to the church of the seven sons of Cóelbad, apparently in a Limerick context. Cf. *GRSH* 64 (Feradach only); DF 712a.

394 If *Gleit|h|nichán* (5) is the same as the father of *Flann . . . toísech Cloinne Murchada* who died in 953 (AFM), then this is a late composition. In character the text is not unlike the tract on 'Four saints' edited by J. G. O'Keeffe in *Ir. texts* 3 (1931) 1-8. K. W. Nicholls points out to me that all the families named have connexions with the area around Annaghdown.

395 (604) *Uí Ḟiachrach*. Cf. *GRSH* 55; DF 704b.

396 (605) *Ceinél Conaill*. In R¹(a), as in M, this entry follows that on Dochonna m. Echach (83). Cf. DF 698b.

397 (625) This entry is closely related to 722.23-26. Compare also 691; 726; *Fél.*² 99; B 84b. The original source is the Appendix to Adamnán's *Vita Columbae*. Here Adamnán's *moccu Céin* is reflected by *mac Coichinn*.

398 *Dál nAraide*. In La the reference to Athracht's brother (e-e) is attached by mistake to the previous pedigree (690.10); Grosjean misread d'Atro*cht* (f) as Datrosi. Cf. *V.Trip* 108; *GRSH* 98 (conflated with 354).

399 (609) At 275 this saint is provided with a local Uí Cheinselaig pedigree. Compare the text of *Baile Finnachta* (*ZCP* 13 (1921) 25-27). Cf. DF 709.1.

400 I cannot identify the families named in this pedigree.

401 (610) *Uí Briúin*. She may be the same Étáin as is noticed under 510. Cf. *GRSH* 59.

402 These are also known as the disciples of Finnian of Clonard. For a discussion of the list by P. Grosjean see *Anal. Bolland.* 73 (1955) 316-22. To his reference add *SG* 47 (cf. 25) and 705.1-10 below; cf. also 712.3-14. Áed mac Crimthainn frequently refers to members of the group as *apstail* (23, 117, 127, 208, 241, 317). Cf. *ZCP* 7 (1910) 299; 10 (1915) 409.

403 *Múscraige Tíre.* The father's name is more generally given as Dub Rea (*M.Tall.* 5, 80; *Fél.*[2] 33; cf. 670.21). Cf. Lc 107Rd.

404 The pedigree appears to be fragmentary. I have no other reference to it.

405 The descent is shared by 406 but I cannot identify it.

406 See note to 405.

407 Found only in H this entry refers to one of the most prominent of the eleventh-century reforming bishops, Domnall Úa hÉnna, who died in 1098. The notice of his death in AU is extremely laudatory. His connexion with the Dál Cais points to a Killaloe provenance for H (see Introduction §14). See also D. Ó Corráin in *Ériu* 24 (1973) 57.

408 I cannot place the descent but this is probably the saint of Athleague; see also B 100b[2] 21 ff. *Fergus* follows *Setna* on a new line as if to begin a new pedigree.

409 *Ceinél Conaill?* Cf. *GRSH* 39?

410 Compare Lc 69V[a] 1-10 (entitled *Leabar Fiathrach*) (cf. B 104cd) from which the here illegible church names are given in the index. B 104 reads: '. . . *Concann o Chill Achaidh. Cruimter oc Belait Oena. Et Finncan o Brig Gabann 7r Ui Fothaigh 7 Firu Mhuidhe. Raidhriu o Thuaim Srutra for bru Ṡuca. Et Failbhi Find o Raith. Dachua o Chill Eo* . . .'. See also note to 78. Cf. DF 715b.

411 *Luigne* (*Corco Fer Trí*). The illegible patronymic probably read *Baíth* (*Báetáin*) (cf. *M.Tall.* 61, C. m. Baeith of Druimm Ráithe, possibly Drumrat, barony of Corann, near Leyney from Luigne, county Sligo).

412 *Luigne.* I have no other reference to this saint's pedigree, but the saint intended is no doubt Findbarr of Druim Coluim Chille (Dromcolumb), barony of Tirerrill, county Sligo.

413 *Luigne.* I have no other reference to this entry.

414 *Eoganachta.* Furudrán is not among the six sons listed for Cairpre Crom in *Anecd.* 3 (1910) 61.

415 *Mugdorna.* The only addition to La, this entry seems related to 496. The maternal name (a-a) is a misreading of Bassar (721.1; 722.14). *Renanus altum* seems corrupt; read *renatus?*

416-661 For a discussion of the provenance, sources and composition of this recension see the Introduction (§15).

416 With the addition in La (c) compare 1.1.2.4 above. Compare also Lc's text of 1.4 at 654 below.

420 Both forms of the paternal name seem incorrect. Compare 196 above and 465 below.

421 Compare 315 where the Cianachta descent is in H[1] only.

422 La's alternative descent (c) is elsewhere the rule; that through Tigernmas is confined to H in 125 above.

424 I have no other reference to this saint whose name appears corrupt.

425 The descent through Eochu is only in LbM in 63 above. See also note to 426.

426 Omitted from the *Recensio Maior,* Dallán's pedigree is elsewhere found in *BNÉ* 1, 265, §229 where, significantly, it again accompanies that of Máedóc (425). See also 633 below. Cf. *GRSH* 67; DF 712c. A conflicting Dál Fiatach descent is also found (*CGH* 407). In the Rawlinson B 502 version of Amra Choluim Chille (*RC* 20 (1899) 134), Dallán's pedigree includes the patronymic *Alla* (corrected to *Calla* by Stokes on the evidence of later manuscripts). I have to thank Máire Herbert for this reference.

431 The reference to Conall Gulban is mistaken. Compare 26 above.

434 In *Gorm, M.Don.,* at July 13, Eirnín is set down as of Inis Chaín. *GRSH* 40 traces Ernán m. Eoghain to Fergus m. Conaill Gulban but Colgan gives his day as Jan. 1 (cf. *Acta SS Hib.* 7-9).

436 In 135 the first version of the descent (b-b) is in Lb only.

437 La's version (a-a) belongs to 438 where the text is missing in both manuscripts. A faulty exemplar is the probable reason for this.

438 The father's name is as in H(LbB)'s version of 185. See also note to 437. Díchu (La[1]) is Diamrán's grandfather in 185.

439 The substitution of *Fraich* for *Finnchaim* of 362 may be due to 442?

443 Of the two descents only La (c-c) agrees with 149.

444 La's reading may be explained as follows. In the exemplar, which Lc abbreviated, the descent read *Scíre ingen Eogain m. Canann m. Ailella m. Fergusa m. Echach Muigmedoin.* Having reached *Ailella,* La continued, through homeoteleuton, with *Cethaig* etc. of the following entry, which it otherwise duly omits.

445 See note to 444.

446 The descent differs from that of 317 but compare 152 (Dabiu m. Comgaill) and *GRSH* 96 (Dabiu . . . qui et Mobius . . .).

448 La's version (c-c) agrees only with R^1 15(37)Ra in 229 above.

449 The 'correct' descent is given at 526 below (cf. 207).

453 See note to 21.

455 The paternal name in 195 is omitted here in favour of the grandfather's name.

458 La's *m.*(a-a) is of course an error.

462 This descent for Cairech |Dergáin|, which makes her a sister of Énna of Árainn (67), is not found in the *Recensio Maior* (110, 325), but cf. *Fél.* 70; *GRSH* 70.

466 Omitted from the *Recensio Maior,* Ciarán's pedigree is elsewhere found in *GRSH* 99.

468 The descent differs from 237 above.

469 La's text (b-b) belongs to 470 which it otherwise duly omits.

470 See note to 469.

473 Compare M's version of 201. For *Maiccaim (Cai)* read *Micain.*

474 This is a conflation of 16 and 42 above, with readings closest to M.

476 *Domáedóc* (cf. Lc 54Vb) is intended for *Domongóc* (40).

481 This agrees only with H's version of 49.

483 No doubt *m.* was omitted before *Imrois* in the common source. La's *m.* (a-a) is a mistake.

486 The initial *c* of *Colcan* was originally taken from the preceding *macc.*

488 Omitted from the *Recensio Maior.* Cf. 722.29 below and *GRSH* 7.

490 For the alternation Findchad/Findchú compare Finnchú of Cell Lerga (Erga) (*Celtica* I (1946) 65) with Finnchad of the same church (*Misc. Celt. Soc.* 80, *SG* 23-4).

491 *Airmedaich* should read *Feradaig* as in 20 and 557. I have no other reference to the saint as Murchan (Murchud).

492 Lc's *Mair* (b) belongs after *Erc* (see 206).

493 La's addition (a) has the effect of giving Brénainn a Conmaicne descent.

495 I have no other example of the article with *Gaibréin.* The three minims shared by *m* and *in* could have brought about the confusion.

497 The text is very much as in M's version of 133.

502 Omitted from the *Recensio Maior.* Cf. *GRSH* 123 (where Colgan notes: *multa in hac desunt*).

507 Omitted from the *Recensio Maior,* Conall Costamail, whose affiliations appear to have been both pagan and secular, has an ancestral role assigned to him in the Conaille genealogies (*CGH* 154).

508 Omitted from the *Recensio Maior,* Dub Dúin of the Cianachta does not appear to be recorded elsewhere. His church gave its name to the parish of Aghanloo, county Derry, formerly in Cianachta Glinne Geimhin (*BCC* §146).

510 In view of the similar descent Étaín is probably identical with the saint of that name at 401 and 610.

512 In La, due perhaps to a faulty exemplar (cf. the corrupt *Eaxpr̄* for *Epscop* in 513), *m. Cormaic* (b-b) is attached to 513.

513 Regarding the corruption (a) see note to 512.

515 For Fintan in place of Findchú (78, 320) see also 707.395.

519 *Chollain* (influenced by *Colla?*) is for *Colgan* (55).

521 The paternal name should read *Ercada* (286).

524 Manchán is mentioned in Lb only at 13 above.

525 This is again related to 13 (cf. 524), with some additions. Lc's *ceithri* (c) includes *Cunter* which is no doubt a corruption of *Cruimther.* For Mianach see also *GRSH* 41 (cf. *M.Tall.* 56).

526 See note to 449.

527 La's *Trea* (a) is the more correct reading (see 76).

531 The saint intended is Mošenóc m. Sencháin m. Sinill (291).

538 Énna for Ernaín is found only in M at 16 above. La's addition of *m. Eogain* (a) is correct.

539 Omitted from the *Recensio Maior,* Garbán is twice entered in this recension (cf. 573). Cf. *GRSH* 55; DF 704b.

545 With La's version of the maternal name (d) compare *BNÉ* 1, 312 §2 (*Ferabla ingine Dima Duibh*).

546 La's readings suggest a faulty exemplar. With *Araide* (b-b) for *Roeide* compare R[1]'s reading at 155 (l).

549 This Berchán is probably identical with Mobí (*al.* Berchan) m. Beonaid (266 etc); see 662.111.

550 The paternal name should read Cáelcharna.

553 Omitted from the *Recensio Maior,* Gregóir's pedigree is elsewhere found in Lc 107Rd; B 145c; R[1] 45(23)V; *GRSH* 78; DF 721c. See also *Fél.* 96; *RC* 42 (1925) 120-1, 140-2, 151; 49 (1932) 183.

554 Also omitted from the *Recensio Maior.* Cf. Lc 108 Rcd; *GRSH* 78; DF 721c.

555 For the paternal name read *Meic Craith* (cf.200).

560 For *Deaga* read *Deicill* (cf. 263)?

561 For *Bronaig* read *Branduib* (240).

564 For *Faibraide* read *Faibrig* (357).

567 For *Dumain* read *Dúnáin* (190).

572 *Ailella* is an error for *Cairill* (382).

573 See note to 539.

591 At 374 above, where it occurs in M only, the saint's name is written Lairen and his descent is traced to Fiachu Araide. Cf. 707.607?

593 The paternal name is more correctly Ailill (m. Dúnlaing) (246).

596 La's *m. Ecain* (b) probably reflects *m. Cáecháin* of 390.

601 Omitted from the *Recensio Maior.*

607 Only in MR[1]'s version of 123 is the paternal descent given as here.

610 A doublet of 510 (see above). The father's name presumably corresponds to *Ligine* (410).

614 If we read *i Conaille* for *7 Conaille,* then the number of sons should be three. Druim Inasclainn, Diarmuid's church, lay in Conaille. On the other hand, *GRSH* (54) has a Cú Aille m. Caolcharna, whence the genitive Conaille.

618 Not in the *Recensio Maior.* See 722.4, the source of this entry, where the reading *Muman* (recte *Breg*) is found only in La (c).

621 Omitted from the *Recensio Maior.* Cf. B 84b 10: *GRSH* 38; DF 700a.

623 In La only and omitted from the *Recensio Maior.* Cf. *GRSH* 41.

624 For *Caithleand* read *Faithlenn* (235).

626 Omitted from the *Recensio Maior. GRSH* 39 and DF 698b have *Droigin* for *Odrain* (*Dogair*) of this entry.

630 Despite its superficially different readings this entry may have been taken from a (corrupt?) copy of 690.8. See also note to 631.

631 The source of this entry was clearly a copy of 690.10.

633 Omitted from the *Recensio Maior,* this is a doublet of 426 above.

634 The saint's name should read *Aíthgen,* that of his father *Ail* (61).

635 This saint may reflect Cruimther Cenannán of 61.2 above. But see also *GRSH* 73, DF 715b.

637 For *Meancra* read *Meic Craith* (200).

638 Possibly *7 Lemain* reflects *ingena Nemnann* of 239.

640 For *Muici* read *Moiche* (278).

641 Here the descent differs from that of 181.7 and 558 above.

642 La's addition of *Baedan* (b), which brings the number of sons to seven, no doubt reflects the *Baethíne* of 243.1.

644 Here *Fiachra* is omitted before *Goll.* Cf. 292 above.

646 Not in the *Recensio Maior.* La's omission (b-b) represents the normal version. Cf. *Misc. Hag. Hib.* 100-1; *GRSH* 118; DF 740a.

647 Omitted from the *Recensio Maior.* For *Dimain* read *Dúnáin.* Cf. *GRSH* 120; DF 743a.

649 Only in H's version of 118 is *Oiblén* given as the father, rather than as the grandfather, of the saint. La's *Fidra* (b) is the more correct reading.

650 For *Thiri Da Glas* read *Droma Glas* (310). La's reading (b-b) is more correct.

652 The source of this entry, which is not in the *Recensio Maior,* was probably a copy of 722.66. La's additions (b, c) are in the text of 722.66.

653 Only three of Dubthach's sons (the last three named here) are listed in 305 above.

654 La adds this entry to 416 above.

655 In La this is joined to 656. With 657-61 this entry is part of a series related to 703 below.

656 See note to 655. For Lc's *Sochar* read with La *Dar* (*Der*) (247).

657-61 See note to 655.

658 For *Dima* read *Gnia* (703.6).

661 At this point, without interruption, La begins its version of the *Recensio Maior*.

662 See *Irish texts* 3 (1931) 40-78, where the text of Cúchoigríche Ó Cléirigh's recension, which forms the main text here, is also edited by P. Grosjean from the Brussels MS, Bibliothéque Royale, No. 2542-2543. In addition to the text given here, Grosjean's edition contains the author's preface, notes and some attestations from another manuscript. With 243 quatrains, numbered 1 (-200-200^{b})-242, Brux. is the longest version of the metrical recension. B (The Book of Ballymote) and Lc (The Book of Lecan) have c.170 and c.176 quatrains respectively (cf. Plummer, *Misc. Hag. Hib.* 227-8 where a slightly greater number of quatrains is given for each). Unlike Brux., neither B nor Lc provides its sections with titles. Both manuscripts, however, introduce sections by using large capitals and Lc regularly adds construe marks in the margins. The notes and calendar information added by Ó Cléirigh to his recension are not published here on account of their practical identity with the notes added under the relevant dates of the Martyrology of Donegal (cf. J.Hennig, *Éigse* 6 (1949) 50-55). A discussion of the interrelationships of the three versions is contained in the Introduction (§17). Marks of lenition on *c* and *t*, which the scribe often omitted, have been added silently to this edition of Brux.

18ef Brux.'s reference to *Síl Luigdech . . . ua Fergusa* is incorrect. The reference should be to *Síl Ninneda . . . m. Fergusa* as in BLc.

22b Adlann († 950) is otherwise in *GRSH* 38; DF 698b.

28 Odrán is otherwise in *GRSH* 43.

29d Malachias is in Brux. only.

45-6 Most of the material in these quatrains is taken from 690 below.

64a Possibly Áedgen m. Lugair (43).

68a Compare 722.9 for Corcair, who is omitted from 37. Cf. *GRSH* 65; DF 711b.

69b B's reading is correct.

74a *Sosar* (*Soror*) derives from the corrupt BLcLb version of 90; L has *Fáeliu soror eius*. Cf. *GRSH* 61, 63.

77bd For Cummin and Aedhan see also *GRSH* 61, 62, 63; DF 711bb.

78 For Triallach and Derbiled see also *Ir. texts* 3 (1931) 4; *GRSH* 62, 63; DF 711bb.

80b For *Ernin* read *Cruitín* (77).

83 Máel Dub is otherwise in *Fél.* 224; *GRSH* 60; DF 710h.

86b For *Damnad* read *Damán* (56).

88a For *Becan* read *Breccan* (722.29).

89 Lommán is given a different descent at 350 and, with less variation, at 694.

104b Conamail is otherwise in *GRSH* 67; DF 712c.

105a *Colla* (*Alla*); *Ailella* may be the correct reading (633).

110cd B gives the correct reading.

111b BLc's *Bocain* is elsewhere only in 549.

112b Colman is in Brux. only.

114b Bairrfinn is otherwise in *GRSH* 74; DF 718c.

115a For Díma see also 670.88 and *GRSH* 75.

131b For *Mioncraith* read *Meic Craith*. Cf. 637.

132, 133 The saints here are taken from 665 below.

135b Sétna m. Nemain is otherwise in *GRSH* 81; DF 721a.

136a Colmán is otherwise in *GRSH* 80; DF 721b.

143d Munnu is otherwise in *GRSH* 84.

154 Brux.'s text is based on Lb which also omits the correct patronymic, *m. Anfothaig* (183).

158b As in Lb, *Meic Iair m.* (253) is omitted before *Eirc*.

183a BLc's reading (d-d) seems more correct.

190a Mochuarócc is otherwise in *GRSH* 110, DF 734b.

200a *Mochta* is an error for *Niatach* (146).

207d *Mochta* (*Luccain*). Compare Lb's reading at 98.2.

219a Beccán is otherwise in *GRSH* 115; DF 740a, 742a.

228b For Fraochnat see also 647.

663 The first of a large number of miscellaneous sections added by Áed mac Crimthainn to his recension of the pedigrees of the saints, this list, like others, is clearly not a random composition. The connecting thread is, however, difficult to unravel on account of the obscurity of the places and saints in the list. The emphasis appears to alternate between Mide (Westmeath), which is represented in 7-10, parts of Kildare (3, 4, 11) and Offaly (5). As such the text mirrors associations found elsewhere. Thus, Eitchén (3), who is attached to Ticknevin, co. Kildare, is more normally connected with Clonfad of the bar. of Farbill in Westmeath (181.7 etc). Also, in the *betha* of Colmán m. Luacháin (K. Meyer ed., Todd Lect. Ser. 17, 1911, §35), Eitchén is brought together with Mochua m. Nemain, the eponym of the church attached here to him.

The inter-association of these places is, of course, also characteristic of Brigit's cult, as her Lives and 670 below show. Fidnat (4), for instance, is entered again in 670.14. A Brigidine connexion may also underlie 1, 6, 11, and it is tempting to assume that, as with 670, the present tract represents a register of churches and saints connected with Ḃrigit's cult.

For another copy of the tract see DF 751b, which is taken from Lb.

663.1 If Kilcrow, bar. of Narragh and Rheban, co. Kildare, is intended, then a Brigidine connexion probably underlies the entry (cf. 670.53.54 etc. for a number of entries concerning churches in that area).

2 I have no other reference to the Moccu Miadchon. Domnach Feimin is identified in *Onom.* with Domnach Mór of Mag Feimin, now Donaghmore near Clonmel.

3 See introductory note above. In *Betha Colmáin Meic Luacháin* §35 it is stated that Cluain Ḟota and Tech Mochua formed a 'single church' (*aenchill*). Compare also the parish of Kilmacnevan which bounds Kilbixy (see 10 below) in Westmeath.

4 See introductory note above. For further references to Ceinél Ucha see *CGH* 21, 23, 49, 341. These references point to Kildare, but I cannot suggest a more exact location.

5 Cf. 708.67.74. Géisill, whence Drummat Géisille, is now Geashil par. in Offaly. It was in the deanery of Offaly but in the dioc. of Kildare. I cannot identify Cell Chalma, but see *Onom.* s.v.

6 The connexions again appear to be with Brigit, through Clothach who shares his feast with Condláed of Kildare (*M.Tall.* 39), and through Mac Caille who, while I cannot identify his *dísert,* placed the veil on Brigit according to Cogitosus (D. Ó hAodha, *Bethu Brigte* (Dublin, 1978) xiii) and who, in 722.16, is named as one of the children of Darerca.

7 P. Walsh, *The Placenames of Westmeath* (Dublin,1957) 224, mentions Kenny church, 'seems = *Ceann eich,* or *Ceanna each,'* in the parish of Mullingar. Also in this parish is the tl. of Clongawny from Cluain Ghamhna, the name of the church in the next entry.

8 *Cf. Betha Colmáin Maic Luacháin* §9: *Gabaiss . . . Treide |ingen Luacháin m. Leda| ⁊ Brogel ⁊ Buidnech hi Cill Cluana Gamna.* Clearly, the reference is to the saint entered here; one or other of the forms of her name, however, is obviously corrupt. Cluain Gamna (cf. 7), now in the par. of Mullingar, lay in Asal (now the bar. of Moyashel) in Westmeath.

9 Asal, now Moyashel, is the area also involved in 7, 8. I cannot identify either the saint or the church.

10 The church is now known as Kilbixy, bar. of Moygoish, co. Westmeath (P. Walsh, *op. cit.* (above 7) 299-302). In the adjoining parish of Kilmacnevan (cf. 3 above) there was a dedication to Brigit (*ibid,* 98, 305).

11 Fid Eoin appears to have lain in the bar. of Carbury, co. Kildare; but see above 161.

12 The reference to Ceinél Ucha (4 above) in *CGH* 21 mentions hUí Ḟolaing (whence Tír Ḟolaing here?). Cf. Róinsech of Tech Maíle Achaid (670.20).

13 I cannot identify the persons or church mentioned here, unless Colmán m. Diarmata, eponymous ancestor of the Clann Cholmáin of Westmeath, is intended.

664 If the equation of Longobardi with Moccu Baird (722.15) is early and genuine, as E. MacNeill (*PRIA* 29C4, p.75n) assumed, then the tradition represented by this entry must predate considerably the earliest extant reference to it, which appears to be *V.Trip.* 80, 82. For Restitutus see also *Lib. Hymn.* 1, 1,4, *M.Tall.* 100. Cf. DF 751b. See also A. Anscombe, 'The Longobardic Origin of St. Sechnall, *Ériu* 4 (1908) 74-90. B's *Sanc* (f) is from a misreading of the suspension over *c* in *sac̄*.

665 With the exception of Senán (Corco Baiscinn; see 228) and Fínán Cam (Corco Duibne; see 211), all the saints here listed either have churches in one or other of the Múscraige territories or belong to that family. In Lc 107Rd (= B 145cd) the pedigrees of Lachtáine, Ciar Ascad and Odrán are given together with that of Grigóir of Rome, of the Corco Duibne (533), under the Uí Chainnig of Múscraige (Introduction §12). Cf. Book of Lismore 147Vb (= 1-7 here); *GRSH* 78-9: DF 720d.

Compare Lb's addition (2^{l}) with *Fél.*^{2} 50, and its other addition (3^{r}) with 666.1 below. The *do* added in BLcLb (4^{c}) makes up the correct syllabic length of the line.

666 Tairbín is also the patronymic accompanying Lachtaíne in the entry on him under Uí Chainnig of the Múscraige in Lc 107Rd (see 665). However, none of the other saints mentioned here accompanies Lachtaíne. P. Power (*Crichad an Chaoilli* (Cork, 1932) 117) identifies Áth na Cell with a ford on the Blackwater near Longfield's Bridge, two miles west of Mallow, but none of the local church-names commemorates the saints listed here. To arrive at seven sons, Sinell Cáelán (g) must be taken as one. Five only of the seven daughters are named. Compare Lb's addition (a) with 212 above. Lc (z) joins this entry to 667. Cf. DF 752a.

667 Through this, and the following entry (668), a connexion is established between Tír Dá Glas (Colum ua Crimthainn) and the Uí Dróna of Carlow: Lemdruimm is now Lorum, the name of a parish in the bar. of Idrone East, co. Carlow. In Lb, 667 follows 668. Cf. DF 752a.

668 See note to 667. Ruidén m. Lainnéin is to be identified with Ruidian (Ruidnén) m. Flainnéin m. Aduair of Síl Ailténe of Uí Dróna (*CGH* 350). Tír Chróinín and Lecc na Sinnach probably refer to places near Lemdruimm (Lorum) in Idrone. I cannot identify Semplán, but for the occurrence of the name in an ecclesiastical context among the Múscraige Tíre of north Tipperary see B 141b 21, b^{3} 47. Cf. DF 752a.

669 While *da mac* only is preceded by a mark of reference, it may be that the three entries should be taken separately. Lb, however, joins 2 to 1. In 3 the names Santán and Sanctán surely referred originally to a single saint. Cf. DF 752a.

670 Preserved only in L and in its three derivative manuscripts, BLcLb (from one of which, i.e. Lb, it was later transcribed by Mac Fhirbhisigh, DF 752a-753b), the list of virgins, not all of whom were females, subject to Brigit was probably compiled by Áed mac Crimthainn himself; he had a close association with Clonenagh, a Fothairt foundation, and would thus have had a great interest in the family's best-known saint (cf. Introduction §2). Much of the topographical detail of the tract now defies identification. It is clear, however, that, as might be expected, the principal areas covered are Kildare and Westmeath/Longford. Churches in places as far apart as Sligo (42, 43) and Wicklow/Wexford (85, 86) are also included, however, and one wonders how their inmates could have been regarded as *subiectae* of Brigit's. At 36 a mark of reference indicates the beginning of a new section (whence Stokes's publication in *Lis.Lives* 336 of 1-35 only), but since the entries which follow are equally connected with the saint, no distinction is made here. Notes are given only where it seemed possible to identify the church. Lb (20a) separates the title, 35 and part of 36 from the remaining text.

670.1 There is a Kilcullen in Kildare but not in the barony of Carbury. Cairpre, now the bar. of Granard, co. Longford, is a more likely location. Cf. *M.Tall.* 13 (= Jan. 28, and thus close to Brigit's feast), *Cainer ingen Chruthnechain m. Laigne i fail Ḟobair.*

2 Unidentified. *Onom.* s. Cluain Chiaráin notes a Clonkeeran in par. Mylerstown, bar. of Carbury, co. Kildare, but the long penultimate syllable is against identification with Cluain Choirinn.

3 The context in which 'Induae'' and 'Indiu' figure in *B.Brigte* (§35) points to Tethbe, as does the descent from Breccán m. Brénainn (*recte* Brénainn m. Breccáin, *CGH* 162), but cf. Kildangan, co. Kildare.

670.4 If the same Fergus as in 5 is intended, then perhaps Bríg is the eponym of Kilbride, par. of Abbeylara (from Lethráith), bar. of Granard, co. Longford.

5 Lethráith, now the par. of Abbeylara, co. Longford (see 4). Cf. *M.Tall* 5, *Ingena Fergnae . . . Brig Corpre*. With the suggested reading *Fuinche* compare *Gorm.*, *M.Don.* Dec.11, Funech of Cluain Brónaig (cf. 6 below).

6 See 5. Possibly a fifth daughter (*cóicir*) of Fergna. Cluain Brónaig is now Clonbroney, bar. of Granard, co. Longford.

7 Unidentified. There may be a connexion between Necht and the mother of Íte who is given in 722.13 as Feidelm, sister of Fedbair of 8 below, and in 722.52 as Necht.

8 See note to 7. In 722.13 Fedbair is assigned to Botha Ech Roichnig, obviously the same place as here. More precisely, her church is given as Cúil Úgaine in Mag Luigne (cf. Bríg of Mag Luinge, 708.13). In *Gorm.* 212, she is placed in Tír Rátha. None of these places has been identified.

11 Uí Bresail is the name of Brigit's own family in Uí Ḟailge (*CGH* 84). Here, however, the reference is to what is now Brazil tl. in the parish of Killossery, co. Dublin. Brazil appears as Obrassell in Norman documents. Also, Lassair and Cell Lasra appear in what seems a Brega context in Brigit's Lives (*B.Brigte* 16, §§44-5: *Lis.Lives* 44-5). Stokes (*Lis.Lives* 377) states 'now Killasher', but I cannot place this. The *garman*-motif occurs in *Lis.Lives* 50 (cf. *Lib.Hymn* 124) without reference to Lassair.

13 P. Walsh (*Placenames* etc. 167) suggests 'Incha Croan' in the bar. of Fartullagh, an area closely connected with the cult of Brigit.

14 See 663.4.

18 There were a number of Fotharta: if 'Lutta virgo' of Druimm Dairbrech (*M.Tall.* 38) is intended, then we possibly have to do with the Fothairt near Brí Éile in co. Offaly (*Onom.* 362: 'druim dairbrech').

21 Ciar ingen Duib Rea is listed in *M.Tall.* 5, 80: in *Fél.*[2] 33 she is identified with Ciar of Cell Chéire, now Kilkeary, co. Tipperary.

25 Tuaim Néill is unidentified but, for Cell Ingen Fiachna, compare 289 above.

26 Perhaps Lusk in co. Dublin?

27 Cf. 76 above. Artrea is in the bar. of Dungannon, co. Tyrone.

28 *M.Tall.* 84 (cf. *Fél.*[2] 159) places these saints in Cell Maignenn (Cell na nIngen) near Dublin.

29 Cf. *B.Brigte* 15 (§42), '. . . *oc Cill Ṡuirdd i ndesciurt Bregh*'. Probably Swords in co. Dublin, but see also Index of Place and Tribal Names.

30 Compare 124 above, which implies that their *bráthair* was Brénainn of Birr. The place-name is unidentified. For Crón see again 68 below. Cf. *M.Tall.* 54.

31 Mag Trega was in Tethbae (*Onom.* 531, 'm. trea').

32 The place is unidentified but compare 47 below.

33 Cluain Moéscnae was in Fir Tulach (Fartullagh), co. Westmeath, (*M.Tall.* 114) and is identified by P. Walsh (*Placenames* etc. 164) with Kylmisken, a local name now obsolete. The place is elsewhere connected with Brigit (*Lib. Hymn.* 119n).

36 Stokes (*Lis.Lives* 336), who was no doubt influenced by the mark of reference preceding this entry, omits 36-88 from his edition of the tract. It is clear, however, from such entries as 38, 78 and 86 that the author's concern continues to lie with saints affiliated to Brigit. To judge by notes q, s-s etc., the derivative versions, BLcLb, derive from a corrupt exemplar. On the other hand, their reading of *mathair* as *mac* (k) may be correct. I cannot identify the churches here but the connexion with Uí Dega points to the deanery of Oday in the bar. of Gorey, co. Wexford or to the barony of Ida, co. Kilkenny.

37 Feib (Feibe) lay in Loígis (*CGH* 90); so the church is probably Donaghmore in the bar. of Clandonagh, near which is Kilbredy, par. of Bordwell, and Kilmartin, par. of Kyle. For Pol and Deineth see also 39.

39 See 37. Perhaps Inis Beoain near Fid Chuilinn (Feighcullen), co. Kildare. Nearby was Kilmeague (Cell Maédóc from Áed(án)).

42 Compare *V.Trip.* 144: '*Epscop Maine . . . 7 Geintene i nEchainuch la Uu Ailella*' (now Aghanagh, bar. of Tirerrill, co. Sligo). Cf. 43.

43 Possibly Shancoe in Tirerrill, co. Sligo, but Kilshanchoe in north co. Kildare is also a possibility Cf. 42.

45 Hogan tentatively places Ceinél Lugair near Gorey, co. Wexford. Conláed was Brigit's *cerd* (82 above and 72 below).

46 Condal (whence Sliab Condala and Cell Chondala?) is Old Connell, co. Kildare.

670.47 Partly a doublet of 32 above and of 76 below. Uí Chuilinn was in Loígis (*CGH* 31-2), somewhere near Mag Réta, later Moyrath, which formed part of the deanery of Offaly in the dioc. of Kildare. There is a Clonfad in the par. of Offerlane, co. Laois.

48 Unidentified, but Cell Derc Daim follows Druimm Urchailli (Dunmurraghill, bar. Ikeathy, co. Kildare) in a list of churches in *Ir. Lit.* 66. K. W. Nicholls mentions Killerrig, co. Carlow, as a possible identification.

49 If Lugnad is for Luigne, then the reference is probably to Clonmore in the bar. of Lune, co. Meath.

50 For Berchán and his three sisters compare 239 above.

51 The church is now Cloncurry, bar. of Offaly East, co. Kildare. It is not far from Kilmoney (52).

52 Cell Muine, now Kilmoney, a townland in the par. of Rathangan, bar. of Offaly East, co. Kildare. See 51.

53 Compare *'i Cill Rois aidchi óenaig Sinchi'* (*CGH* 339). Now Kilrush, bar. of Offaly West, co. Kildare.

54 Compare 7 above. Tech Airthir, which is unidentified, lay in Uí Ercáin, around Glassely (56) in south Kildare. For Fínán's sisters see *V.Trip.* 188, 350.

56 Now Glassely, bar. of Narragh and Reban East, co. Kildare.

57 Probably Nurney, near Kilrush (53), bar of Offaly West, co. Kildare.

58 For Rónán see 325. The church is unidentified.

61 Kilkea near Moone, co. Kildare?

63 Compare *Caput Litoris,* a lake on the river Life connected with Brigit (*Heist VSH* 87).

64 Cf. Coolcor, par. of Carbury, north Kildare, or Coolcor in par. of Granard, co. Longford, which appears to be the Cúil Chorrae mentioned, with Brigit, in *V. Trip.* 310 (= Bieler, *The Patrician Texts in the Book of Armagh* 136). Bieler (*ibid.* 256) places it near 'Slatey, co. Leix' (sic! read Sleatey, co. Carlow?). *Onom.* 319 places it in co. Westmeath.

67 Now Timahoe, al.Fossy, in the bar. of Cullenagh, co. Laois.

68 Marcach is no doubt connected with Sliab Mairce (cf. Cróine of Dísert Mairge, 708.60), now Slievemargie, a bar. in cos. Laois and Kilkenny.

69 Now, according to K. W. Nicholls, Killadreenan in the par. and bar. of Newcastle, co. Wicklow.

70 *M.Tall.* 53 places a saint Dartinne in Cell Aird of Uí Ercáin in south Kildare.

72 This entry is shared with RLc[1] and R's *Nannine* (x) seems preferable to *Muninne* (cf. *Moninne*) which usually refers to a female. While Ceinél Lugair appears to have had Wexford connexions (45 above), Molaisse Moccu Lugair was attached to Min Drochait, now Mendrehid in the par. of Aghaboe, co. Laois. Cf. *Ir. texts* 3 (1931) 81.

73 *Martar* (more usually *Martre*) is possibly to be taken as a placename. With Sárnat of Cell Bairnig compare Sárnat of Beirrech in Fotharta, now the par. of Barragh, co. Carlow.

74 Cell Chúile Dumae lay in Laígis Chúile (*Onom.* 186).

76 Affrica is already mentioned in 47 above in a Laois context. Also, the name was borne by two abbesses of Kildare (AU 743, 834).

78 The milking of the cows thrice in one day is related of Brigit herself in *Lis. Lives* 11.1680-88 and *Lib. Hymn.* 117. In the latter source, Broccán's *Hymnus in laudem sanctae Brigidae,* the preceding quatrain has the line: *laithe buana di mad-bocht.*

79 There is a townland of Rathbride in the par. of Tully, bar. of Offaly East, co. Kildare, which would suit the affiliation to the Fothairt of Mag Ítha given to Uí Chormaic in *CGH* 84.

82 Domnach Eochaille is mentioned with Cell Deirce Daim (48 above) and other Kildare churches in *Ir. lit.* 66. Near Athy, in the par. of Monasterevin, there is a townland of Oghill.

85 *Onom.* suggests Delgany in co. Wicklow for Deirgne. Sruthair Guaire (86), now Shrule near Gorey in co. Wexford, is attached, with Deirgne, to a saint called Mogóróc (707.633-4, 722.89).

86 See note to 85. Mogobbóc Moccu Láime is assigned to Ráith Lámraige or Cell Lámraige, now Killamery, co. Kilkenny.

87 There is a parish of Rosconnel on the bounds of three baronies in cos. Laois and Kilkenny.

671 For other versions of the list see *V.Trip.* 264-6 (= *B. Phátr.* 155), 574 (from Lb 220); cf. DF 695a. A metrical version, with numerous additions, is in 672 below. Not all those listed in the text are elsewhere associated with Patrick (e.g. Sinell of Cell Airis (7), the only other reference to him being *M.Tall.* 7). Nevertheless, the fact that the list does accompany one of the surviving manuscript witnesses to the *Vita Tripartita* suggests that this text was its pricipal source. Thus, while there is considerable variation in the names of the saints concerned, Patrick's three smiths, artisans and embroideresses are also given in that order in the catalogue of miracles which occurs in the body of the *Vita Tripartita* (*V.Trip.* 248-52). Also, the names of the embroideresses as given here, *Lupait, Erc ingen Dáre ⁊ Crumthiris* occur in successive passages in *V.Trip.* 232-4, albeit without reference either to each other or to embroidery. There are several pointers to a south Derry/north Tyrone authorship for the text. The church assigned to Cóemán (6), Cell Riatai, if it is not to be identified with Cell Rath of *V.Trip.* 200, is likely to be Kilrea in the barony of Loughinsolin, co. Derry; Patrick was patron of this church (*Celtica* 1 (1950) 82). Similarly, while none of the persons named in 8-10 are mentioned in *V.Trip.*, two of their churches (8, 10) are included in a list of south Derry/north Tyrone churches allegedly founded by Patrick (*V.Trip* 154). Finally, Tamlachta Arda (15), which does not figure as such in *V.Trip.*, is now Tamlaght Ard or Magilligan, co. Derry. Page-references to *V.Trip.* are as follows: Sechnall (80, 150, 220, 238); Mochta (226); Erc (44); Mac Caírthinn (156); Beinén (36, 58, 98 etc.); Essiu, Bite, Tassach (250); Lupait, Erc (Ercnat), Cruimthiris (232-4); Odrán (218); Ródán (98, 108). With Lb's addition (3) compare *V.Trip.* 572 and Lb 220b. In 11 the name of the first smith is omitted in L but contained in B¹Lc (c); compare *V.Trip.* 250, 574.

672 Only in Lc. Marks of lenition have been restored silently; otherwise, restored letters are in square brackets. The attribution to Flann [Mainistrech] in the heading and in the quatrain following the poem's *dúnadh* (29) is no doubt false. A clue to the real poet's period may be contained in the allusions in 2 but, unfortunately, these are obscure. As it stands the text appears corrupt in many places and the variants given below from the eighteenth century copy in RIA 23 E 26, 240 may in fact derive ultimately from Lc. The only other copy known to me is that incorporated by the Four Masters in their annals (AFM s.a. 448) but, as the notes show, this is a separate recension. The poet's sources seem largely undiscoverable, at least as far as quatrains 9-11, 14-28 are concerned, although verifiable Patrician connexions are apparent here and there. With the exceptions of 5a and 8d, quatrains 5-8, 12, 13 are based on a copy of 671 closest to that represented by B¹Lc, whose order is followed in 8ab (= 671.15 vis-a-vis 671.10), and whose inclusion of Mac Cecht (= 671.11, note c) is matched in 13b. In 13d, however, B¹Lc's *Tasan* gives way to the usual *Tasach*.

Variants from RIA 23 E 26, 240: Title *Flann Mainisdrech cc .i. abb Mainistreach Buite m. Broinaigh.* 2d *ni fed.* 3b *nocha nfine.* 4a *gan feall.* 5a *Mac Cuill.* 7a *Meascan bine.* 7c *ua binn roinn.* 16b *cheileabhair.* 18d *Blocdha m. Murfodaigh.* 20d *cuacholl.* 23b *Tarcuire a iasguire.* 30c *co mbeadh.*

672.2-4 Omitted in AFM.

3d .h. Deochain, the deacon's descendant, refers to Patrick

5a Mac Caille is mentioned in *V.Trip* but, as was usual, in connexion with Brigit. The more usual bishop Sechnall (671.1) is named in AFM.

6c The corresponding designation in 671.7 is *aistire*.

7c The name Colum was probably fabricated by the poet. AFM reads Cruimthir Bescnait (cf. 671.10).

8-11 Omitted in AFM.

9 In *M.Don.* Oct. 27 Colmán Ua Fiachrach accompanies Bishop Erc and Moaba m. Ernain (cf. 26 below).

12 This follows 13 in AFM which also reads *m. Braga* for *in broda* (12d).

12d AFM adds *Ippis, Tigris is Erca, agus Liamhain la Eibeachta, Padraig ros forran an dechra, dóibh ro ba tearbh fhearta.*

13b See introductory note.

13d Aissmiti (Aesbuite AFM) is a fusion of Essiu and Biti (671.12); Tairill is a fabrication.

14-23 Omitted in AFM.

17b For the name Derball compare *V.Trip.* 208.

18d For b-b read M*ur*fodaide?

23b The *a* of *ar* (f-f) is preceded by *t* with a dot underneath.

672.24a AFM reads *mac da siar Banban co mblaidh.*

24cd AFM reads *rapa rogot ar oglach, Mochonnoc a chomhgarmach.*

AFM adds *Cribri is Lasra na Leand, ingheana glana Glegrand macraidh car sai abhir as Erc, ra tharngair re na tri uidheacht.*

25bd AFM reads *Loga* and *Machui* for *Lugna* and *Mac hÍ* respectively.

26ab AFM omits. Cf. 9 above.

27 For Gornias and German see *V.Trip.* 8, 16. For *Gornias* AFM reads *Cairniuch.*

27cd-30 AFM omits.

28d See also *Lis.Lives* 5, ll. 136-40.

29d AFM adds a *dúnadh,* i.e. *In trinóid is trean ar chuch, dailea duind maith morgrath, righ ran foem tre aittin mbuic, ra soer do phattir Padruig.*

30 *r* of *fochraic* is written as *u.*

673 In L only, where it is added in the lower margin. For other versions see *M.Tall.* 98 (also from L 367), *M.Don.* 74, AFM s.a. 917 (with Comgall given as the author's name).

674-689 A number of the entries in this biblical and classical section of the Corpus, i.e. 675-77, 679-81, 687-89, are omitted in L which treats the section as an addendum. Their inclusion here, however, using B's readings as the main text, is justified not only by the fact that they form an integral part of the introductory section of the Corpus in BLc[1], but also by their apparent presence in the no longer extant earlier part of the Corpus as preserved in the Book of Glendalough, now Rawlinson B 502. The evidence for this is contained in NLI G 2 (first intercalated leaf) which shares with BLc[1] almost all the additional entries (see below) while invariably showing a closer affinity to Lc[1] than to B (see *ZCP* 39 (1982) 29-32). We may infer that the section was originally composed by the redactor of the Rawlinson B 502 recension, and while his version is represented more or less completely by BLc[1], that it was selectively and independently used by Áed mac Crimthainn and by the scribe of the intercalated leaf in NLI G 2. The sources of the pedigrees are varied. In 680, for instance, as well as in 684-6, there is verbal evidence to confirm that a copy of the Bible was used. The section has also much in common with the tract of *Sex Aetates Mundi* (see 676, 678, 681) and it may be no coincidence that a copy of this text occupies an important place in Rawlinson B 502.

674 The pedigree corresponds to Luke 3. 23-38. Comparison with the biblical version shows that L's readings are often inferior to those of the other manuscripts.

675 Omitted in L. Compare Matthew I. 1-17 and, for the earlier section, Luke 3. 23-38; cf. Genesis 5. 1-32.

676 Only in BLc[1]; cf. NLI G 2 (intercalated leaf). Nin's pedigree is also given in part in *IT* 4 (1909) 2, p.2 (*In Cath Catharda*) and in B 6b 56. Cf. R 43Va, where it is given in full but somewhat differently.

677 Only in BLc[1]; cf. NLI G 2 (intercalated leaf). Some generations of Alexander's pedigree are elsewhere given in B 3b 34.

678 Compare 1 Samuel 1 which gives the pedigree as far as Suub (Suph). The same book of the Bible appears to have been used in the composition of 682 below. Compare also 1 Chronicles 6. See also 684. Cf. R 43R *in marg. sup.*

679 Only in BLc[1]; cf. NLI G 2 (intercalated leaf). The usual Greek descent through Tantal son of Zeus gives way here to a 'Roman' descent through Mercury. Cf. *Gen. tracts* 175-76. Compare also B 3b 24ff, 4a 10ff and G. Calder, *Imtheachta Aeniasa. The Irish Aeneid* (ITS 6, London, 1907) 92-4, where Vergil VII. 48 is very much 'improved' upon by the Irish adaptor. For the children of Tantalus see also *RC* 44 (1927) 14-33.

680 Only in BLc[1]; *not* in NLI G 2 (intercalated leaf). 1 Chronicles 5.26 appears to be the source, at least of the Latin addition. For Sennacherib see Isaiah 37.37-8. (For use of the same book of the Bible see 684-6 below). To Tiglath-pileser is attributed the deportation of population to Assyria (2 Kings 15.29). For Pul see *ibid.* 15.19. By right, Asarodan (Esarhaddon) is Sennacherib's son (*ibid.* 19.37).

681 Only in BLc[1]: *not* in NLI G 2 (intercalated leaf). *Merech Baladon m. Baladon* (e-e) is correct (Isaiah 39.1). Again the context is Assyrian. Cf. R 43Va.

682 Compare 1 Samuel 9.1, which gives the pedigree as far as Aphia. The remaining names may represent Urijah son of Shemaiah (Jeremiah 26.20)?

683 Hestras, *al,* Ezra, the prophet, is among those given special mention in the passage on the Babylonian Captivity in *V.Trip.* 4. For his pedigree see Ezra 7.1-6.

684 With B(Lc[1])'s addition (d) compare 678 above. The original source of the present entry, and of 685, 686, is 1 Chronicles 6, which likewise places Asaph at his right hand. See also 680.

685 Compare 1 Chronicles 6 and see notes to 680, 684.

686 Compare 1 Chronicles 6 and see notes to 680, 684.

687 Only in BLc[1]; cf. NLI G 2 (intercalated leaf). For Laimiach's (Lamech's) pedigree see Genesis 4.17-22.

688 Only in BLc[1]; cf. NLI G 2 (intercalated leaf). Compare Exodus 6. 14-19.

689 In B entry 671 intervenes between this and the foregoing. In M Britus's pedigrees occur separately in the body of the text; an unusually large initial introduces the first one, however. In La, where the entry has been joined to Cairnech's pedigree by P.Grosjean (*Ir. texts* 3 (1931) 97), the arrangement is different. Sections 1, 2 seem to be based on *Lebor Bretnach* §9, §5 respectively (edited by A.G. Van Hamel, Dublin, [1932], pp. 6-7, 16-17); the Latin sentence in section 1 (cf. Genesis 9.22-3, 25) is found in Van Hamel's version II of *Lebor Bretnach*. Sections 3, 4, on the other hand, correspond to, and have probably been taken from, the 'British' section of Patrick's pedigree (1 above). For other versions see G. Calder, *Imtheachta Aeniasa. The Irish Aeneid* (ITS 6, London, 1907) 148 (cf. 92-4); *Gen. tracts* 175 and NLI G 2 (intercalated leaf).

690 In LbLc[1]MR[1]HLa (see also DF 753b) the tract on the saints of Clann Lugdach survives in part only. A metrical version is contained in 662.45-61. Outside the Corpus, in B 87d-88e, a large number of the pedigrees in this section (1-7, 12, 14) form part of a secular genealogical tract, an earlier version of which probably served as Áed mac Crimthainn's main source for the composition of this text. Thus the arrangement of entries 1-7 corresponds to the lay-out of the tract in B. Also, the bulk of the remaining entries could have been taken from Áed's other source, the Book of Glendalough, since Lc[1] contains six of them (8, 9, 12, 14, 16, 17) grouped together in its section on Ceinél Lóegaire saints (RLc[1] 21-8). The list of Áth Truim saints in Tírechán's *Additamenta* (*V. Trip.* 336) includes a few of the saints listed here. (Now see D. Ó Corráin in idem ed. *Irish Antiquity* (Cork, 1981) 329-30). With the fact that many of the churches mentioned lie on or near Loch Éirne compare the statement in B 87e[b] that the original patrimony of Clann Lugdach extended *'ó Lochaib Éirne co Bladma'*. Not all the saints listed here belonged to the Clann Lugdach in the strict sense, however.

1 Cf. B 87d; *GRSH* 49; DF 705b.

2 Cf. B 87d; *GRSH* 51; DF 706a. In *M.Don.* 2 this saint is confused with Fainche ingen Rónáin (= *GRSH* 46).

3 Cf. B 87d; *GRSH* 49; DF 706b, 753b.

4 Judging by the couplet, which corresponds to *Fél.*[2] 43(= Feb. 17), and by the context, *Corpmac* (s) is the better reading. Cf. 722.74; B 87d; DF 753b. In *GRSH* 93, Ceannfaoladh, Ceallach, Conall and Coirbre are made sons of Rumann Duach *'righfhile Erenn'*.

5 Cf. 325 above; B 88a; *GRSH* 50; DF 706b.

6 Cf. B 88a; *GRSH* 49; DF 706b.

7 Cf. B 88b; *GRSH* 53; DF 706b.

8 Cf. *GRSH* 50; DF 705c.

9 Cf. *GRSH* 49; DF 707d. See also *V.Trip.* 336.

10 Cf. *GRSH* 50, 52, 53; DF 705c. For Rónnat see also 71 above.

11 Cf. *GRSH* 52; DF 706a.

12 Cf. B 88e; *GRSH* 51; DF 707b.

13 Cf. *GRSH* 49, 52; DF 705b. For Ossán see also *V.Trip.* 336. Lb 20a misplaces this entry.

14 Cf. B 88d; *GRSH* 52; DF 706b.

15 Cf. *GRSH* 50; DF 707b.

16 La's mostly illegible 241 probably belongs here. Cf. 539, 573 above; *GRSH* 55; DF 704b.

17 Cf. 22 above; *GRSH* 50; DF 705c.

18 Cf. GRSH 51; DF 707c.

691 Cf. 397 above and 722.23, 726 below. Compare also *CGH* 99 and . *él.*[2] 99.

692 Following the scribe's mark of reference, I have incorporated this entry in its proper place at 722. 4-13. The scribe of the common source of BLcLb had copied only a small part of the entry at this point before breaking off, on noticing that it duplicated 722.4-13. M, which duplicates most of L's entries in this section of the Corpus, omits 692.

693 Since this entry, as contained in LM, is in substantial agreement with 722.16, its text is omitted here: its variants, however, are entered below with the designation L^1M^1.

694 This entry, which, excepting the saint's assignment here to Áth Truim as against Loch Gile of the earlier entry, agrees closely with the text of 350 (from Lc^1 only), may have been triggered by the occurrence of Lommán's name in 693. For Lommán of Áth Truim see *V.Trip.* 44. See also the note to 350.

695 J. O'Donovan (*The Tribes and Customs of Hy-Many* Ir. Arch. Soc., Dublin, 1843, p.92n) states that Fidh Manach was co-extensive with the parish of Kilbride, bar. of Ballintober, county Roscommon. However, K. W. Nicholls would place it in north-east Galway. B 102a (= Lc 68Ra) refers to Corco Raighi of Fid Manach in the same context as the Uí Thomrair of Cell Mac nAingin, i.e. the church of the sons of Aingen (Angan).

696 Note that the initial component element of each name, *all-, dess-, less-, mid-* is a point of direction. With Midabair compare *M.Tall.* 116. With Allabair compare *PRIA* 28C12, 245.

697 Sections 1,3 (ab) correspond to 132.1.2 above. With sections 2, 4 compare 722.34 below. With section 3 (cd) compare *Plummer VSH* 2, 22. I know of no other source of the quatrains.

698 Compare 722.68. Ráith Scannlaige in Termonn Brigte may denote Ráith Brigte, now Rathbride in the par. of Tully, bar. of Offaly East (Uí Ḟailge), co. Kildare. Ráith Brigte lay in Crích Hua Cormaic (670.79) and Áed Rón's descendants are named Uí Chormaic (*CGH* 58).

699 Cf. 722.65. The poem also occurs in the notes to *Fél.*^{2} 89; there, however, the mother's name is given as Créd.

700 This is a metrical version of 290.2.1.3. *Flainn* (3) reads *Crimthainn* (290.3).

701 Only in L. As the scribe's mark of reference implies, this is a metrical version of 209, which already contains the first line and the ascription to Colum Cille. Lc's addition to 209 (q) does not form part of the poem here. See now D. Ó Cróinín's edition in *Ériu* 32 (1981) 112-3.

702 This is a metrical version of 722.92, where, however, Manchán of Liath (2d) is omitted from the L text and added from BLc^1(i). The poem's *dúnadh* is at 4d. Colgan added a somewhat corrupt and disarranged version of the poem from an *alius vetustus codex* |i.e. L?| to *GRSH* 103.

703 This entry on the original names of Irish saints has already been published by Stokes (*Lis.Lives* 300-01) and Grosjean (*Ir. texts* 4 (1934) 99-100), the latter with additions from Egerton 92 27Ra (cf. *Ir. texts* 3 (1931) 81-2). Using Egerton, Grosjean was able to fill out some of L's lacunae. Here, using M (q-q), a full text is published for the first time. Of those named I cannot identify Eogan (19). M's statement (r-r) that Maedóc was a name for Fintan must be an error. Egerton adds *Fota m. Fiachna* to the Cuimmíne of 9.

704 Commenting on this list, which he published with 705-6, 709-11 in *Ir. texts* 3 (1931) 22-39, in *Anal. Bolland.* 77 (1959) 174, P. Grosjean states: *'se rencontre pour la première fois . . . dans LL . . . et il parait remonter plus haut: c'est une compilation de noms puisés çà et la dans divers documents notablement plus anciens.* Grosjean's *çà et la* is no doubt correct; with some exceptions however, i.e. 1-32, 'traditional' bishops, 124-144, a series of homonymous bishops which might just as well have been included under 707, and other isolated entries, e.g. 115, 184, 188 etc., the entries here, as in 705-6, 709-11, do not appear to represent saints of the early period. The impression is that Áed mac Crimthainn, the probable author (see 705), was drawing on lists similar to those used in the composition of the entries for certain days in the L version of the *Martyrology of Tallaght,* e.g. October 21, which lists the *monachi* of Taghmon and April 17, which provides a list of Donnán's family at Egg. Many of the names in 704 and in the following lists occur also in the martyrology lists, and the assumption is that we have to do in both types of list with Irish examples of the widespread European practice of preserving within monasteries *libri memoriales* which, as well as commemorating the monastery's lay and clerical benefactors, also remembered the members of the community as such. Using such documents (cf. K. Hughes, *The Church in Early Irish Society* (London, 1966) 61n, 66), Áed would have had no trouble in compiling the specialised lists represented by 704 etc. Tírechán (*V.Trip.* 304) had already provided a model for the specialisation featured in them but his lists of *episcopi* and *diaconi* are very meagre by comparison. With the exception of 705, which contains some clusters of names beginning with the same letter, the lists are devoid of any sense of alphabetical arrangement. P.Grosjean provided each entry with a number and this is followed in the present work; his very few inaccuracies are silently corrected.

704.1-2 For the two Patricks see also *M.Tall.* 65 and the additions in RBLc[1] at 707.911. See also P.Grosjean, 'S. Patrice d'Irlande et quelques homonymes dans les anciens martyrologes', *The Journal of Ecclesiastical History* 1 (1950) 151-71.

4-7 Secundinus, Benignus and Brón are also in the list in *V.Trip.* 304. Tassach was one of Patrick's household (671 above).

9-13 Consecutively, the churches represented are Clones, Ardstraw, Connor, Louth, Monasterboyce and Duleek.

22-5 A Munster grouping representing Emly, Ardmore, Lismore and Scattery.

124-144 The groups of saints of one name appear more suited to 707 below.

705 See introductory note to 704. The inclusion of a group of saints named Fintan (25-36), apparently from the Book of Glendalough's version of 707.440 *add*, suggests that Áed mac Crimthainn, who used this source (Introduction §3), was the compiler of this and, by implication, of the other lists, i.e. 704, 706, 709, 710, 711. Here also, possibly as far as number 44, the entries concern recognizably early saints. From 45-150 the author is at pains to arrange the saints according to the initial letters of their names but not in alphabetical order.

1-10 With the omission of Ruadán and Ninnid, this is the list of the 'twelve apostles' of Ireland (402 above).

25-36 These saints Fintan correspond exactly to the saints of that name added in RBLc[1] to the *Comainmnigud*-list (707.440 *add*). See above.

51-90 Grosjean's variants from B at this point belong more correctly at 237-277.

706 See introductory note to 704. For a very much shorter, prior but unrelated list of deacons see *V.Trip.* 305.

707-8 Unlike 704-6, 709-11, sections 707-8 occur in RB and Lc[1] as well as in L. D.T.Brosnan in his careful publication of the lists in *Archivium Hibernicum* 1 (1912) 314-65 based his text on L with variants from RB; he was unaware, it seems, of the Lc[1] version but, with the exception of some significant additions which are noted below, this agrees closely with RB.

Together with the section of biblical and classical pedigrees (674-89) and the tract on the mothers of the saints, this text was taken over by B and Lc[1] from the same copy of R. Thus BLc[1] share a number of readings against R and, in reproducing the invocation added by R's scribe to his copy of 707-08 (which completes the hagiographical part of the manuscript), they omit a word in common. R's version of the text, which is followed by BLc[1], is earlier and, generally speaking, better than that of L: for this reason, its readings are indexed here when the versions diverge significantly. L sometimes telescopes two or three or even four entries into one. Thus its 707.355 corresponds to four separate saints Ciarán in RBLc[1]. Similarly, at 707.33.34 (and elsewhere), the use of *dá* 'two' enables L to avoid duplicating the entries on Áed of Áth Truim and Cluain Domail which are twice written out in R. In some cases, however, L's text is superior. Thus, as Brosnan (p.330n) points out, R's lists of saints Findchú and Findlug are confused with that of Fintan. Similarly, at 707.726, R reads *Mochóemóc m. Airdne* for the correct *Mochóemóc Airdne*. On the basis of these and other irregularities in R's text, L's scribe, if he did use R, occasionally corrected the errors of his source.

On the other hand, there are a number of unusual readings in L which could be explained by reference to R. Thus, at 163, R's *Dullduib* (with the *b* written somewhat like *l*) becomes *Dulduil* in L. Similarly, at 266, R's *Calath* (= *Colmán Alath*) may be compared with L's *Colmán Calath*. Also, as we have already seen, L's list of *sacerdotes* (705 above) includes several saints Fintan who are elsewhere found only in R's (cf. BLc[1]'s) list of homonymous saints Fintan.

The likelihood is that, as with other lists of its kind, e.g. 704, 705 etc., the list of homonymous saints was first composed either by or for the scribe of its earliest extant copy, here R, using earlier materials. (Colgan (*Acta SS.Hib.* 5) attributes this and the other similar lists to Óengus, *céile Dé*). That some of the earlier materials may ultimately have been of considerable antiquity is shown by the large sprinkling of *moccu* forms among the entries. On the other hand, these probably derive here directly from intermediate texts, which in turn used earlier materials. One such text undoubtedly took the form of a martyrology.

NOTES

Comparison of the lists with surviving copies of the Irish Calendar of Saints, particularly with the earliest example, the Martyrology of Tallaght (*M.Tall.*), reveals in places a striking correspondence. Taking the list of saints Áedán, we find that of sixteen entries (1-16) six (10-13, 15,16) correspond closely, indeed sometimes verbally, with *M.Tall.* (19/7, 11/4, 12/2, 3/8, 29/3, 1/4); two (3, 9) agree with *M.Don.* (2/11, 21/11) where there is a lacuna in *M.Tall.*, and one (5) is found in *M.Don.* (7/8) but not in *M.Tall.* More or less the same result is obtained from an examination of the saints named Áed (17-34) of whom six (17-19, 25, 27, 31) are paralleled by entries in *M.Tall.* (31/1, 28/2, 11/4, 31/1, 7/2, 17/12) and two by entries in *M.Don.* (1/11, 2/6). While this large measure of agreement is not maintained throughout (Brénainn (35-51), and Barrḟind (52-8) reveal four and no correspondences respectively), there can be little doubt but that a martyrology served as one of the principal sources of the text.

Here and there we find evidence to suggest that this source is unlikely to have been *M.Tall.*, at least in its extant form (but see the note to 707.763). Thus, as already stated, *M.Don.* occasionally agrees with our text independently of *M.Tall.* Similarly, at 78 (Colum Moccu Airte), the parallel entry in *M.Tall.* (7/6), Mocholmóc Dromma Móir, is glossed Moccu Arta only in *Gorm.* and *M.Don.* Again, at 375 (Finnio Gilldae), the source was hardly *M.Tall.* (28/9) which separates Finnio from Gildae; in *Fél.* (28/9), on the other hand, the corresponding line reads *in dá Finnio Geldae.*

In view of its nature, the text could hardly do other than swarm with examples of duplication. In my 'Cainnech al. Colum Cille, Patron of Ossory', *Folia Gadelica* (Cork, 1982) 20-35, I draw attention to some examples. Suffice it here to remark that Findbarr (378-84) and its hypocoristic Finnian (373-77), Mochonna (679-706) and its diminutive Mochonóc (626-31) and Ultán (943-48) and its hypocoristic Tua (933-5) are each given a separate list.

707.4 L's *inorois* probably takes its form from a misreading of R's *indrois,* if this was the source.

70 In *M.Tall.* 72 the church is named Ros Toirc.

122 Read Maccu Ansi. Cf. Mac Neill, *PRIA* 29C4 (1911) 75.

440 R(BLc^1)'s additions occur in L at 705.24-36.

484 Lc^1's addition reflects the tendency of the scribe to add local colour to his text. Cf. 591.

529 Having already added Balla at 484, Lc^1's scribe here substitutes Crannan, the name of a place in the bar. of Carra, co. Mayo (?), for Balla of his exemplar.

591 Lc^1's Echros again refers to a local north Connacht church.

619 The *g* of R's *Glaisreain* may reflect the *g* of *Tige* which precedes it. Read *Laisreain?*

717 L's *-moc* is added below the line, as an afterthought?

763 *Aircsirend* probably belongs to the previous entry, the likely source being the calendar entry for March 11 which, in *M.Tall.*, reads: *Findcain aircisiremh* |glossed *in cruciatibus diuturnis*| *Mosenoc ⁊ Senani Bethrech.*

708.7-9 These three entries are also added in the lower margin of M 56Ra.

709 See introductory note to 704.

710 See introductory note to 704. A number of the entries here (e.g. 2, 5, 20, 35, 37, 41-3, 51, 56-7, 76) seem to refer to early saints.

711 See introductory note to 704. The commentary at 87 may be compared to 81 of the main Corpus. As with the addition at 28, the information given relates to west Leinster, Áed mac Crimthainn's place of origin.

712 A previous edition of this list from L is found in *Lis.Lives* 298-9. (cf. J.H. Todd, *Leabhar Imuinn. The Book of Hymns* 1 (Ir.Arch.Soc., Dublin, 1855) 69-70). Its core is made up on the one hand of the twelve biblical apostles (2-14), who number thirteen here on account of the inclusion of Paulus (3), and on the other hand of the twelve apostles of Ireland (3-14; see 402 above) who, unusually (but cf. 705.7), include Comgall of Bennchor. For the rest, the correspondences reveal various shades of appropriateness. Thus underlying 1 is the notion of precursorship, 2 that of headship and 3-14 that of apostleship. Interestingly, a roughly similar arrangement of the apostles is observed in the genealogical tract at Lc 166Vd and in the prayer written into the margin of Lb 102 (cf. *Fél.*^{2} 186); compare also K. Meyer, *Hibernica Minora* (Oxford, 1894) 46 and R 44Rb. Brigit's standing as Ireland's Mary was already well established (15). Cóemgen's abandonment of the world for a *dísert,* or hermitage (17), is emphasized in his Lives although, unlike here, his *vita* describes him as *alter Antonius* (*Heist VSH* 361). This latter parallels Féichíne of Fore in the following entry (18); so, perhaps, the positions were reversed in the exemplar because Féichíne's feast (January 20) follows that of Paulus *heremita* (*M.Tall.* 10). Lon Garad (19) was noted for his learning (*Fél.*[2] 141-2). *Éices* (20) pairs off neatly with *Hymnodicus,* if this is the correct reading. Iob (21) is elsewhere compared to Finnian (*Heist VSH* 106). Manchán's choice of fellow (22) may have been influenced by the existence of a Mainchéne Sapiens (*M.Tall.* 4). Ciarán of Saigir (23) is reputed to have studied in Rome for twenty years (*Heist VSH* 347) around the time of Clemens's pontificate (cf. *ibid* 121-2). Mochutu's *alias,* Carthach, suits him for correspondence with a saint of Carthage (25), just as Nessán's standing as deacon links him to Laurentius (26). Between Buite and Beda there may be no more connexion than their similarity of name. The connexion between Adamnán (30) and Silvester was established (on grounds of their common excellence at preaching?) at least as early as the date of the composition of *Fís Adamnáin* (*IT* 1 (1880) 193). The names Bonifatius (31) and Laisrén (Molaisse) fall together in the *M.Tall.* list for October 25. Garald (32) and Paucomius share the title of *monachus,* as do Caimmíne (33) and Pastor; also, one of Pastor's feasts (Aug. 10) is shared by Cuimmíne, abbot of Druimm Bó. Finally, the place of honour among the saints of Ireland is reserved for Fintan of Clonenagh (34) *caput monachorum totius Hiberniae* and fellow of Benedict, which title is elsewhere preserved in *Fél.* 100, 168. This strongly argues a Clonenagh authorship for the list, a copy of which would then have been readily available to Áed mac Crimthainn who had strong ties with the monastery (Introduction §2). Bairre (35) was no doubt an addition to the list (made, perhaps, by Áed?). The implicit recognition of Bairre's Connacht pedigree may be noted; the basis of the equivalence with Augustine of Canterbury is unknown to me, however.

713 *Óentu* as used here (cf. 665.9, 716.4, 722.11) may denote something like *confraternitas* or *Gebetsverbrüderung,* the various saints representing churches which had joined together in an arrangement or agreement of mutual prayer, a practice which was widely observed in Europe from the eighth century onwards. Another such 'community' is reflected in 724 below, the membership of which is made up of all those listed here with some additions. In 724 the unity revolves around the churches of Tallaght and Derrynavlan both of which are also featured prominently here. The concentration, however, in both lists is on Munster churches represented here by Dairinis (2), now Molana near Youghal, Derrynavlan (3, 4), Killaloe (5), Terryglass (6) and Cúl Chollainge in north Cork. Araid (7) was a name for east Limerick, and Feidlimid, who replaces Máel Ruain as the pivotal figure of 724, may be assigned to Cashel. From outside Munster we find, besides Tallaght (11, 12), Castledermot (10) and Dysart at Lough Ennel in county Westmeath, which is represented by Máel Tuile (1). I have no other reference to the *ballán*-poem attributed to Cormac m. Cuilennáin (13). His possible authorship of the quatrains in 14, 15 cannot be controlled for lack of linguistic evidence. For a discussion of the entry see R. Flower in W. Bell, N.D. Emerson ed. *The Church of Ireland A.D. 432-1932* (Dublin, 1932) 70-1.

714 Already edited in *Archivium Hibernicum* 4 (1915) 204-07 by L. Gwynn, who collated the text with that of Harleian 4280, this poem has now been re-edited by J. Carney, *Celtica* 15 (1983) 25-41. See also *Misc. Hag. Hib.* 198, §67.

715 Edited by J. Vendryes in *RC* 31 (1910) 309-11 from another manuscript. Plummer (*Misc. Hag. Hib.* 202, §81) draws attention to a comparable passage in *Heist VSH* 331. Grosjean, *Anal.Bolland.* 48 (1930) 102n, adds references to other manuscripts, and edits the text in *Études Celtiques* 2 (1937) 280-82. Bishop Moinenn is said to have been Brénainn's *comharba* (*Fél.*[2] 59). Cf. *BNÉ* 1, 87 (§179), *Plummer VSH* 1, 143 (§88n).

716 Edited by H. Gaidoz (see *Misc. Hag. Hib.* 202, §80) and W. Stokes (*Lis.Lives* 349), this entry corresponds to *BNÉ* 1, 45, §§4-7 and *Lis.Lives* 99-100 (= 11.3331-72).

717 See *Misc. Hag. Hib.* 213, §131 for other references. Edited by P. Grosjean, *Anal. Bolland.* 51 (1933) 125-30. *M.Tall.* 33, which is related to this entry, gives the number of disciples as 'lii'.

718 See *Misc. Hag. Hib.* 219, §156 for other references. In *Conchubrani Vita Sanctae Monennae* (*PRIA* 28C12 (1910) 202-51) §3 Patrick's veiling of Moninne (cf. 6 here) is referred to.

719 This piece is attributed to Cóemán of Cluain mac Treóin in the Rawl. B 512 text, which identifies Sinchell as Ócsinchell of Cell Achaid. K. Meyer (*Hibernica minora* (Oxford, 1894) 41-2) edits it from Rawlinson B 512 with variants from L.

720 See *Misc. Hag. Hib.* 216, §145 for further references: add M 53Vb to the list of manuscripts.

721 The division into paragraphs follows that made by P. Grosjean in his edition of the text, 'Deux Textes Inédits sur S. Ibar', in *Anal. Bolland.* 77 (1959) 426-50 (442-3).

722 See *Misc. Hag. Hib.* 230, §195; add M 54Vab-55Vb to the list of manuscripts, and amend '*Note that* (3) (4) . . . to read *Note that* (2) (3) (4) . . .'. Colgan (*GRSH* 112n; cf. *Acta SS. Hib.* 5 *et passim*) refers to this tract as *Liber de Matribus Sanctorum Hiberniae* and attributes it, most implausibly, to Óengus, *céile Dé*. It has never been edited, except for three entries of Welsh interest (76, 89, 94) which P.C. Bartrum included in his *Early Welsh Genealogical Tracts* (Cardiff, 1966) 32-4. L's text is the earliest extant version. Unlike the main body of the Corpus, however, L is not followed by the scribes of B and Lc (here Lc[1]), who are in substantial agreement with M. Thus, when L errs, the correct reading is usually found in BLc[1]M; e.g. 25(a), 58(a), 77(b), 89(b-b, c), 94(f) and 97(b). Also there are two entries in BLc[1]M (105-6) which L omits. Compare also L's Bassar (14; cf. 721.1) with BLc[1]M's apparently more correct Lassar. More important, however, is the lack of correspondence between L and BLc[1] in the placing of this tract. In L it follows the main Corpus as an addition; in BLc[1] it forms part of the introduction to the Corpus. Indeed, in both of the later manuscripts, it leads off the hagiographical section, and is preceded in Lc[1] by the heading; *Incipit Senchas Naom Erend anso sis.* As has been shown, however (674-89 above; cf. *ZCP* 39 (1982) 29-32), BLc[1]'s source appears to have used the Book of Glendalough, now Rawl. B 502, in the composition of its introductory section. That this also extended to its version of 722 is likely on several grounds. Firstly, BLc[1]M's source pre-dated L, which drew on it occasionally in its recension of the main Corpus (see notes to 27, 31, 59, 74, 81 below). Secondly, an addition to BLc[1]M at 59 (t) below repeats verbatim a passage in Rawl. B 502, the greater part of which is omitted at that point in L. It may be inferred, therefore, that the now missing folios of Rawl. B 502 also contained a copy of the 'Mothers of Irish Saints' the text of which is preserved in BLc[1], and in M, although this latter may also have occasionally used L (see 20 below).

Biographers of saints sometimes made use of this tract. Compare *Anecd.* 3 (1910) 3 §5 (Farannán) with 6-10; *BNÉ* I, 24, §4 (Berach) with 101, and *ibid.* 125, §§5-6 (Cóemgein) with 19-20. It was also used as a source by authors of the various recensions of the tract on the pedigrees of the saints. Thus the entries, 380, 397, which were added to MLa, are based on 64 and 23-6 below respectively. Likewise, M's addition (c) to 363 is derived from 30 below. Similarly, the redactor of the *recensio minor* supplied his 652 from 66 below.

As has already been stated, there is also evidence to suggest that Áed mac Crimthainn borrowed extensively from the tract in his recension of the main Corpus. Thus entries 157 (k-k), 160, 162, 163 above correspond, wholly or partly, to 33, 32, 31, 28, 27 of 722 below. Of the entries in the main Corpus three (160, 162, 163) are wholly omitted in RLc[1], and the same applies to the relevant detail in 157 (k-k). Consequently, since R is also likely to have contained a copy of 722, as I argue above, the borrowing cannot have been in the other direction. Other correspondences between the tract and the main Corpus are noted below.

The sources of the tract itself were probably very varied, if not always as '*anciennes*' as Grosjean thought (*Anal. Bolland.* 78 (1960) 378n). One must suspect the presence of some *ad hoc* fabrication. Thus the quatrain in 69 which yielded Cuillenn mother of Colgu m. Áeda must surely refer to Colgu, son of Fáilbe Flann, king of Caisel (*CGH* 216, 360). Similarly, a form such as Sin (22) is too close to that of the saint's father Sinell to be above suspicion, and the same may apply to Sinell, sister of senṠinchell (90).

The arrangement of the entries, with pride of place as usual going to Patrick, Brigit and their relatives (1-13, 15-16), supplies no clear evidence of provenance but the BLc[1] version, which reflects the lost Book of Glendalough (R) version, ends with 722.102, a Glendalough entry. Doublets, of which there are several, are noted below.

722.1 For the first maternal name I have no other evidence; for Coinches see the note to 1.1 above.

2 *Cille* (n), which is only in L, must be mistaken (see 23 below). For Caillín see *B.Fenagh* 10n. *Dethidu filia Massani* is the corrupt (?) form given to the name of Daig's mother in *Heist VSH* 389.

722.3 Cf. 728.

4-13 See 692 above. Having already excerpted 4-13 from his exemplar of the 'Mothers of Irish Saints', Áed mac Crimthainn was content with a cross-reference to 345d at this point. The copyist of the common source of BLc (cf.Lb), when he came to L 354d, does not appear to have noticed that he was duplicating material he had already copied as part of this tract until he broke off in the middle of a passage at 6 (x) below.

4 Cf. 2.1 and 618 above.

5 See also 2.1 of the main Corpus. Cf. *B.Brigte* §1; *Lis.Lives* 35.

6-10 The author of *Betha Farannáin* (*Anecd.* 3 (1910) 1-7) used these entries as a source for his §§5-6.

6 B[1]Lc 46 VbLb break off at *beo* (x) for the reason given above (4-13); in this way Lb contains 4-6 (x) only of this tract. Here also the common source of BLcLb concludes its recension, B rounding off its copy with the statement *Finit amen finit don naemhseanchas* (cf. Introduction §5). Cumman's encounter with Patrick is otherwise unrecorded.

7 Excepting Moninne (cf. *PRIA* 28C12 (1910) 208, f2, 244), the concentration here is on saints of north-east Connacht.

8 At March 25 (= p.27) *M.Tall.* notes: *Cammini sancti Cumman nomen matris eius.* Senán's mother is elsewhere variously named Coimgell (*Lis.Lives* 54) and Fionnmhaith (*Ir. texts* 4 (1934) 93).

9 Again (cf.7) the saints mostly belong to north-east Connacht. Scíre (9) and Eirn(in)e (8) are described as the children of Eogan in 37 above.

10 Tuathal Máelgarb (†544 (549) AU) and Ailill m. Mochta are also mentioned above (6) as the two non-saints descended from Cumman. I have no other reference to Ailill but Tuathal's pedigree (AU 534) traces him to the Ceinél Cairpre (whence, among other places, Carbury in north-east Connacht). Furthermore, at AU 534, 536, Tuathal is joined by Mochta, a saint who is elsewhere (*M.Tall.* 26, where, significantly, he is followed by Scire *uirgo* (9 above)), but not here, set down as the son of Cumman. This coincidence may explain the form Ailill m. Mochta? For Tuathal's relationship to Cumman see also the *Banṡenchas* (*RC* 47 (1930) 305, 48 (1931) 217).

11 Cf. *Anecd.* 3 (1910) 4 §6. Carn Tráchta Eochaille is now Beltra Strand, near Ballysadare, co. Sligo.

13 Cf. 670.8.

14 Note the disagreement between L (Bassar) and BLc[1]M (Lassair) as regards the mother's name. L's form may have been influenced by 721.1. See Grosjean *Anal. Bolland.* 77 (1959) 445-6.

15 The shadowy figure of Lupait (*V.Trip.* 12, 16) is nowhere else brought into connexion with the Moccu Baird (cf. 664). (In *V.Trip.* 82 they are described as the sons of Darerca (16)). Lupait's otherwise only recorded pregnancy, which brought about her death through Patrick's intervention, resulted in the birth of Áedán, 'saint of Inis Lothair' (*V.Trip.* 234).

16 The variants from the duplicate version in LM (693) are marked L[1]M[1] here. Despite the assertion that the bishops number fifteen (a-a) (sixteen in L[1]M[1]), seventeen are named. *Fél.*[2] 48-9 (= *Fél.* 68) gives the number as seventeen but names only Mac Cairthinn, who is omitted here, Móel (= Mel) and the two nuns. In *V.Trip.* 82 the nuns are again named together with four of the bishops, Crummaíne, Muinis, Mel and Ríóc, and Darerca is said to have had seven sons (cf. 15) and two daughters.

17 Cf. *Fél.* 222-24; *Ir. texts* 3 (1931) 5 (§11).

18 The entry on Mella is placed elsewhere in B (212b 47), Lc[1](34Rb 46) and M(55Ra 55). For Cainnech see also *Heist VSH* 182; *Plummer VSH* 1, 152.

19 This and 20 were used as a source by the author of Cóemgen's first Irish Life (*BNÉ* 1, 125, §6); cf. *Plummer VSH* 1, 234. See also *CGH* 35 (added from L) and *Fél.*[2] 98 (= *Fél.* 144).

20 See note to 19. The entry is placed elsewhere in B (213ab), Lc[1] (34Va 41) and M, (55Rb 53 = M[1]) which, presumably drawing on L, also includes the entry at this point. Cf. *Heist VSH* 225, §1 (Minchlu) and *CGH* 35.

21 Cf. (340), 733.2; *Cáin Ad.* 6 (§§8, 12); *Arch. Hib.* 4 (1915) 214; *Fél.*[2] 146-7; B 84b. Note the similarity between the names of the parents.

22 Cf. 132.2, as far as *mathair* (e-e), which may derive from this entry.

23-26 These served as the source for 397 above which is in MLa only. The original source is the Appendix to Adamnán's *Vita Columbae* (Anderson, Anderson pp. 546-8;

Reeves 246-7). This shows BLc's *nEnáin* to be the correct reading at 25 (a), and *Moccu* to have been omitted before *Céin* in 26. Also, BLc[1](M)'s Latin addition at 25 (b-b) reflects Adamnán's *quorum unus Colmaan dicebatur*. Cf. 651; 691 (h); 726; *RC* 20 (1899) §143; B 84b; *Lib. Hymn.* 1, 182; Rawl. B 505, 117V; *ZCP* 10 (1915) 343.

722.27 Áed mac Crimthainn copied this entry into the main Corpus at 162. However, his use of *ur* in place of *brú* (d) here means that he was using a BLc[1]M type exemplar (see also 31).

28 Cf. 163 above; *RC* 48 (1931) 224.

29 Cf. A.G. Van Hamel, *Lebor Bretnach* (Dublin, n.d.) 40; *RC* 48 (1931) 224. See also *Éigse* 15 (1974) 177.

30 Cf. 363 (c) where this entry is added in M only, drawing, to judge by the spelling Collo, on its own copy of 722.30. Cf. B 195a 38-40.

31 This and 32 were copied into L at 160.2 from a BLc[1] type exemplar, to judge by the omission of 31 (e-e). See also 27.

32 Cf. 160.2. See previous note. The omission (c-c) (cf. 33, a-a) in Lc[1] is due to haplography.

33 Cf. 157.1. (k-k).

34 Cf. 697.2.

35 Cf. *Heist VSH* 340, §1 (Gemma); *Fél.* 116.

37 Cf. *Heist VSH* 198, 247; *Plummer VSH* 2, 226; Lc 60Rb 32; B 82a 52. (In LcB her father is named Braccán m. Maine).

38 Cf. *Fél.*[2] 117.

40 Cf. B 166b 40ff; *Acta SS. Hib.* 649.

41 Cf. *Heist VSH* 332 (Briga).

42 This follows 44 in BLc[1]M. Cf. *Heist VSH* 107; *Plummer VSH* 1, 262; *Fél.*[2] 72 (= *Fél.* 110).

43 This is written twice in M. The only name put forward elsewhere for the mother of Brénainn of Clonfert (if he is intended here) is Cara (*Plummer VSH* 1, 98; *Heist VSH* 324).

45 The name given to the mother of Féichín of Fore in his Irish Life is Lasair (*RC* 12 (1891) 320).

46 A doublet of 60 below. Cf. *BNÉ* 1, 183; *Heist VSH* 234.

47 Cf. *Heist VSH* 131, 382; *Plummer VSH* 2, 206.

48 Cóemán m. Nise (whence Ness) may be intended, but Ness is given as the name of Mochóemóc's mother in *Plummer VSH* 2, 164.

49 Elsewhere (B 167a 40-1) 'Tuleth ingen Maine' is his mother.

50 A doublet of 86 below, where the mother's name reads Subthain. Cf. *Fél.* 118.

51 Cf. *B.Moling* 5 (Emnait); *Plummer VSH* 2, 190n.

53 Cf. Lb's addition at 93 (a) above.

54 Cf. K. Meyer, *Betha Colmáin Maic Luacháin* (RIA Todd Lect. Ser. 17, Dublin, 1911) 6, §5.

55 Elsewhere, *ZCP* 10 (1915) 343, 'Cognag' is Baíthín's mother.

56 Cf. *Lis. Lives* 75 (= 1.2509); *Heist VSH* 96.

57 Cf. 125.2; M 18Vb; *Lis.Lives* 119; *Plummer VSH* 1, 200; *Heist VSH* 78. In the latter, Darerca is identified with Patrick's sister (of whom *multi sancti nati sunt*); cf. 722.16 above which includes a Ciarán.

58 BLc[1]M give the correct reading at (a). Cf. *Heist VSH* 404 (Ness); *Fél.*[2] 142 (= *Fél.* 198); Chron. Scot. |508| which, rightly, establishes a link between *mac|c nise|* and the no doubt invented form Cness.

59 Cf. 191.2, which is only in LBLc (cf. La). Again, as in 27, 31 above, there is clear evidence to show that L's text (at 191.2) is drawn from a BLc[1]M type copy of this entry whose variants (n), (o-o), (p), (q) are reflected in L. Cf. *Fél.*[2] 121; DF 740b; *Plummer VSH* 2, 65-6. For Ailbe; cf. *Heist VSH* 118; *Plummer VSH* 1, 47. The addition in BLc[1]M at (t), if we except its final sentence, duplicates a passage in Rawl.B 502 151a 52-5 (= *CGH* 225). The corresponding passage in L (321d) is much shorter. This again argues a close connexion between Rawl. B 502 and the text of the source of BLc[1]M here (cf. introductory note).

60 A doublet of 46 above.

62 Cf. 126 (n), where this entry is added in substance by M[1]R[1]La[1]. Cf. also *BNÉ* 1, 291 (Med) and *Plummer VSH* 1, 170 (Med, wrongly corrected to Med|b|). See also *Ir. texts* 4, (1934) 93.

722.64 This may be the source of 380 above which is in M only. Cf. *RC* 47 (1930) 306, 48 (1931) 218 (Brigit).

65 Cf. 699.1-4; *Fél.*^{2} 89 (Créd).

66 Cf. 652 which used this as a source. For a discussion of the entry, see S. Ó Coileáin, 'The structure of a literary cycle', *Ériu* 25 (1974) 88-125; pp. 92 ff.

67 Cf. *CGH* 35 (ingen Lóchéne).

68 Cf. 698.

69 A chapter in Adamnán's *V.Columbae* (1 17; 23ab) is devoted to Colcu's mother who remains nameless. Here she is confused with the mother of Colgu m. Fáilbe Ḟlainn, king of Caisel, who died in 678.

71 M is partly illegible here. Judging by *Anecd.* 2 (1908) 36, §22, Fidlin m. Irlamain's church lay somewhere in west Leinster.

72 A doublet of 102 which reads Cóemóc for Cóeltigern. Cf. L 385a.

73 Since both entries refer to an abbot of Iona, BLc^{1}M's placing of 73 after 70 probably reflects the text's original arrangement.

74 Cf. 690.4 in which L also omits ⁊ *Ossain* (see BLc^1 (c-c) here). This again implies that L had access to a BLc^1 type exemplar of 722.

75 Cf. *Fél.*^{2} 83 (= *Fél.* 128).

76 Also printed by Bartrum, *op.cit.*, 32; cf. *ibid.* 56, §13 which refers to . . . *m. Sawyl Benuchel* (*Benisel*). In B 214a 23 (= B^1), Lc 35Ra 3 and M 55Vb 18 (= M^1) this entry is repeated. Cf. *Fél.*^{2} 85; *Lib. Hymn.* 1, 129.

77 L's *Enan* (from *c̊nan*?) should read *Cronan* (cf. 243.1.2).

78 In BLc^{1}M (a, b) there is confusion with the mother mentioned in 58 above.

79 For Cainech see also 721.2; 722.14. In 287.3 (cf. *BNÉ* 1, 3) Abbán's mother is named Mella (cf. 80?). See also 97 below.

80 Cf. 188 (g-g). In 722.92 (i) BLc^1 add Manchán Léith to the sons of Brónach. See also previous note.

81 Cf. 211 (b-b), where L's omission of *ingen Chéin* again suggests a BLc^{1}M type source. Cf. *Fél.* 112; *Heist VSH* 153; *Plummer VSH* 2, 87.

83 *Ir. lit.* 68 refers to *secht nóebepscoip Milcon Fiaich*. Unlike the prose (d), Damrad is given a feminine declension in the verse (j).

84 Judging by 313.2 (j), BLc^1's *Rune* (b) is more correct.

85 Regarding Libae compare 67 (f-f) of the main Corpus. *Plummer VSH* 2, 60 names Énna's mother as Bríg daughter of Ainmire. Cf. *Fél.* 100; Rawl. B 505, 90R.

86 A doublet of 50 above, which reads *Suaibsech*. Cf. *Fél.*^{2} (= Subthan).

88 This is preceded in BLc^{1}M by 105 below.

89 Already printed by Bartrum, *op.cit.*, 32-3. BLc^{1}M (b-b, c) represent the more correct readings.

91 Cf. *Fél.* 78, which gives *Uthenni* (read *Eithne*) *ingen Ḟeidlimid* as his mother together with the names of six brothers.

92 Cf. 702 above. With the addition in BLc^1 (i) compare 722.80.

93 Áed Rón, king of Ulaid, was slain at the battle of Fochard in 736 (AU). Provided *m.* be emended to read *ua,* this entry may refer to *'Diarmait huae Aedha Roin, anchorita et religionis doctor totius Hiberniae',* who died in 826 (AU); cf. *Fél.*^{2} 106.

94 Already printed by Bartrum, *op.cit.* 33. BLc^{1}M's reading *Muicce* (f) is correct.

96 This is preceded in BLc^{1}M by 106 below and the doublet of 76 above. At 287.3 the mother is named Mella, sister of Coémgen. See also 722.79.

97 Again, BLc^{1}M's *Findtain* (b) is no doubt the correct reading. For Rígnach see also *Lis.Lives* 79-80. (= ll. 2661-71); *Heist VSH* 102.

99 For a discussion of this entry see P.Grosjean. 'The pedigree of Saint Caelainn', *Journal of Celtic Studies* 1 (1950) 193-98; p. 193-4.

100 Cf. *Lib. Hymn.* 1, 22.

101 *BNÉ* 1, 24, §4 is clearly based on this entry.

102 A doublet of 72, which substitutes Cóeltigern for Cóemóc.

104 For Máel Aithgin m. Forannáin see also 51 of the main Corpus. Here (e) M's text of the *náemshenchas* ends with the words: *Finid amen Finid Faelan Mac A Gabann na Scel doscrib in caidirrni seo da thigerrna carad companaig .i. don Easpog Ua Cellaig* (.i. *Muirchertach* (above line)), ⁊ *co fogna do* ⁊ *na tabradh da charaid in caidirrne seo* (see Introduction §11).

105 Omitted in L, this entry precedes 722.88 in BLc^{1}M.

722.106 Omitted in L, this entry precedes 722.96 above in BLc[1]M. The reference is to Servanus of Cuilennros (Culross) in Scotland (see W. J. Watson, *The History of the Celtic Placenames of Scotland* (Edinburgh and London, 1926; repr. Shannon, 1973) 209n). Servanus's *vita* (W. M. Metcalfe, *Pinkerton's Lives of the Scottish Saints* 2 (Paisley, 1889) 119-30; p. 119) names his mother as *Alpia filia regis Arabiae*'. M's Cluain Imrois (e) represents an attempt to deal with an unfamiliar name.

723 This poem is given a context in *Fél.*[2] 144 where the first line only is written down. To M. O'Dalys edition (*Éigse* 2 (1940) 183-86) from L add that of P. Grosjean, 'Notes d'hagiographie celtique', *Anal. Bolland.* 69 (1951) 77-106; pp. 102-06, from a Brussels manuscript, and D. Greene and F. O'Connor, *A Golden Treasury of Irish Poetry* (London, 1967) no. 28.

724 See note to 713. The *óentu* (10d) reflected here comprises the whole membership of that in 713 and, in addition, eleven other saints, many of whom cannot be identified. Lobrán (26) represents Dísert Lobráin in the diocese of Emly; Molling (3a), St. Mullins in co. Carlow. Rechtgniad (4a) may be for Rechtnia abbot of Clonmacnoise (†784 AU). For Mochonna (4c) of Daire see *M.Tall.* 21. I cannot identify the others. Daire Eidnech (8b) is another name for Daire na bhFlann, Derrynavlan, near Caisel, and Druim Abrat (12a) of the additional quatrain may be another name for Ard Fínáin, Ardfinan, on the river Suir. For a discussion of the entry see K. Hughes in N. K. Chadwick etc. ed., *Studies in the Early British Church* (Cambridge, 1958) 263-4.

725 When editing 704, P.Grosjean omitted this marginal note; but see *Anal. Bolland.* 61 (1943) 98. The illegible final word may be expected to have read (. . .) |aid| for metrical reasons; Cell Achaid is a possibility.

726 Also omitted by P.Grosjean when editing 705. From *Ferg* . . . to *Noe* is apparently in verse form. See *Fél.* 146. Cf. 397, 625, 691, 722.23-26.

727-734 For a previous edition of these sections by D.T. Brosnan see *Archivium Hibernicum* I (1912) 361-65.

727 Cf. K. Meyer, 'Ein mittelirisches Gedicht auf Brendan den Meerfahrer, *Sitzungsberichte der königlich preussischen Akademie der Wissenschaften* 25 (1912) 436-43; H.P.A. Oskamp, 'Mochen, mochen, a Brénaind', *Éigse* 13 (1970) 92-8.

728 Cf. 722.3. The places mentioned are mostly in the barony of Carbury, co. Kildare.

730 Cf. 298.1.2

731 Another *óentu*-text (cf. 713, 724). Compare also *Fél.*[2] 87 (*Óentu Choinning is Barrai ⁊ Brénaind díb línaib*). Also edited by P.Grosjean in *Anal. Bolland.* 55 (1937) 284-5.

732 Cf. P.Grosjean, 'S. Caelani cum ave colloquium' *Anal. Bolland.* 47 (1929) 39-43; *idem, ibid.* 49 (1931) 98.

733 Compare the slightly different pedigree given Adamnán at 340 above. For Rónnat see also 722.21. K. Meyer prints a copy of the poem made by M. Ó Cléirigh *'as seinleabhar dorcha'* (probably L) in *Cáin Ad.* 34.

734 A Brénainn of Druimm Liss is listed above (707.47). For another edition and discussion see P.Grosjean in *Anal. Bolland.* 55 (1937) 96-104.

735 Omitted by C. Plummer (who refers to it in *VSH* 1, lxiii) from his edition of *Ir.lit.* Cf. 379; *Fél.*[2] 102 (= *Fél.* 150). K.W. Nicholls draws my attention to Cell Moccu Birn, now Killickabawn, bar. of Newcastle, co. Wicklow, of which Nem was the probable eponym.

736 This is the upper portion of a Corco Loígde pedigree (cf. *CGH* 256) which was interpolated for no apparent reason into the RLc[1] version of the Corpus.

737 In M only. Of the saints here listed only Báetán and Furodrán (1b) are elsewhere assigned to Lann Léire (*M.Tall.* 51). Brigit (5a), and Cairell (5b) are connected with Fochard and Tír Rois respectively in the north Louth-Monaghan area (whence the other saints as well?).

738 Possibly, *ceide* (1a, 4b) and *duirthech* (2a, 3a) should be written with large initials to denote names of churches rather than parts of a particular church. A poem on the Lent of the Apostles follows in M (53Vb). See also *M.Tall.* 118-20, from L 363 *in marg. infer.*

INDEX OF SAINTS' NAMES

Separate indexes serve (a) the names of saints and mothers of saints, (b) other Irish personal names and (c) the biblical and classical names of entries 674-689.1.2; the biblical or early christian names found elsewhere in the text (e.g. 1, (208), 689.3.4, 712) are entered in the main indexes. Generally, but not always, the spelling of headwords follows that adopted by M. A. O'Brien in *CGH*. The use of hyphens, however, is avoided, and palatalization is normally shown (e.g. Beinén, Eithne etc.). The 'profession' assigned to a saint (artisan, cobbler, cook, etc.) or his place in orders (presbyter, deacon, priest, bishop) does not influence the alphabetical arrangement. Exceptions, however, are such designations as *ailithir* (i.e. pilgrim) and *láech* (i.e. laic), which are often felt as part of the saint's name, e.g. Colmán ailithir. Round brackets, e.g. (416), 722.(6), refer to the *varia lectiones*. Asterisked entries have not been normalised. The following abbreviations are used: aps. (apstal, apostolus), dech. (dechoin), diac. (diaconus), eps. (episcopus), m. (mac), sac. (sacart, sacerdos).

INDEX OF OTHER IRISH PERSONAL NAMES

INDEX OF BIBLICAL AND CLASSICAL NAMES

(These names are drawn from entries 674-689.1.2 of the Corpus. As far as possible, account has been taken of the official forms in establishing the nominative endings of the head-words, but there is no serious departure from the Irish text. Generally, the more correct forms of BLc[1] and M are preferred.)

INDEX OF PLACE AND TRIBAL NAMES

In identifying the place names, I have been mostly guided by such authorities as *Onom.* and the relevant indexes to *M.Tall.* and AI. These sources are seldom cited, however, except when I choose to give them responsibility for the identifications. I have also been greatly assisted by K. W. Nicholls, who provided a large number of identifications; these are indicated by the letters K.W.N. between parentheses. Some of the identifications are my own but, for obvious reasons, the evidence for them is not included. On account of their very small number (four in all) the place and tribal names of the biblical and classical section (674-89) are incorporated in the main index. The following abbreviations are used: bar. (barony), co. (county), dean. (deanery), dioc. (diocese), par. (parish), r. (river), tl. (townland). Where possible, identifications refer to the tl. or civil par. which took its name from the place mentioned in the text.

APPENDIXES

The tables of entries which follow are for purposes of reference when reading the introduction; La's table will be found in the printed text (*Ir. texts* 3, 94 - 104, §§206 - 329). The biblical and classical pedigrees are disregarded since they form a special section in almost all the recensions in which they occur.

APPENDIX 1:

Table of entries in M, with the parallel entries of the other Ormond texts and of the other recensions (excepting the metrical recension).

M	R[1]	La	H	Rec. Min.	L	RLc[1]	H[1]
1. Pátraic	1		1	416	1	1	1
2. Brigit	4	267-8	3	427	2	2	
3. Cianán	73		84	455	195	60	37
4. Fínán Lobar	36		87	447	193	52	
5. Tola	38	307	51	449 526	207		
6. Berech	78			430	25		24
7. Cummaíne Fota	23	209	20	451	232	169	
8. Ultán m. Ernaíne		308	50	528	194	54	
9. Míte	59	250 309	69		93	68	
10. Luaithrinn	60		74	530	197	69	32
11. Mochóemóc m. Beoáin	61		58	439		205	7
12. Samthann	62		55	438	185	179	
13. Máedóc Ferna	39	226	64	425	63	153	
14. Dáire ingen Chathaír	63 103	219		452	39	96	
15. Becc m. Dé		225		453	21		
16. Colum Cille	121		4	418	8	3	13
17. Ciarán m. Branduib	43	229					
18. Domongart		230	85	537	162		
19. Iarlaithe m. Trena	44	231	89	540	150	89	
20. Máel Ruain	45	232	10	565	316	142	
21. Crónán m. Odráin	6	210	78	570	225	137	
22. Bairrfind m. Muiredaig	46	222		433	27		
23. Molaisse m. Nadfraích	47	224	29	475	117	170	
24. Ruadán Lothra	2	208		504	208		
25. Luarach		243	90	615 541	79	141	
26. Óengus m. Ingobann	76	244	66 91	649 544	118	206	
27. Ruanach; cf. 132		245		543 616	11 31		
28. Colmán Ailithir	24	252	77		223	135	
29. Mac Í i.e. Colmán			68		302		11
30. Motheimneóc	51	327 246	71		224	132	
31. Findchú Brig Gobann	64			490 515	78		23
32. Sílán m. Fáilbe		247	73	574	221	134	
33. Munnu m. Tulcháin	69	248		546	155	146	
34. Fachtna		249 328	75	518	222		

M	R[1]	La	H	Rec. Min.	L	RLc[1]	H[1]
35. Áedán m. Colmáin	65	251		617			
36. Rónán m. Beraig		253		534	325	28	
37. Rícell	106	254			690.10		
38. Cormac m. Dímma	52	255	76		227	136	
39. Báetán		235					
40. Senán m. Fintain	26	256	7	417	299	71	
41. Cainner ingen Chóeláin	107	257		630	690.8	21	
42. Connad 7 Obba ingena Colmáin	108	258		631	690.10		
43. Rónnat ingen Ḟiachna	109	259			690.10	100	
44. Molua m. Carthaig; cf. 118	3 33	326	72		116	133	
45. Dalbach cf. 119	48	310		561	240		
46. Furudrán cf. 120		289		519	55		
47. Findlug m. Dímmáin				639			
48. Beccán m. Sáráin			81		115	139	
49. Colmán m. Rónáin	25	290			33		
50. Fiachu m. Eogain; cf. 54.	87 93	223 294		575	30		
51. Breccán m. Ubáin	88	295			34	79	
52. Beccán m. Lugdach; cf. 147.	53 89	296			32		
53. Maine m. Eichin	92	297		511	28		
54. Fiachu m. Fergusa; cf. 50.	87 93	223 294		575	30		
55. Óengus m. Ailella	90				44		
56. Sinell m. Tigernaig	91			532	46		
57. Dathí m. Conamla				460	148		29
58. Beoaid m. Olchon				514	214		
59. Trea ingen Cháerthainn	110		2	527	76	64	
60. Cumman ingen Ailleáin			13	420 465	196	65	
61. Moninne ingen Mochta				523	98	66	
62. Fiacc m. Ercada			15	477 521	286	159	
63. Senán m. Geircinn	13	207	92	450	228	143	
64. Manchán Léith	54	273		577	188		
65. Eogan m. Eirc; cf. 107.	67			520 559	251		
66. Beccán m. Murchada	95	213 215	16	432 478 578	199	72	
67. Molanga Saingil					205		
68. Énán m. Eirnín	58 94	216	18	474 514	42	183	
69. Áithgen m. Lugair					43	73	
70. Máel Dóid m. Fíngein			22	480 579	50	75	
71. Máel Ruba	70		21	479	17	74	
72. Colmán m. Áeda	96		24	481	49	76	
73. Mochuta m. Lugada				445			
74. Colmán m. Eogain	97		25	482 582	60	88	
75. Glúnṡalach					119	208	
76. Declán		288	32 70	470 483	107	187	
77. Dabeóc m. Luainín		311	33	501	184		

M	R^1	La	H	Rec. Min.	L	$RLc^1 1$	H^1
78. Mac Caírthinn m. Cainnig			35	485	95	77	
79. Colmán m. Fergusa (Fergna)	118		36	468	237	78	
80. Cóemán m. Taicce					147		
81. Moluóc m. Luchta				590	121		
82. Muirdebair					106		
83. Daig m. Cairill			38	469	19 82		
84. Tigernach m. Cairpre		305	37	505	244	48	
85. Cuanna m. Fualascaig				583	51	83	
86. Rónán Find m. Sáráin	27	304	40	487	48	56	
87. Mac Nise m. Faibrig	118		8	564		144	
88. Muru m. Feradaig	120		42	491 557	20		
89. Colmán Ela	28		9	454	311	186	
90. Mocholmóc m. Conratháin	30	306	43		99		
91. Cóemán m. Taláin			44		131		
92. Cóemán Brecc			46	492 584	206		
93. Buite m. Brónaig		329	47	429	231	174	
94. Áed m. Eogain			48	498 563 645	285	160	
95. Commán m. Ainmerech			49		138		
96. Fergna m. Ainmerech						82	
97. Molaisse m. Cairill			52	437 585	143	57 228	
98. Diarmait Dísirt Diarmata; cf. 186			53		142	229	
99. Findbarr m. Áeda			54	517 586	6		
100. Mac Liac m. Cernaig	80	324	59	619 650	310	227	
101. Momáedóc Feda Dúin	31	325	60		242		
102. Fergus m. Énna					108	84	
103. Ciarán Saigre	7		61	461	288	173	
104. Conláed Cerd	78		62	440 499	252	192	
105. Trí meic Duib							
106. Eogan m. Cainnig; cf. 65	67		57	587	251		
107. Crummaíne Lecna	56	217	63	456 588		189	
108. Cairpre m. Déicill; cf. 168					104		
109. Mochua m. Lonáin	74		67	522	5	212	
110. Mochua Balla	75						
111. Cormac m. Cuilennáin	77						
112. Barra m. Aimirgin	41	220	34	484	314	167	21
113. Lairén m. Colmáin							
114. Finnian m. Fintain	19	275	93	516	122	29	
115. Scáth ingen Tigernaig							
116. Dašinchell	42	228			282	154	
117. Ciarán m. Beonaid	68 122		23	422 613	125	33	3
118. Molua m. Carthaig; cf. 44	33	326	72		116	133	
119. Dalbach; cf. 45	48	310		561	240		
120. Furudrán and Báetán; cf. 46		289		519	55		
121. Scíre ingen Eogain	111			444	37	178	

M	R[1]	La	H	Rec. Min.	L	RLc[1]	H[1]
122. Énna Toraige			14	538	16	67	
123. Erc Sláine	57	274	94	513 576	130	36	
124. Colmán m. Duach	16	272		503			
125. Cuan m. Odráin							
126. Cuimmine Cadan*	81	221		603			
127. Braccán Airne	17	211		600			
128. Áelchu		212					
129. Bríg ingen Chobthaig	114	281					
130. Colum Cilli, Áedh co feraib etc.							
131. Lommán m. Erannáin				620	10	44	
132. Ruanach; cf. 27		245		543 616	11 31		
133. Brénainn m. Findloga	11		28	493	127	46	5
134. Saints Berchán (11 entries)				548-9 551 560 562	261-71		
135. Britus etc.		237			689.1		
136. Molua m. Sinill	40	323		542	77	20	
137. Flannán	5	206	11	471 568	230	165	
138. Dímma Dub m. Óengusa	10	233	80		226	138	
139. Liadain ingen Diarmata	104	214	79	571	198	70	
140. Cóemgen	32	236	45	458	250	175	
141. Cairnech		237					
142. Brittus					689.2.		
143. Coimgall m. Cairill		239		572			22
144. Énna Airne	15	240	86	569	67	140	
145. Gabrán m. Óengusa	105	241	88	539 573	690.16	24	
146. Carthach m. Finn; cf. 178	83	242			126	188	
147. Beccán m. Luigdech; cf. 52	52 89	296			32		
148. Colum Tíre Dá Glas	12	273	27	457	241	47	
149. Moling	29		6	547	249	59	
150. Fidmuine				545			
151. Brénainn and Domaingen		218					
152. Molaca m. Duibdligid	65 102	299			217	115	
153. Fergna m. Fintain*				494		184	
154. Sárnat ingen Áeda	113	303		602			
155. Crónán m. Óengusa;† cf. 171	22			589	24	148	18
156. Ailenn ingen Eogain							
157. List of Uí Bairrche Saints							
158. List of Dál Meisin Corb Saints		270			181	176-7	
159. Cainnech	82	301	31	607	123	30	
160. Ingena Cormaic		279		656	247	50	
161. Ingena Cairpre		280			248	51	
162. Cóelchú		282					
163. List of saints' aliases		283-7		658-61	703		
164. Modíchu m. Amairgin		261		608	314		
165. Séigín m. Senaig					274		
166. Fáilbe m. Echach	71	262			274		

*also in Lb. †In Lc[1] only of RLc[1].

M	R[1]	La	H	Rec. Min.	L	RLc[1]	H[1]
167. Ingena Ailella; cf. 181	72	263-4		593	246		
168. Cairpre m. Déicill; cf. 108					104		
169. Molaisse† m. Décláin	20	277		581		171	
170. Diarmait† m. Lugna	21	278	96	533		147	
171. Crónán† m. Óengusa; cf. 155	22			589	24	148	18
172. Commán m. Fáelchon	100			467	109	91	
173. Cairell m. Curnáin				464			
174. Édamair ingen Eogain	112			595			
175. List of Uí Ailella saints	98-9 101	312-21		596-9			
176. Faithlech m. Findloga etc.	117	298					
177. Fergus m. Colmáin		302		604			
178. Mochuta; cf. 146	83	271			126	188	
179. Dachonna Essa	84			627	83	86	
180. Dachonna m. Tigernaig	85			605			
181. Ingena Ailella; cf. 167	72	263-4		593	246		
182. Berchán m. Micáin		265		473 556	201		
183. Crimthann ainm Coluim Chille etc.		266		625 651	397		
184. Attracht ingen Taláin	115	260					
185. Diarmait Dísirt Diarmata; cf. 98			53		142	229	
186. Áed m. Bricc	9		65	441 509	9	18	
187. Eithern Epscop				497	133		
188. Ultán m. Rónáin						207	
189. Finnachta Luimnig etc.	116	300		609			
190. Mac Finn							
191. Étaín Tuama Noa		292		510 610			
192. Fintan m. Echach etc.					160		
193. Crónán Ua hEilmíne etc.					161		
194. Derinnill Chethirchíchech					162		
195. Máel Uma m. Báetáin					163		
196. Trí meic Cendḟota etc.					164		
197. Cuach ingen Chóelbad etc.					165		
198. Teora náem etc.					166		
199. Colum ingen Lugna					167		
200. Domma etc.					168		
201. Secht n-epscoip etc.					169		
202. Díucaill and Colmán etc.					170		
203. Finus Ailithir etc.					171		
204. Mac Erca etc.					159		
205. Cellán and Garbán etc.					172		
206. Brigit and Cumman etc.					173		
207. Guaire and Cumman etc.					174		
208. Munnu and Mechar etc.					175		
209. Ultán 7 Máel Dub etc.					176		
210. Cruimthir Lugnaith etc.					177		
211. Tír Féicc etc.					178		
212. Teora ingena Maine etc.					179		
213. Athracht ingen Tigernaig					180		
214. Saints of Dál Meisin Corb					181		
215. Mechar and Mursan					663		

†In Lc[1] only of RLc[1].

M	R[1]	La	H	Rec. Min.	L	RLc[1]	H[1]
216. Secht meic Reistitiúit etc.					664		
217. Nónbur Síl Chonaire etc.					665		
218. Patrick's Household					671		
219. Áed m. Guaire etc.					690		
220. Mel and Melchú					693		
221. Lommán m. Dalláin					694		
222. Trí meic Angáin					695		
223. Allabair etc.					696		
224. De choimlib Dál Cais etc.					697		
225. Scannlach etc.					698		
226. Bráthair Fursu etc.					702		
227. Trea etc.					699		
228. Caimmíne etc.					700		
229. Mochen a Brénainn etc.					725.3		
230. Lann Léire etc.							
231. At iad 'sin cheide chruaid etc.							
232. Longarad etc.					720		
233. Poem on the apostles							

APPENDIX 2:
Table of entries in RLc[1].

RLc[1] (1-78 in Lc[1] only)

1. Pátraic.
2. Brigit.
3. Colum Cille.
4. Baithíne m. Brénainn.
5. Laisrén m. Feradaig.
6. Séigíne m. Fiachna.
7. Cuimmíne m. Arnaíne.
8. Fáilbe m. Pípáin.
9. Adamnán.
10. Dúnchad m. Cinn Ḟáelad.
11. Dorbaíne Fota.
12. Fáelchú m. Dorbaíne.
13. Cillíne Droichtech.
14. Sléibíne m. Congaile.
15. Flann m. Maíle Dúin.
16. Máel Brigte m. Tornáin.
17. Dubthach m. Dubáin.
18. Áed m. Bricc.
19. Colmán m. Foirtcheirn.
20. Secht meic Muiredaig.
21. Cainner ingen Chóeláin.
22. Áed Mór and Áed Becc.
23. hIlladan m. Echach.
24. Garbán m. Óengusa.
25. Máel Tuile m. Nóchaire.
26. Serc ingen Echach.
27. Colmán m. Echach.

RLc[1] (1-78 in Lc[1] only)

28. Rónán m. Beraig.
29. Finnén Cluana Iraird.
30. Cainnech.
31. Comgall Bennchair.
32. Brénainn Birra.
33. Ciarán Cluana Mac Nóis.
34. Findbarr Maige Bile.
35. Secht meic Trichim.
36. Erc m. Dega.
37. hUi|d|riu m. Cuain.
38. Áed m. Maíl Odráin.
39. Mártain m. Dúnáin.
40. Mochuta.
41. Colmán m. Óengusa.
42. Secht meic Lugada.
43. Lommán m. Dalláin.
44. Lommán m. Erannáin.
45. Dobarchú m. Onchon.
46. Brénainn m. Findloga.
47. Colum Tíre Dá Glas.
48. Tigernach Cluana Eois.
49. Ingena Ailella.
50. Ingena Cormaic.
51. Ingena Cairpre.
52. Fínán m. Conaill.
53. Muirgen ingen Libáin.
54. Ultán m. Bruidge.

RLc[1]

55. Fachtna etc. m. Brónaig.
56. Rónán Find m. Sáráin.
57. Molaisse m. Cairill.
58. Colcu m. Áeda.
59. Moling.
60. Cianán m. Sétna.
61. Cuanna m. Miduirn.
62. Tigernán m. Ninneda.
63. Diarmait m. Fergaile.
64. Trea ingen Chaírthinn.
65. Cumman ingen Ailléain.
66. Moninne ingen Mochta.
67. Ernán Toraige.
68. Míte ingen Chinn Ḟáelad.
69. Luaithrinn.
70. Liadain ingen Diarmata.
71. Senán m. Fintain.
72. Beccán m. Murchada.
73. Áedgein m. Lugair.
74. Máel Ruba m. Elganaig.
75. Máel Doid m. Fíngin.
76. Colmán m. Áeda.
77. Mac Caírthinn m. Cainnig.
78. Colmán Imroma.
79. Breccán* m. Ubáin.
80. Mac Laisre m. Ubáin.
81. Cormac m. Echach.
82. Fergna m. Ainmirech.
83. Cuana m. Fualascaig.
84. Fergus etc. m. Énda.
85. Comgall etc. m. Echach.
86. Dachonna etc. m. Echach.
87. Dochuailén.
88. Colmán m. Eogain.
89. Iarlaithe m. Trena.
90. Fethgne.
91. Commán m. Fáelchon.
92. Attracht† ingen Sáráin.
93. Ernaíne etc. m. Eogain.
94. Aíthgen Boithe Domnaig.
95. Cróine ingen Diarmata.
96. Dáire ingen Chathaír.
97. Fainiu etc. ingen Nadfraích.
98. Darchaírthinn ingen Énna.
99. Cairech Dergáin.
100. Rónnat ingen Ḟiachna.
101. Brigit ingen Áeda.
102. Sinche ingen Annuda.
103. Lann ingen Beicce.
104. Boga etc. ingen Ḟiangalaig.
105. Fainche ingen Bleidíne.
106. Fainche ingen Óengusa.
107. Secht n-ingena Léiníne etc.
108. Fiachraich m. Colmáin.
109. Flann Febla.
110. Colmán Cille m. Eogain.
111. Dúilech Clochair.

*R begins here. †In Lc[1] only.

RLc[1]

112. Mobí etc. m. Nadfraích.
113. Fínán Dromma Abrat.
114. Bairrḟind Metíne.
115. Molaca m. Duibdligid.
116. Mochuille m. Díucaill.
117. Cuanu m. Cailchín.
118. Conall m. Fiachna.
119. Áed Cóel m. Feradaig.
120. Moluga m. Lainneóin.
121. Forannán m. Rónáin.
122. Dobiú m. Comgaill.
123. Colmán m. Lugna.
124. Tiú m. Fínáin.
125. Colmán m. Raithíne.
126. Sechnasach m. Fínáin.
127. Sinell m. Áeda.
128. Ercc m. Fergna.
129. Breccán m. Cinn Barca.
130. Fergus m. Óengusa.
131. Colmán m. Conaill.
132. Motheimneóc.
133. Molua m. Carthaig.
134. Sílán m. Fáilbe.
135. Colmán m. Grillíne.
136. Cormac Ua Liatháin.
137. Crónán m. Odráin.
138. Dímma Dub m. Óengusa.
139. Breccán m. Sáráin.
140. Énna Áirne.
141. Lúrach m. Cuanach.
142. Máel Ruain Tamlachta.
143. Senán m. Geirrcinn.
144. Mac Nise m. Faibrig.
145. Beoán etc. m. Nesáin.
146. Munnu m. Tulcháin.
147. Diarmait† m. Lugna.
148. Crónán† m. Óengusa.
149. Colco† m. Áeda.
150. Baithíne m. Finnaich.
151. Erc Sláine m. Dega.
152. Ercca m. Ercca.
153. Máedóc Ferna.
154. Sinchell m. Cenannáin.
155. Sinchell m. Corcáin.
156. Benén m. Seiscnéin.
157. Fintan Cluana Eidnech.
158. Domongóc Toraige.
159. Fiacc Sléibte.
160. Áed m. Eogain.
161. Abbán.
162. Fursu Cráibthech.
163. Domongart m. Echach.
164. Colmán m. Luacháin.
165. Flannán etc. m. Tairdelbaig.
166. Féichín Fobair.
167. Bairre etc. m. Aimirgin.
168. Óengus Láimidan.
169. Cuimmíne Fota.
170. Molaisse m. Nadfraích.

RLc[1]
171. Molaisse† m. Décláin.
172. Dáire Doimthig.
173. Ciarán Saigre.
174. Buite m. Brónaig.
175. Cóemgen Glinne Dá Locha.
176. Eichen m. Maine.
177. Áedán m. Maine.
178. Scíre ingen Eogain.
179. Samthann Cluana Brónaig.
180. Trí ingena Cainnig.
181. Cumman etc. ingen Áeda.
182. Senán Achaid Choil.
183. Énán m. Eiríne.
184. Fergna m. ind Ḟiled.
185. Fiachna Find m. Cobthaig.
186. Colmán m. Beognae.
187. Déclán Airde Móire.
188. Carthach i.e. Mochuta.
189. Crumaíne Lecna.
190. Dronán m. Fiangalaig.
191. Feirgil m. Maíle Dúin.
192. Conláed Cráibthech.
193. Ailbe m. Olcain.
194. Foircetal m. Táil.
195. Faithlenn m. Áeda Damáin.
196. Mochromma Dísertach.
197. Feidlimed m. Crimthainn.
198. Mobriccu m. Siláin.
199. Secht meic Dubthain.
200. Fínán m. Fergna.

RLc[1]
201. Caimmíne Inse Celtra.
202. Comgán m. Diarmata.
203. Secht meic Restitiuit.
204. Iarlaithe m. Loga.
205. Mochóemóc Léith.
206. Óengus m. in Gobann.
207. Ultán m. Crónáin.
208. Glúnṡalach m. Costamail.
209. Secht meic Draigin.
210. Mothenóc m. Mugna.
211. Fiachra m. Dáire.
212. Mochua m. Lonáin.
213. Diarmait m. Siabair.
214. Máel Anfaid m. Anfodaig.
215. Séigíne etc. m. Crónáin.
216. Ibar m. Lugna.
217. Colmán etc. ic Dún Baile.
218. Crothu etc. i Cill Criú.
219. Martra m. Tinne.
220. Cuanu m. Dúnadaig.
221. Díucaill etc. i Cluain Trelecc.
222. Cellán etc. ic Findchoire.
223. Brigit etc. in nAchad Togarta.
224. Munnu etc. ic Rus Achaid Liac.
225. Nannine etc. la Pátraicc.
226. Bairre† m. Amairgein.
227. Mac Liac† i.e. Diucaill.
228. Molaisse† Leithglinne.
229. Diarmait† m. Áeda Róin.

†In Lc[1] only.

APPENDIX 3:
Table of entries in R[1]; (bracketed entries denote interpolations).

R[1]
1. Pátraic.
2. Ruadán Lothra.
(3. |Molua| m. Carthaig), cf. 33.
4. Brigit.
5. Flannán.
6. Crónán m. Odráin.
7. Ciarán Saigre.
(8. Odrán m. Meic Raith.)
9. Áed m. Bricc.
10. Dímma Dub m. Óengusa.
11. Brénainn m. Findloga.
12. Colum Tíre Dá Glas.
13. Senán m. Geirrcinn.
14. Fursu Cráibdech.
15. Énna Áirne.
16. Colmán Mór m. Duach.
17. Braccán Áirne.
(18. Finnén Maige Bile.)
19. Finnén Cluana Iraird.
20. Molaise m. Décláin.

R[1]
21. Diarmait Inse Clothrann.
22. Crónán m. Óengusa.
23. Cuimmíne Fota.
24. Colmán Ailither.
25. Colmán m. Rónáin.
26. Senán m. Fintain.
27. Rónán Find m. Sáráin.
28. Colmán Ela.
29. Moling.
30. Mocholmóc m. Conratháin.
31. Máedóc Feda Dúin.
32. Cóemgen.
33. Molua m. Carthaig. Cf. 3.
(34. Lachtaíne m. Toirbín.)
(35. Ciar Ascad ingen Cholla.)
36. Fínán Lobar.
37. Beinén m. Seiscnéin.
38. Tola m. Dúnchada.
39. Máedóc Ferna.
40. Molua m. Sinill.

R[1]

41. Bairre.
42. Daṡinchell m. Cenannáin.
43. Ciarán m. Branduib.
44. Iarlaithe m. Trena.
45. Máel Ruain.
46. Bairrḟind m. Muiredaig.
47. Molaise m. Nadfroích.
48. Dalbach Cúile Collaing.
49. Sinchell Máel m. Corcáin.
50. Scuithíne Sléibe Mairge.
51. Motheimneóc.
52. Cormac m. Dímma.
53. Braccán m. Luigdech. Cf. 89.
54. Manchán m. Síláin.
55. Colcu m. Áeda.
56. Crummaíne Lecna.
57. Erc Sláine.
58. Énán m. Eirnín. Cf. 94.
59. Míte ingen Chinn Ḟáelad.
60. Luaithrinn.
61. Mochóemóc m. Beoáin.
62. Samthann.
63. Dáire ingen Chathair. Cf. 103.
64. Findchú m. Sétna.
65. Áedán m. Colmáin.
66. Molaca m. Duib Dligid. Cf. 102.
67. Eogan Arda Srath.
68. Ciarán m. Beoaid. Cf. 122.
69. Munnu m. Tulcháin.
70. Máel Ruba.
71. Fáilbe m. Cenannáin.
72. Ingena Ailella.
73. Cianán m. Sétna.
74. Mochua m. Lonáin.
75. Mochua Balla.
(76. Óengus m. Óengobann).
77. Cormac m. Cuilennáin.
78. Beirech m. Nemairgin.
79. Conláed Cerd.
80. Mac Liac m. Cernaig.
81. Cuimmíne Cadan.
82. Cainnech.
83. Mochuta.

R[1]

84. Dachonna etc. m. Echach.
85. Dachonna m. Tigernaig.
86. Eogan m. Cormaic.
87. Fiachna m. Eogain. Cf. 93.
88. Braccán m. Ubáin.
89. Braccán m. Lugdach. Cf. 53.
90. Óengus m. Ailella.
91. Cruimthir Sinell m. Tigernáin.
92. Maine m. Eichin.
93. Fiachna m. Fergusa. Cf. 87.
94. Énán m. Eirnín. Cf. 58.
95. Beccán m. Murchada.
96. Colmán m. Áeda.
97. Colmán m. Eogain.
98. Mainchín m. Coíl.
99. Senach m. Coíl.
100. Commán m. Fáelchon.
101. Imráitech.
102. Molaca m. Duib Dligid. Cf. 66.
103. Dáire ingen Chathaír. Cf. 63.
104. Liadain ingen Diarmata.
105. Garbán m. Óengusa.
106. Riagail ingen Athrachta.
107. Cainner ingen Chóeláin.
108. Connad & Obba ingena Colmáin.
109. Rónnat ingen Ḟiachna.
110. Trea ingen Chaírthinn.
111. Scíre ingen Eogain.
112. Ádamair ingen Eogain.
113. Sárnat ingen Áeda.
114. Bríg ingen Chobthaig.
115. Athracht ingen Taláin.
116. Succait etc.
117. Faithlech m. Findloga etc.
118. Colmán Imrama.
119. Mac Nise m. Fabraig.
120. Muru m. Feradaig.
121. Colum Cille.
122. Ciarán Cluana Mac Nóis. Cf. 68.
123. Máelán m. Dáire.
124. Brandam m. Echach.
125. Brénainn Birra.

APPENDIX 4:
Table of entries in H.

H

1. Pátraic.
2. Trea ingen Chaírthinn.
3. Brigit.
4. Colum Cille.
5. Comgall Bennchoir.
6. Moling Luachair.
7. Senán m. Fintain.
8. Mac Nise m. Faibrig.

H

9. Colmán Ela.
10. Máel Ruain.
11. Flannán.
12. Domnall Ua hÉnne.
13. Cumman ingen Ailléin.
14. Ernaín m. Colmáin.
15. Fiacc m. Erchada.
16. Beccán m. Murchada.

H
17. Féichíne m. Caíl Charna.
18. Énán m. Eirnín.
19. Damongóc m. Sáráin.
20. Cuimmíne m. Fiachna.
21. Máel Ruba.
22. Máel Dóid.
23. Ciarán m. Beoid.
24. Colmán m. Guaire.
25. Colmán m. Eogain.
26. Finnén Maige Bile.
27. Colum Tíre Dá Glas.
28. Brénainn m. Findloga.
29. Molaisse m. Nadfraích.
30. Ninnid m. Echach.
31. Cainnech.
32. Déclán. Cf. 70.
33. Dabeóc m. Luaininn.
34. Bairre.
35. Mac Caírthinn m. Cainnig.
36. Colmán Imrama.
37. Tigernach m. Cairpre.
38. Daig m. Cairill.
39. Ailbe m. Olchain.
40. Rónán m. Sáráin.
41. Trí ingena Cainnig.
42. Muru m. Feradaig.
43. Mocholmóc m. Conratháin.
44. Cóemán m. Taláin.
45. Cóemgen.
46. Cóemán Brecc.
47. Buite.
48. Áed m. Eogain.
49. Comán m. Ainmerech.
50. Ultán m. Ernaíne.
51. Tola m. Dúnchada.
52. Molaise m. Cairill.
53. Diarmait m. Áeda Róin.
54. Findbarr m. Áeda.
55. Samthann.
56. Fintan m. Gaibréin.

H
57. Eogan m. Cainnig.
58. Mochóemóc m. Beoáin.
59. Mac Liac m. Cernaig.
60. Momédóc m. Midgna.
61. Ciarán m. Luaigne.
62. Conláed Cerd.
63. Crummaíne m. Cormaic.
64. Máedóc Ferna.
65. Áed m. Bricc.
66. Óengus m. Oíbléin. Cf. 91.
67. Mochua m. Lonáin.
68. Macc Í i.e. Conna.
69. Míte ingen Chinn Ḟáelad.
70. Déclán. Cf. 32.
71. Motheimneóc.
72. Molua m. Carthaig.
73. Sillán m. Oiche.
74. Luaithrinn.
75. Fachtna m. Móenaig.
76. Cormac m. Dímma.
77. Colmán Ailithir.
78. Crónán m. Odráin.
79. Liadain ingen Diarmata.
80. Dímma Dub m. Óengusa.
81. Breccán m. Sáráin.
82. Adomnán m. Rónáin.
83. Baíthín m. Brénainn.
84. Cianán m. Sétna.
85. Domongart m. Echach.
86. Énna m. Conaill.
87. Fínán Lobar.
88. Garbán m. Óengusa.
89. Iarlaithe m. Trena.
90. Lúrach m. Cuanach.
91. Óengus m. Óengobann. Cf. 66.
92. Senán m. Geirrcinn.
93. Finnén Cluana Iraird.
94. Erc Sláine m. Dega.
95. Brénainn m. Nemain.
96. Diarmait m. Lugna.

APPENDIX 5:
Table of entries in H[1].

H[1]
1. Pátraic.
2. Comgall m. Sétna.
3. Ciarán m. Beonaid.
4. Lugaid m. Luigech.
5. Brénainn m. Findloga.
6. Cruimther Fróech.
7. Mochóemóc m. Beoáin.
8. Caillín m. Niatach.
9. Feilic m. Beochraide.
10. Iarlaithe m. Loga.

H[1]
11. Colmán m. Conna.
12. Móenacán m. Duib Dá Dos.
13. Colum Cille.
14. Baíthín m. Brénainn.
15. Cuan Átha Escrach.
16. Baíthín m. Cuanach.
17. Adamnán m. Rónáin.
18. Crónán m. Óengusa.
19. Ninned m. Echach.
20. Molua m. Sinill.

H^1

21. Bairre.
22. Comgall m. Cairill.
23. Findchú m. Sétna.
24. Berach m. Nemaingin.
25. Meithen Chóel.
26. Meithen Ḟind.
27. Mes Ráeda ingen Branáin.
28. Colcu m. Áeda.
29. Cruimthir Dathí m. Conamla.

H^1

30. Féichín m. Coíl Charna.
31. Mobí Clárainech.
32. Luaithrinn.
33. Colmán m. B[aíth].
34. Cruimthir Findbarr m. Bresail.
35. Cruimthir Sárán m. Brónaig.
36. Furudrán m. Cairpre Chroimm.
37. Cian Bithbeo m. Sétna.